morningglories

volumethree

P.E.

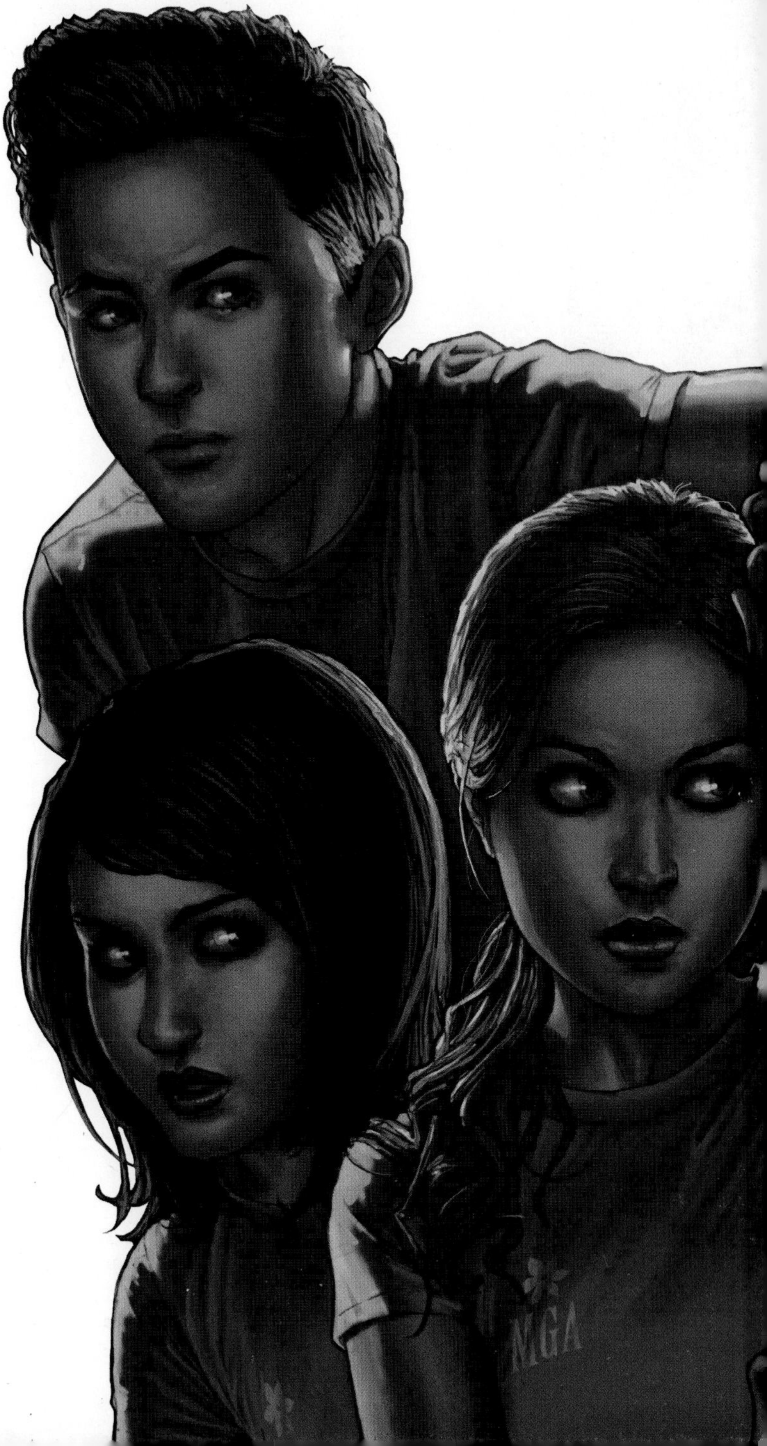
MGA

MGA

WORDS
NICK SPENCER

ART
JOE EISMA

RODIN ESQUEJO
COVERS

ALEX SOLLAZZO - JOHNNY LOWE - TIM DANIEL
COLORS   LETTERS   DESIGN

IMAGE COMICS, INC.
Robert Kirkman - chief operating officer
Erik Larsen - chief financial officer
Todd McFarlane - president
Marc Silvestri - chief executive officer
Jim Valentino - vice-president

Eric Stephenson - publisher
Todd Martinez - sales & licensing coordinator
Jennifer de Guzman - pr & marketing director
Branwyn Bigglestone - accounts manager
Emily Miller - accounting assistant
Jamie Parreno - marketing assistant
Jenna Savage - administrative assistant
Sarah deLaine - events coordinator
Kevin Yuen - digital rights coordinator
Jonathan Chan - production manager
Drew Gill - art director
Monica Garcia - production artist
Vincent Kukua - production artist
Jana Cook - production artist
www.imagecomics.com

thirteen

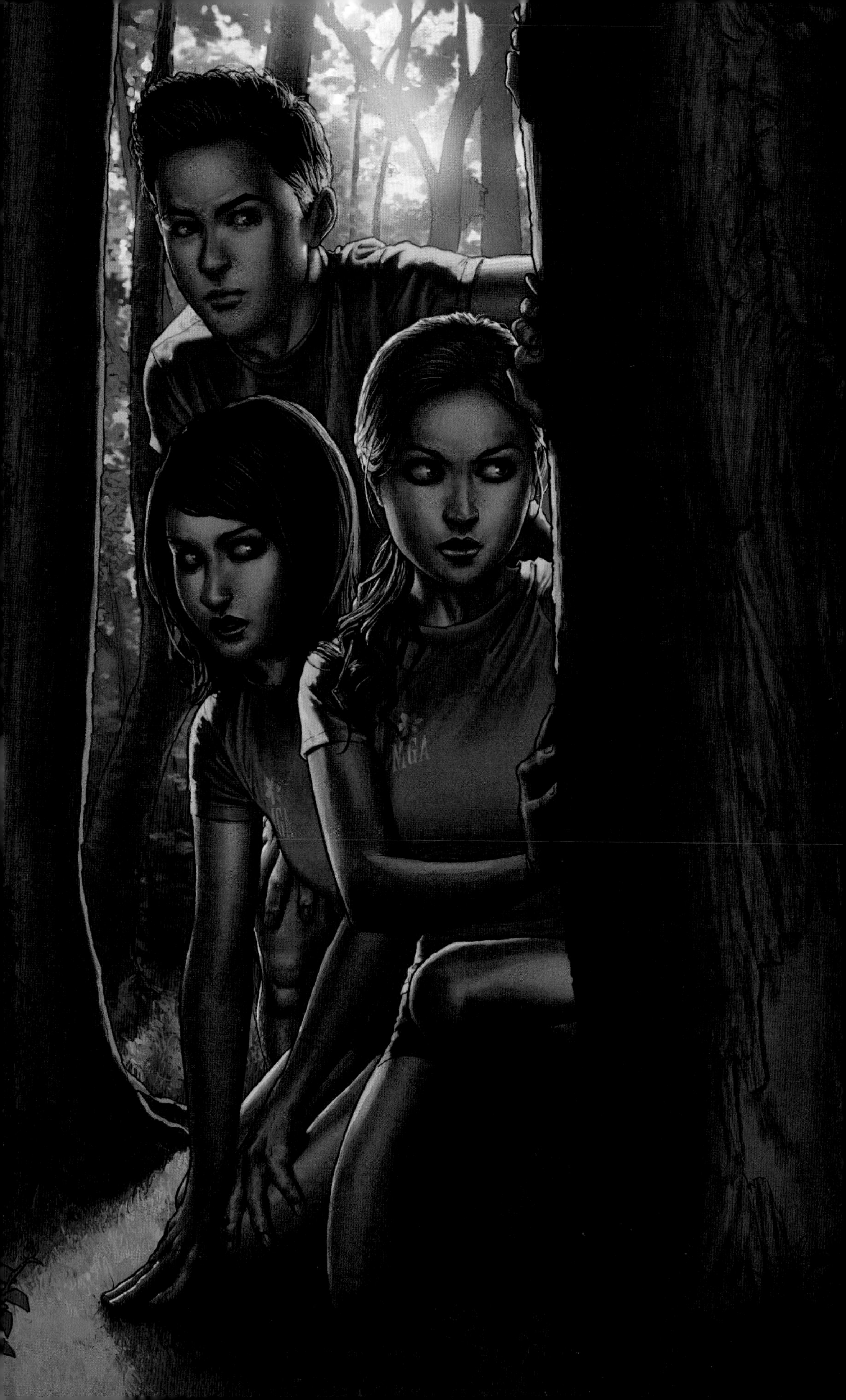
MGA

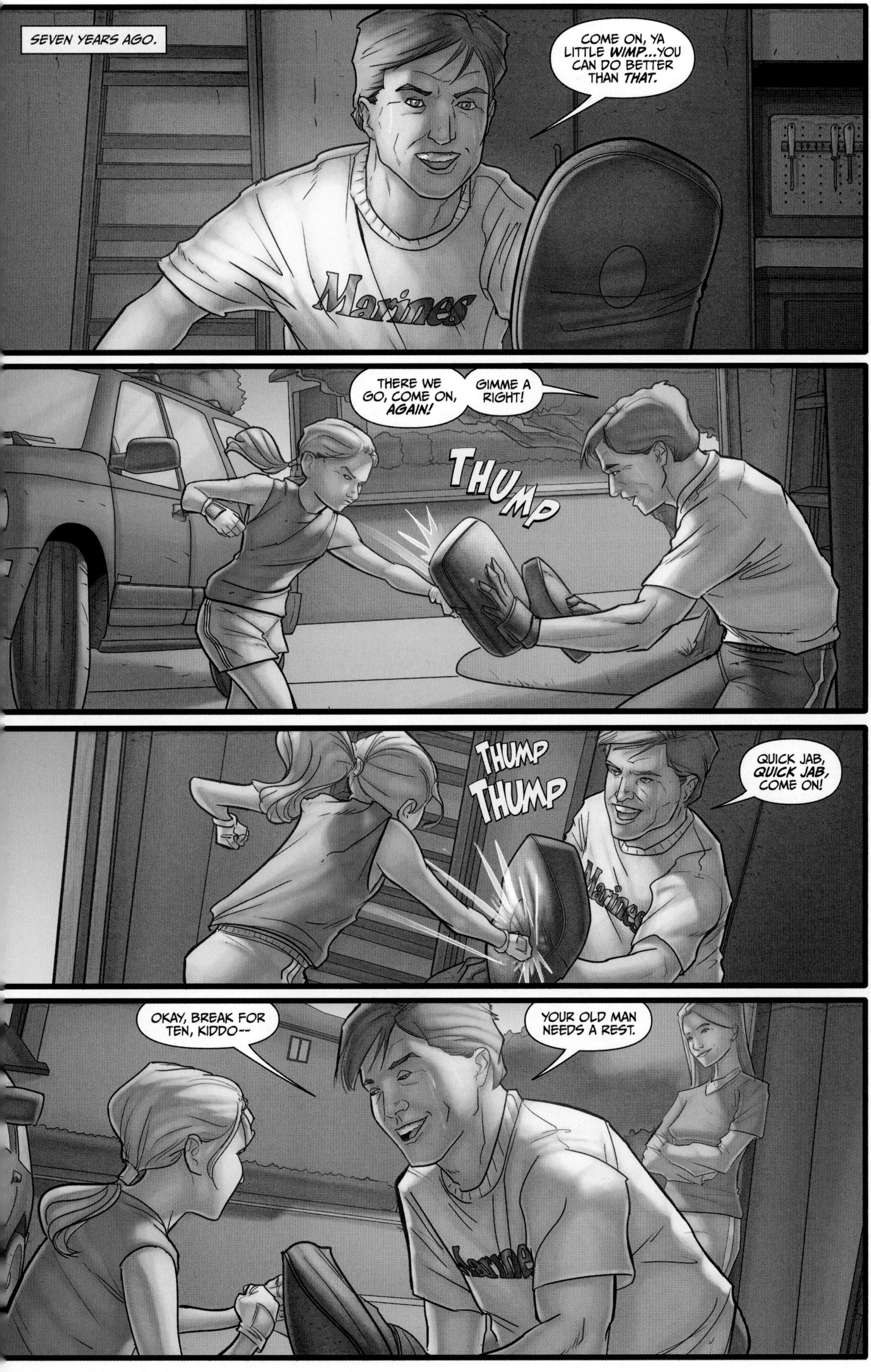
SEVEN YEARS AGO.
COME ON, YA LITTLE WIMP...YOU CAN DO BETTER THAN THAT.
Marines
THERE WE GO, COME ON, AGAIN!
GIMME A RIGHT!
THUMP
THUMP THUMP
QUICK JAB, QUICK JAB, COME ON!
OKAY, BREAK FOR TEN, KIDDO--
YOUR OLD MAN NEEDS A REST.

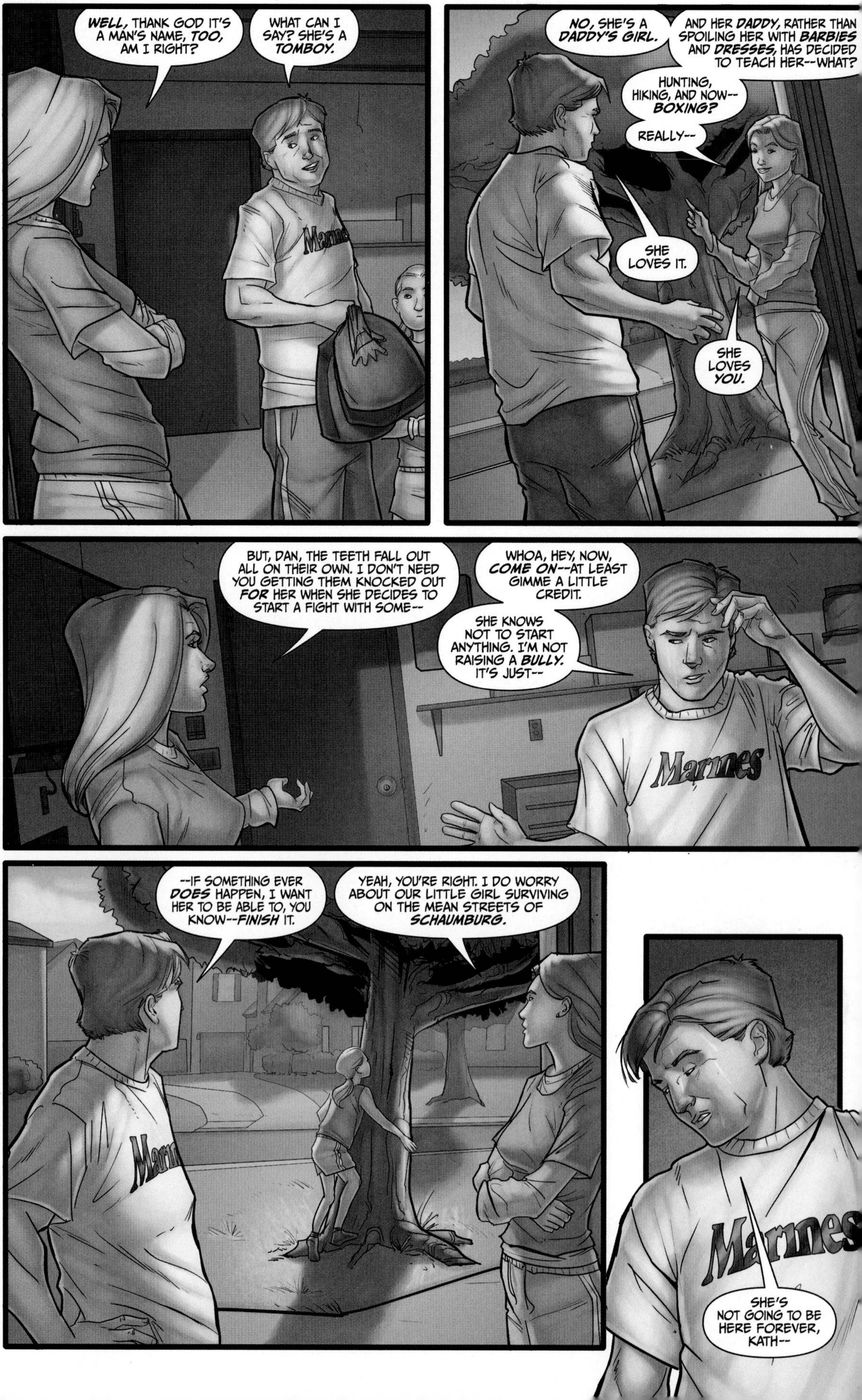
WELL, THANK GOD IT'S A MAN'S NAME, TOO, AM I RIGHT?
WHAT CAN I SAY? SHE'S A TOMBOY.
NO, SHE'S A DADDY'S GIRL.
AND HER DADDY, RATHER THAN SPOILING HER WITH BARBIES AND DRESSES, HAS DECIDED TO TEACH HER--WHAT?
HUNTING, HIKING, AND NOW--BOXING?
REALLY--
SHE LOVES IT.
SHE LOVES YOU.
BUT, DAN, THE TEETH FALL OUT ALL ON THEIR OWN. I DON'T NEED YOU GETTING THEM KNOCKED OUT FOR HER WHEN SHE DECIDES TO START A FIGHT WITH SOME--
WHOA, HEY, NOW, COME ON--AT LEAST GIMME A LITTLE CREDIT.
SHE KNOWS NOT TO START ANYTHING. I'M NOT RAISING A BULLY. IT'S JUST--
Marines
--IF SOMETHING EVER DOES HAPPEN, I WANT HER TO BE ABLE TO, YOU KNOW--FINISH IT.
YEAH, YOU'RE RIGHT. I DO WORRY ABOUT OUR LITTLE GIRL SURVIVING ON THE MEAN STREETS OF SCHAUMBURG.
SHE'S NOT GOING TO BE HERE FOREVER, KATH--

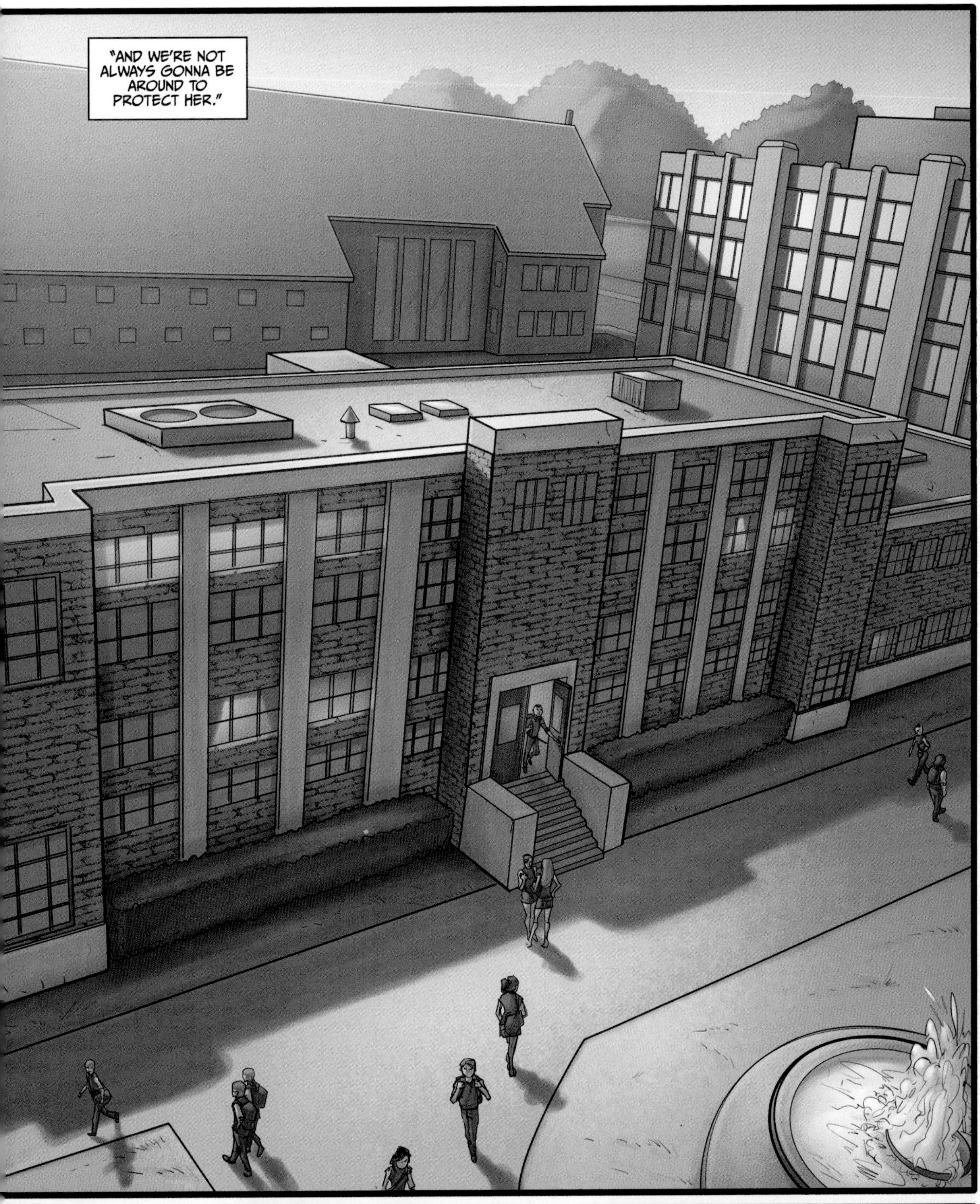
"AND WE'RE NOT ALWAYS GONNA BE AROUND TO PROTECT HER."

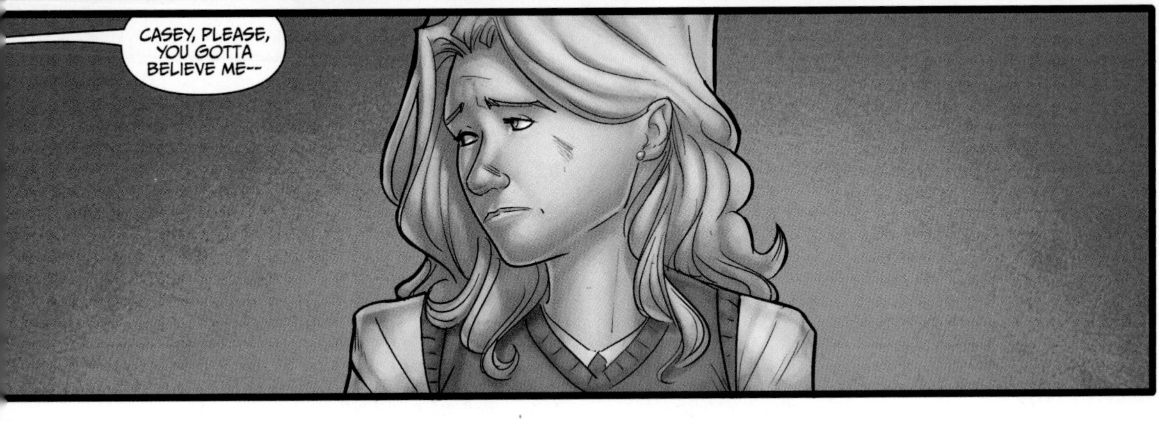
CASEY, PLEASE, YOU GOTTA BELIEVE ME--

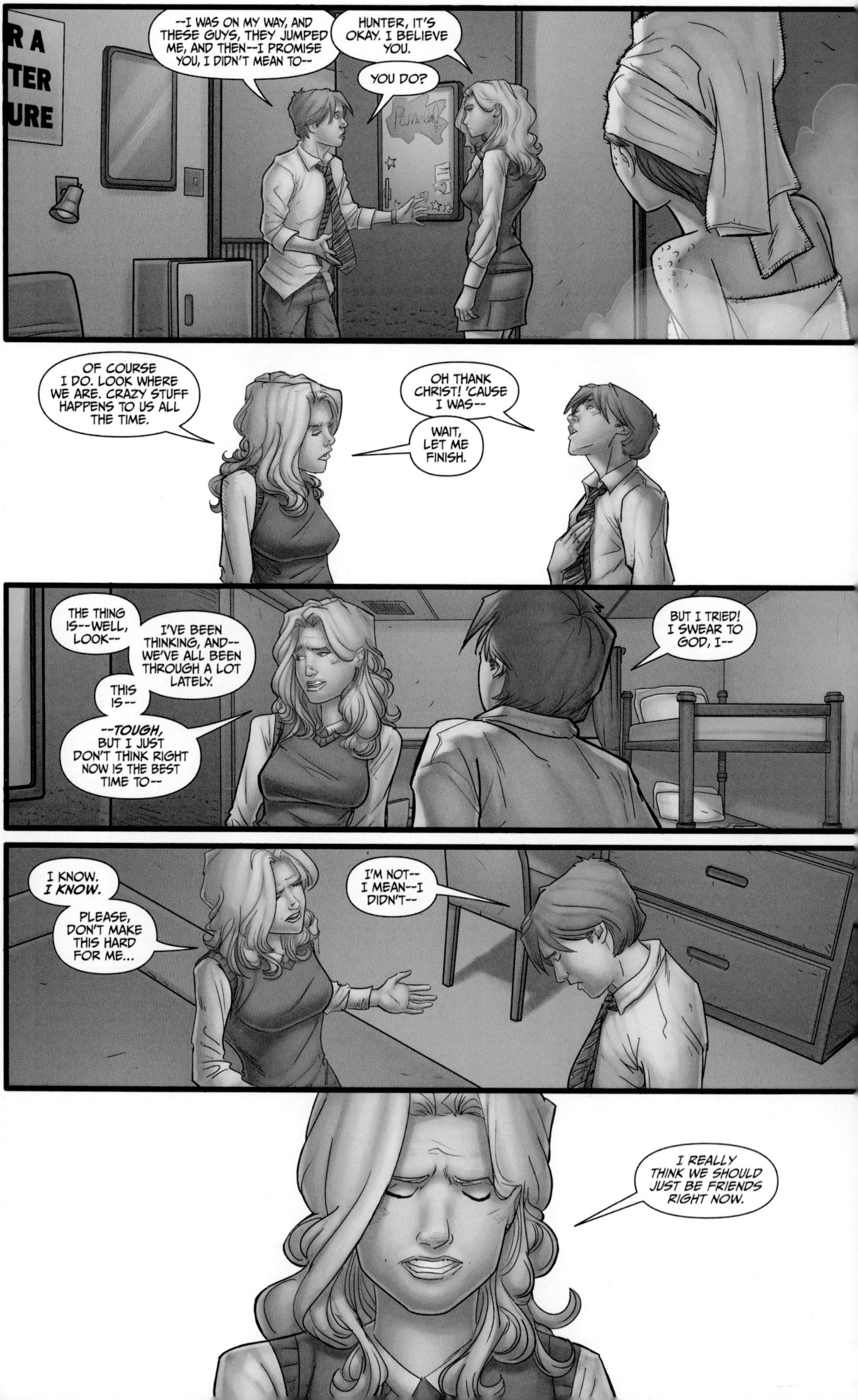

R A
TER
URE
--I WAS ON MY WAY, AND THESE GUYS, THEY JUMPED ME, AND THEN--I PROMISE YOU, I DIDN'T MEAN TO--
HUNTER, IT'S OKAY. I BELIEVE YOU.
YOU DO?
Pamela
OF COURSE I DO. LOOK WHERE WE ARE. CRAZY STUFF HAPPENS TO US ALL THE TIME.
OH THANK CHRIST! 'CAUSE I WAS--
WAIT, LET ME FINISH.
THE THING IS--WELL, LOOK--
I'VE BEEN THINKING, AND--WE'VE ALL BEEN THROUGH A LOT LATELY.
THIS IS--
--TOUGH, BUT I JUST DON'T THINK RIGHT NOW IS THE BEST TIME TO--
BUT I TRIED! I SWEAR TO GOD, I--
I KNOW. I KNOW.
PLEASE, DON'T MAKE THIS HARD FOR ME...
I'M NOT--I MEAN--I DIDN'T--
I REALLY THINK WE SHOULD JUST BE FRIENDS RIGHT NOW.

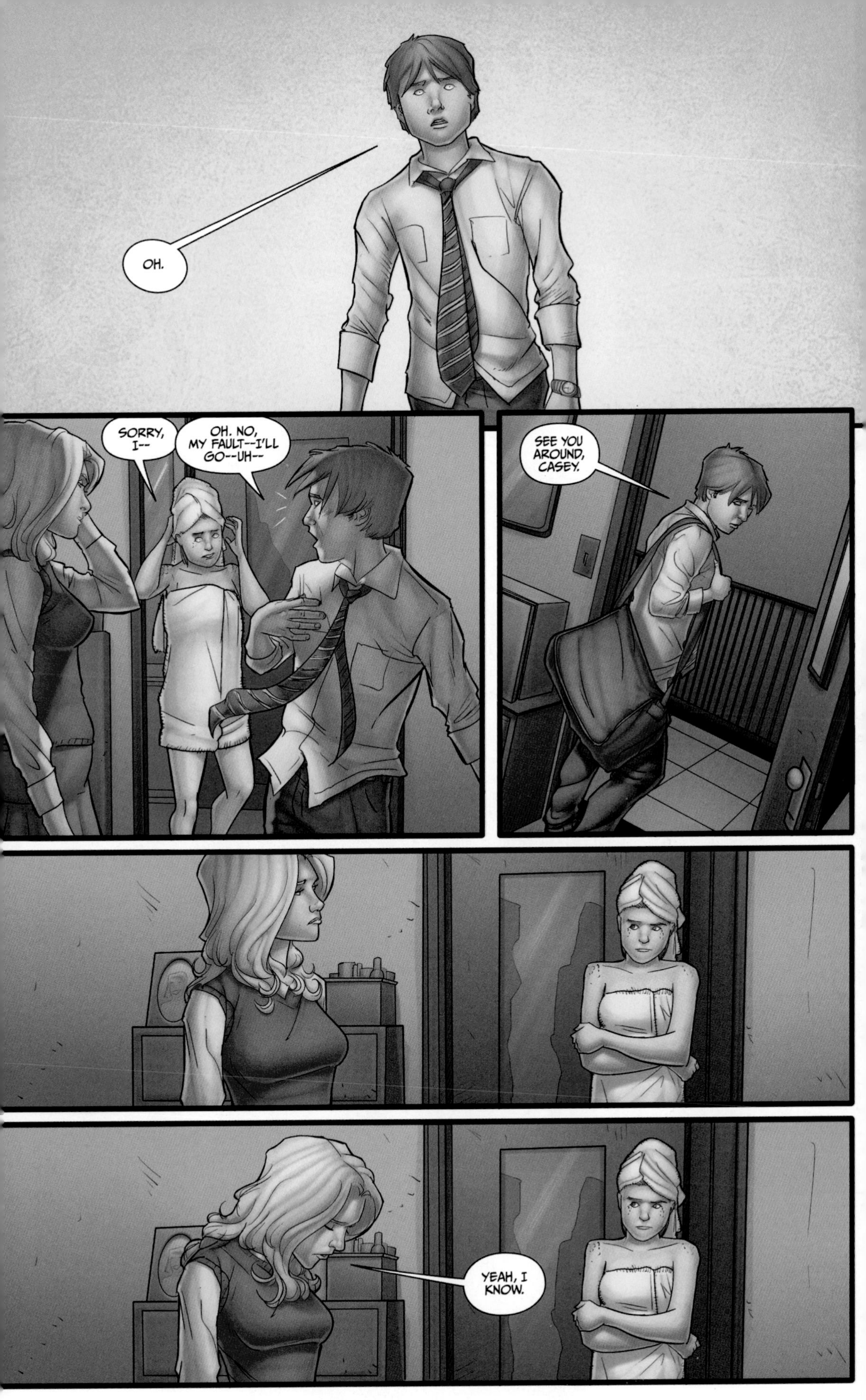
OH.
SORRY, I--
OH. NO, MY FAULT--I'LL GO--UH--
SEE YOU AROUND, CASEY.
YEAH, I KNOW.

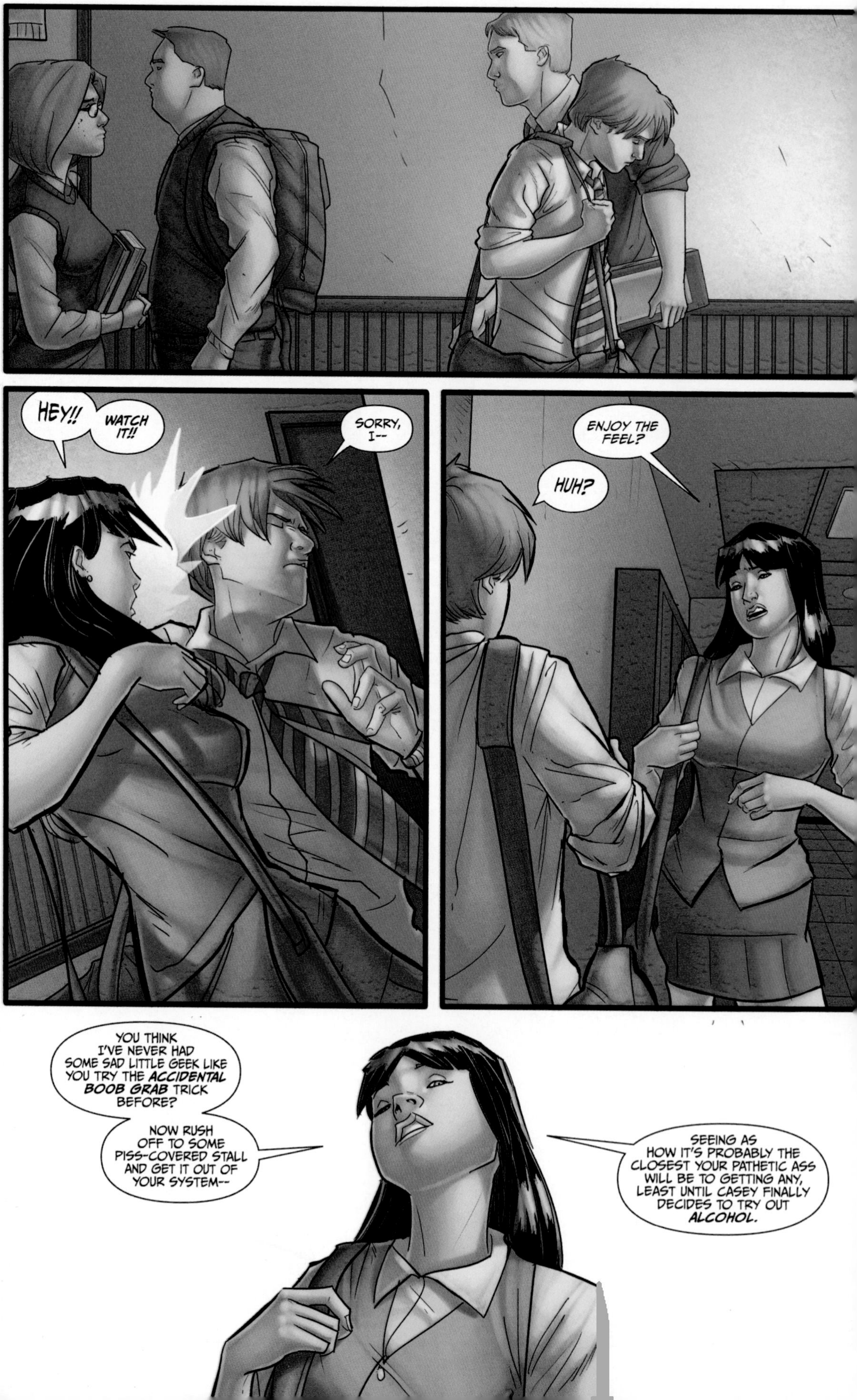

HEY!!
WATCH IT!!
SORRY, I--
ENJOY THE FEEL?
HUH?
YOU THINK I'VE NEVER HAD SOME SAD LITTLE GEEK LIKE YOU TRY THE ACCIDENTAL BOOB GRAB TRICK BEFORE?
NOW RUSH OFF TO SOME PISS-COVERED STALL AND GET IT OUT OF YOUR SYSTEM--
SEEING AS HOW IT'S PROBABLY THE CLOSEST YOUR PATHETIC ASS WILL BE TO GETTING ANY, LEAST UNTIL CASEY FINALLY DECIDES TO TRY OUT ALCOHOL.

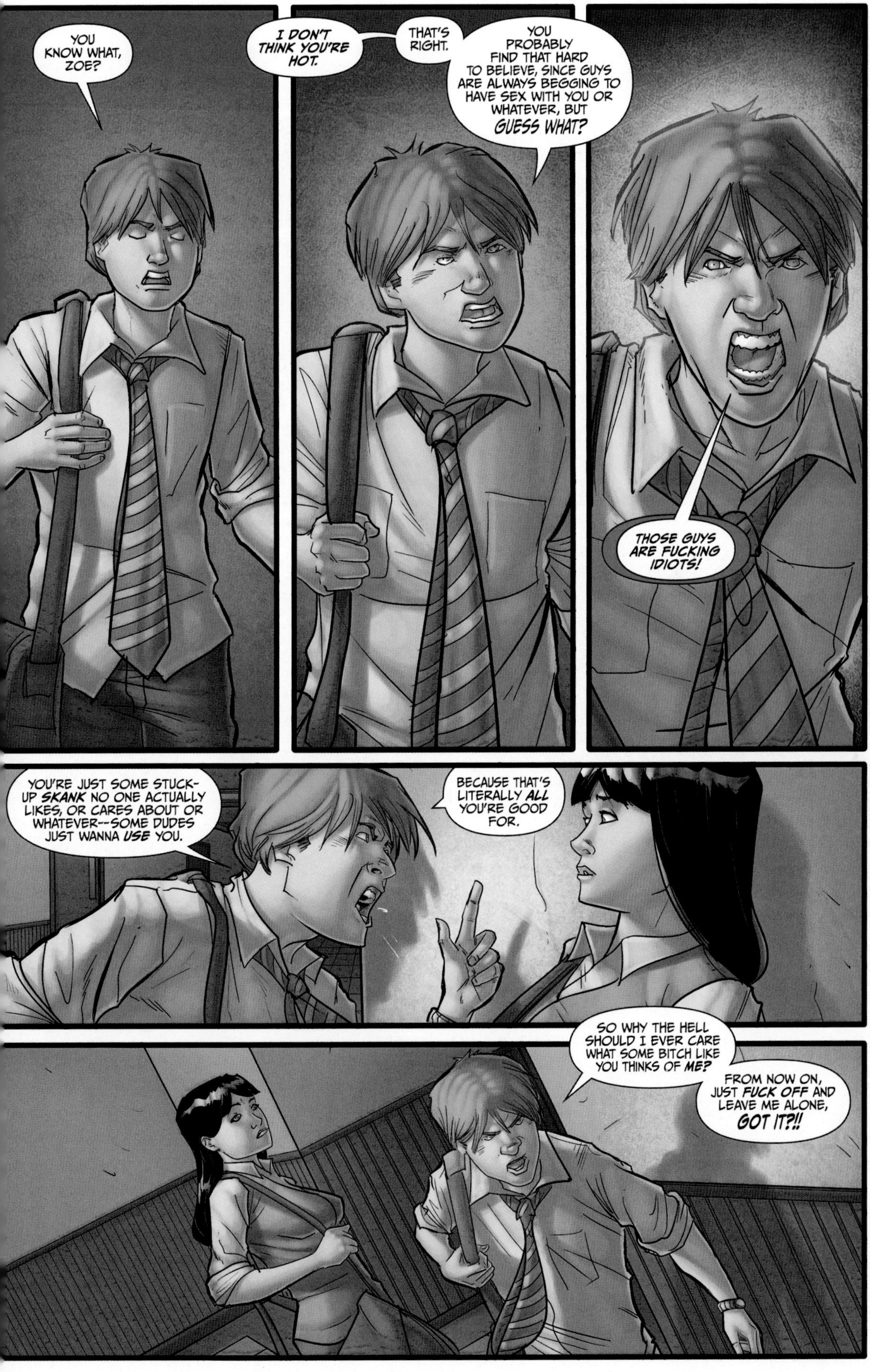
YOU KNOW WHAT, ZOE?
I DON'T THINK YOU'RE HOT.
THAT'S RIGHT.
YOU PROBABLY FIND THAT HARD TO BELIEVE, SINCE GUYS ARE ALWAYS BEGGING TO HAVE SEX WITH YOU OR WHATEVER, BUT GUESS WHAT?
THOSE GUYS ARE FUCKING IDIOTS!
YOU'RE JUST SOME STUCK-UP SKANK NO ONE ACTUALLY LIKES, OR CARES ABOUT OR WHATEVER--SOME DUDES JUST WANNA USE YOU.
BECAUSE THAT'S LITERALLY ALL YOU'RE GOOD FOR.
SO WHY THE HELL SHOULD I EVER CARE WHAT SOME BITCH LIKE YOU THINKS OF ME?
FROM NOW ON, JUST FUCK OFF AND LEAVE ME ALONE, GOT IT?!!

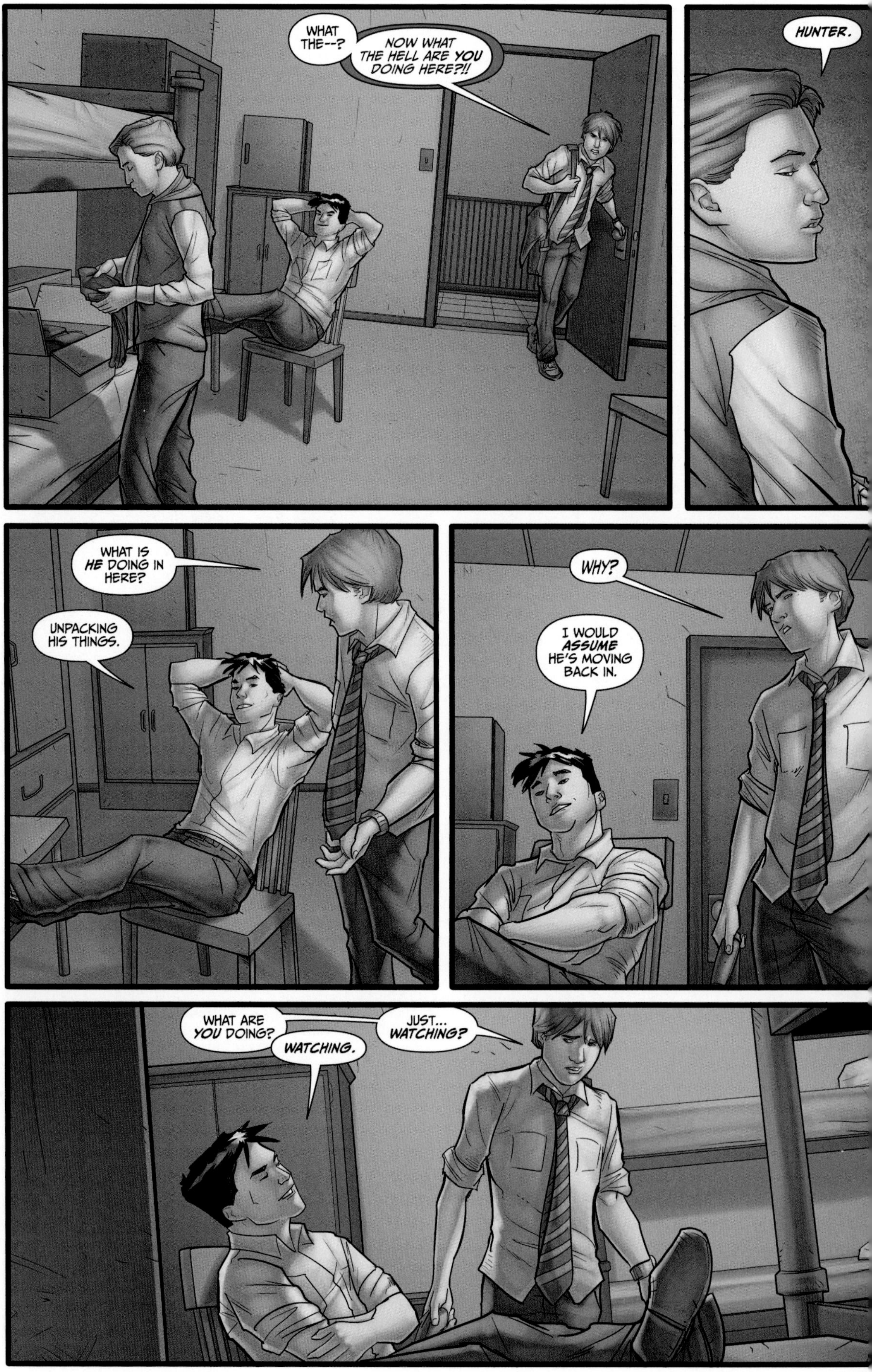
WHAT THE--?
NOW WHAT THE HELL ARE YOU DOING HERE?!!
HUNTER.
WHAT IS HE DOING IN HERE?
UNPACKING HIS THINGS.
WHY?
I WOULD ASSUME HE'S MOVING BACK IN.
WHAT ARE YOU DOING?
WATCHING.
JUST... WATCHING?

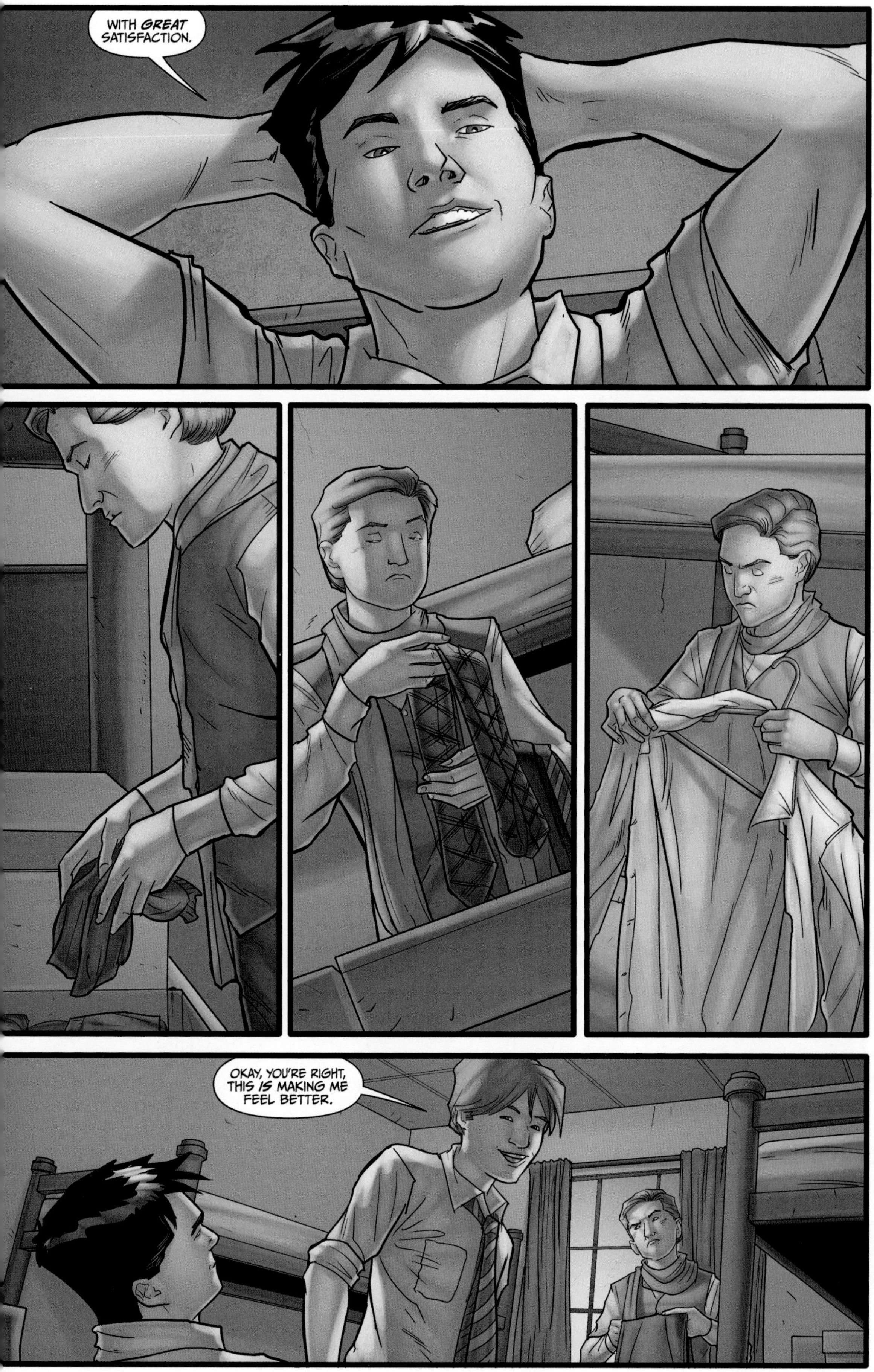
WITH GREAT SATISFACTION.
OKAY, YOU'RE RIGHT, THIS IS MAKING ME FEEL BETTER.

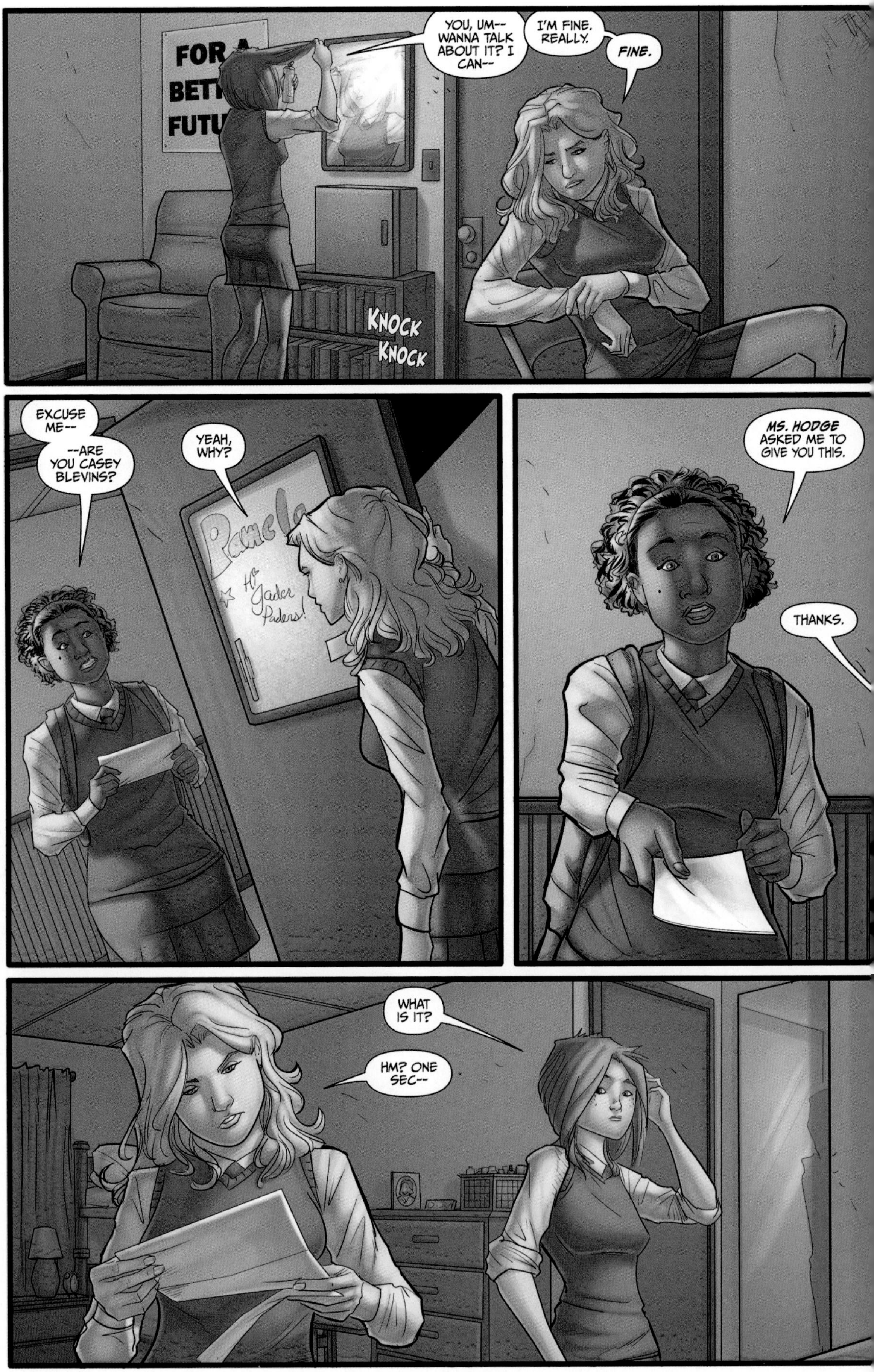
FOR A
BETT
FUTU
YOU, UM-- WANNA TALK ABOUT IT? I CAN--
I'M FINE. REALLY.
FINE.
KNOCK
KNOCK
EXCUSE ME--
--ARE YOU CASEY BLEVINS?
YEAH, WHY?
Pamela
Hi Jader Paders!
MS. HODGE ASKED ME TO GIVE YOU THIS.
THANKS.
WHAT IS IT?
HM? ONE SEC--

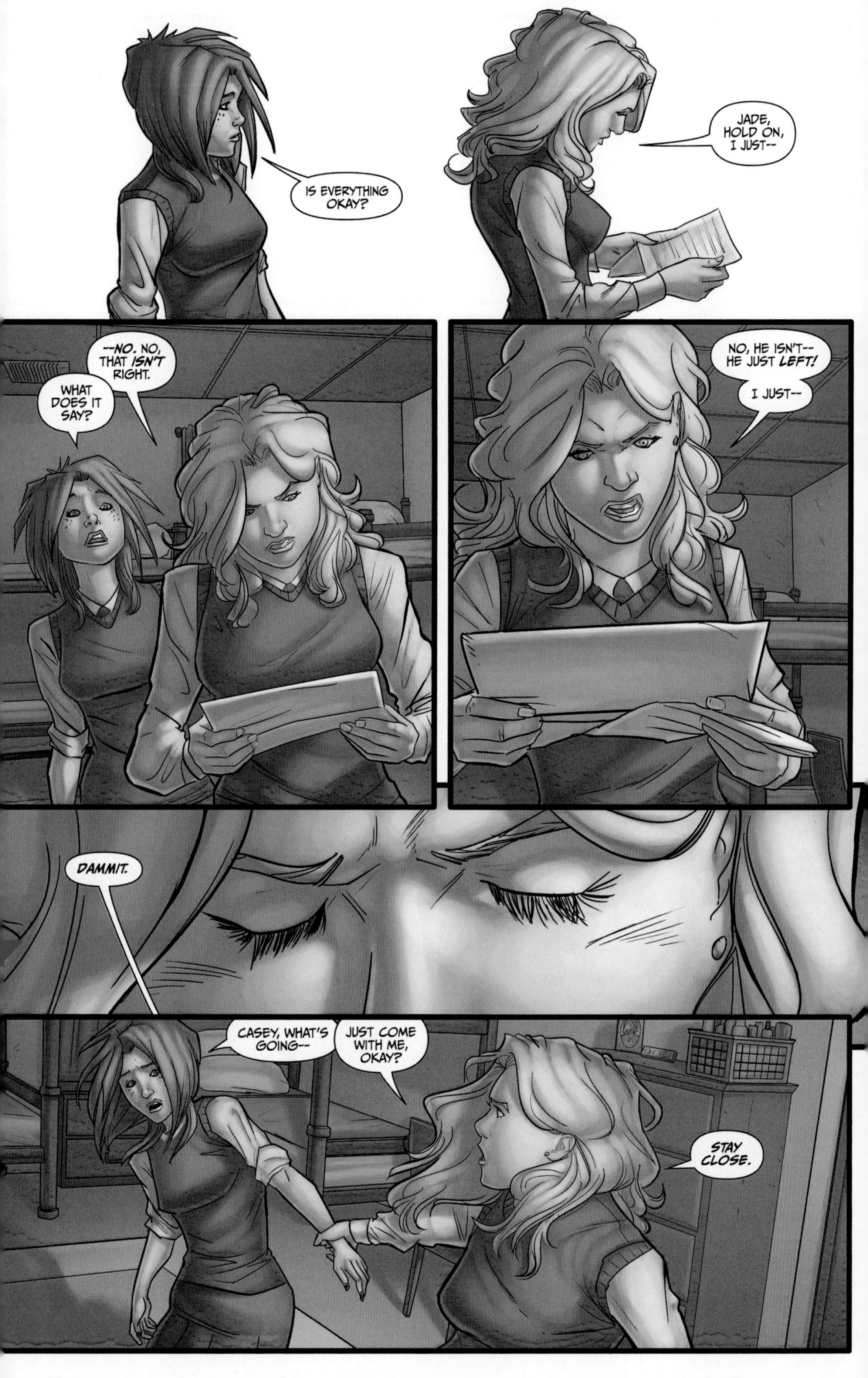
IS EVERYTHING OKAY?
JADE, HOLD ON, I JUST--
WHAT DOES IT SAY?
--NO. NO, THAT ISN'T RIGHT.
NO, HE ISN'T-- HE JUST LEFT!
I JUST--
DAMMIT.
CASEY, WHAT'S GOING--
JUST COME WITH ME, OKAY?
STAY CLOSE.

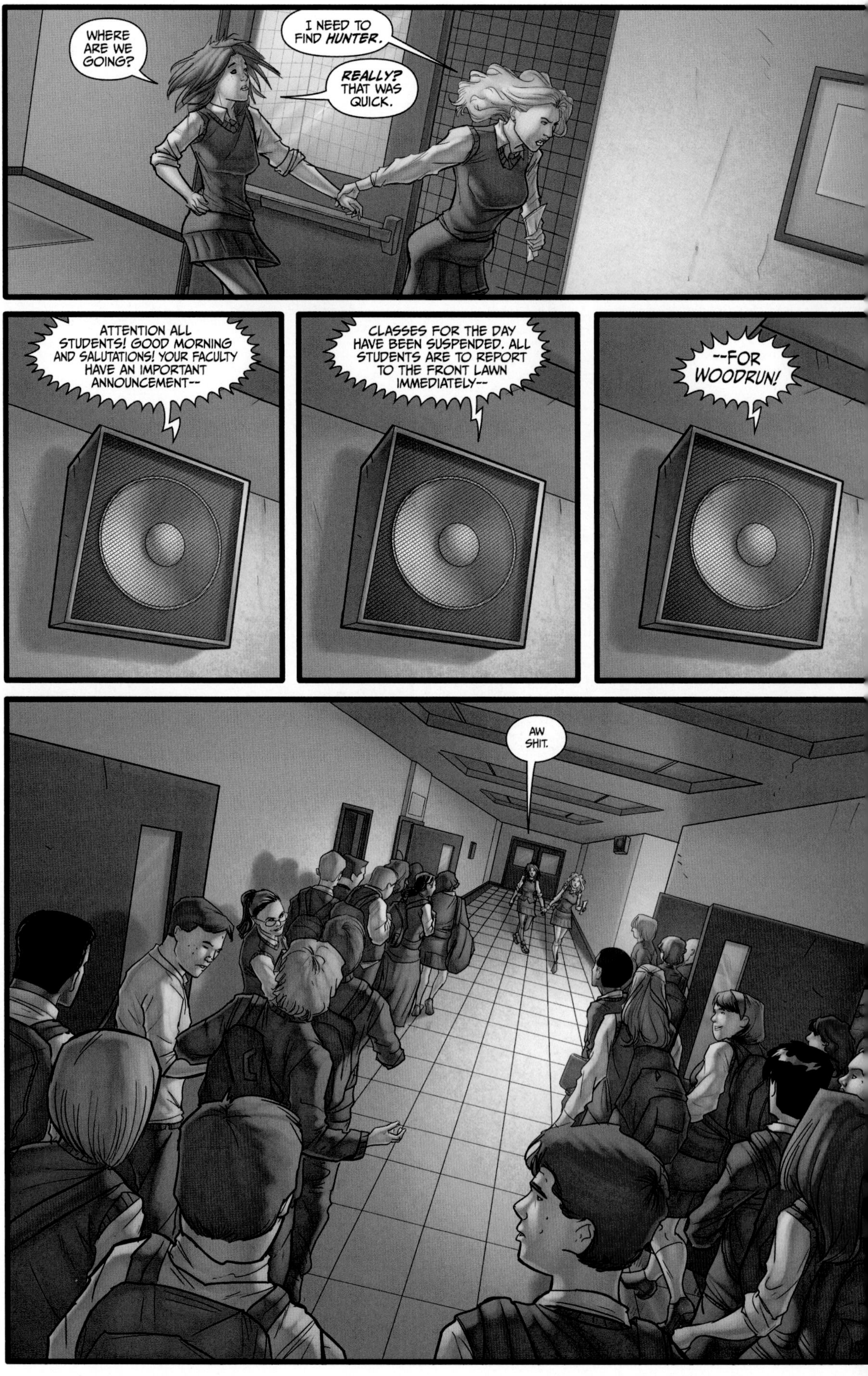
WHERE ARE WE GOING?
I NEED TO FIND *HUNTER*.
REALLY? THAT WAS QUICK.
ATTENTION ALL STUDENTS! GOOD MORNING AND SALUTATIONS! YOUR FACULTY HAVE AN IMPORTANT ANNOUNCEMENT--
CLASSES FOR THE DAY HAVE BEEN SUSPENDED. ALL STUDENTS ARE TO REPORT TO THE FRONT LAWN IMMEDIATELY--
--FOR WOODRUN!
AW SHIT.

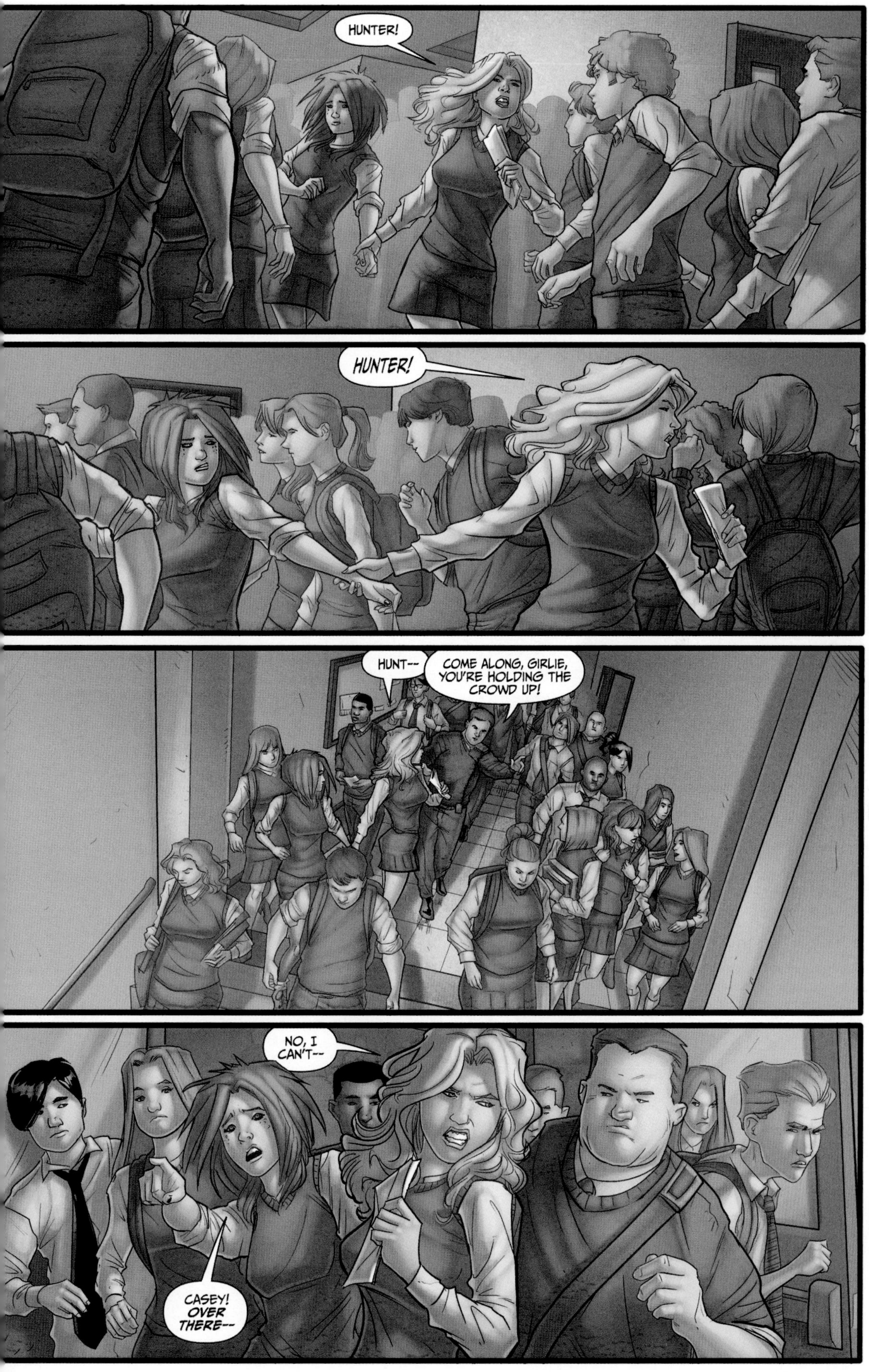
HUNTER!
HUNTER!
HUNT--
COME ALONG, GIRLIE, YOU'RE HOLDING THE CROWD UP!
NO, I CAN'T--
CASEY! OVER THERE--

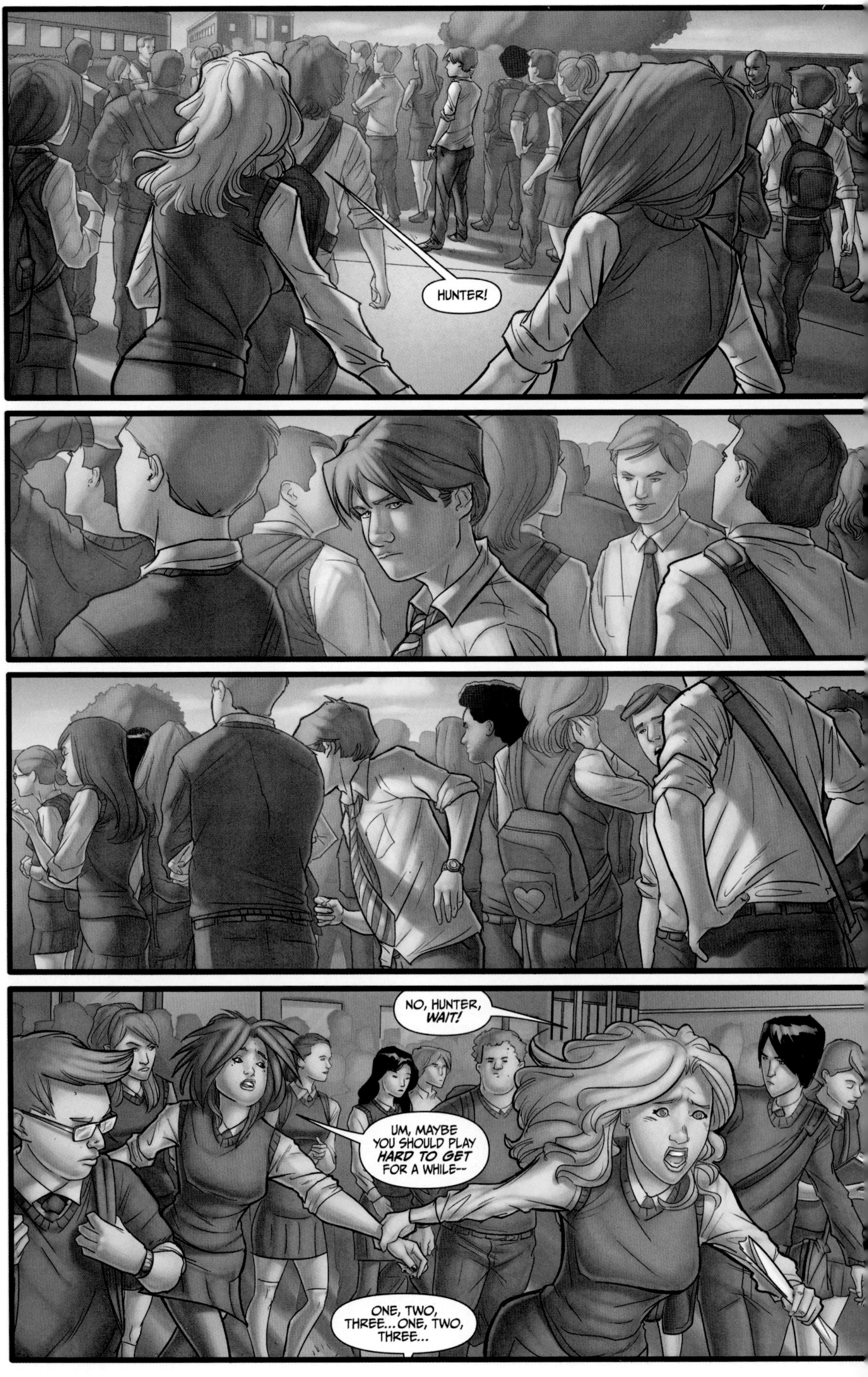
HUNTER!
NO, HUNTER, WAIT!
UM, MAYBE YOU SHOULD PLAY HARD TO GET FOR A WHILE--
ONE, TWO, THREE...ONE, TWO, THREE...

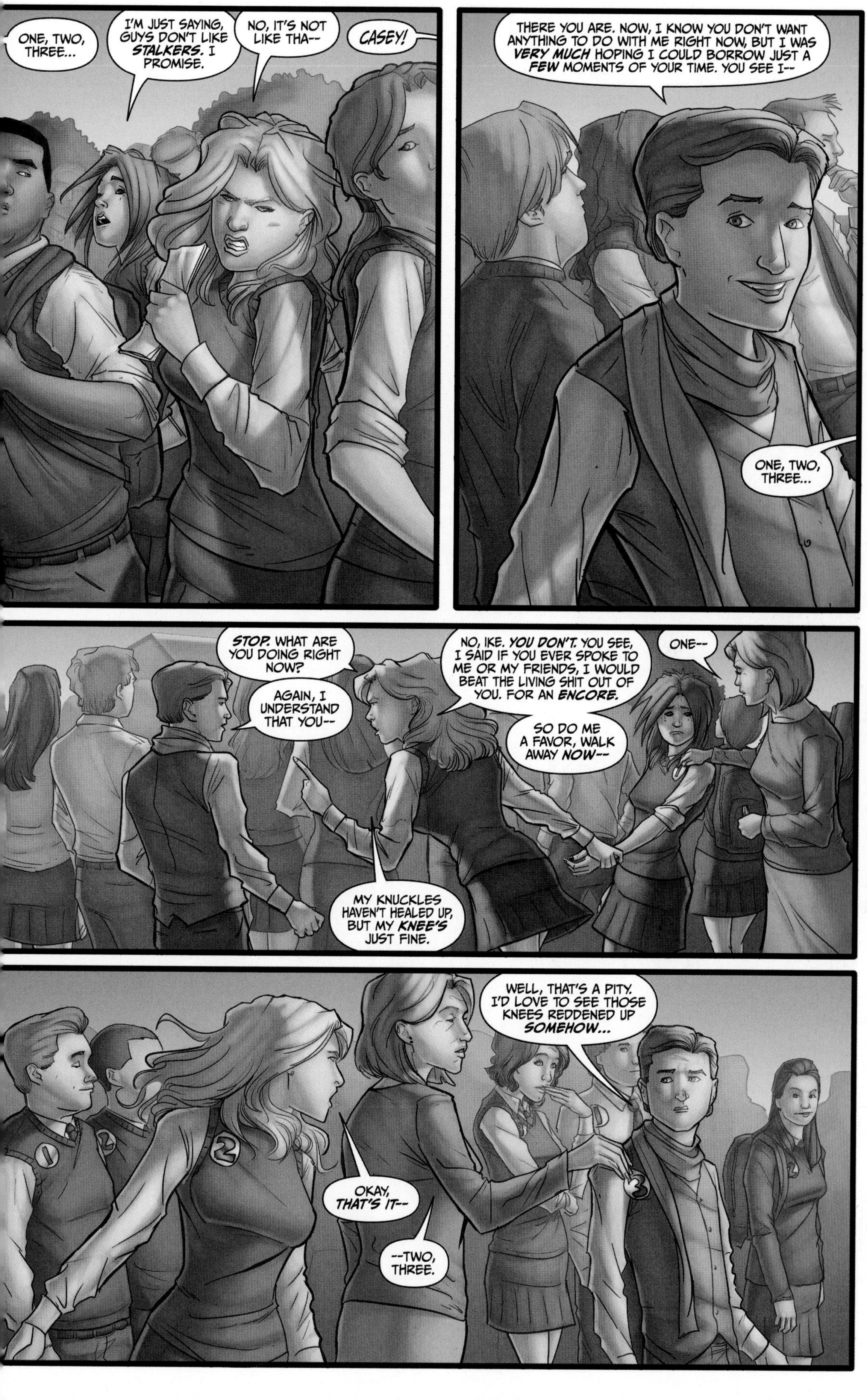
ONE, TWO, THREE...
I'M JUST SAYING, GUYS DON'T LIKE STALKERS. I PROMISE.
NO, IT'S NOT LIKE THA--
CASEY!
THERE YOU ARE. NOW, I KNOW YOU DON'T WANT ANYTHING TO DO WITH ME RIGHT NOW, BUT I WAS VERY MUCH HOPING I COULD BORROW JUST A FEW MOMENTS OF YOUR TIME. YOU SEE I--
ONE, TWO, THREE...
STOP. WHAT ARE YOU DOING RIGHT NOW?
AGAIN, I UNDERSTAND THAT YOU--
NO, IKE. YOU DON'T. YOU SEE, I SAID IF YOU EVER SPOKE TO ME OR MY FRIENDS, I WOULD BEAT THE LIVING SHIT OUT OF YOU. FOR AN ENCORE.
SO DO ME A FAVOR, WALK AWAY NOW--
ONE--
MY KNUCKLES HAVEN'T HEALED UP, BUT MY KNEE'S JUST FINE.
WELL, THAT'S A PITY. I'D LOVE TO SEE THOSE KNEES REDDENED UP SOMEHOW...
OKAY, THAT'S IT--
--TWO, THREE.

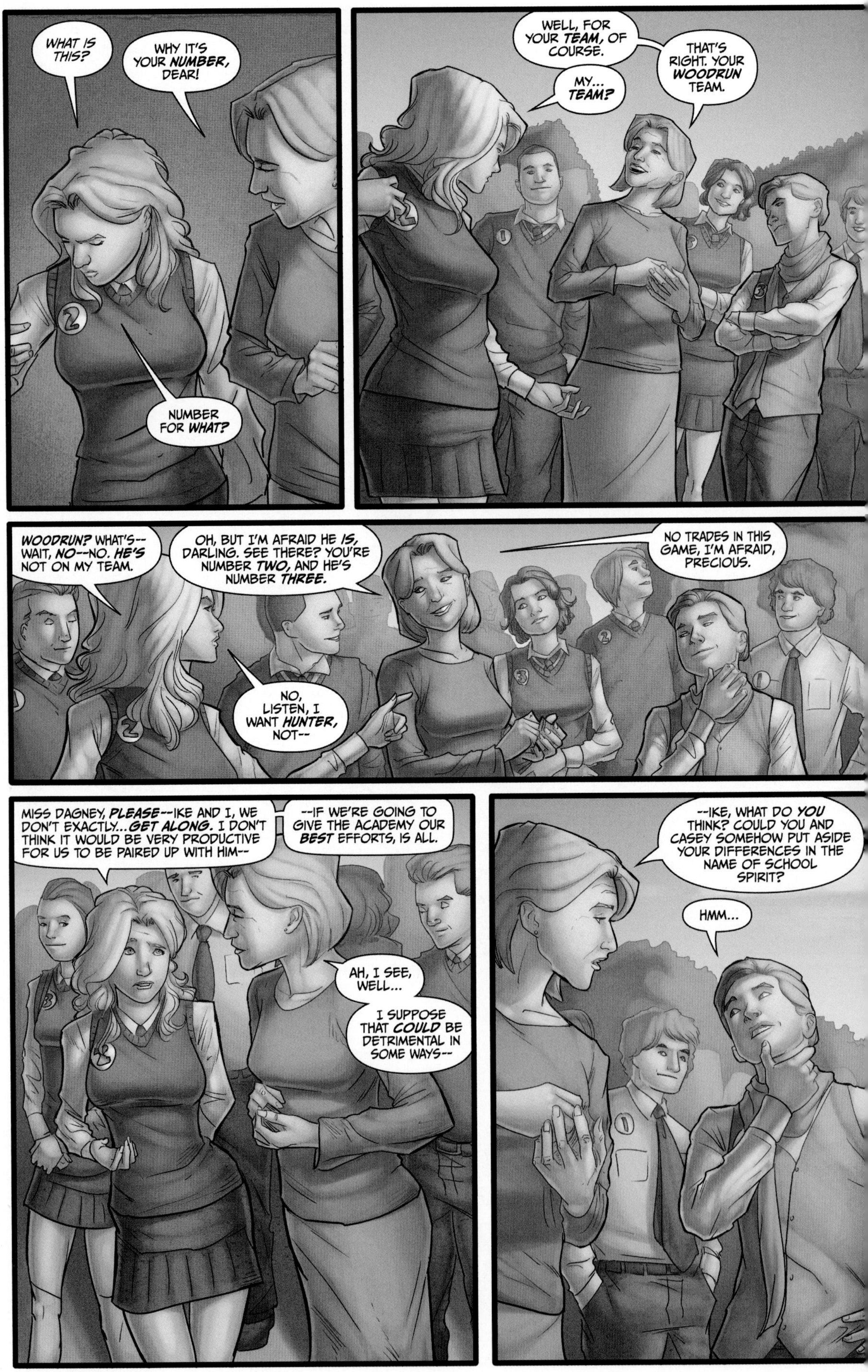

WHAT IS THIS?
WHY IT'S YOUR NUMBER, DEAR!
NUMBER FOR WHAT?
WELL, FOR YOUR TEAM, OF COURSE.
MY... TEAM?
THAT'S RIGHT. YOUR WOODRUN TEAM.
WOODRUN? WHAT'S-- WAIT, NO--NO. HE'S NOT ON MY TEAM.
OH, BUT I'M AFRAID HE IS, DARLING. SEE THERE? YOU'RE NUMBER TWO, AND HE'S NUMBER THREE.
NO, LISTEN, I WANT HUNTER, NOT--
NO TRADES IN THIS GAME, I'M AFRAID, PRECIOUS.
MISS DAGNEY, PLEASE--IKE AND I, WE DON'T EXACTLY...GET ALONG. I DON'T THINK IT WOULD BE VERY PRODUCTIVE FOR US TO BE PAIRED UP WITH HIM--
--IF WE'RE GOING TO GIVE THE ACADEMY OUR BEST EFFORTS, IS ALL.
AH, I SEE, WELL...
I SUPPOSE THAT COULD BE DETRIMENTAL IN SOME WAYS--
--IKE, WHAT DO YOU THINK? COULD YOU AND CASEY SOMEHOW PUT ASIDE YOUR DIFFERENCES IN THE NAME OF SCHOOL SPIRIT?
HMM...

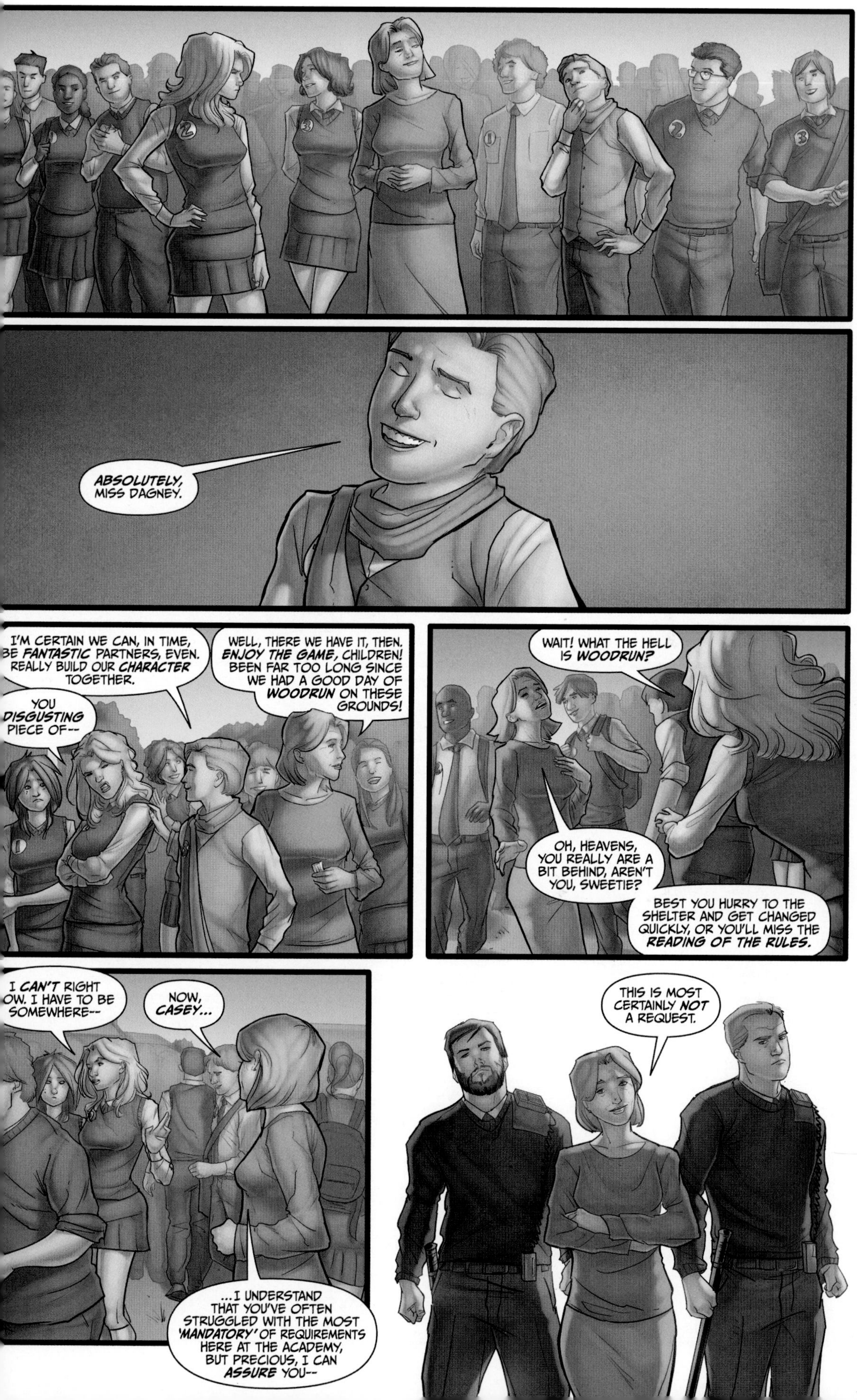
ABSOLUTELY, MISS DAGNEY.
I'M CERTAIN WE CAN, IN TIME, BE FANTASTIC PARTNERS, EVEN. REALLY BUILD OUR CHARACTER TOGETHER.
YOU DISGUSTING PIECE OF--
WELL, THERE WE HAVE IT, THEN. ENJOY THE GAME, CHILDREN! BEEN FAR TOO LONG SINCE WE HAD A GOOD DAY OF WOODRUN ON THESE GROUNDS!
WAIT! WHAT THE HELL IS WOODRUN?
OH, HEAVENS, YOU REALLY ARE A BIT BEHIND, AREN'T YOU, SWEETIE?
BEST YOU HURRY TO THE SHELTER AND GET CHANGED QUICKLY, OR YOU'LL MISS THE READING OF THE RULES.
I CAN'T RIGHT OW. I HAVE TO BE SOMEWHERE--
NOW, CASEY...
...I UNDERSTAND THAT YOU'VE OFTEN STRUGGLED WITH THE MOST 'MANDATORY' OF REQUIREMENTS HERE AT THE ACADEMY, BUT PRECIOUS, I CAN ASSURE YOU--
THIS IS MOST CERTAINLY NOT A REQUEST.

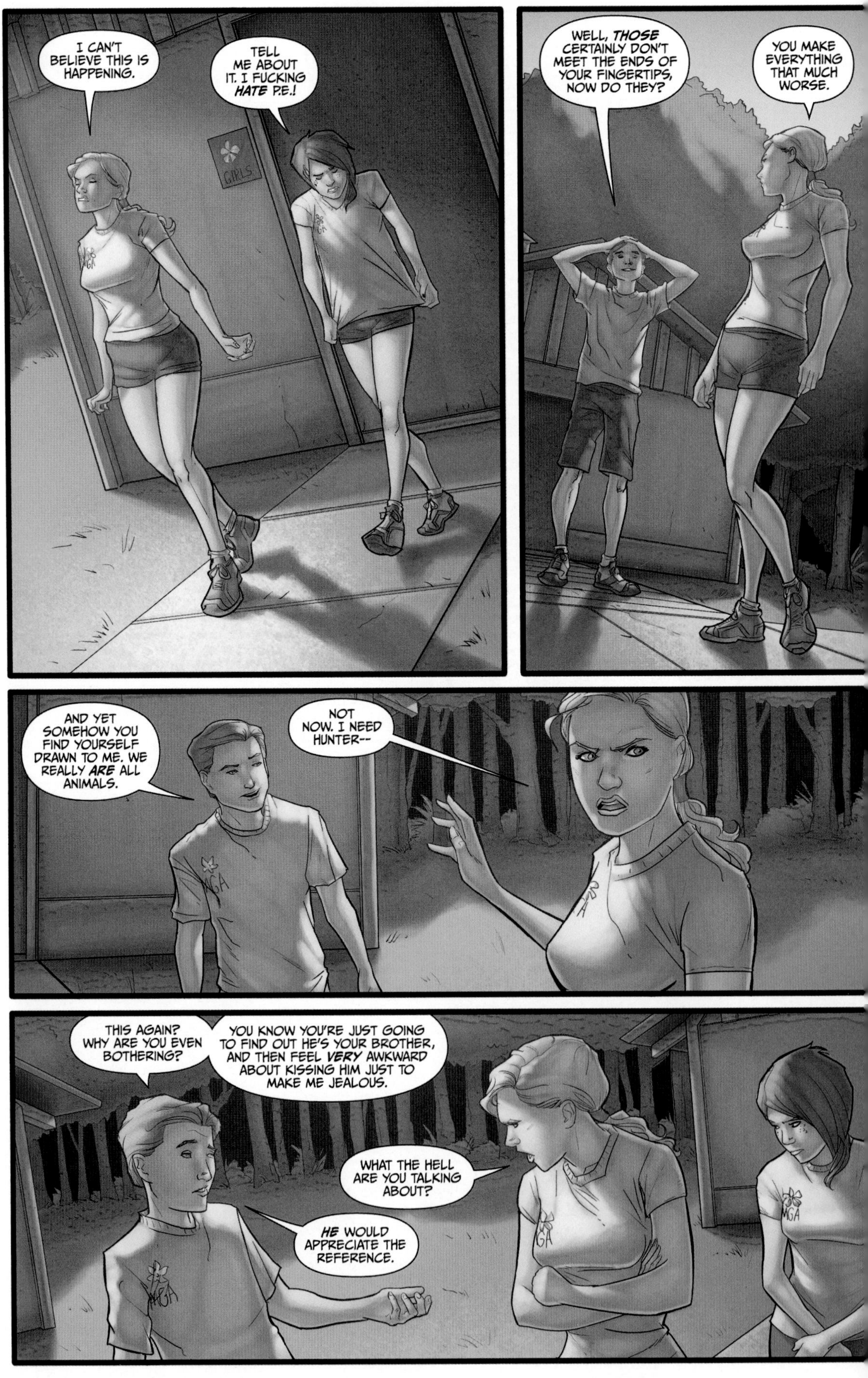
I CAN'T BELIEVE THIS IS HAPPENING.
TELL ME ABOUT IT. I FUCKING *HATE* P.E.!
WELL, *THOSE* CERTAINLY DON'T MEET THE ENDS OF YOUR FINGERTIPS, NOW DO THEY?
YOU MAKE EVERYTHING THAT MUCH WORSE.
AND YET SOMEHOW YOU FIND YOURSELF DRAWN TO ME. WE REALLY *ARE* ALL ANIMALS.
NOT NOW. I NEED HUNTER--
THIS AGAIN? WHY ARE YOU EVEN BOTHERING?
YOU KNOW YOU'RE JUST GOING TO FIND OUT HE'S YOUR BROTHER, AND THEN FEEL *VERY* AWKWARD ABOUT KISSING HIM JUST TO MAKE ME JEALOUS.
WHAT THE HELL ARE YOU TALKING ABOUT?
HE WOULD APPRECIATE THE REFERENCE.

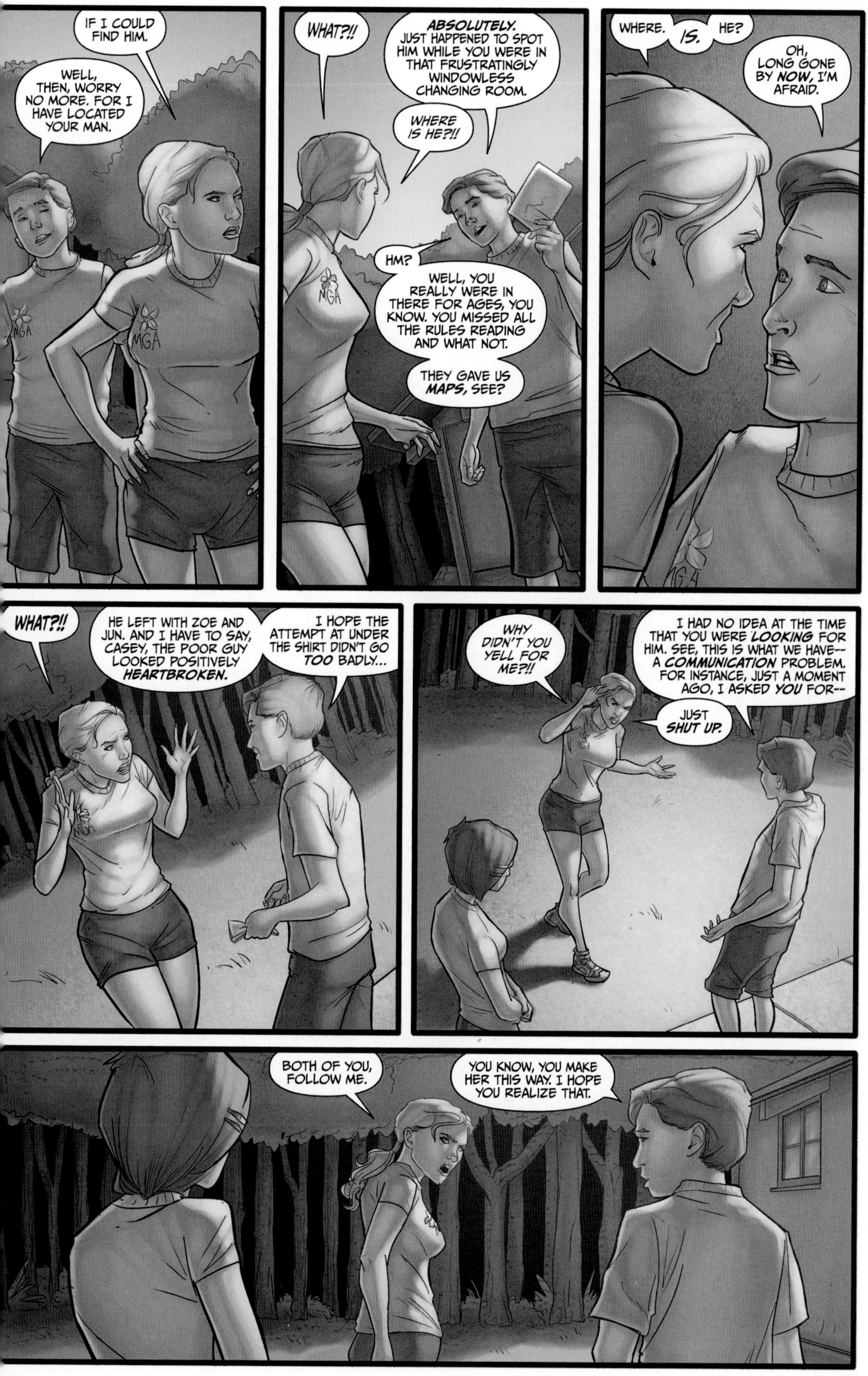
IF I COULD FIND HIM.
WELL, THEN, WORRY NO MORE. FOR I HAVE LOCATED YOUR MAN.
WHAT?!!
ABSOLUTELY. JUST HAPPENED TO SPOT HIM WHILE YOU WERE IN THAT FRUSTRATINGLY WINDOWLESS CHANGING ROOM.
WHERE IS HE?!!
HM?
WELL, YOU REALLY WERE IN THERE FOR AGES, YOU KNOW. YOU MISSED ALL THE RULES READING AND WHAT NOT.
THEY GAVE US MAPS, SEE?
MGA
WHERE. IS. HE?
OH, LONG GONE BY NOW, I'M AFRAID.
WHAT?!!
HE LEFT WITH ZOE AND JUN. AND I HAVE TO SAY, CASEY, THE POOR GUY LOOKED POSITIVELY HEARTBROKEN.
I HOPE THE ATTEMPT AT UNDER THE SHIRT DIDN'T GO TOO BADLY...
WHY DIDN'T YOU YELL FOR ME?!!
I HAD NO IDEA AT THE TIME THAT YOU WERE LOOKING FOR HIM. SEE, THIS IS WHAT WE HAVE-- A COMMUNICATION PROBLEM. FOR INSTANCE, JUST A MOMENT AGO, I ASKED YOU FOR--
JUST SHUT UP.
BOTH OF YOU, FOLLOW ME.
YOU KNOW, YOU MAKE HER THIS WAY. I HOPE YOU REALIZE THAT.

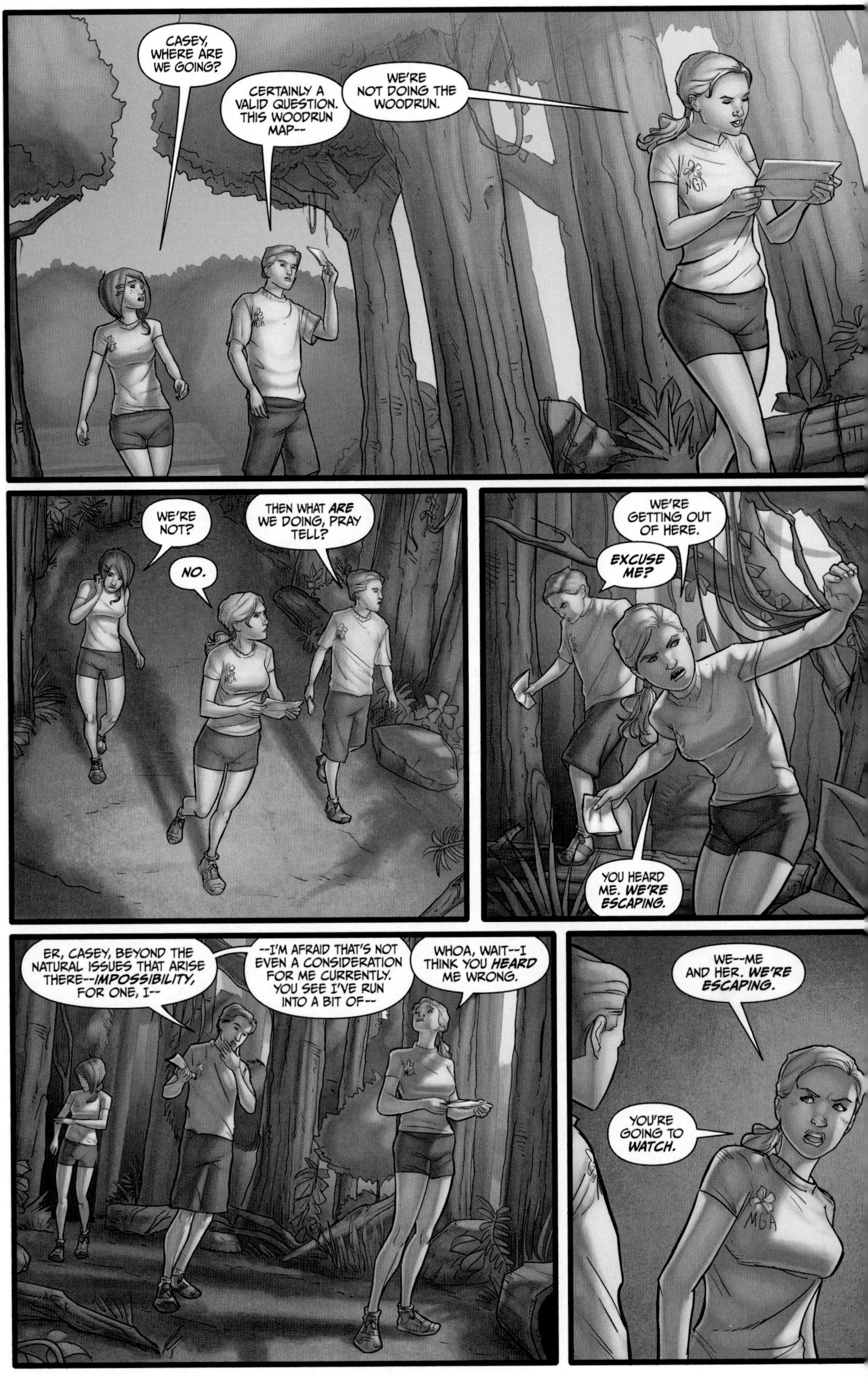
CASEY, WHERE ARE WE GOING?
CERTAINLY A VALID QUESTION. THIS WOODRUN MAP--
WE'RE NOT DOING THE WOODRUN.
WE'RE NOT?
THEN WHAT ARE WE DOING, PRAY TELL?
NO.
WE'RE GETTING OUT OF HERE.
EXCUSE ME?
YOU HEARD ME. WE'RE ESCAPING.
ER, CASEY, BEYOND THE NATURAL ISSUES THAT ARISE THERE--IMPOSSIBILITY, FOR ONE, I--
--I'M AFRAID THAT'S NOT EVEN A CONSIDERATION FOR ME CURRENTLY. YOU SEE I'VE RUN INTO A BIT OF--
WHOA, WAIT--I THINK YOU HEARD ME WRONG.
WE--ME AND HER. WE'RE ESCAPING.
YOU'RE GOING TO WATCH.

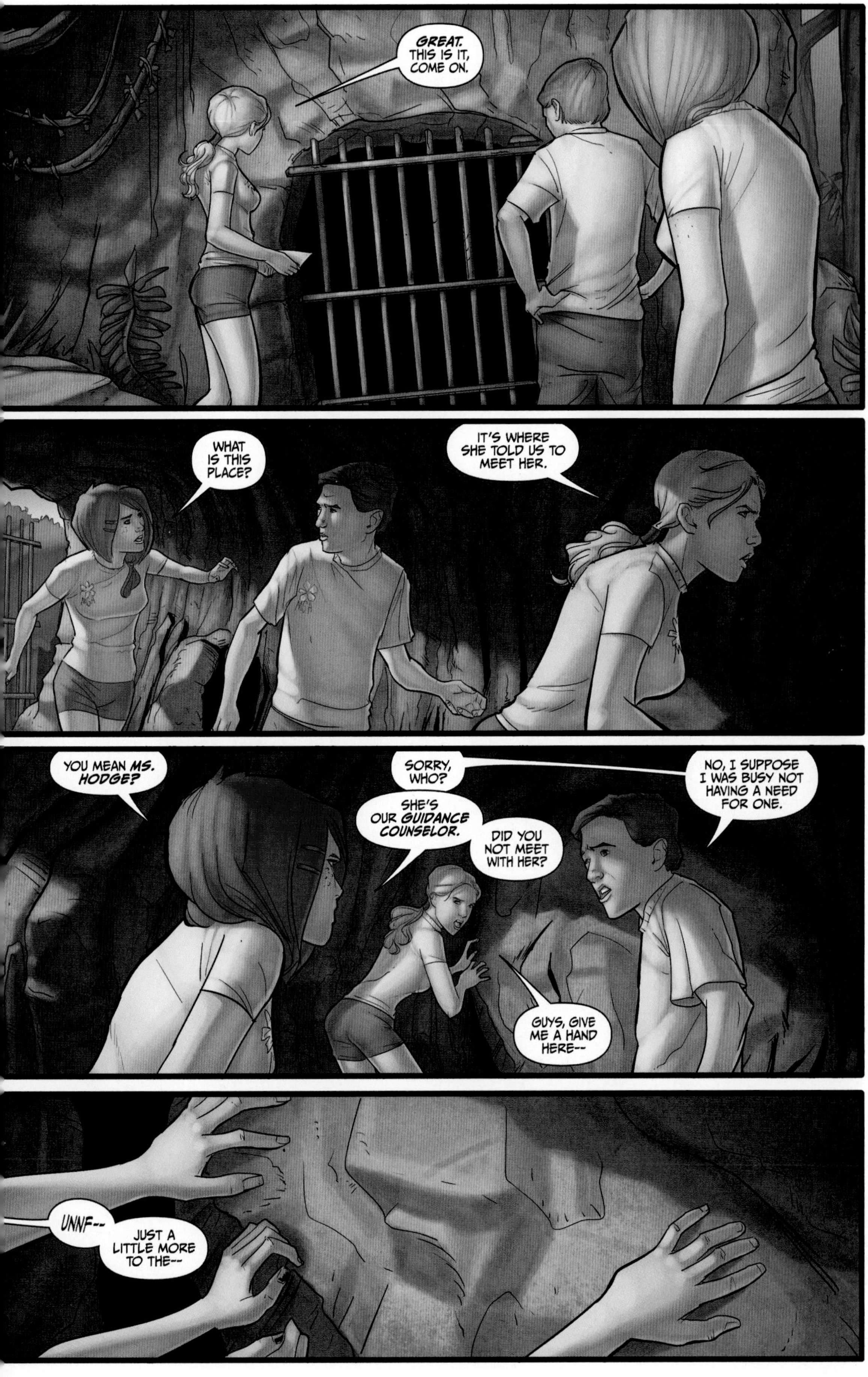
GREAT. THIS IS IT, COME ON.
WHAT IS THIS PLACE?
IT'S WHERE SHE TOLD US TO MEET HER.
YOU MEAN MS. HODGE?
SORRY, WHO?
SHE'S OUR GUIDANCE COUNSELOR.
DID YOU NOT MEET WITH HER?
NO, I SUPPOSE I WAS BUSY NOT HAVING A NEED FOR ONE.
GUYS, GIVE ME A HAND HERE--
UNNF--
JUST A LITTLE MORE TO THE--

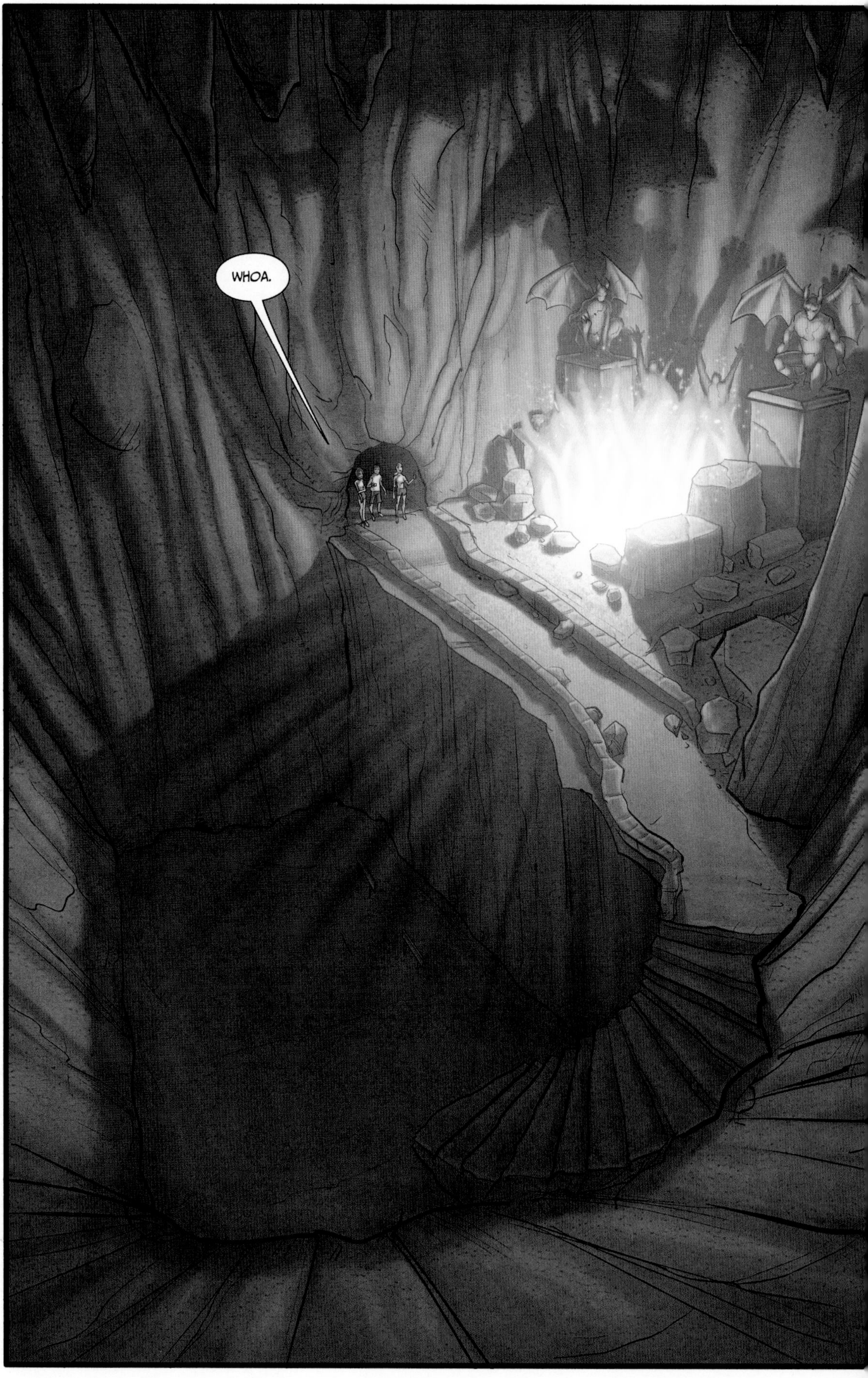
WHOA.

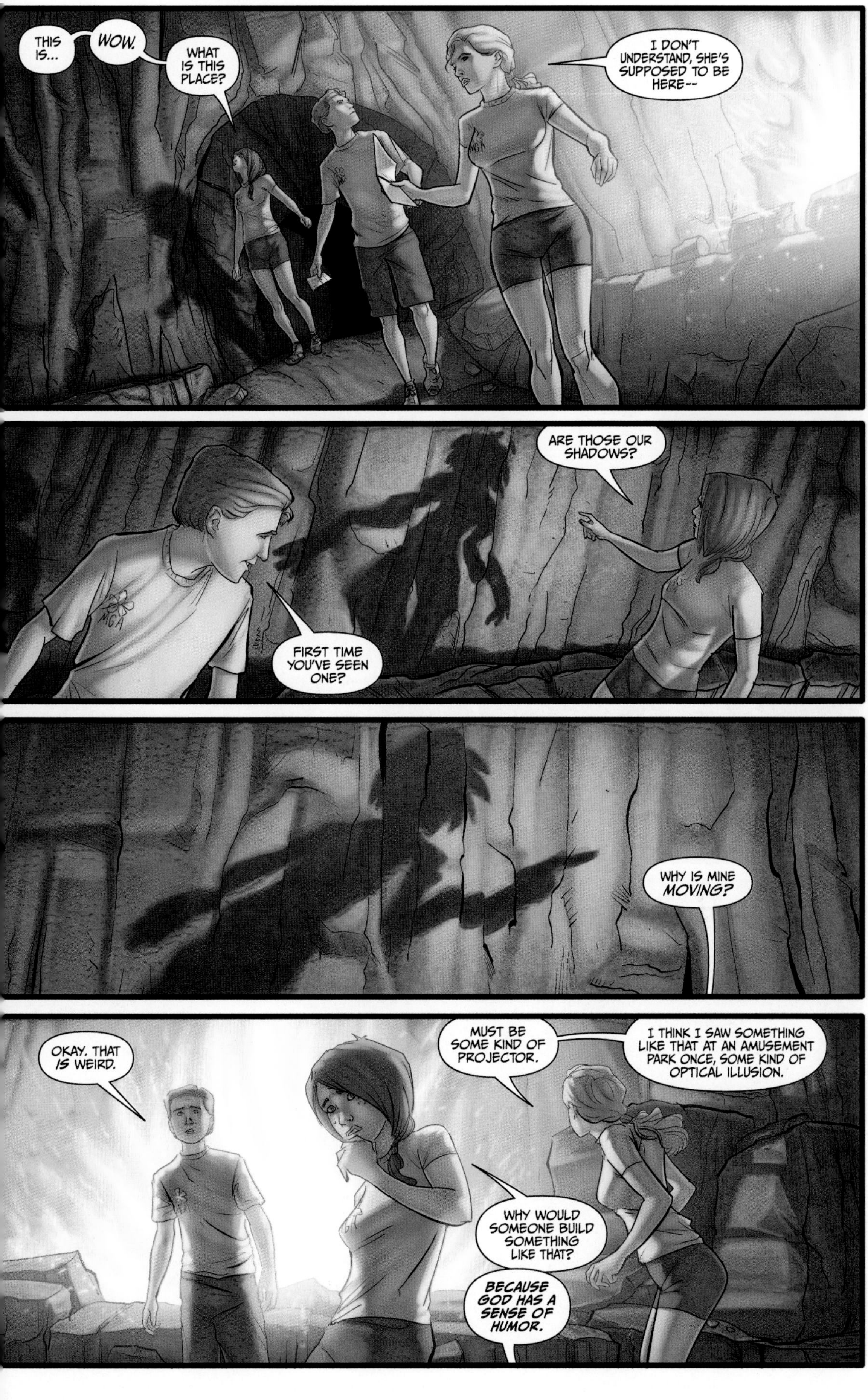
THIS IS...
WOW.
WHAT IS THIS PLACE?
I DON'T UNDERSTAND, SHE'S SUPPOSED TO BE HERE--
ARE THOSE OUR SHADOWS?
FIRST TIME YOU'VE SEEN ONE?
WHY IS MINE *MOVING?*
OKAY. THAT *IS* WEIRD.
MUST BE SOME KIND OF PROJECTOR.
I THINK I SAW SOMETHING LIKE THAT AT AN AMUSEMENT PARK ONCE, SOME KIND OF OPTICAL ILLUSION.
WHY WOULD SOMEONE BUILD SOMETHING LIKE THAT?
BECAUSE GOD HAS A SENSE OF HUMOR.

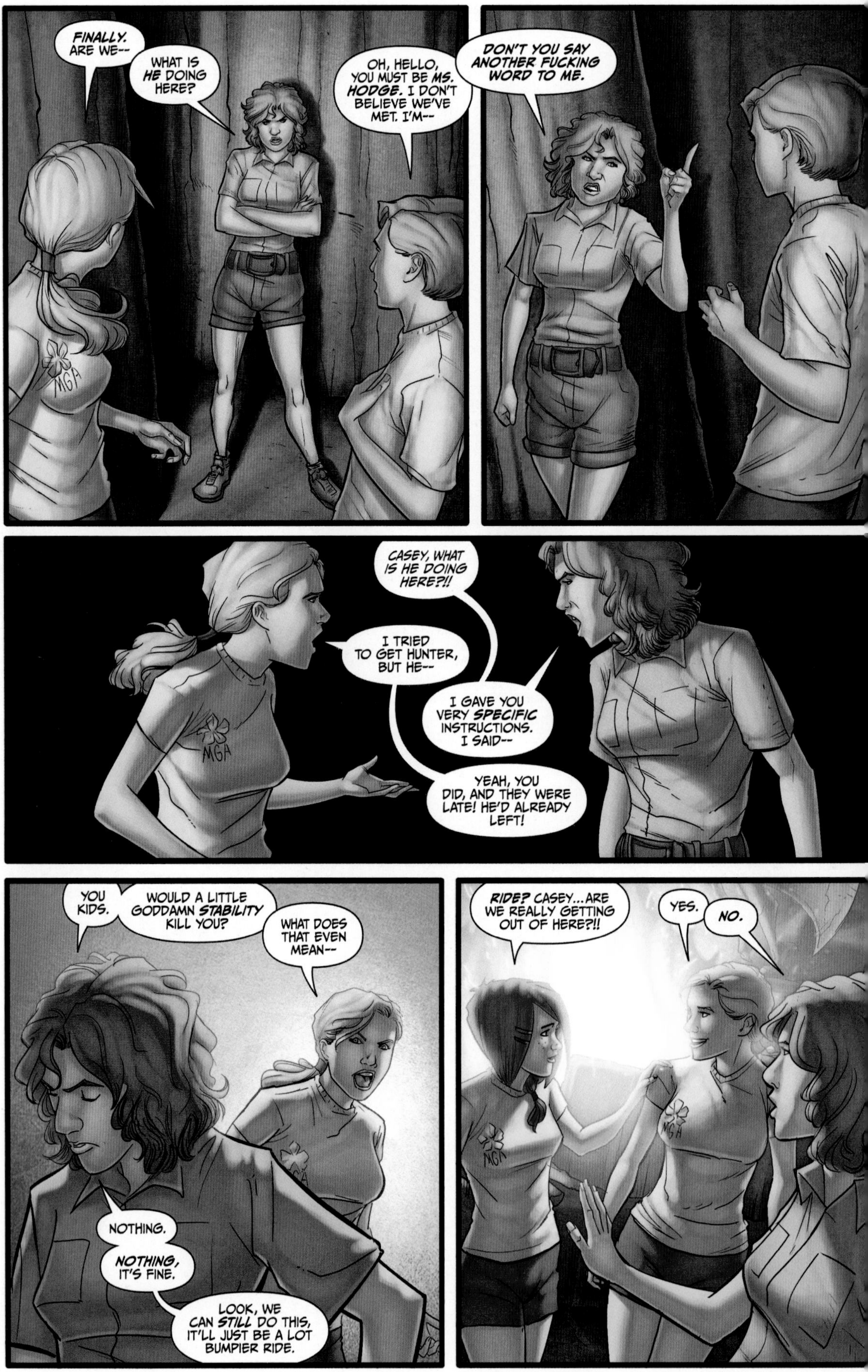

FINALLY. ARE WE--
WHAT IS HE DOING HERE?
OH, HELLO, YOU MUST BE MS. HODGE. I DON'T BELIEVE WE'VE MET. I'M--
DON'T YOU SAY ANOTHER FUCKING WORD TO ME.
CASEY, WHAT IS HE DOING HERE?!!
I TRIED TO GET HUNTER, BUT HE--
I GAVE YOU VERY SPECIFIC INSTRUCTIONS. I SAID--
YEAH, YOU DID, AND THEY WERE LATE! HE'D ALREADY LEFT!
YOU KIDS.
WOULD A LITTLE GODDAMN STABILITY KILL YOU?
WHAT DOES THAT EVEN MEAN--
NOTHING.
NOTHING, IT'S FINE.
LOOK, WE CAN STILL DO THIS, IT'LL JUST BE A LOT BUMPIER RIDE.
RIDE? CASEY...ARE WE REALLY GETTING OUT OF HERE?!!
YES.
NO.

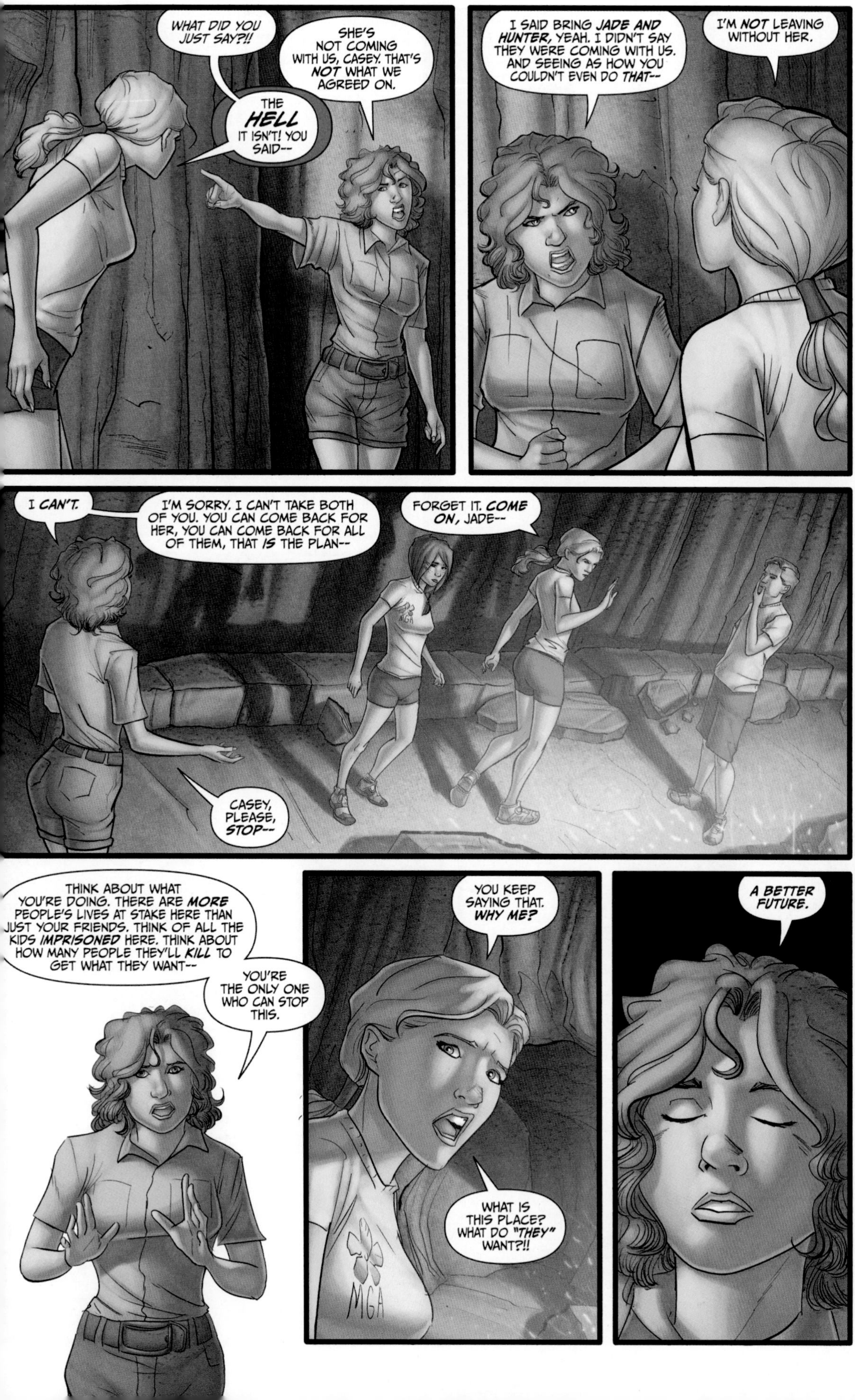
WHAT DID YOU JUST SAY?!!
SHE'S NOT COMING WITH US, CASEY. THAT'S NOT WHAT WE AGREED ON.
THE HELL IT ISN'T! YOU SAID--
I SAID BRING JADE AND HUNTER, YEAH. I DIDN'T SAY THEY WERE COMING WITH US. AND SEEING AS HOW YOU COULDN'T EVEN DO THAT--
I'M NOT LEAVING WITHOUT HER.
I CAN'T.
I'M SORRY. I CAN'T TAKE BOTH OF YOU. YOU CAN COME BACK FOR HER, YOU CAN COME BACK FOR ALL OF THEM, THAT IS THE PLAN--
FORGET IT. COME ON, JADE--
CASEY, PLEASE, STOP--
THINK ABOUT WHAT YOU'RE DOING. THERE ARE MORE PEOPLE'S LIVES AT STAKE HERE THAN JUST YOUR FRIENDS. THINK OF ALL THE KIDS IMPRISONED HERE. THINK ABOUT HOW MANY PEOPLE THEY'LL KILL TO GET WHAT THEY WANT--
YOU'RE THE ONLY ONE WHO CAN STOP THIS.
YOU KEEP SAYING THAT. WHY ME?
WHAT IS THIS PLACE? WHAT DO "THEY" WANT?!!
A BETTER FUTURE.

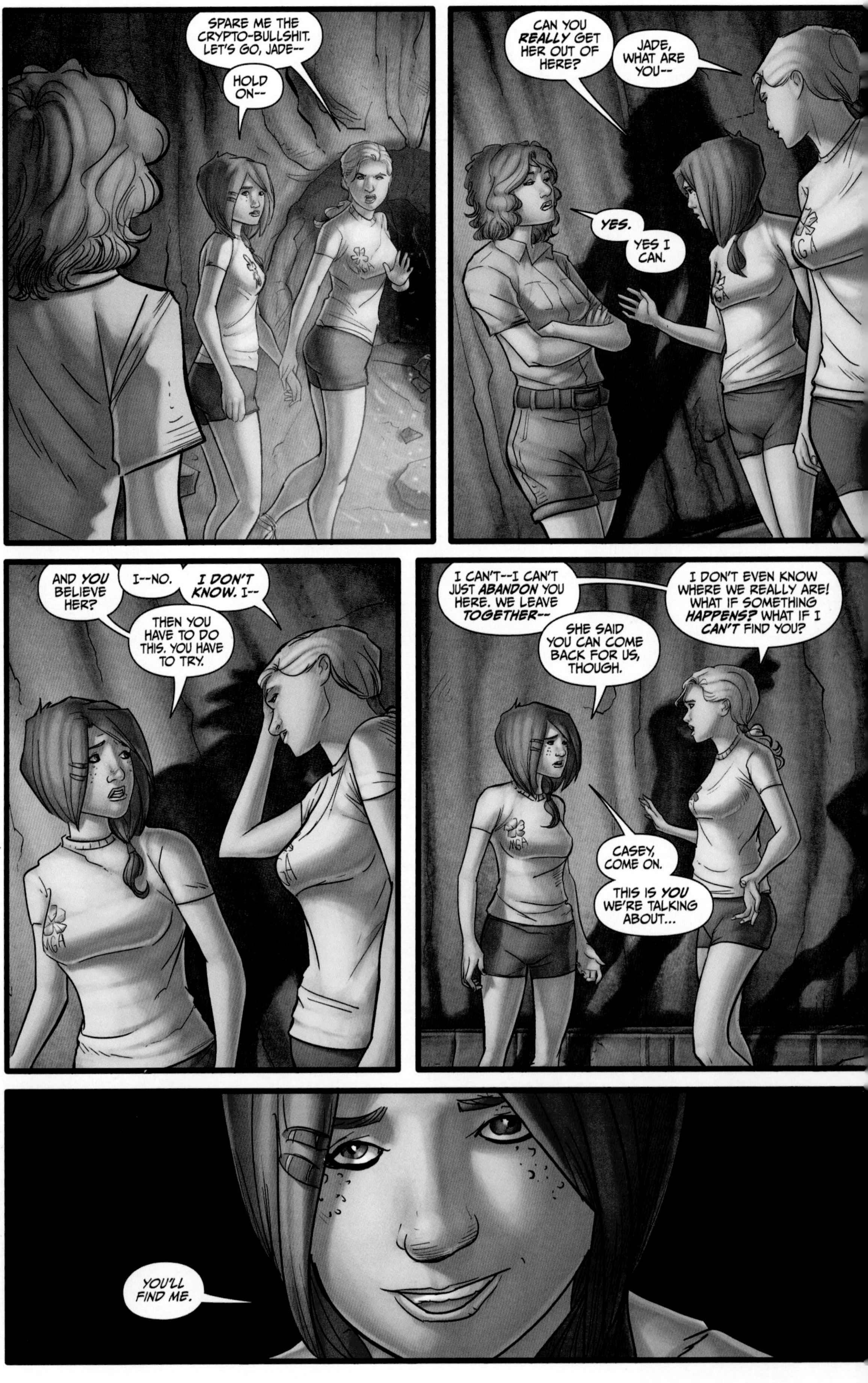
SPARE ME THE CRYPTO-BULLSHIT. LET'S GO, JADE--
HOLD ON--
CAN YOU REALLY GET HER OUT OF HERE?
JADE, WHAT ARE YOU--
YES.
YES I CAN.
AND YOU BELIEVE HER?
I--NO.
I DON'T KNOW. I--
THEN YOU HAVE TO DO THIS. YOU HAVE TO TRY.
I CAN'T--I CAN'T JUST ABANDON YOU HERE. WE LEAVE TOGETHER--
I DON'T EVEN KNOW WHERE WE REALLY ARE! WHAT IF SOMETHING HAPPENS? WHAT IF I CAN'T FIND YOU?
SHE SAID YOU CAN COME BACK FOR US, THOUGH.
CASEY, COME ON.
THIS IS YOU WE'RE TALKING ABOUT...
YOU'LL FIND ME.

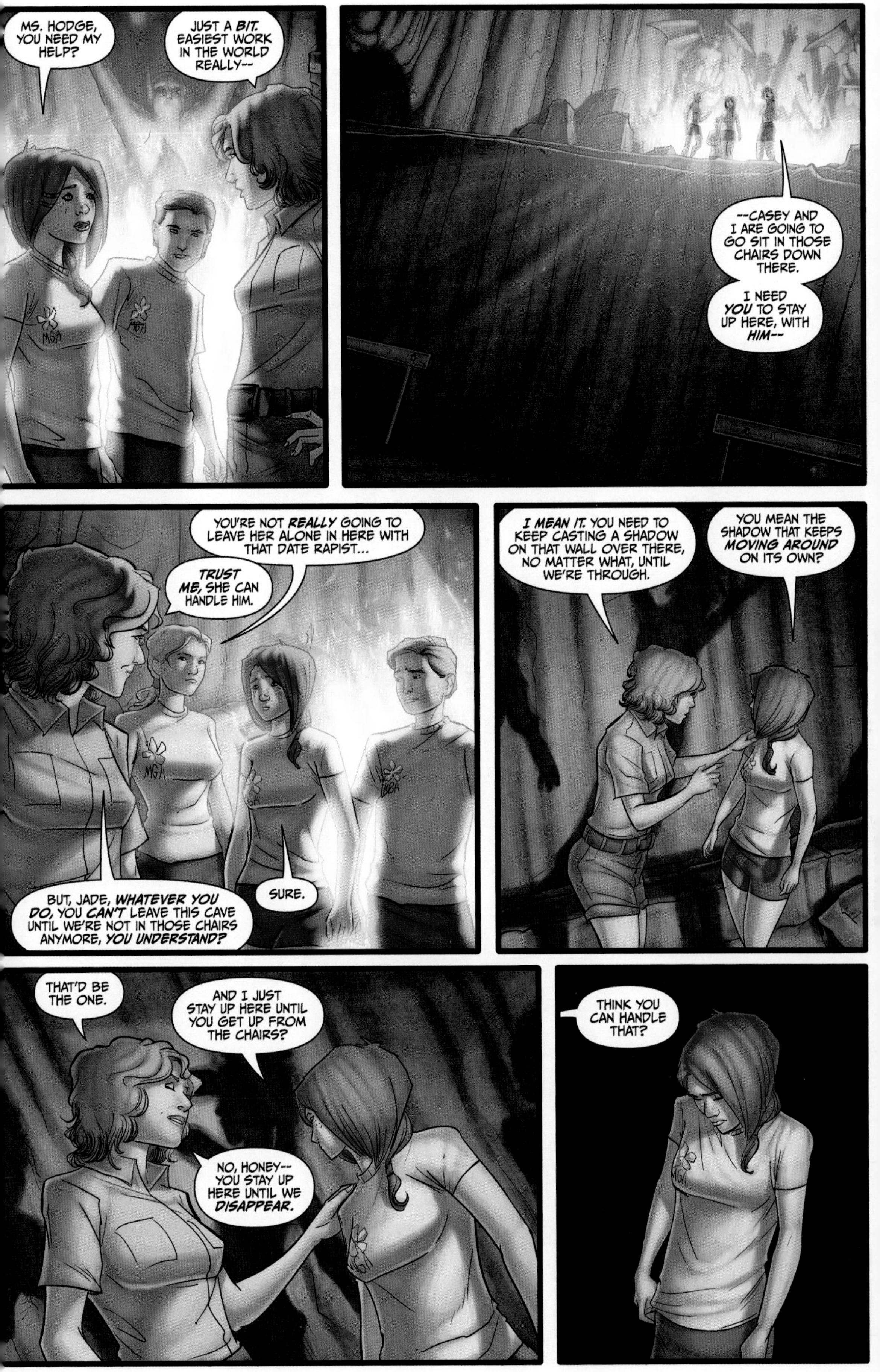

MS. HODGE, YOU NEED MY HELP?
JUST A BIT. EASIEST WORK IN THE WORLD REALLY--
--CASEY AND I ARE GOING TO GO SIT IN THOSE CHAIRS DOWN THERE.
I NEED YOU TO STAY UP HERE, WITH HIM--
YOU'RE NOT REALLY GOING TO LEAVE HER ALONE IN HERE WITH THAT DATE RAPIST...
TRUST ME, SHE CAN HANDLE HIM.
BUT, JADE, WHATEVER YOU DO, YOU CAN'T LEAVE THIS CAVE UNTIL WE'RE NOT IN THOSE CHAIRS ANYMORE, YOU UNDERSTAND?
SURE.
I MEAN IT. YOU NEED TO KEEP CASTING A SHADOW ON THAT WALL OVER THERE, NO MATTER WHAT, UNTIL WE'RE THROUGH.
YOU MEAN THE SHADOW THAT KEEPS MOVING AROUND ON ITS OWN?
THAT'D BE THE ONE.
AND I JUST STAY UP HERE UNTIL YOU GET UP FROM THE CHAIRS?
NO, HONEY-- YOU STAY UP HERE UNTIL WE DISAPPEAR.
THINK YOU CAN HANDLE THAT?

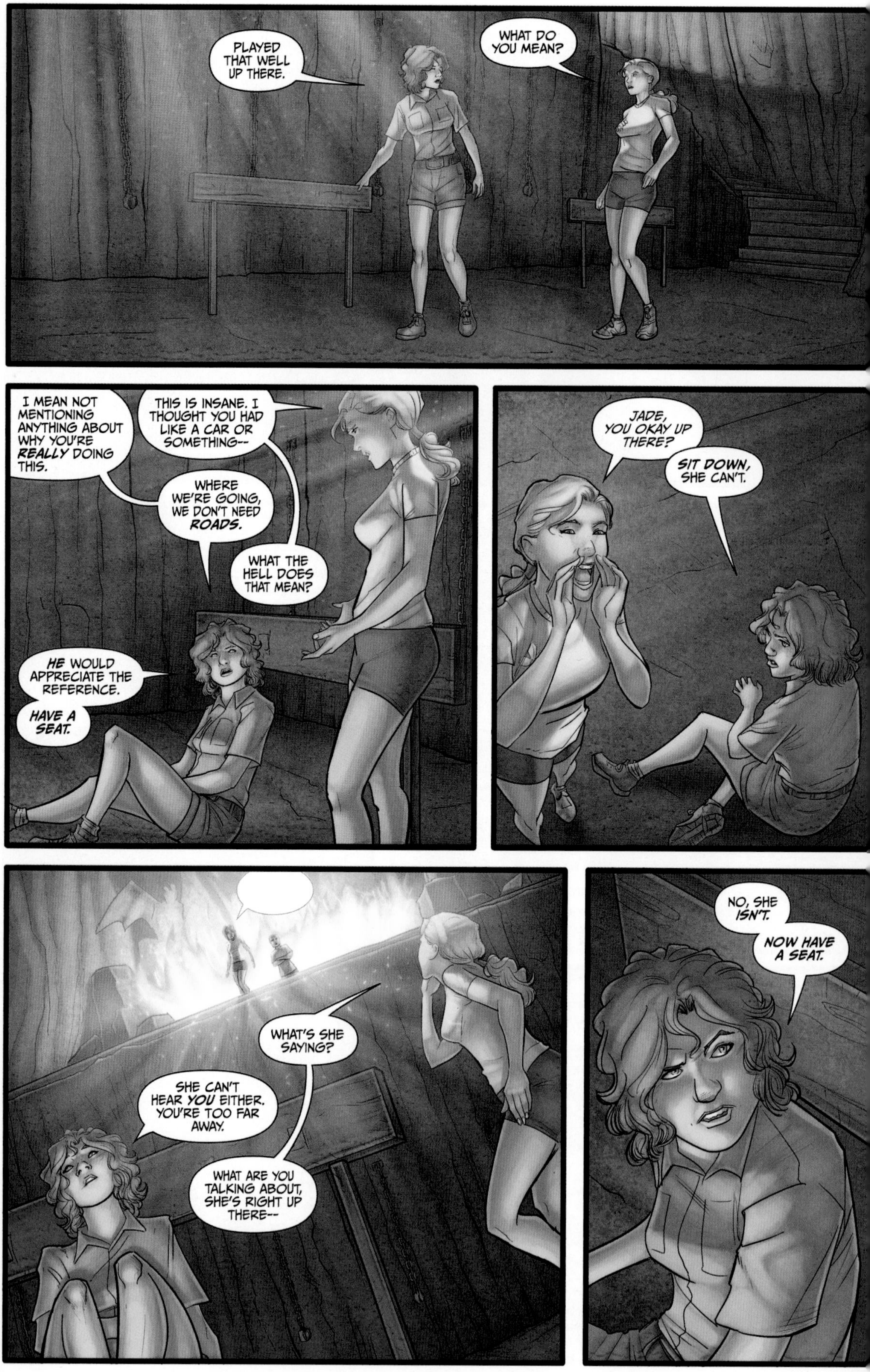
PLAYED THAT WELL UP THERE.
WHAT DO YOU MEAN?
I MEAN NOT MENTIONING ANYTHING ABOUT WHY YOU'RE REALLY DOING THIS.
THIS IS INSANE. I THOUGHT YOU HAD LIKE A CAR OR SOMETHING--
WHERE WE'RE GOING, WE DON'T NEED ROADS.
WHAT THE HELL DOES THAT MEAN?
HE WOULD APPRECIATE THE REFERENCE.
HAVE A SEAT.
JADE, YOU OKAY UP THERE?
SIT DOWN, SHE CAN'T.
WHAT'S SHE SAYING?
SHE CAN'T HEAR YOU EITHER. YOU'RE TOO FAR AWAY.
WHAT ARE YOU TALKING ABOUT, SHE'S RIGHT UP THERE--
NO, SHE ISN'T.
NOW HAVE A SEAT.

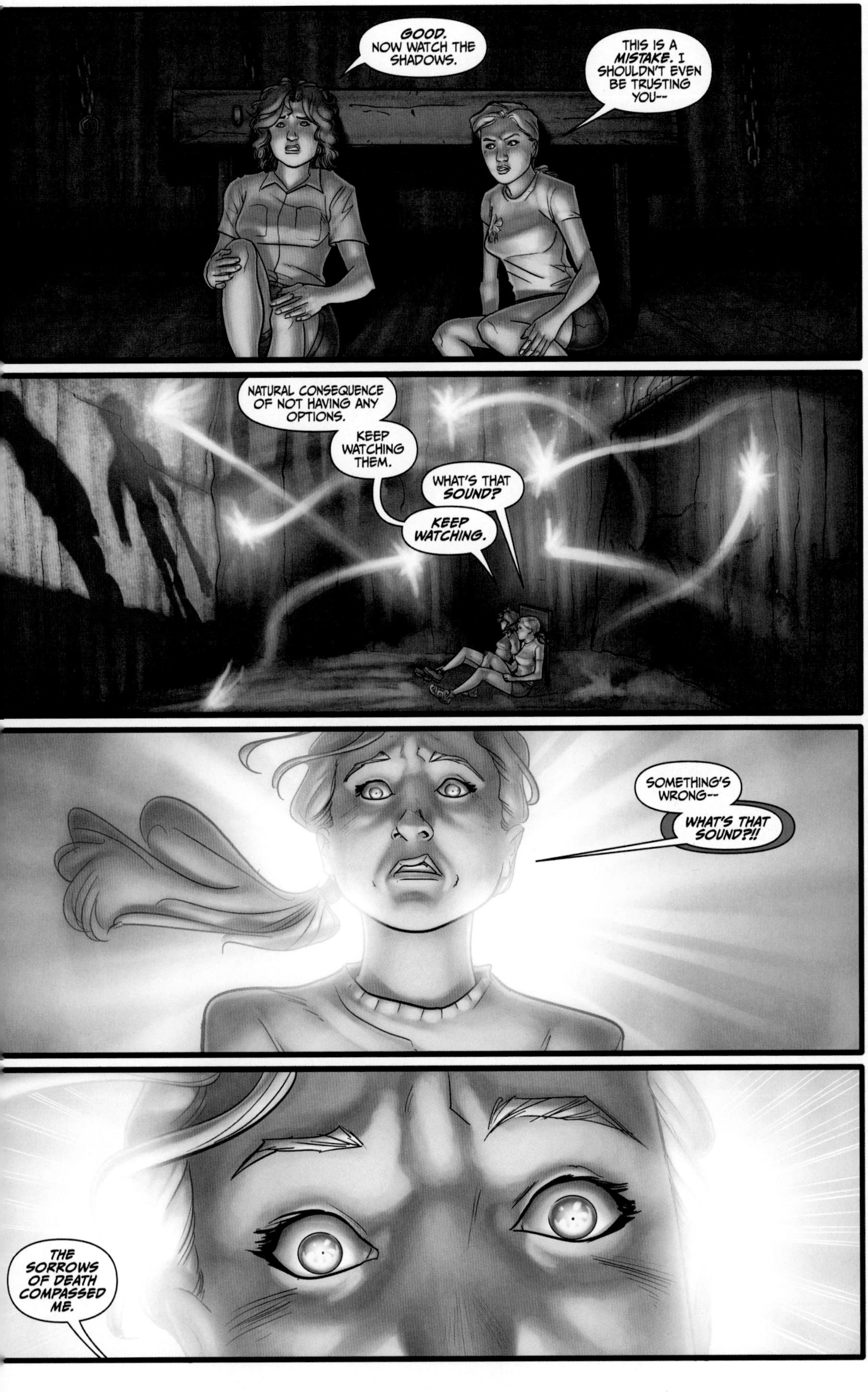
GOOD. NOW WATCH THE SHADOWS.
THIS IS A MISTAKE. I SHOULDN'T EVEN BE TRUSTING YOU--
NATURAL CONSEQUENCE OF NOT HAVING ANY OPTIONS.
KEEP WATCHING THEM.
WHAT'S THAT SOUND?
KEEP WATCHING.
SOMETHING'S WRONG--
WHAT'S THAT SOUND?!!
THE SORROWS OF DEATH COMPASSED ME.

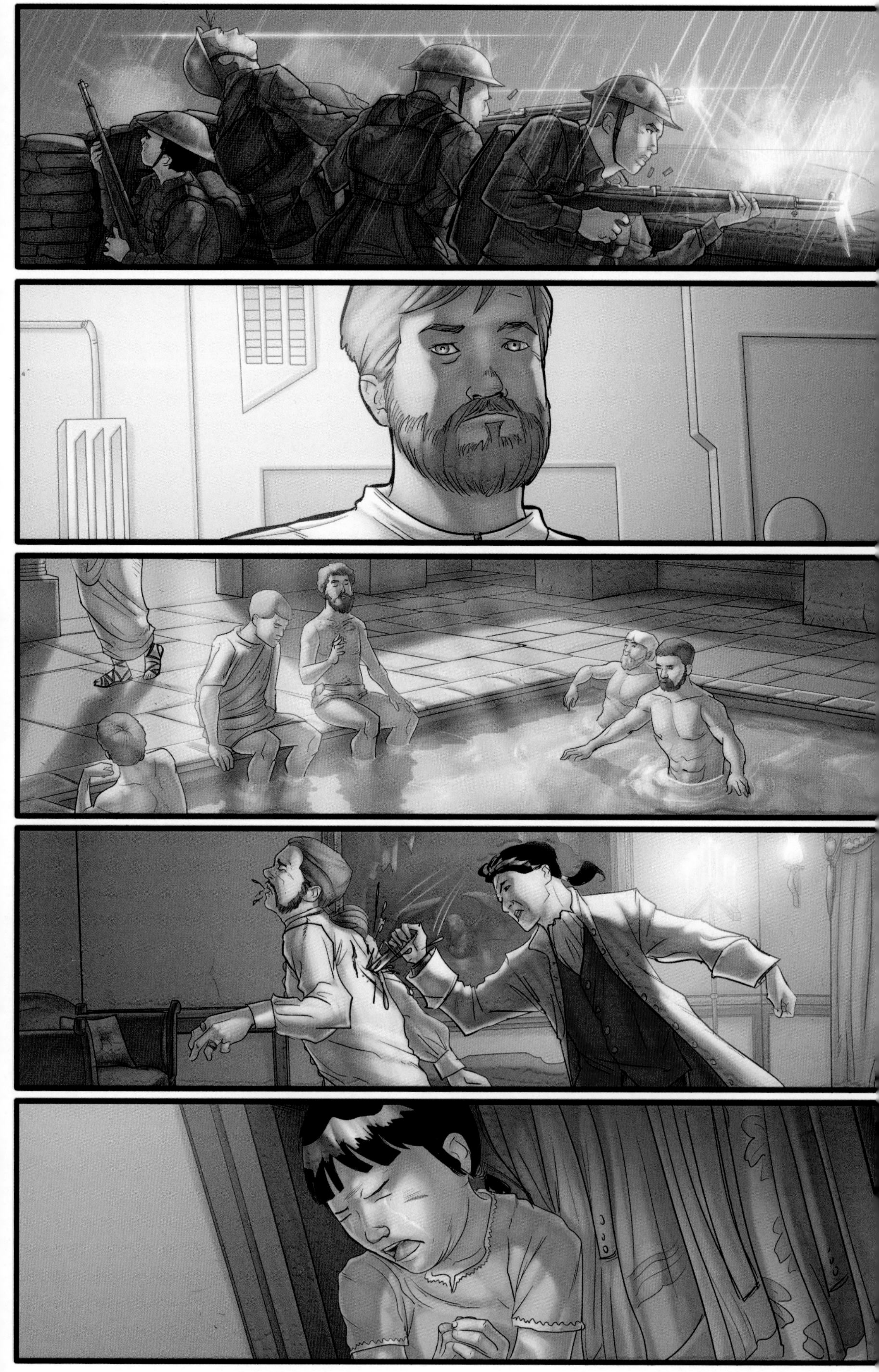

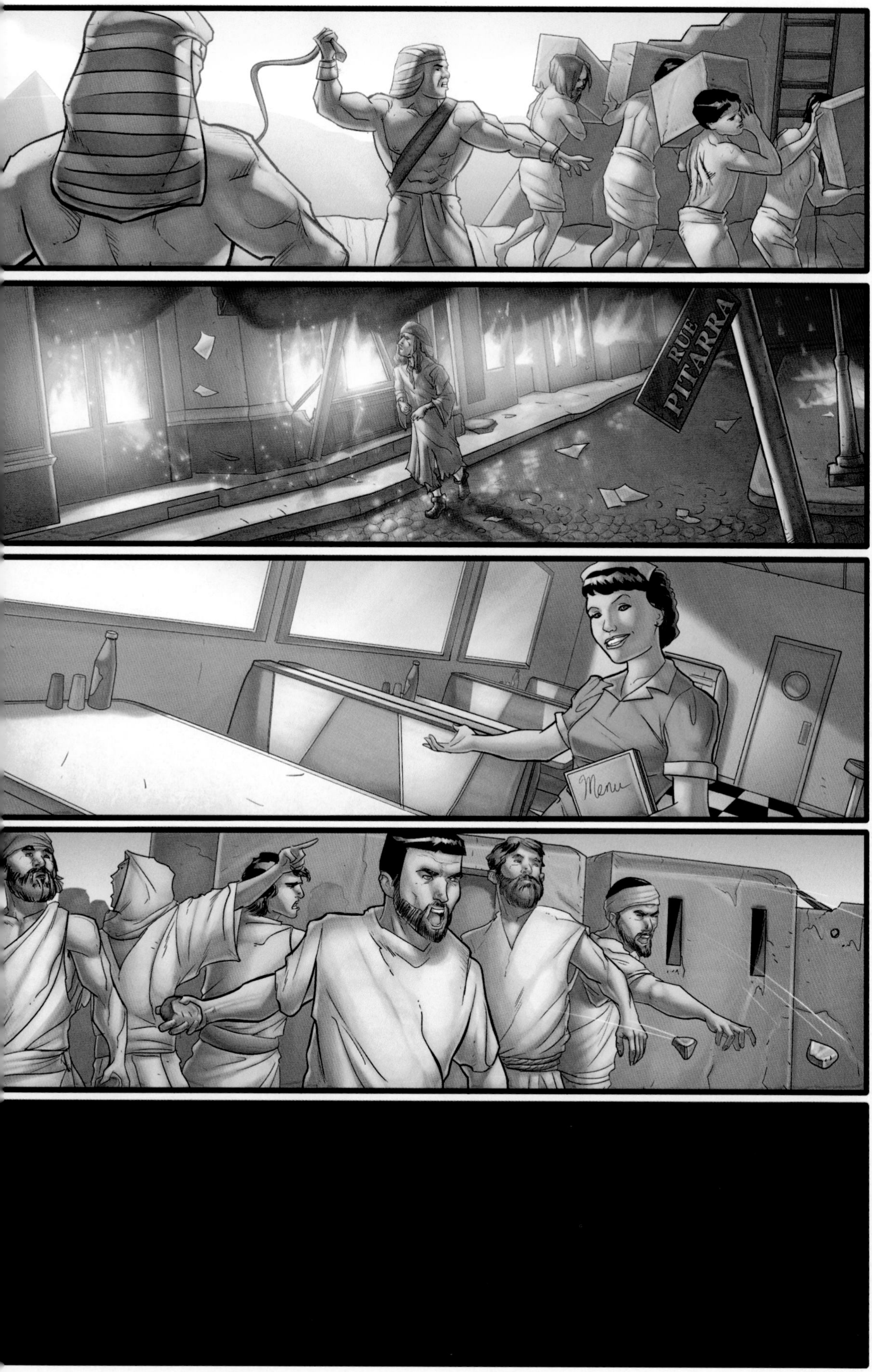
RUE
PITARRA
Menu

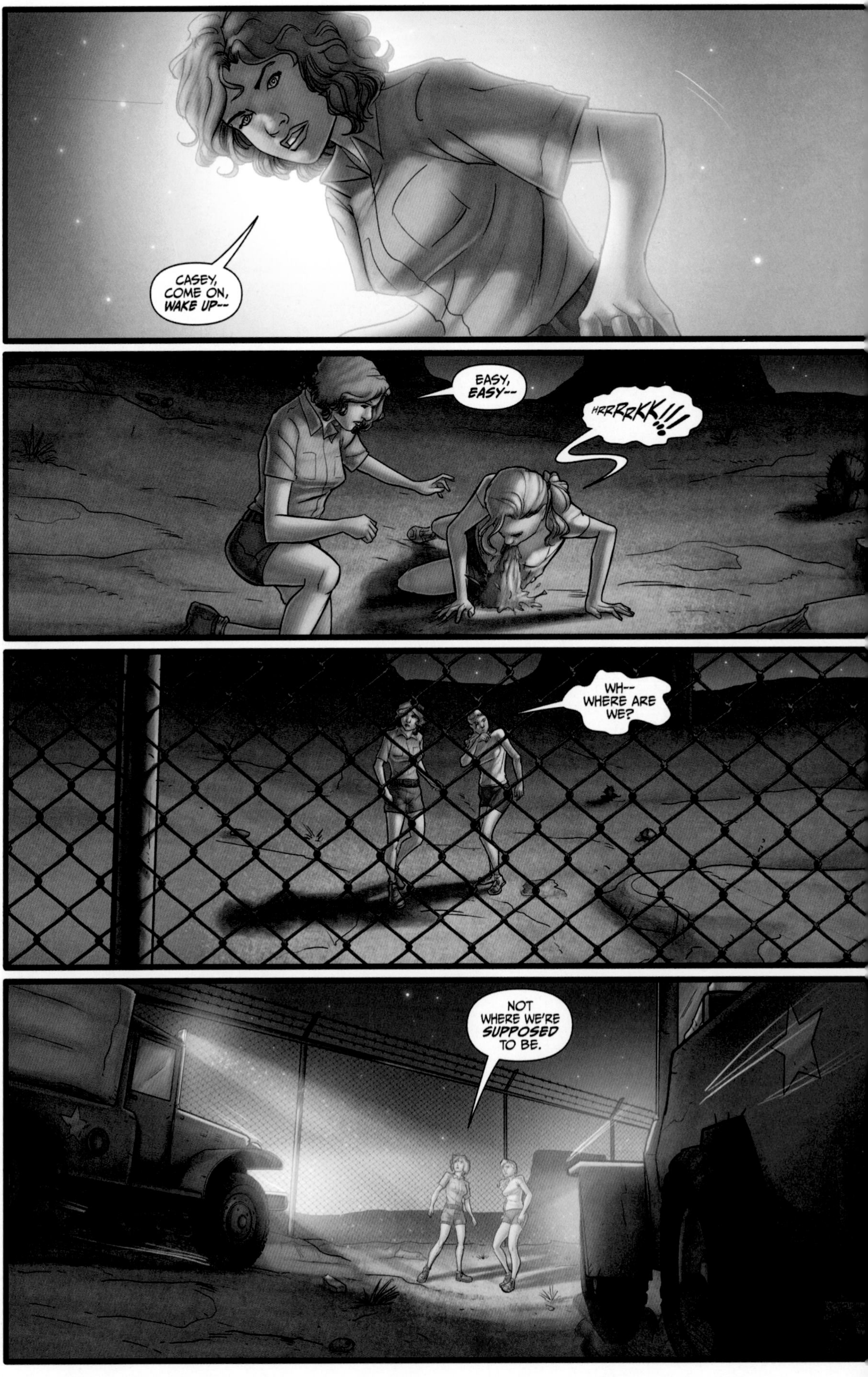
CASEY, COME ON, WAKE UP--
EASY, EASY--
HRRRRKK!!!
WH-- WHERE ARE WE?
NOT WHERE WE'RE SUPPOSED TO BE.

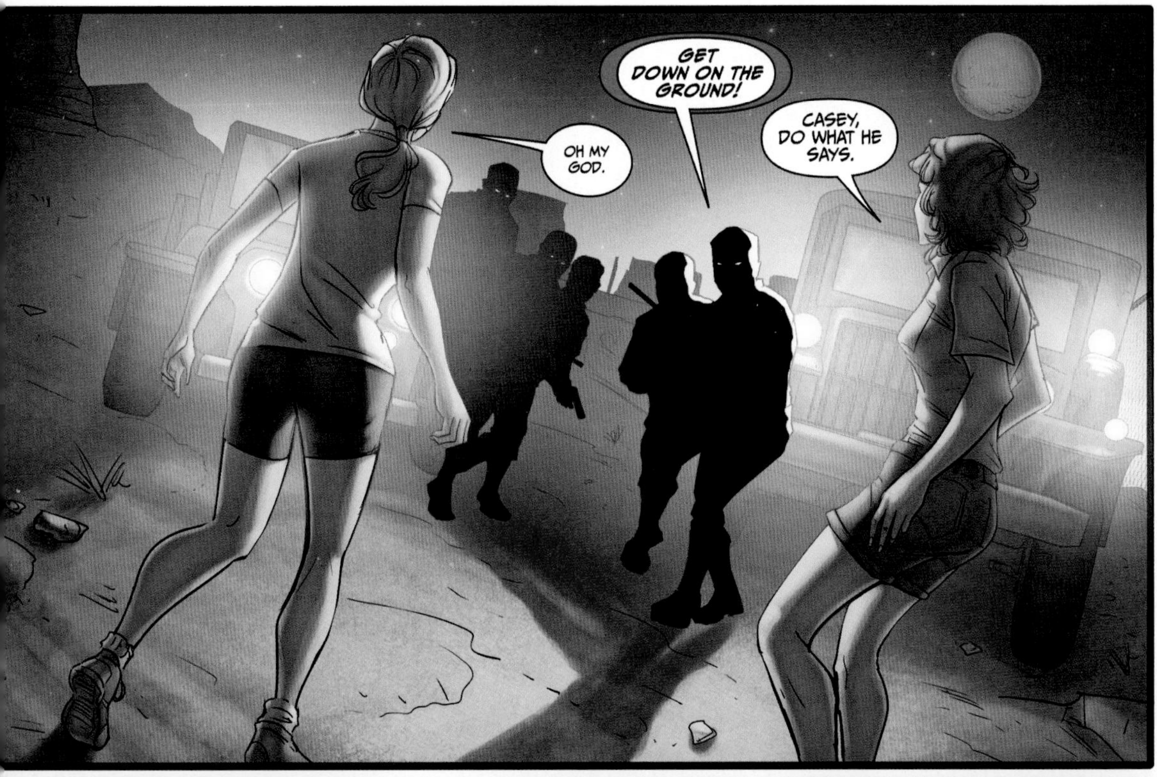
GET DOWN ON THE GROUND!
OH MY GOD.
CASEY, DO WHAT HE SAYS.

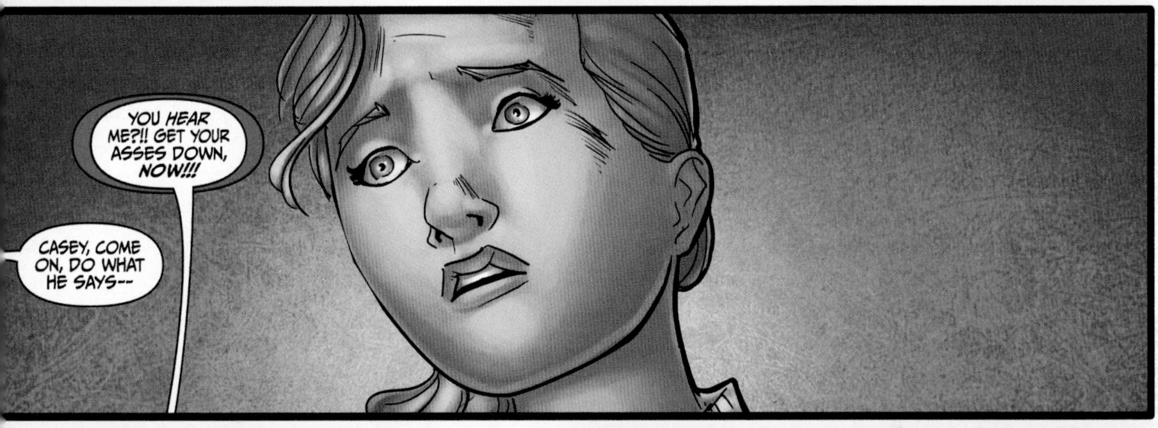
YOU HEAR ME?!! GET YOUR ASSES DOWN, NOW!!!
CASEY, COME ON, DO WHAT HE SAYS--

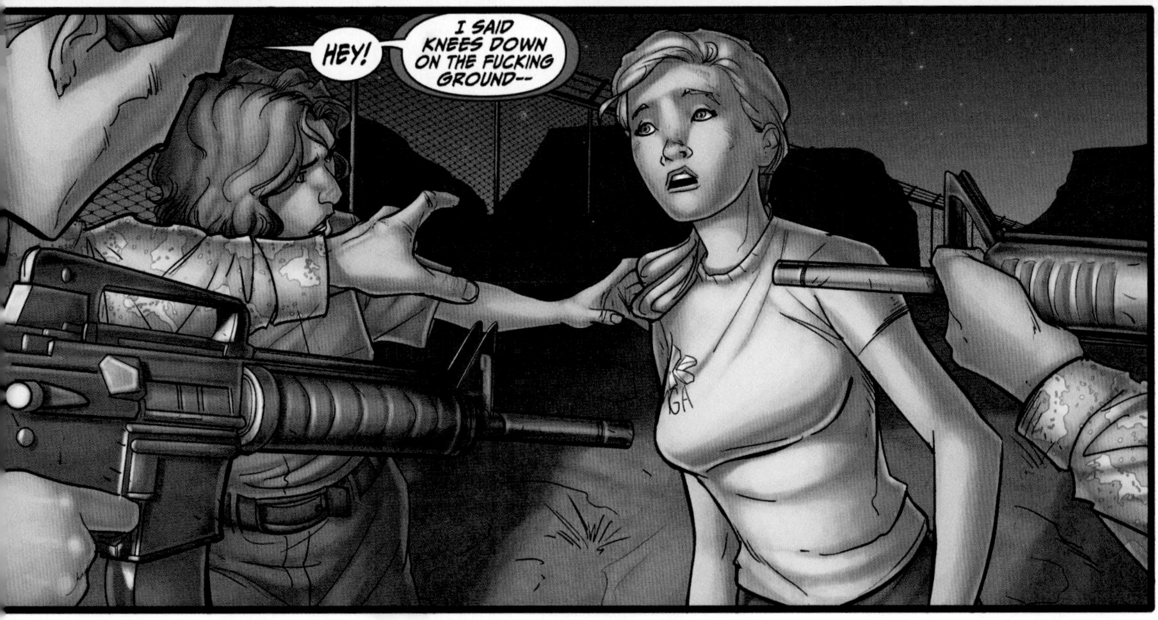
HEY!
I SAID KNEES DOWN ON THE FUCKING GROUND--

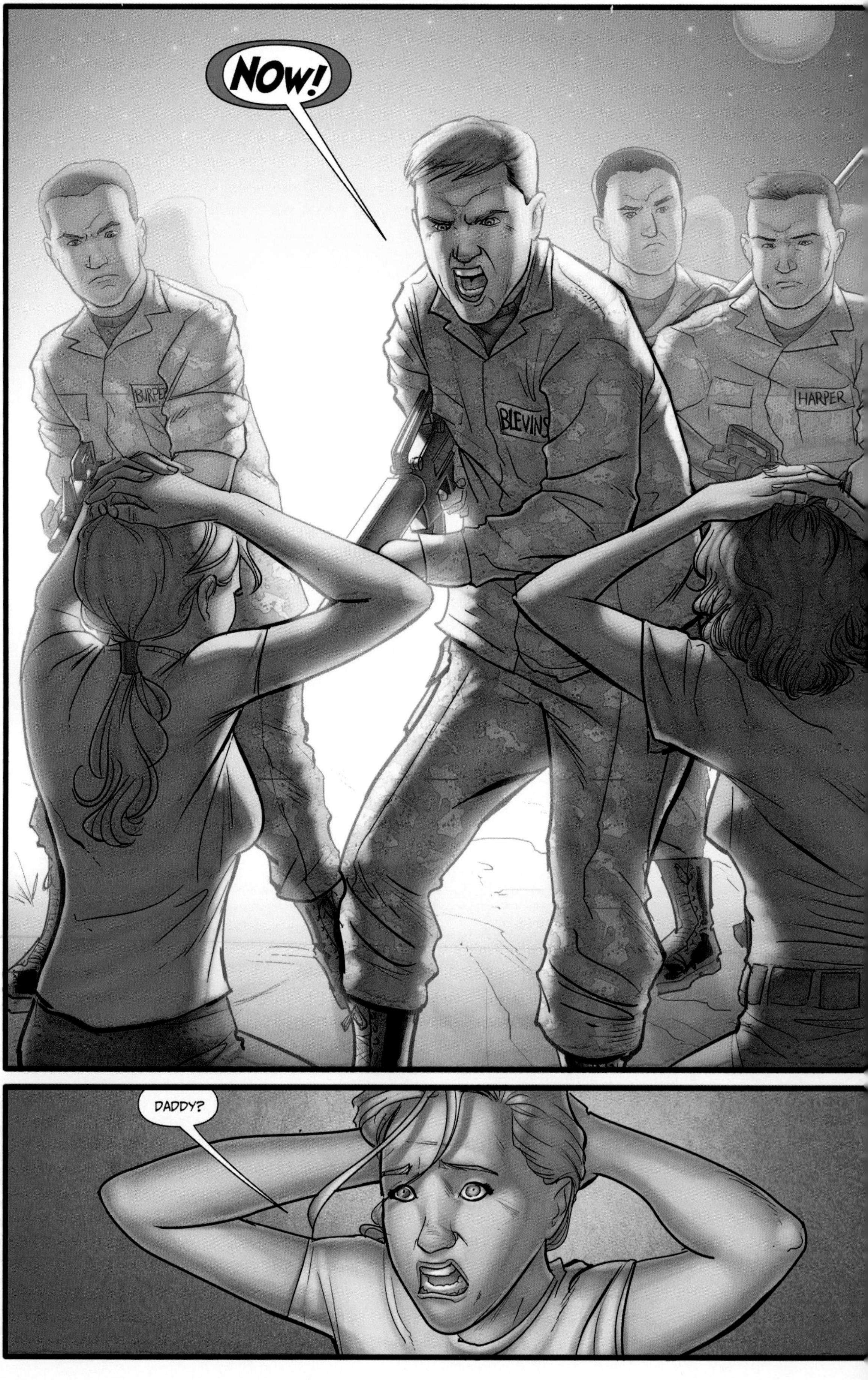
NOW!
BLEVINS
HARPER
DADDY?

fourteen

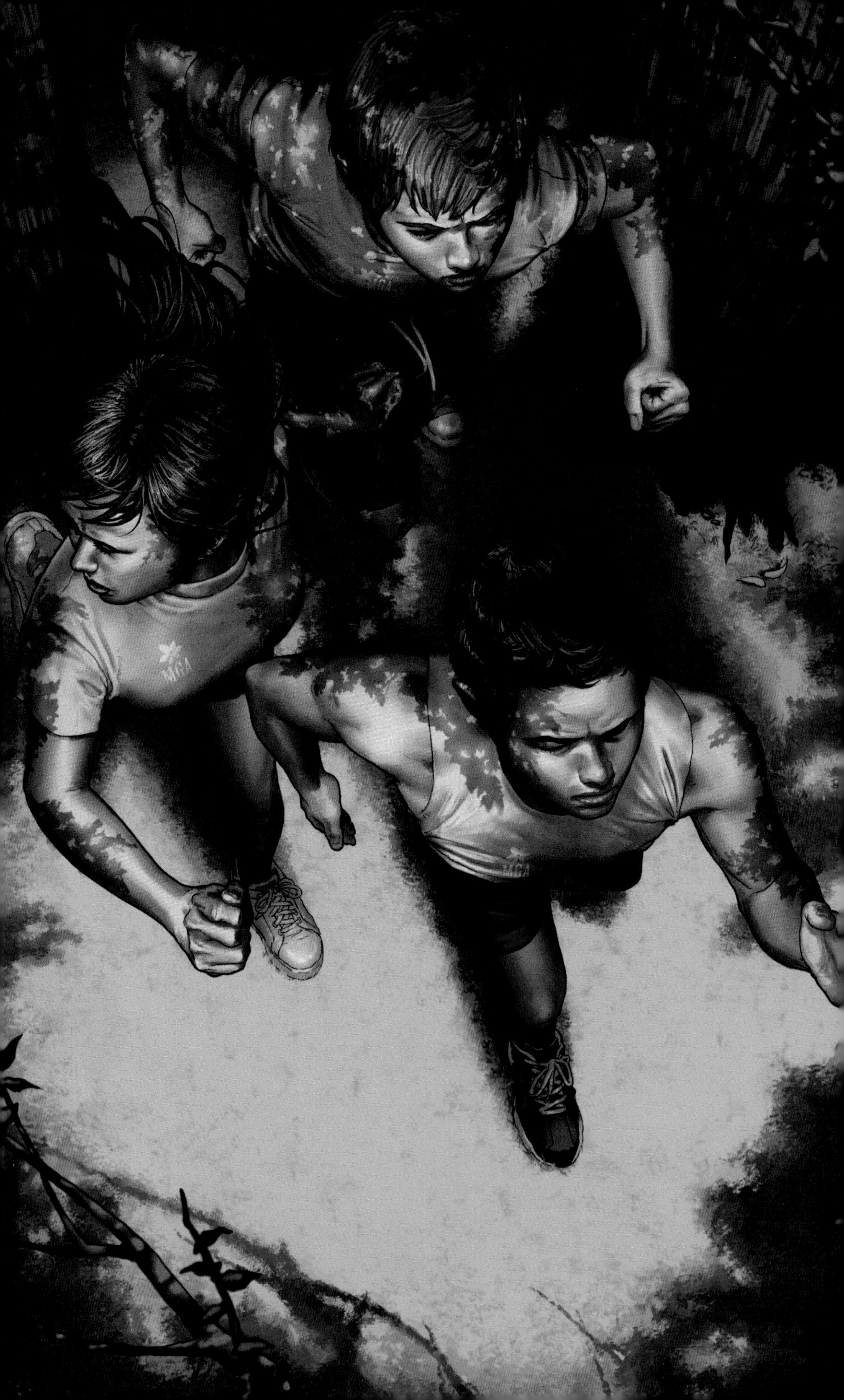
MGA

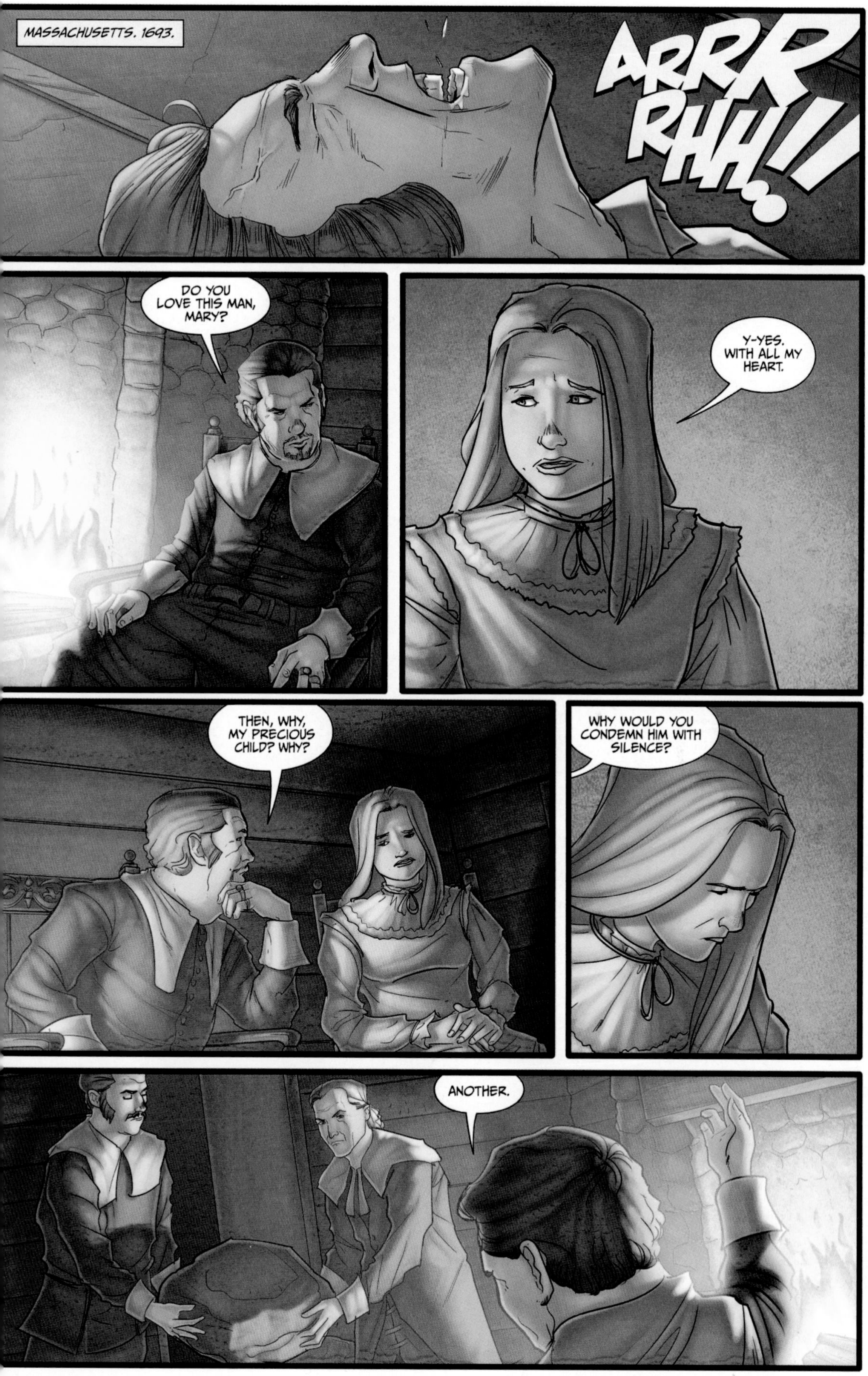
MASSACHUSETTS. 1693.
ARRRRHH!!
DO YOU LOVE THIS MAN, MARY?
Y-YES. WITH ALL MY HEART.
THEN, WHY, MY PRECIOUS CHILD? WHY?
WHY WOULD YOU CONDEMN HIM WITH SILENCE?
ANOTHER.

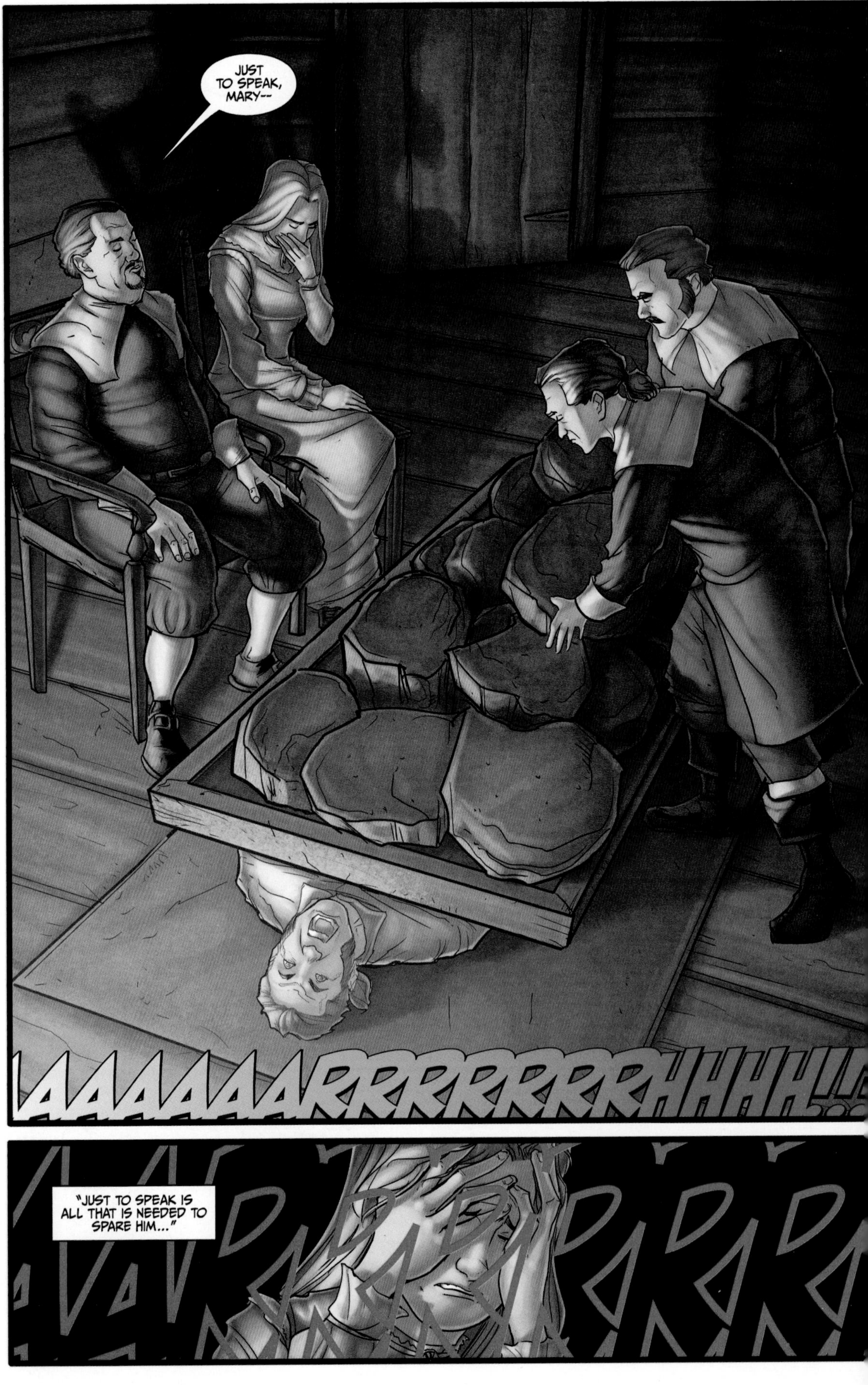
JUST TO SPEAK, MARY--
AAAAAARRRRRRRRRHHHH!!
"JUST TO SPEAK IS ALL THAT IS NEEDED TO SPARE HIM..."

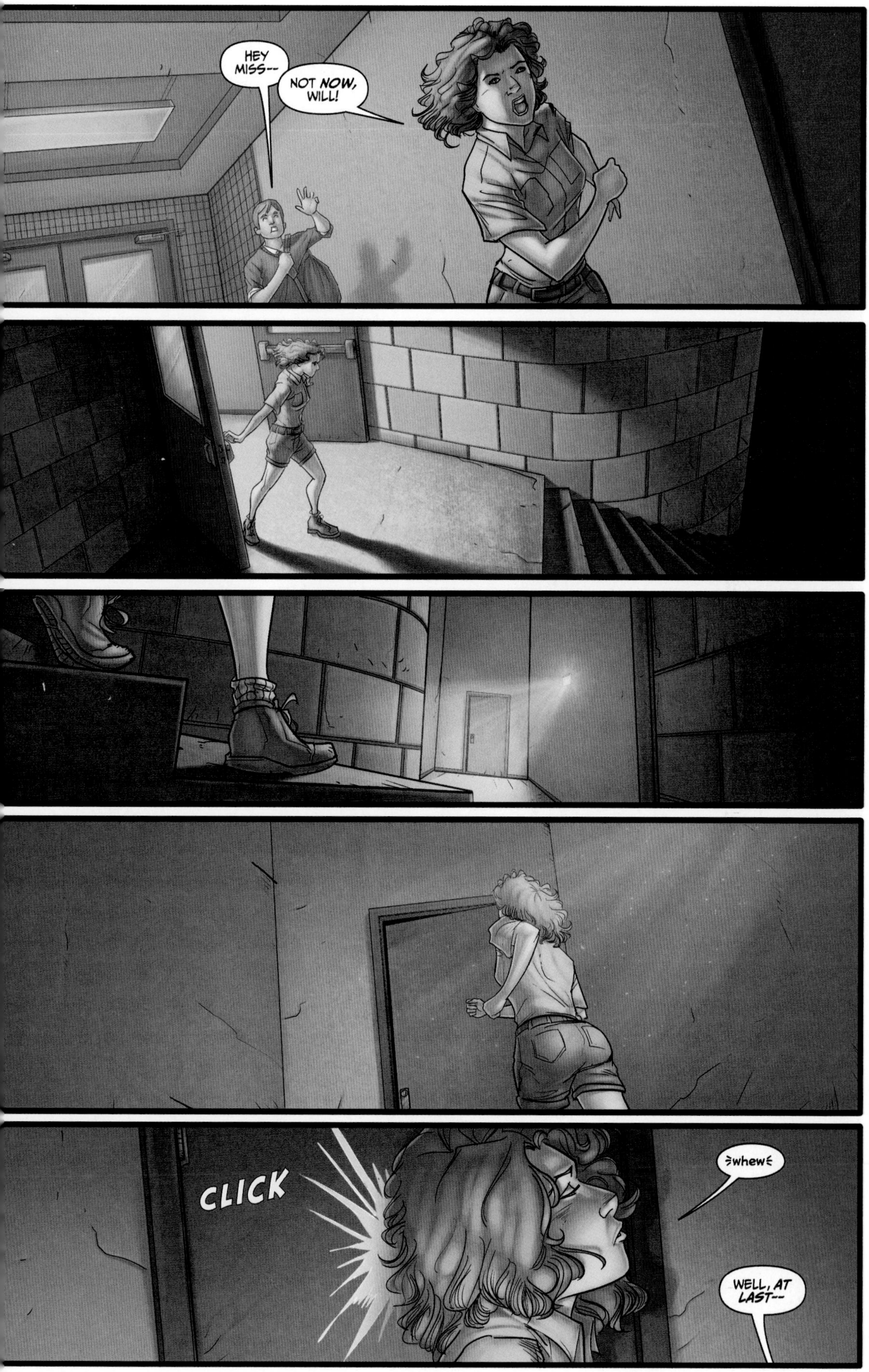
HEY MISS--
NOT *NOW*, WILL!
CLICK
whew
WELL, *AT LAST*--

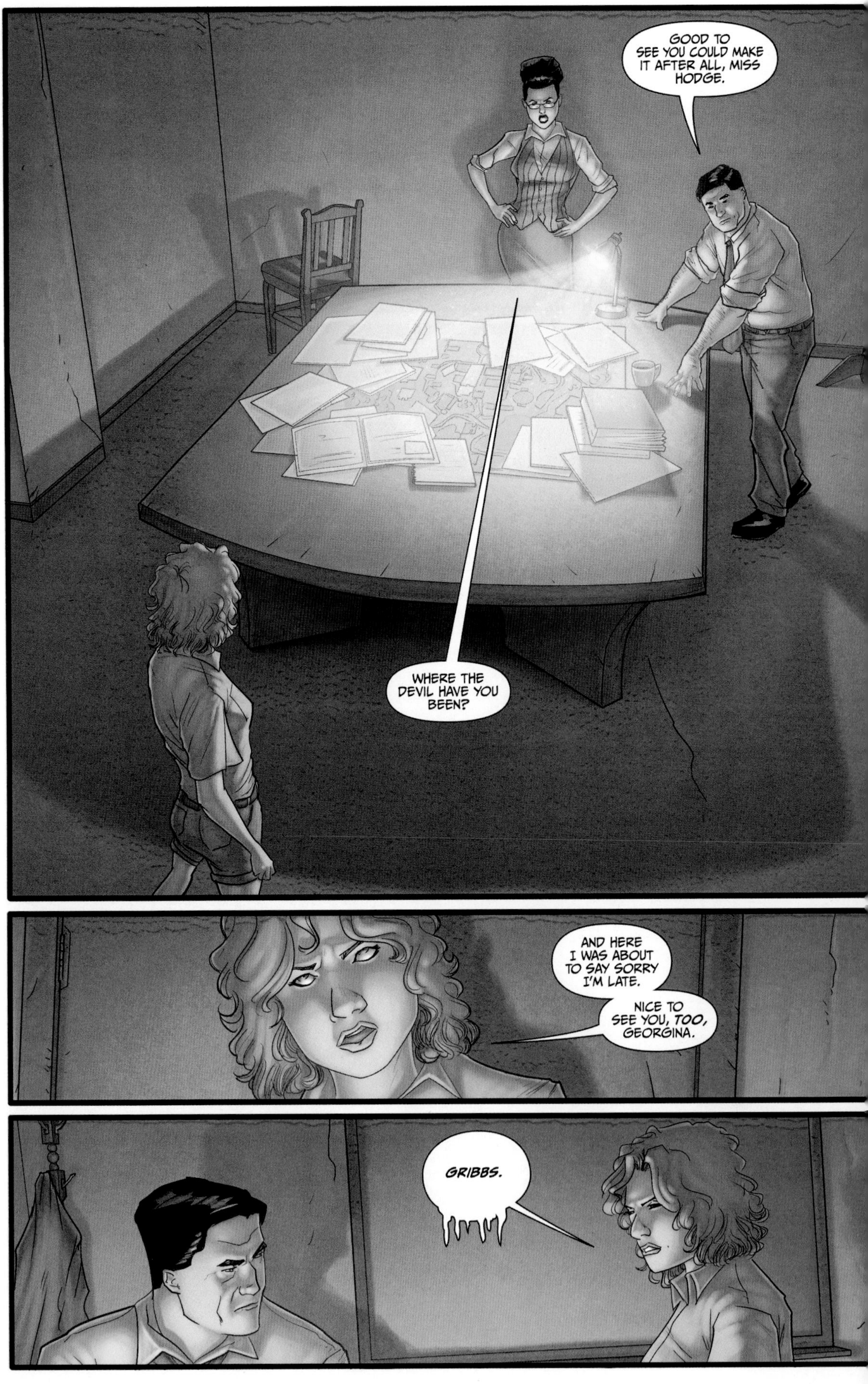
GOOD TO SEE YOU COULD MAKE IT AFTER ALL, MISS HODGE.
WHERE THE DEVIL HAVE YOU BEEN?
AND HERE I WAS ABOUT TO SAY SORRY I'M LATE.
NICE TO SEE YOU, *TOO,* GEORGINA.
GRIBBS.

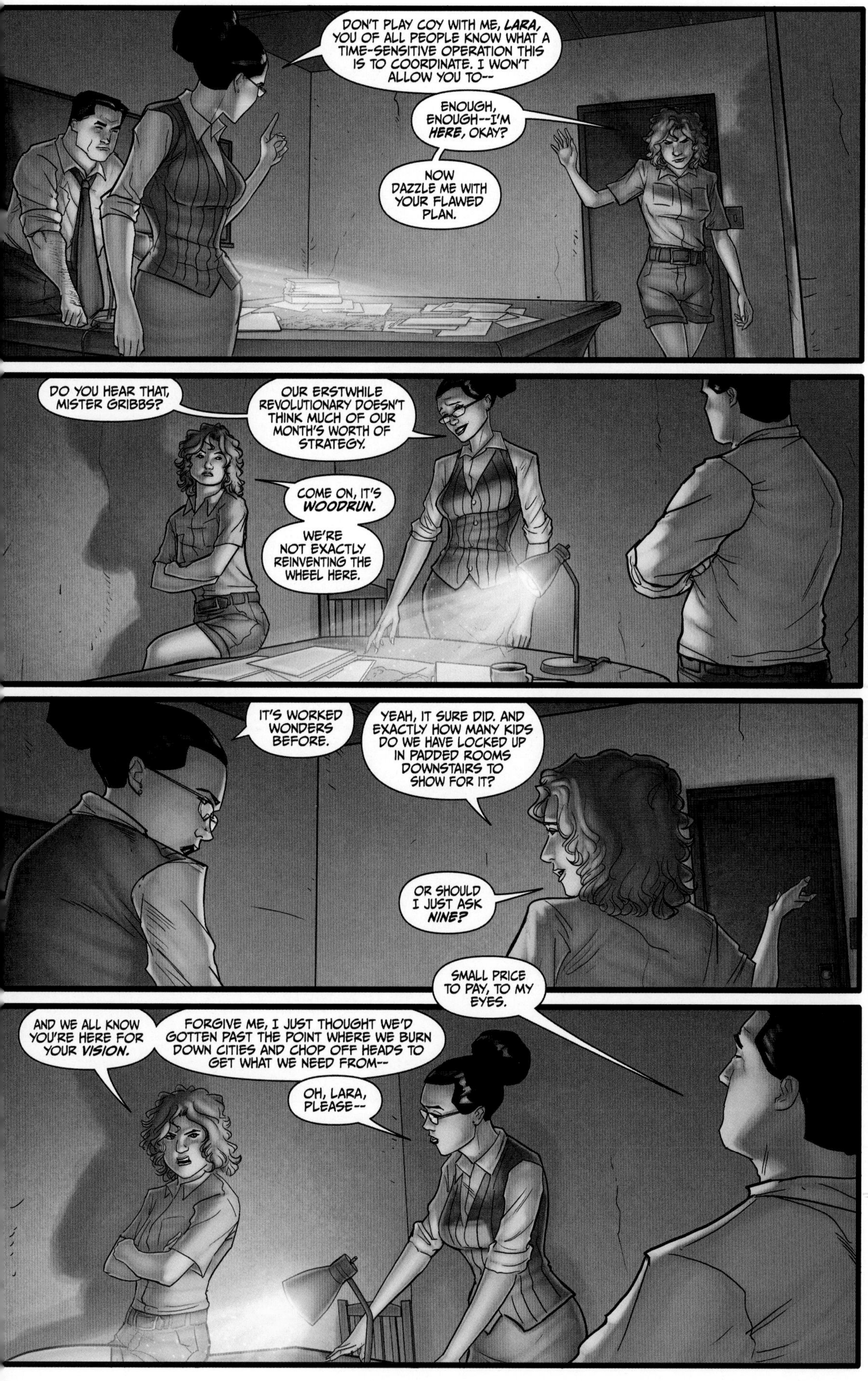
DON'T PLAY COY WITH ME, *LARA,* YOU OF ALL PEOPLE KNOW WHAT A TIME-SENSITIVE OPERATION THIS IS TO COORDINATE. I WON'T ALLOW YOU TO--
ENOUGH, ENOUGH--I'M *HERE,* OKAY?
NOW DAZZLE ME WITH YOUR FLAWED PLAN.
DO YOU HEAR THAT, MISTER GRIBBS?
OUR ERSTWHILE REVOLUTIONARY DOESN'T THINK MUCH OF OUR MONTH'S WORTH OF STRATEGY.
COME ON, IT'S *WOODRUN.*
WE'RE NOT EXACTLY REINVENTING THE WHEEL HERE.
IT'S WORKED WONDERS BEFORE.
YEAH, IT SURE DID. AND EXACTLY HOW MANY KIDS DO WE HAVE LOCKED UP IN PADDED ROOMS DOWNSTAIRS TO SHOW FOR IT?
OR SHOULD I JUST ASK *NINE?*
SMALL PRICE TO PAY, TO MY EYES.
AND WE ALL KNOW YOU'RE HERE FOR YOUR *VISION.*
FORGIVE ME, I JUST THOUGHT WE'D GOTTEN PAST THE POINT WHERE WE BURN DOWN CITIES AND CHOP OFF HEADS TO GET WHAT WE NEED FROM--
OH, LARA, PLEASE--

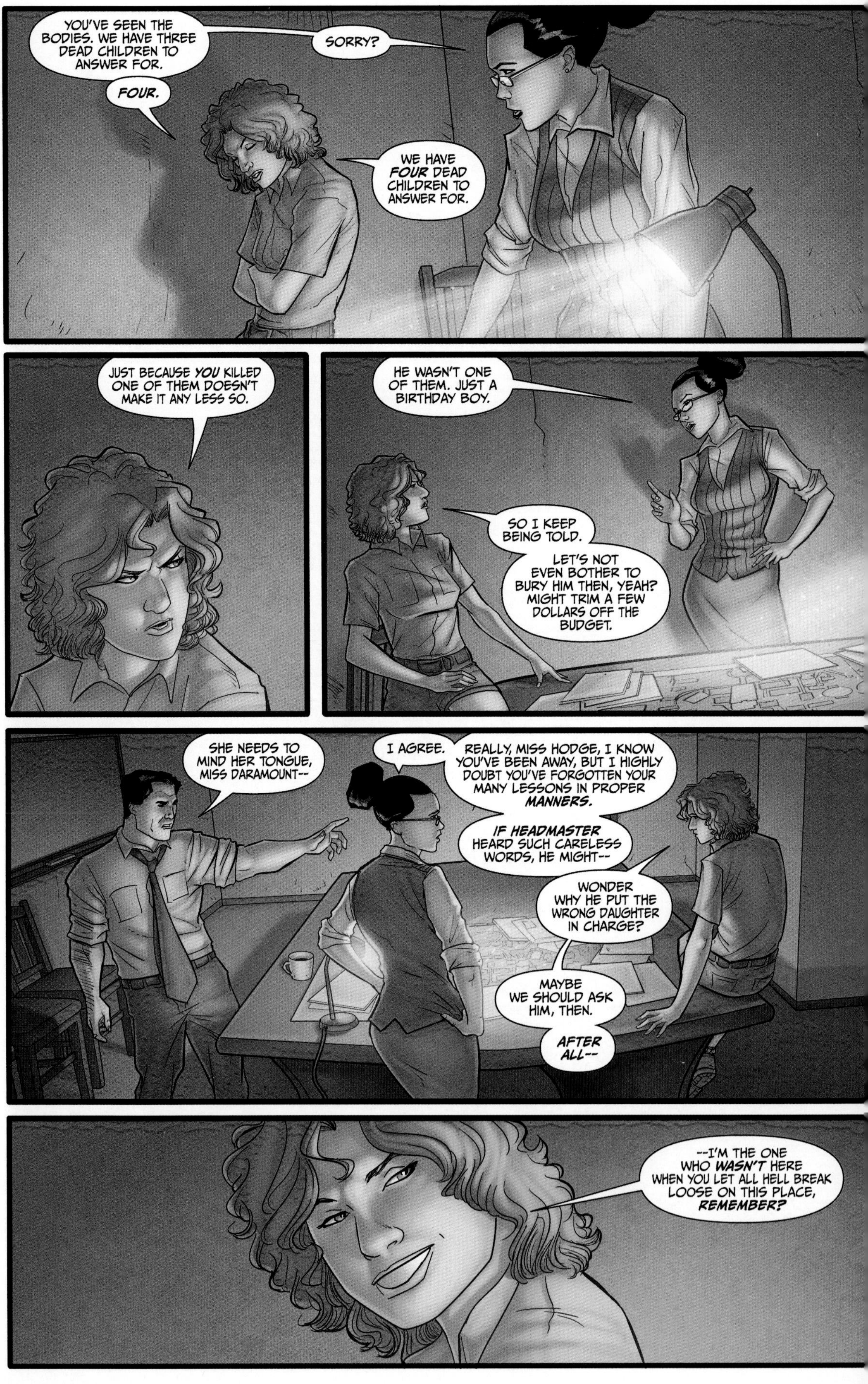

YOU'VE SEEN THE BODIES. WE HAVE THREE DEAD CHILDREN TO ANSWER FOR.
SORRY?
FOUR.
WE HAVE FOUR DEAD CHILDREN TO ANSWER FOR.
JUST BECAUSE YOU KILLED ONE OF THEM DOESN'T MAKE IT ANY LESS SO.
HE WASN'T ONE OF THEM. JUST A BIRTHDAY BOY.
SO I KEEP BEING TOLD.
LET'S NOT EVEN BOTHER TO BURY HIM THEN, YEAH? MIGHT TRIM A FEW DOLLARS OFF THE BUDGET.
SHE NEEDS TO MIND HER TONGUE, MISS DARAMOUNT--
I AGREE.
REALLY, MISS HODGE, I KNOW YOU'VE BEEN AWAY, BUT I HIGHLY DOUBT YOU'VE FORGOTTEN YOUR MANY LESSONS IN PROPER MANNERS.
IF HEADMASTER HEARD SUCH CARELESS WORDS, HE MIGHT--
WONDER WHY HE PUT THE WRONG DAUGHTER IN CHARGE?
MAYBE WE SHOULD ASK HIM, THEN.
AFTER ALL--
--I'M THE ONE WHO WASN'T HERE WHEN YOU LET ALL HELL BREAK LOOSE ON THIS PLACE, REMEMBER?

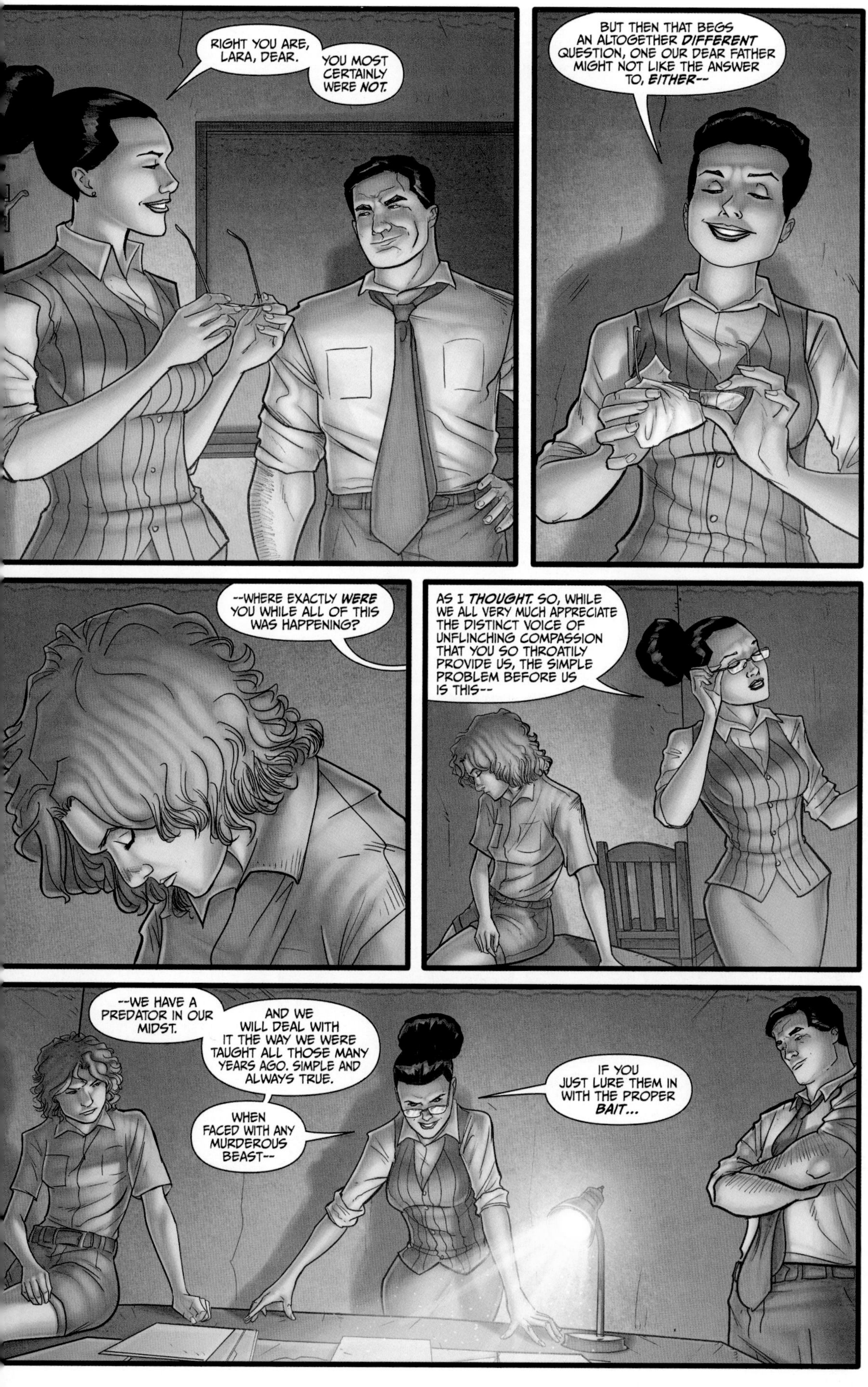
RIGHT YOU ARE, LARA, DEAR.
YOU MOST CERTAINLY WERE *NOT.*
BUT THEN THAT BEGS AN ALTOGETHER *DIFFERENT* QUESTION, ONE OUR DEAR FATHER MIGHT NOT LIKE THE ANSWER TO, *EITHER--*
--WHERE EXACTLY *WERE* YOU WHILE ALL OF THIS WAS HAPPENING?
AS I *THOUGHT.* SO, WHILE WE ALL VERY MUCH APPRECIATE THE DISTINCT VOICE OF UNFLINCHING COMPASSION THAT YOU SO THROATILY PROVIDE US, THE SIMPLE PROBLEM BEFORE US IS THIS--
--WE HAVE A PREDATOR IN OUR MIDST.
AND WE WILL DEAL WITH IT THE WAY WE WERE TAUGHT ALL THOSE MANY YEARS AGO. SIMPLE AND ALWAYS TRUE.
WHEN FACED WITH ANY MURDEROUS BEAST--
IF YOU JUST LURE THEM IN WITH THE PROPER *BAIT...*

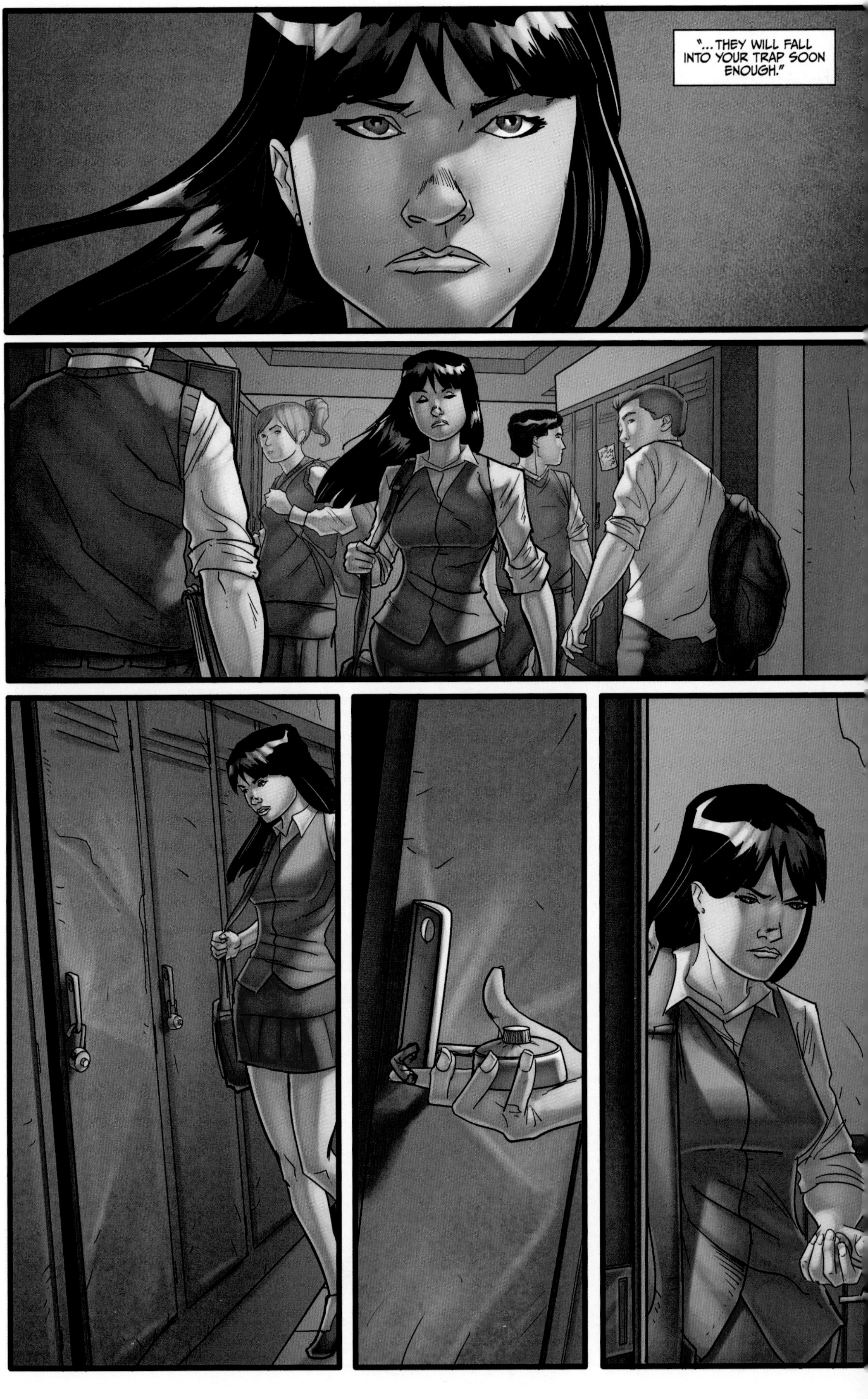
"...THEY WILL FALL INTO YOUR TRAP SOON ENOUGH."

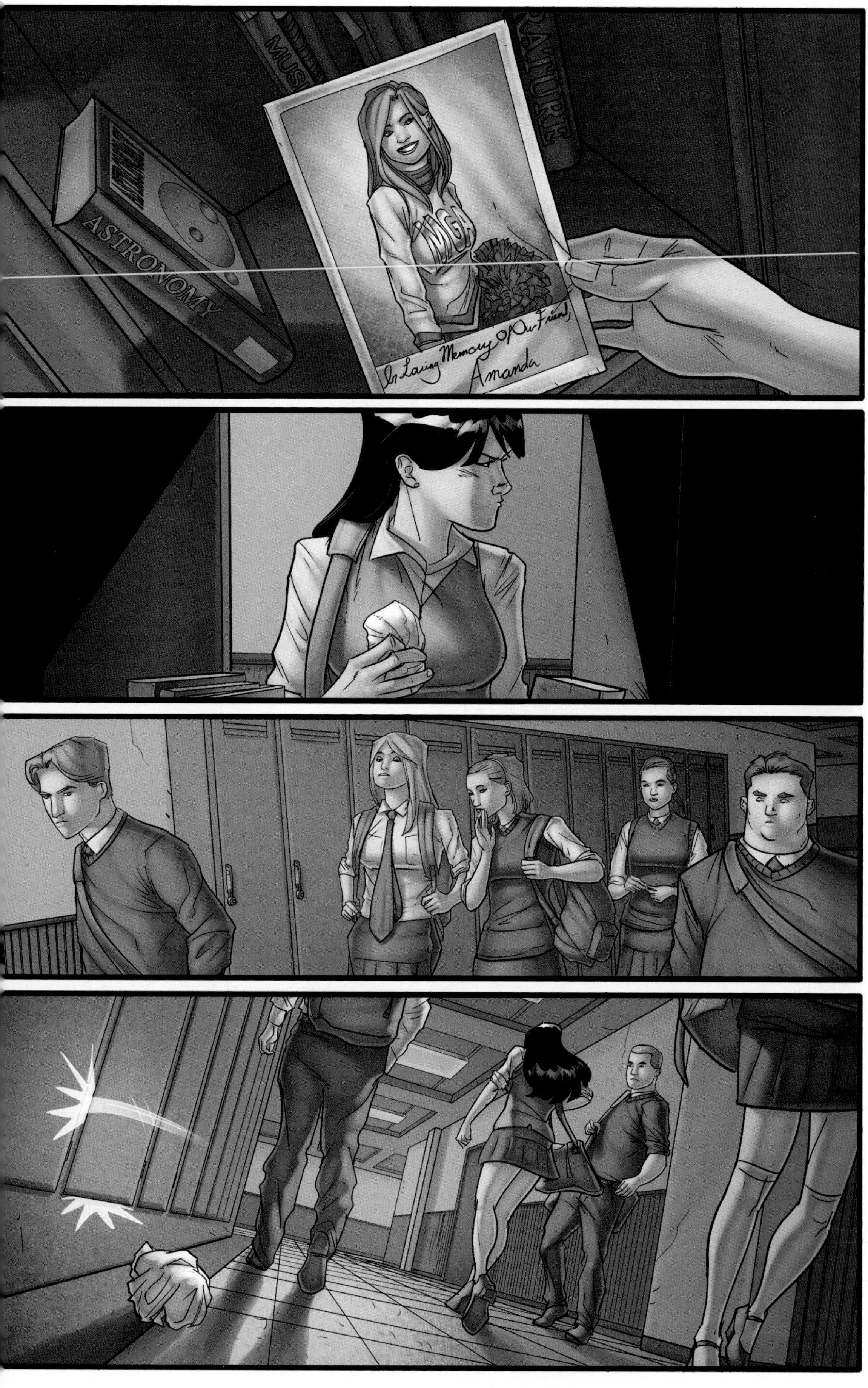
ASTRONOMY
In Loving Memory Of Our Friend,
Amanda

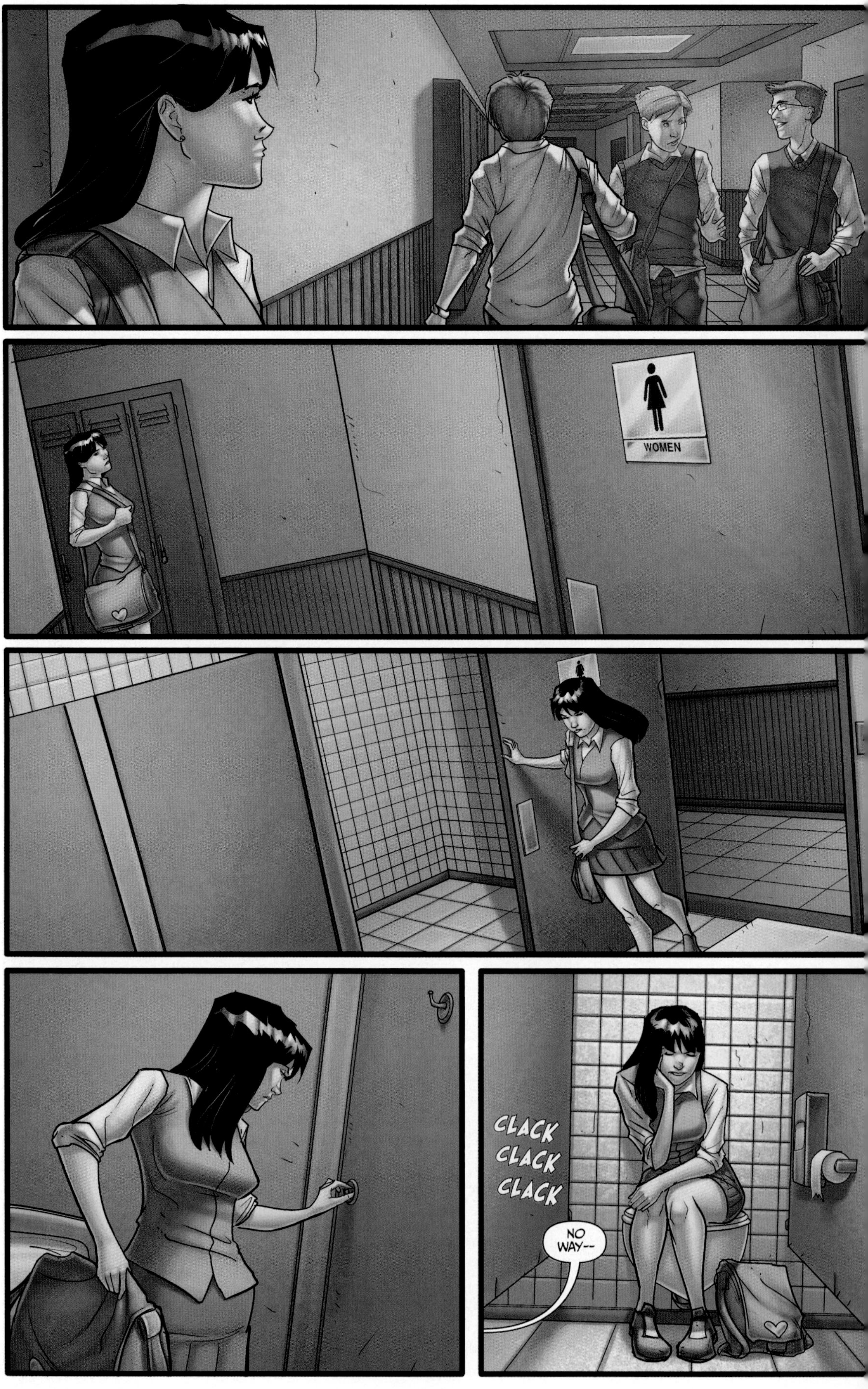
WOMEN
CLACK
CLACK
CLACK
NO WAY--

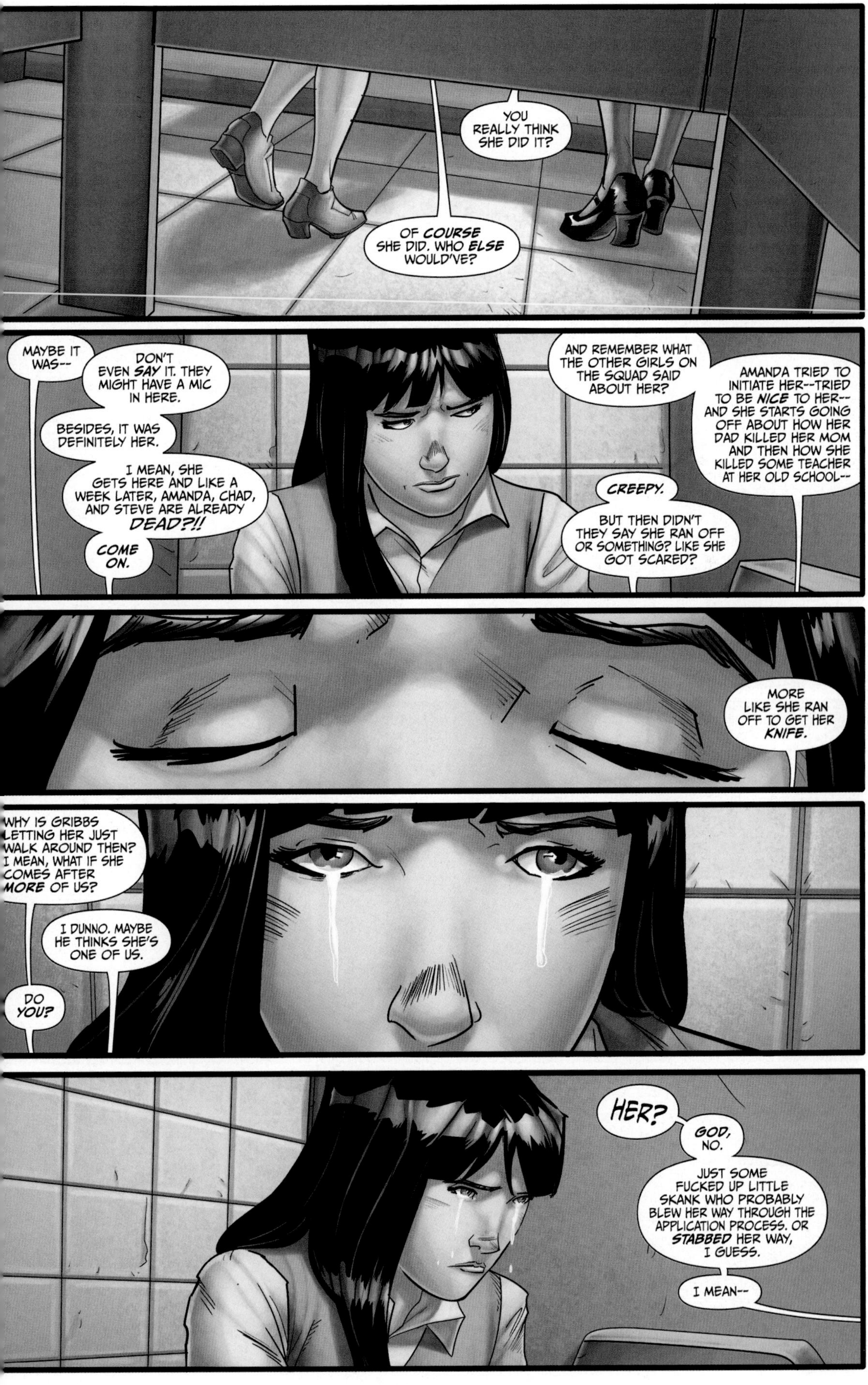

YOU REALLY THINK SHE DID IT?
OF COURSE SHE DID. WHO ELSE WOULD'VE?
MAYBE IT WAS--
DON'T EVEN SAY IT. THEY MIGHT HAVE A MIC IN HERE.
BESIDES, IT WAS DEFINITELY HER.
I MEAN, SHE GETS HERE AND LIKE A WEEK LATER, AMANDA, CHAD, AND STEVE ARE ALREADY DEAD?!!
COME ON.
AND REMEMBER WHAT THE OTHER GIRLS ON THE SQUAD SAID ABOUT HER?
AMANDA TRIED TO INITIATE HER--TRIED TO BE NICE TO HER--AND SHE STARTS GOING OFF ABOUT HOW HER DAD KILLED HER MOM AND THEN HOW SHE KILLED SOME TEACHER AT HER OLD SCHOOL--
CREEPY.
BUT THEN DIDN'T THEY SAY SHE RAN OFF OR SOMETHING? LIKE SHE GOT SCARED?
MORE LIKE SHE RAN OFF TO GET HER KNIFE.
WHY IS GRIBBS LETTING HER JUST WALK AROUND THEN? I MEAN, WHAT IF SHE COMES AFTER MORE OF US?
I DUNNO. MAYBE HE THINKS SHE'S ONE OF US.
DO YOU?
HER?
GOD, NO.
JUST SOME FUCKED UP LITTLE SKANK WHO PROBABLY BLEW HER WAY THROUGH THE APPLICATION PROCESS. OR STABBED HER WAY, I GUESS.
I MEAN--

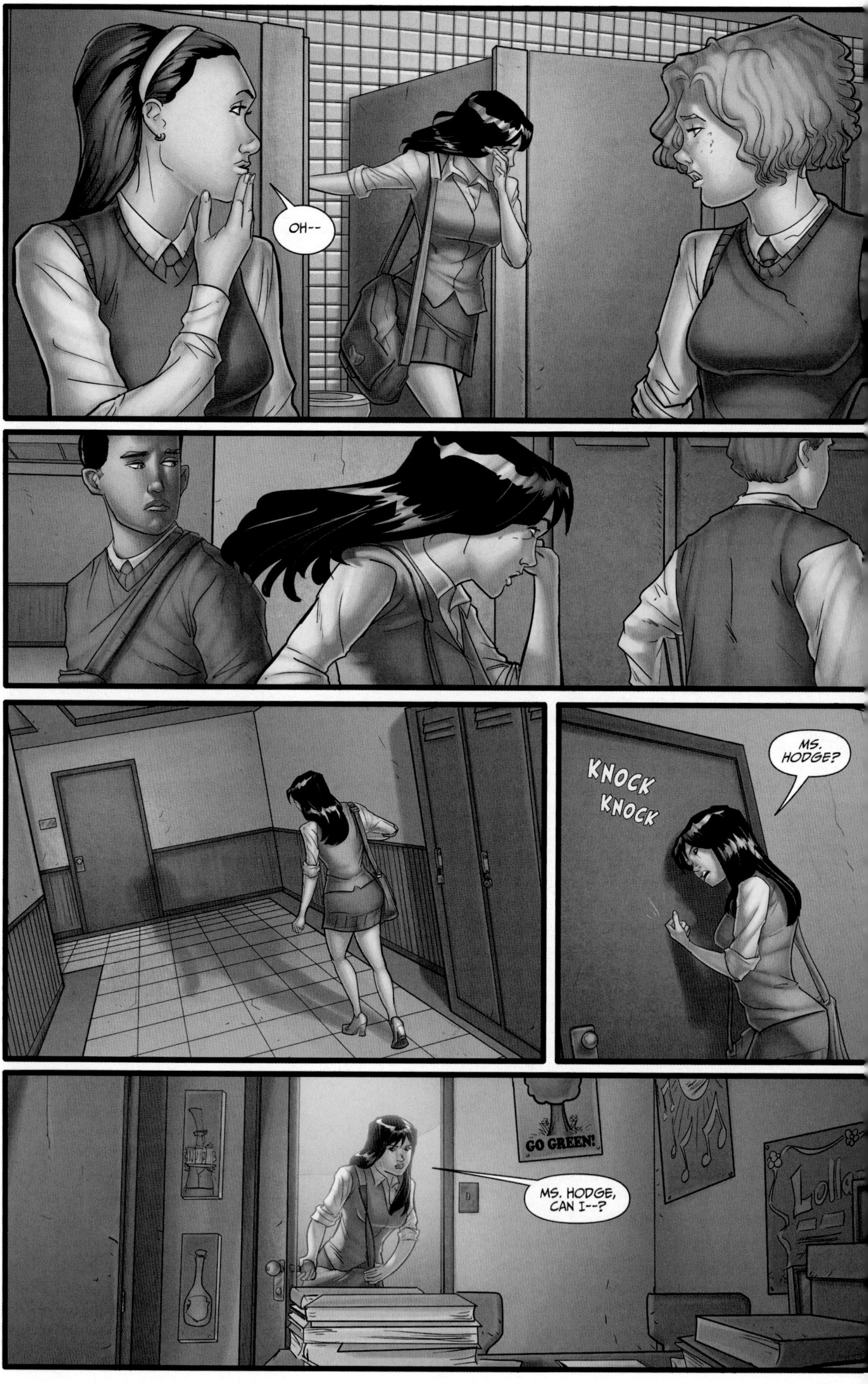
OH--
KNOCK
KNOCK
MS. HODGE?
GO GREEN!
MS. HODGE, CAN I--?

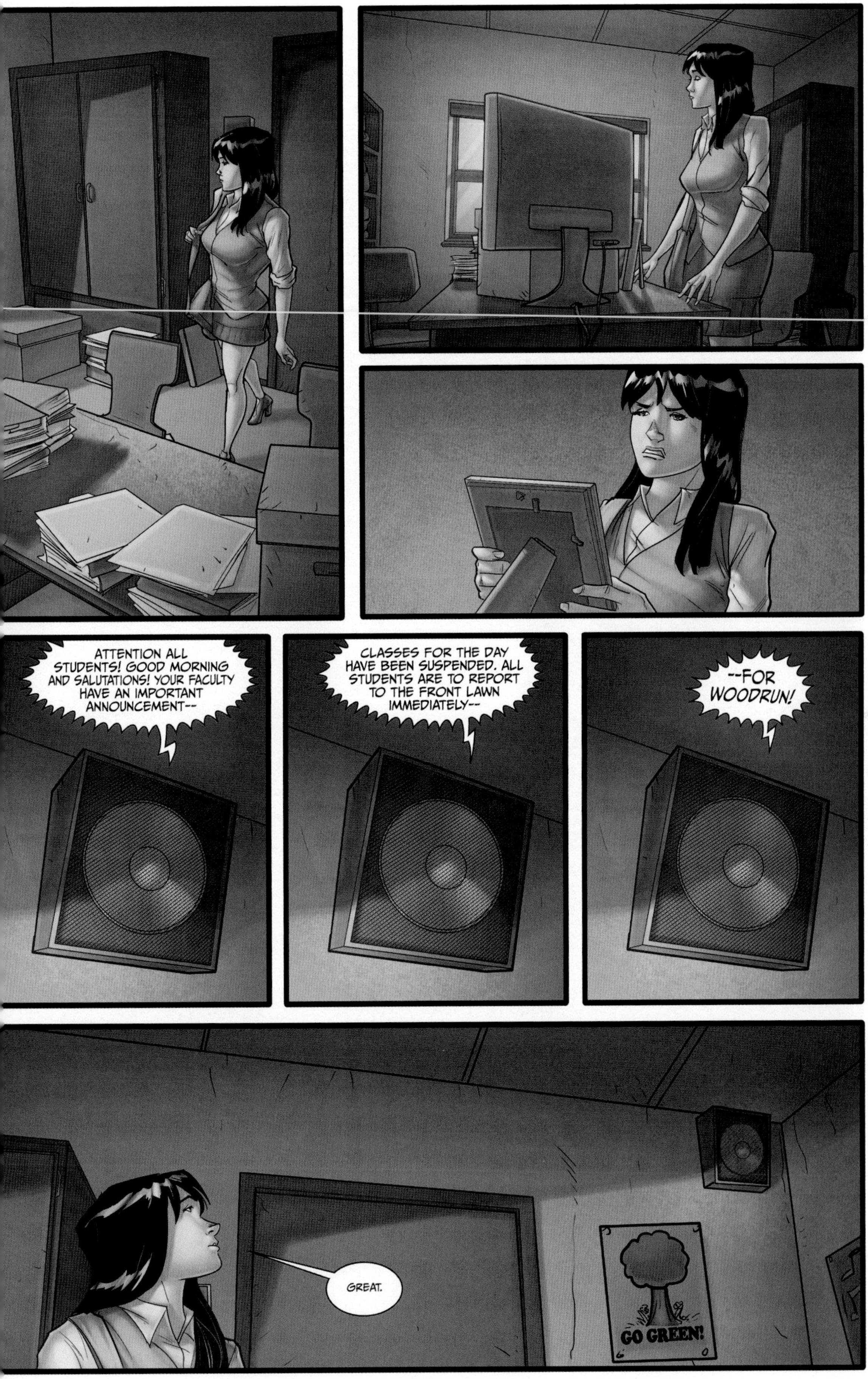
ATTENTION ALL STUDENTS! GOOD MORNING AND SALUTATIONS! YOUR FACULTY HAVE AN IMPORTANT ANNOUNCEMENT--
CLASSES FOR THE DAY HAVE BEEN SUSPENDED. ALL STUDENTS ARE TO REPORT TO THE FRONT LAWN IMMEDIATELY--
--FOR WOODRUN!
GREAT.
GO GREEN!

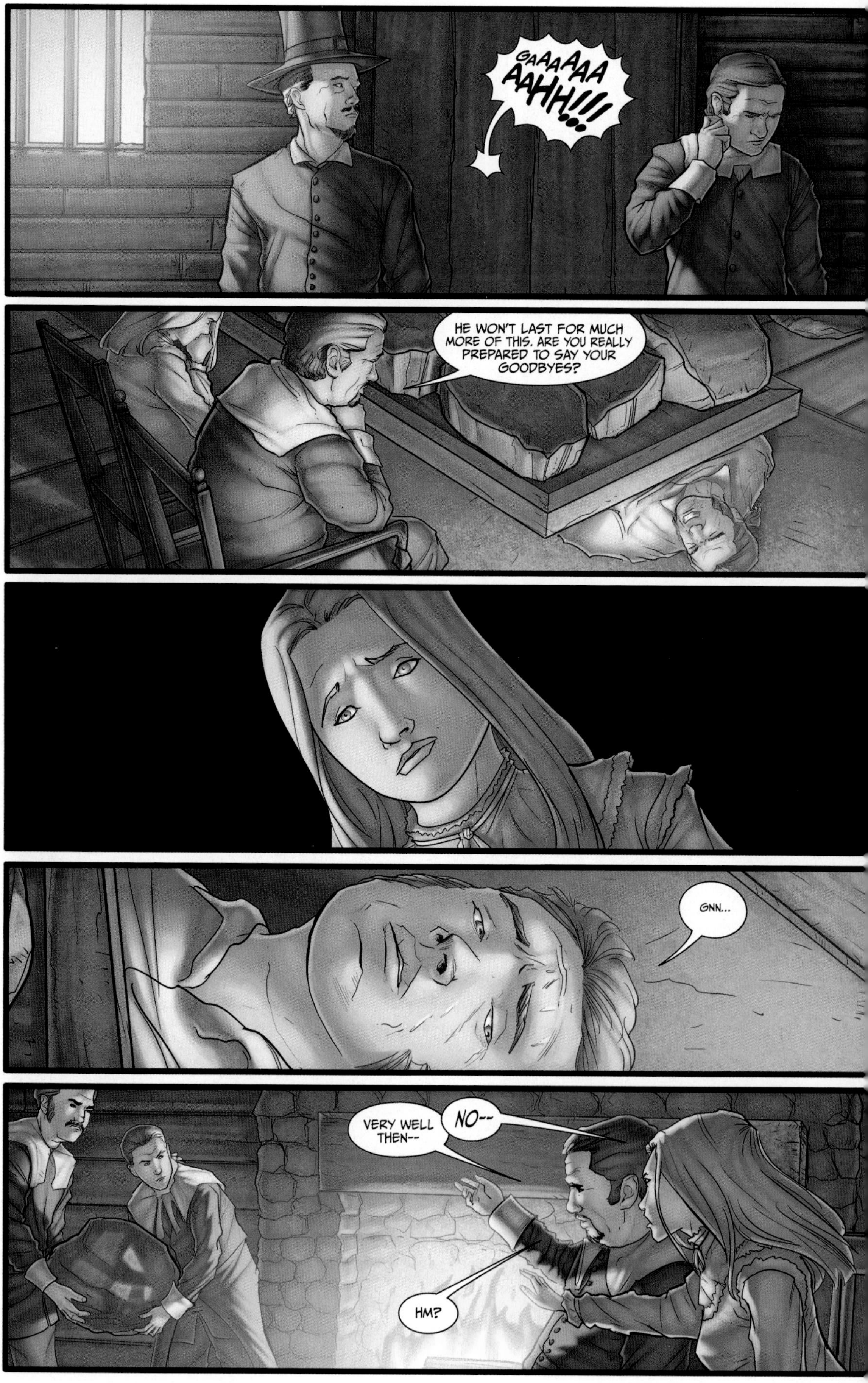
GAAAAAA AAHH!!!
HE WON'T LAST FOR MUCH MORE OF THIS. ARE YOU REALLY PREPARED TO SAY YOUR GOODBYES?
GNN...
VERY WELL THEN--
NO--
HM?

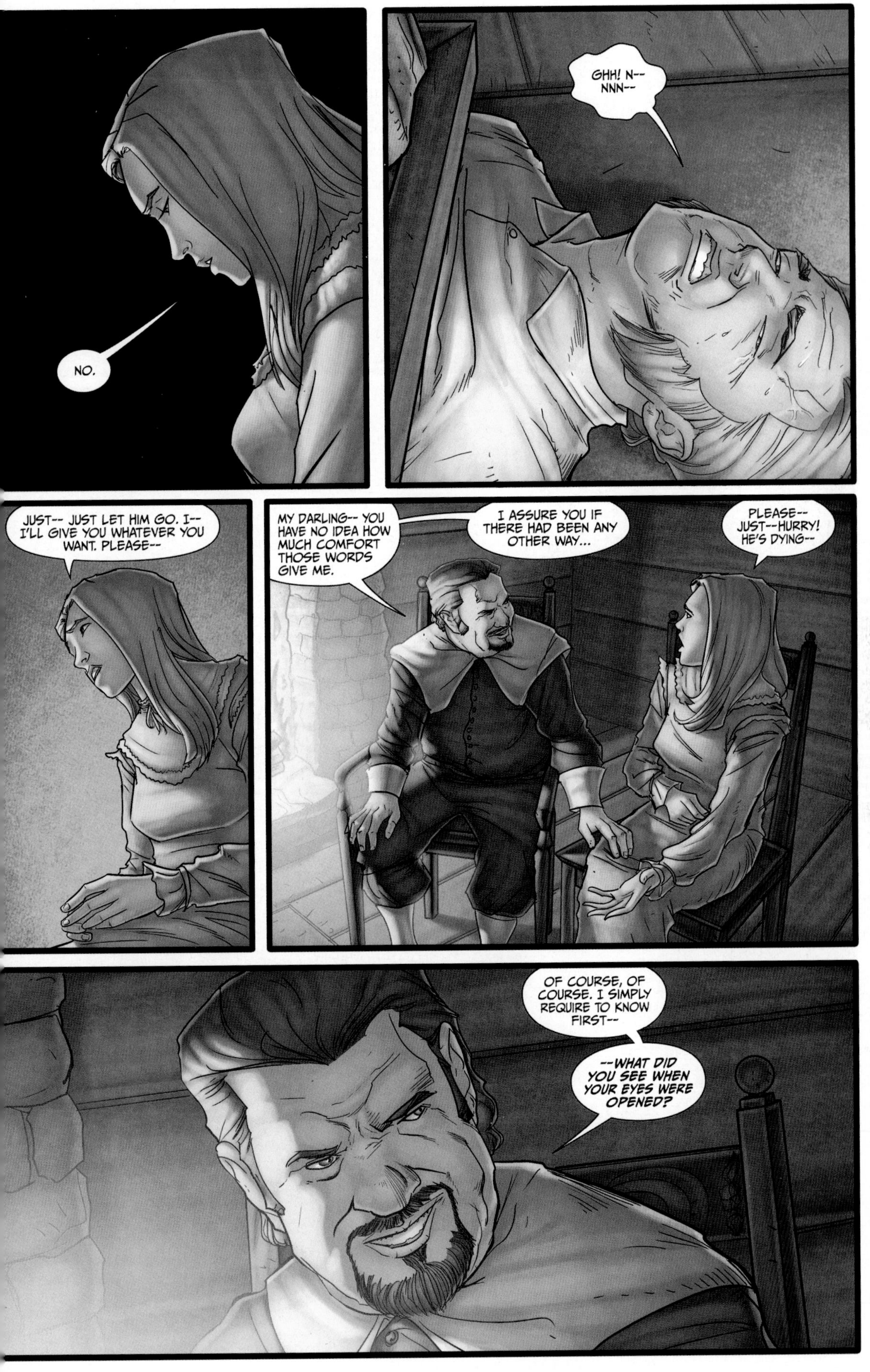
NO.
GHH! N-- NNN--
JUST-- JUST LET HIM GO. I-- I'LL GIVE YOU WHATEVER YOU WANT. PLEASE--
MY DARLING-- YOU HAVE NO IDEA HOW MUCH COMFORT THOSE WORDS GIVE ME.
I ASSURE YOU IF THERE HAD BEEN ANY OTHER WAY...
PLEASE-- JUST--HURRY! HE'S DYING--
OF COURSE, OF COURSE. I SIMPLY REQUIRE TO KNOW FIRST--
--WHAT DID YOU SEE WHEN YOUR EYES WERE OPENED?

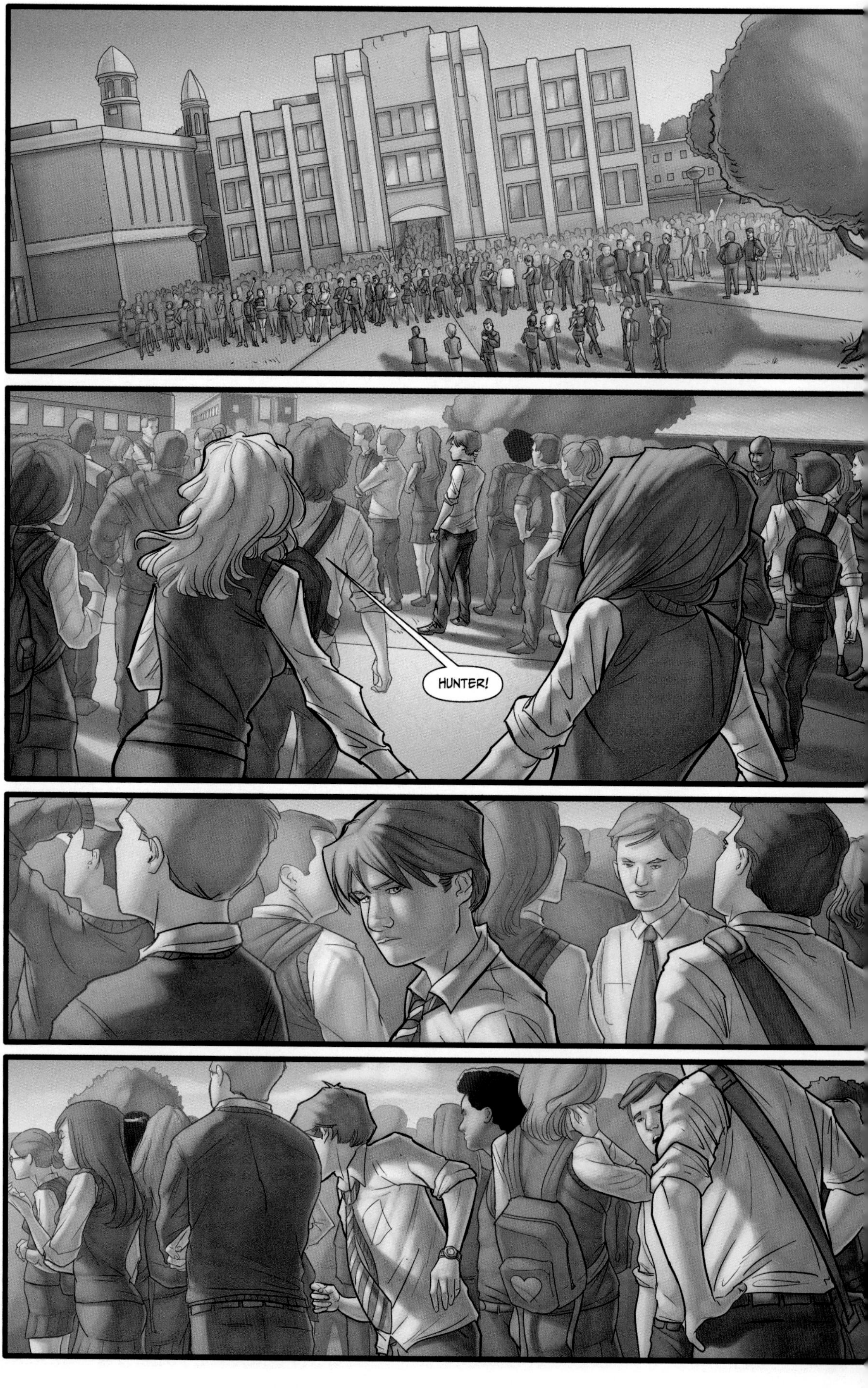
HUNTER!

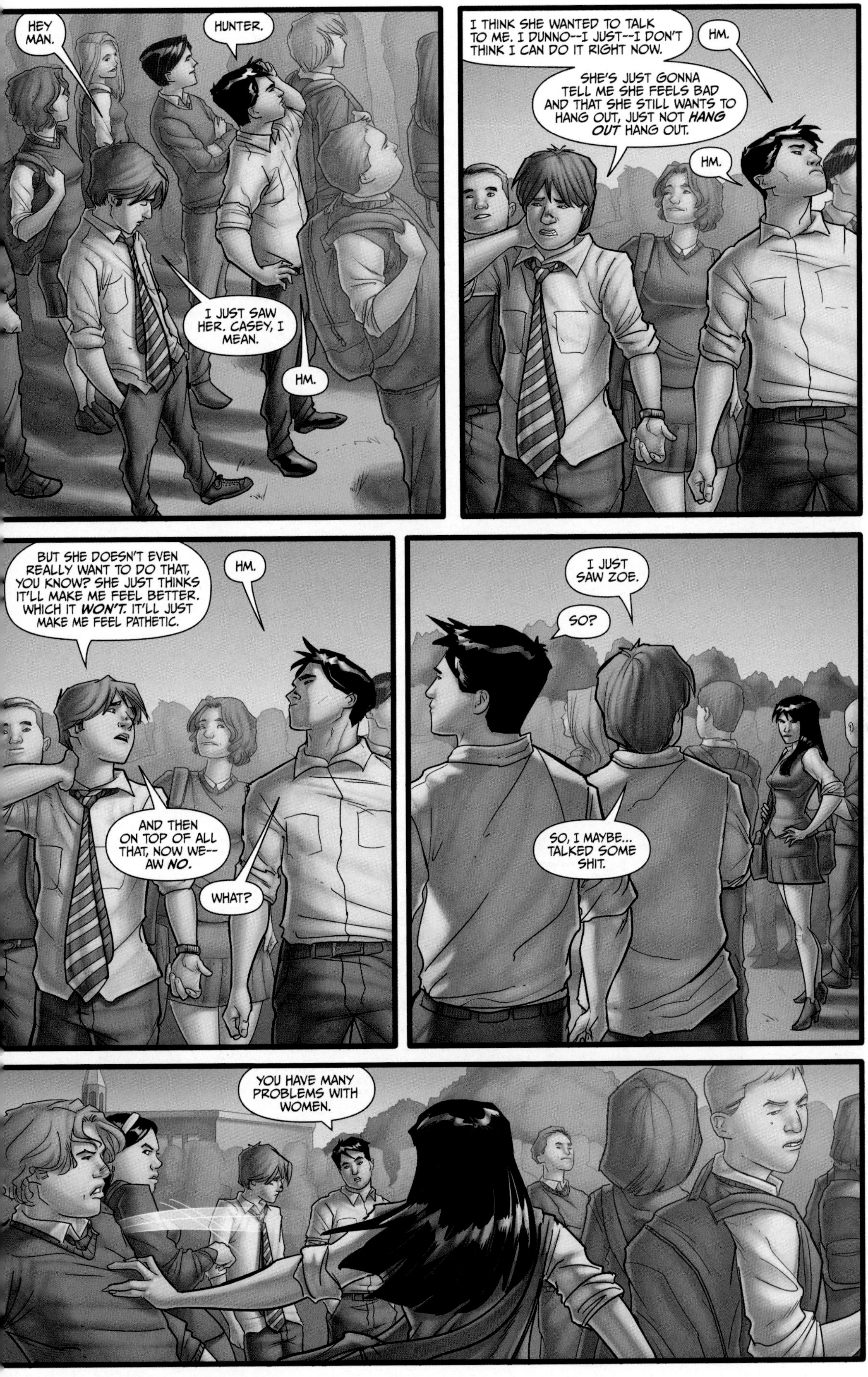
HEY MAN.
HUNTER.
I JUST SAW HER. CASEY, I MEAN.
HM.
I THINK SHE WANTED TO TALK TO ME. I DUNNO--I JUST--I DON'T THINK I CAN DO IT RIGHT NOW.
HM.
SHE'S JUST GONNA TELL ME SHE FEELS BAD AND THAT SHE STILL WANTS TO HANG OUT, JUST NOT *HANG OUT* HANG OUT.
HM.
BUT SHE DOESN'T EVEN REALLY WANT TO DO THAT, YOU KNOW? SHE JUST THINKS IT'LL MAKE ME FEEL BETTER. WHICH IT *WON'T.* IT'LL JUST MAKE ME FEEL PATHETIC.
HM.
AND THEN ON TOP OF ALL THAT, NOW WE-- AW *NO.*
WHAT?
I JUST SAW ZOE.
SO?
SO, I MAYBE... TALKED SOME SHIT.
YOU HAVE MANY PROBLEMS WITH WOMEN.

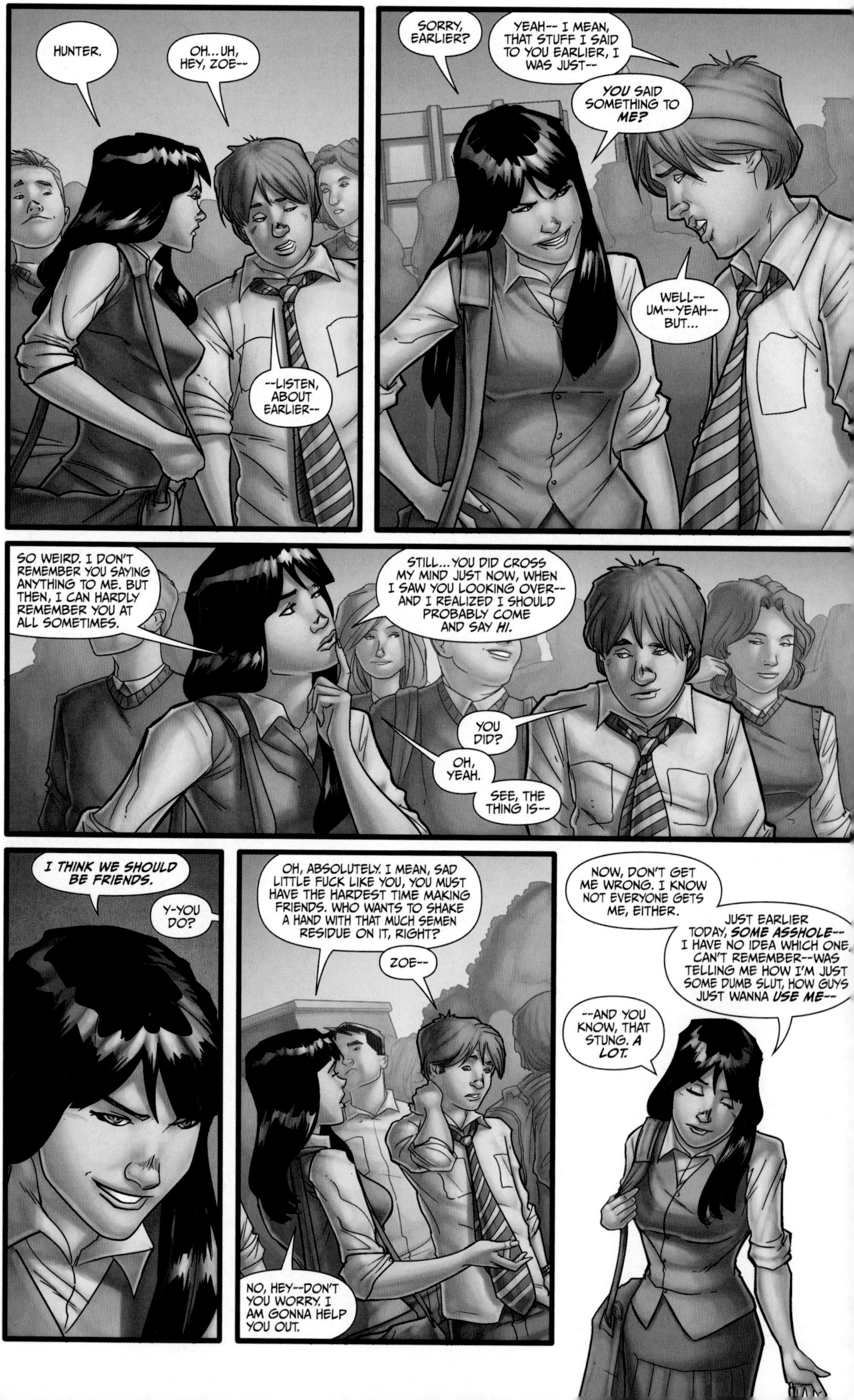
HUNTER.
OH... UH, HEY, ZOE--
--LISTEN, ABOUT EARLIER--
SORRY, EARLIER?
YEAH-- I MEAN, THAT STUFF I SAID TO YOU EARLIER, I WAS JUST--
YOU SAID SOMETHING TO ME?
WELL-- UM--YEAH-- BUT...
SO WEIRD. I DON'T REMEMBER YOU SAYING ANYTHING TO ME. BUT THEN, I CAN HARDLY REMEMBER YOU AT ALL SOMETIMES.
STILL... YOU DID CROSS MY MIND JUST NOW, WHEN I SAW YOU LOOKING OVER-- AND I REALIZED I SHOULD PROBABLY COME AND SAY HI.
YOU DID?
OH, YEAH.
SEE, THE THING IS--
I THINK WE SHOULD BE FRIENDS.
Y-YOU DO?
OH, ABSOLUTELY. I MEAN, SAD LITTLE FUCK LIKE YOU, YOU MUST HAVE THE HARDEST TIME MAKING FRIENDS. WHO WANTS TO SHAKE A HAND WITH THAT MUCH SEMEN RESIDUE ON IT, RIGHT?
ZOE--
NO, HEY--DON'T YOU WORRY. I AM GONNA HELP YOU OUT.
NOW, DON'T GET ME WRONG. I KNOW NOT EVERYONE GETS ME, EITHER.
JUST EARLIER TODAY, SOME ASSHOLE-- I HAVE NO IDEA WHICH ONE, CAN'T REMEMBER--WAS TELLING ME HOW I'M JUST SOME DUMB SLUT, HOW GUYS JUST WANNA USE ME--
--AND YOU KNOW, THAT STUNG. A LOT.

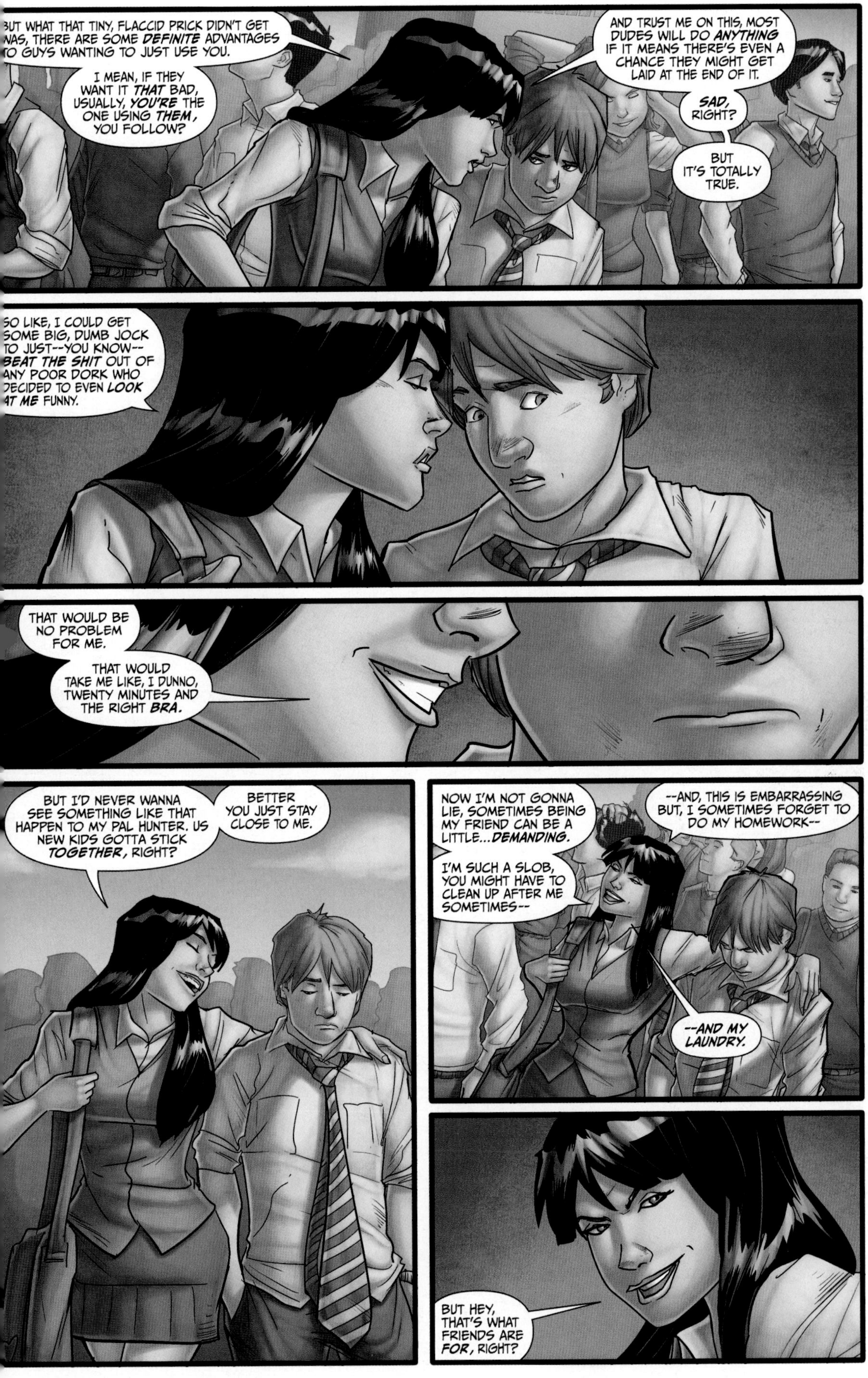

BUT WHAT THAT TINY, FLACCID PRICK DIDN'T GET WAS, THERE ARE SOME DEFINITE ADVANTAGES TO GUYS WANTING TO JUST USE YOU.
I MEAN, IF THEY WANT IT THAT BAD, USUALLY, YOU'RE THE ONE USING THEM, YOU FOLLOW?
AND TRUST ME ON THIS, MOST DUDES WILL DO ANYTHING IF IT MEANS THERE'S EVEN A CHANCE THEY MIGHT GET LAID AT THE END OF IT.
SAD, RIGHT?
BUT IT'S TOTALLY TRUE.
SO LIKE, I COULD GET SOME BIG, DUMB JOCK TO JUST--YOU KNOW-- BEAT THE SHIT OUT OF ANY POOR DORK WHO DECIDED TO EVEN LOOK AT ME FUNNY.
THAT WOULD BE NO PROBLEM FOR ME.
THAT WOULD TAKE ME LIKE, I DUNNO, TWENTY MINUTES AND THE RIGHT BRA.
BUT I'D NEVER WANNA SEE SOMETHING LIKE THAT HAPPEN TO MY PAL HUNTER. US NEW KIDS GOTTA STICK TOGETHER, RIGHT?
BETTER YOU JUST STAY CLOSE TO ME.
NOW I'M NOT GONNA LIE, SOMETIMES BEING MY FRIEND CAN BE A LITTLE...DEMANDING.
I'M SUCH A SLOB, YOU MIGHT HAVE TO CLEAN UP AFTER ME SOMETIMES--
--AND, THIS IS EMBARRASSING BUT, I SOMETIMES FORGET TO DO MY HOMEWORK--
--AND MY LAUNDRY.
BUT HEY, THAT'S WHAT FRIENDS ARE FOR, RIGHT?

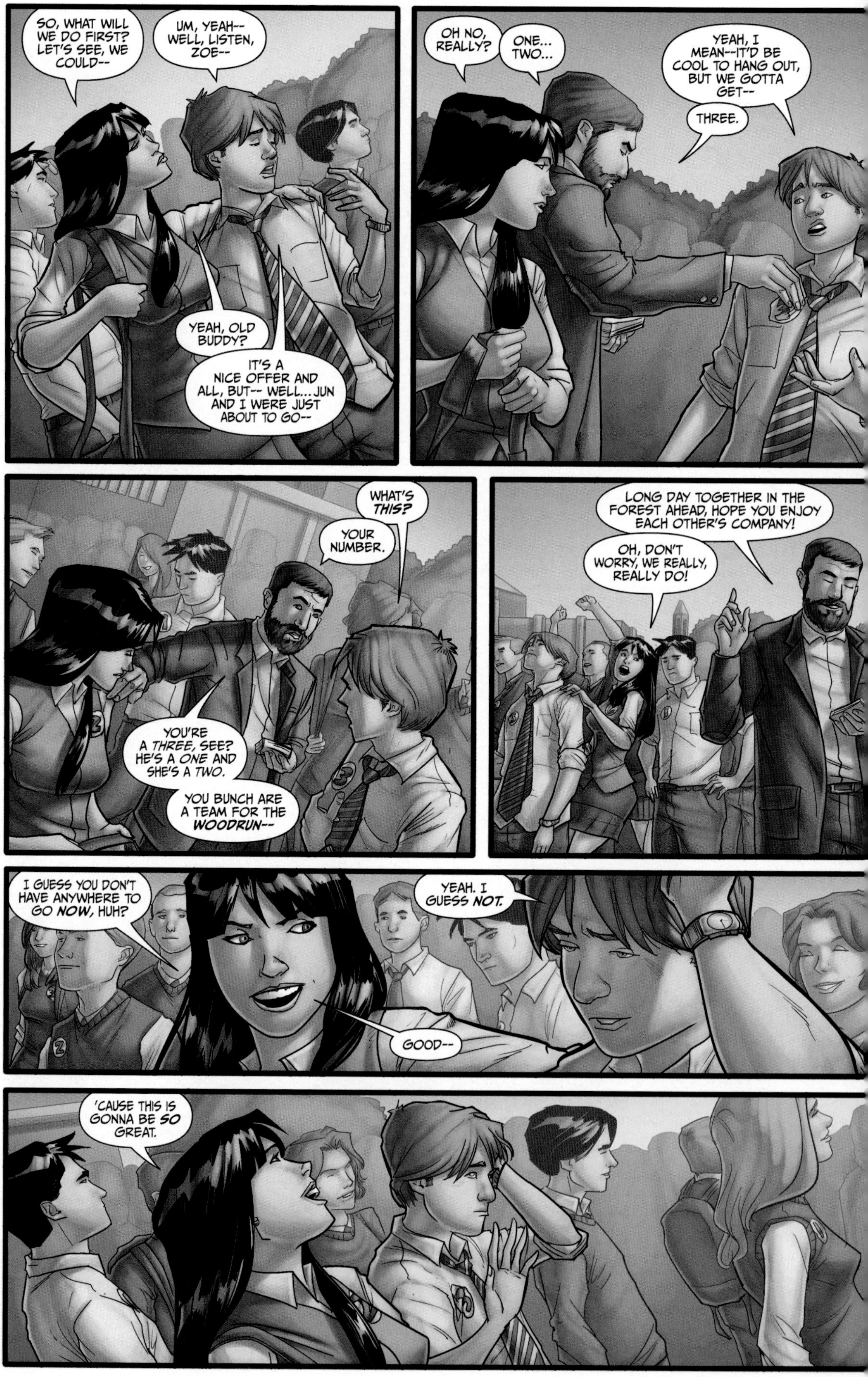

SO, WHAT WILL WE DO FIRST? LET'S SEE, WE COULD--
UM, YEAH-- WELL, LISTEN, ZOE--
YEAH, OLD BUDDY?
IT'S A NICE OFFER AND ALL, BUT-- WELL... JUN AND I WERE JUST ABOUT TO GO--
OH NO, REALLY?
ONE... TWO...
YEAH, I MEAN--IT'D BE COOL TO HANG OUT, BUT WE GOTTA GET--
THREE.
WHAT'S *THIS?*
YOUR NUMBER.
YOU'RE A *THREE,* SEE? HE'S A *ONE* AND SHE'S A *TWO.*
YOU BUNCH ARE A TEAM FOR THE ***WOODRUN--***
LONG DAY TOGETHER IN THE FOREST AHEAD, HOPE YOU ENJOY EACH OTHER'S COMPANY!
OH, DON'T WORRY, WE REALLY, REALLY DO!
I GUESS YOU DON'T HAVE ANYWHERE TO GO **NOW,** HUH?
YEAH. I GUESS **NOT.**
GOOD--
'CAUSE THIS IS GONNA BE ***SO*** GREAT.

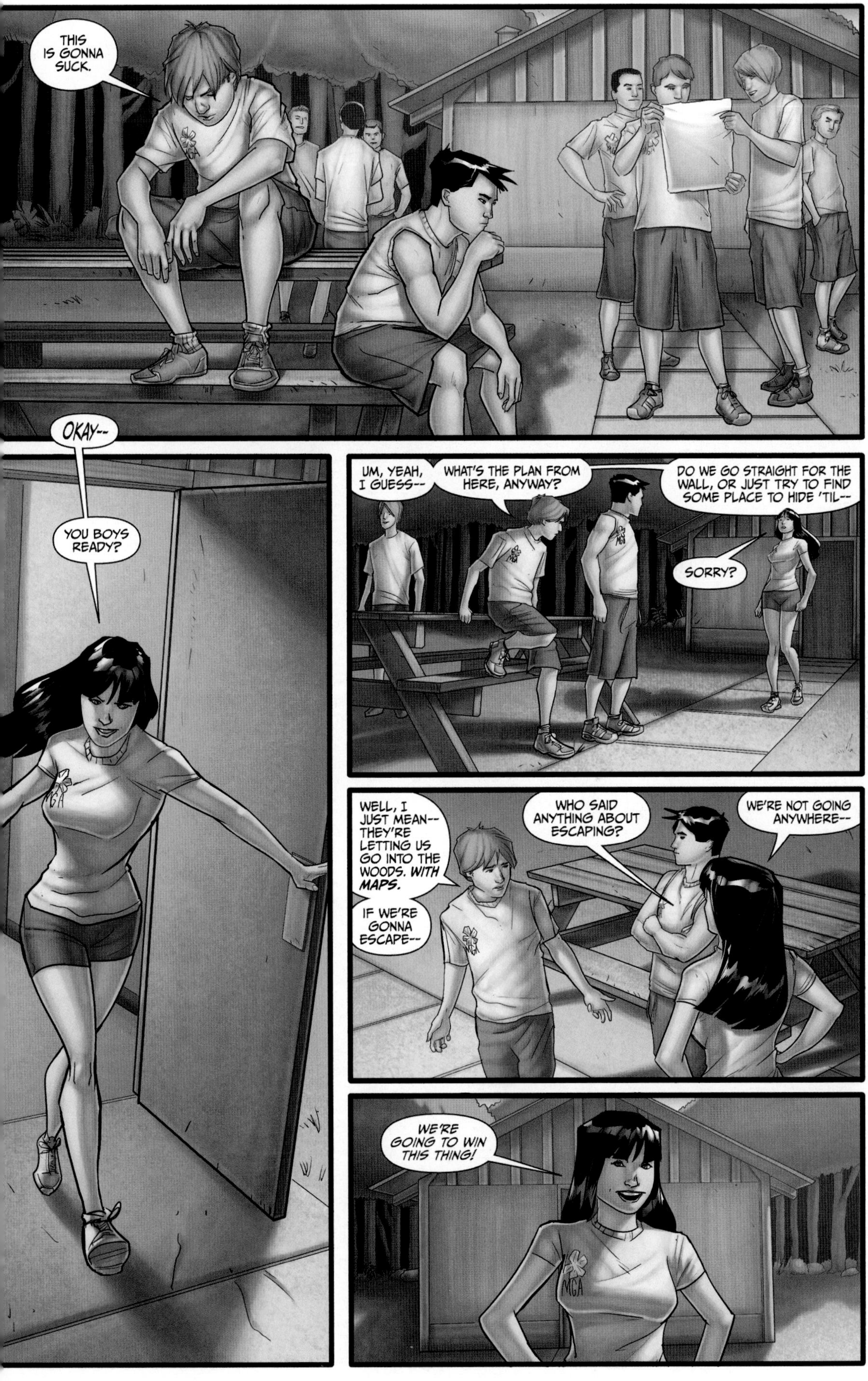
THIS IS GONNA SUCK.
OKAY--
YOU BOYS READY?
UM, YEAH, I GUESS--
WHAT'S THE PLAN FROM HERE, ANYWAY?
DO WE GO STRAIGHT FOR THE WALL, OR JUST TRY TO FIND SOME PLACE TO HIDE 'TIL--
SORRY?
WELL, I JUST MEAN-- THEY'RE LETTING US GO INTO THE WOODS. WITH MAPS.
IF WE'RE GONNA ESCAPE--
WHO SAID ANYTHING ABOUT ESCAPING?
WE'RE NOT GOING ANYWHERE--
WE'RE GOING TO WIN THIS THING!

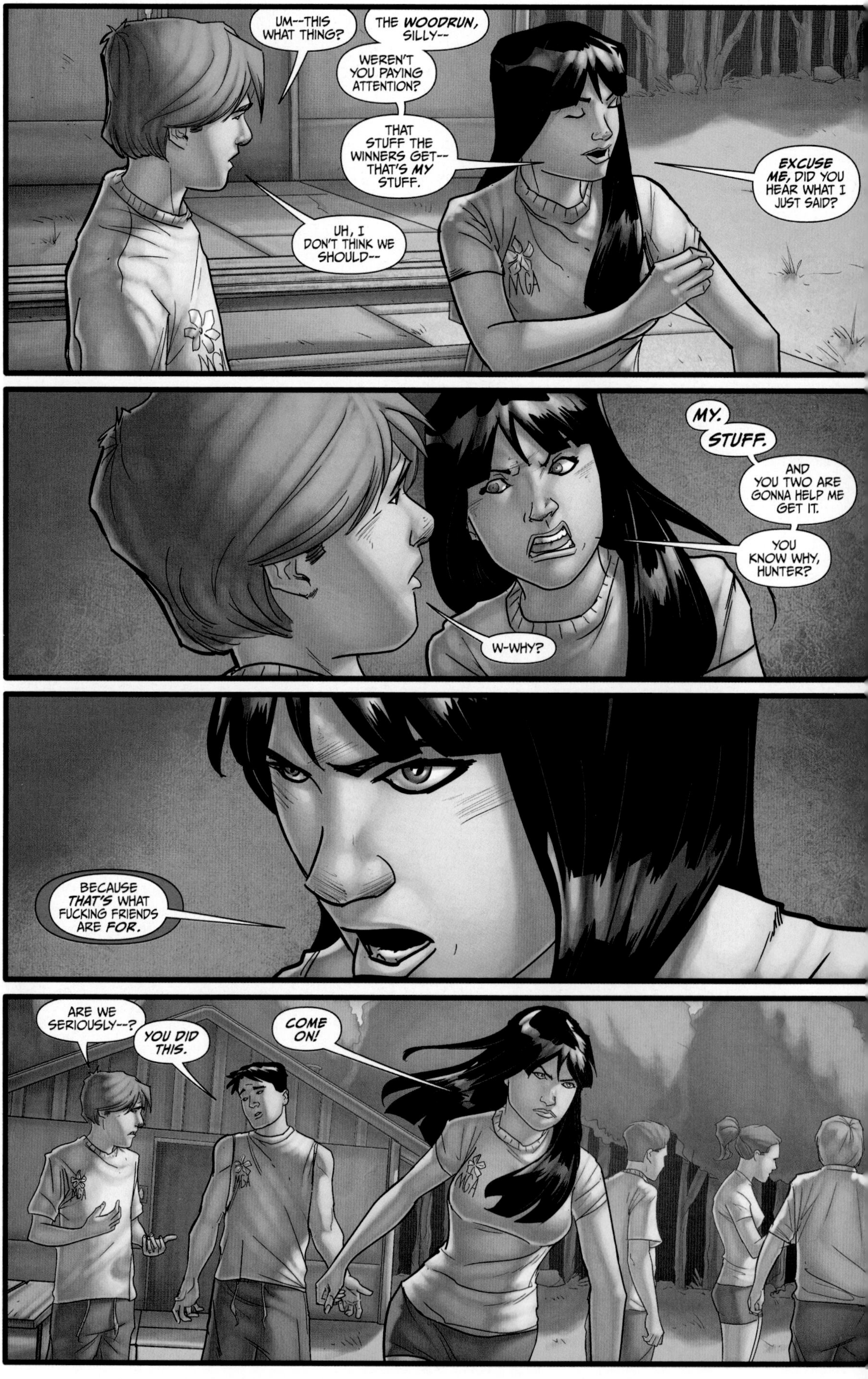
UM--THIS WHAT THING?
THE *WOODRUN,* SILLY--
WEREN'T YOU PAYING ATTENTION?
THAT STUFF THE WINNERS GET-- THAT'S *MY* STUFF.
UH, I DON'T THINK WE SHOULD--
EXCUSE ME, DID YOU HEAR WHAT I JUST SAID?
MY. STUFF.
AND YOU TWO ARE GONNA HELP ME GET IT.
YOU KNOW WHY, HUNTER?
W-WHY?
BECAUSE ***THAT'S*** WHAT FUCKING FRIENDS ARE ***FOR.***
ARE WE SERIOUSLY--?
YOU DID THIS.
COME ON!

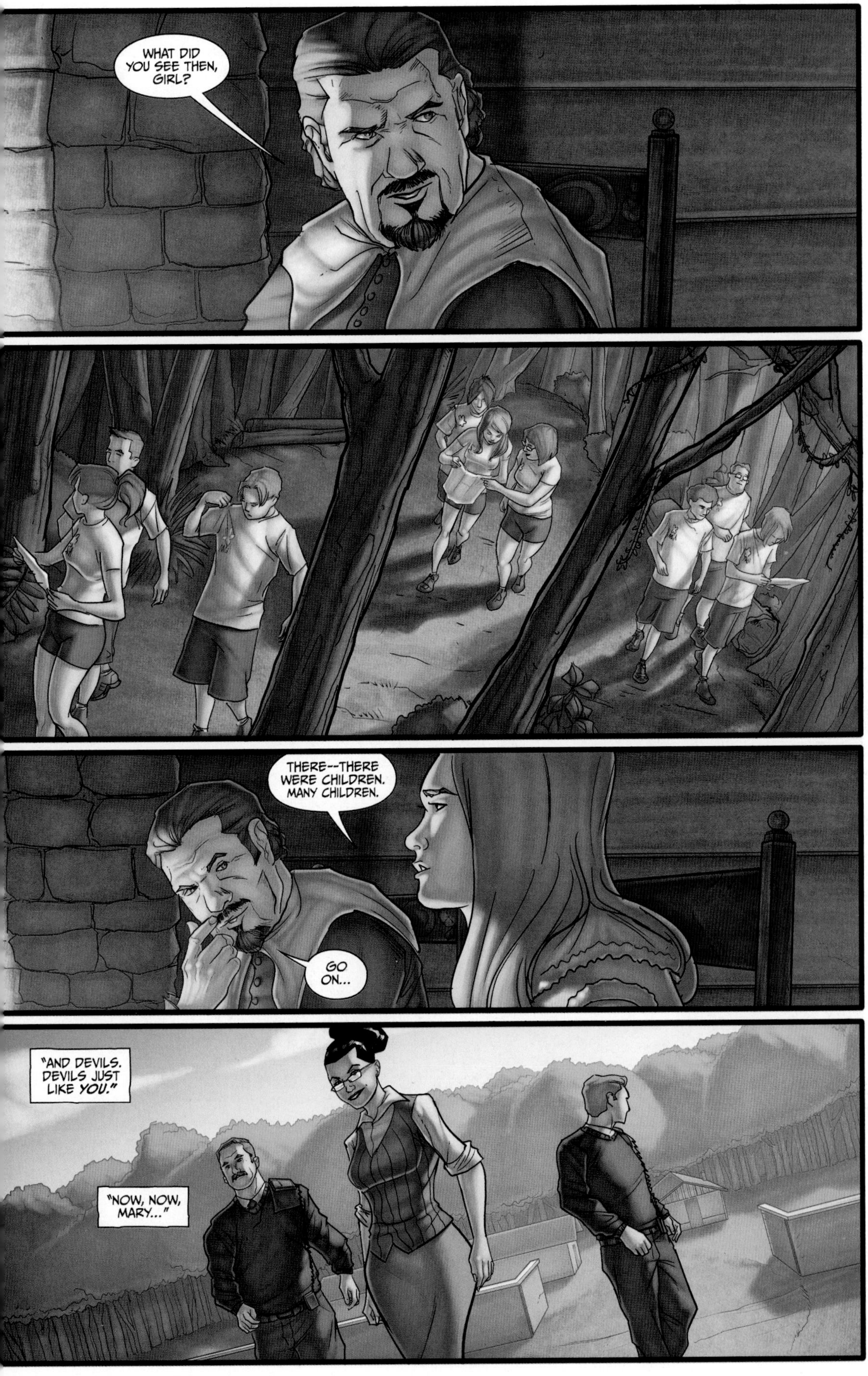
WHAT DID YOU SEE THEN, GIRL?
THERE--THERE WERE CHILDREN. MANY CHILDREN.
GO ON...
"AND DEVILS. DEVILS JUST LIKE *YOU*."
"NOW, NOW, MARY..."

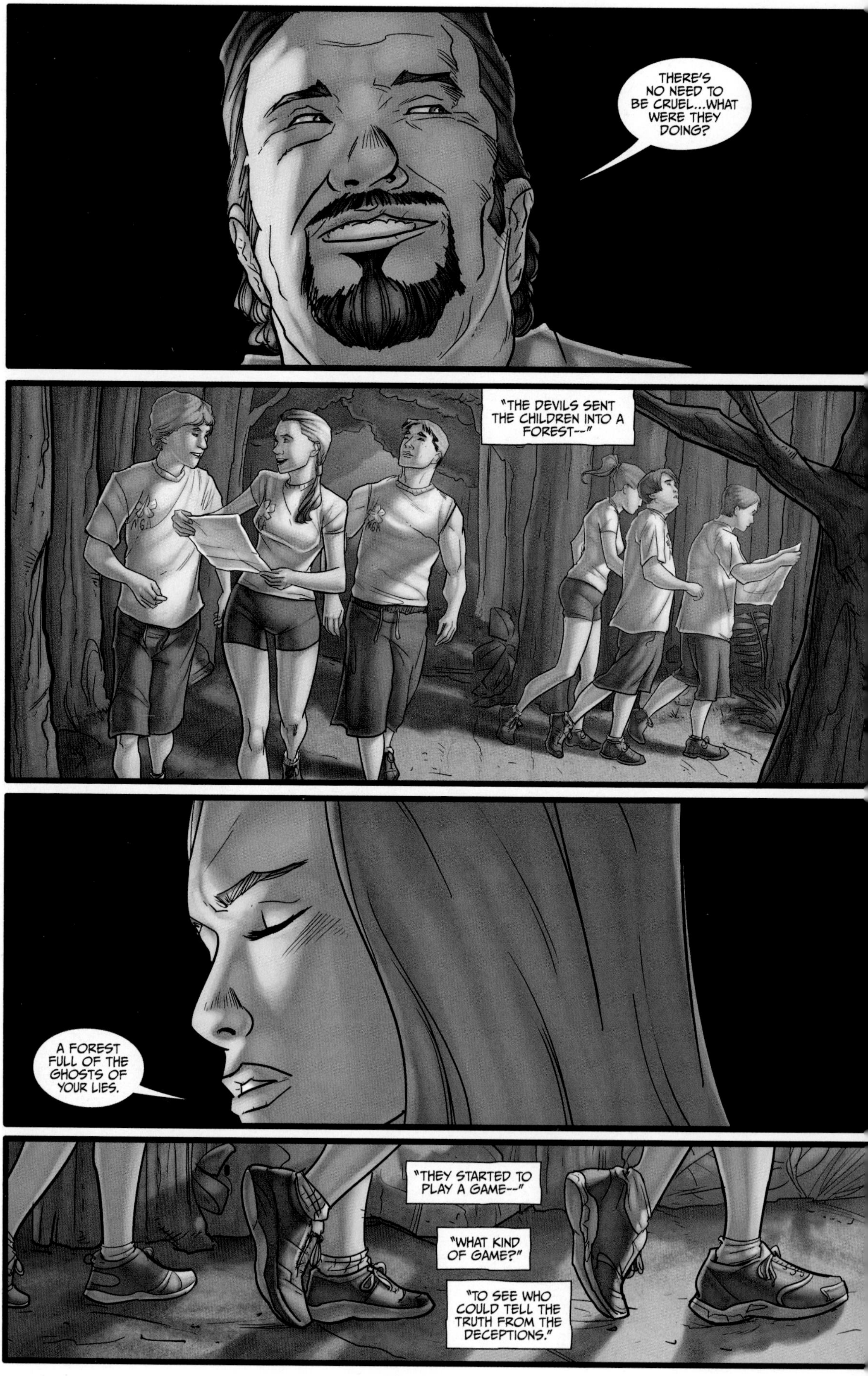
THERE'S NO NEED TO BE CRUEL...WHAT WERE THEY DOING?
"THE DEVILS SENT THE CHILDREN INTO A FOREST--"
A FOREST FULL OF THE GHOSTS OF YOUR LIES.
"THEY STARTED TO PLAY A GAME--"
"WHAT KIND OF GAME?"
"TO SEE WHO COULD TELL THE TRUTH FROM THE DECEPTIONS."

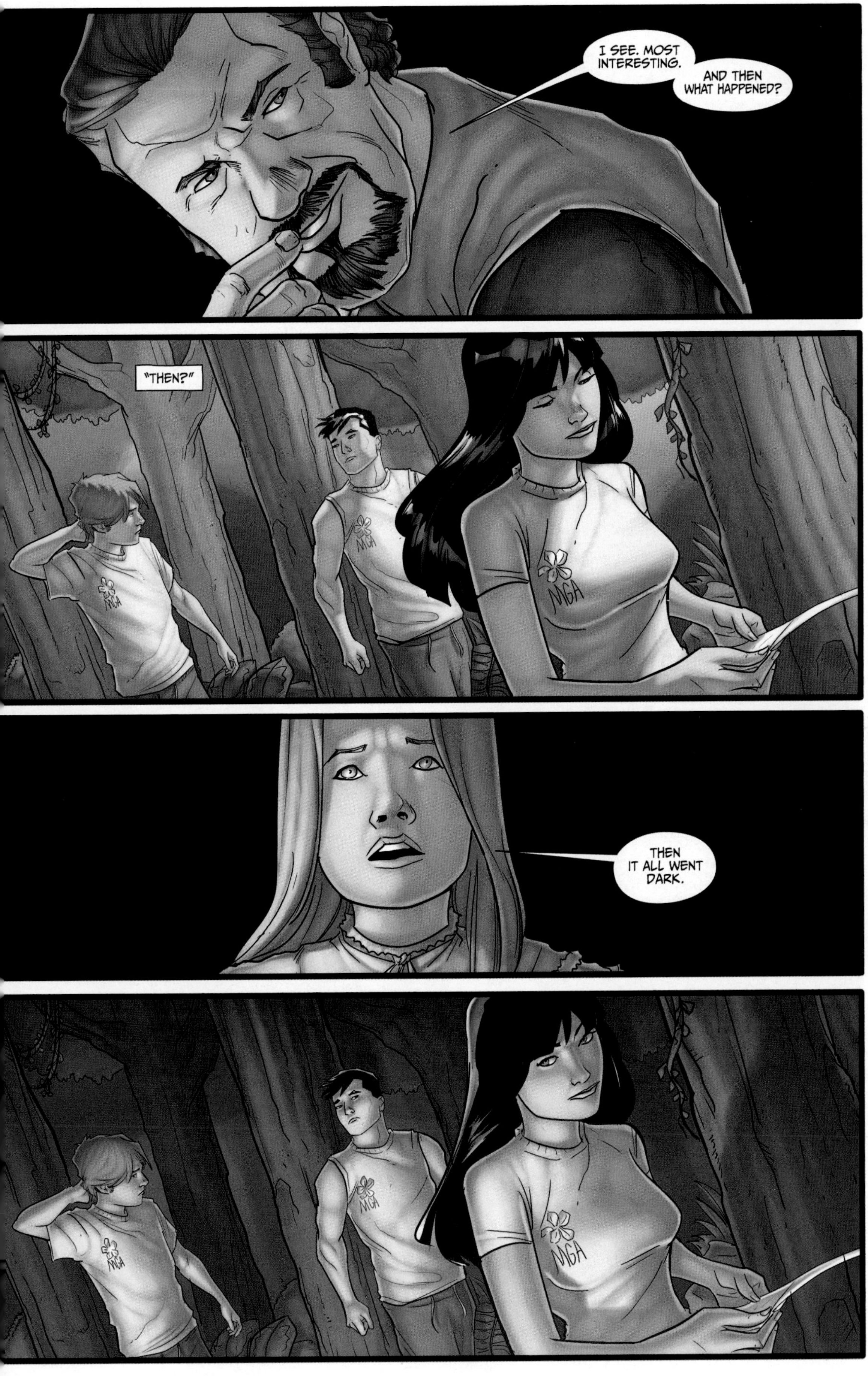
I SEE. MOST INTERESTING.
AND THEN WHAT HAPPENED?
"THEN?"
THEN IT ALL WENT DARK.

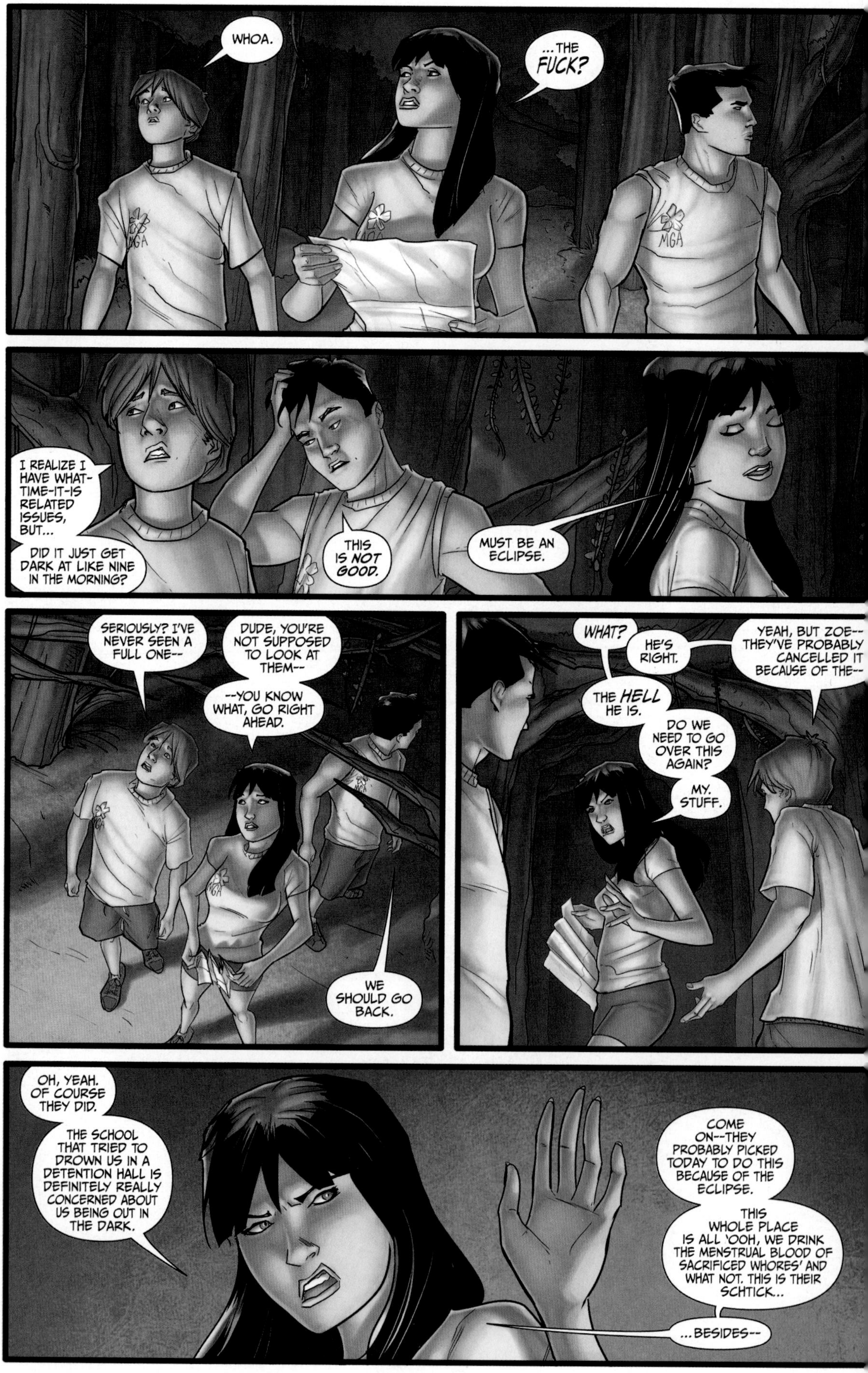
WHOA.
...THE FUCK?
I REALIZE I HAVE WHAT-TIME-IT-IS RELATED ISSUES, BUT...
DID IT JUST GET DARK AT LIKE NINE IN THE MORNING?
THIS IS NOT GOOD.
MUST BE AN ECLIPSE.
SERIOUSLY? I'VE NEVER SEEN A FULL ONE--
DUDE, YOU'RE NOT SUPPOSED TO LOOK AT THEM--
--YOU KNOW WHAT, GO RIGHT AHEAD.
WE SHOULD GO BACK.
WHAT?
HE'S RIGHT.
YEAH, BUT ZOE--THEY'VE PROBABLY CANCELLED IT BECAUSE OF THE--
THE HELL HE IS.
DO WE NEED TO GO OVER THIS AGAIN?
MY. STUFF.
OH, YEAH. OF COURSE THEY DID.
THE SCHOOL THAT TRIED TO DROWN US IN A DETENTION HALL IS DEFINITELY REALLY CONCERNED ABOUT US BEING OUT IN THE DARK.
COME ON--THEY PROBABLY PICKED TODAY TO DO THIS BECAUSE OF THE ECLIPSE.
THIS WHOLE PLACE IS ALL 'OOH, WE DRINK THE MENSTRUAL BLOOD OF SACRIFICED WHORES' AND WHAT NOT. THIS IS THEIR SCHTICK...
...BESIDES--

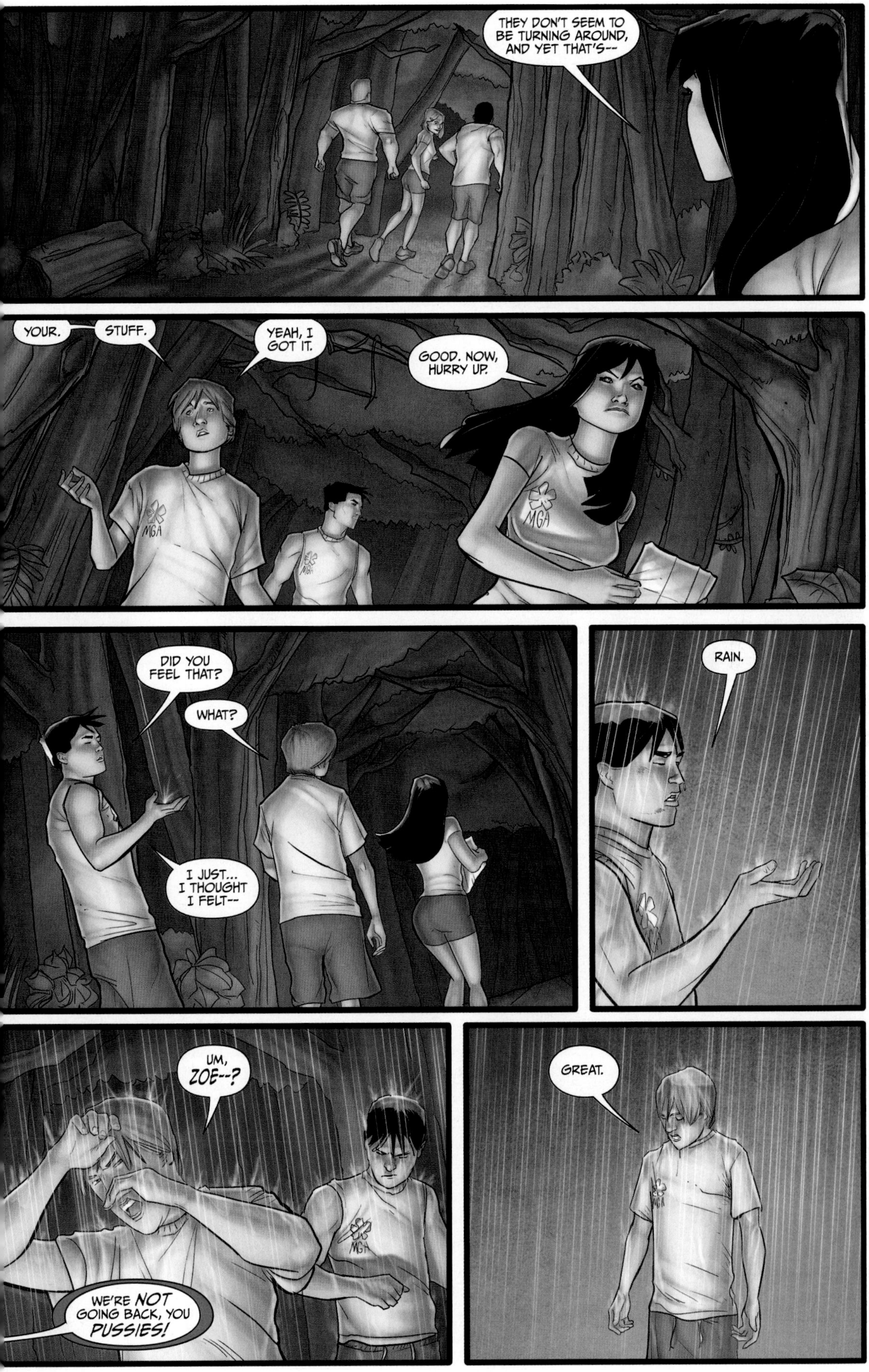
THEY DON'T SEEM TO BE TURNING AROUND, AND YET THAT'S--
YOUR.
STUFF.
YEAH, I GOT IT.
GOOD. NOW, HURRY UP.
DID YOU FEEL THAT?
WHAT?
I JUST... I THOUGHT I FELT--
RAIN.
UM, ZOE--?
WE'RE NOT GOING BACK, YOU PUSSIES!
GREAT.

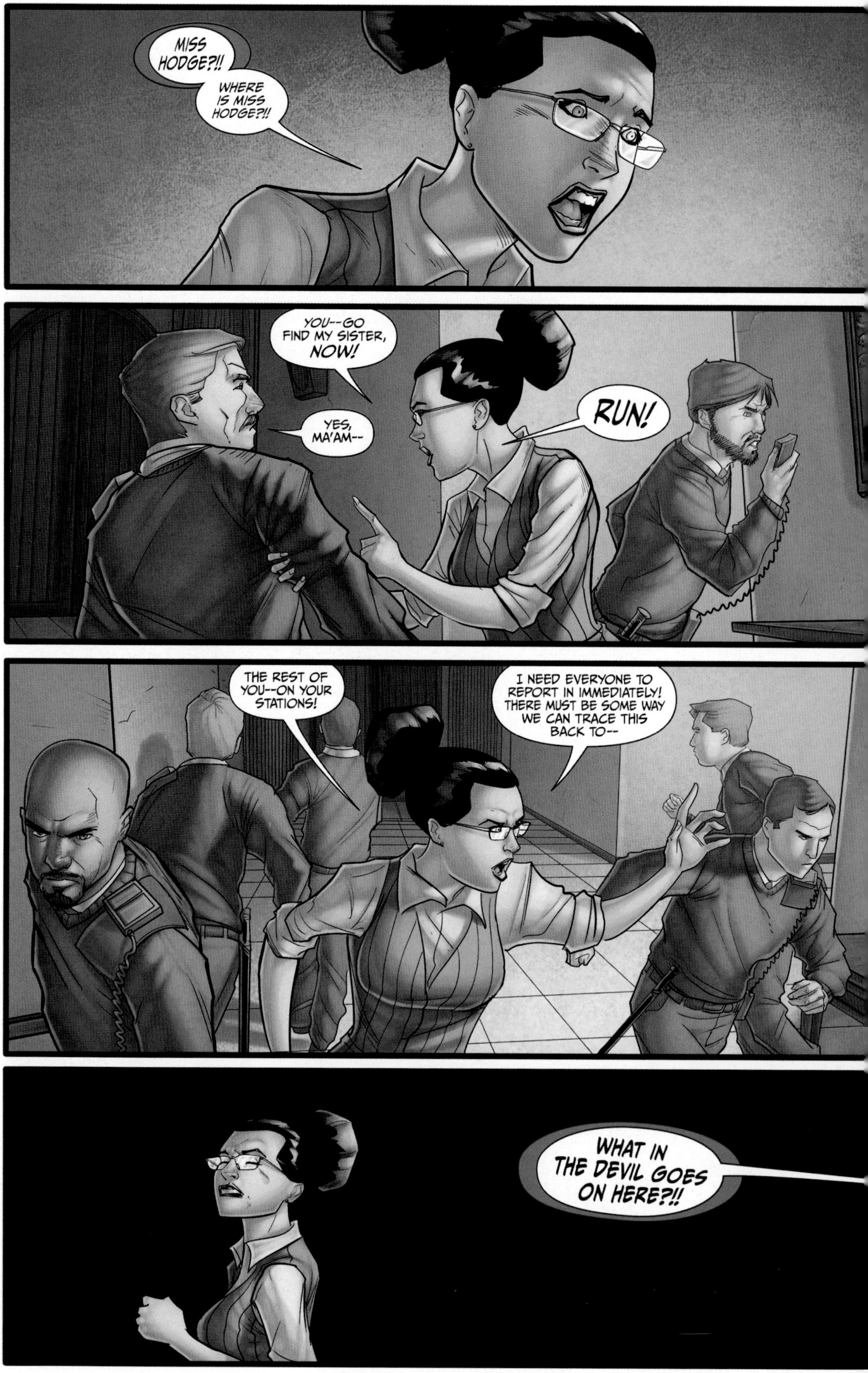
MISS HODGE?!!
WHERE IS MISS HODGE?!!
YOU--GO FIND MY SISTER, NOW!
YES, MA'AM--
RUN!
THE REST OF YOU--ON YOUR STATIONS!
I NEED EVERYONE TO REPORT IN IMMEDIATELY! THERE MUST BE SOME WAY WE CAN TRACE THIS BACK TO--
WHAT IN THE DEVIL GOES ON HERE?!!

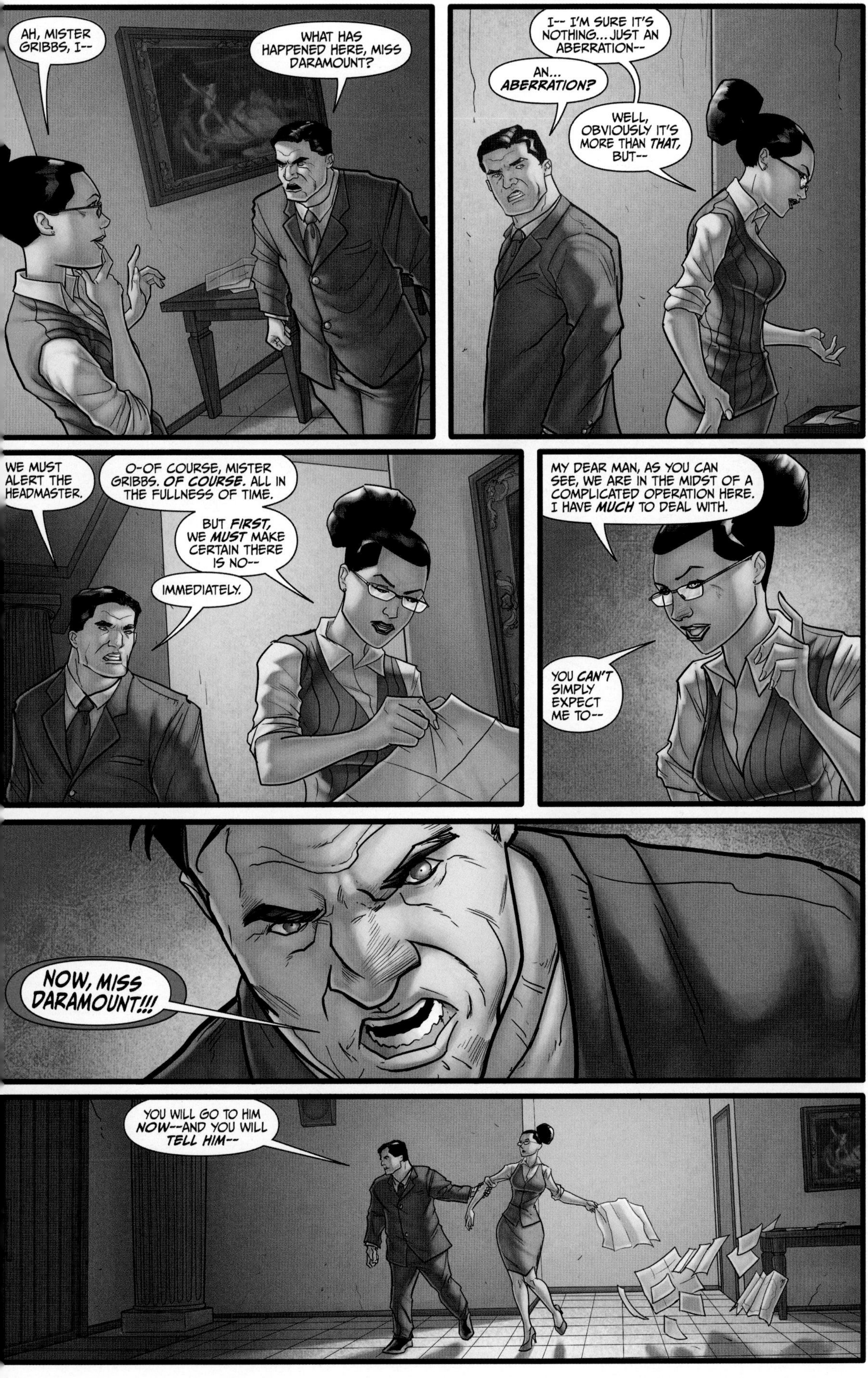

AH, MISTER GRIBBS, I--
WHAT HAS HAPPENED HERE, MISS DARAMOUNT?
I-- I'M SURE IT'S NOTHING... JUST AN ABERRATION--
AN... *ABERRATION?*
WELL, OBVIOUSLY IT'S MORE THAN *THAT,* BUT--
WE MUST ALERT THE HEADMASTER.
O-OF COURSE, MISTER GRIBBS. *OF COURSE.* ALL IN THE FULLNESS OF TIME.
BUT *FIRST,* WE *MUST* MAKE CERTAIN THERE IS NO--
IMMEDIATELY.
MY DEAR MAN, AS YOU CAN SEE, WE ARE IN THE MIDST OF A COMPLICATED OPERATION HERE. I HAVE *MUCH* TO DEAL WITH.
YOU *CAN'T* SIMPLY EXPECT ME TO--
NOW, MISS DARAMOUNT!!!
YOU WILL GO TO HIM *NOW*--AND YOU WILL *TELL HIM*--

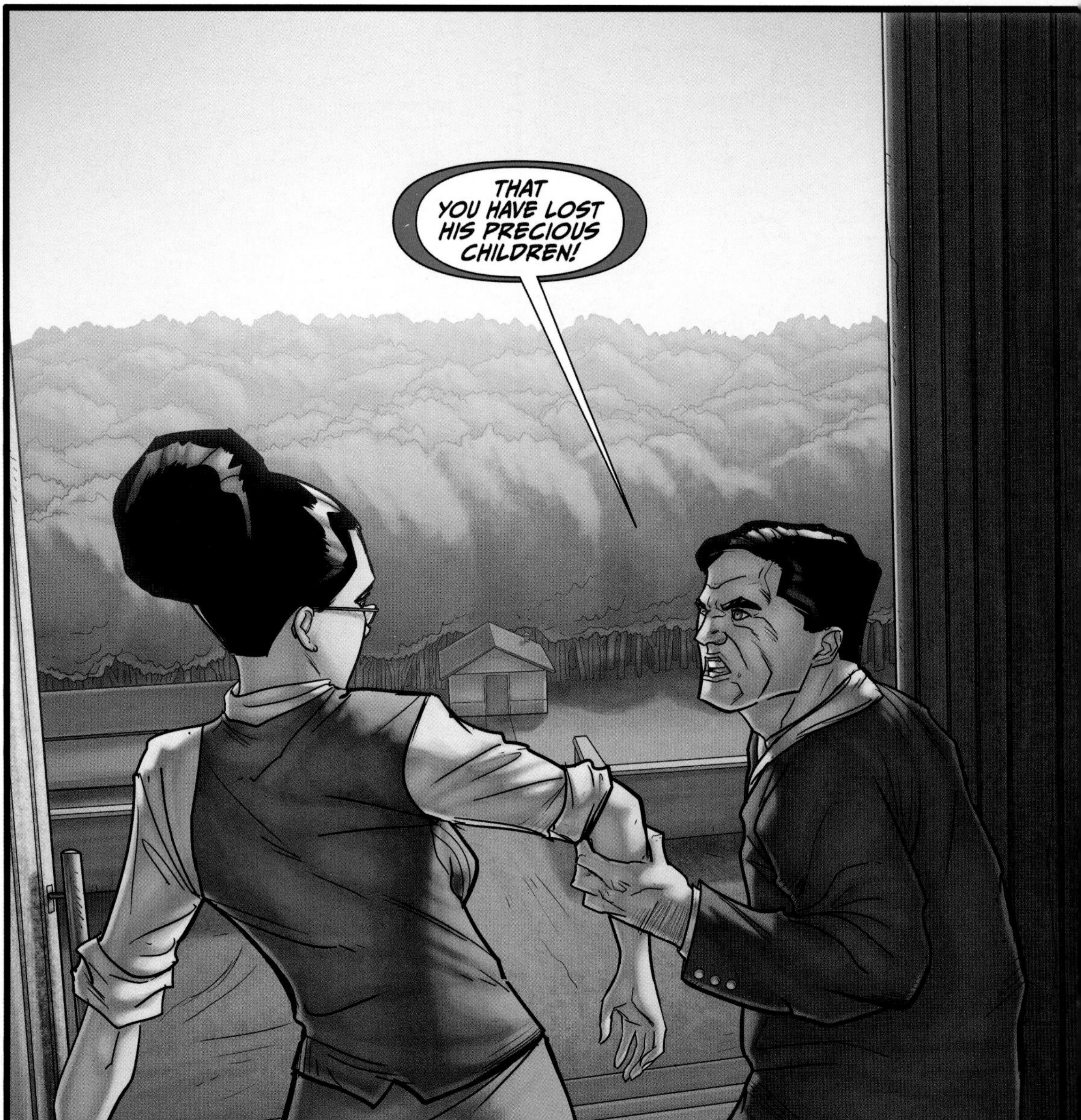
THAT YOU HAVE LOST HIS PRECIOUS CHILDREN!

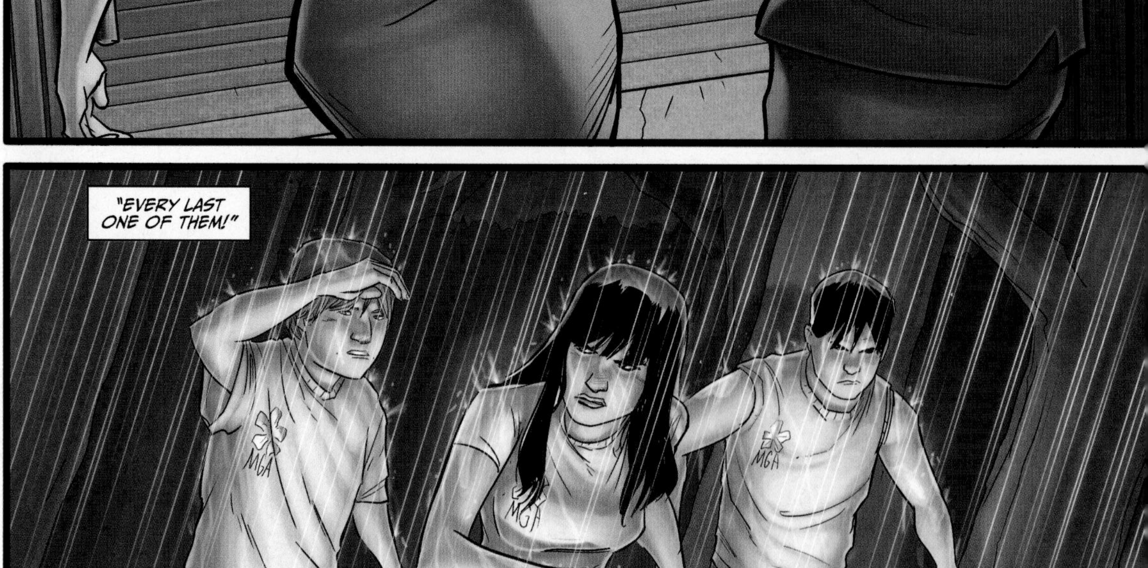
"EVERY LAST ONE OF THEM!"
MGA
MGA
MGA

fifteen

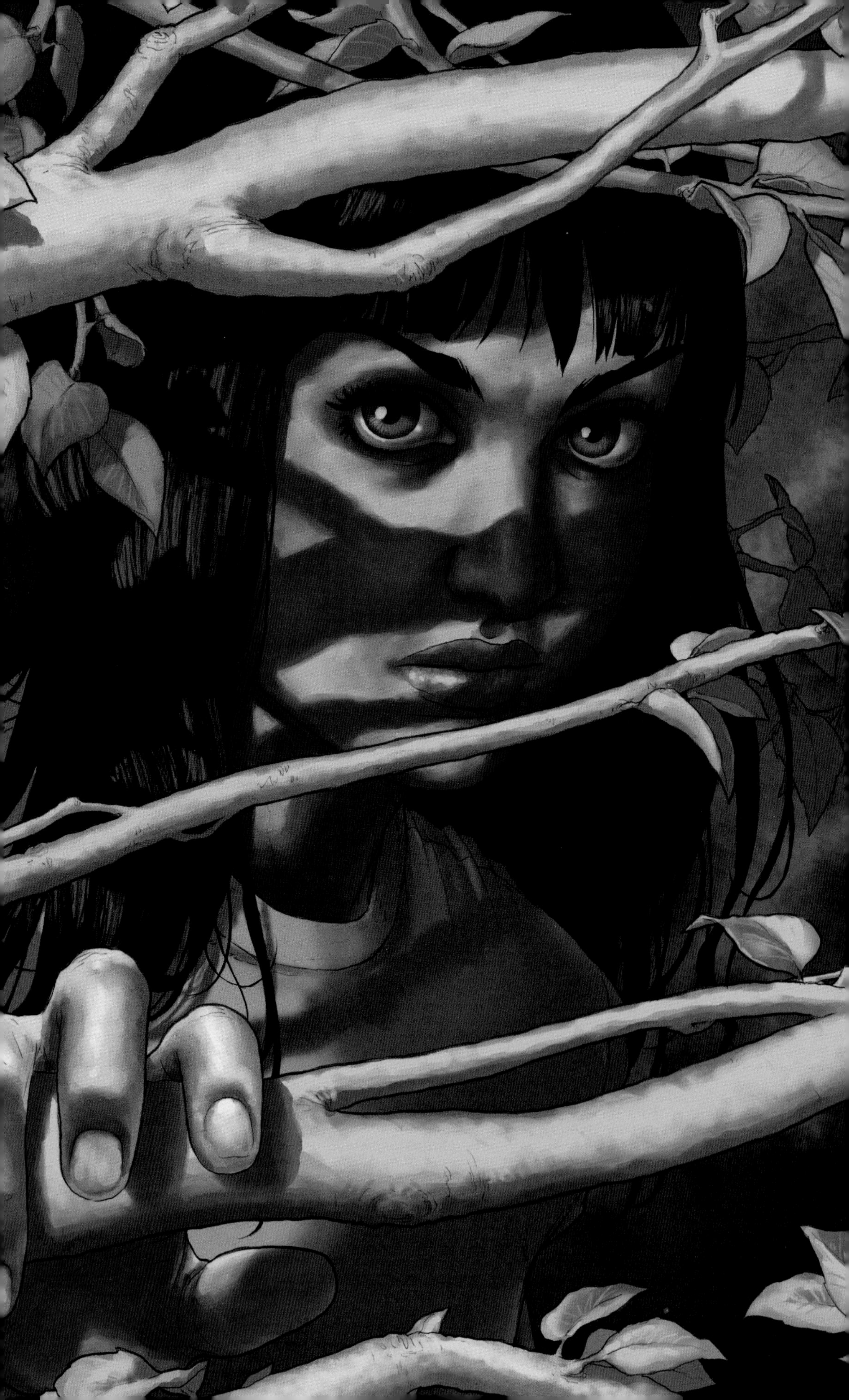

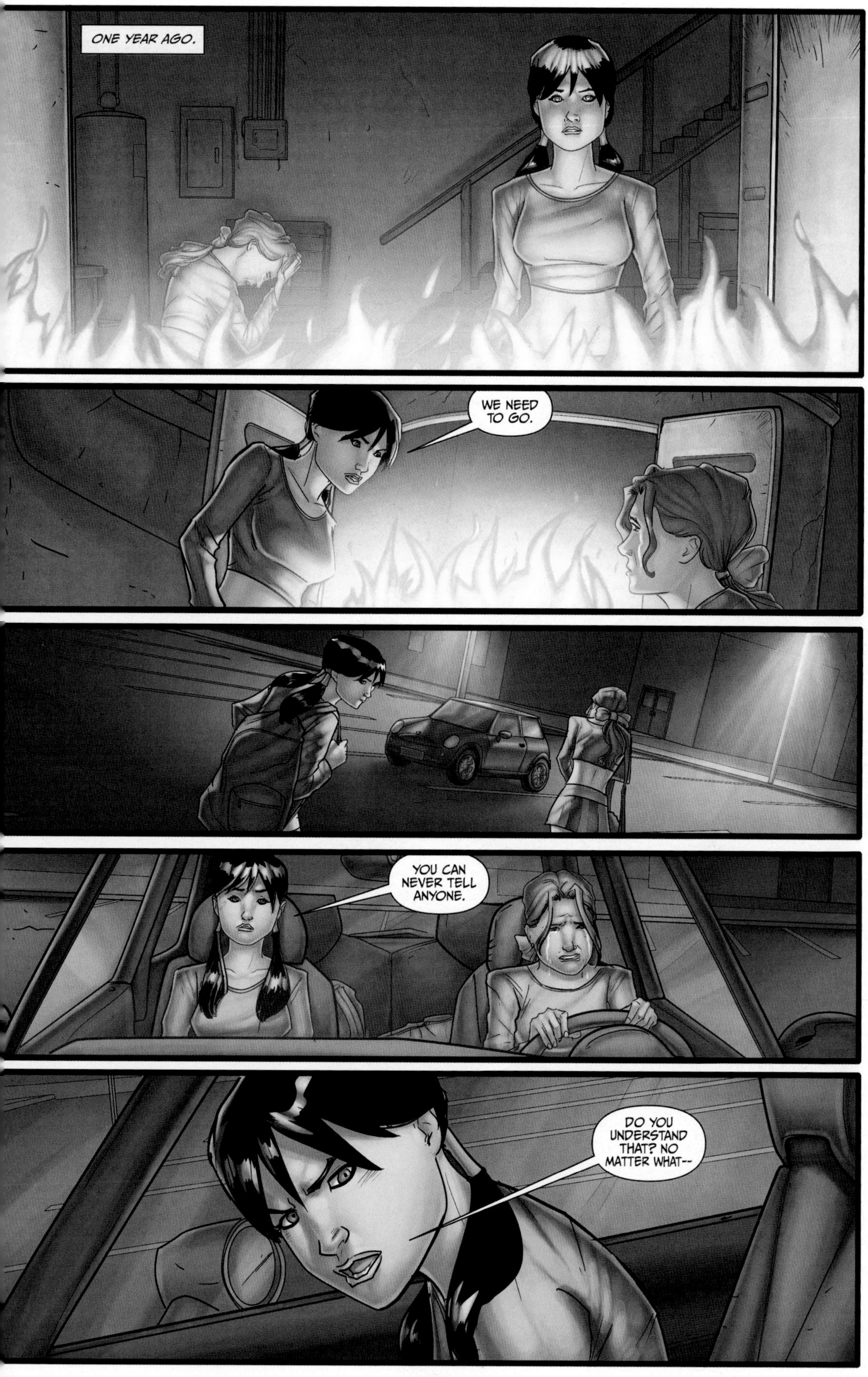
ONE YEAR AGO.
WE NEED TO GO.
YOU CAN NEVER TELL ANYONE.
DO YOU UNDERSTAND THAT? NO MATTER WHAT--

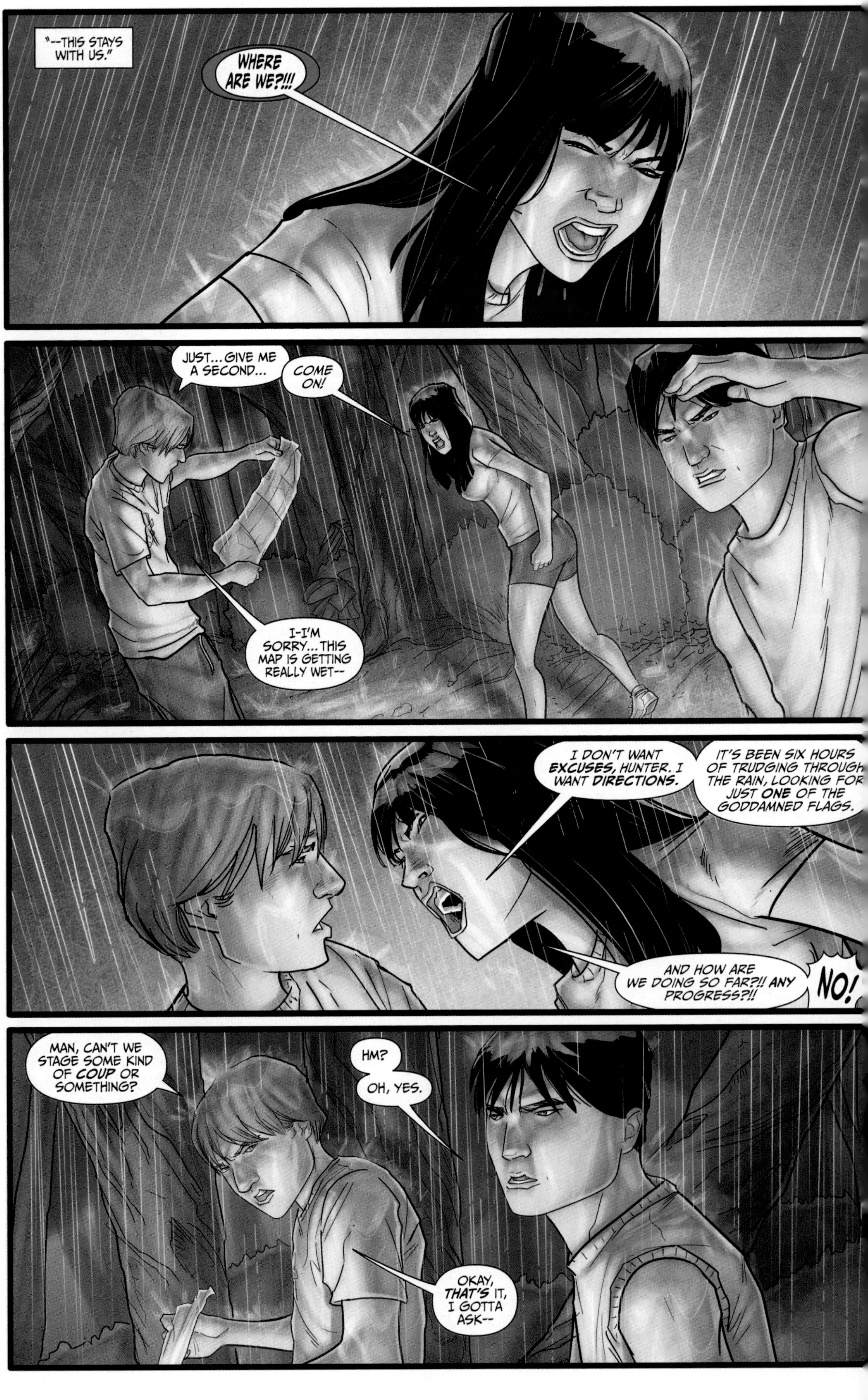
"--THIS STAYS WITH US."
WHERE ARE WE?!!!
JUST... GIVE ME A SECOND...
COME ON!
I-I'M SORRY... THIS MAP IS GETTING REALLY WET--
I DON'T WANT EXCUSES, HUNTER. I WANT DIRECTIONS.
IT'S BEEN SIX HOURS OF TRUDGING THROUGH THE RAIN, LOOKING FOR JUST ONE OF THE GODDAMNED FLAGS.
AND HOW ARE WE DOING SO FAR?!! ANY PROGRESS?!!
NO!
MAN, CAN'T WE STAGE SOME KIND OF COUP OR SOMETHING?
HM?
OH, YES.
OKAY, THAT'S IT, I GOTTA ASK--

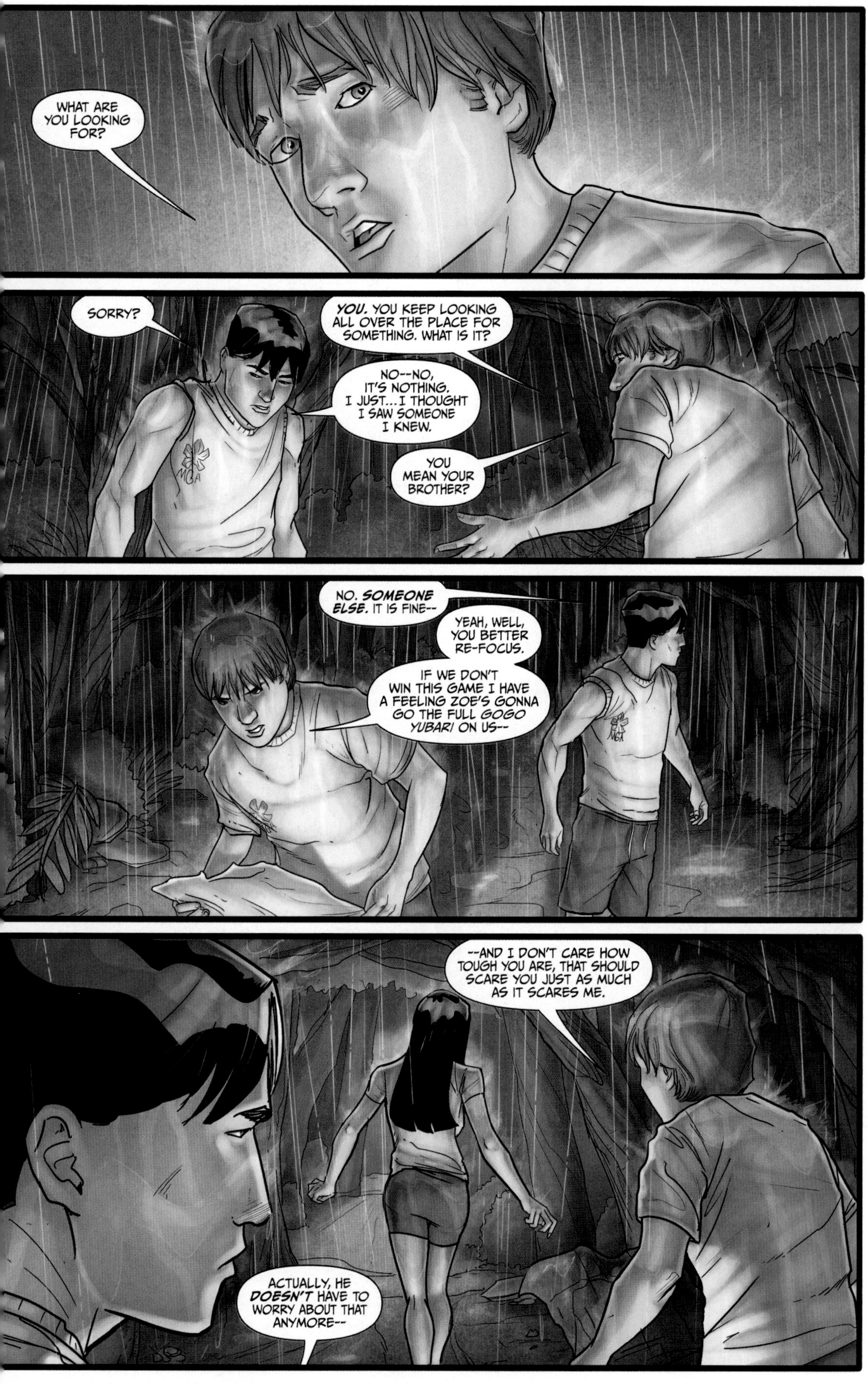
WHAT ARE YOU LOOKING FOR?
SORRY?
YOU. YOU KEEP LOOKING ALL OVER THE PLACE FOR SOMETHING. WHAT IS IT?
NO--NO, IT'S NOTHING. I JUST...I THOUGHT I SAW SOMEONE I KNEW.
YOU MEAN YOUR BROTHER?
NO. SOMEONE ELSE. IT IS FINE--
YEAH, WELL, YOU BETTER RE-FOCUS.
IF WE DON'T WIN THIS GAME I HAVE A FEELING ZOE'S GONNA GO THE FULL GOGO YUBARI ON US--
--AND I DON'T CARE HOW TOUGH YOU ARE, THAT SHOULD SCARE YOU JUST AS MUCH AS IT SCARES ME.
ACTUALLY, HE DOESN'T HAVE TO WORRY ABOUT THAT ANYMORE--

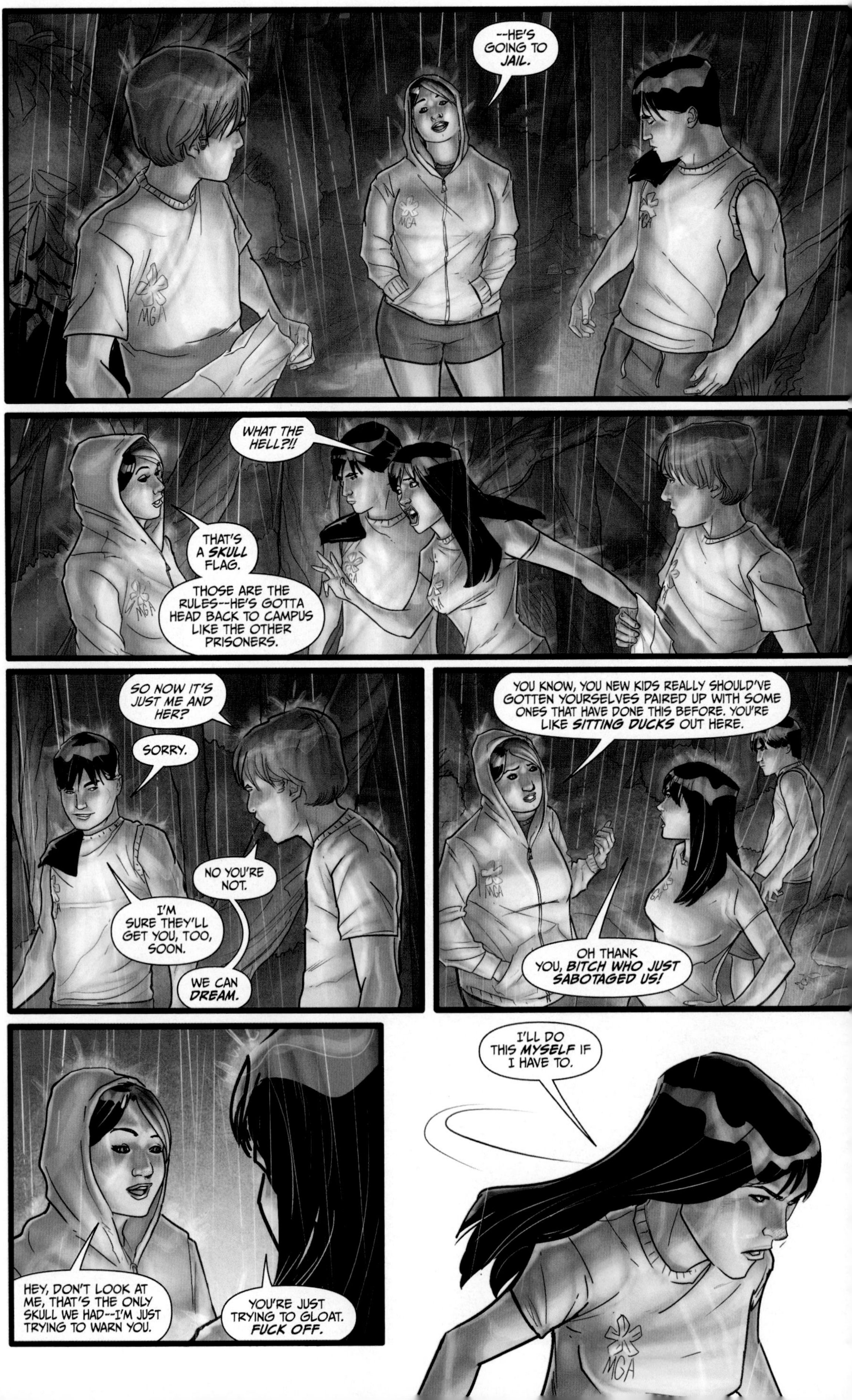

--HE'S GOING TO JAIL.
WHAT THE HELL?!!
THAT'S A SKULL FLAG.
THOSE ARE THE RULES--HE'S GOTTA HEAD BACK TO CAMPUS LIKE THE OTHER PRISONERS.
SO NOW IT'S JUST ME AND HER?
SORRY.
NO YOU'RE NOT.
I'M SURE THEY'LL GET YOU, TOO, SOON.
WE CAN DREAM.
YOU KNOW, YOU NEW KIDS REALLY SHOULD'VE GOTTEN YOURSELVES PAIRED UP WITH SOME ONES THAT HAVE DONE THIS BEFORE. YOU'RE LIKE SITTING DUCKS OUT HERE.
OH THANK YOU, BITCH WHO JUST SABOTAGED US!
HEY, DON'T LOOK AT ME, THAT'S THE ONLY SKULL WE HAD--I'M JUST TRYING TO WARN YOU.
YOU'RE JUST TRYING TO GLOAT. FUCK OFF.
I'LL DO THIS MYSELF IF I HAVE TO.

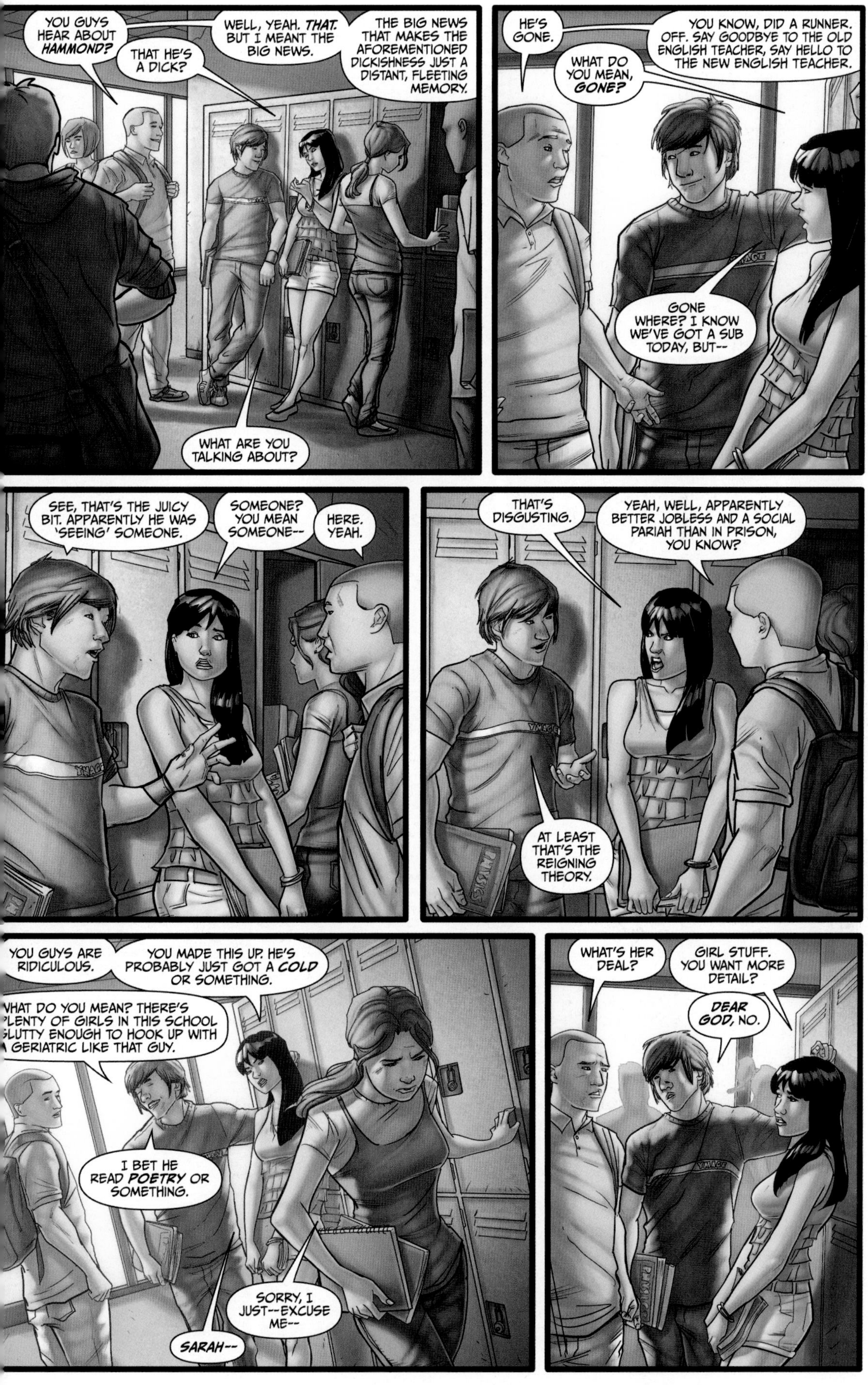
YOU GUYS HEAR ABOUT HAMMOND?
THAT HE'S A DICK?
WELL, YEAH. THAT. BUT I MEANT THE BIG NEWS.
THE BIG NEWS THAT MAKES THE AFOREMENTIONED DICKISHNESS JUST A DISTANT, FLEETING MEMORY.
WHAT ARE YOU TALKING ABOUT?
HE'S GONE.
WHAT DO YOU MEAN, GONE?
YOU KNOW, DID A RUNNER. OFF. SAY GOODBYE TO THE OLD ENGLISH TEACHER, SAY HELLO TO THE NEW ENGLISH TEACHER.
GONE WHERE? I KNOW WE'VE GOT A SUB TODAY, BUT--
SEE, THAT'S THE JUICY BIT. APPARENTLY HE WAS 'SEEING' SOMEONE.
SOMEONE? YOU MEAN SOMEONE--
HERE. YEAH.
THAT'S DISGUSTING.
YEAH, WELL, APPARENTLY BETTER JOBLESS AND A SOCIAL PARIAH THAN IN PRISON, YOU KNOW?
AT LEAST THAT'S THE REIGNING THEORY.
YOU GUYS ARE RIDICULOUS.
YOU MADE THIS UP. HE'S PROBABLY JUST GOT A COLD OR SOMETHING.
WHAT DO YOU MEAN? THERE'S PLENTY OF GIRLS IN THIS SCHOOL SLUTTY ENOUGH TO HOOK UP WITH A GERIATRIC LIKE THAT GUY.
I BET HE READ POETRY OR SOMETHING.
SORRY, I JUST--EXCUSE ME--
SARAH--
WHAT'S HER DEAL?
GIRL STUFF. YOU WANT MORE DETAIL?
DEAR GOD, NO.

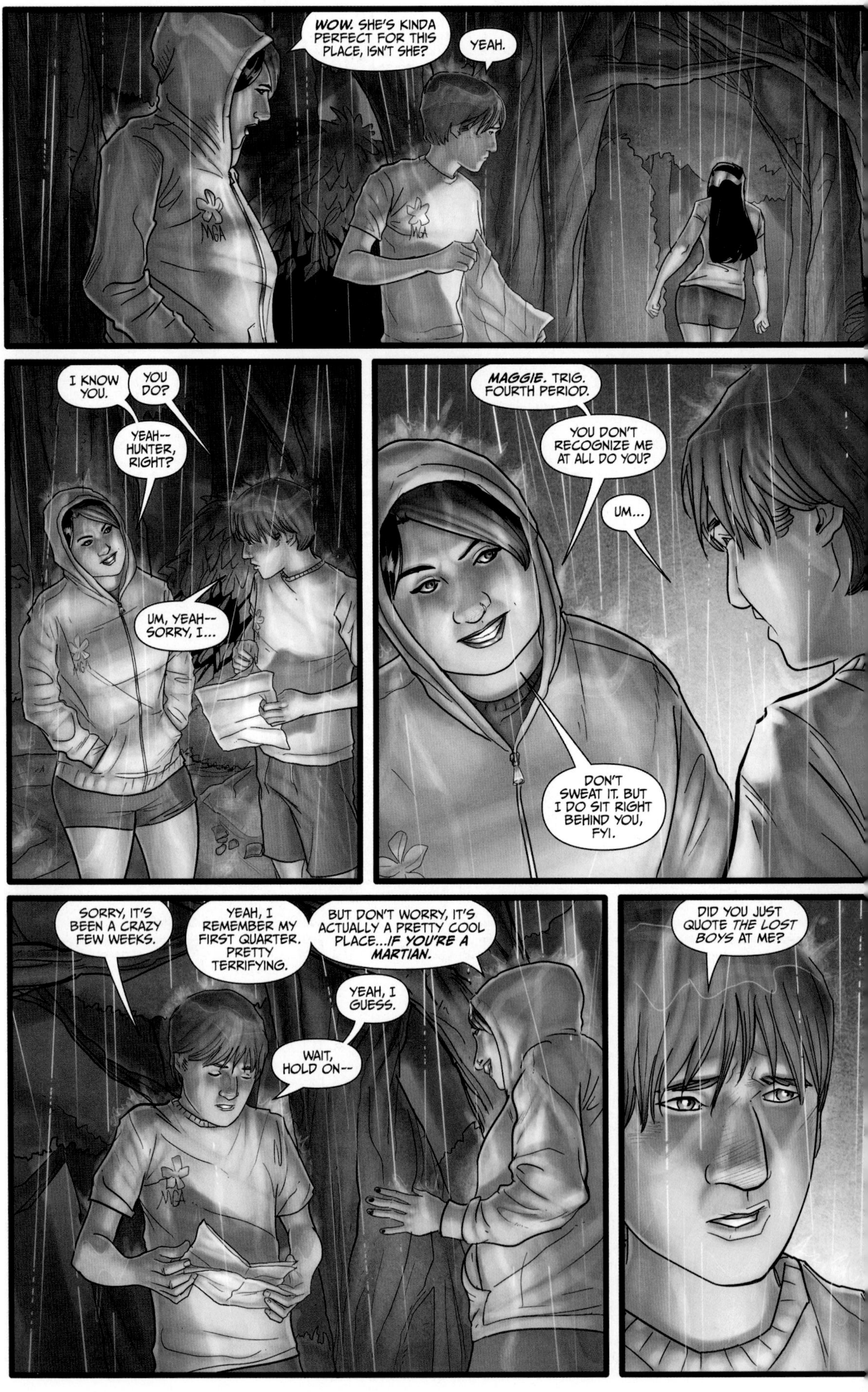
WOW. SHE'S KINDA PERFECT FOR THIS PLACE, ISN'T SHE?
YEAH.
I KNOW YOU.
YOU DO?
YEAH--HUNTER, RIGHT?
UM, YEAH--SORRY, I...
MAGGIE. TRIG. FOURTH PERIOD.
YOU DON'T RECOGNIZE ME AT ALL DO YOU?
UM...
DON'T SWEAT IT. BUT I DO SIT RIGHT BEHIND YOU, FYI.
SORRY, IT'S BEEN A CRAZY FEW WEEKS.
YEAH, I REMEMBER MY FIRST QUARTER. PRETTY TERRIFYING.
BUT DON'T WORRY, IT'S ACTUALLY A PRETTY COOL PLACE...IF YOU'RE A MARTIAN.
YEAH, I GUESS.
WAIT, HOLD ON--
DID YOU JUST QUOTE THE LOST BOYS AT ME?

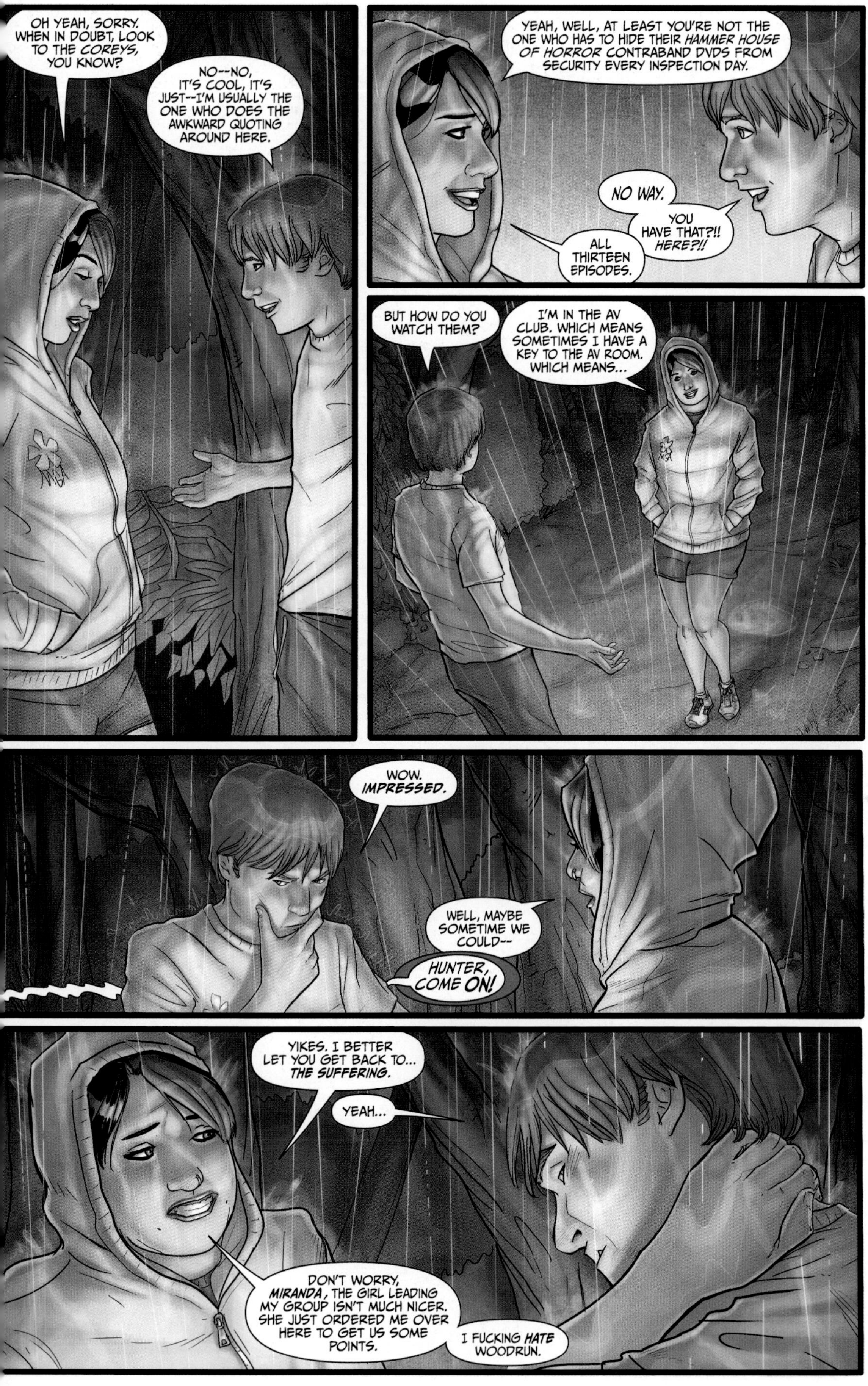
OH YEAH, SORRY. WHEN IN DOUBT, LOOK TO THE *COREYS*, YOU KNOW?
NO--NO, IT'S COOL, IT'S JUST--I'M USUALLY THE ONE WHO DOES THE AWKWARD QUOTING AROUND HERE.
YEAH, WELL, AT LEAST YOU'RE NOT THE ONE WHO HAS TO HIDE THEIR *HAMMER HOUSE OF HORROR* CONTRABAND DVDS FROM SECURITY EVERY INSPECTION DAY.
NO WAY.
YOU HAVE THAT?!! *HERE?!!*
ALL THIRTEEN EPISODES.
BUT HOW DO YOU WATCH THEM?
I'M IN THE AV CLUB. WHICH MEANS SOMETIMES I HAVE A KEY TO THE AV ROOM. WHICH MEANS...
WOW. ***IMPRESSED.***
WELL, MAYBE SOMETIME WE COULD--
HUNTER, COME *ON!*
YIKES. I BETTER LET YOU GET BACK TO... ***THE SUFFERING.***
YEAH...
DON'T WORRY, ***MIRANDA***, THE GIRL LEADING MY GROUP ISN'T MUCH NICER. SHE JUST ORDERED ME OVER HERE TO GET US SOME POINTS.
I FUCKING ***HATE*** WOODRUN.

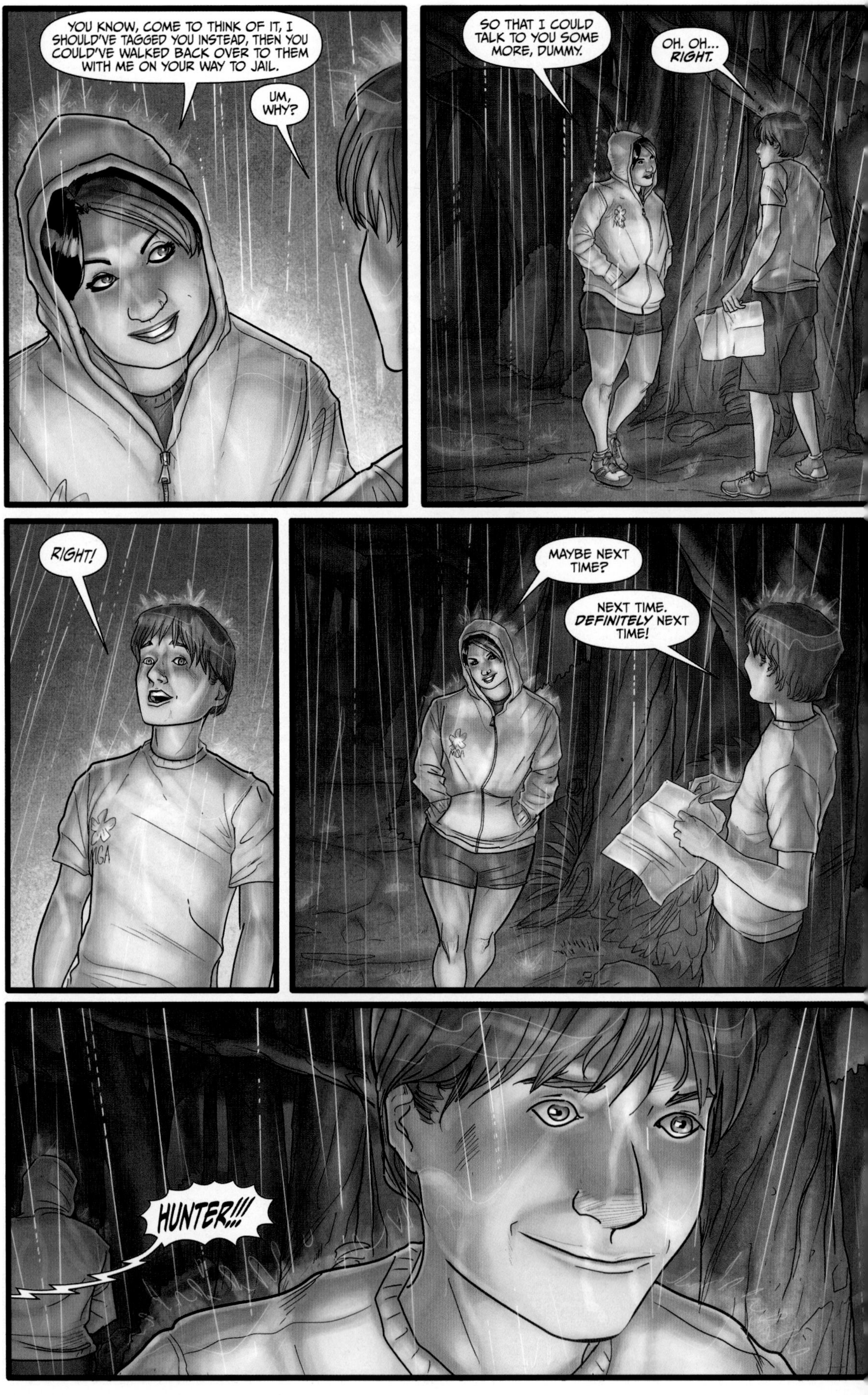
YOU KNOW, COME TO THINK OF IT, I SHOULD'VE TAGGED YOU INSTEAD, THEN YOU COULD'VE WALKED BACK OVER TO THEM WITH ME ON YOUR WAY TO JAIL.
UM, WHY?
SO THAT I COULD TALK TO YOU SOME MORE, DUMMY.
OH. OH... *RIGHT.*
RIGHT!
MAYBE NEXT TIME?
NEXT TIME. *DEFINITELY* NEXT TIME!
HUNTER!!!

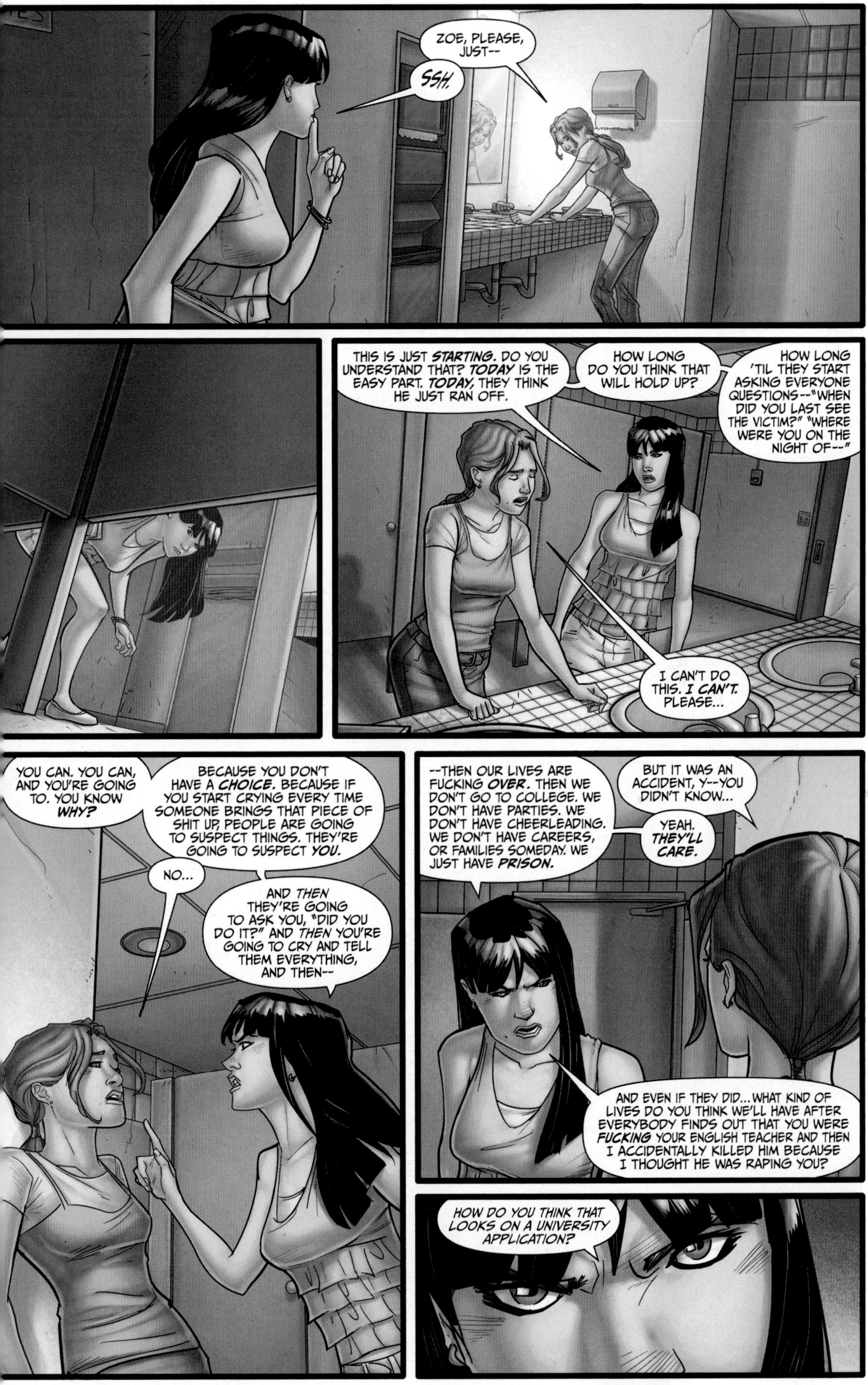
ZOE, PLEASE, JUST--
SSH.
THIS IS JUST STARTING. DO YOU UNDERSTAND THAT? TODAY IS THE EASY PART. TODAY, THEY THINK HE JUST RAN OFF.
HOW LONG DO YOU THINK THAT WILL HOLD UP?
HOW LONG 'TIL THEY START ASKING EVERYONE QUESTIONS--"WHEN DID YOU LAST SEE THE VICTIM?" "WHERE WERE YOU ON THE NIGHT OF--"
I CAN'T DO THIS. I CAN'T. PLEASE...
YOU CAN. YOU CAN, AND YOU'RE GOING TO. YOU KNOW WHY?
BECAUSE YOU DON'T HAVE A CHOICE. BECAUSE IF YOU START CRYING EVERY TIME SOMEONE BRINGS THAT PIECE OF SHIT UP, PEOPLE ARE GOING TO SUSPECT THINGS. THEY'RE GOING TO SUSPECT YOU.
NO...
AND THEN THEY'RE GOING TO ASK YOU, "DID YOU DO IT?" AND THEN YOU'RE GOING TO CRY AND TELL THEM EVERYTHING, AND THEN--
--THEN OUR LIVES ARE FUCKING OVER. THEN WE DON'T GO TO COLLEGE. WE DON'T HAVE PARTIES. WE DON'T HAVE CHEERLEADING. WE DON'T HAVE CAREERS, OR FAMILIES SOMEDAY. WE JUST HAVE PRISON.
BUT IT WAS AN ACCIDENT, Y--YOU DIDN'T KNOW...
YEAH. THEY'LL CARE.
AND EVEN IF THEY DID...WHAT KIND OF LIVES DO YOU THINK WE'LL HAVE AFTER EVERYBODY FINDS OUT THAT YOU WERE FUCKING YOUR ENGLISH TEACHER AND THEN I ACCIDENTALLY KILLED HIM BECAUSE I THOUGHT HE WAS RAPING YOU?
HOW DO YOU THINK THAT LOOKS ON A UNIVERSITY APPLICATION?

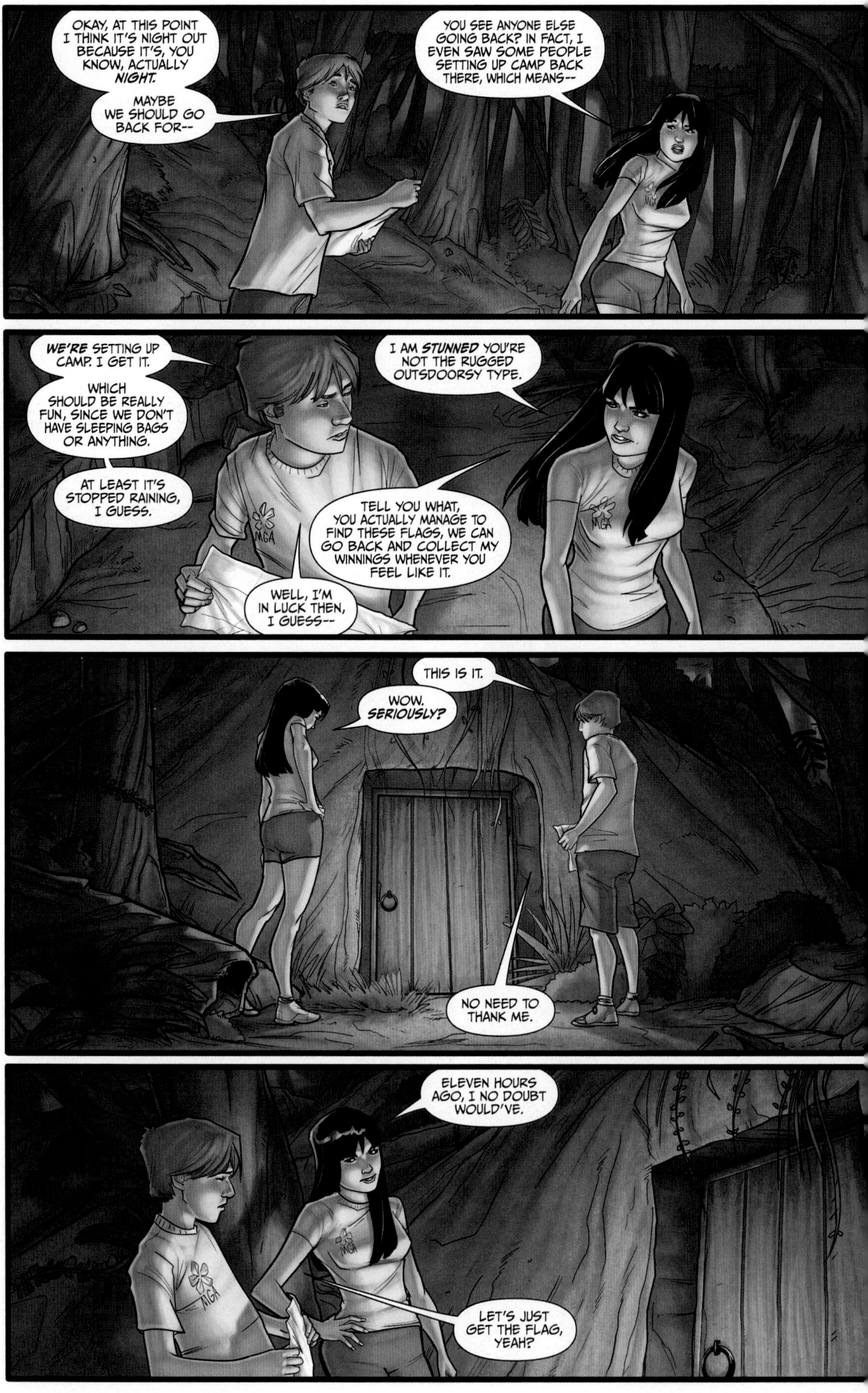
OKAY, AT THIS POINT I THINK IT'S NIGHT OUT BECAUSE IT'S, YOU KNOW, ACTUALLY *NIGHT.*
MAYBE WE SHOULD GO BACK FOR--
YOU SEE ANYONE ELSE GOING BACK? IN FACT, I EVEN SAW SOME PEOPLE SETTING UP CAMP BACK THERE, WHICH MEANS--
WE'RE SETTING UP CAMP. I GET IT.
WHICH SHOULD BE REALLY FUN, SINCE WE DON'T HAVE SLEEPING BAGS OR ANYTHING.
AT LEAST IT'S STOPPED RAINING, I GUESS.
I AM *STUNNED* YOU'RE NOT THE RUGGED OUTSDOORSY TYPE.
TELL YOU WHAT, YOU ACTUALLY MANAGE TO FIND THESE FLAGS, WE CAN GO BACK AND COLLECT MY WINNINGS WHENEVER YOU FEEL LIKE IT.
WELL, I'M IN LUCK THEN, I GUESS--
THIS IS IT.
WOW. *SERIOUSLY?*
NO NEED TO THANK ME.
ELEVEN HOURS AGO, I NO DOUBT WOULD'VE.
LET'S JUST GET THE FLAG, YEAH?

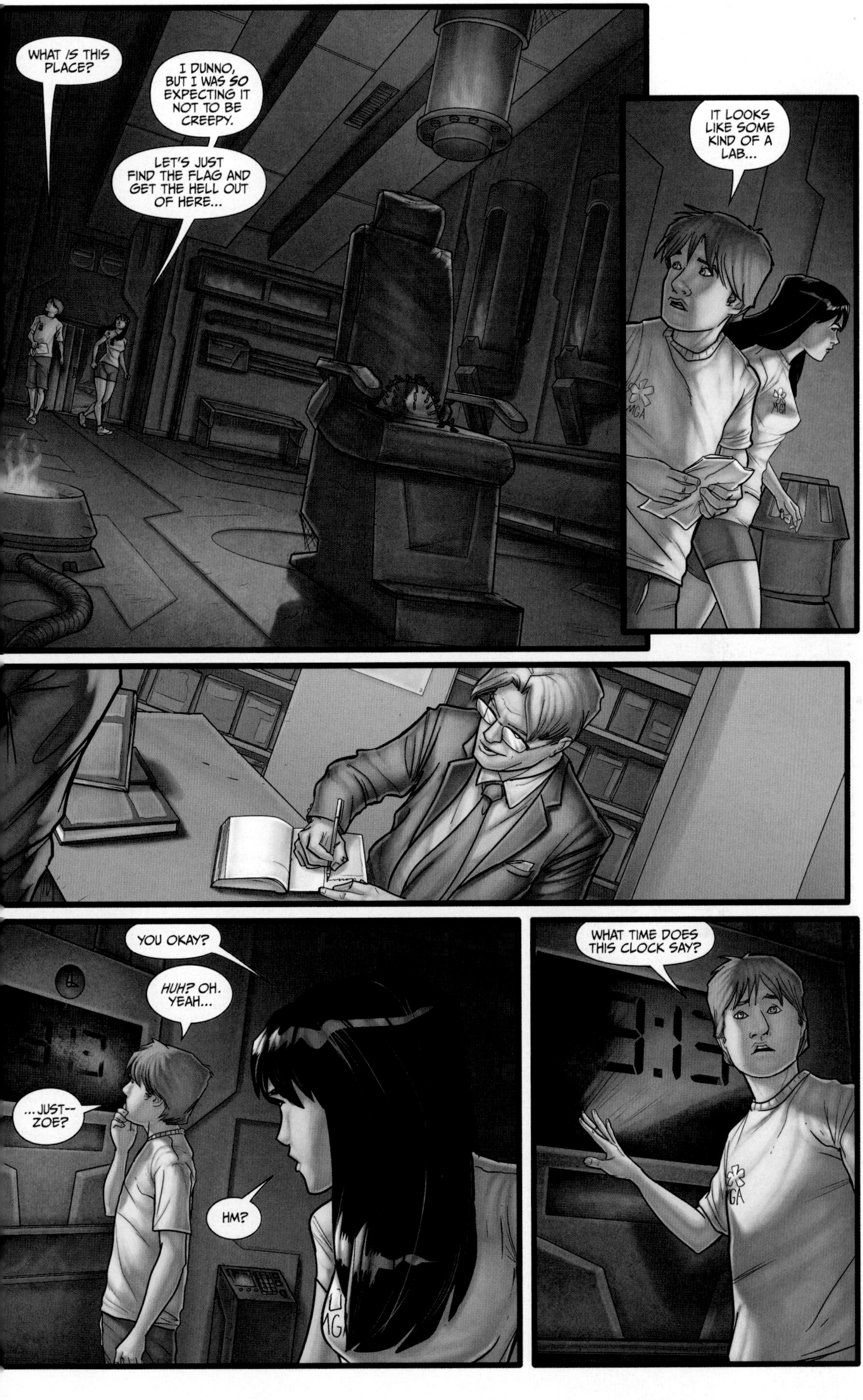
WHAT IS THIS PLACE?
I DUNNO, BUT I WAS SO EXPECTING IT NOT TO BE CREEPY.
LET'S JUST FIND THE FLAG AND GET THE HELL OUT OF HERE...
IT LOOKS LIKE SOME KIND OF A LAB...
YOU OKAY?
HUH? OH. YEAH...
...JUST-- ZOE?
HM?
WHAT TIME DOES THIS CLOCK SAY?

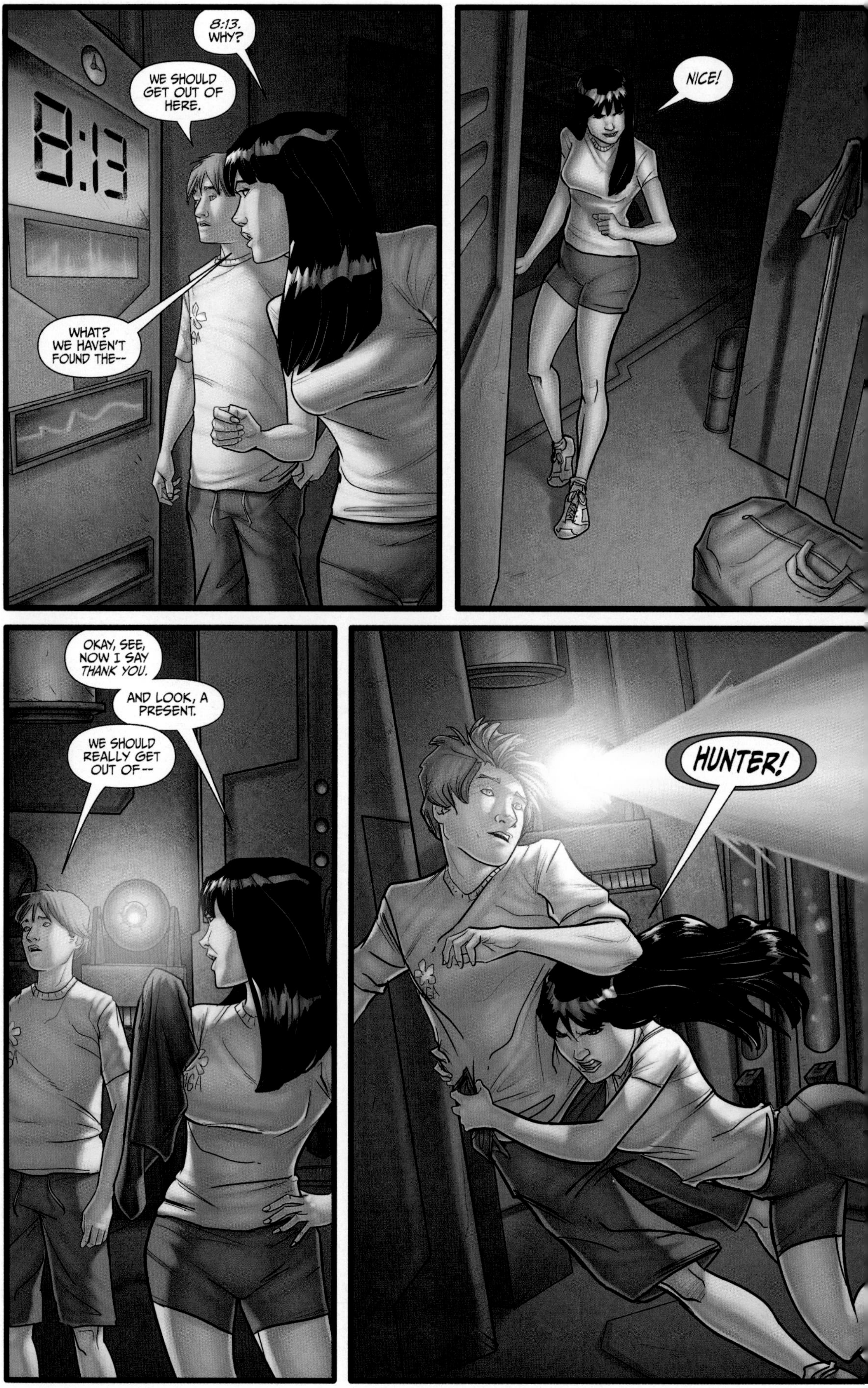
8:13. WHY?
WE SHOULD GET OUT OF HERE.
8:13
WHAT? WE HAVEN'T FOUND THE--
NICE!
OKAY, SEE, NOW I SAY *THANK YOU.*
AND LOOK, A PRESENT.
WE SHOULD REALLY GET OUT OF--
HUNTER!

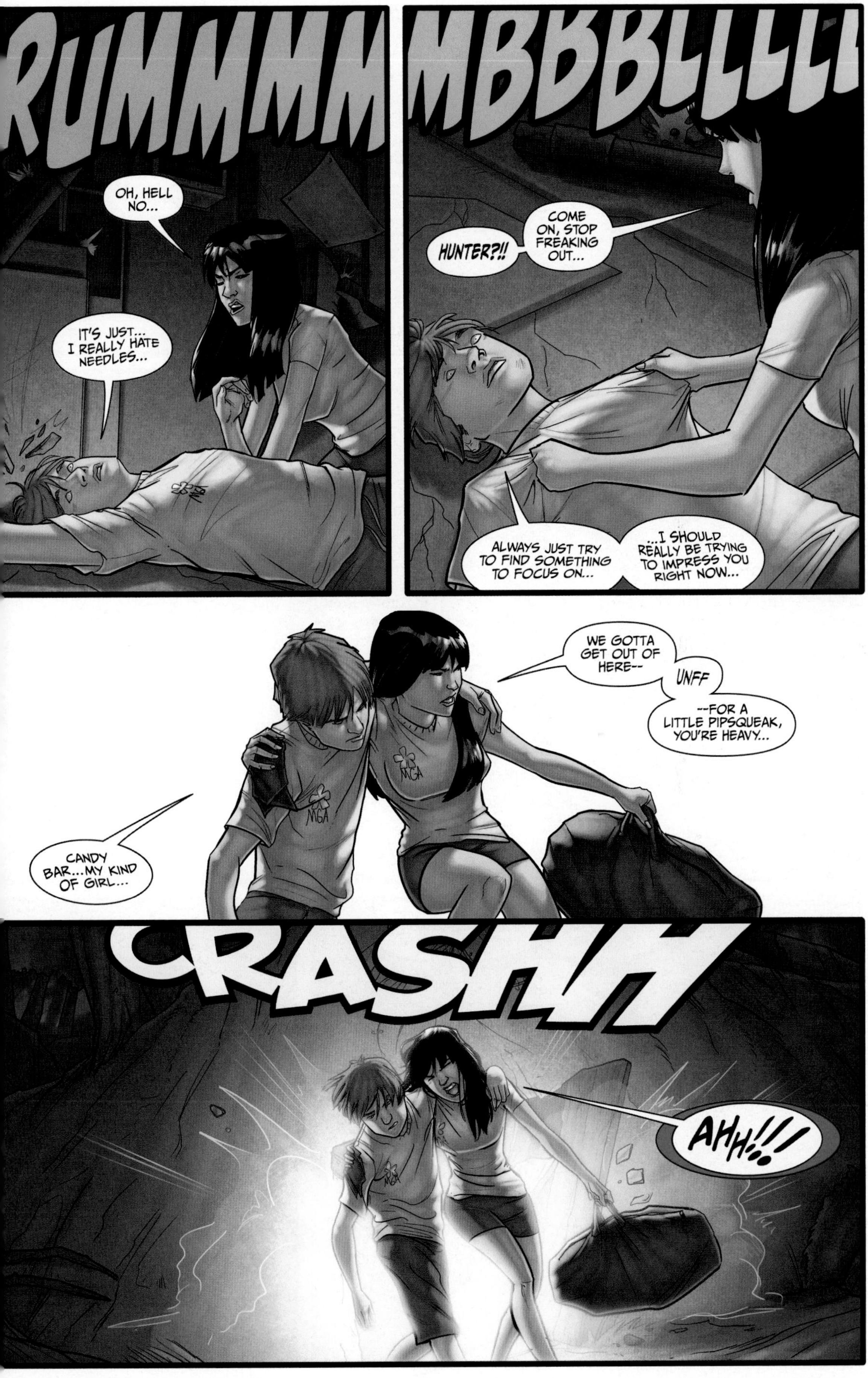
RUMMMMMMBBBLLLLL
OH, HELL NO...
IT'S JUST... I REALLY HATE NEEDLES...
HUNTER?!!
COME ON, STOP FREAKING OUT...
ALWAYS JUST TRY TO FIND SOMETHING TO FOCUS ON...
...I SHOULD REALLY BE TRYING TO IMPRESS YOU RIGHT NOW...
WE GOTTA GET OUT OF HERE--
UNFF
--FOR A LITTLE PIPSQUEAK, YOU'RE HEAVY...
CANDY BAR...MY KIND OF GIRL...
CRASHH
AHH!!!

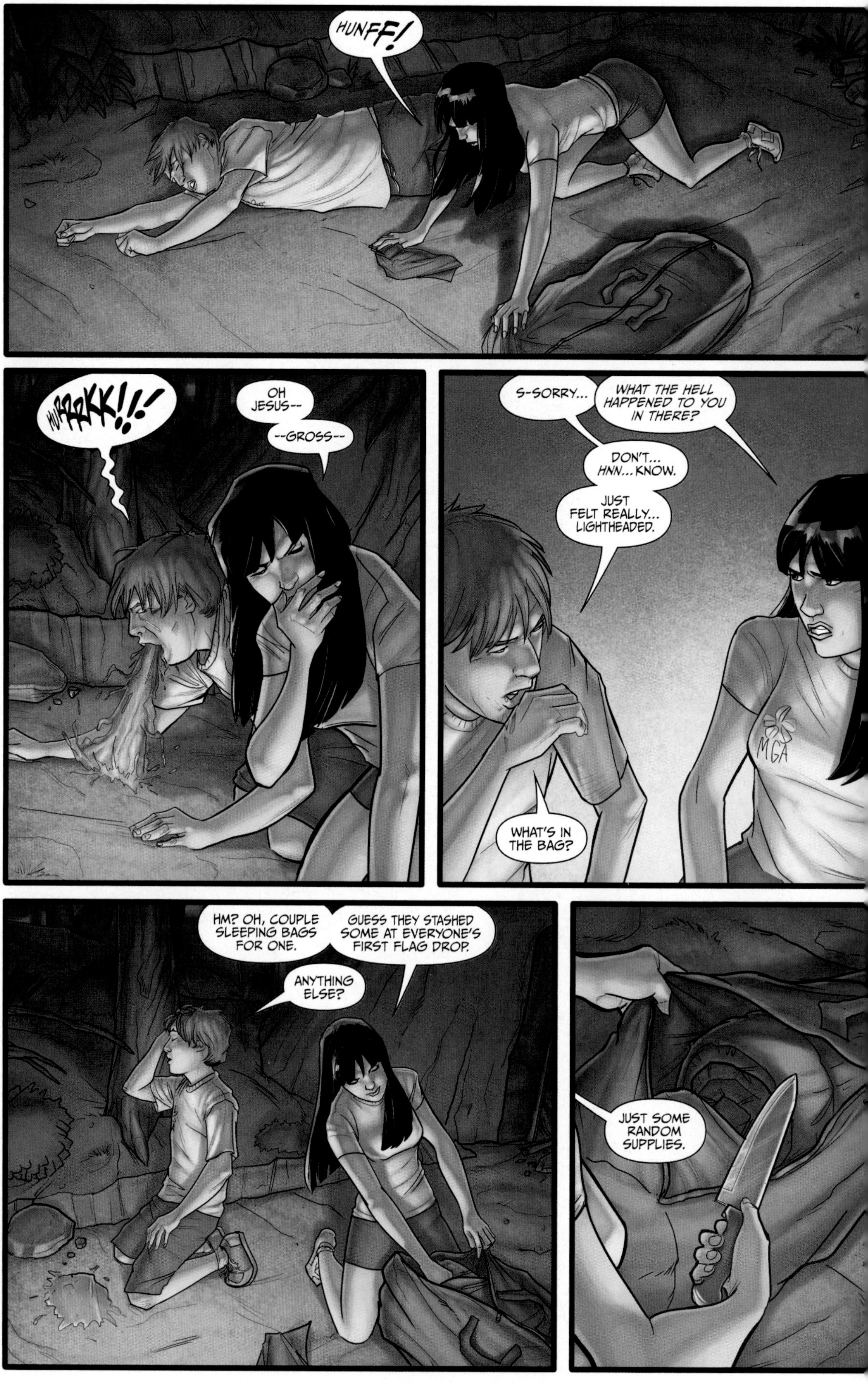
HUNFF!
HURRRKK!!!
OH JESUS--
--GROSS--
S-SORRY...
WHAT THE HELL HAPPENED TO YOU IN THERE?
DON'T... HNN... KNOW.
JUST FELT REALLY... LIGHTHEADED.
MGA
WHAT'S IN THE BAG?
HM? OH, COUPLE SLEEPING BAGS FOR ONE.
GUESS THEY STASHED SOME AT EVERYONE'S FIRST FLAG DROP.
ANYTHING ELSE?
JUST SOME RANDOM SUPPLIES.

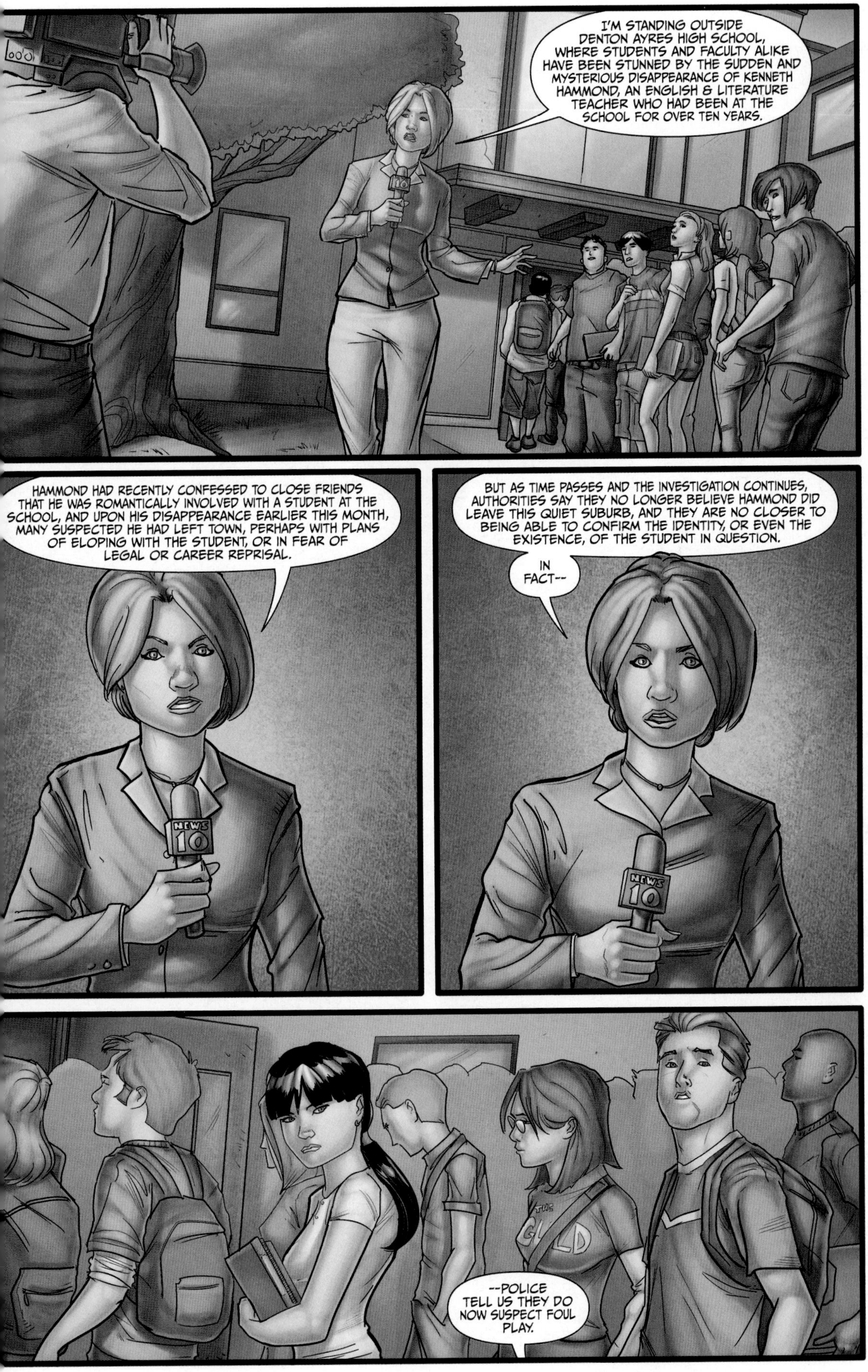
I'M STANDING OUTSIDE DENTON AYRES HIGH SCHOOL, WHERE STUDENTS AND FACULTY ALIKE HAVE BEEN STUNNED BY THE SUDDEN AND MYSTERIOUS DISAPPEARANCE OF KENNETH HAMMOND, AN ENGLISH & LITERATURE TEACHER WHO HAD BEEN AT THE SCHOOL FOR OVER TEN YEARS.
HAMMOND HAD RECENTLY CONFESSED TO CLOSE FRIENDS THAT HE WAS ROMANTICALLY INVOLVED WITH A STUDENT AT THE SCHOOL, AND UPON HIS DISAPPEARANCE EARLIER THIS MONTH, MANY SUSPECTED HE HAD LEFT TOWN, PERHAPS WITH PLANS OF ELOPING WITH THE STUDENT, OR IN FEAR OF LEGAL OR CAREER REPRISAL.
NEWS 10
BUT AS TIME PASSES AND THE INVESTIGATION CONTINUES, AUTHORITIES SAY THEY NO LONGER BELIEVE HAMMOND DID LEAVE THIS QUIET SUBURB, AND THEY ARE NO CLOSER TO BEING ABLE TO CONFIRM THE IDENTITY, OR EVEN THE EXISTENCE, OF THE STUDENT IN QUESTION.
IN FACT--
NEWS 10
--POLICE TELL US THEY DO NOW SUSPECT FOUL PLAY.

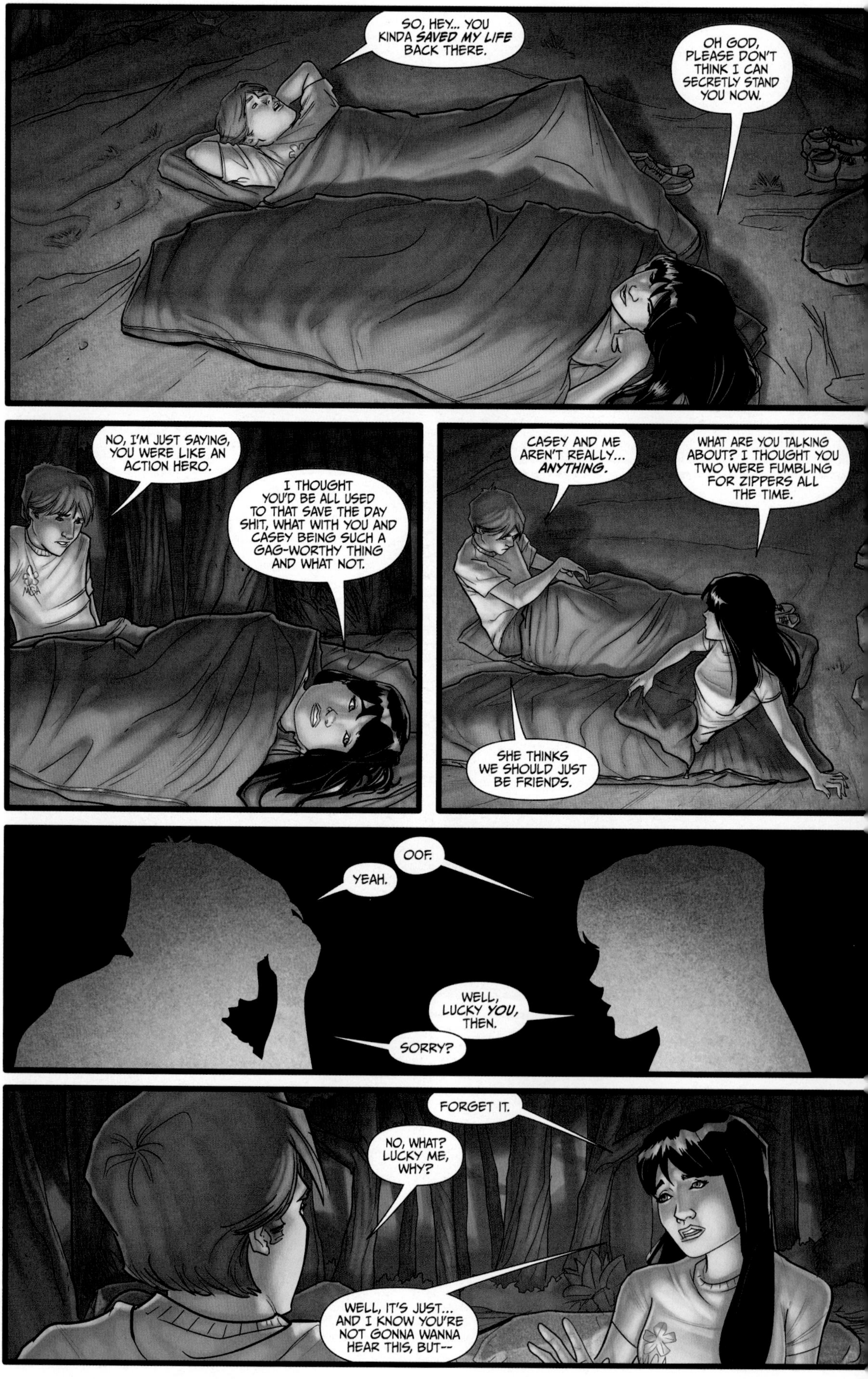
SO, HEY... YOU KINDA SAVED MY LIFE BACK THERE.
OH GOD, PLEASE DON'T THINK I CAN SECRETLY STAND YOU NOW.
NO, I'M JUST SAYING, YOU WERE LIKE AN ACTION HERO.
I THOUGHT YOU'D BE ALL USED TO THAT SAVE THE DAY SHIT, WHAT WITH YOU AND CASEY BEING SUCH A GAG-WORTHY THING AND WHAT NOT.
CASEY AND ME AREN'T REALLY... ANYTHING.
WHAT ARE YOU TALKING ABOUT? I THOUGHT YOU TWO WERE FUMBLING FOR ZIPPERS ALL THE TIME.
SHE THINKS WE SHOULD JUST BE FRIENDS.
OOF.
YEAH.
WELL, LUCKY YOU, THEN.
SORRY?
FORGET IT.
NO, WHAT? LUCKY ME, WHY?
WELL, IT'S JUST... AND I KNOW YOU'RE NOT GONNA WANNA HEAR THIS, BUT--

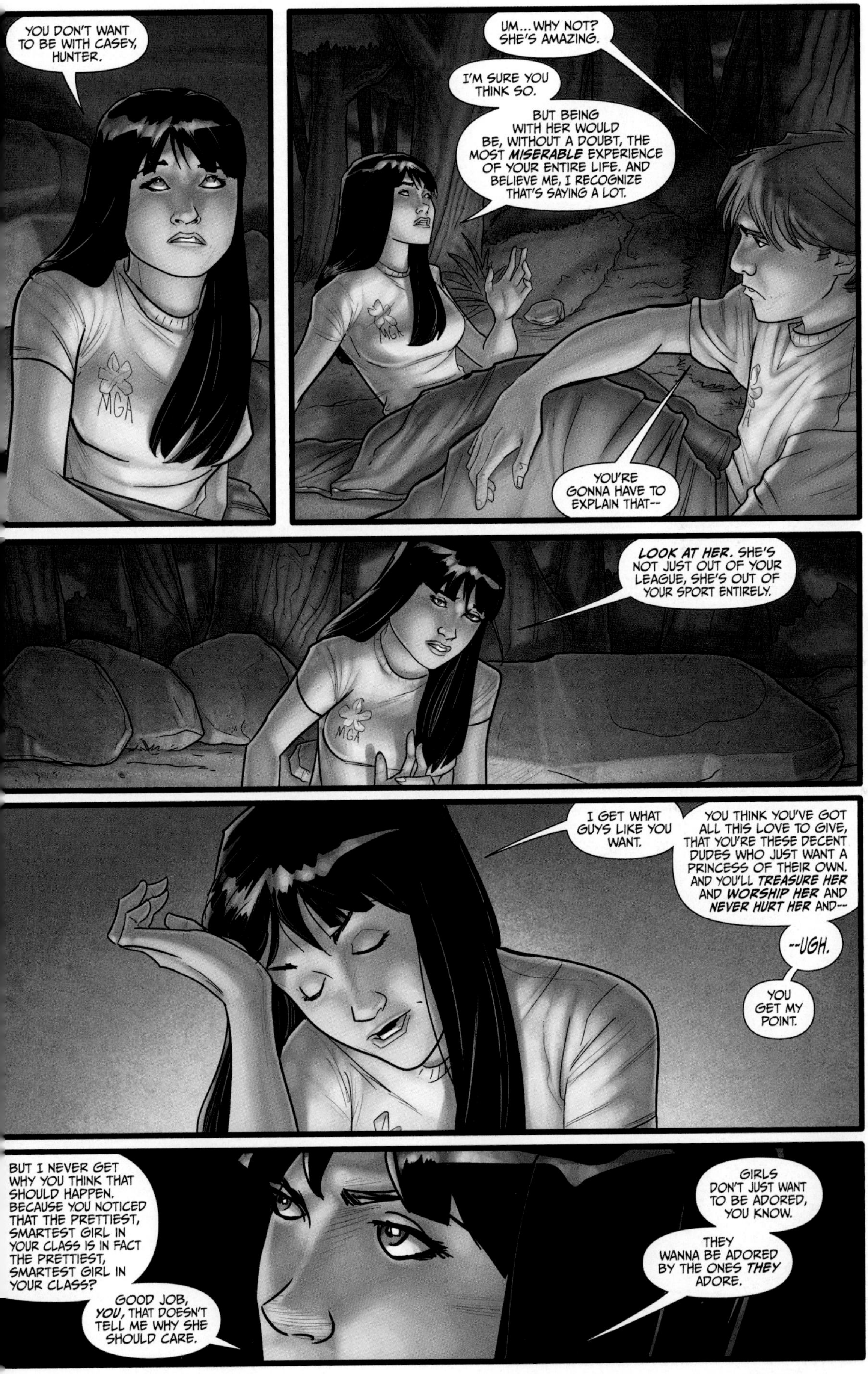
YOU DON'T WANT TO BE WITH CASEY, HUNTER.
UM... WHY NOT? SHE'S AMAZING.
I'M SURE YOU THINK SO.
BUT BEING WITH HER WOULD BE, WITHOUT A DOUBT, THE MOST MISERABLE EXPERIENCE OF YOUR ENTIRE LIFE. AND BELIEVE ME, I RECOGNIZE THAT'S SAYING A LOT.
YOU'RE GONNA HAVE TO EXPLAIN THAT--
LOOK AT HER. SHE'S NOT JUST OUT OF YOUR LEAGUE, SHE'S OUT OF YOUR SPORT ENTIRELY.
MGA
I GET WHAT GUYS LIKE YOU WANT.
YOU THINK YOU'VE GOT ALL THIS LOVE TO GIVE, THAT YOU'RE THESE DECENT DUDES WHO JUST WANT A PRINCESS OF THEIR OWN. AND YOU'LL TREASURE HER AND WORSHIP HER AND NEVER HURT HER AND--
--UGH.
YOU GET MY POINT.
BUT I NEVER GET WHY YOU THINK THAT SHOULD HAPPEN. BECAUSE YOU NOTICED THAT THE PRETTIEST, SMARTEST GIRL IN YOUR CLASS IS IN FACT THE PRETTIEST, SMARTEST GIRL IN YOUR CLASS?
GOOD JOB, YOU, THAT DOESN'T TELL ME WHY SHE SHOULD CARE.
GIRLS DON'T JUST WANT TO BE ADORED, YOU KNOW.
THEY WANNA BE ADORED BY THE ONES THEY ADORE.

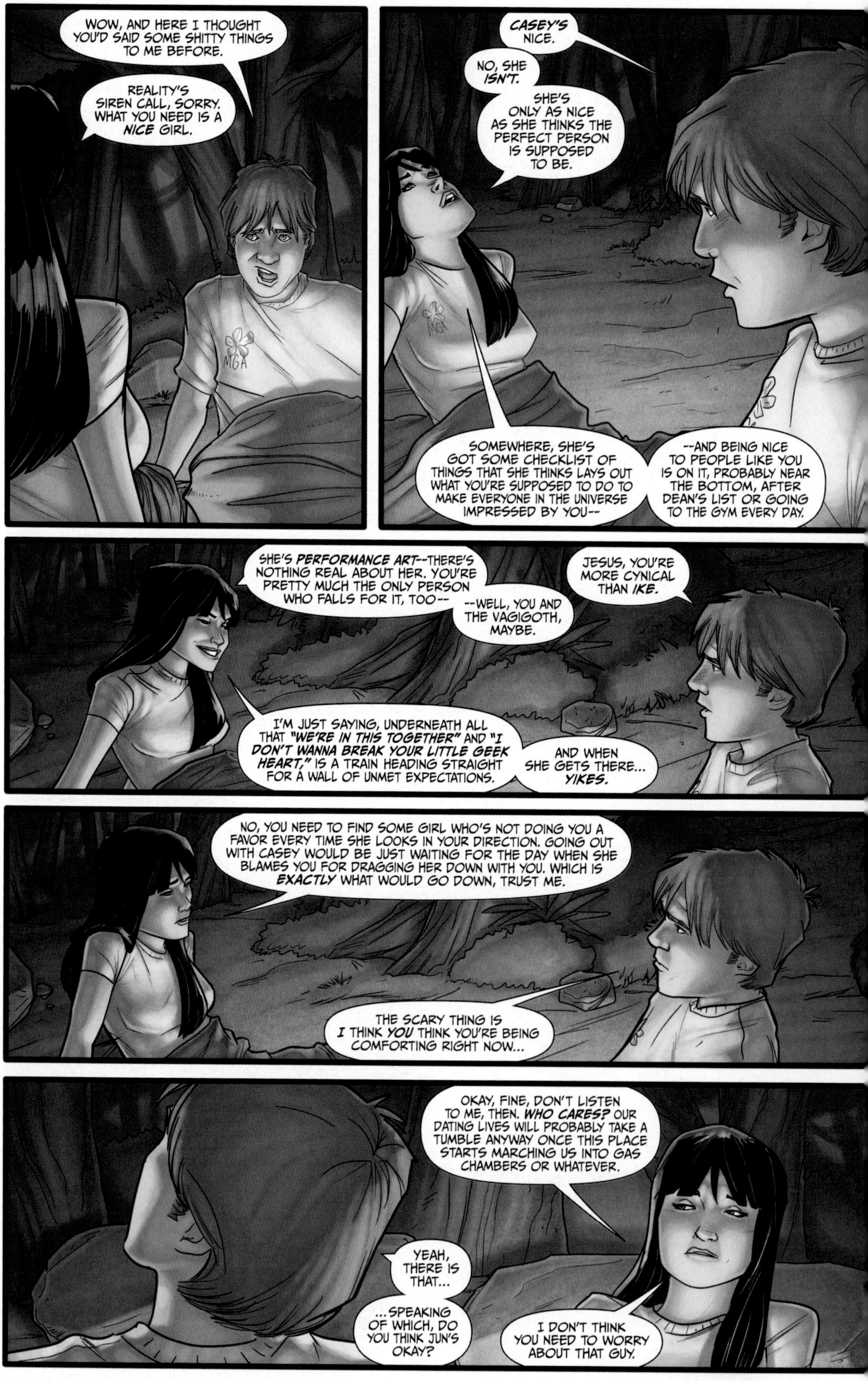
WOW, AND HERE I THOUGHT YOU'D SAID SOME SHITTY THINGS TO ME BEFORE.
REALITY'S SIREN CALL, SORRY. WHAT YOU NEED IS A *NICE* GIRL.
CASEY'S NICE.
NO, SHE *ISN'T.*
SHE'S ONLY AS NICE AS SHE THINKS THE PERFECT PERSON IS SUPPOSED TO BE.
SOMEWHERE, SHE'S GOT SOME CHECKLIST OF THINGS THAT SHE THINKS LAYS OUT WHAT YOU'RE SUPPOSED TO DO TO MAKE EVERYONE IN THE UNIVERSE IMPRESSED BY YOU--
--AND BEING NICE TO PEOPLE LIKE YOU IS ON IT, PROBABLY NEAR THE BOTTOM, AFTER DEAN'S LIST OR GOING TO THE GYM EVERY DAY.
SHE'S *PERFORMANCE ART*--THERE'S NOTHING REAL ABOUT HER. YOU'RE PRETTY MUCH THE ONLY PERSON WHO FALLS FOR IT, TOO--
--WELL, YOU AND THE VAGIGOTH, MAYBE.
JESUS, YOU'RE MORE CYNICAL THAN *IKE.*
I'M JUST SAYING, UNDERNEATH ALL THAT *"WE'RE IN THIS TOGETHER"* AND *"I DON'T WANNA BREAK YOUR LITTLE GEEK HEART,"* IS A TRAIN HEADING STRAIGHT FOR A WALL OF UNMET EXPECTATIONS.
AND WHEN SHE GETS THERE... *YIKES.*
NO, YOU NEED TO FIND SOME GIRL WHO'S NOT DOING YOU A FAVOR EVERY TIME SHE LOOKS IN YOUR DIRECTION. GOING OUT WITH CASEY WOULD BE JUST WAITING FOR THE DAY WHEN SHE BLAMES YOU FOR DRAGGING HER DOWN WITH YOU. WHICH IS *EXACTLY* WHAT WOULD GO DOWN, TRUST ME.
THE SCARY THING IS *I* THINK *YOU* THINK YOU'RE BEING COMFORTING RIGHT NOW...
OKAY, FINE, DON'T LISTEN TO ME, THEN. *WHO CARES?* OUR DATING LIVES WILL PROBABLY TAKE A TUMBLE ANYWAY ONCE THIS PLACE STARTS MARCHING US INTO GAS CHAMBERS OR WHATEVER.
YEAH, THERE IS THAT...
...SPEAKING OF WHICH, DO YOU THINK JUN'S OKAY?
I DON'T THINK YOU NEED TO WORRY ABOUT THAT GUY.

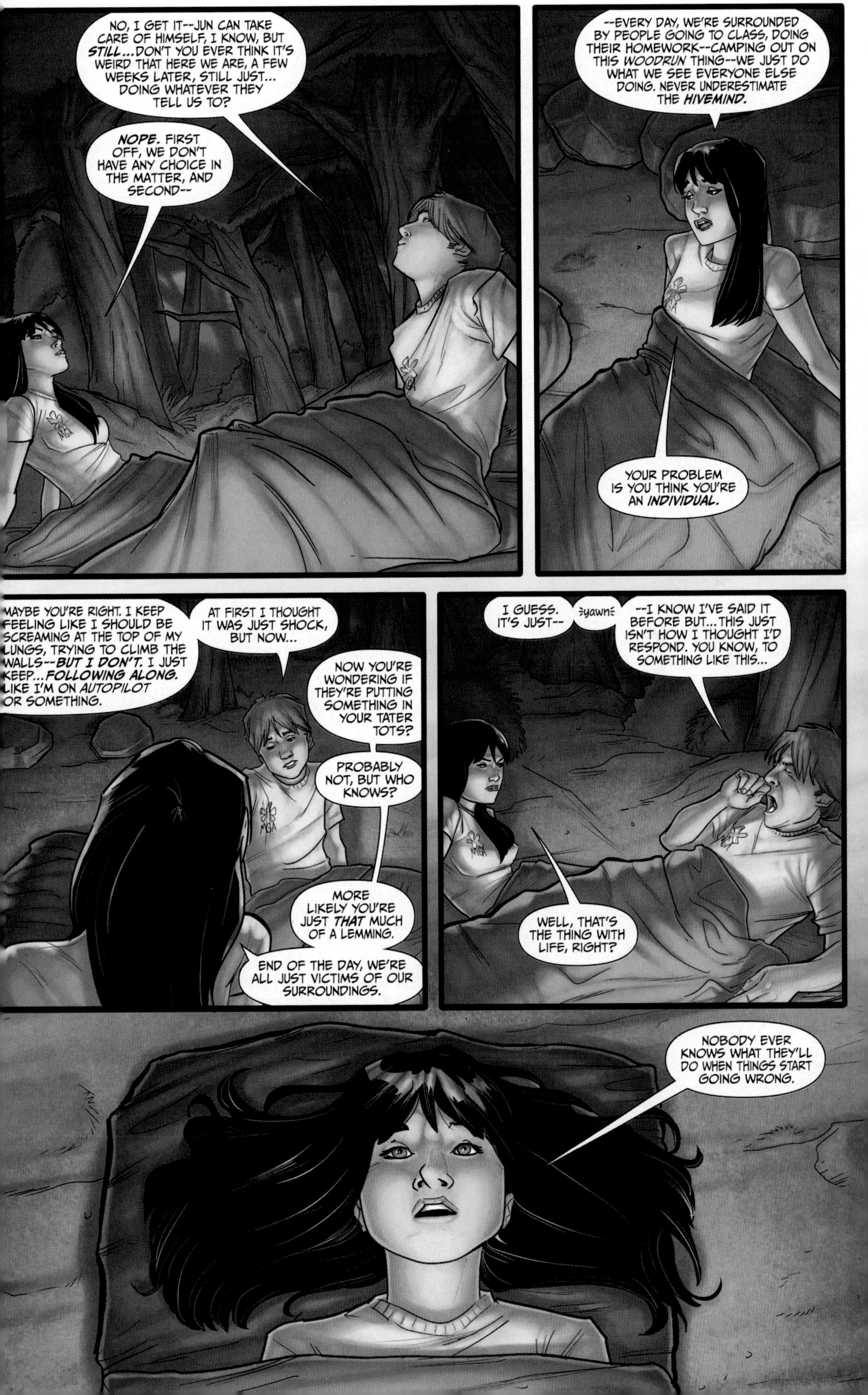
NO, I GET IT--JUN CAN TAKE CARE OF HIMSELF, I KNOW, BUT STILL...DON'T YOU EVER THINK IT'S WEIRD THAT HERE WE ARE, A FEW WEEKS LATER, STILL JUST... DOING WHATEVER THEY TELL US TO?
NOPE. FIRST OFF, WE DON'T HAVE ANY CHOICE IN THE MATTER, AND SECOND--
--EVERY DAY, WE'RE SURROUNDED BY PEOPLE GOING TO CLASS, DOING THEIR HOMEWORK--CAMPING OUT ON THIS WOODRUN THING--WE JUST DO WHAT WE SEE EVERYONE ELSE DOING. NEVER UNDERESTIMATE THE HIVEMIND.
YOUR PROBLEM IS YOU THINK YOU'RE AN INDIVIDUAL.
MAYBE YOU'RE RIGHT. I KEEP FEELING LIKE I SHOULD BE SCREAMING AT THE TOP OF MY LUNGS, TRYING TO CLIMB THE WALLS--BUT I DON'T. I JUST KEEP...FOLLOWING ALONG. LIKE I'M ON AUTOPILOT OR SOMETHING.
AT FIRST I THOUGHT IT WAS JUST SHOCK, BUT NOW...
NOW YOU'RE WONDERING IF THEY'RE PUTTING SOMETHING IN YOUR TATER TOTS?
PROBABLY NOT, BUT WHO KNOWS?
MORE LIKELY YOU'RE JUST THAT MUCH OF A LEMMING.
END OF THE DAY, WE'RE ALL JUST VICTIMS OF OUR SURROUNDINGS.
I GUESS. IT'S JUST--
yawn
--I KNOW I'VE SAID IT BEFORE BUT...THIS JUST ISN'T HOW I THOUGHT I'D RESPOND. YOU KNOW, TO SOMETHING LIKE THIS...
WELL, THAT'S THE THING WITH LIFE, RIGHT?
NOBODY EVER KNOWS WHAT THEY'LL DO WHEN THINGS START GOING WRONG.

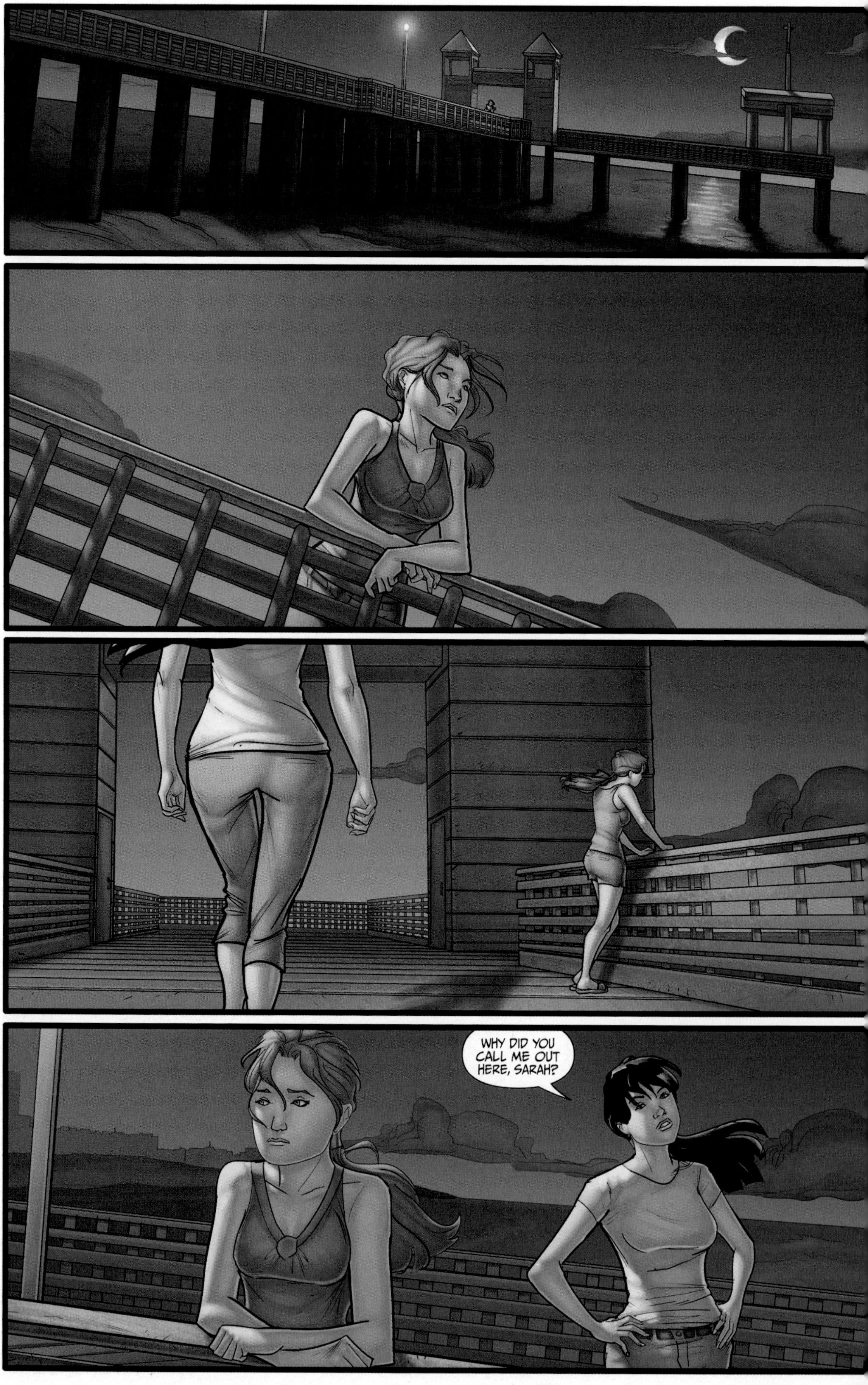
WHY DID YOU
CALL ME OUT
HERE, SARAH?

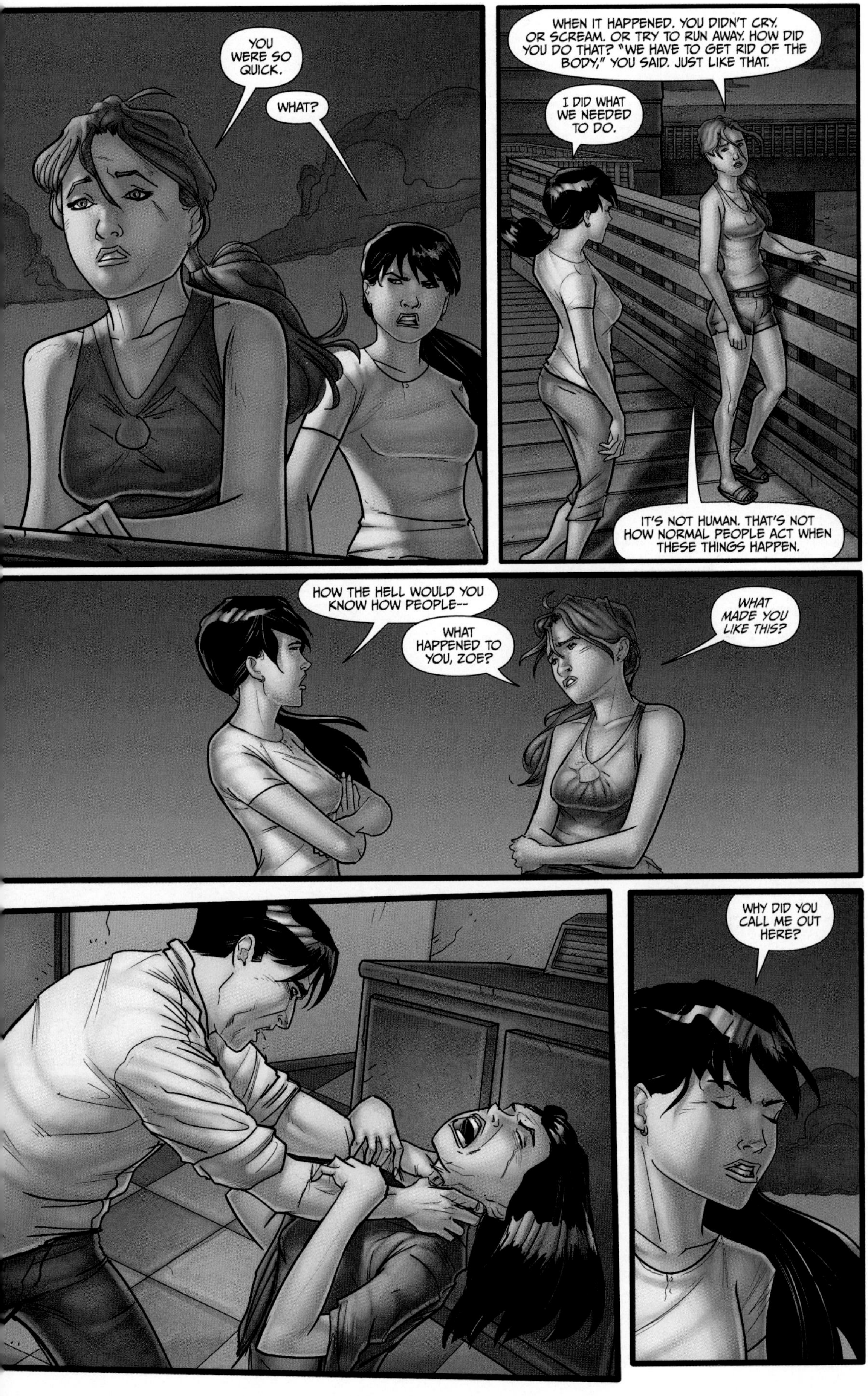
YOU WERE SO QUICK.
WHAT?
WHEN IT HAPPENED. YOU DIDN'T CRY. OR SCREAM. OR TRY TO RUN AWAY. HOW DID YOU DO THAT? "WE HAVE TO GET RID OF THE BODY," YOU SAID. JUST LIKE THAT.
I DID WHAT WE NEEDED TO DO.
IT'S NOT HUMAN. THAT'S NOT HOW NORMAL PEOPLE ACT WHEN THESE THINGS HAPPEN.
HOW THE HELL WOULD YOU KNOW HOW PEOPLE--
WHAT HAPPENED TO YOU, ZOE?
WHAT MADE YOU LIKE THIS?
WHY DID YOU CALL ME OUT HERE?

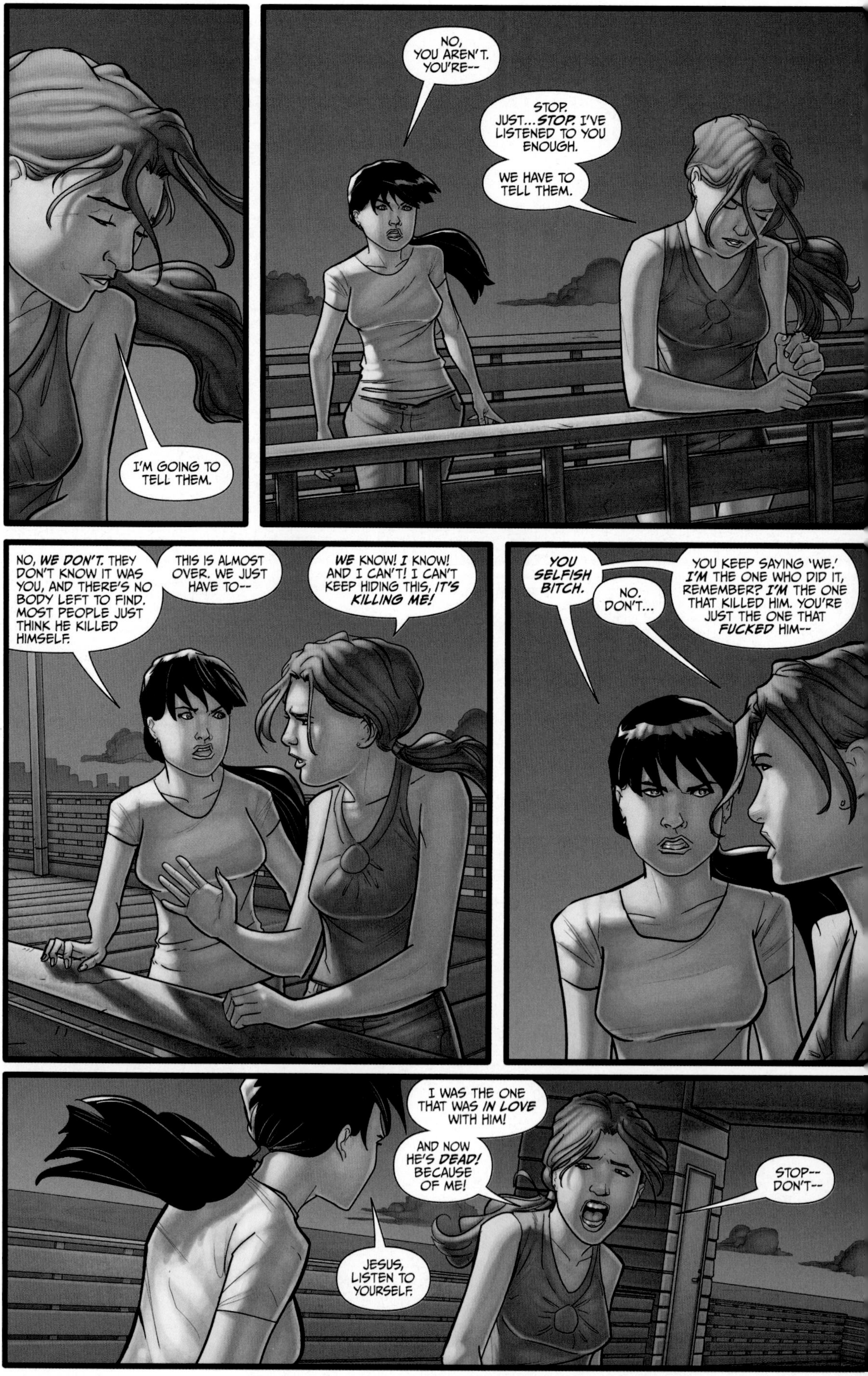
I'M GOING TO TELL THEM.
NO, YOU AREN'T. YOU'RE--
STOP. JUST...STOP. I'VE LISTENED TO YOU ENOUGH.
WE HAVE TO TELL THEM.
NO, WE DON'T. THEY DON'T KNOW IT WAS YOU, AND THERE'S NO BODY LEFT TO FIND. MOST PEOPLE JUST THINK HE KILLED HIMSELF.
THIS IS ALMOST OVER. WE JUST HAVE TO--
WE KNOW! I KNOW! AND I CAN'T! I CAN'T KEEP HIDING THIS, IT'S KILLING ME!
YOU SELFISH BITCH.
NO. DON'T...
YOU KEEP SAYING 'WE.' I'M THE ONE WHO DID IT, REMEMBER? I'M THE ONE THAT KILLED HIM. YOU'RE JUST THE ONE THAT FUCKED HIM--
I WAS THE ONE THAT WAS IN LOVE WITH HIM!
AND NOW HE'S DEAD! BECAUSE OF ME!
JESUS, LISTEN TO YOURSELF.
STOP-- DON'T--

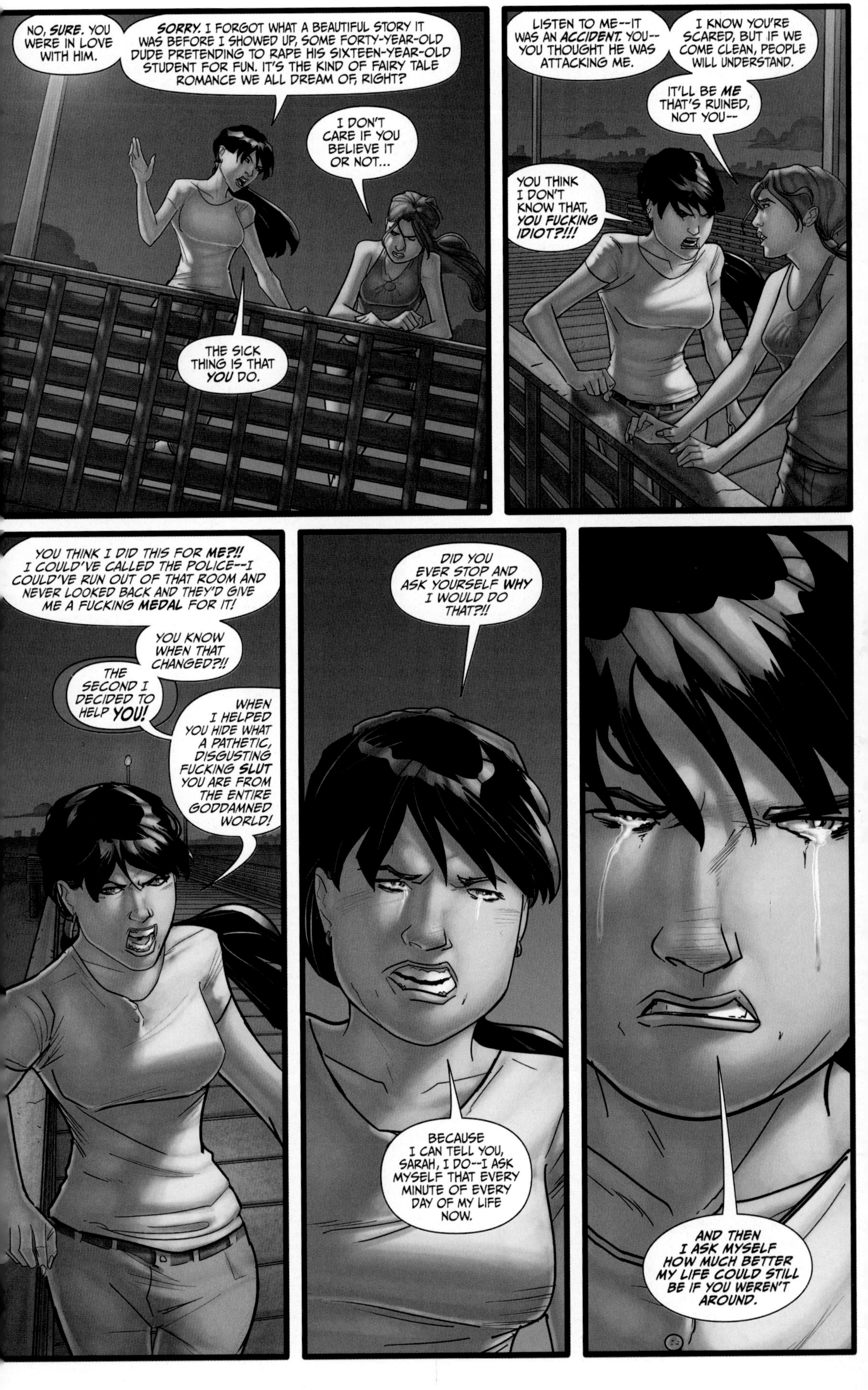

NO, SURE. YOU WERE IN LOVE WITH HIM.
SORRY. I FORGOT WHAT A BEAUTIFUL STORY IT WAS BEFORE I SHOWED UP, SOME FORTY-YEAR-OLD DUDE PRETENDING TO RAPE HIS SIXTEEN-YEAR-OLD STUDENT FOR FUN. IT'S THE KIND OF FAIRY TALE ROMANCE WE ALL DREAM OF, RIGHT?
I DON'T CARE IF YOU BELIEVE IT OR NOT...
THE SICK THING IS THAT YOU DO.
LISTEN TO ME--IT WAS AN ACCIDENT. YOU--YOU THOUGHT HE WAS ATTACKING ME.
I KNOW YOU'RE SCARED, BUT IF WE COME CLEAN, PEOPLE WILL UNDERSTAND.
IT'LL BE ME THAT'S RUINED, NOT YOU--
YOU THINK I DON'T KNOW THAT, YOU FUCKING IDIOT?!!!
YOU THINK I DID THIS FOR ME?!! I COULD'VE CALLED THE POLICE--I COULD'VE RUN OUT OF THAT ROOM AND NEVER LOOKED BACK AND THEY'D GIVE ME A FUCKING MEDAL FOR IT!
YOU KNOW WHEN THAT CHANGED?!!
THE SECOND I DECIDED TO HELP YOU!
WHEN I HELPED YOU HIDE WHAT A PATHETIC, DISGUSTING FUCKING SLUT YOU ARE FROM THE ENTIRE GODDAMNED WORLD!
DID YOU EVER STOP AND ASK YOURSELF WHY I WOULD DO THAT?!!
BECAUSE I CAN TELL YOU, SARAH, I DO--I ASK MYSELF THAT EVERY MINUTE OF EVERY DAY OF MY LIFE NOW.
AND THEN I ASK MYSELF HOW MUCH BETTER MY LIFE COULD STILL BE IF YOU WEREN'T AROUND.

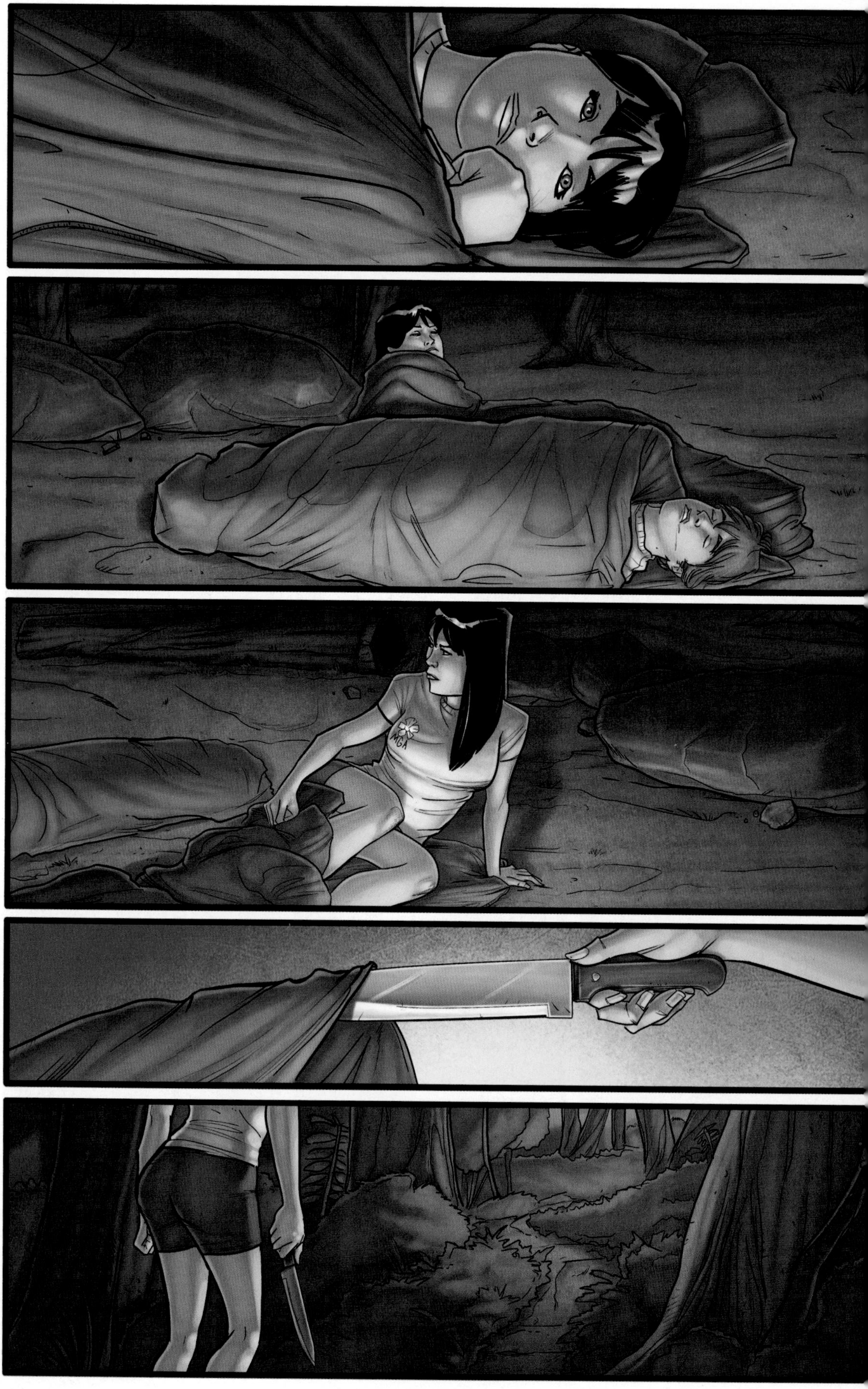

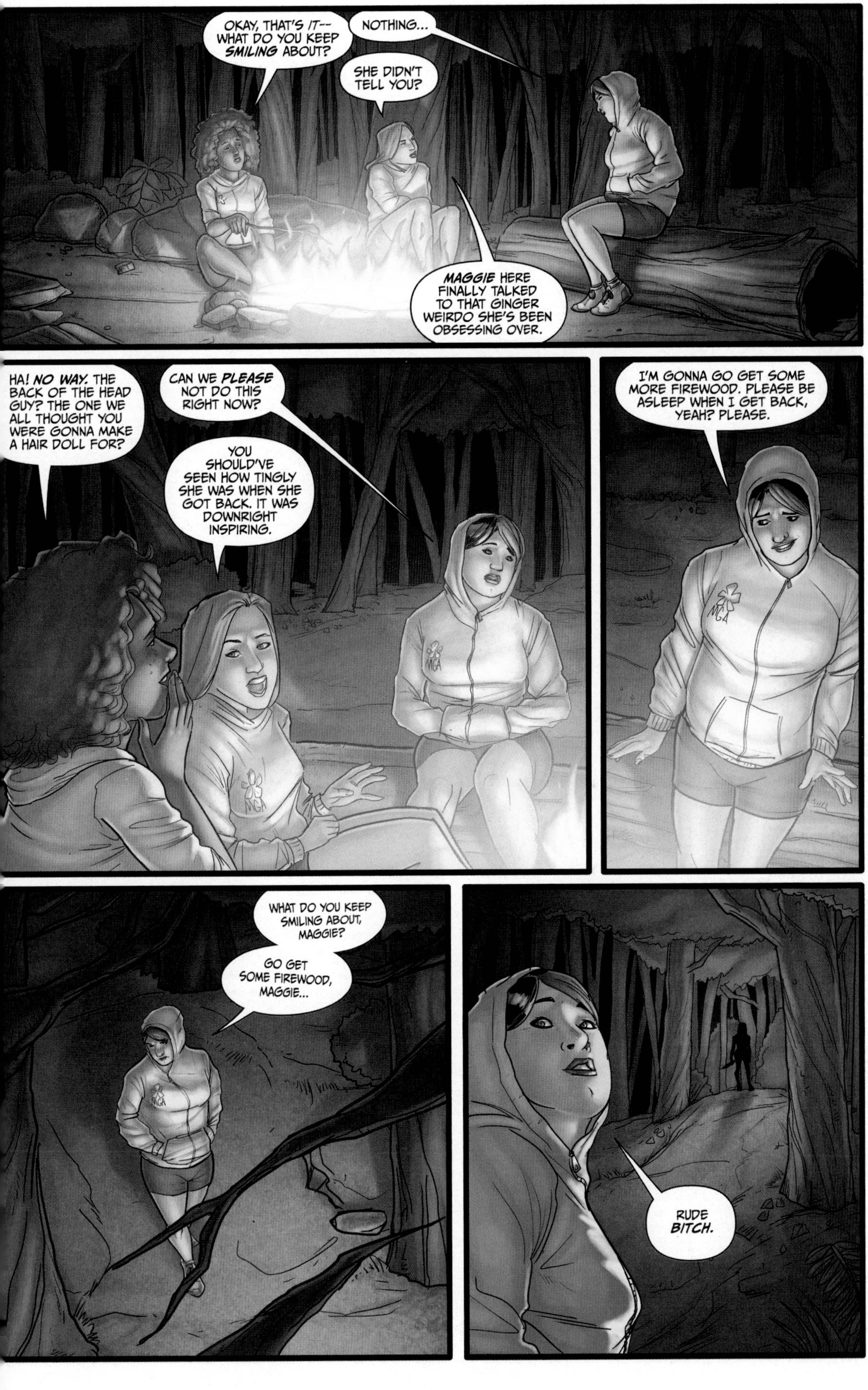
OKAY, THAT'S IT-- WHAT DO YOU KEEP SMILING ABOUT?
NOTHING...
SHE DIDN'T TELL YOU?
MAGGIE HERE FINALLY TALKED TO THAT GINGER WEIRDO SHE'S BEEN OBSESSING OVER.
HA! NO WAY. THE BACK OF THE HEAD GUY? THE ONE WE ALL THOUGHT YOU WERE GONNA MAKE A HAIR DOLL FOR?
CAN WE PLEASE NOT DO THIS RIGHT NOW?
YOU SHOULD'VE SEEN HOW TINGLY SHE WAS WHEN SHE GOT BACK. IT WAS DOWNRIGHT INSPIRING.
I'M GONNA GO GET SOME MORE FIREWOOD. PLEASE BE ASLEEP WHEN I GET BACK, YEAH? PLEASE.
WHAT DO YOU KEEP SMILING ABOUT, MAGGIE?
GO GET SOME FIREWOOD, MAGGIE...
RUDE BITCH.

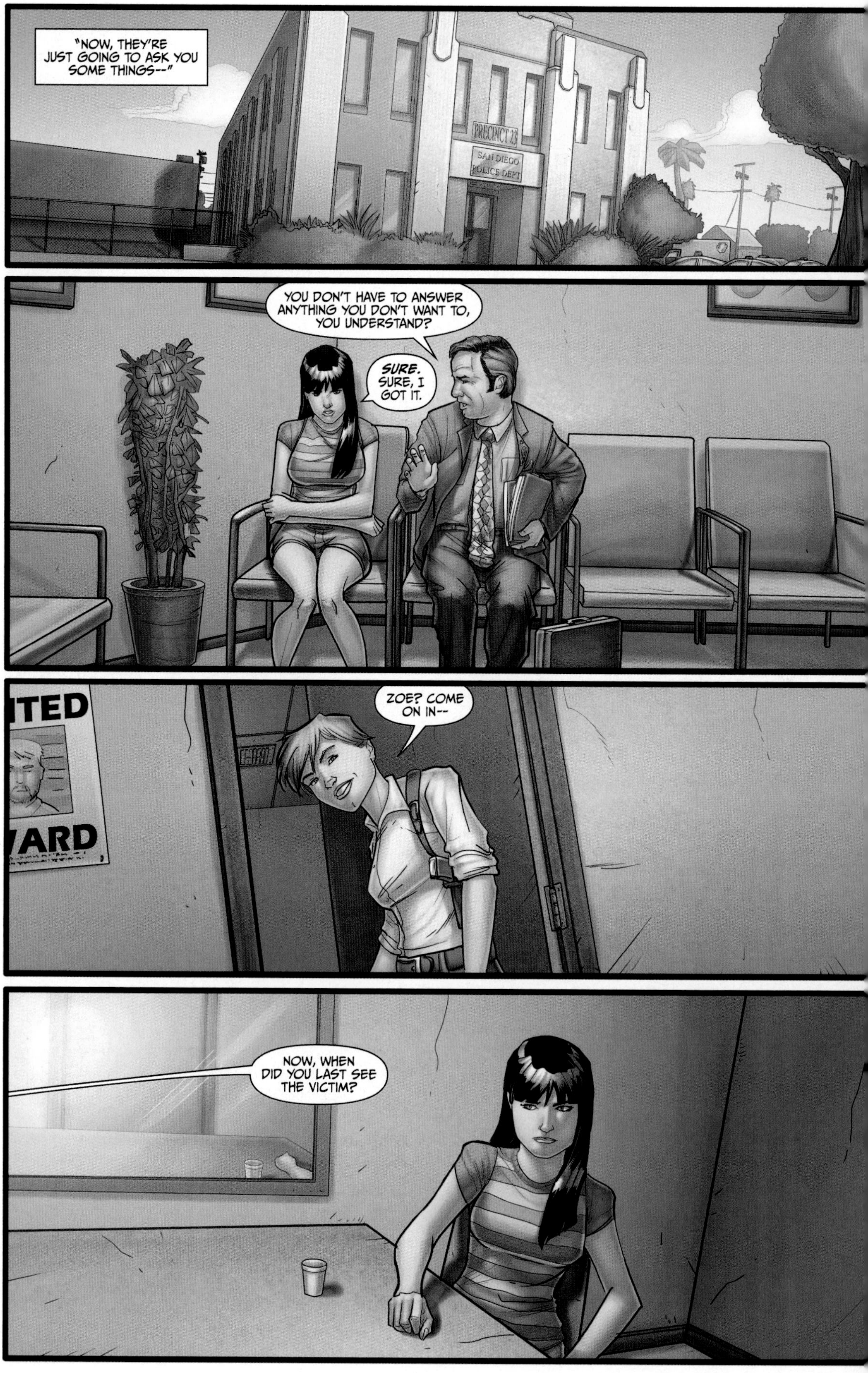
"NOW, THEY'RE JUST GOING TO ASK YOU SOME THINGS--"
SAN DIEGO POLICE DEPT
YOU DON'T HAVE TO ANSWER ANYTHING YOU DON'T WANT TO, YOU UNDERSTAND?
SURE. SURE, I GOT IT.
ZOE? COME ON IN--
NOW, WHEN DID YOU LAST SEE THE VICTIM?

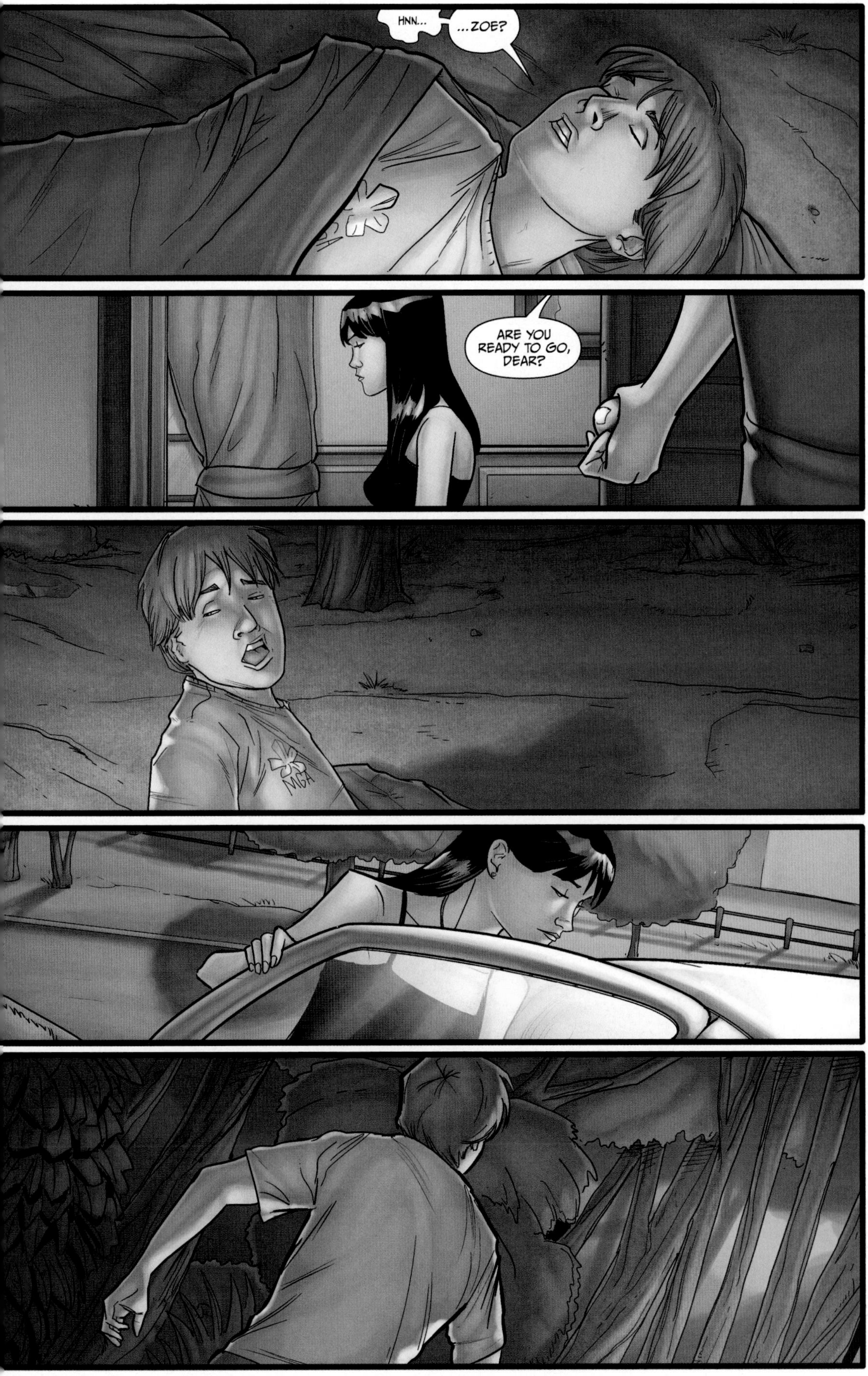
HNN...
...ZOE?
ARE YOU READY TO GO, DEAR?
MGA

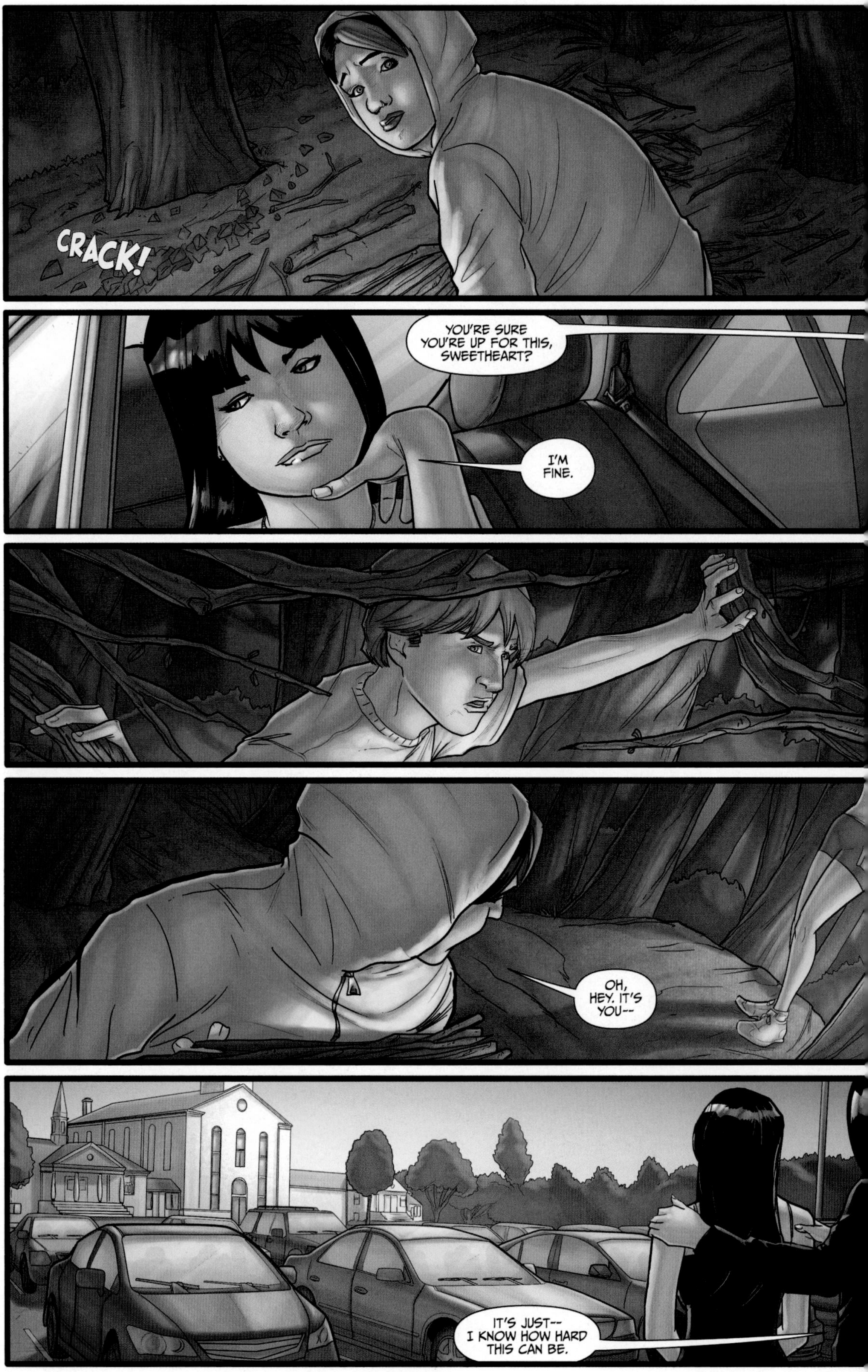
CRACK!
YOU'RE SURE YOU'RE UP FOR THIS, SWEETHEART?
I'M FINE.
OH, HEY. IT'S YOU--
IT'S JUST-- I KNOW HOW HARD THIS CAN BE.

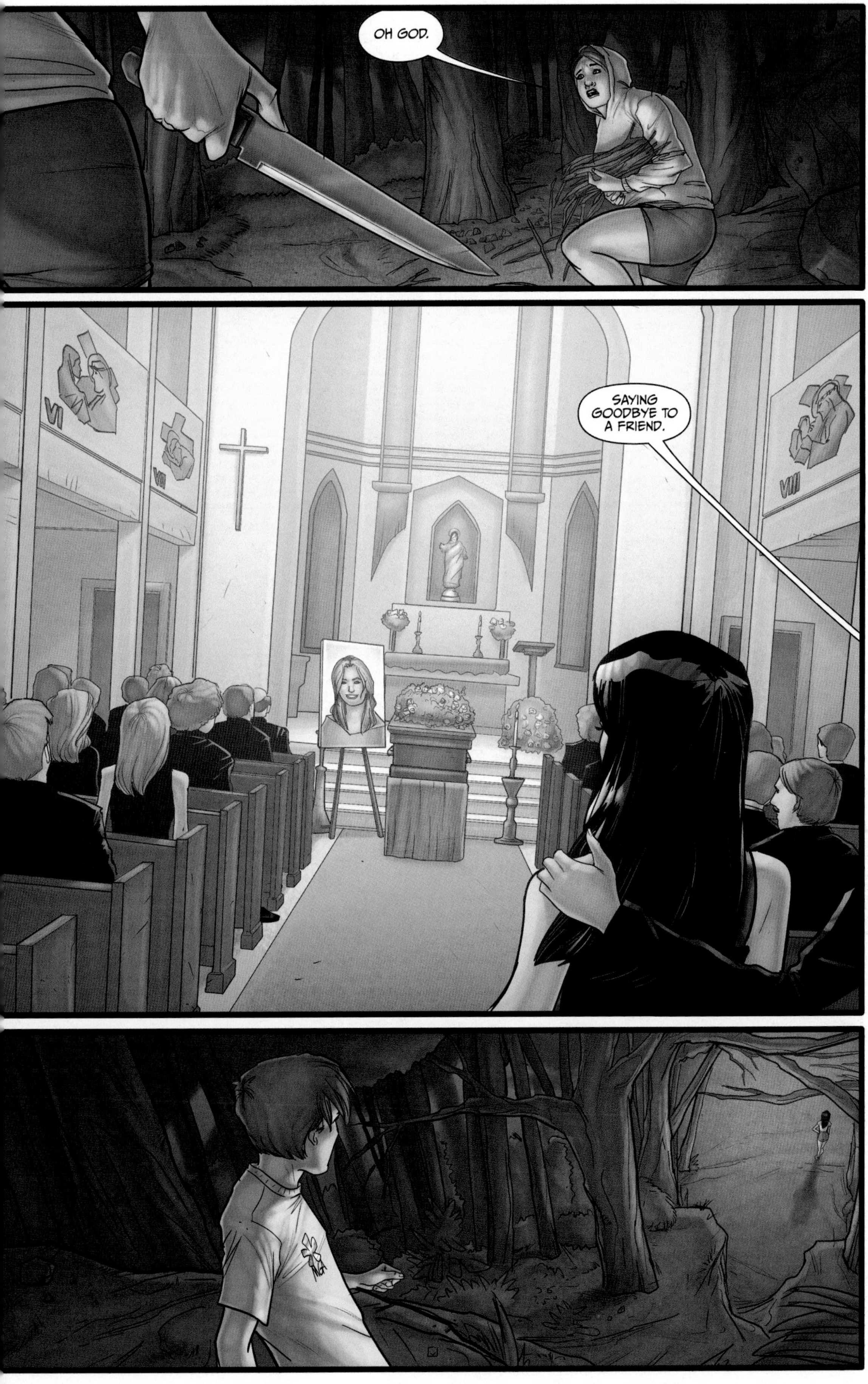
OH GOD.
SAYING GOODBYE TO A FRIEND.

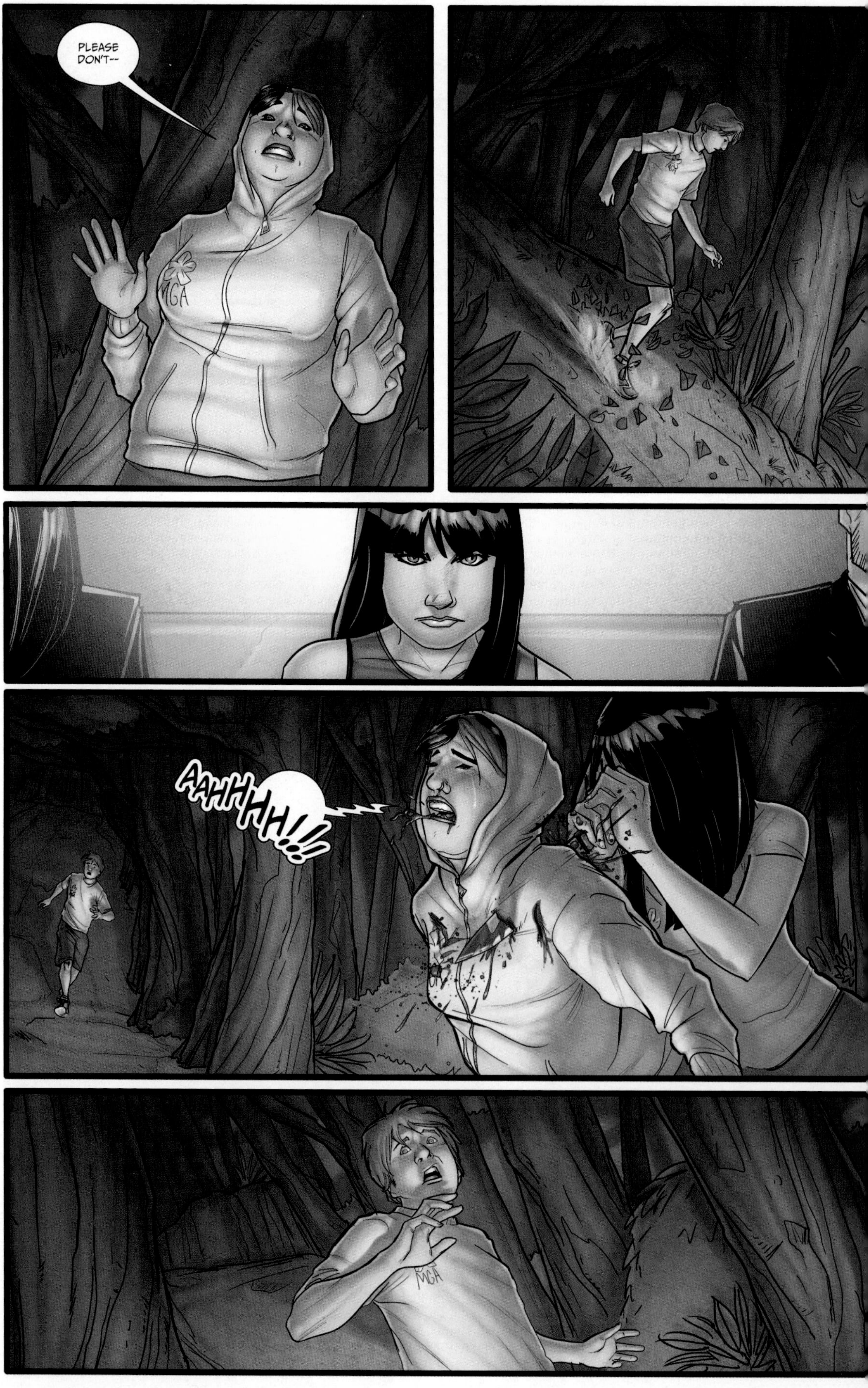
PLEASE DON'T--
AAHHHH!!!

sixteen

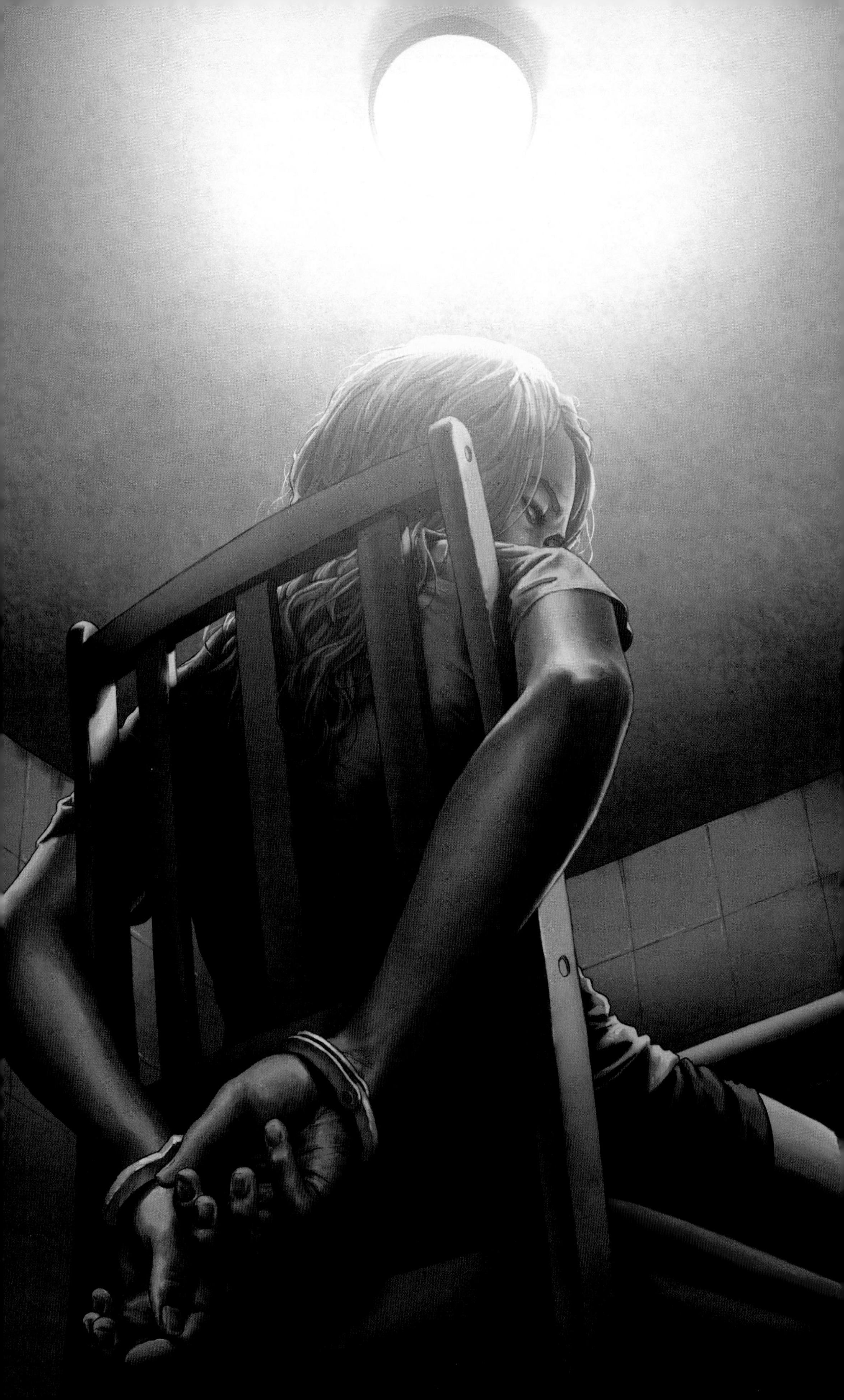

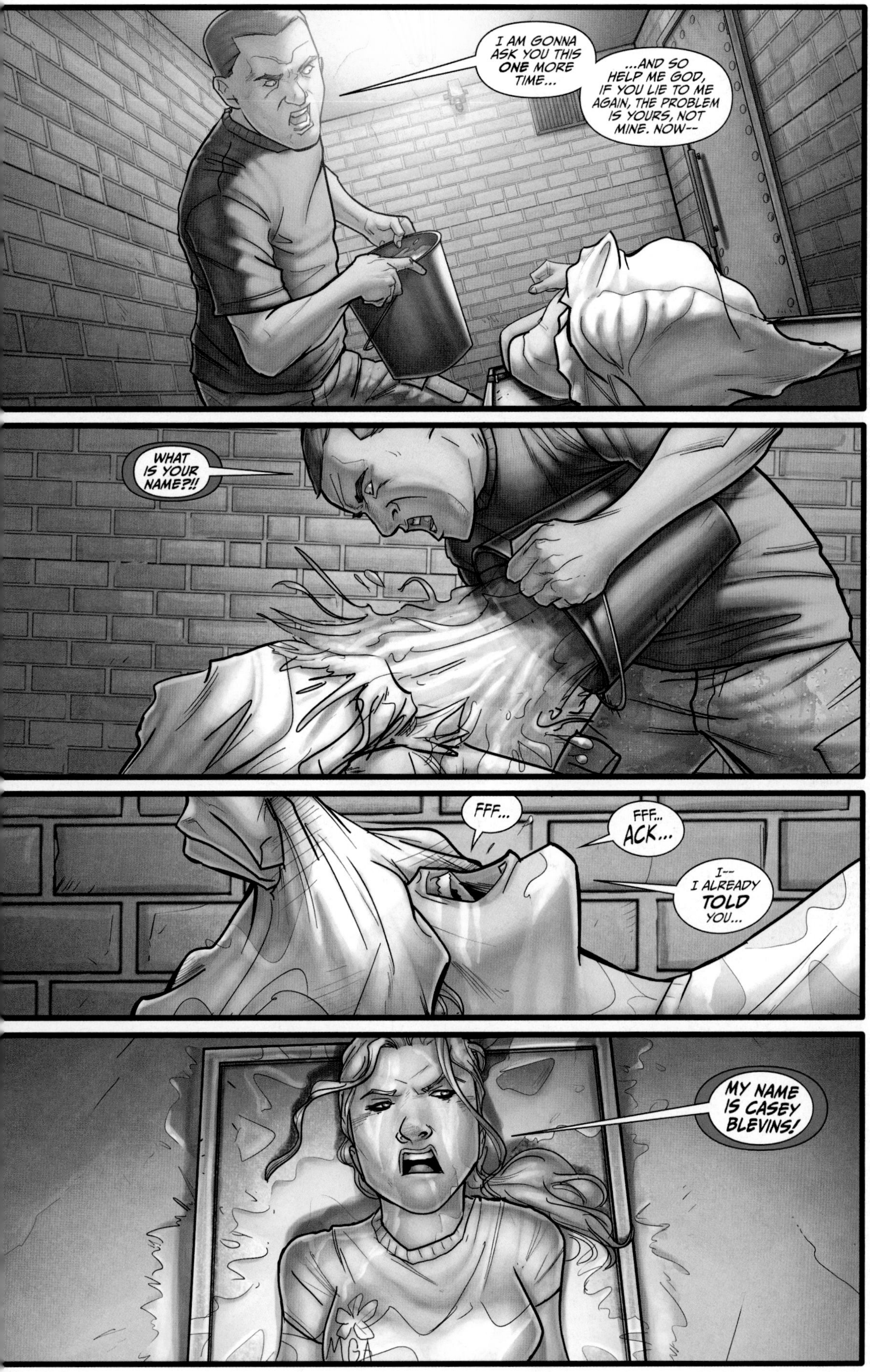
I AM GONNA ASK YOU THIS **ONE** MORE TIME...
...AND SO HELP ME GOD, IF YOU LIE TO ME AGAIN, THE PROBLEM IS YOURS, NOT MINE. NOW--
WHAT IS YOUR NAME?!!
FFF...
FFF... ACK...
I-- I ALREADY **TOLD** YOU...
MY NAME IS CASEY BLEVINS!

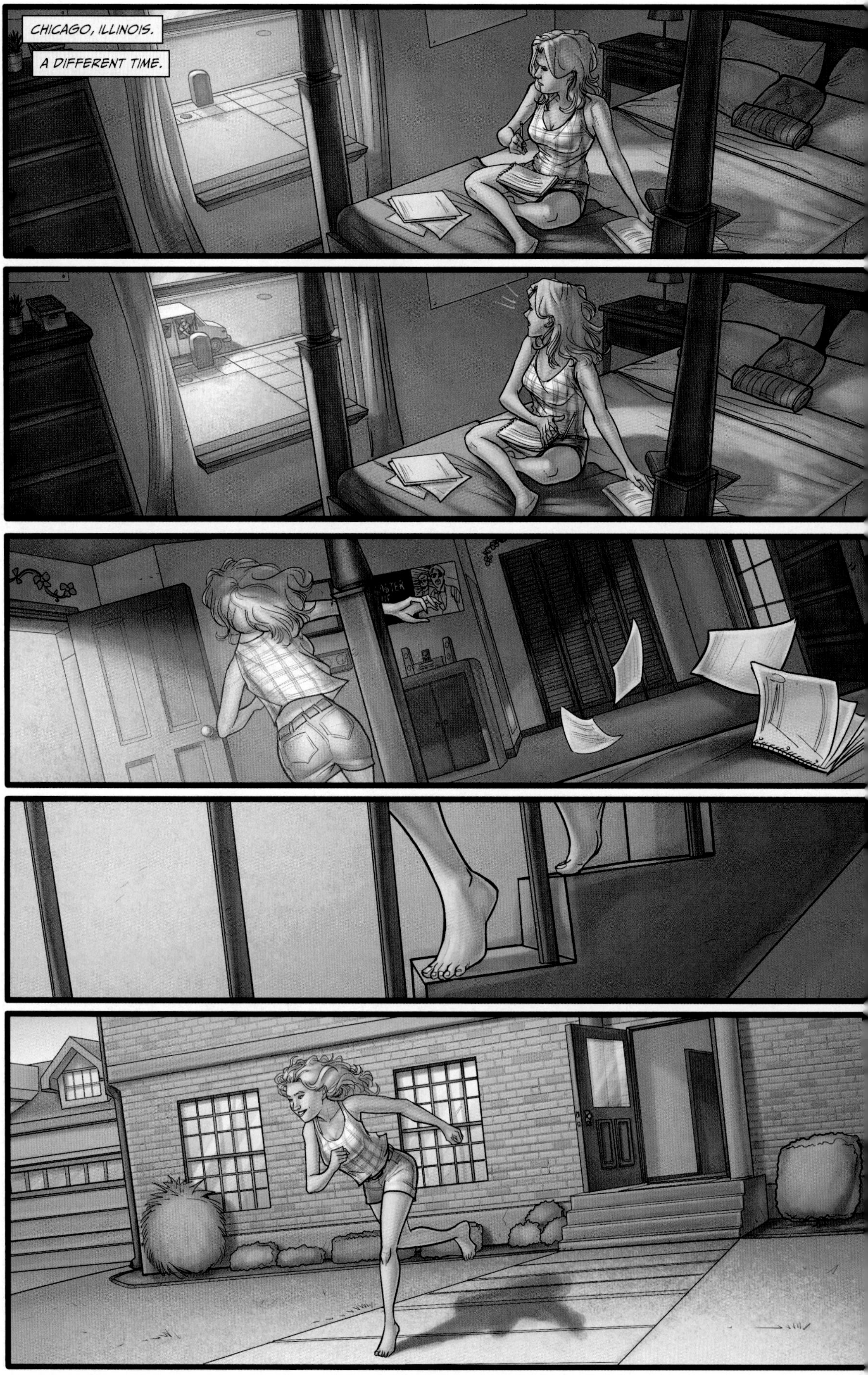
CHICAGO, ILLINOIS.
A DIFFERENT TIME.

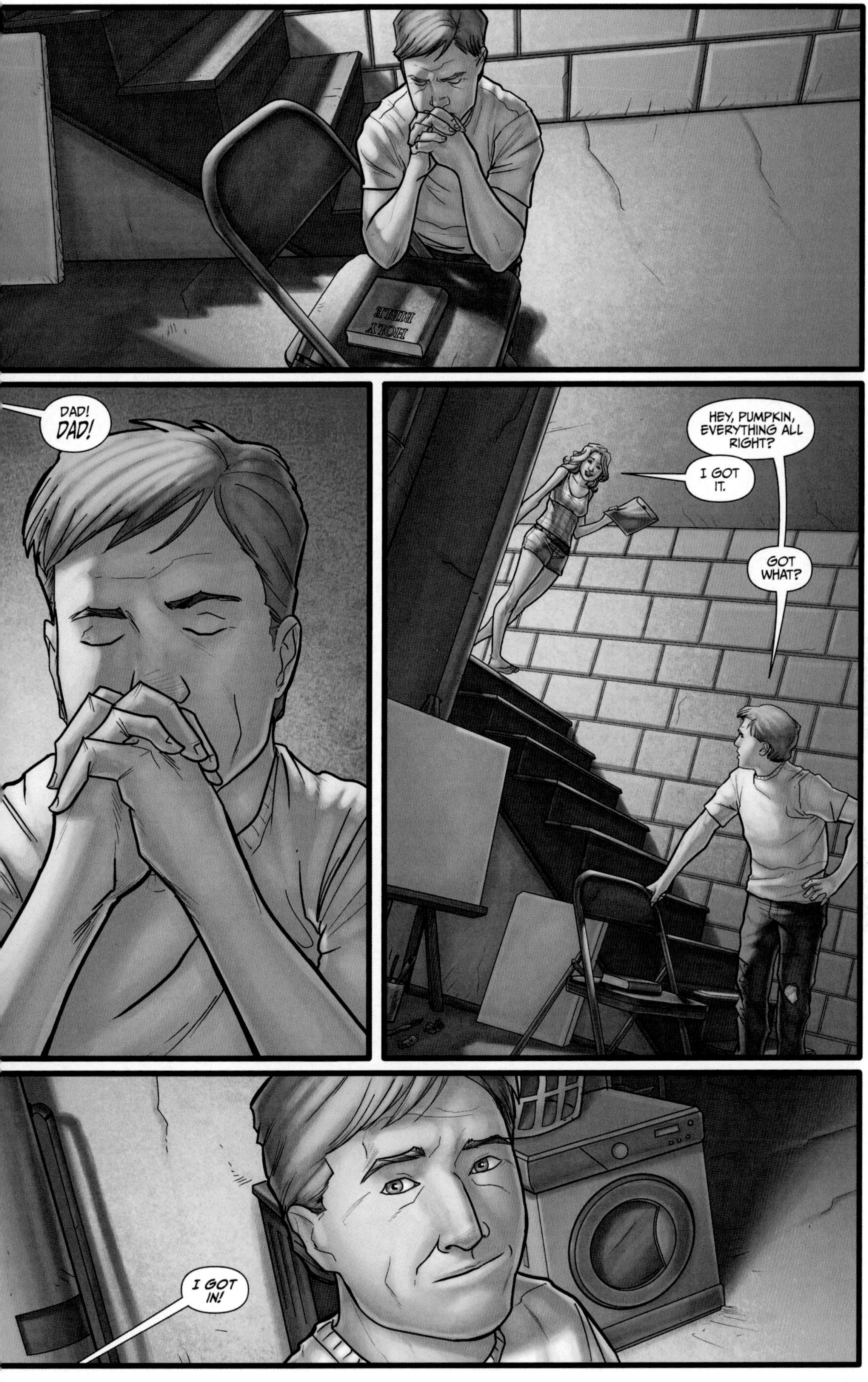
HOLY BIBLE
DAD! DAD!
HEY, PUMPKIN, EVERYTHING ALL RIGHT?
I GOT IT.
GOT WHAT?
I GOT IN!

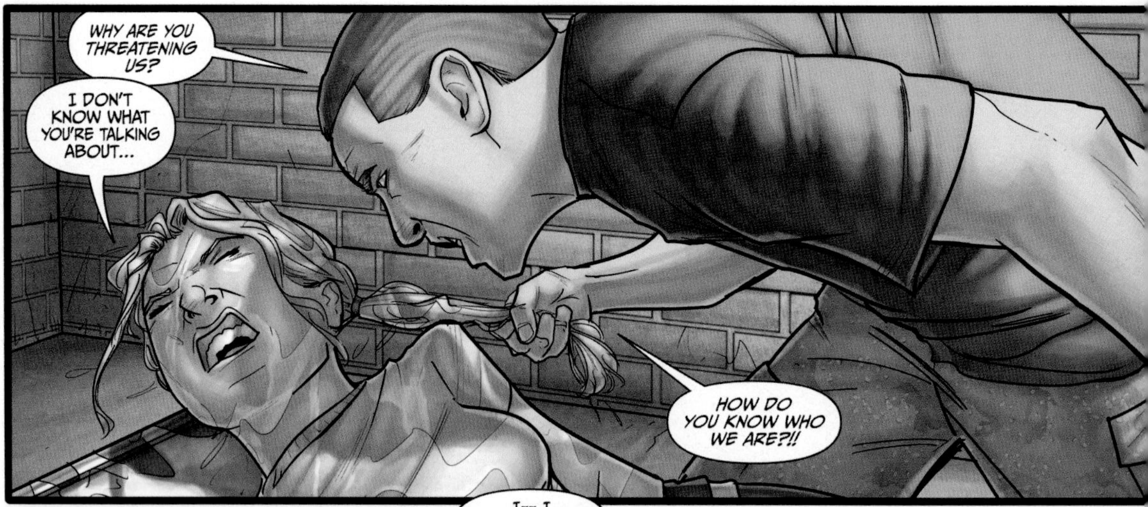
WHY ARE YOU THREATENING US?
I DON'T KNOW WHAT YOU'RE TALKING ABOUT...
HOW DO YOU KNOW WHO WE ARE?!!

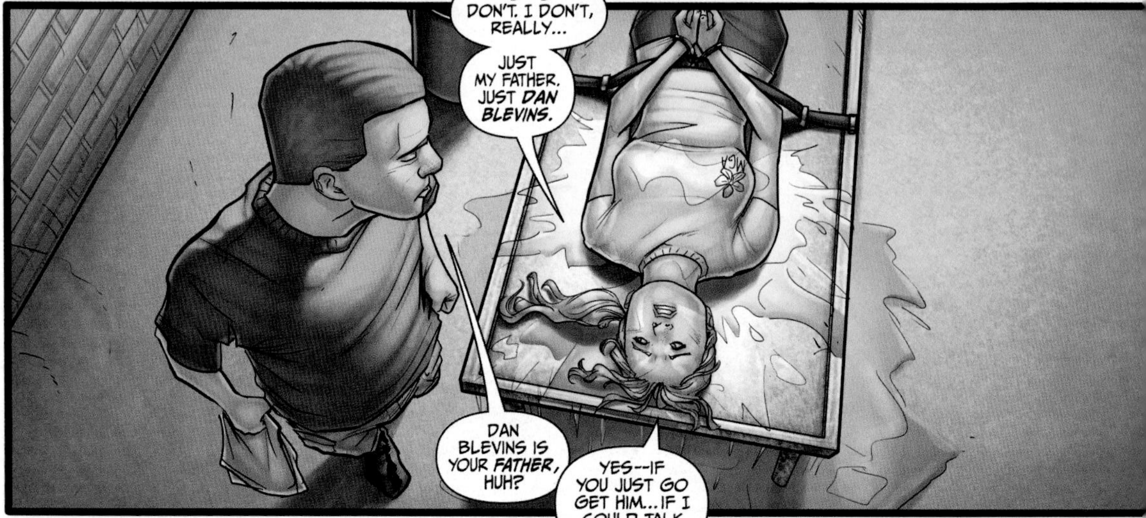
I-- I DON'T. I DON'T, REALLY...
JUST MY FATHER. JUST DAN BLEVINS.
DAN BLEVINS IS YOUR FATHER, HUH?
YES--IF YOU JUST GO GET HIM...IF I COULD TALK TO HIM--

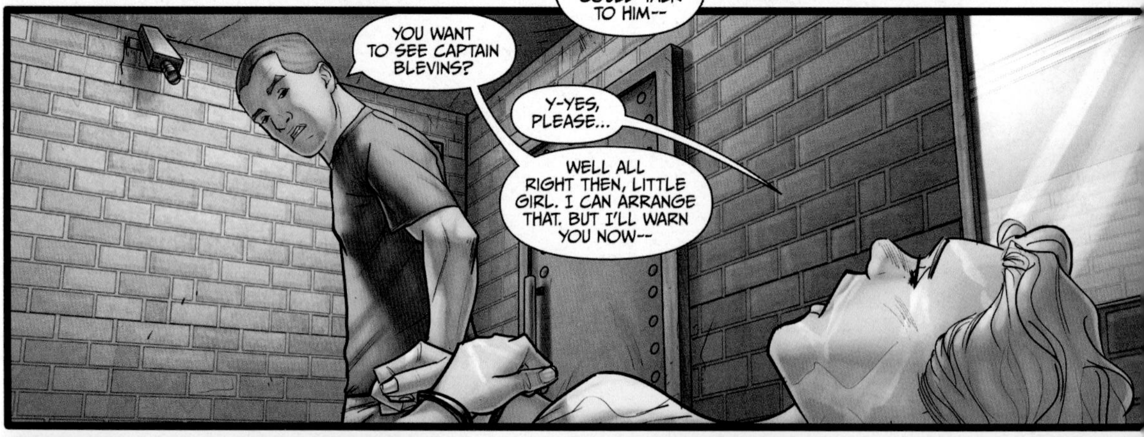
YOU WANT TO SEE CAPTAIN BLEVINS?
Y-YES, PLEASE...
WELL ALL RIGHT THEN, LITTLE GIRL. I CAN ARRANGE THAT. BUT I'LL WARN YOU NOW--

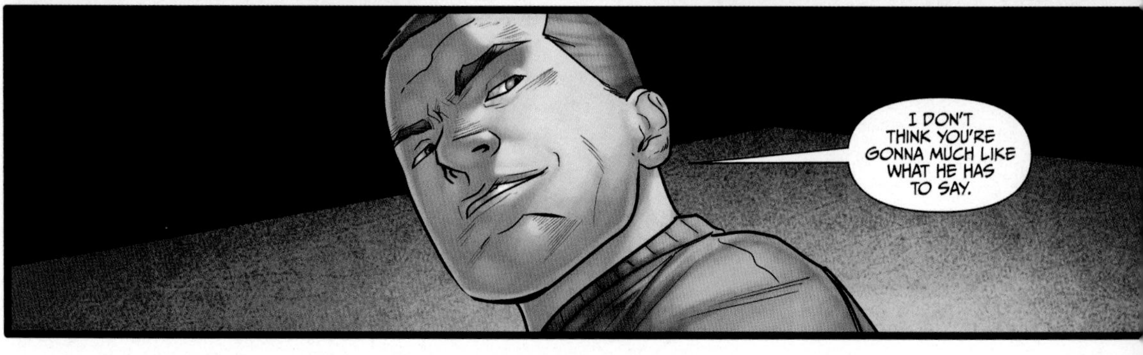
I DON'T THINK YOU'RE GONNA MUCH LIKE WHAT HE HAS TO SAY.

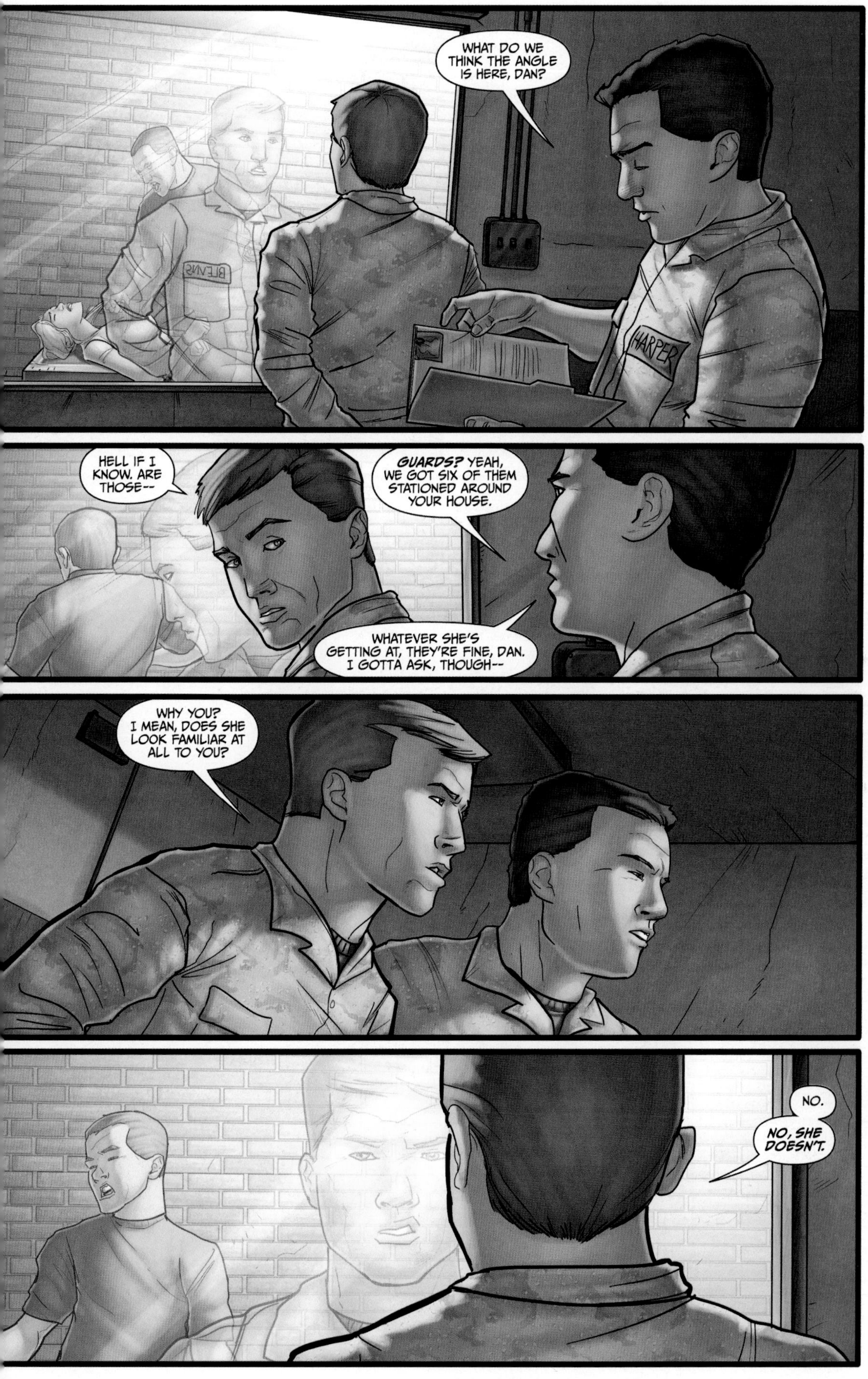
WHAT DO WE THINK THE ANGLE IS HERE, DAN?
BLEVINS
HARPER
HELL IF I KNOW. ARE THOSE--
GUARDS? YEAH, WE GOT SIX OF THEM STATIONED AROUND YOUR HOUSE.
WHATEVER SHE'S GETTING AT, THEY'RE FINE, DAN. I GOTTA ASK, THOUGH--
WHY YOU? I MEAN, DOES SHE LOOK FAMILIAR AT ALL TO YOU?
NO.
NO, SHE DOESN'T.

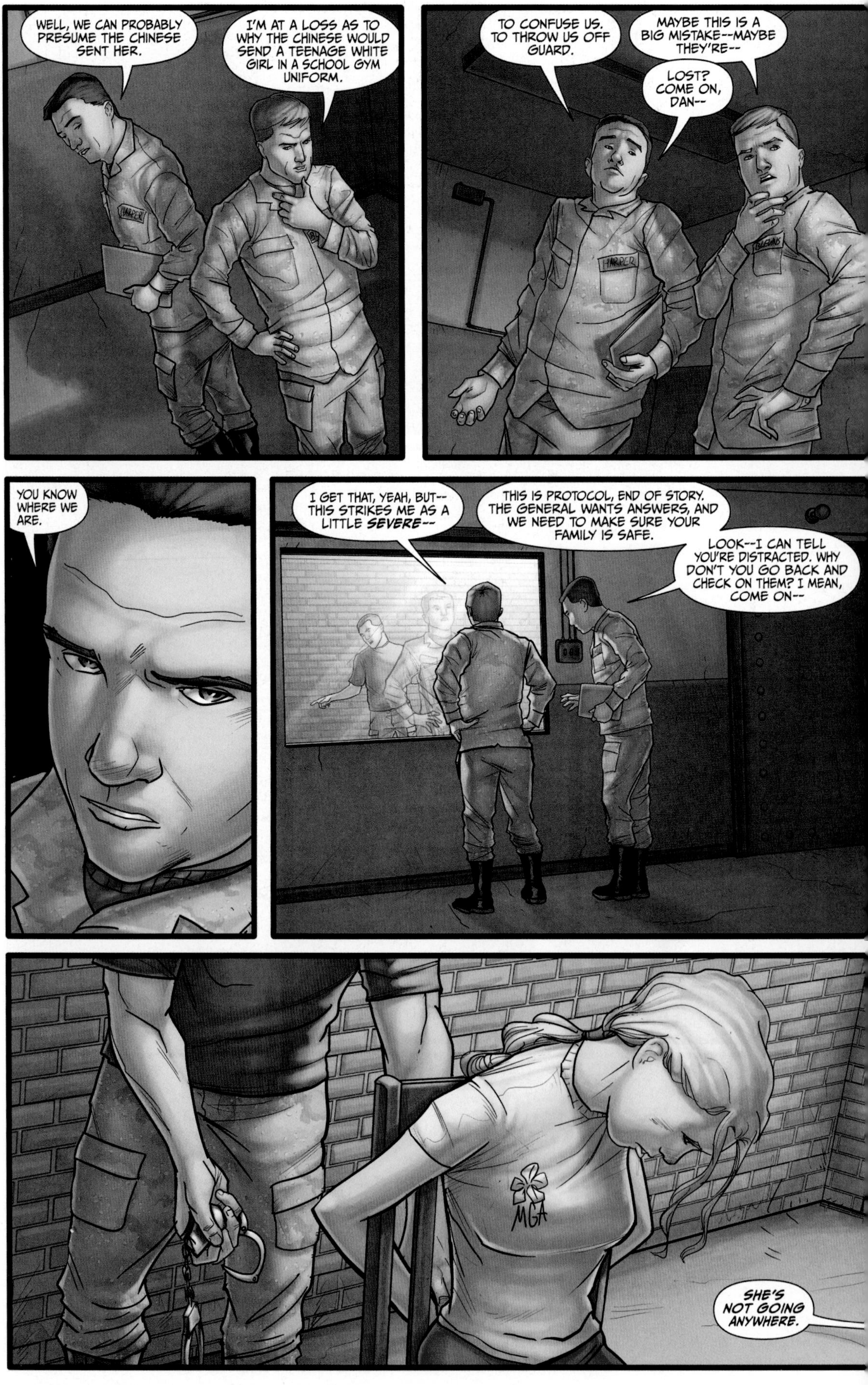

WELL, WE CAN PROBABLY PRESUME THE CHINESE SENT HER.
I'M AT A LOSS AS TO WHY THE CHINESE WOULD SEND A TEENAGE WHITE GIRL IN A SCHOOL GYM UNIFORM.
TO CONFUSE US. TO THROW US OFF GUARD.
MAYBE THIS IS A BIG MISTAKE--MAYBE THEY'RE--
LOST? COME ON, DAN--
HARPER
BLEVINS
YOU KNOW WHERE WE ARE.
I GET THAT, YEAH, BUT-- THIS STRIKES ME AS A LITTLE *SEVERE*--
THIS IS PROTOCOL, END OF STORY. THE GENERAL WANTS ANSWERS, AND WE NEED TO MAKE SURE YOUR FAMILY IS SAFE.
LOOK--I CAN TELL YOU'RE DISTRACTED. WHY DON'T YOU GO BACK AND CHECK ON THEM? I MEAN, COME ON--
MGA
SHE'S NOT GOING ANYWHERE.

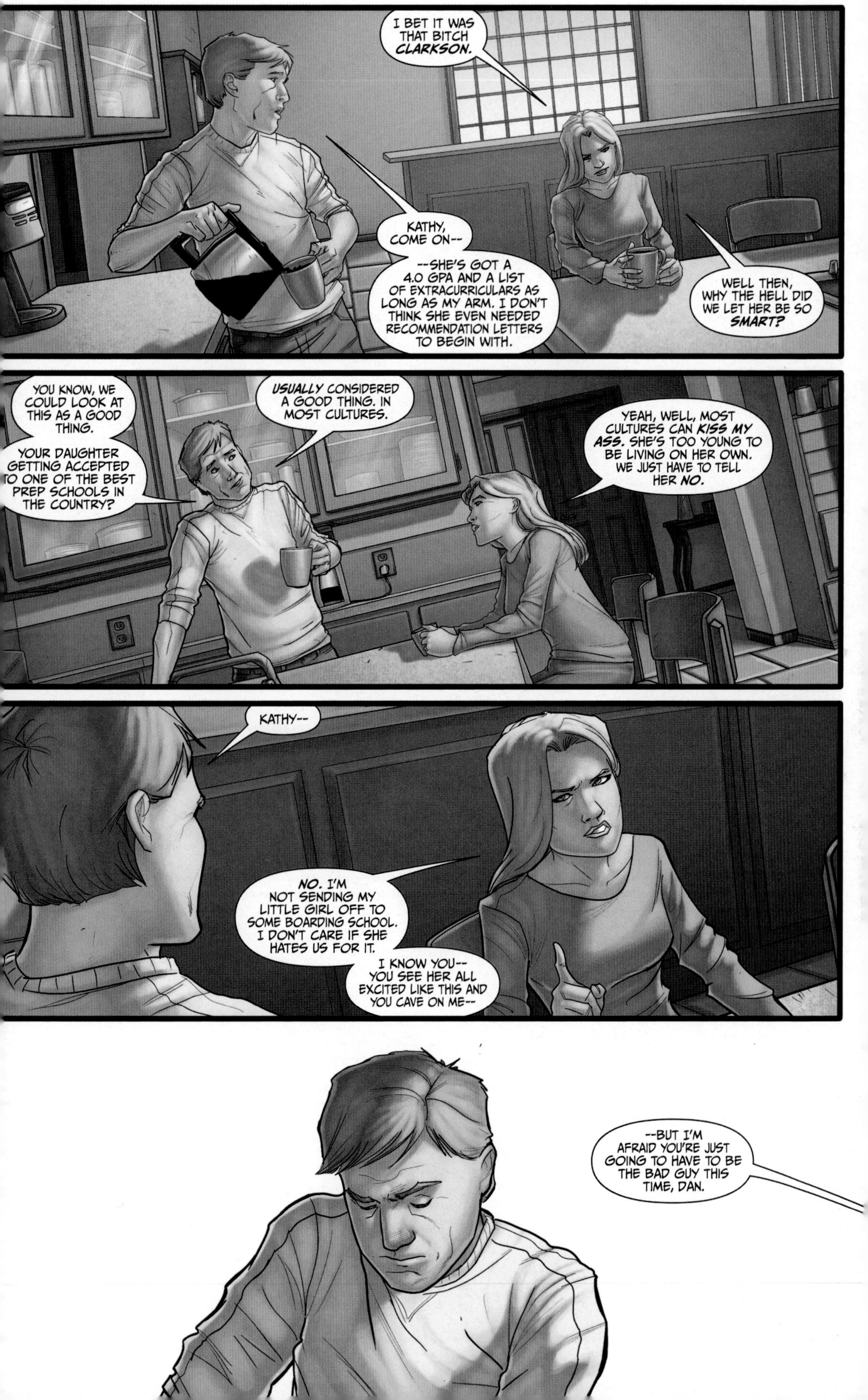
I BET IT WAS THAT BITCH CLARKSON.
KATHY, COME ON--
--SHE'S GOT A 4.0 GPA AND A LIST OF EXTRACURRICULARS AS LONG AS MY ARM. I DON'T THINK SHE EVEN NEEDED RECOMMENDATION LETTERS TO BEGIN WITH.
WELL THEN, WHY THE HELL DID WE LET HER BE SO SMART?
YOU KNOW, WE COULD LOOK AT THIS AS A GOOD THING.
YOUR DAUGHTER GETTING ACCEPTED TO ONE OF THE BEST PREP SCHOOLS IN THE COUNTRY?
USUALLY CONSIDERED A GOOD THING. IN MOST CULTURES.
YEAH, WELL, MOST CULTURES CAN KISS MY ASS. SHE'S TOO YOUNG TO BE LIVING ON HER OWN. WE JUST HAVE TO TELL HER NO.
KATHY--
NO. I'M NOT SENDING MY LITTLE GIRL OFF TO SOME BOARDING SCHOOL. I DON'T CARE IF SHE HATES US FOR IT.
I KNOW YOU-- YOU SEE HER ALL EXCITED LIKE THIS AND YOU CAVE ON ME--
--BUT I'M AFRAID YOU'RE JUST GOING TO HAVE TO BE THE BAD GUY THIS TIME, DAN.

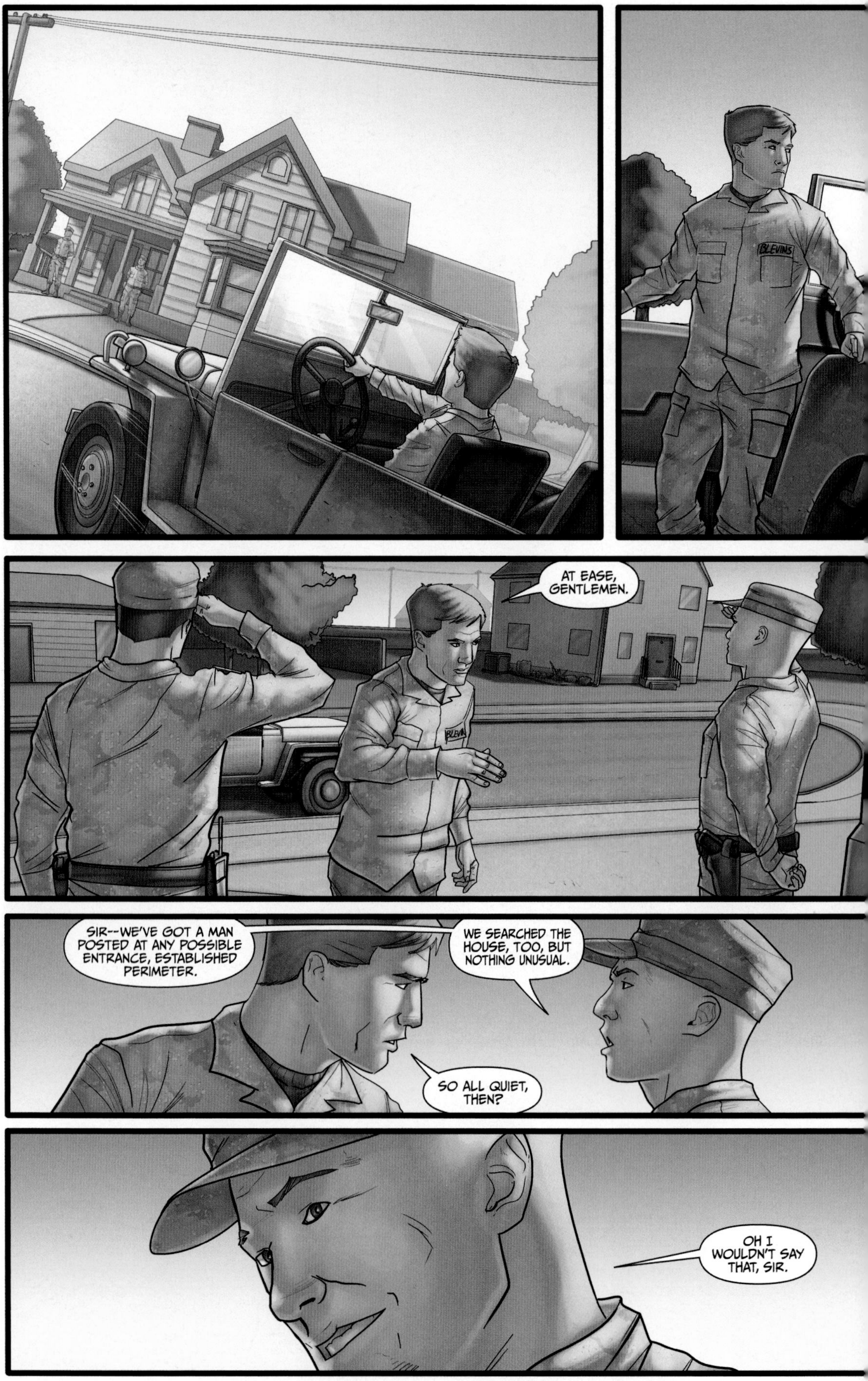
BLEVINS
BLEVINS
AT EASE, GENTLEMEN.
SIR--WE'VE GOT A MAN POSTED AT ANY POSSIBLE ENTRANCE, ESTABLISHED PERIMETER.
WE SEARCHED THE HOUSE, TOO, BUT NOTHING UNUSUAL.
SO ALL QUIET, THEN?
OH I WOULDN'T SAY THAT, SIR.

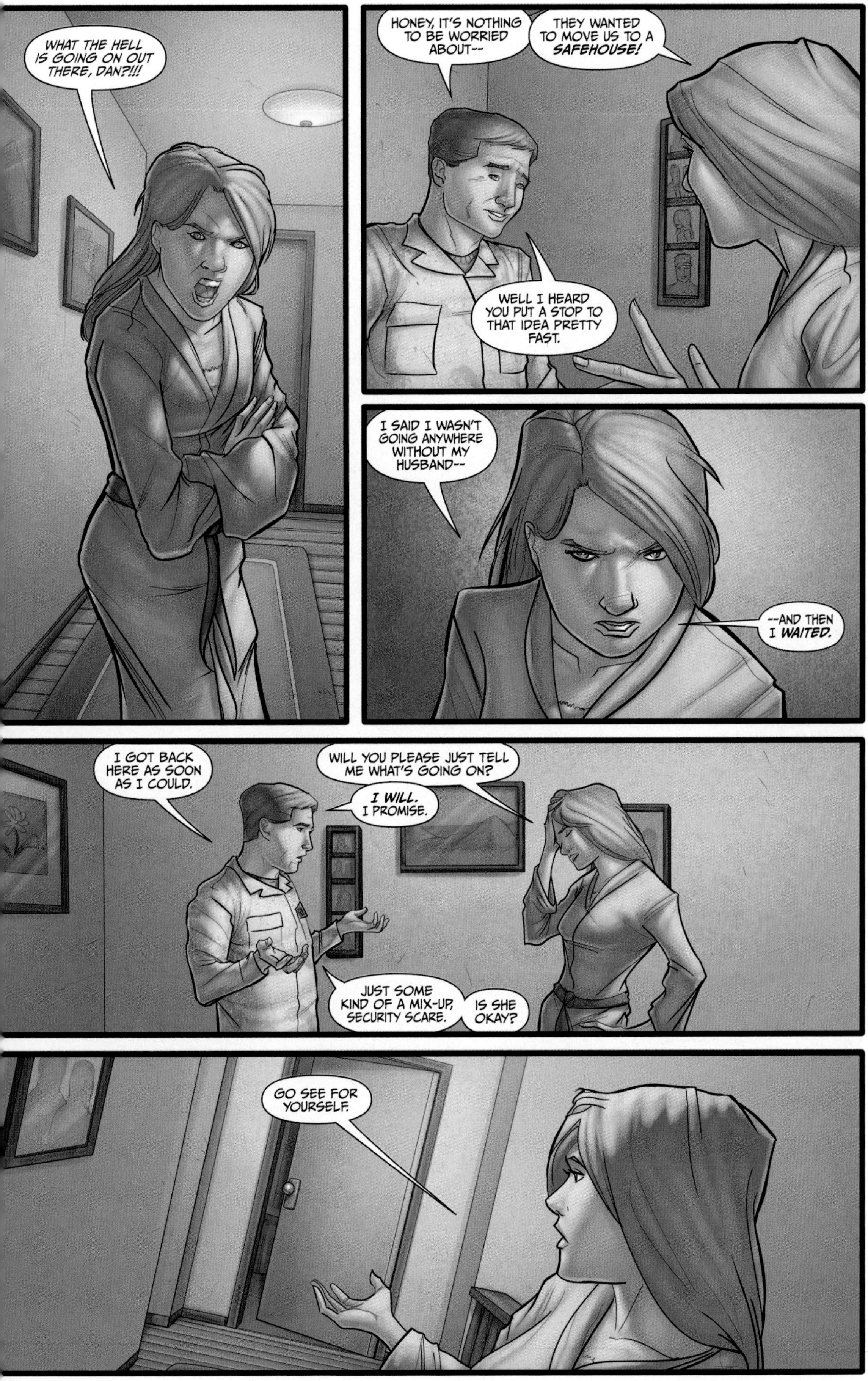
WHAT THE HELL IS GOING ON OUT THERE, DAN?!!!
HONEY, IT'S NOTHING TO BE WORRIED ABOUT--
THEY WANTED TO MOVE US TO A SAFEHOUSE!
WELL I HEARD YOU PUT A STOP TO THAT IDEA PRETTY FAST.
I SAID I WASN'T GOING ANYWHERE WITHOUT MY HUSBAND--
--AND THEN I WAITED.
I GOT BACK HERE AS SOON AS I COULD.
WILL YOU PLEASE JUST TELL ME WHAT'S GOING ON?
I WILL. I PROMISE.
JUST SOME KIND OF A MIX-UP, SECURITY SCARE.
IS SHE OKAY?
GO SEE FOR YOURSELF.

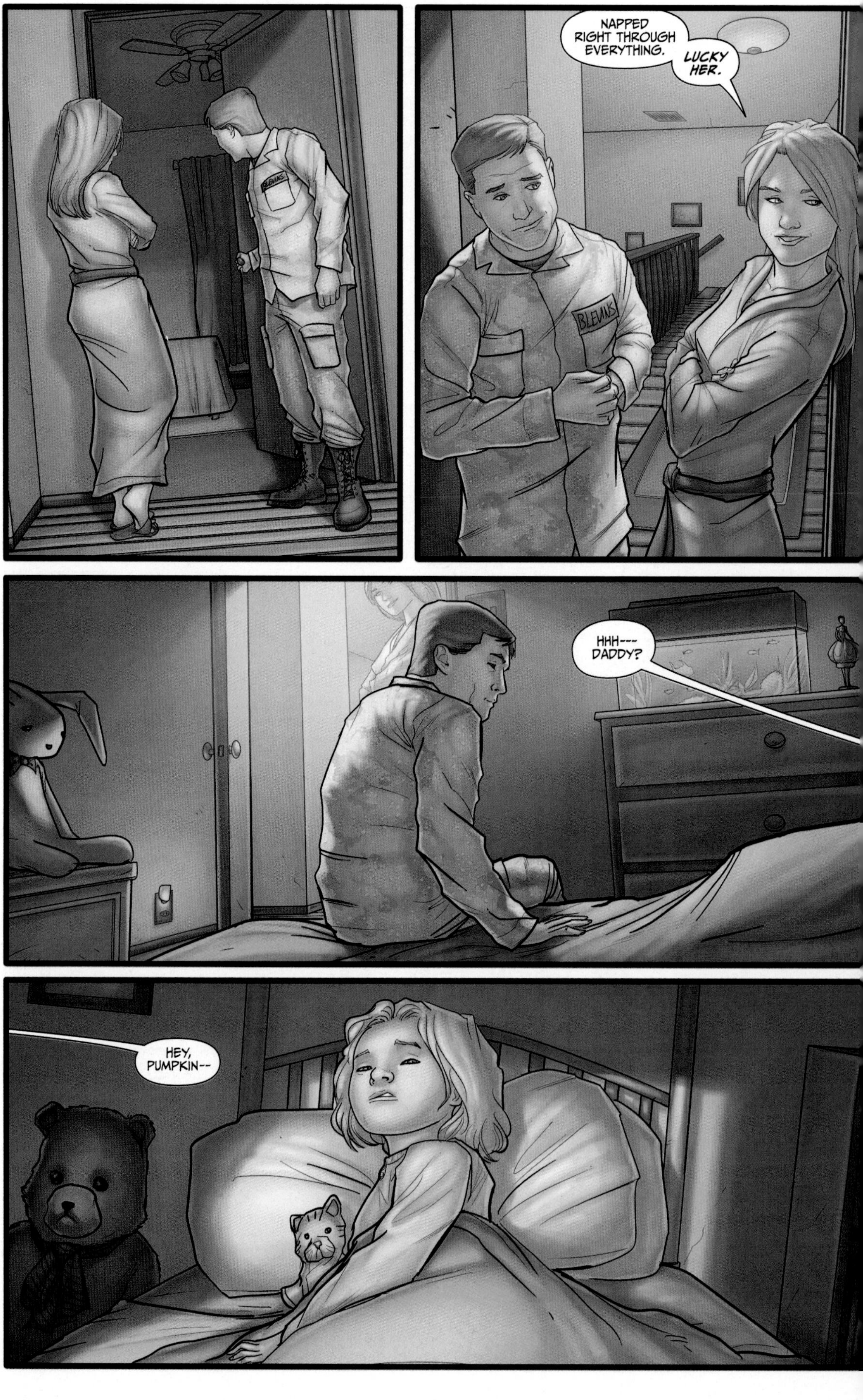

BLEVINS
NAPPED RIGHT THROUGH EVERYTHING.
LUCKY HER.
BLEVINS
HHH--- DADDY?
HEY, PUMPKIN--

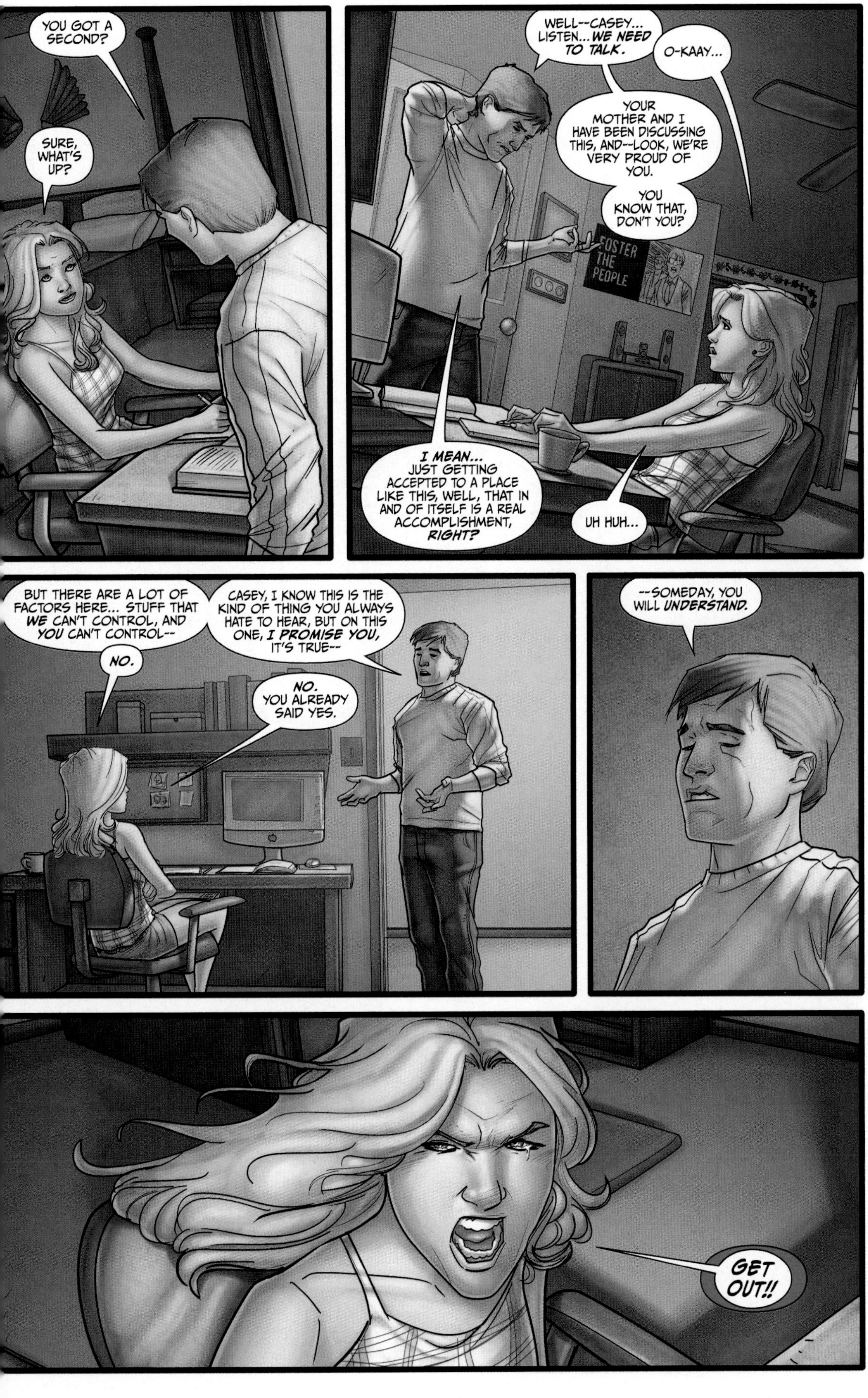

YOU GOT A SECOND?
SURE, WHAT'S UP?
WELL--CASEY... LISTEN... *WE NEED TO TALK.*
O-KAAY...
YOUR MOTHER AND I HAVE BEEN DISCUSSING THIS, AND--LOOK, WE'RE VERY PROUD OF YOU.
YOU KNOW THAT, DON'T YOU?
FOSTER THE PEOPLE
I MEAN... JUST GETTING ACCEPTED TO A PLACE LIKE THIS, WELL, THAT IN AND OF ITSELF IS A REAL ACCOMPLISHMENT, *RIGHT?*
UH HUH...
BUT THERE ARE A LOT OF FACTORS HERE... STUFF THAT *WE* CAN'T CONTROL, AND *YOU* CAN'T CONTROL--
NO.
CASEY, I KNOW THIS IS THE KIND OF THING YOU ALWAYS HATE TO HEAR, BUT ON THIS ONE, *I PROMISE YOU,* IT'S TRUE--
NO. YOU ALREADY SAID YES.
--SOMEDAY, YOU WILL *UNDERSTAND.*
GET OUT!!

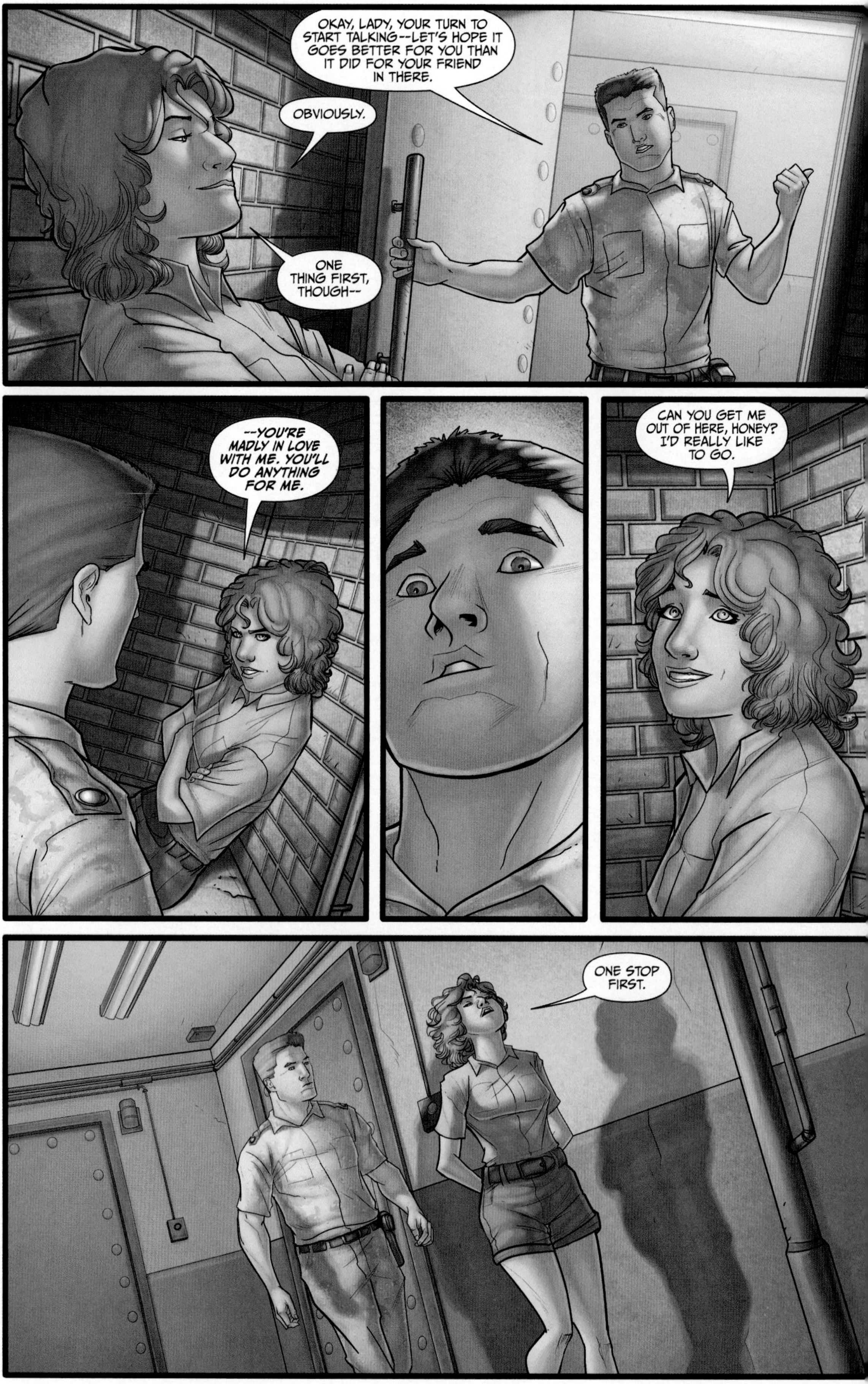
OKAY, LADY, YOUR TURN TO START TALKING--LET'S HOPE IT GOES BETTER FOR YOU THAN IT DID FOR YOUR FRIEND IN THERE.
OBVIOUSLY.
ONE THING FIRST, THOUGH--
--YOU'RE MADLY IN LOVE WITH ME. YOU'LL DO ANYTHING FOR ME.
CAN YOU GET ME OUT OF HERE, HONEY? I'D REALLY LIKE TO GO.
ONE STOP FIRST.

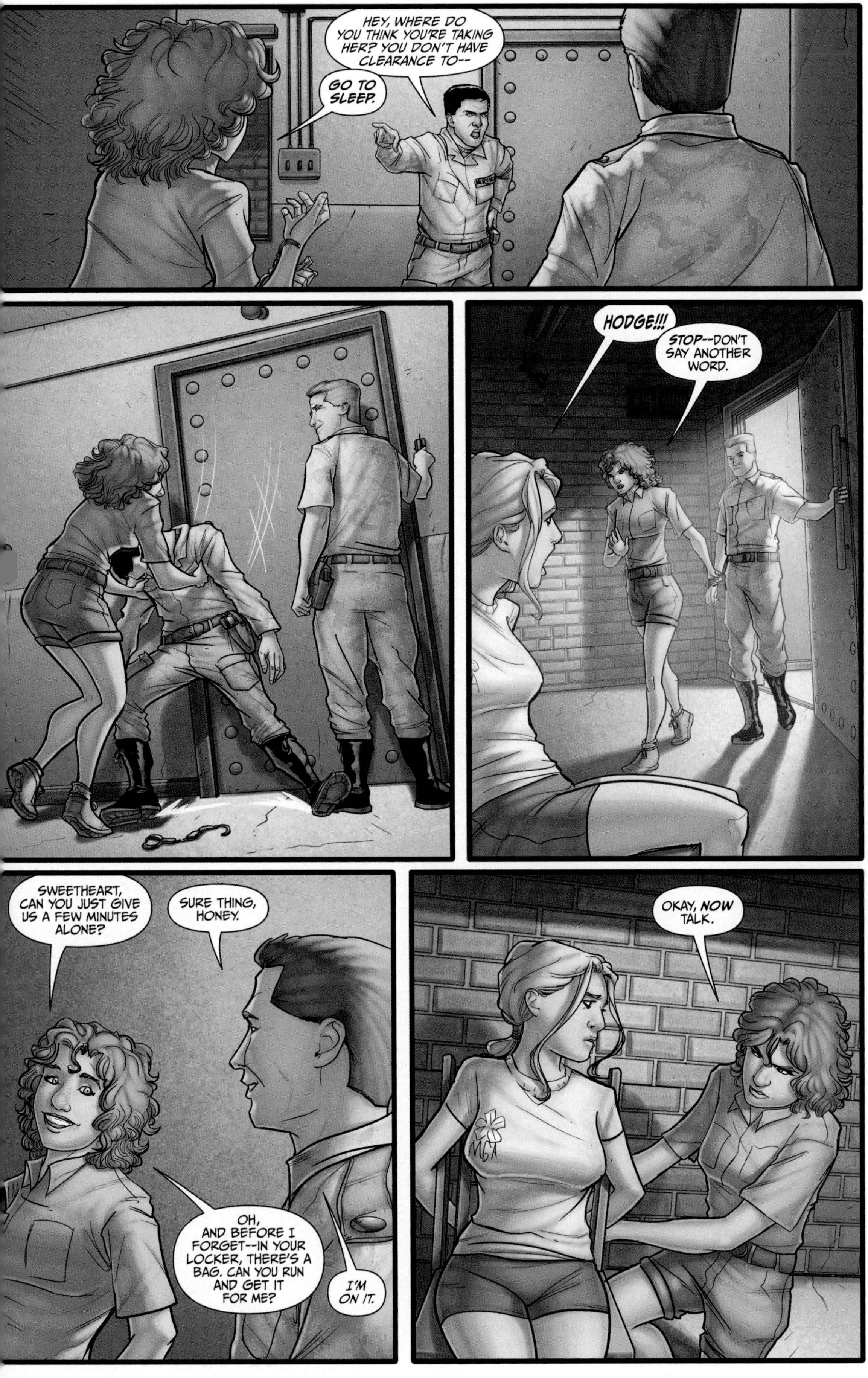
HEY, WHERE DO YOU THINK YOU'RE TAKING HER? YOU DON'T HAVE CLEARANCE TO--
GO TO SLEEP.
HODGE!!!
STOP--DON'T SAY ANOTHER WORD.
SWEETHEART, CAN YOU JUST GIVE US A FEW MINUTES ALONE?
SURE THING, HONEY.
OH, AND BEFORE I FORGET--IN YOUR LOCKER, THERE'S A BAG. CAN YOU RUN AND GET IT FOR ME?
I'M ON IT.
OKAY, NOW TALK.

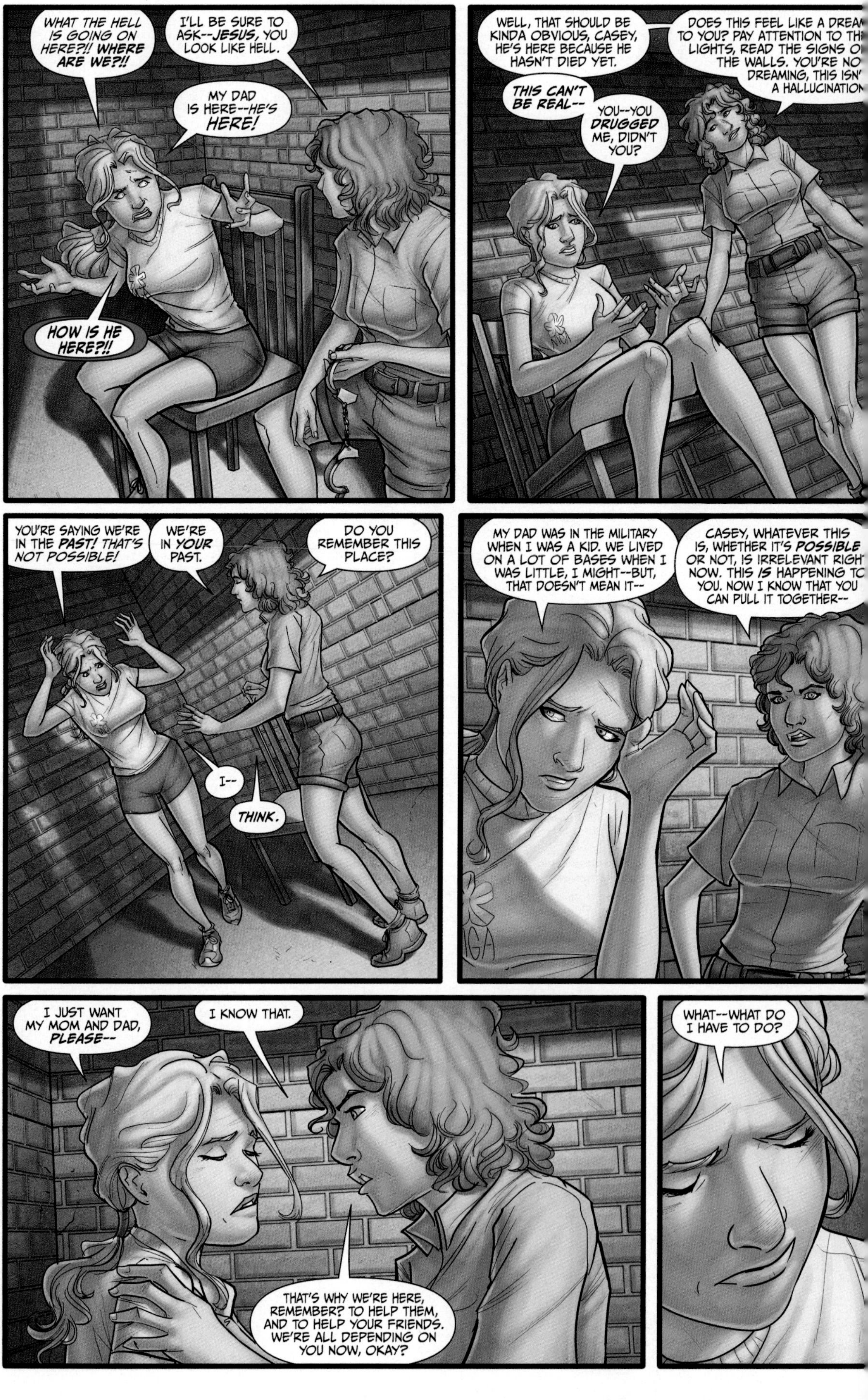

WHAT THE HELL IS GOING ON HERE?!! WHERE ARE WE?!!
I'LL BE SURE TO ASK--JESUS, YOU LOOK LIKE HELL.
MY DAD IS HERE--HE'S HERE!
HOW IS HE HERE?!!
WELL, THAT SHOULD BE KINDA OBVIOUS, CASEY, HE'S HERE BECAUSE HE HASN'T DIED YET.
DOES THIS FEEL LIKE A DREA TO YOU? PAY ATTENTION TO TH LIGHTS, READ THE SIGNS O THE WALLS. YOU'RE NO DREAMING, THIS ISN' A HALLUCINATIO
THIS CAN'T BE REAL--
YOU--YOU DRUGGED ME, DIDN'T YOU?
YOU'RE SAYING WE'RE IN THE PAST! THAT'S NOT POSSIBLE!
WE'RE IN YOUR PAST.
DO YOU REMEMBER THIS PLACE?
I--
THINK.
MY DAD WAS IN THE MILITARY WHEN I WAS A KID. WE LIVED ON A LOT OF BASES WHEN I WAS LITTLE, I MIGHT--BUT, THAT DOESN'T MEAN IT--
CASEY, WHATEVER THIS IS, WHETHER IT'S POSSIBLE OR NOT, IS IRRELEVANT RIGH NOW. THIS IS HAPPENING TO YOU. NOW I KNOW THAT YOU CAN PULL IT TOGETHER--
I JUST WANT MY MOM AND DAD, PLEASE--
I KNOW THAT.
THAT'S WHY WE'RE HERE, REMEMBER? TO HELP THEM, AND TO HELP YOUR FRIENDS. WE'RE ALL DEPENDING ON YOU NOW, OKAY?
WHAT--WHAT DO I HAVE TO DO?

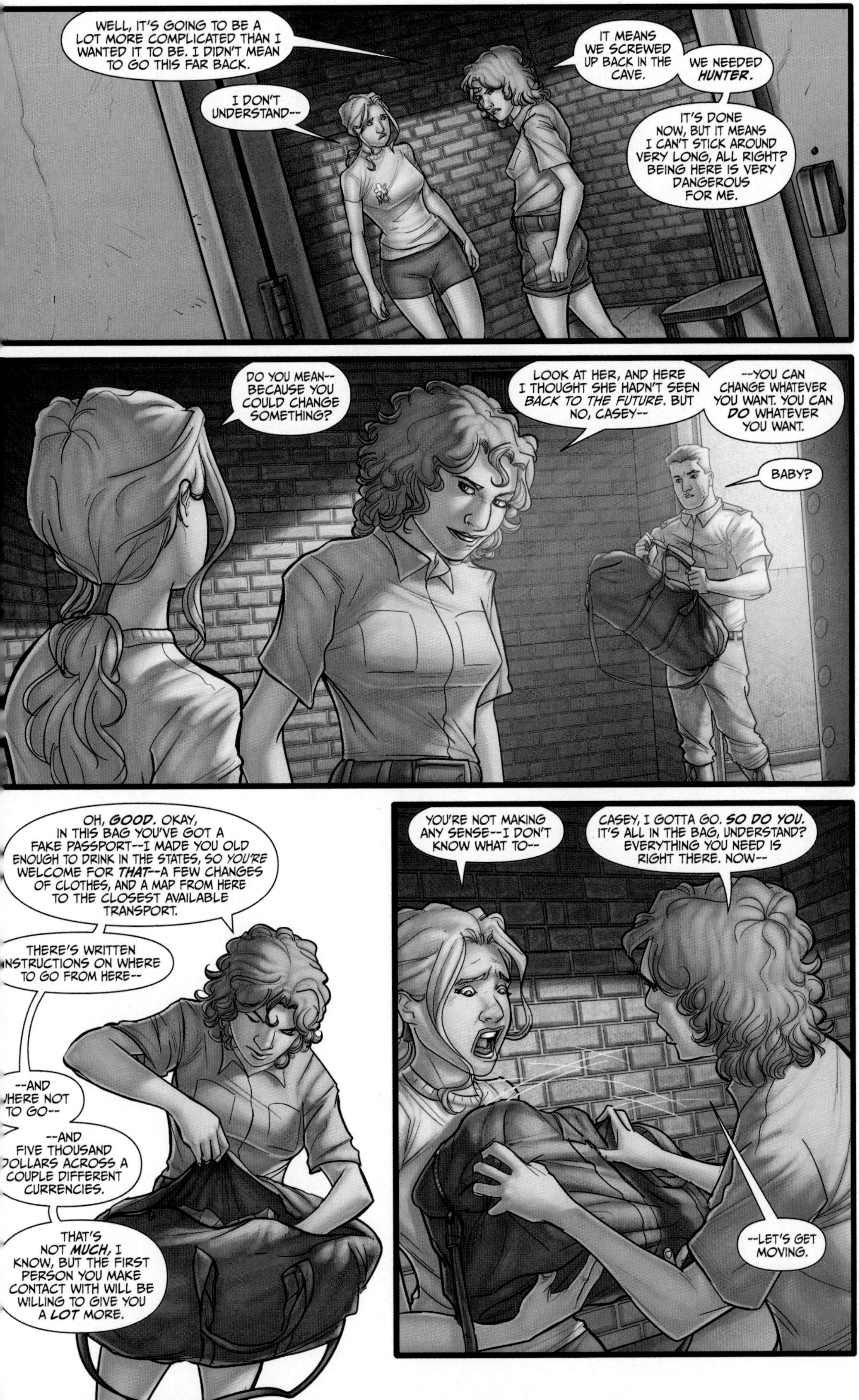
WELL, IT'S GOING TO BE A LOT MORE COMPLICATED THAN I WANTED IT TO BE. I DIDN'T MEAN TO GO THIS FAR BACK.
I DON'T UNDERSTAND--
IT MEANS WE SCREWED UP BACK IN THE CAVE.
WE NEEDED HUNTER.
IT'S DONE NOW, BUT IT MEANS I CAN'T STICK AROUND VERY LONG, ALL RIGHT? BEING HERE IS VERY DANGEROUS FOR ME.
DO YOU MEAN-- BECAUSE YOU COULD CHANGE SOMETHING?
LOOK AT HER, AND HERE I THOUGHT SHE HADN'T SEEN BACK TO THE FUTURE. BUT NO, CASEY--
--YOU CAN CHANGE WHATEVER YOU WANT. YOU CAN DO WHATEVER YOU WANT.
BABY?
OH, GOOD. OKAY, IN THIS BAG YOU'VE GOT A FAKE PASSPORT--I MADE YOU OLD ENOUGH TO DRINK IN THE STATES, SO YOU'RE WELCOME FOR THAT--A FEW CHANGES OF CLOTHES, AND A MAP FROM HERE TO THE CLOSEST AVAILABLE TRANSPORT.
THERE'S WRITTEN INSTRUCTIONS ON WHERE TO GO FROM HERE--
--AND WHERE NOT TO GO--
--AND FIVE THOUSAND DOLLARS ACROSS A COUPLE DIFFERENT CURRENCIES.
THAT'S NOT MUCH, I KNOW, BUT THE FIRST PERSON YOU MAKE CONTACT WITH WILL BE WILLING TO GIVE YOU A LOT MORE.
YOU'RE NOT MAKING ANY SENSE--I DON'T KNOW WHAT TO--
CASEY, I GOTTA GO. SO DO YOU. IT'S ALL IN THE BAG, UNDERSTAND? EVERYTHING YOU NEED IS RIGHT THERE. NOW--
--LET'S GET MOVING.

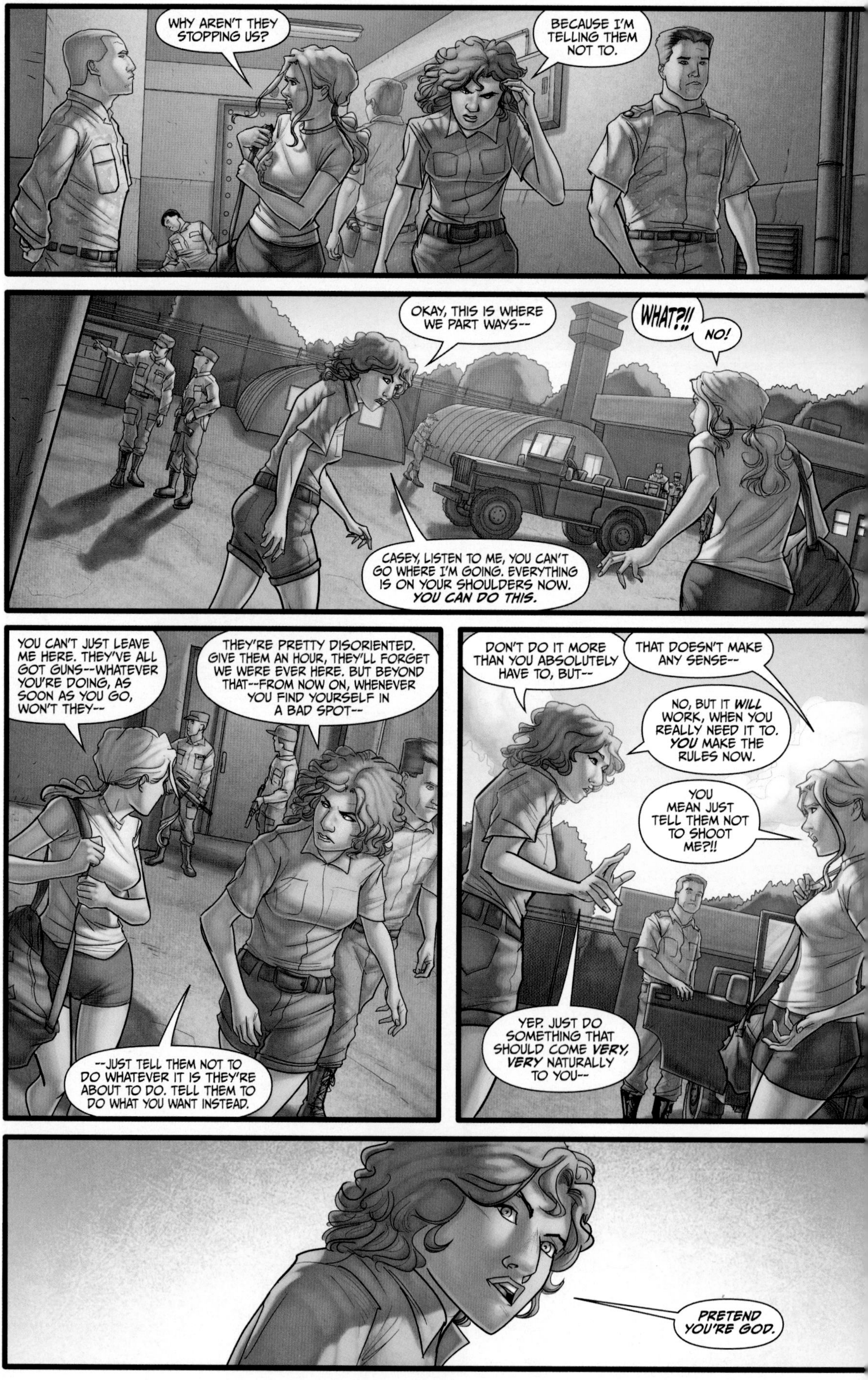
WHY AREN'T THEY STOPPING US?
BECAUSE I'M TELLING THEM NOT TO.
OKAY, THIS IS WHERE WE PART WAYS--
WHAT?!!
NO!
CASEY, LISTEN TO ME, YOU CAN'T GO WHERE I'M GOING. EVERYTHING IS ON YOUR SHOULDERS NOW. YOU CAN DO THIS.
YOU CAN'T JUST LEAVE ME HERE. THEY'VE ALL GOT GUNS--WHATEVER YOU'RE DOING, AS SOON AS YOU GO, WON'T THEY--
THEY'RE PRETTY DISORIENTED. GIVE THEM AN HOUR, THEY'LL FORGET WE WERE EVER HERE. BUT BEYOND THAT--FROM NOW ON, WHENEVER YOU FIND YOURSELF IN A BAD SPOT--
--JUST TELL THEM NOT TO DO WHATEVER IT IS THEY'RE ABOUT TO DO. TELL THEM TO DO WHAT YOU WANT INSTEAD.
DON'T DO IT MORE THAN YOU ABSOLUTELY HAVE TO, BUT--
THAT DOESN'T MAKE ANY SENSE--
NO, BUT IT WILL WORK, WHEN YOU REALLY NEED IT TO. YOU MAKE THE RULES NOW.
YOU MEAN JUST TELL THEM NOT TO SHOOT ME?!!
YEP. JUST DO SOMETHING THAT SHOULD COME VERY, VERY NATURALLY TO YOU--
PRETEND YOU'RE GOD.

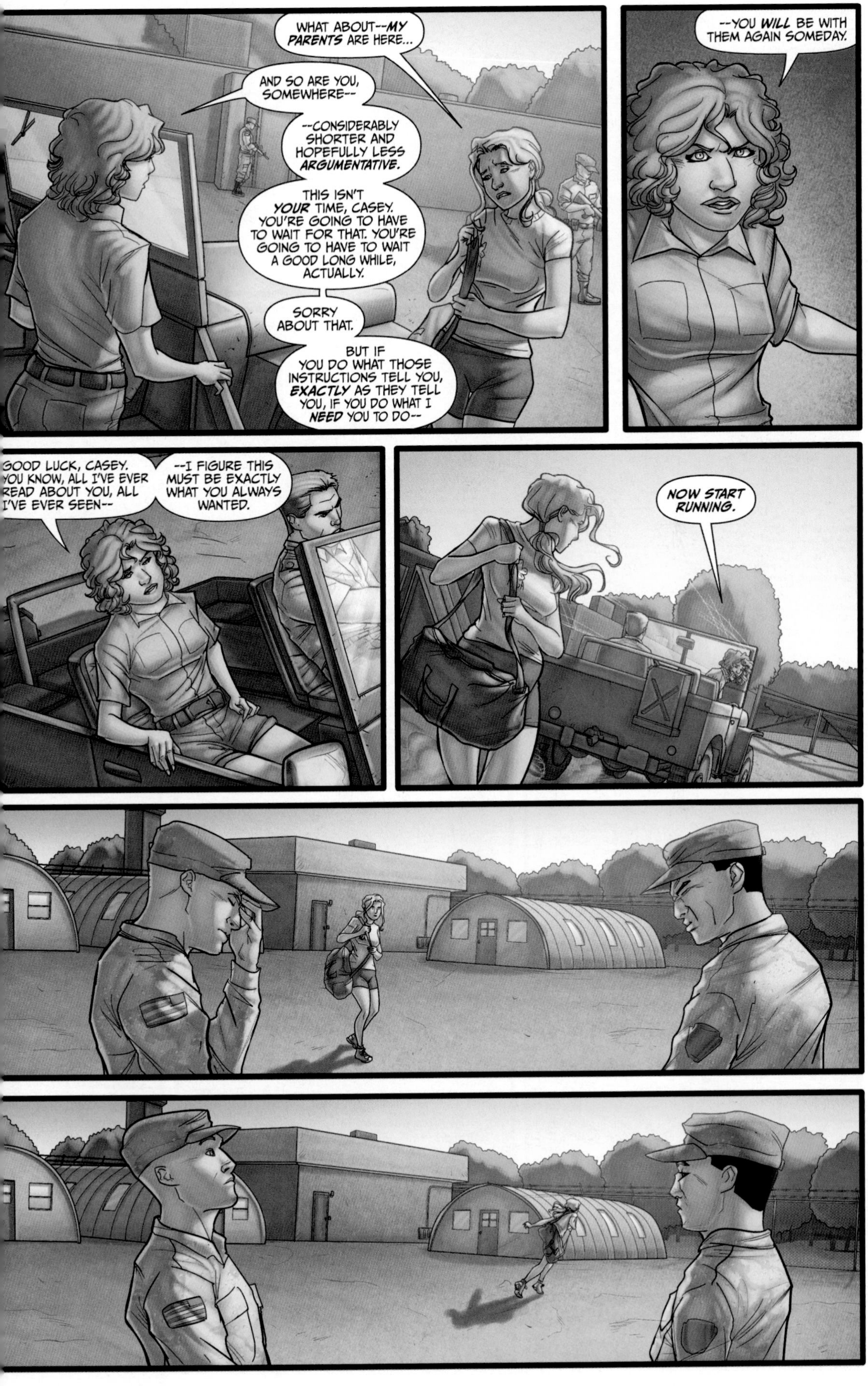
WHAT ABOUT--MY PARENTS ARE HERE...
AND SO ARE YOU, SOMEWHERE--
--CONSIDERABLY SHORTER AND HOPEFULLY LESS ARGUMENTATIVE.
THIS ISN'T YOUR TIME, CASEY. YOU'RE GOING TO HAVE TO WAIT FOR THAT. YOU'RE GOING TO HAVE TO WAIT A GOOD LONG WHILE, ACTUALLY.
SORRY ABOUT THAT.
BUT IF YOU DO WHAT THOSE INSTRUCTIONS TELL YOU, EXACTLY AS THEY TELL YOU, IF YOU DO WHAT I NEED YOU TO DO--
--YOU WILL BE WITH THEM AGAIN SOMEDAY.
GOOD LUCK, CASEY. YOU KNOW, ALL I'VE EVER READ ABOUT YOU, ALL I'VE EVER SEEN--
--I FIGURE THIS MUST BE EXACTLY WHAT YOU ALWAYS WANTED.
NOW START RUNNING.

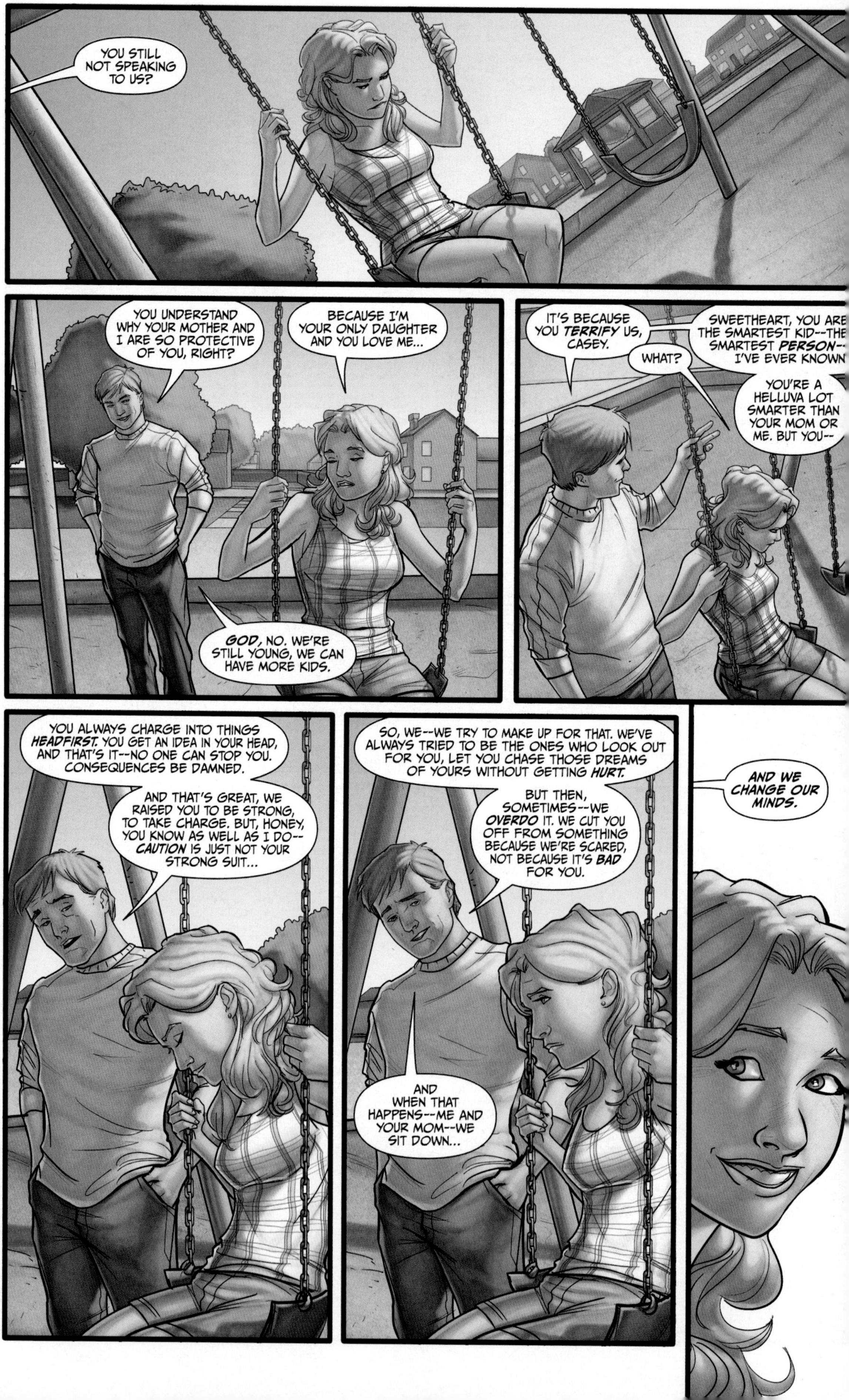

YOU STILL NOT SPEAKING TO US?
YOU UNDERSTAND WHY YOUR MOTHER AND I ARE SO PROTECTIVE OF YOU, RIGHT?
BECAUSE I'M YOUR ONLY DAUGHTER AND YOU LOVE ME...
GOD, NO. WE'RE STILL YOUNG, WE CAN HAVE MORE KIDS.
IT'S BECAUSE YOU *TERRIFY* US, CASEY.
WHAT?
SWEETHEART, YOU ARE THE SMARTEST KID--THE SMARTEST *PERSON*-- I'VE EVER KNOWN.
YOU'RE A HELLUVA LOT SMARTER THAN YOUR MOM OR ME. BUT YOU--
YOU ALWAYS CHARGE INTO THINGS *HEADFIRST.* YOU GET AN IDEA IN YOUR HEAD, AND THAT'S IT--NO ONE CAN STOP YOU. CONSEQUENCES BE DAMNED.
AND THAT'S GREAT, WE RAISED YOU TO BE STRONG, TO TAKE CHARGE. BUT, HONEY, YOU KNOW AS WELL AS I DO-- *CAUTION* IS JUST NOT YOUR STRONG SUIT...
SO, WE--WE TRY TO MAKE UP FOR THAT. WE'VE ALWAYS TRIED TO BE THE ONES WHO LOOK OUT FOR YOU, LET YOU CHASE THOSE DREAMS OF YOURS WITHOUT GETTING *HURT.*
BUT THEN, SOMETIMES--WE *OVERDO* IT. WE CUT YOU OFF FROM SOMETHING BECAUSE WE'RE SCARED, NOT BECAUSE IT'S *BAD* FOR YOU.
AND WHEN THAT HAPPENS--ME AND YOUR MOM--WE SIT DOWN...
AND WE CHANGE OUR MINDS.

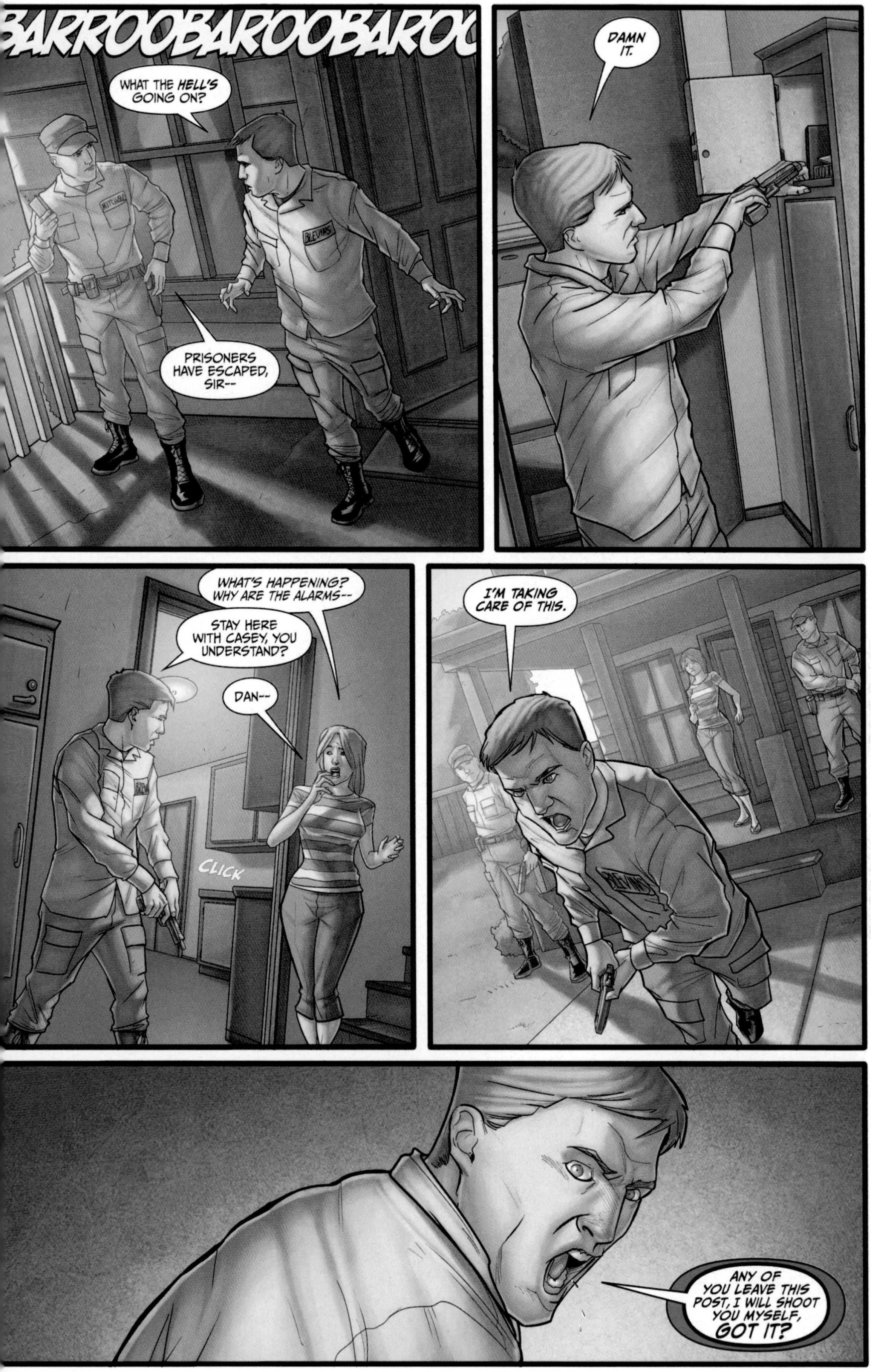
BARROOBARROOBAROO
WHAT THE HELL'S GOING ON?
PRISONERS HAVE ESCAPED, SIR--
MITCHELL
BLEVINS
DAMN IT.
WHAT'S HAPPENING? WHY ARE THE ALARMS--
STAY HERE WITH CASEY, YOU UNDERSTAND?
DAN--
CLICK
I'M TAKING CARE OF THIS.
BLEVINS
ANY OF YOU LEAVE THIS POST, I WILL SHOOT YOU MYSELF, GOT IT?

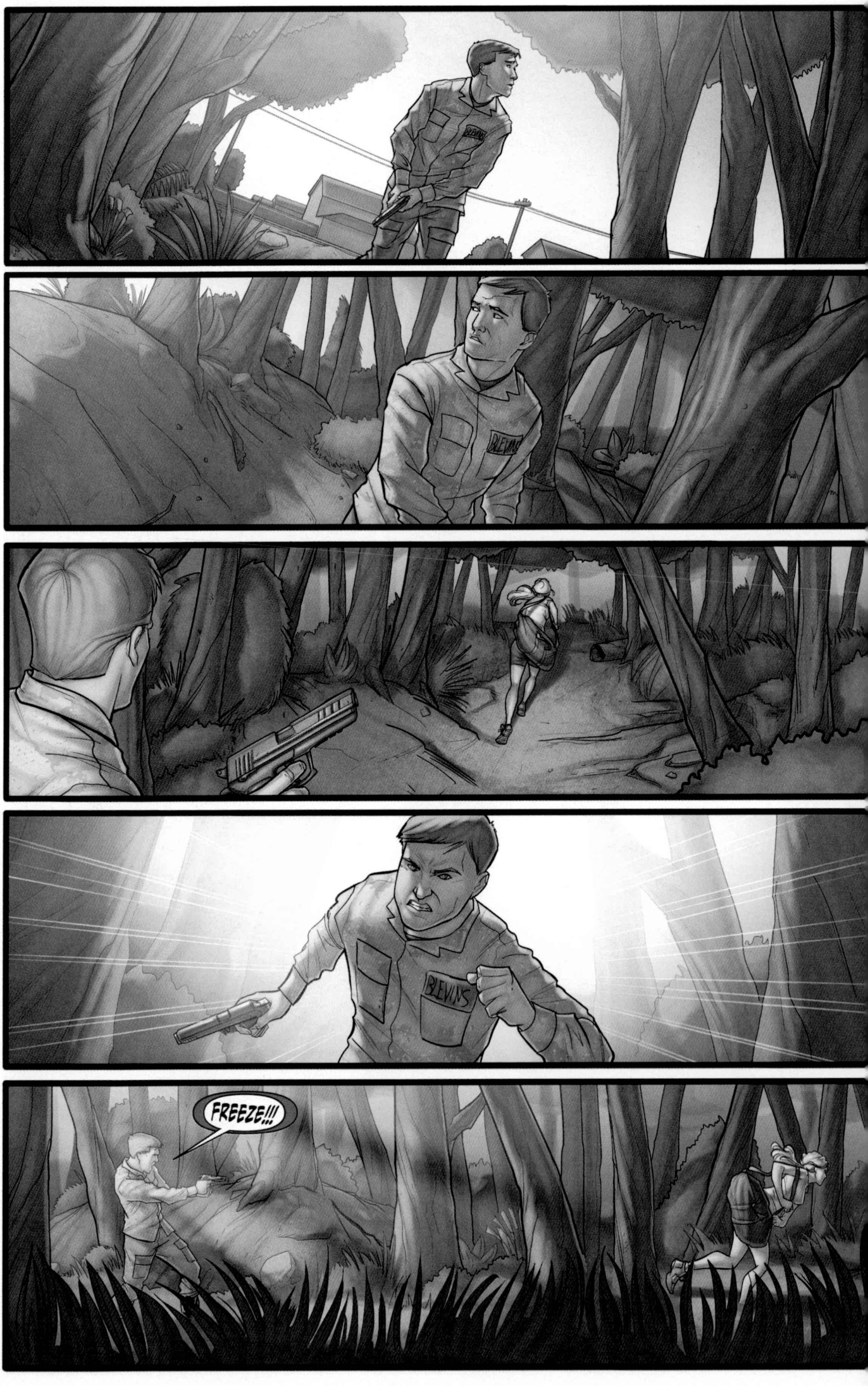
BLEVINS
BLEVINS
FREEZE!!!

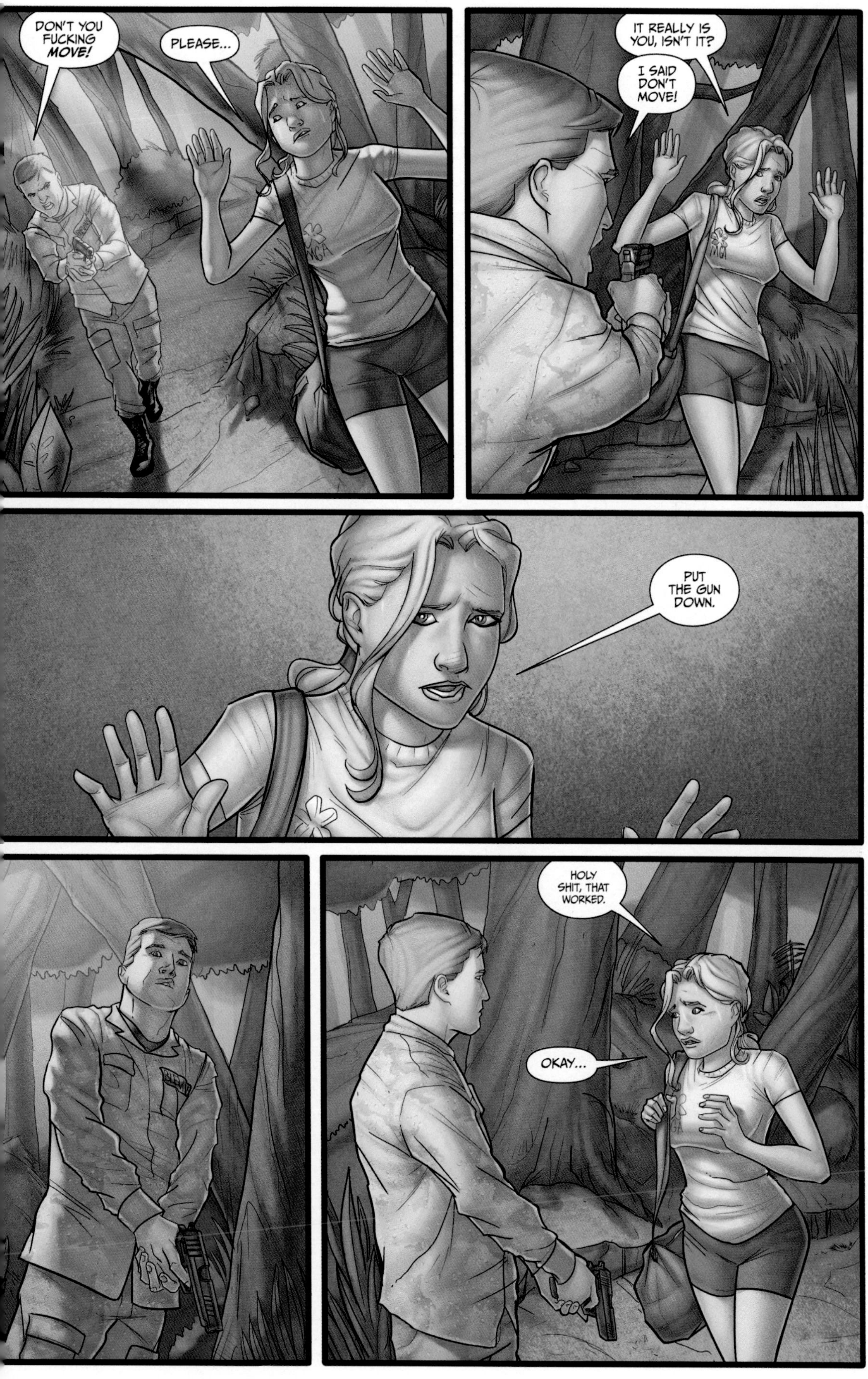
DON'T YOU FUCKING *MOVE!*
PLEASE...
IT REALLY IS YOU, ISN'T IT?
I SAID DON'T MOVE!
PUT THE GUN DOWN.
HOLY SHIT, THAT WORKED.
OKAY...

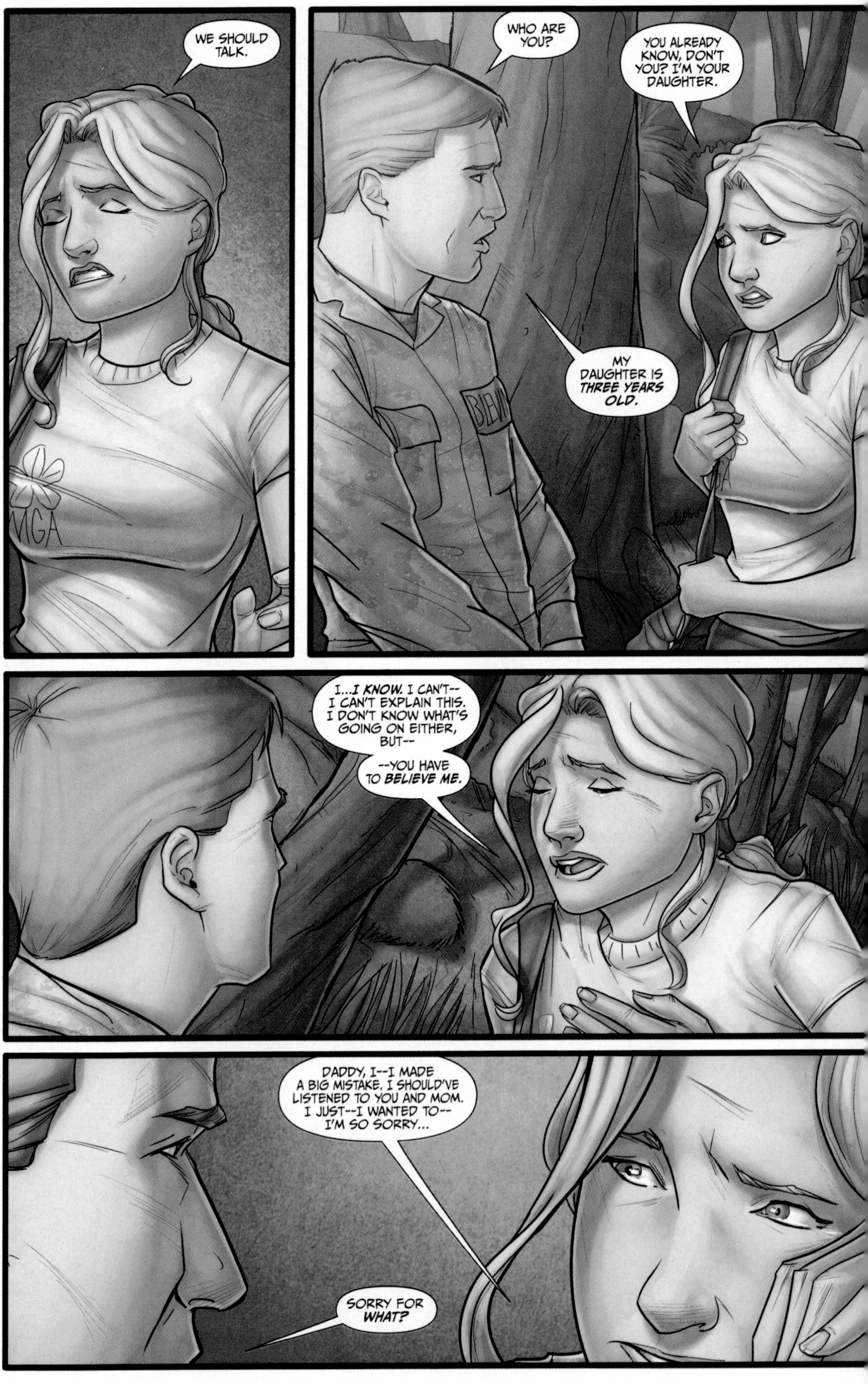
WE SHOULD TALK.
WHO ARE YOU?
YOU ALREADY KNOW, DON'T YOU? I'M YOUR DAUGHTER.
MY DAUGHTER IS *THREE YEARS OLD.*
I...*I KNOW.* I CAN'T-- I CAN'T EXPLAIN THIS. I DON'T KNOW WHAT'S GOING ON EITHER, BUT--
--YOU HAVE TO *BELIEVE ME.*
DADDY, I--I MADE A BIG MISTAKE. I SHOULD'VE LISTENED TO YOU AND MOM. I JUST--I WANTED TO-- I'M SO SORRY...
SORRY FOR *WHAT?*

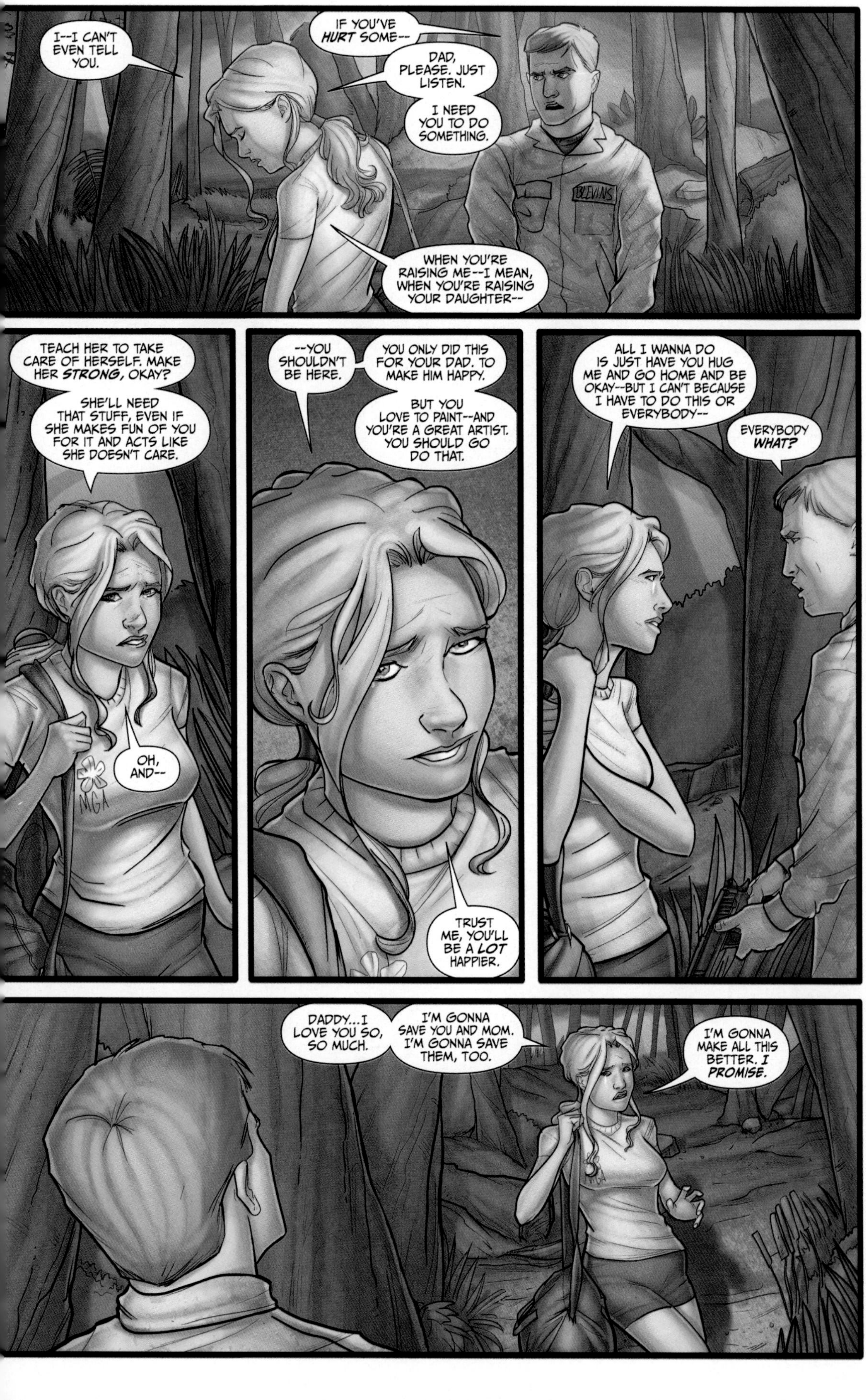
I--I CAN'T EVEN TELL YOU.
IF YOU'VE *HURT* SOME--
DAD, PLEASE. JUST LISTEN.
I NEED YOU TO DO SOMETHING.
BLEVINS
WHEN YOU'RE RAISING ME--I MEAN, WHEN YOU'RE RAISING YOUR DAUGHTER--
TEACH HER TO TAKE CARE OF HERSELF. MAKE HER *STRONG*, OKAY?
SHE'LL NEED THAT STUFF, EVEN IF SHE MAKES FUN OF YOU FOR IT AND ACTS LIKE SHE DOESN'T CARE.
OH, AND--
MGA
--YOU SHOULDN'T BE HERE.
YOU ONLY DID THIS FOR YOUR DAD. TO MAKE HIM HAPPY.
BUT YOU LOVE TO PAINT--AND YOU'RE A GREAT ARTIST. YOU SHOULD GO DO THAT.
TRUST ME, YOU'LL BE A *LOT* HAPPIER.
ALL I WANNA DO IS JUST HAVE YOU HUG ME AND GO HOME AND BE OKAY--BUT I CAN'T BECAUSE I HAVE TO DO THIS OR EVERYBODY--
EVERYBODY *WHAT?*
DADDY...I LOVE YOU SO, SO MUCH.
I'M GONNA SAVE YOU AND MOM. I'M GONNA SAVE THEM, TOO.
I'M GONNA MAKE ALL THIS BETTER. *I PROMISE.*
MGA

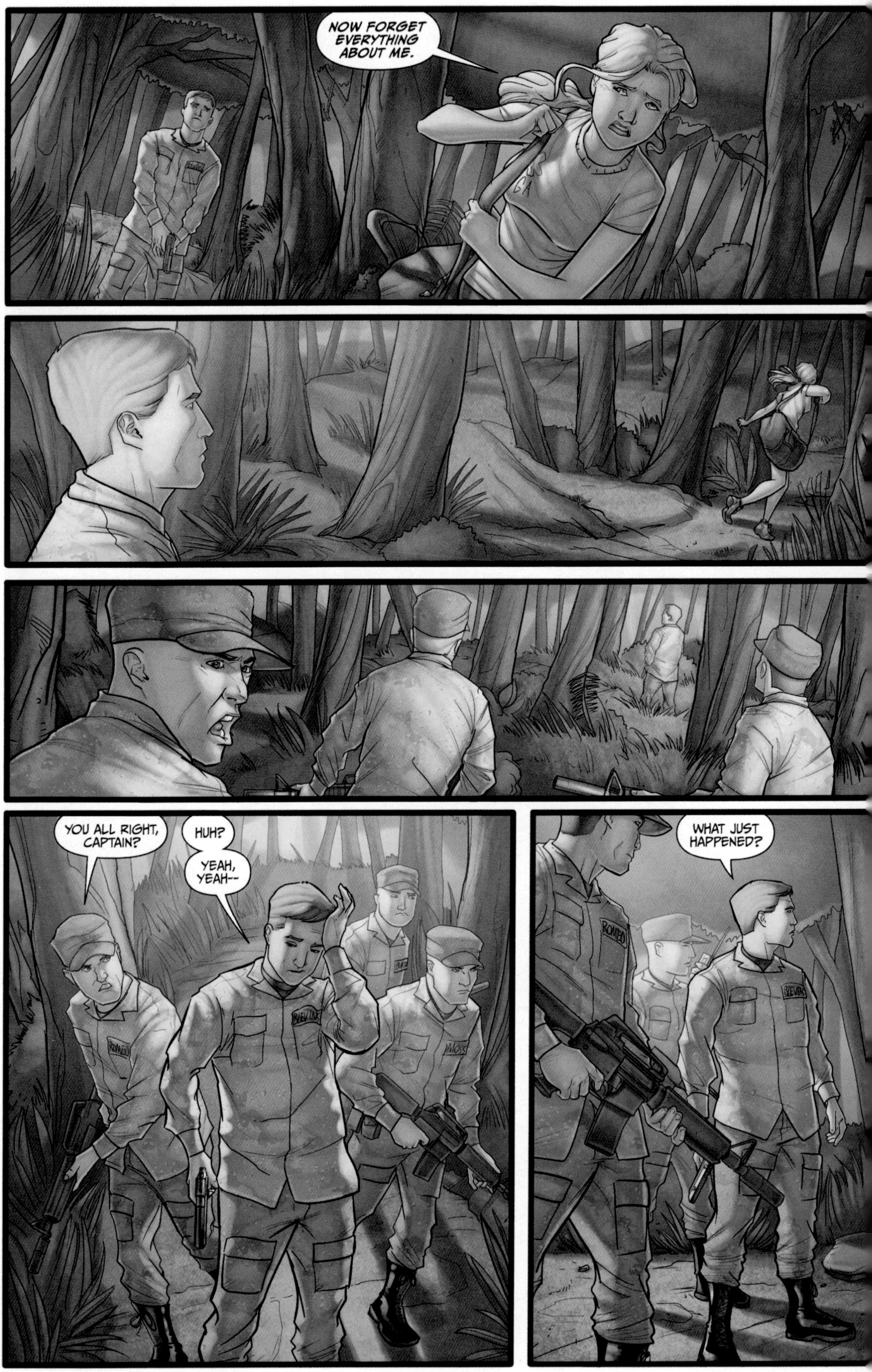
NOW FORGET EVERYTHING ABOUT ME.
YOU ALL RIGHT, CAPTAIN?
HUH?
YEAH, YEAH--
WHAT JUST HAPPENED?

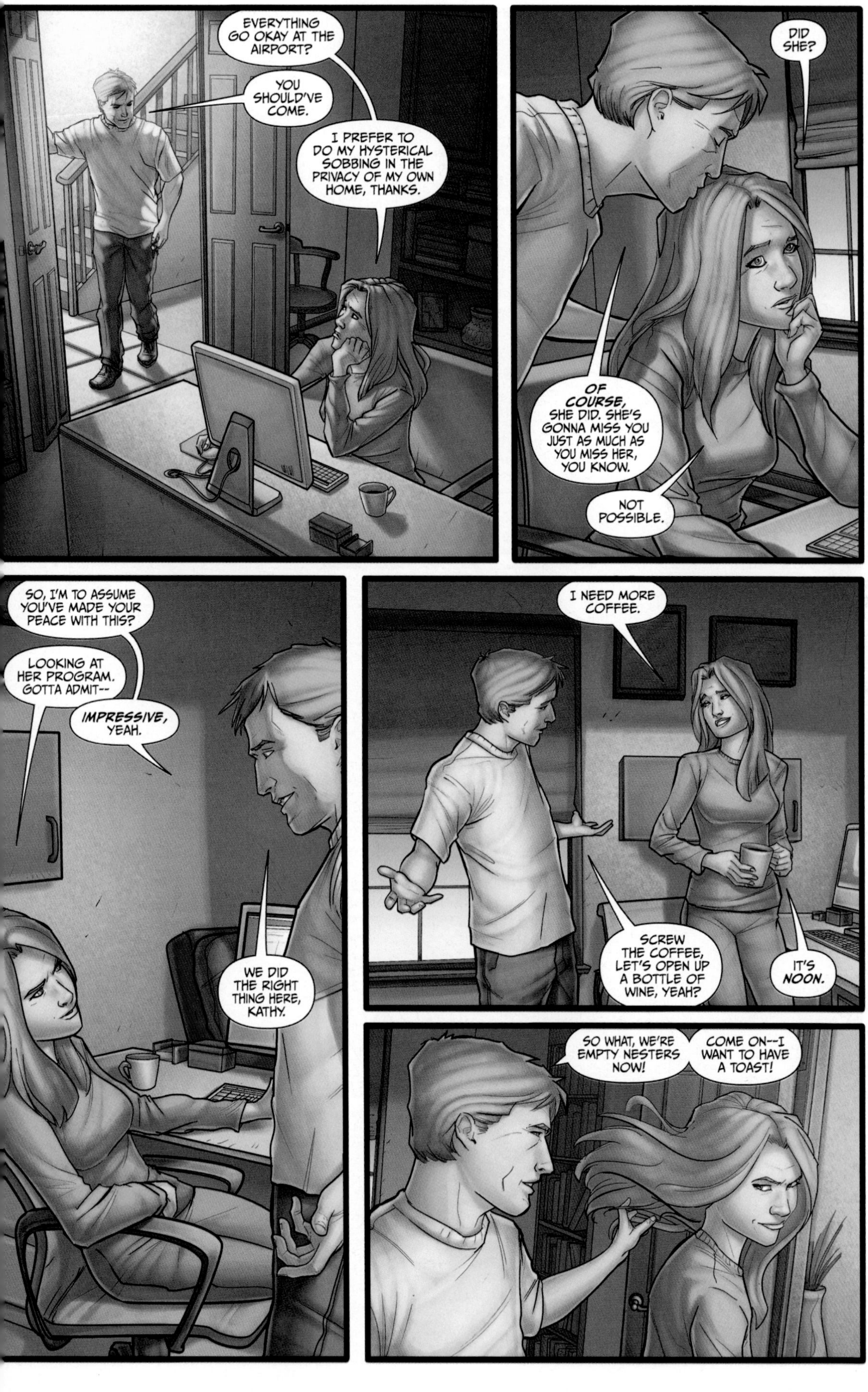
EVERYTHING GO OKAY AT THE AIRPORT?
YOU SHOULD'VE COME.
I PREFER TO DO MY HYSTERICAL SOBBING IN THE PRIVACY OF MY OWN HOME, THANKS.
DID SHE?
OF COURSE, SHE DID. SHE'S GONNA MISS YOU JUST AS MUCH AS YOU MISS HER, YOU KNOW.
NOT POSSIBLE.
SO, I'M TO ASSUME YOU'VE MADE YOUR PEACE WITH THIS?
LOOKING AT HER PROGRAM. GOTTA ADMIT--
IMPRESSIVE, YEAH.
WE DID THE RIGHT THING HERE, KATHY.
I NEED MORE COFFEE.
SCREW THE COFFEE, LET'S OPEN UP A BOTTLE OF WINE, YEAH?
IT'S *NOON.*
SO WHAT, WE'RE EMPTY NESTERS NOW!
COME ON--I WANT TO HAVE A TOAST!

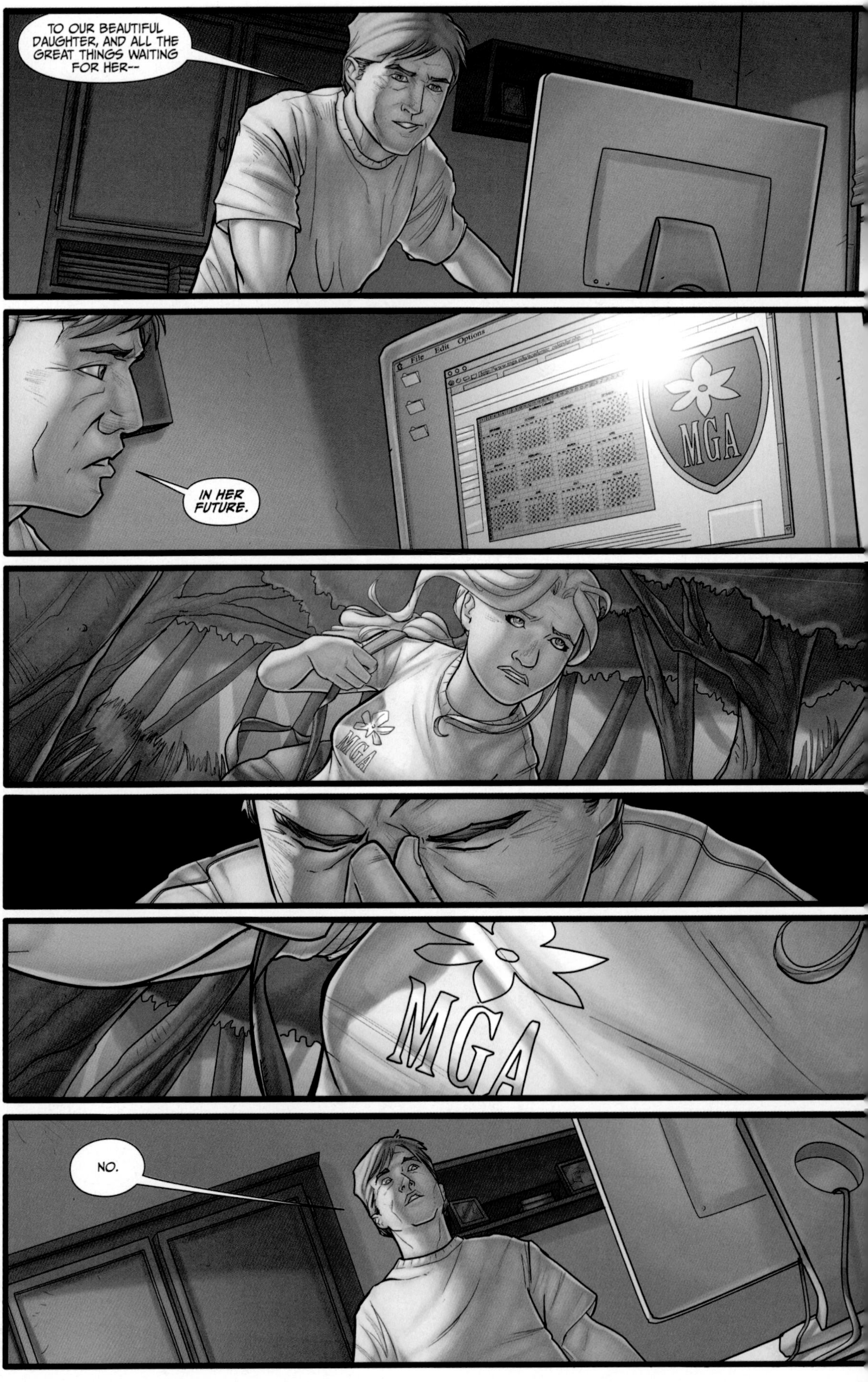
TO OUR BEAUTIFUL DAUGHTER, AND ALL THE GREAT THINGS WAITING FOR HER--
IN HER FUTURE.
NO.

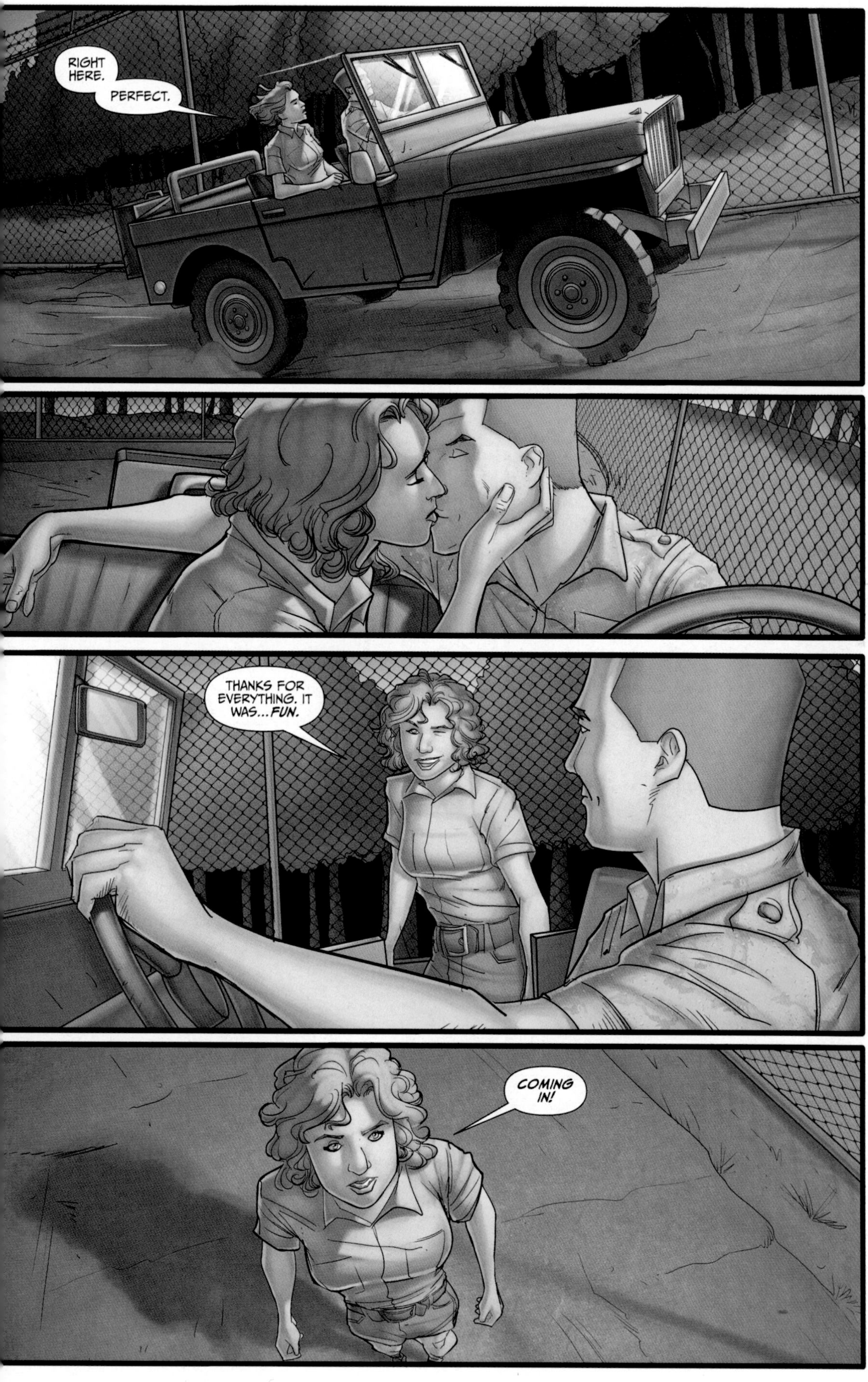
RIGHT HERE.
PERFECT.
THANKS FOR EVERYTHING. IT WAS... *FUN.*
COMING IN!

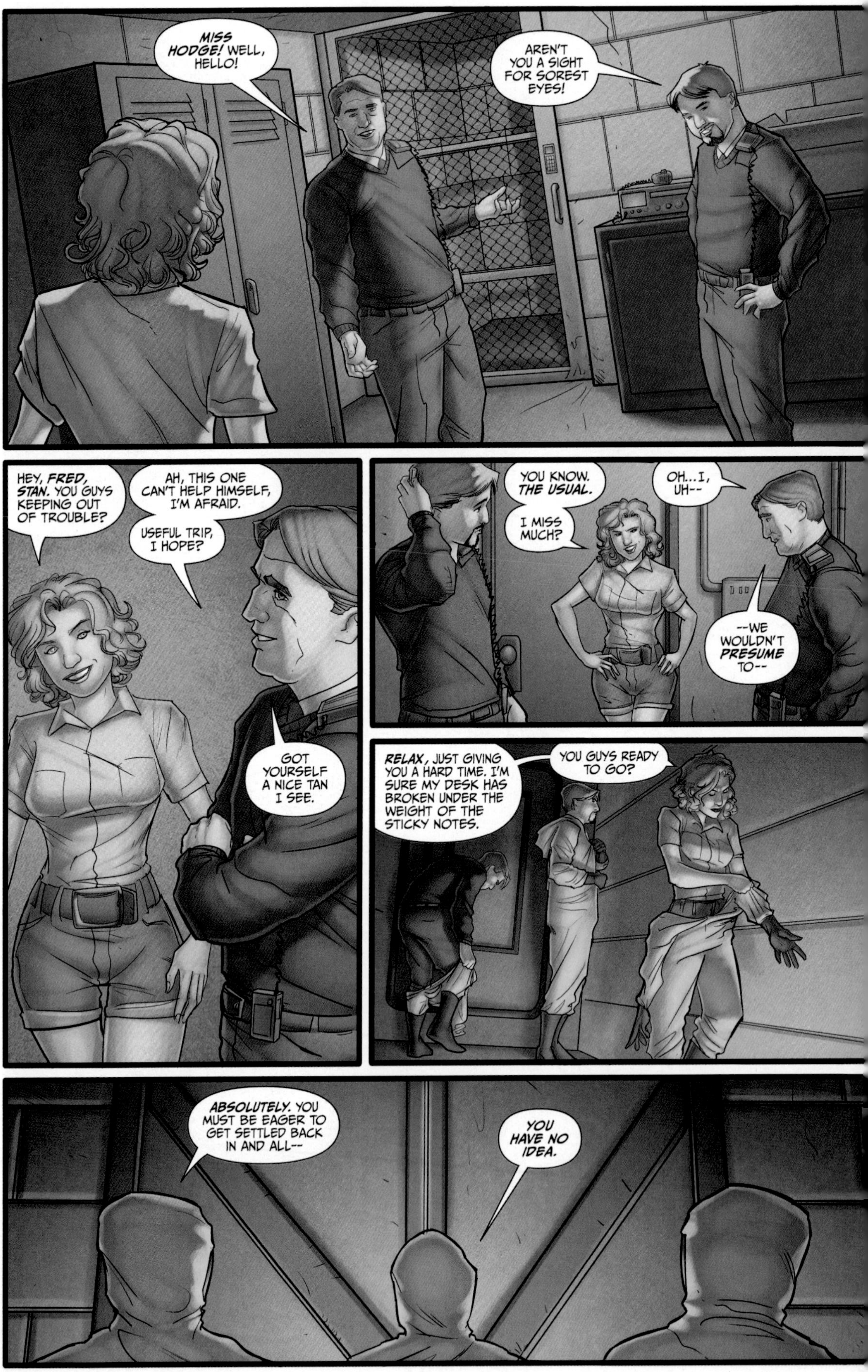
MISS HODGE! WELL, HELLO!
AREN'T YOU A SIGHT FOR SOREST EYES!
HEY, FRED, STAN. YOU GUYS KEEPING OUT OF TROUBLE?
AH, THIS ONE CAN'T HELP HIMSELF, I'M AFRAID.
USEFUL TRIP, I HOPE?
GOT YOURSELF A NICE TAN I SEE.
YOU KNOW. THE USUAL.
I MISS MUCH?
OH...I, UH--
--WE WOULDN'T PRESUME TO--
RELAX, JUST GIVING YOU A HARD TIME. I'M SURE MY DESK HAS BROKEN UNDER THE WEIGHT OF THE STICKY NOTES.
YOU GUYS READY TO GO?
ABSOLUTELY. YOU MUST BE EAGER TO GET SETTLED BACK IN AND ALL--
YOU HAVE NO IDEA.

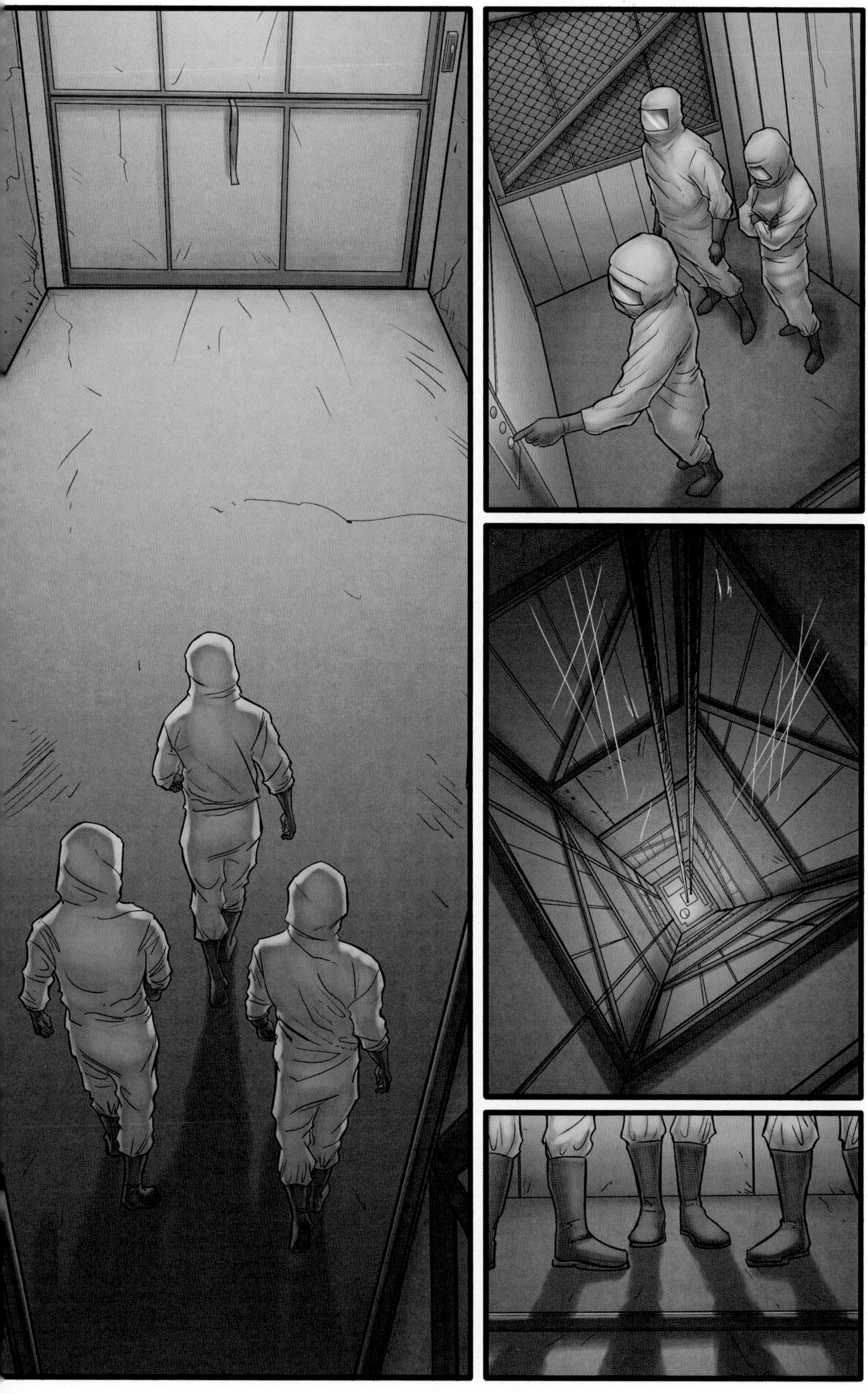

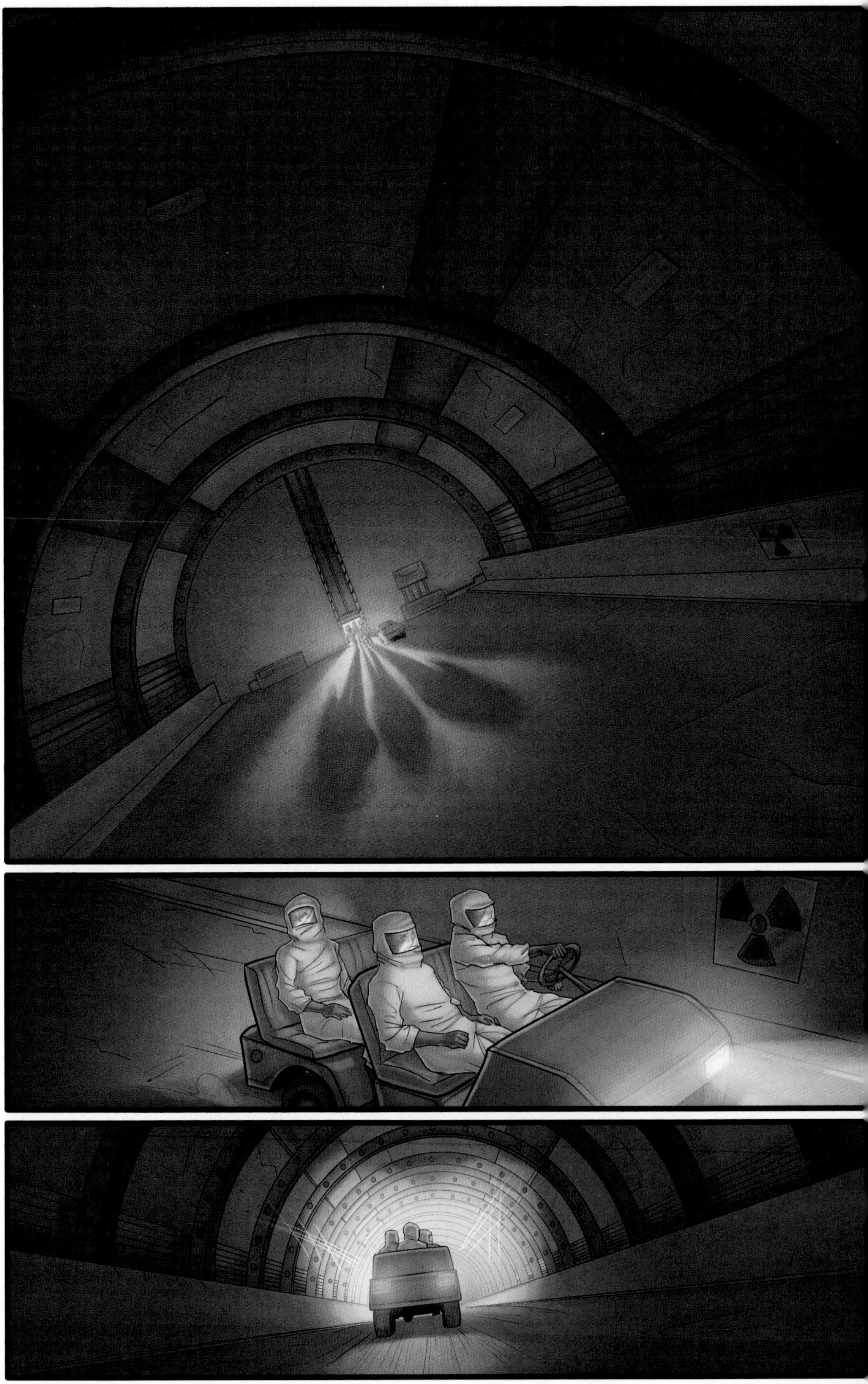

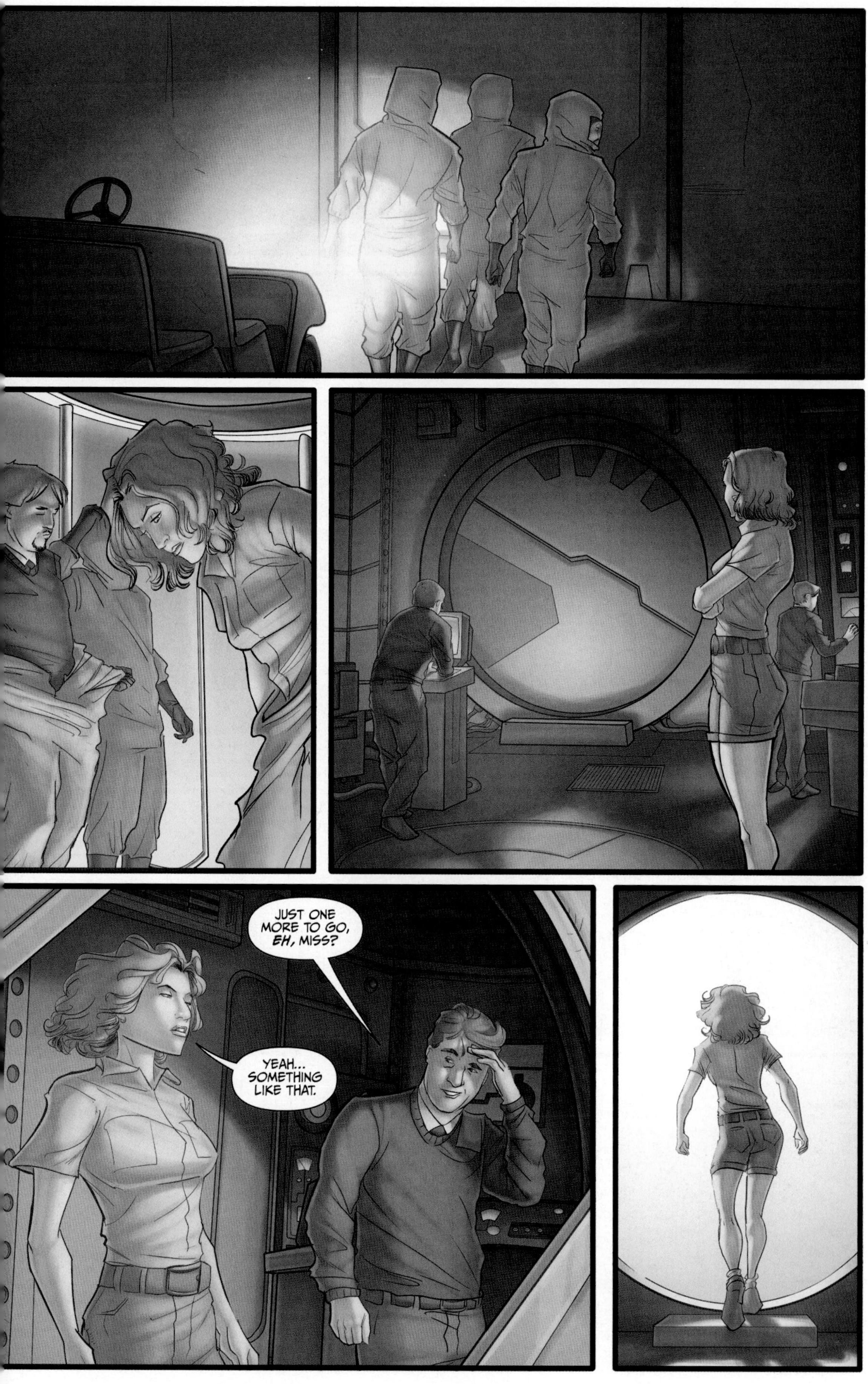
JUST ONE MORE TO GO, *EH*, MISS?
YEAH... SOMETHING LIKE THAT.

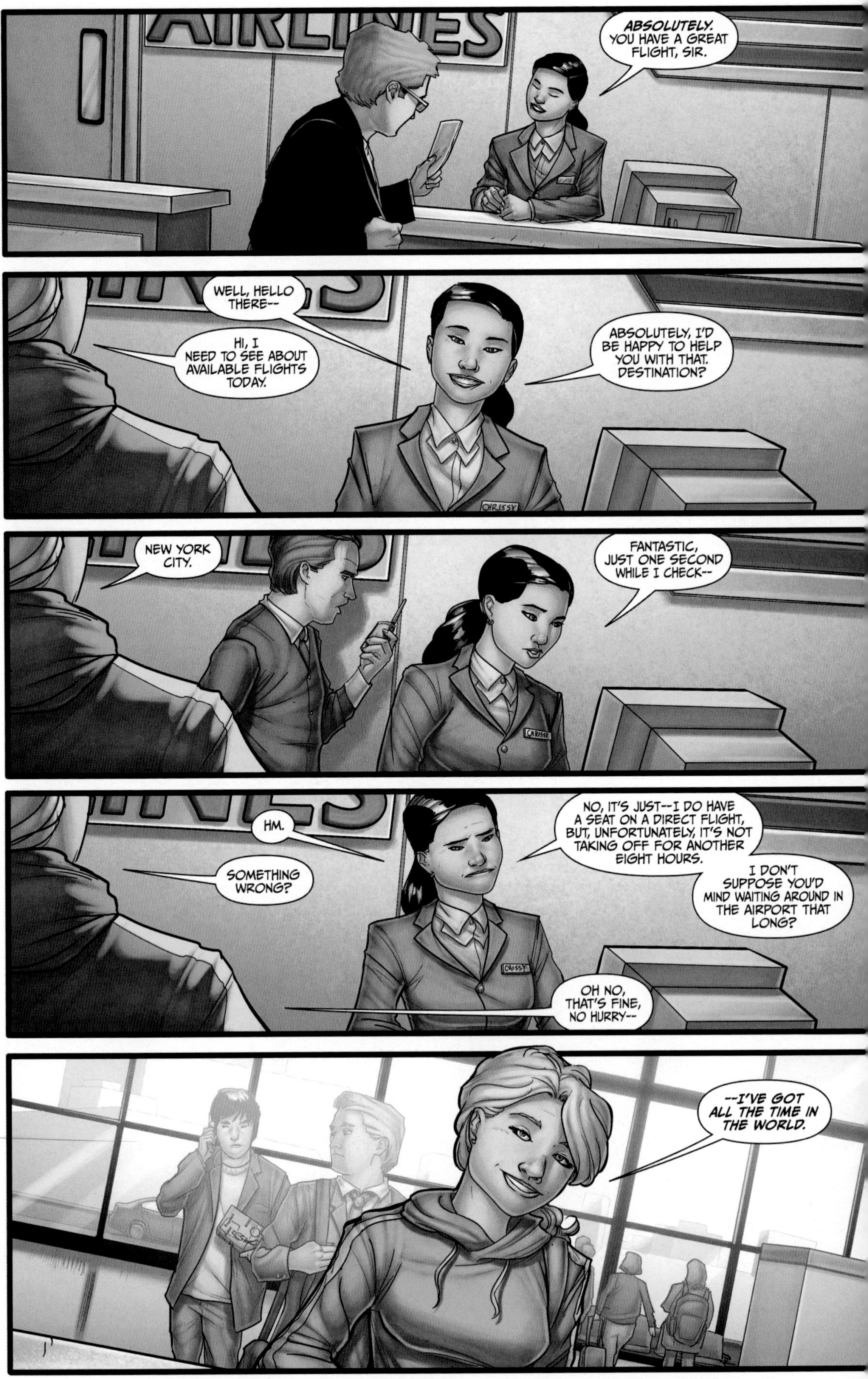
ABSOLUTELY. YOU HAVE A GREAT FLIGHT, SIR.
AIRLINES
WELL, HELLO THERE--
HI, I NEED TO SEE ABOUT AVAILABLE FLIGHTS TODAY.
ABSOLUTELY, I'D BE HAPPY TO HELP YOU WITH THAT. DESTINATION?
NEW YORK CITY.
FANTASTIC, JUST ONE SECOND WHILE I CHECK--
HM.
SOMETHING WRONG?
NO, IT'S JUST--I DO HAVE A SEAT ON A DIRECT FLIGHT, BUT, UNFORTUNATELY, IT'S NOT TAKING OFF FOR ANOTHER EIGHT HOURS.
I DON'T SUPPOSE YOU'D MIND WAITING AROUND IN THE AIRPORT THAT LONG?
OH NO, THAT'S FINE, NO HURRY--
--I'VE GOT ALL THE TIME IN THE WORLD.

seventeen

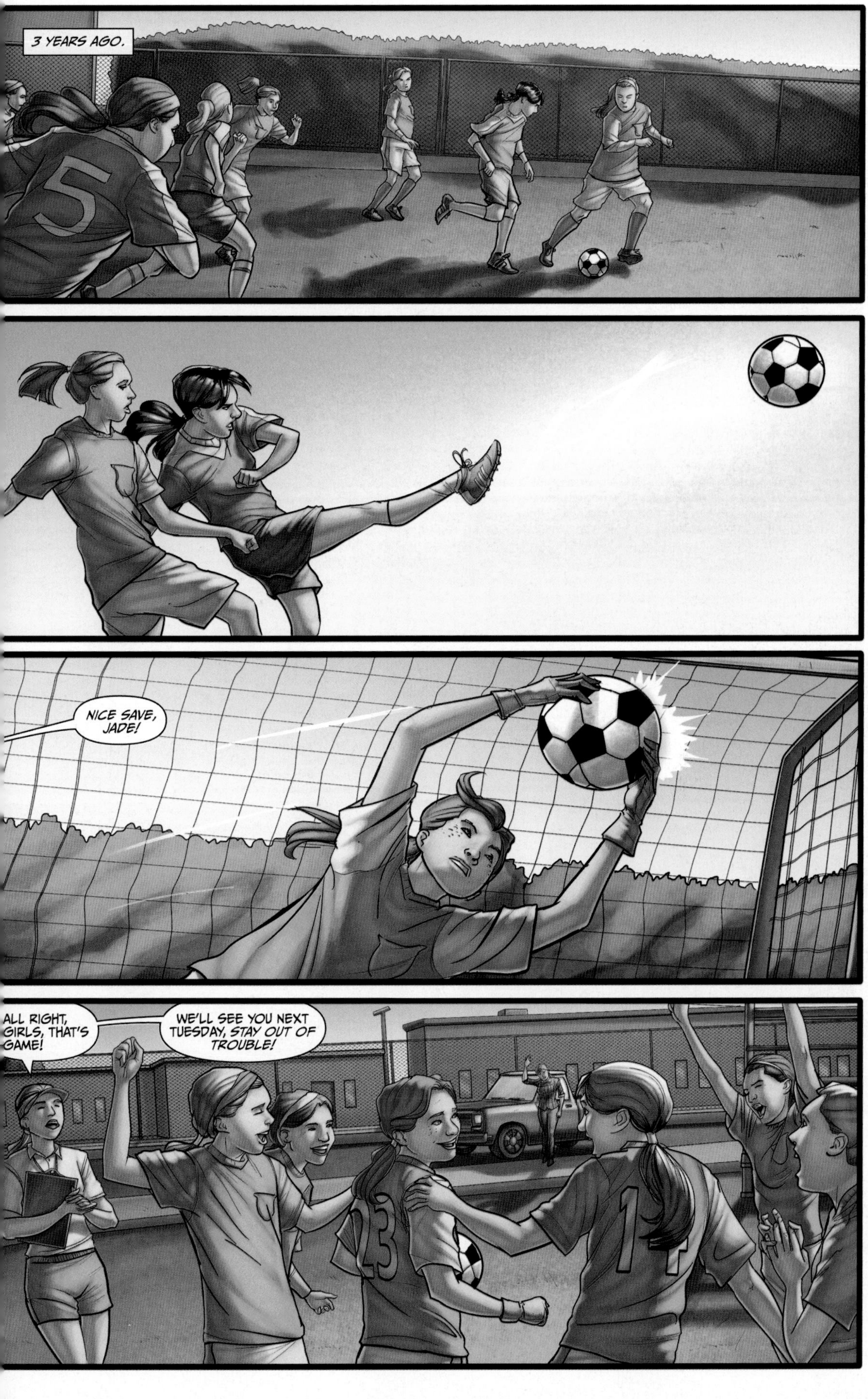
3 YEARS AGO.
NICE SAVE, JADE!
ALL RIGHT, GIRLS, THAT'S GAME!
WE'LL SEE YOU NEXT TUESDAY, STAY OUT OF TROUBLE!

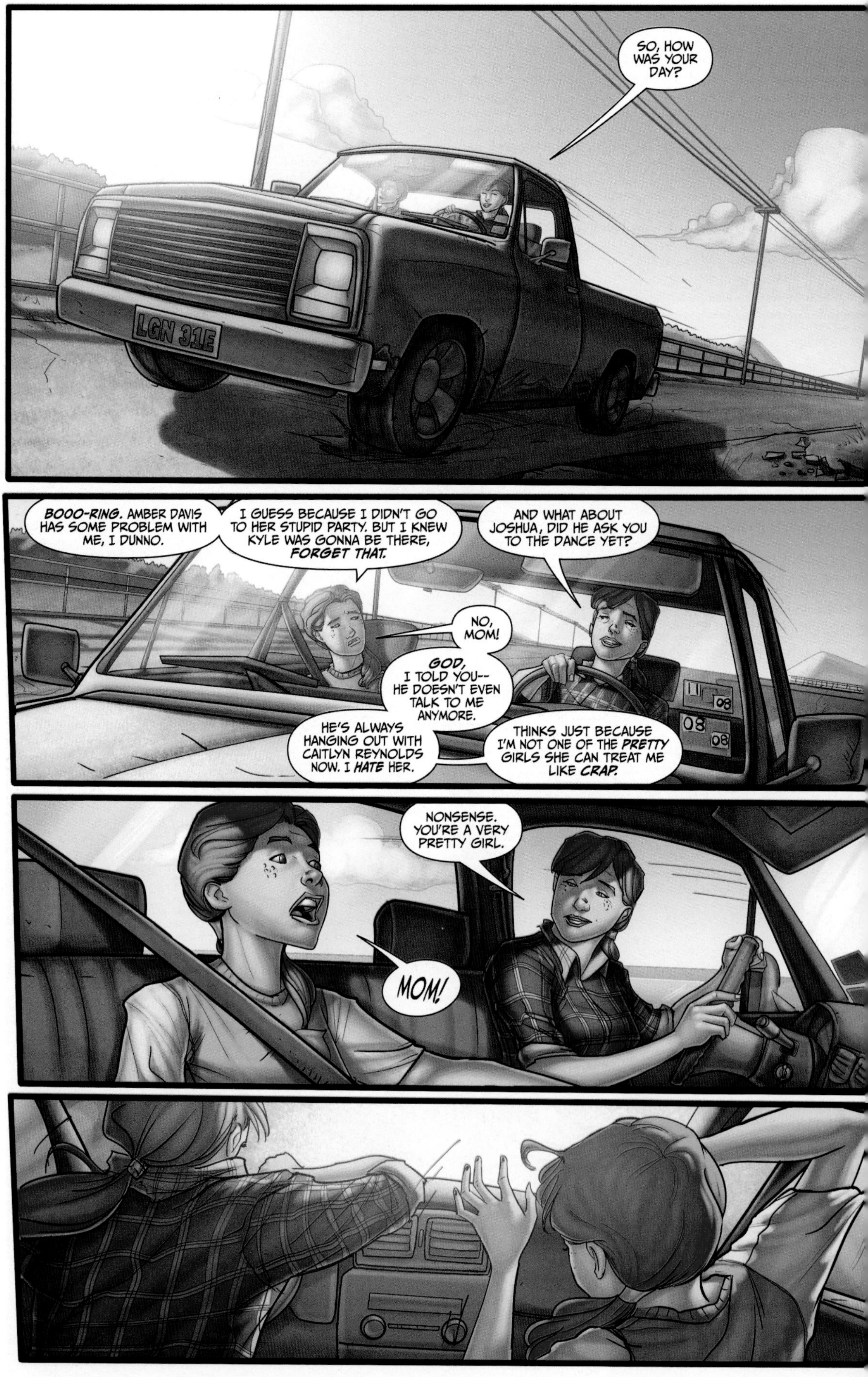
SO, HOW WAS YOUR DAY?
LGN 31E
BOOO-RING. AMBER DAVIS HAS SOME PROBLEM WITH ME, I DUNNO.
I GUESS BECAUSE I DIDN'T GO TO HER STUPID PARTY. BUT I KNEW KYLE WAS GONNA BE THERE, FORGET THAT.
AND WHAT ABOUT JOSHUA, DID HE ASK YOU TO THE DANCE YET?
NO, MOM!
GOD, I TOLD YOU-- HE DOESN'T EVEN TALK TO ME ANYMORE.
HE'S ALWAYS HANGING OUT WITH CAITLYN REYNOLDS NOW. I HATE HER.
THINKS JUST BECAUSE I'M NOT ONE OF THE PRETTY GIRLS SHE CAN TREAT ME LIKE CRAP.
NONSENSE. YOU'RE A VERY PRETTY GIRL.
MOM!

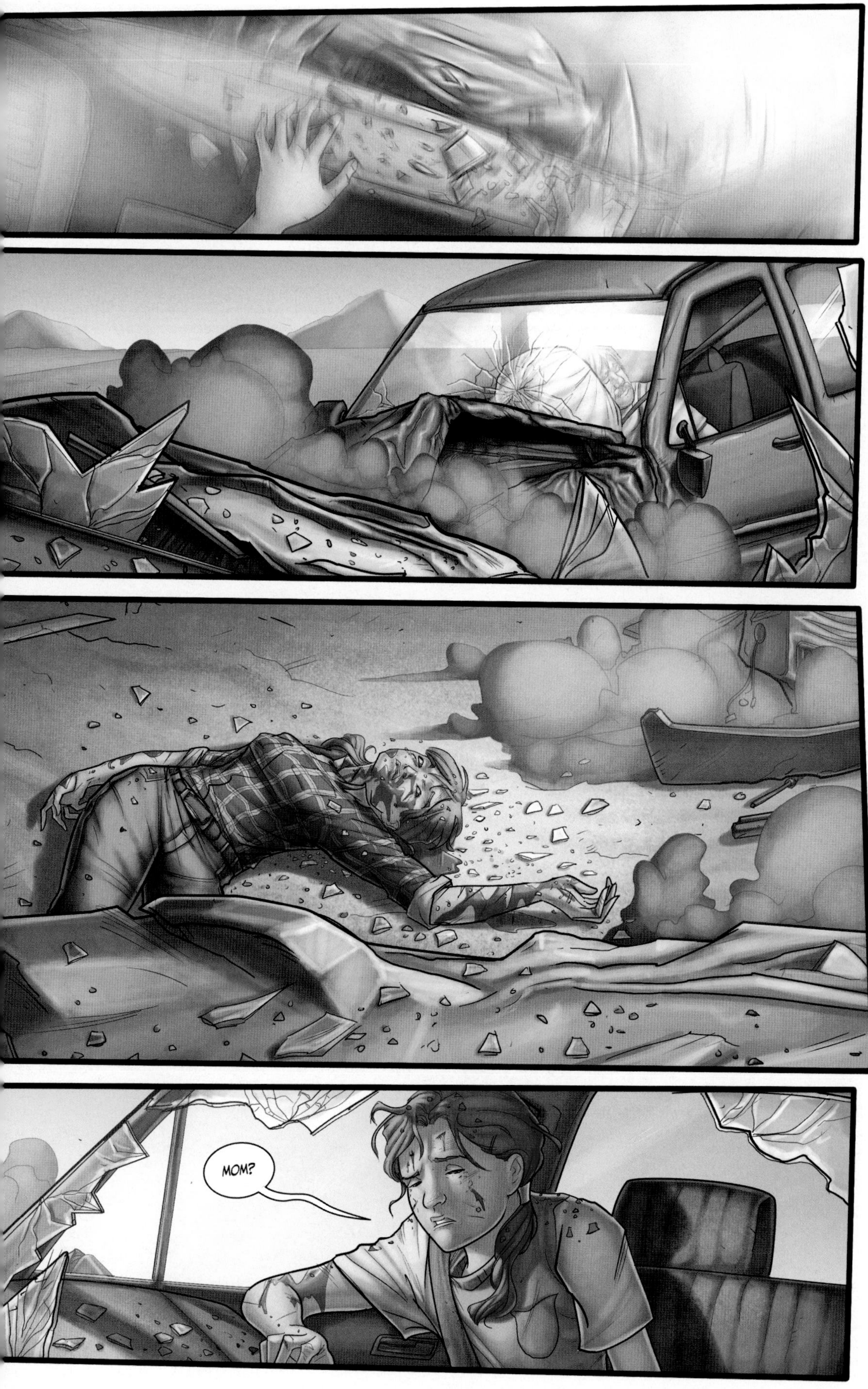
MOM?

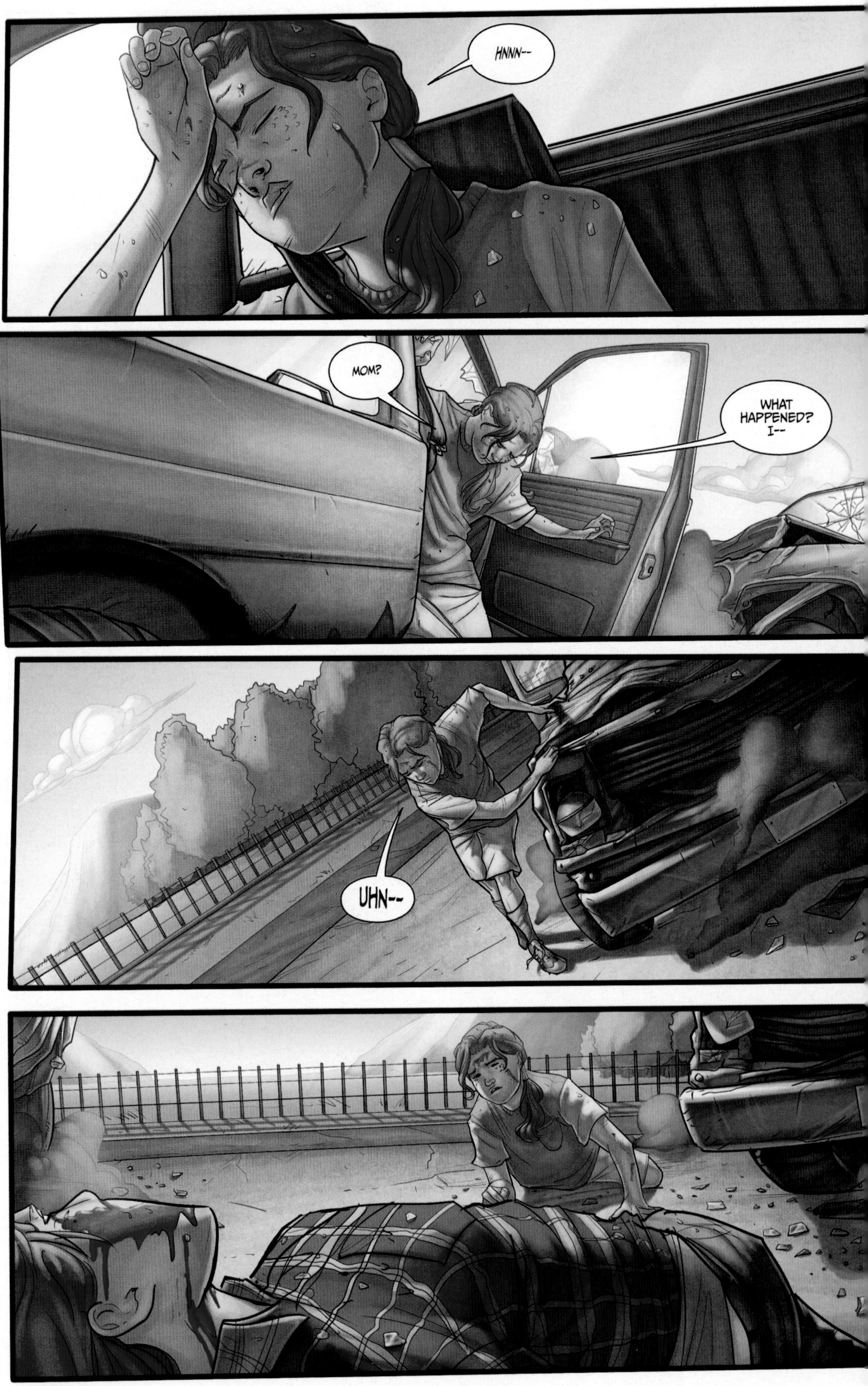
HNNN--
MOM?
WHAT HAPPENED? I--
UHN--

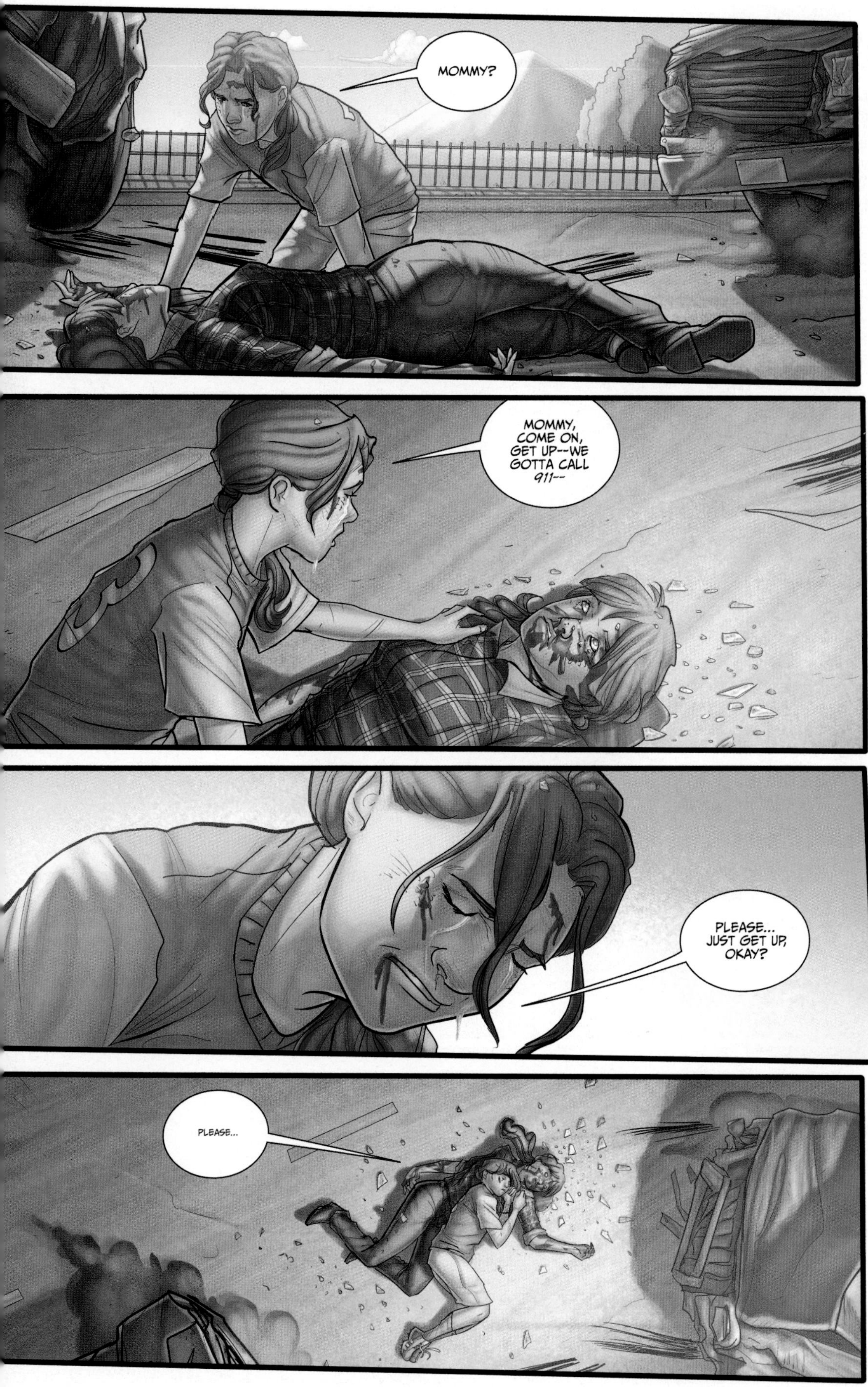
MOMMY?
MOMMY, COME ON, GET UP--WE GOTTA CALL 911--
PLEASE... JUST GET UP, OKAY?
PLEASE...

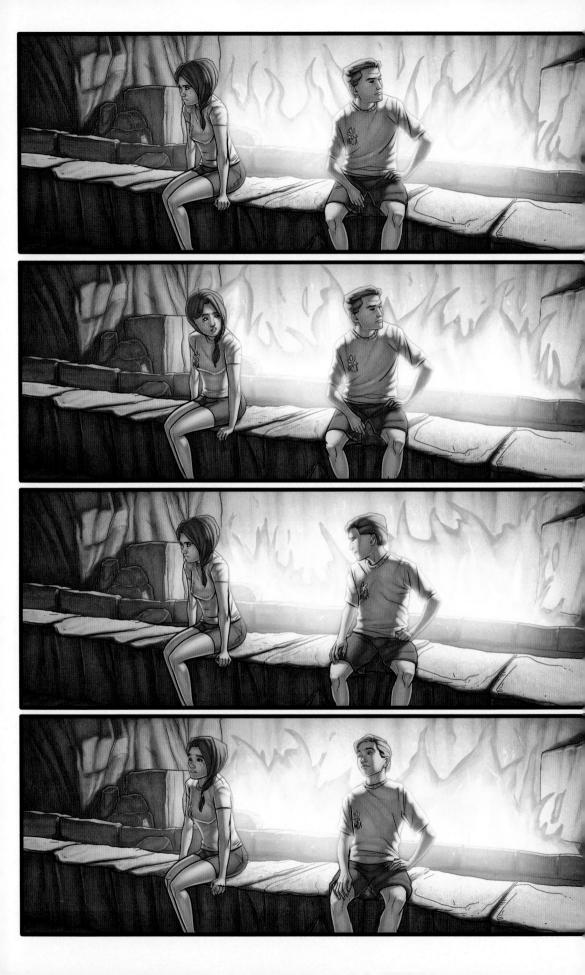

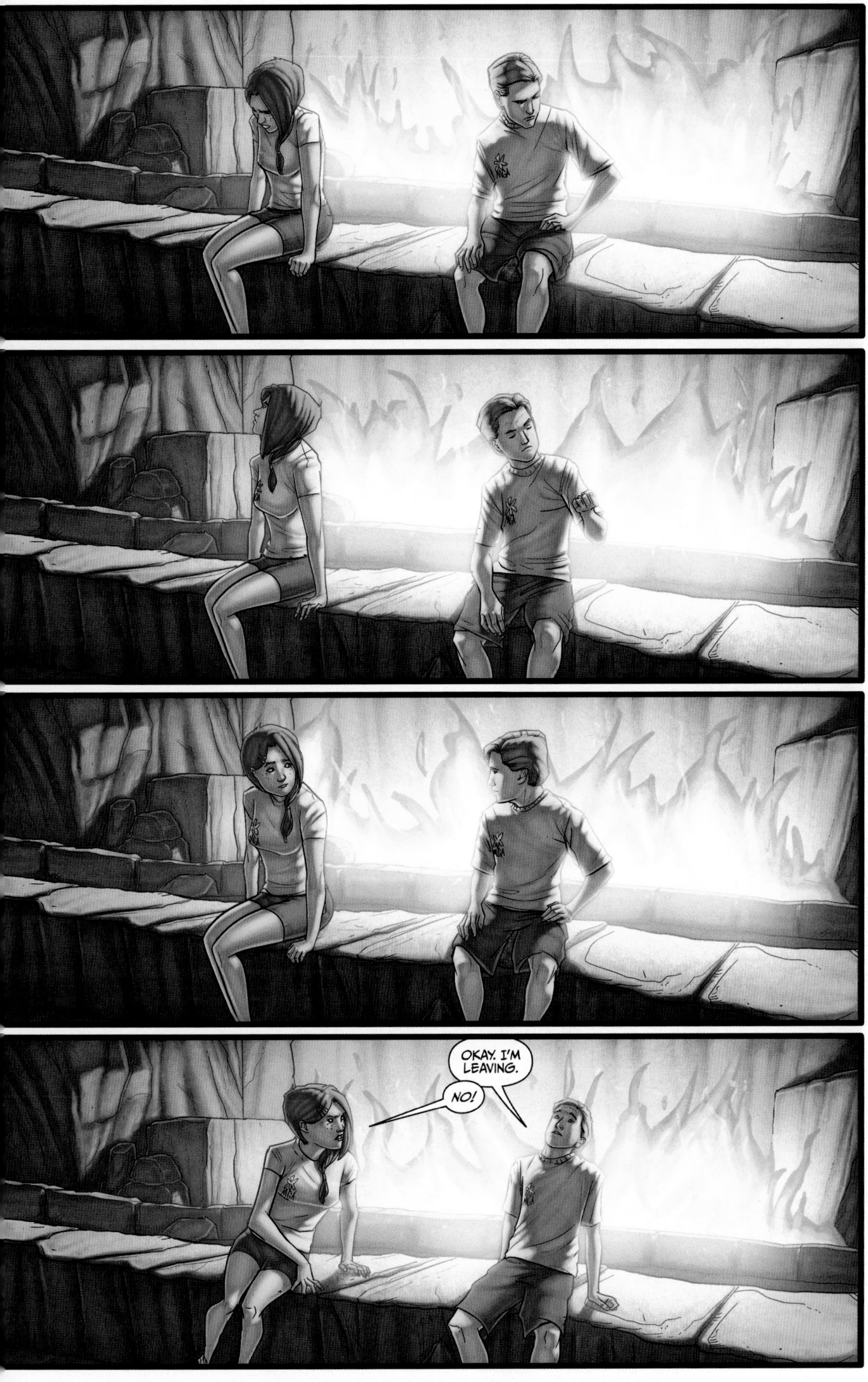
OKAY. I'M LEAVING.
NO!

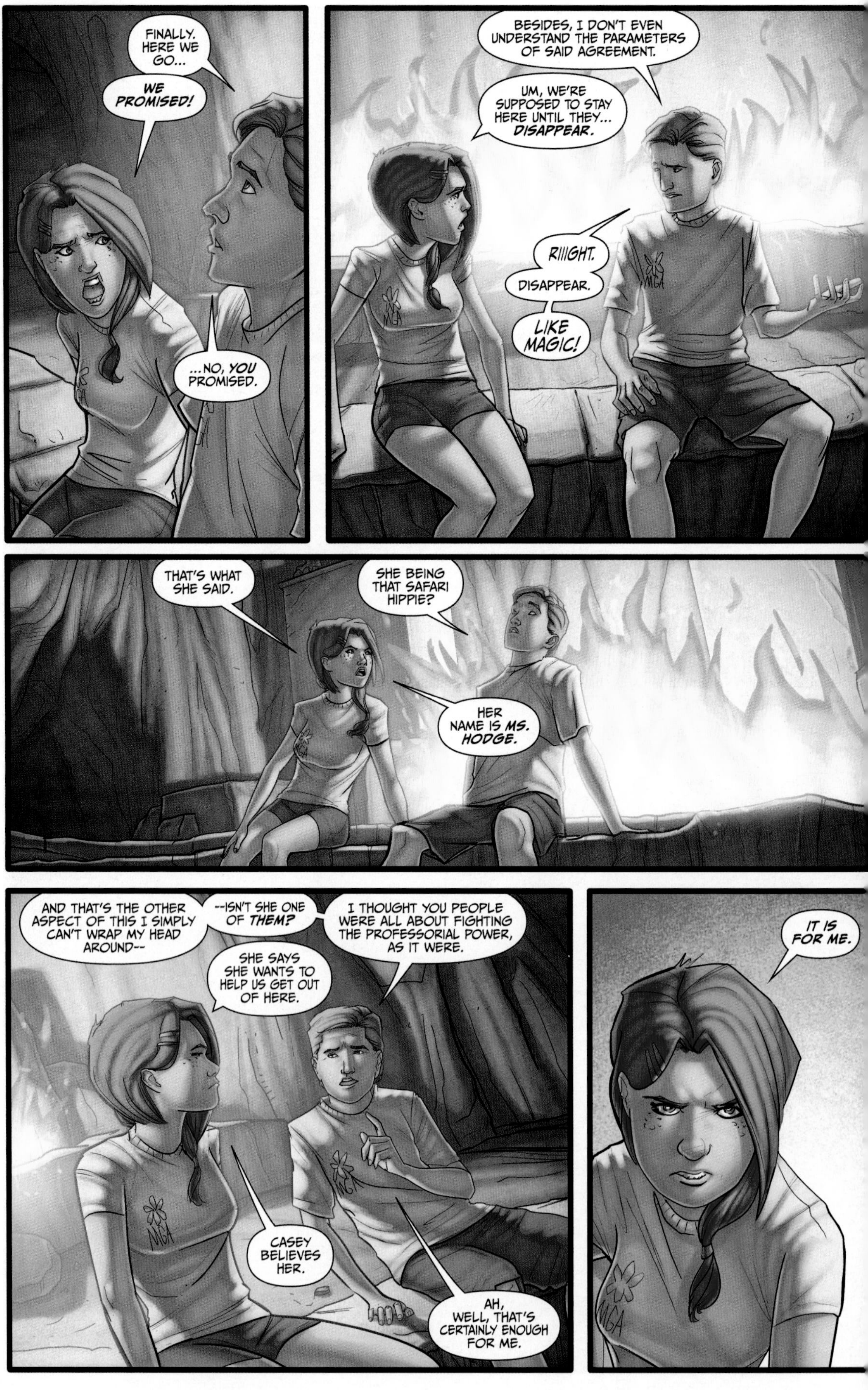
FINALLY. HERE WE GO...
WE PROMISED!
...NO, YOU PROMISED.
BESIDES, I DON'T EVEN UNDERSTAND THE PARAMETERS OF SAID AGREEMENT.
UM, WE'RE SUPPOSED TO STAY HERE UNTIL THEY... DISAPPEAR.
RIIIGHT.
DISAPPEAR.
LIKE MAGIC!
THAT'S WHAT SHE SAID.
SHE BEING THAT SAFARI HIPPIE?
HER NAME IS MS. HODGE.
AND THAT'S THE OTHER ASPECT OF THIS I SIMPLY CAN'T WRAP MY HEAD AROUND--
--ISN'T SHE ONE OF THEM?
I THOUGHT YOU PEOPLE WERE ALL ABOUT FIGHTING THE PROFESSORIAL POWER, AS IT WERE.
SHE SAYS SHE WANTS TO HELP US GET OUT OF HERE.
CASEY BELIEVES HER.
AH, WELL, THAT'S CERTAINLY ENOUGH FOR ME.
IT IS FOR ME.

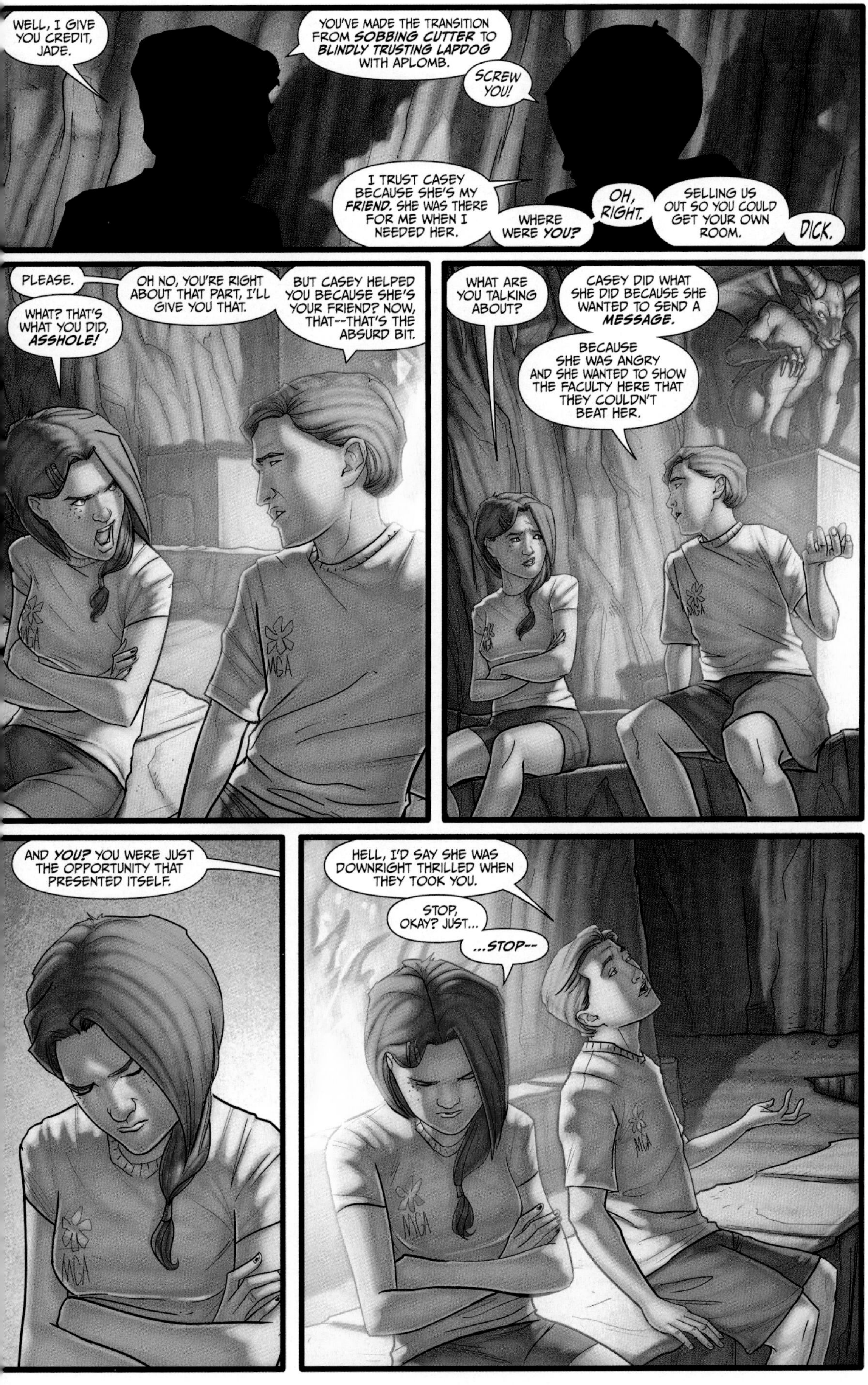
WELL, I GIVE YOU CREDIT, JADE.
YOU'VE MADE THE TRANSITION FROM **SOBBING CUTTER** TO **BLINDLY TRUSTING LAPDOG** WITH APLOMB.
SCREW YOU!
I TRUST CASEY BECAUSE SHE'S MY *FRIEND.* SHE WAS THERE FOR ME WHEN I NEEDED HER.
WHERE WERE *YOU?*
OH, RIGHT.
SELLING US OUT SO YOU COULD GET YOUR OWN ROOM.
DICK.
PLEASE.
WHAT? THAT'S WHAT YOU DID, ***ASSHOLE!***
OH NO, YOU'RE RIGHT ABOUT THAT PART, I'LL GIVE YOU THAT.
BUT CASEY HELPED YOU BECAUSE SHE'S YOUR FRIEND? NOW, THAT--THAT'S THE ABSURD BIT.
WHAT ARE YOU TALKING ABOUT?
CASEY DID WHAT SHE DID BECAUSE SHE WANTED TO SEND A ***MESSAGE.***
BECAUSE SHE WAS ANGRY AND SHE WANTED TO SHOW THE FACULTY HERE THAT THEY COULDN'T BEAT HER.
AND *YOU?* YOU WERE JUST THE OPPORTUNITY THAT PRESENTED ITSELF.
HELL, I'D SAY SHE WAS DOWNRIGHT THRILLED WHEN THEY TOOK YOU.
STOP, OKAY? JUST...
...STOP--

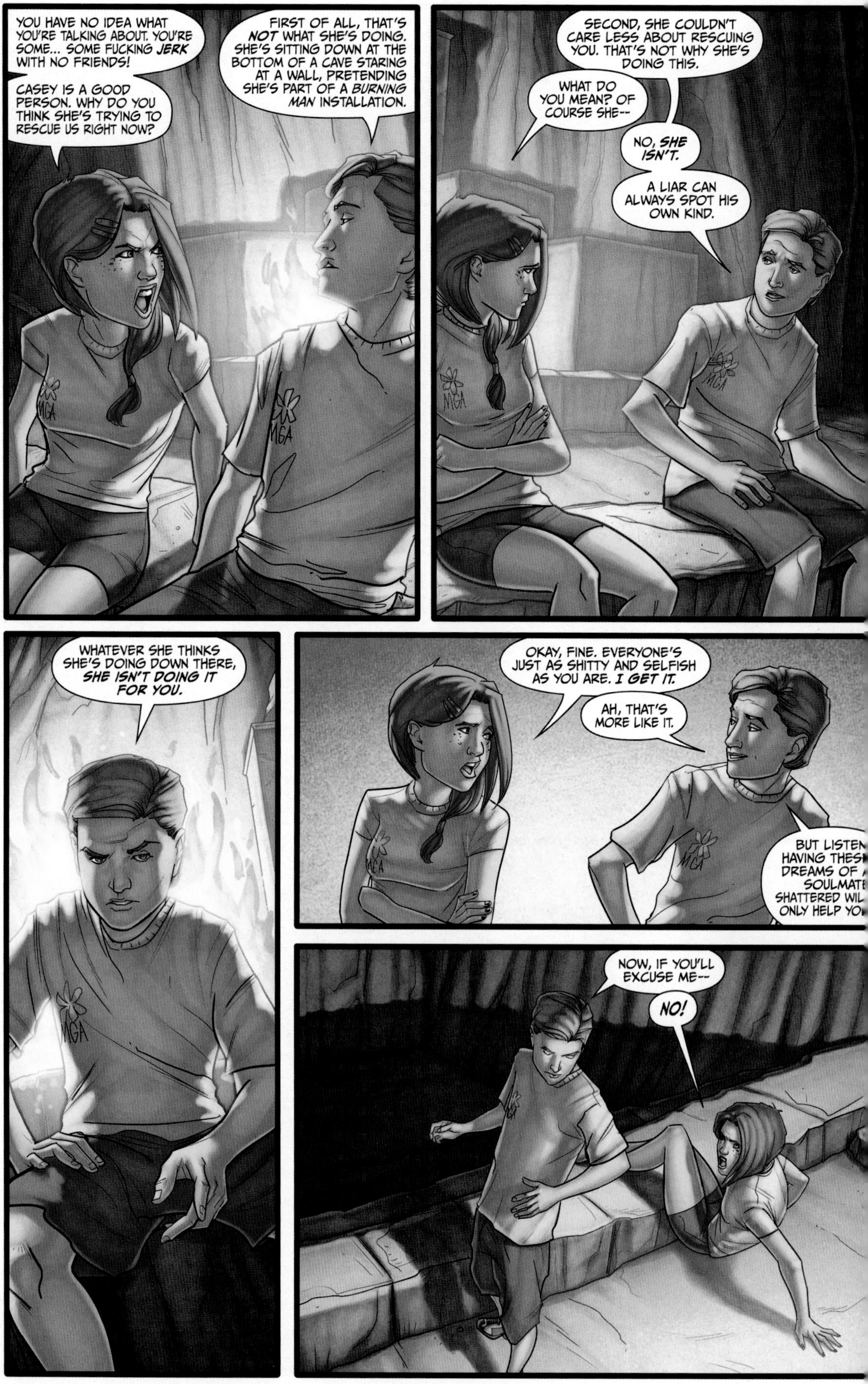

YOU HAVE NO IDEA WHAT YOU'RE TALKING ABOUT. YOU'RE SOME... SOME FUCKING JERK WITH NO FRIENDS!
CASEY IS A GOOD PERSON. WHY DO YOU THINK SHE'S TRYING TO RESCUE US RIGHT NOW?
FIRST OF ALL, THAT'S NOT WHAT SHE'S DOING. SHE'S SITTING DOWN AT THE BOTTOM OF A CAVE STARING AT A WALL, PRETENDING SHE'S PART OF A BURNING MAN INSTALLATION.
SECOND, SHE COULDN'T CARE LESS ABOUT RESCUING YOU. THAT'S NOT WHY SHE'S DOING THIS.
WHAT DO YOU MEAN? OF COURSE SHE--
NO, SHE ISN'T.
A LIAR CAN ALWAYS SPOT HIS OWN KIND.
WHATEVER SHE THINKS SHE'S DOING DOWN THERE, SHE ISN'T DOING IT FOR YOU.
OKAY, FINE. EVERYONE'S JUST AS SHITTY AND SELFISH AS YOU ARE. I GET IT.
AH, THAT'S MORE LIKE IT.
NOW, IF YOU'LL EXCUSE ME--
NO!

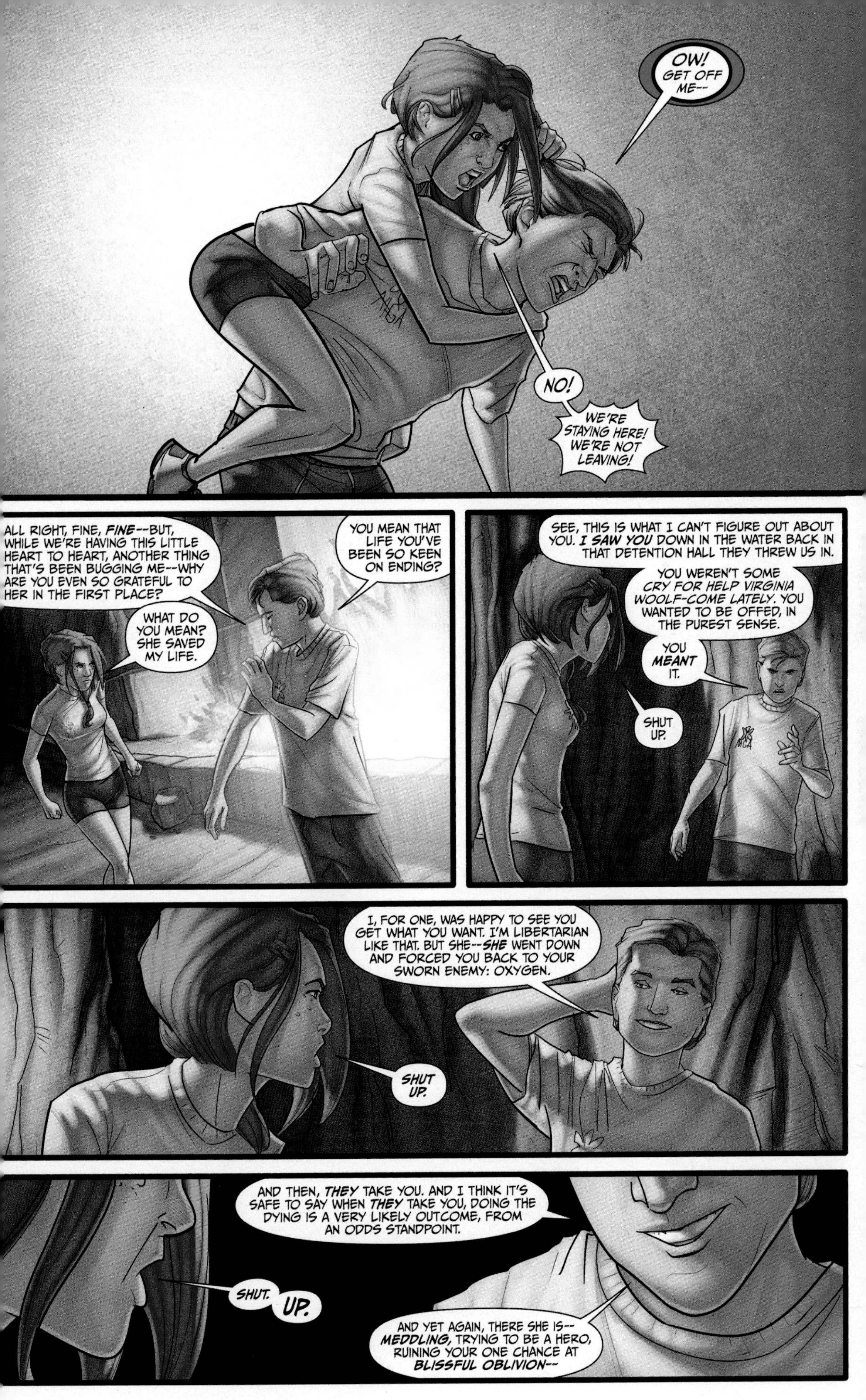
OW! GET OFF ME--
NO!
WE'RE STAYING HERE! WE'RE NOT LEAVING!
ALL RIGHT, FINE, FINE--BUT, WHILE WE'RE HAVING THIS LITTLE HEART TO HEART, ANOTHER THING THAT'S BEEN BUGGING ME--WHY ARE YOU EVEN SO GRATEFUL TO HER IN THE FIRST PLACE?
WHAT DO YOU MEAN? SHE SAVED MY LIFE.
YOU MEAN THAT LIFE YOU'VE BEEN SO KEEN ON ENDING?
SEE, THIS IS WHAT I CAN'T FIGURE OUT ABOUT YOU. I SAW YOU DOWN IN THE WATER BACK IN THAT DETENTION HALL THEY THREW US IN.
YOU WEREN'T SOME CRY FOR HELP VIRGINIA WOOLF-COME LATELY. YOU WANTED TO BE OFFED, IN THE PUREST SENSE.
YOU MEANT IT.
SHUT UP.
I, FOR ONE, WAS HAPPY TO SEE YOU GET WHAT YOU WANT. I'M LIBERTARIAN LIKE THAT. BUT SHE--SHE WENT DOWN AND FORCED YOU BACK TO YOUR SWORN ENEMY: OXYGEN.
SHUT UP.
AND THEN, THEY TAKE YOU. AND I THINK IT'S SAFE TO SAY WHEN THEY TAKE YOU, DOING THE DYING IS A VERY LIKELY OUTCOME, FROM AN ODDS STANDPOINT.
SHUT.
UP.
AND YET AGAIN, THERE SHE IS-- MEDDLING, TRYING TO BE A HERO, RUINING YOUR ONE CHANCE AT BLISSFUL OBLIVION--

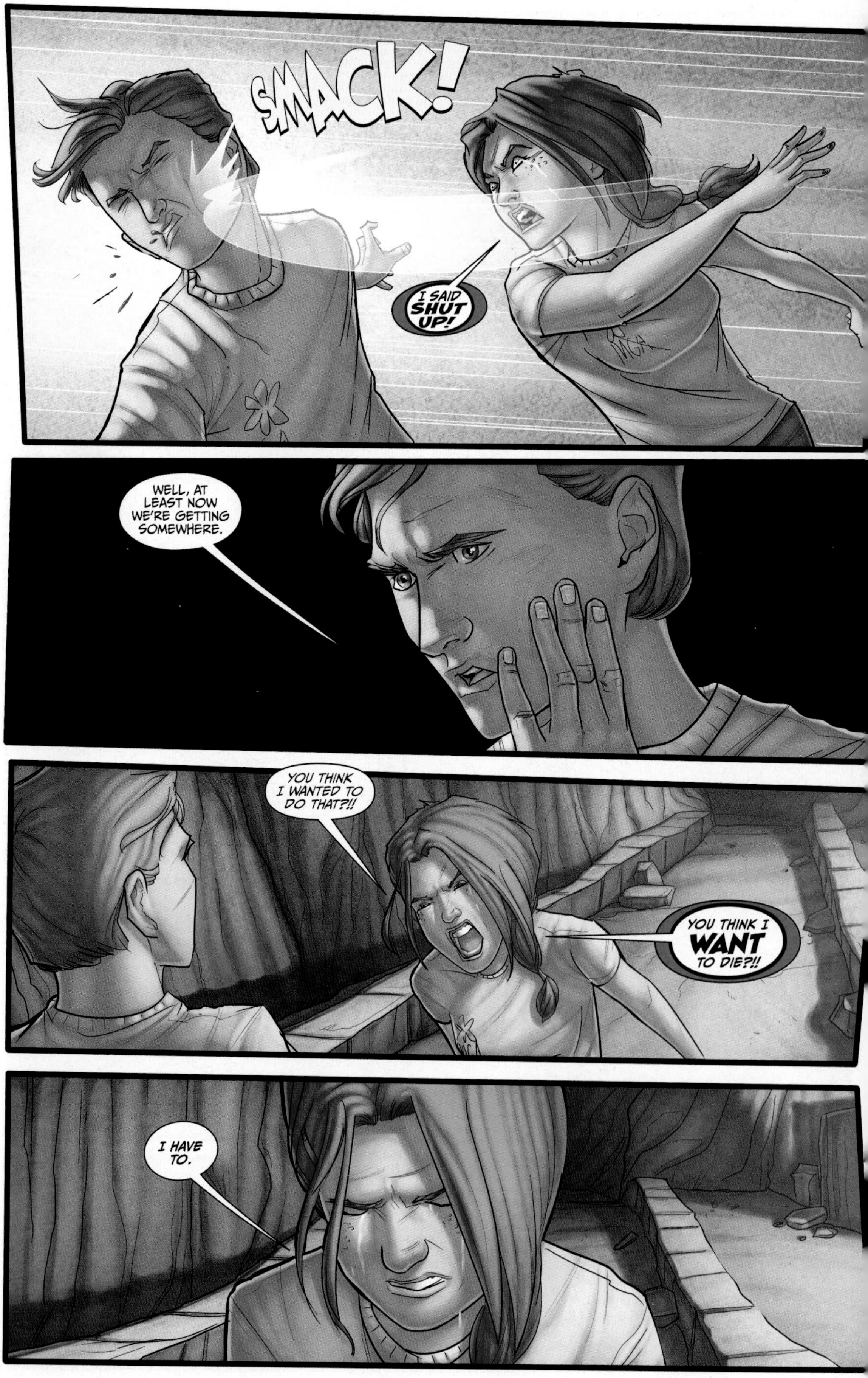
SMACK!
I SAID SHUT UP!
WELL, AT LEAST NOW WE'RE GETTING SOMEWHERE.
YOU THINK I WANTED TO DO THAT?!!
YOU THINK I WANT TO DIE?!!
I HAVE TO.

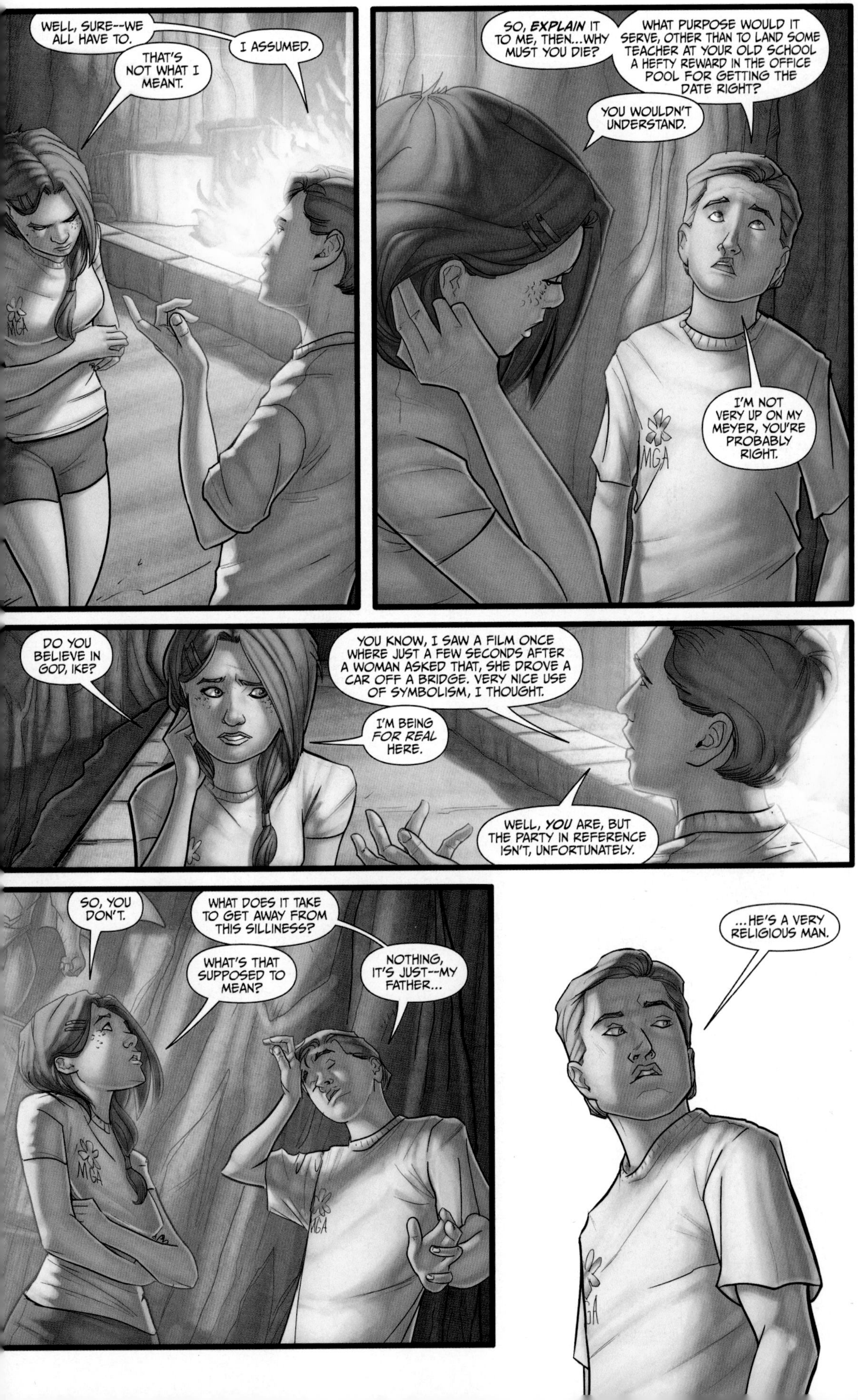

WELL, SURE--WE ALL HAVE TO.
I ASSUMED.
THAT'S NOT WHAT I MEANT.
SO, EXPLAIN IT TO ME, THEN...WHY MUST YOU DIE?
WHAT PURPOSE WOULD IT SERVE, OTHER THAN TO LAND SOME TEACHER AT YOUR OLD SCHOOL A HEFTY REWARD IN THE OFFICE POOL FOR GETTING THE DATE RIGHT?
YOU WOULDN'T UNDERSTAND.
I'M NOT VERY UP ON MY MEYER, YOU'RE PROBABLY RIGHT.
DO YOU BELIEVE IN GOD, IKE?
YOU KNOW, I SAW A FILM ONCE WHERE JUST A FEW SECONDS AFTER A WOMAN ASKED THAT, SHE DROVE A CAR OFF A BRIDGE. VERY NICE USE OF SYMBOLISM, I THOUGHT.
I'M BEING FOR REAL HERE.
WELL, YOU ARE, BUT THE PARTY IN REFERENCE ISN'T, UNFORTUNATELY.
SO, YOU DON'T.
WHAT DOES IT TAKE TO GET AWAY FROM THIS SILLINESS?
WHAT'S THAT SUPPOSED TO MEAN?
NOTHING, IT'S JUST--MY FATHER...
...HE'S A VERY RELIGIOUS MAN.

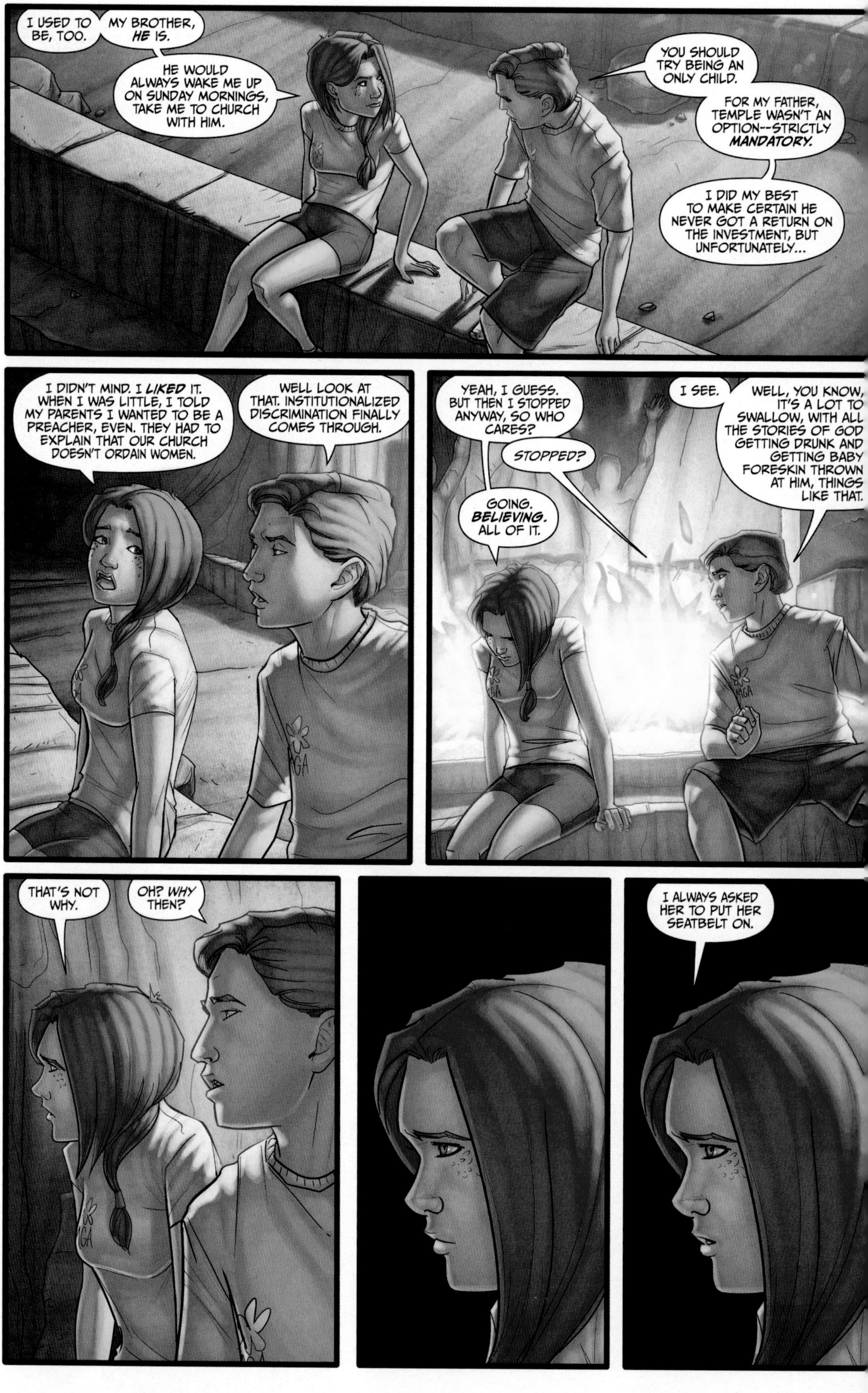
I USED TO BE, TOO.
MY BROTHER, *HE* IS.
HE WOULD ALWAYS WAKE ME UP ON SUNDAY MORNINGS, TAKE ME TO CHURCH WITH HIM.
YOU SHOULD TRY BEING AN ONLY CHILD.
FOR MY FATHER, TEMPLE WASN'T AN OPTION--STRICTLY ***MANDATORY.***
I DID MY BEST TO MAKE CERTAIN HE NEVER GOT A RETURN ON THE INVESTMENT, BUT UNFORTUNATELY...
I DIDN'T MIND. I ***LIKED*** IT. WHEN I WAS LITTLE, I TOLD MY PARENTS I WANTED TO BE A PREACHER, EVEN. THEY HAD TO EXPLAIN THAT OUR CHURCH DOESN'T ORDAIN WOMEN.
WELL LOOK AT THAT. INSTITUTIONALIZED DISCRIMINATION FINALLY COMES THROUGH.
YEAH, I GUESS. BUT THEN I STOPPED ANYWAY, SO WHO CARES?
STOPPED?
GOING. ***BELIEVING.*** ALL OF IT.
I SEE.
WELL, YOU KNOW, IT'S A LOT TO SWALLOW, WITH ALL THE STORIES OF GOD GETTING DRUNK AND GETTING BABY FORESKIN THROWN AT HIM, THINGS LIKE THAT.
THAT'S NOT WHY.
OH? *WHY* THEN?
I ALWAYS ASKED HER TO PUT HER SEATBELT ON.

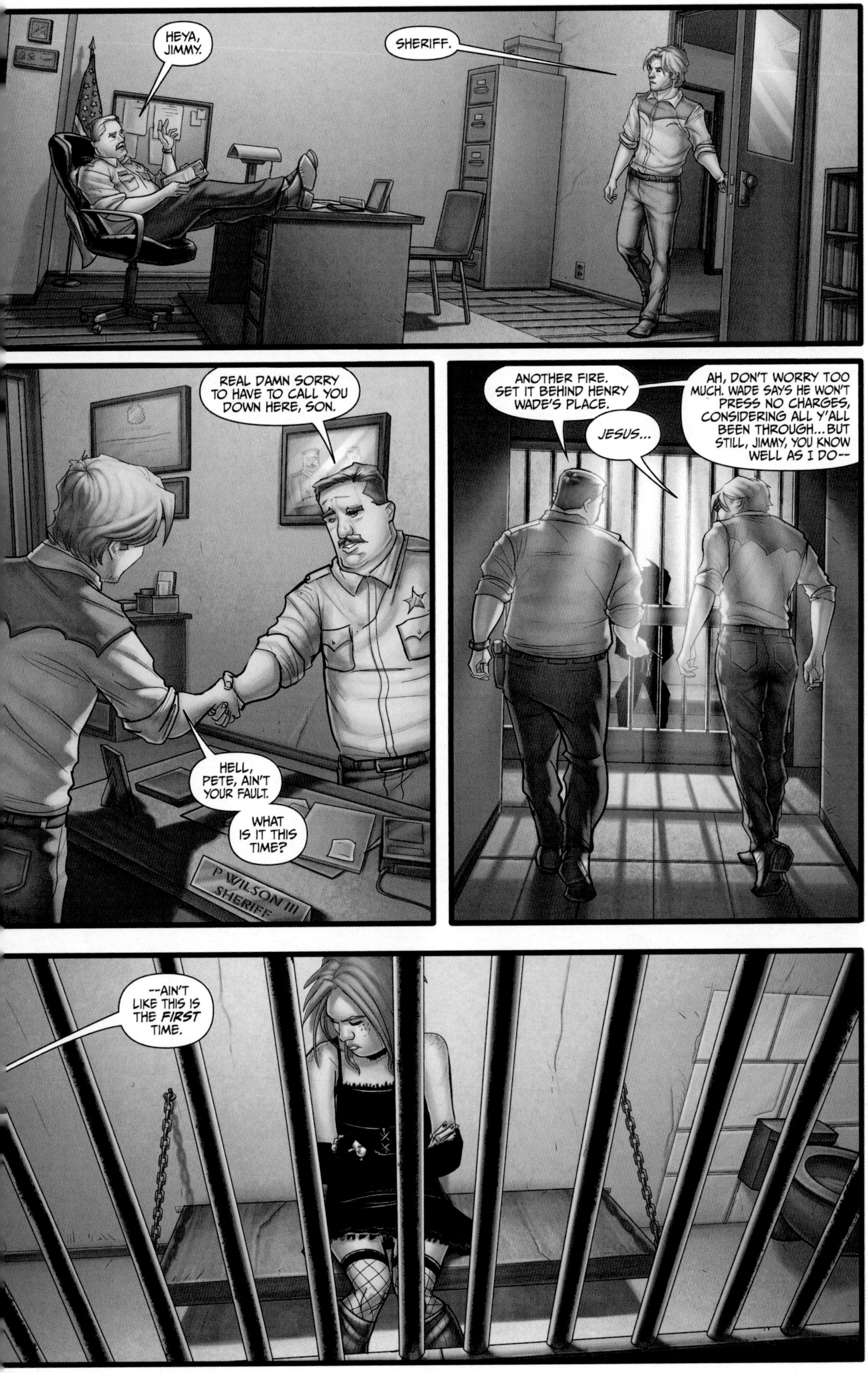
HEYA, JIMMY.
SHERIFF.
REAL DAMN SORRY TO HAVE TO CALL YOU DOWN HERE, SON.
HELL, PETE, AIN'T YOUR FAULT.
WHAT IS IT THIS TIME?
P WILSON III SHERIFF
ANOTHER FIRE. SET IT BEHIND HENRY WADE'S PLACE.
JESUS...
AH, DON'T WORRY TOO MUCH. WADE SAYS HE WON'T PRESS NO CHARGES, CONSIDERING ALL Y'ALL BEEN THROUGH...BUT STILL, JIMMY, YOU KNOW WELL AS I DO--
--AIN'T LIKE THIS IS THE *FIRST* TIME.

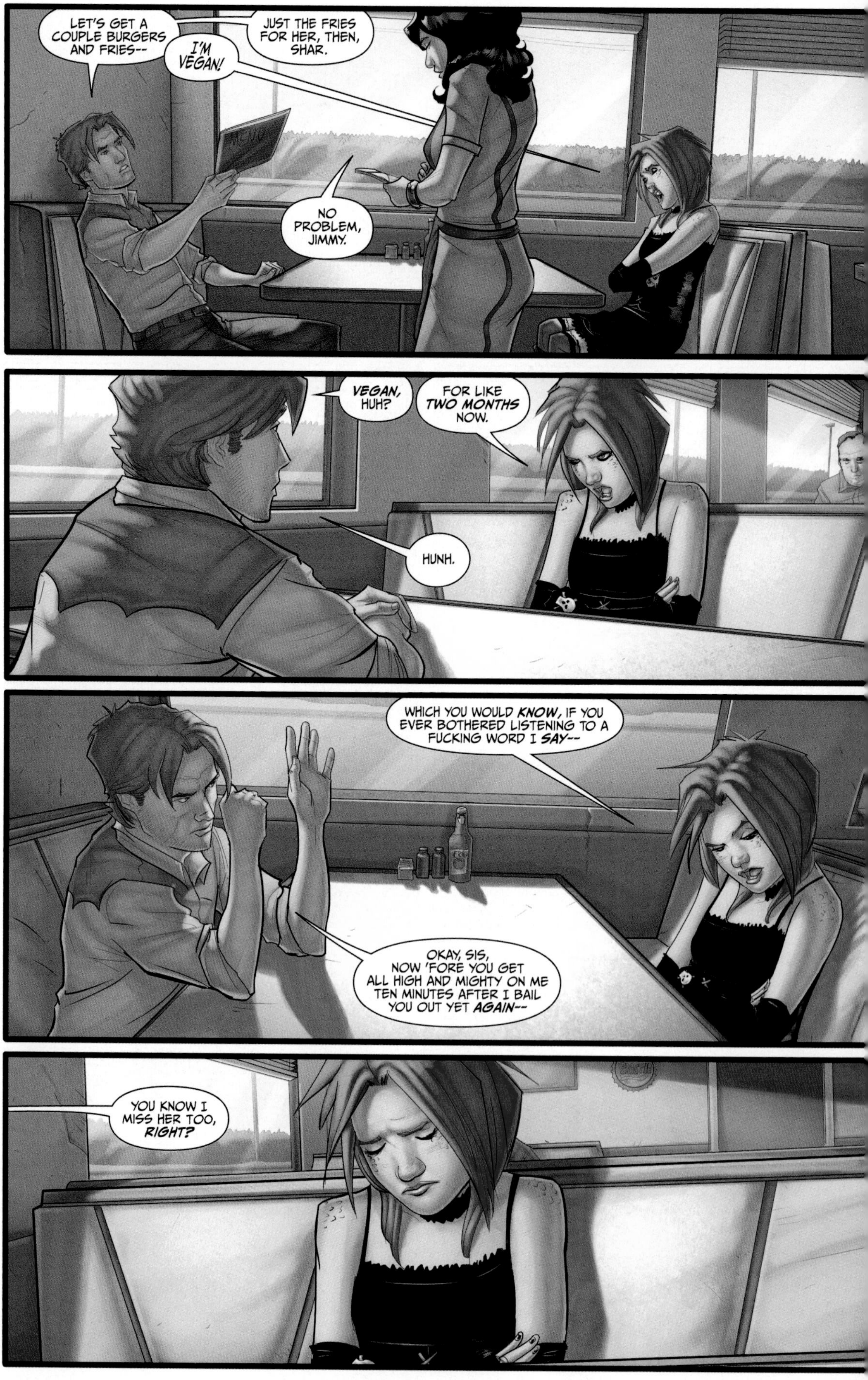
LET'S GET A COUPLE BURGERS AND FRIES--
I'M VEGAN!
JUST THE FRIES FOR HER, THEN, SHAR.
NO PROBLEM, JIMMY.
VEGAN, HUH?
FOR LIKE TWO MONTHS NOW.
HUNH.
WHICH YOU WOULD KNOW, IF YOU EVER BOTHERED LISTENING TO A FUCKING WORD I SAY--
OKAY, SIS, NOW 'FORE YOU GET ALL HIGH AND MIGHTY ON ME TEN MINUTES AFTER I BAIL YOU OUT YET AGAIN--
YOU KNOW I MISS HER TOO, RIGHT?

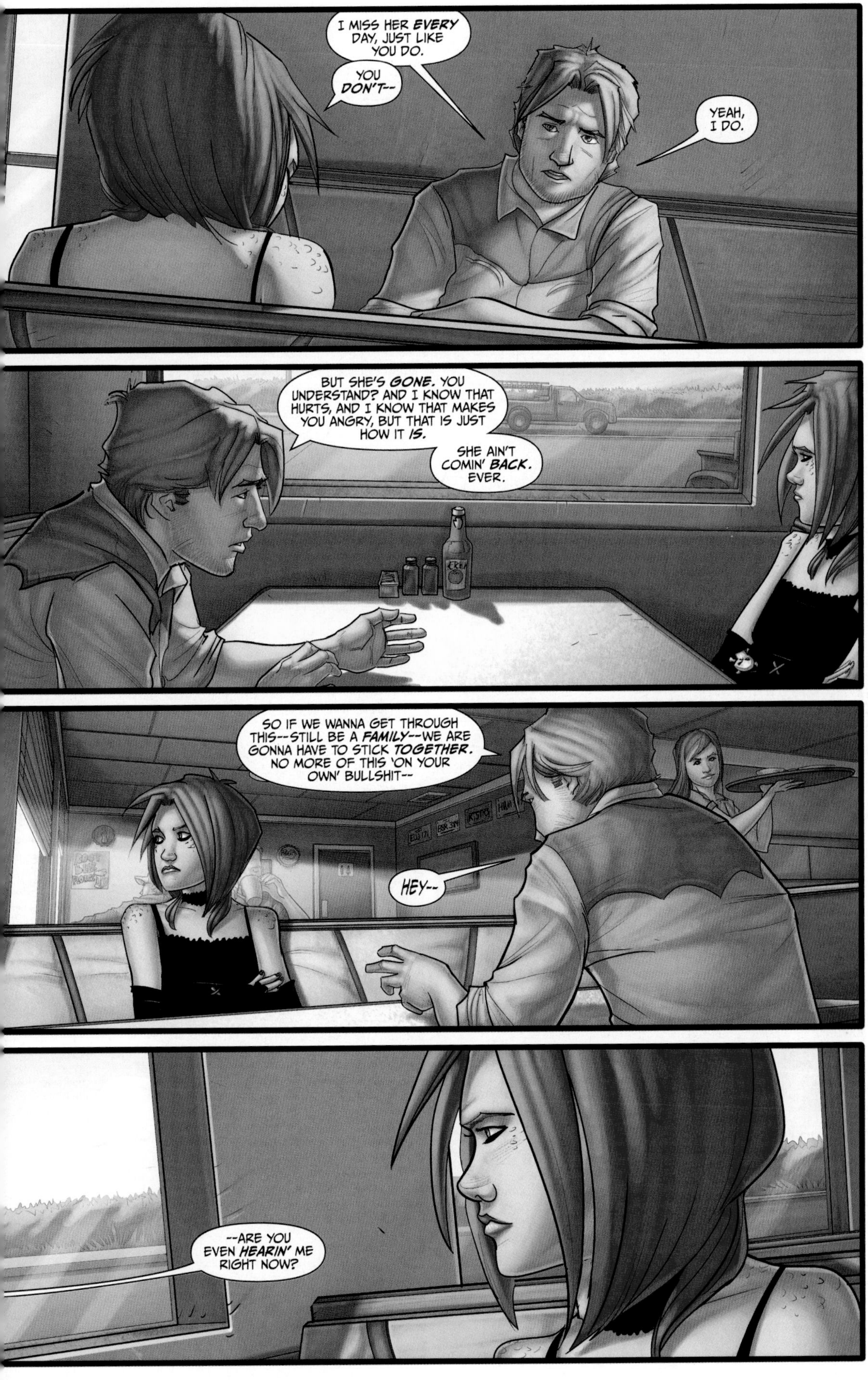
I MISS HER EVERY DAY, JUST LIKE YOU DO.
YOU DON'T--
YEAH, I DO.
BUT SHE'S GONE. YOU UNDERSTAND? AND I KNOW THAT HURTS, AND I KNOW THAT MAKES YOU ANGRY, BUT THAT IS JUST HOW IT IS.
SHE AIN'T COMIN' BACK. EVER.
SO IF WE WANNA GET THROUGH THIS--STILL BE A FAMILY--WE ARE GONNA HAVE TO STICK TOGETHER. NO MORE OF THIS 'ON YOUR OWN' BULLSHIT--
HEY--
--ARE YOU EVEN HEARIN' ME RIGHT NOW?

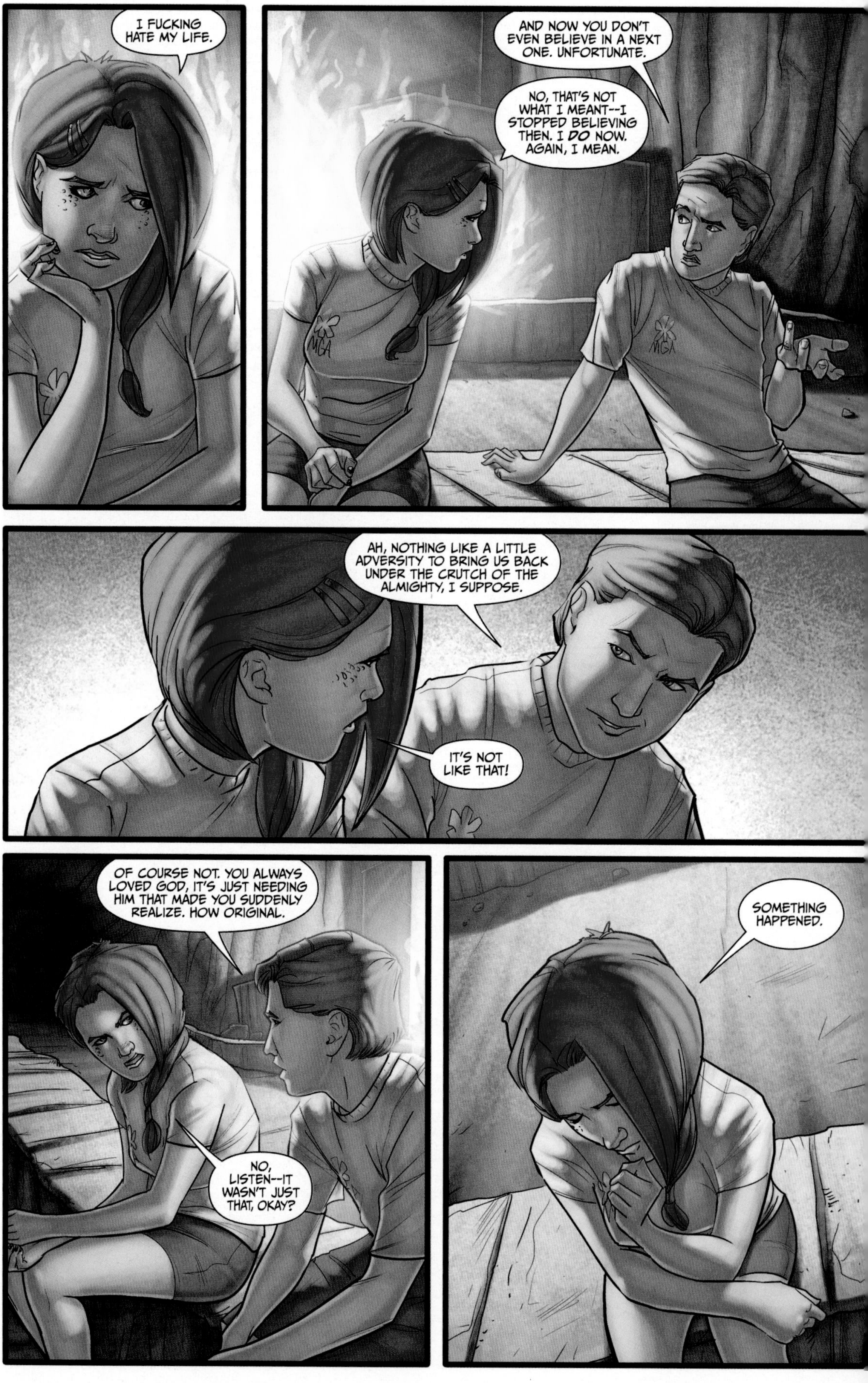
I FUCKING HATE MY LIFE.
AND NOW YOU DON'T EVEN BELIEVE IN A NEXT ONE. UNFORTUNATE.
NO, THAT'S NOT WHAT I MEANT--I STOPPED BELIEVING THEN. I *DO* NOW. AGAIN, I MEAN.
AH, NOTHING LIKE A LITTLE ADVERSITY TO BRING US BACK UNDER THE CRUTCH OF THE ALMIGHTY, I SUPPOSE.
IT'S NOT LIKE THAT!
OF COURSE NOT. YOU ALWAYS LOVED GOD, IT'S JUST NEEDING HIM THAT MADE YOU SUDDENLY REALIZE. HOW ORIGINAL.
NO, LISTEN--IT WASN'T JUST THAT, OKAY?
SOMETHING HAPPENED.

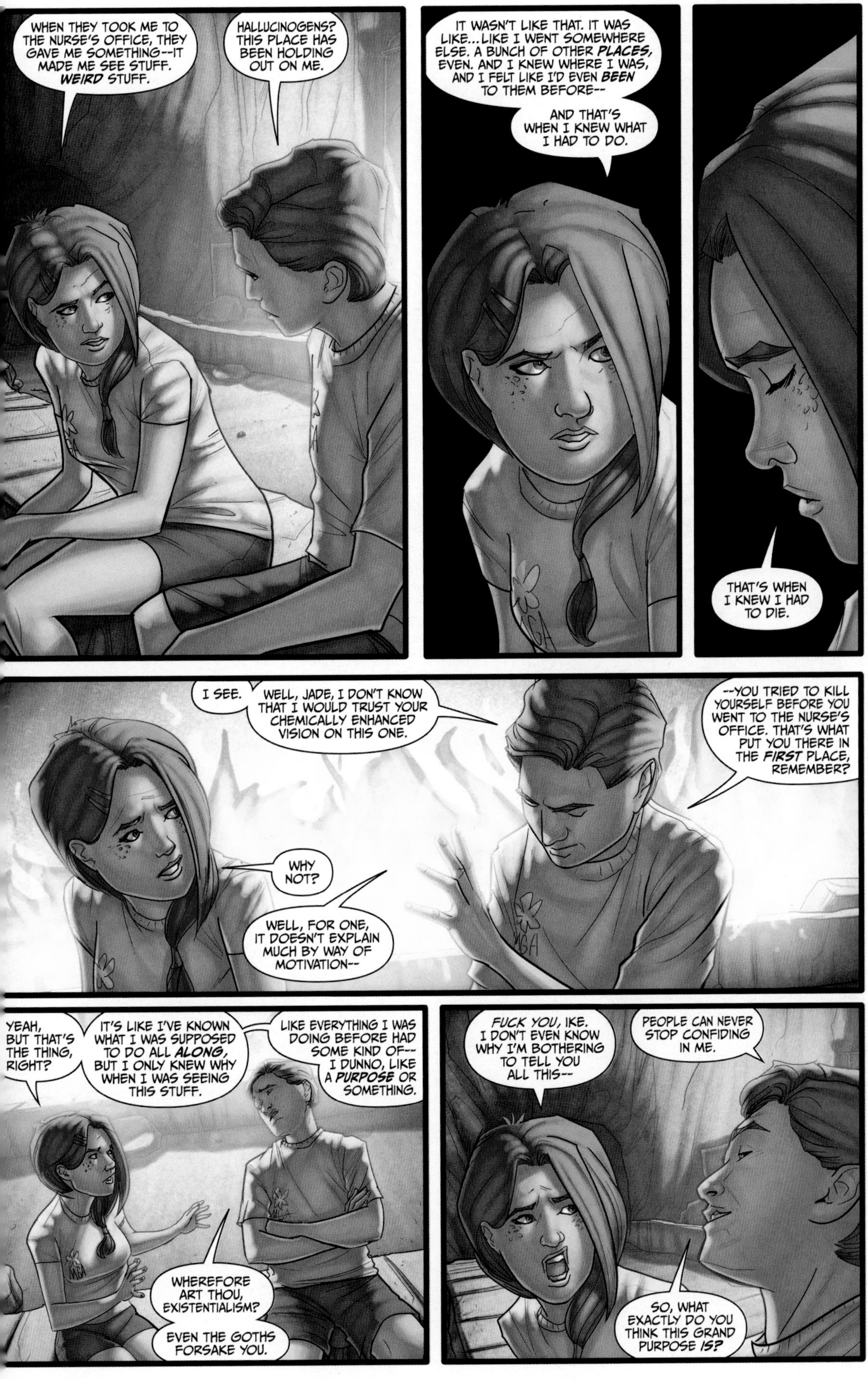
WHEN THEY TOOK ME TO THE NURSE'S OFFICE, THEY GAVE ME SOMETHING--IT MADE ME SEE STUFF. WEIRD STUFF.
HALLUCINOGENS? THIS PLACE HAS BEEN HOLDING OUT ON ME.
IT WASN'T LIKE THAT. IT WAS LIKE... LIKE I WENT SOMEWHERE ELSE. A BUNCH OF OTHER PLACES, EVEN. AND I KNEW WHERE I WAS, AND I FELT LIKE I'D EVEN BEEN TO THEM BEFORE--
AND THAT'S WHEN I KNEW WHAT I HAD TO DO.
THAT'S WHEN I KNEW I HAD TO DIE.
I SEE.
WELL, JADE, I DON'T KNOW THAT I WOULD TRUST YOUR CHEMICALLY ENHANCED VISION ON THIS ONE.
--YOU TRIED TO KILL YOURSELF BEFORE YOU WENT TO THE NURSE'S OFFICE. THAT'S WHAT PUT YOU THERE IN THE FIRST PLACE, REMEMBER?
WHY NOT?
WELL, FOR ONE, IT DOESN'T EXPLAIN MUCH BY WAY OF MOTIVATION--
YEAH, BUT THAT'S THE THING, RIGHT?
IT'S LIKE I'VE KNOWN WHAT I WAS SUPPOSED TO DO ALL ALONG, BUT I ONLY KNEW WHY WHEN I WAS SEEING THIS STUFF.
LIKE EVERYTHING I WAS DOING BEFORE HAD SOME KIND OF-- I DUNNO, LIKE A PURPOSE OR SOMETHING.
WHEREFORE ART THOU, EXISTENTIALISM?
EVEN THE GOTHS FORSAKE YOU.
FUCK YOU, IKE. I DON'T EVEN KNOW WHY I'M BOTHERING TO TELL YOU ALL THIS--
PEOPLE CAN NEVER STOP CONFIDING IN ME.
SO, WHAT EXACTLY DO YOU THINK THIS GRAND PURPOSE IS?

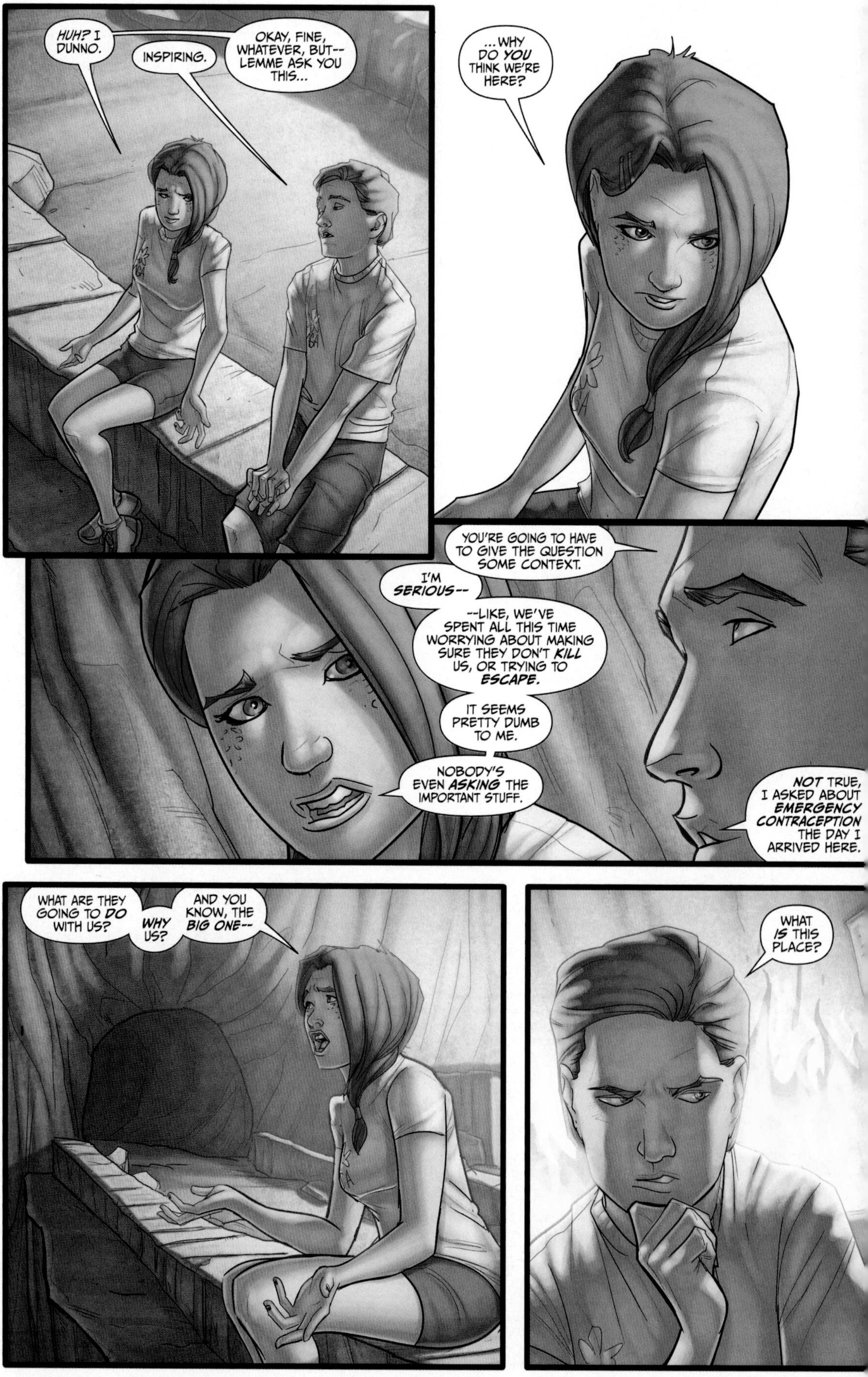
HUH? I DUNNO.
INSPIRING.
OKAY, FINE, WHATEVER, BUT-- LEMME ASK YOU THIS...
...WHY DO YOU THINK WE'RE HERE?
YOU'RE GOING TO HAVE TO GIVE THE QUESTION SOME CONTEXT.
I'M SERIOUS--
--LIKE, WE'VE SPENT ALL THIS TIME WORRYING ABOUT MAKING SURE THEY DON'T KILL US, OR TRYING TO ESCAPE.
IT SEEMS PRETTY DUMB TO ME.
NOBODY'S EVEN ASKING THE IMPORTANT STUFF.
NOT TRUE, I ASKED ABOUT EMERGENCY CONTRACEPTION THE DAY I ARRIVED HERE.
WHAT ARE THEY GOING TO DO WITH US?
WHY US?
AND YOU KNOW, THE BIG ONE--
WHAT IS THIS PLACE?

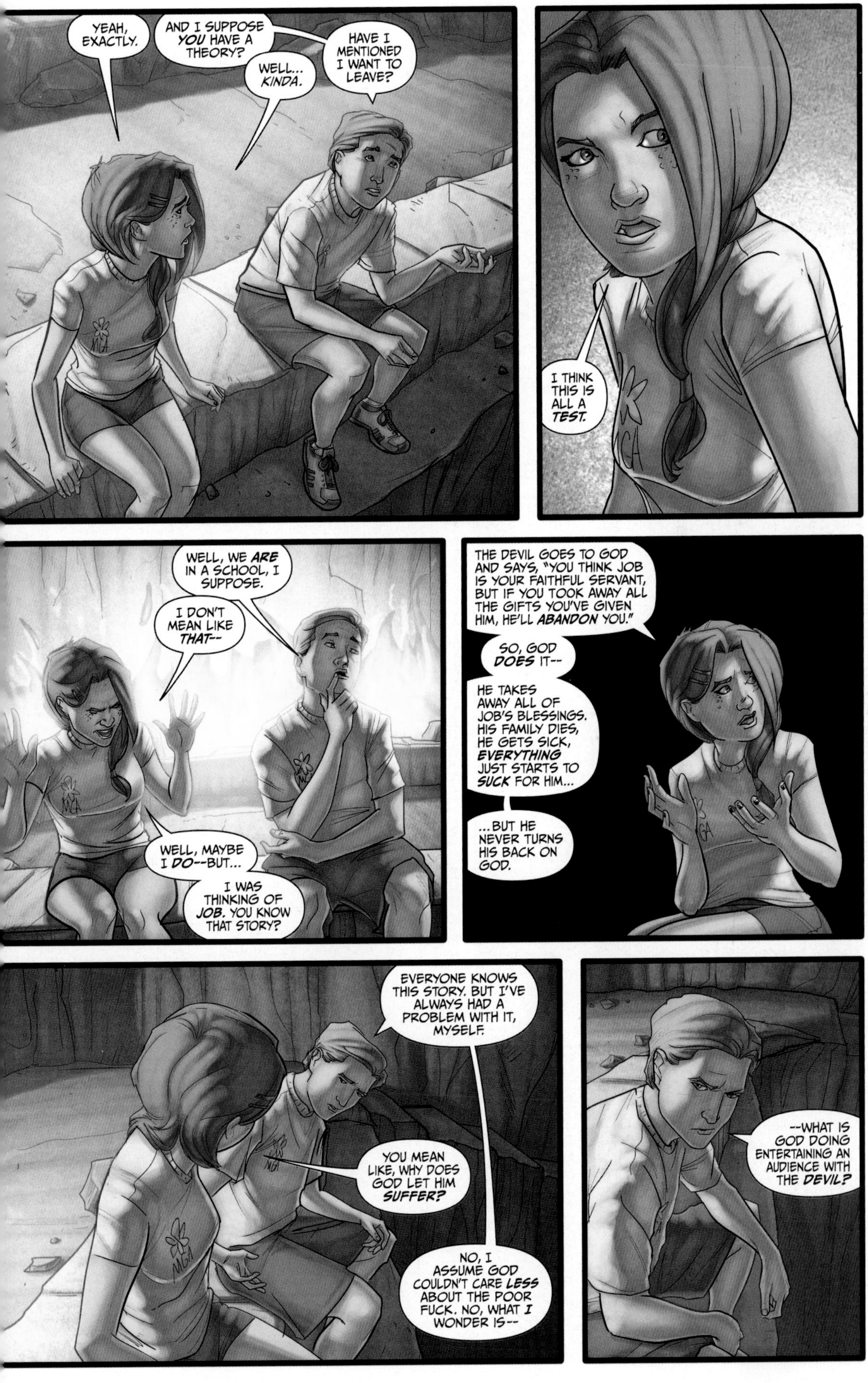
YEAH, EXACTLY.
AND I SUPPOSE *YOU* HAVE A THEORY?
HAVE I MENTIONED I WANT TO LEAVE?
WELL... *KINDA.*
I THINK THIS IS ALL A *TEST.*
WELL, WE *ARE* IN A SCHOOL, I SUPPOSE.
I DON'T MEAN LIKE *THAT*--
WELL, MAYBE I *DO*--BUT...
I WAS THINKING OF *JOB.* YOU KNOW THAT STORY?
THE DEVIL GOES TO GOD AND SAYS, "YOU THINK JOB IS YOUR FAITHFUL SERVANT, BUT IF YOU TOOK AWAY ALL THE GIFTS YOU'VE GIVEN HIM, HE'LL *ABANDON* YOU."
SO, GOD *DOES* IT--
HE TAKES AWAY ALL OF JOB'S BLESSINGS. HIS FAMILY DIES, HE GETS SICK, *EVERYTHING* JUST STARTS TO *SUCK* FOR HIM...
...BUT HE NEVER TURNS HIS BACK ON GOD.
EVERYONE KNOWS THIS STORY. BUT I'VE ALWAYS HAD A PROBLEM WITH IT, MYSELF.
YOU MEAN LIKE, WHY DOES GOD LET HIM *SUFFER?*
NO, I ASSUME GOD COULDN'T CARE *LESS* ABOUT THE POOR FUCK. NO, WHAT *I* WONDER IS--
--WHAT IS GOD DOING ENTERTAINING AN AUDIENCE WITH THE *DEVIL?*

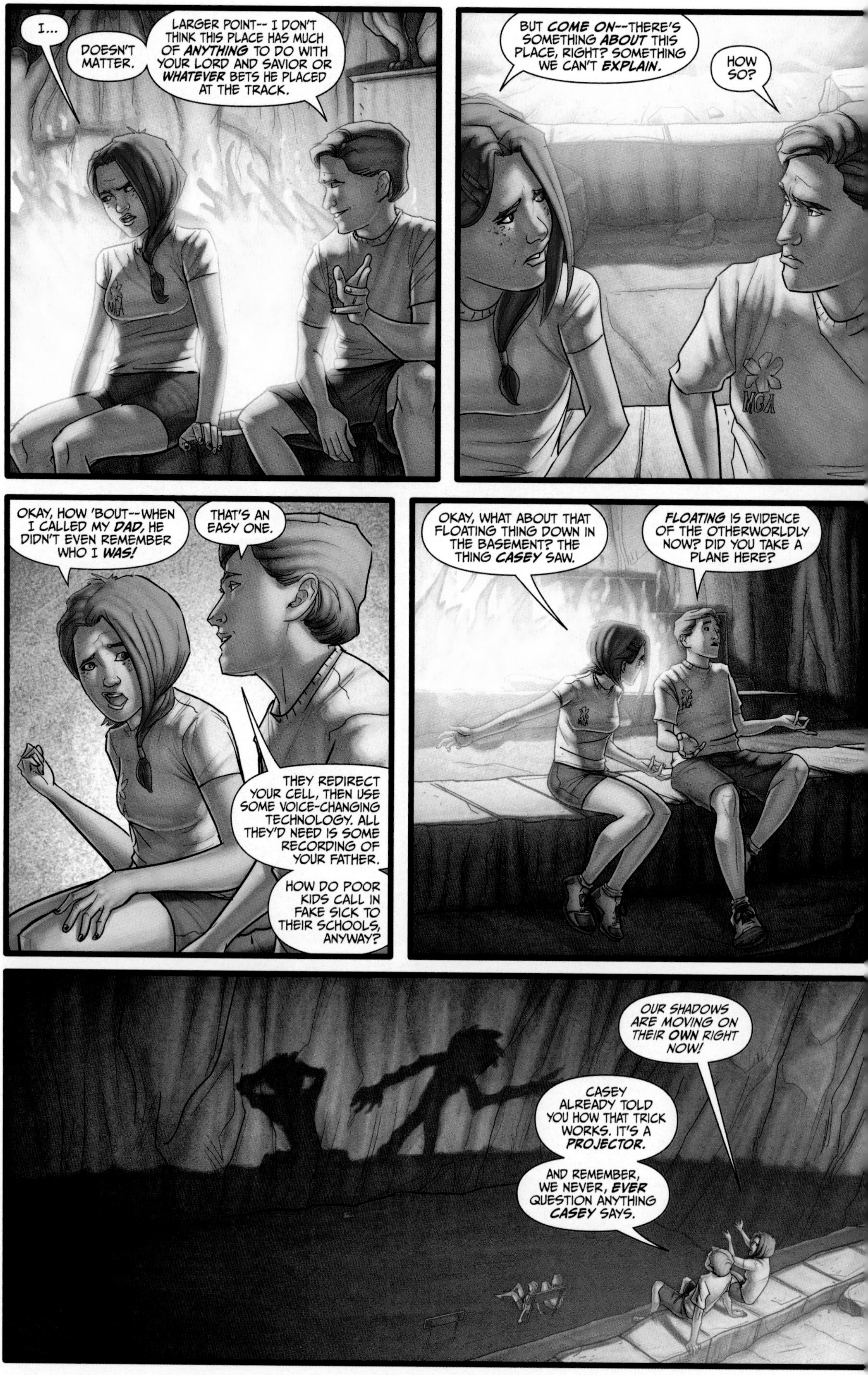
I...
DOESN'T MATTER.
LARGER POINT-- I DON'T THINK THIS PLACE HAS MUCH OF ANYTHING TO DO WITH YOUR LORD AND SAVIOR OR WHATEVER BETS HE PLACED AT THE TRACK.
BUT COME ON--THERE'S SOMETHING ABOUT THIS PLACE, RIGHT? SOMETHING WE CAN'T EXPLAIN.
HOW SO?
OKAY, HOW 'BOUT--WHEN I CALLED MY DAD, HE DIDN'T EVEN REMEMBER WHO I WAS!
THAT'S AN EASY ONE.
THEY REDIRECT YOUR CELL, THEN USE SOME VOICE-CHANGING TECHNOLOGY. ALL THEY'D NEED IS SOME RECORDING OF YOUR FATHER.
HOW DO POOR KIDS CALL IN FAKE SICK TO THEIR SCHOOLS, ANYWAY?
OKAY, WHAT ABOUT THAT FLOATING THING DOWN IN THE BASEMENT? THE THING CASEY SAW.
FLOATING IS EVIDENCE OF THE OTHERWORLDLY NOW? DID YOU TAKE A PLANE HERE?
OUR SHADOWS ARE MOVING ON THEIR OWN RIGHT NOW!
CASEY ALREADY TOLD YOU HOW THAT TRICK WORKS. IT'S A PROJECTOR.
AND REMEMBER, WE NEVER, EVER QUESTION ANYTHING CASEY SAYS.

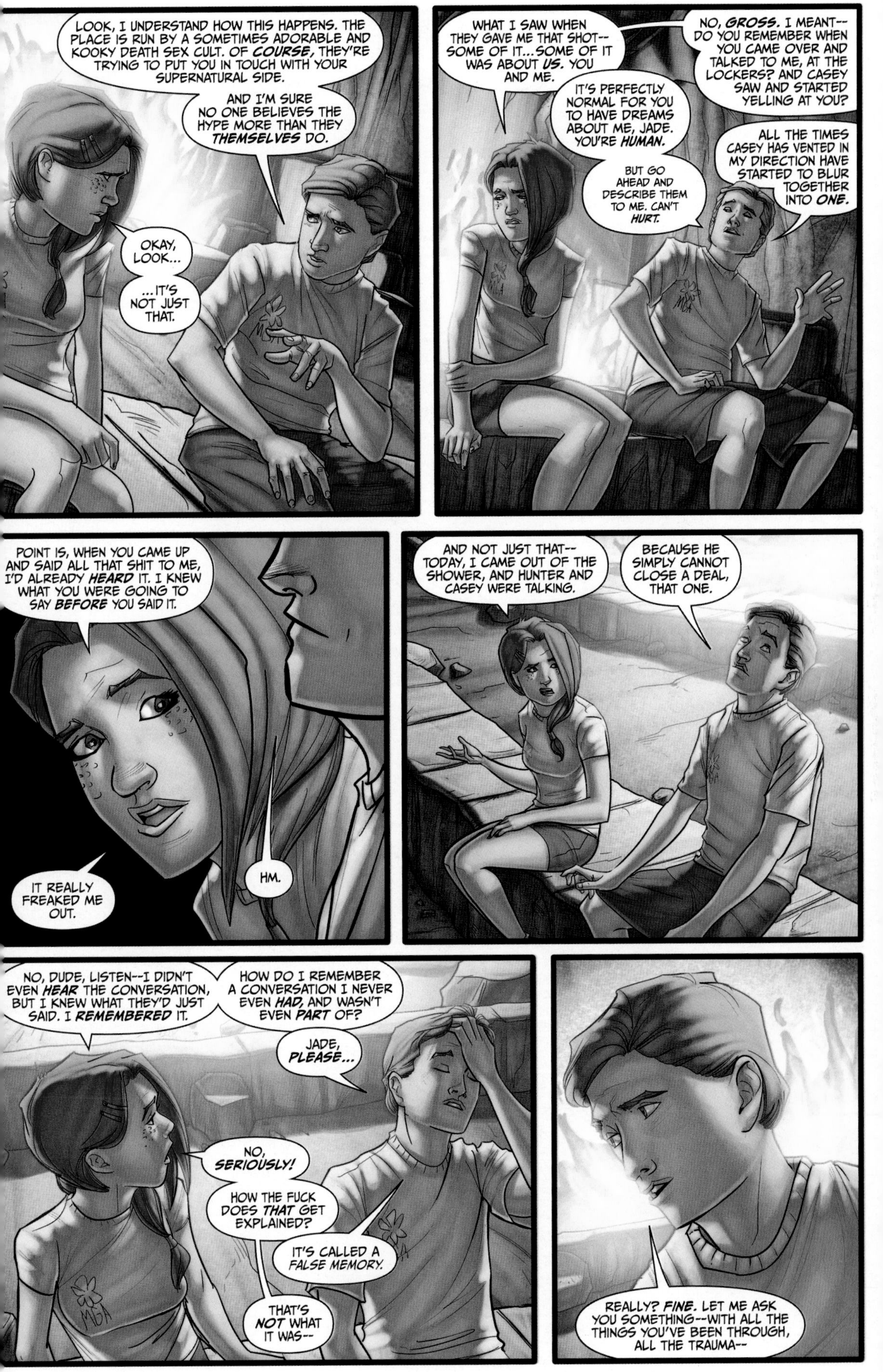
LOOK, I UNDERSTAND HOW THIS HAPPENS. THE PLACE IS RUN BY A SOMETIMES ADORABLE AND KOOKY DEATH SEX CULT. OF COURSE, THEY'RE TRYING TO PUT YOU IN TOUCH WITH YOUR SUPERNATURAL SIDE.
AND I'M SURE NO ONE BELIEVES THE HYPE MORE THAN THEY THEMSELVES DO.
OKAY, LOOK...
...IT'S NOT JUST THAT.
WHAT I SAW WHEN THEY GAVE ME THAT SHOT--SOME OF IT...SOME OF IT WAS ABOUT US. YOU AND ME.
IT'S PERFECTLY NORMAL FOR YOU TO HAVE DREAMS ABOUT ME, JADE. YOU'RE HUMAN.
BUT GO AHEAD AND DESCRIBE THEM TO ME. CAN'T HURT.
NO, GROSS. I MEANT--DO YOU REMEMBER WHEN YOU CAME OVER AND TALKED TO ME, AT THE LOCKERS? AND CASEY SAW AND STARTED YELLING AT YOU?
ALL THE TIMES CASEY HAS VENTED IN MY DIRECTION HAVE STARTED TO BLUR TOGETHER INTO ONE.
POINT IS, WHEN YOU CAME UP AND SAID ALL THAT SHIT TO ME, I'D ALREADY HEARD IT. I KNEW WHAT YOU WERE GOING TO SAY BEFORE YOU SAID IT.
IT REALLY FREAKED ME OUT.
HM.
AND NOT JUST THAT--TODAY, I CAME OUT OF THE SHOWER, AND HUNTER AND CASEY WERE TALKING.
BECAUSE HE SIMPLY CANNOT CLOSE A DEAL, THAT ONE.
NO, DUDE, LISTEN--I DIDN'T EVEN HEAR THE CONVERSATION, BUT I KNEW WHAT THEY'D JUST SAID. I REMEMBERED IT.
HOW DO I REMEMBER A CONVERSATION I NEVER EVEN HAD, AND WASN'T EVEN PART OF?
JADE, PLEASE...
NO, SERIOUSLY!
HOW THE FUCK DOES THAT GET EXPLAINED?
IT'S CALLED A FALSE MEMORY.
THAT'S NOT WHAT IT WAS--
REALLY? FINE. LET ME ASK YOU SOMETHING--WITH ALL THE THINGS YOU'VE BEEN THROUGH, ALL THE TRAUMA--

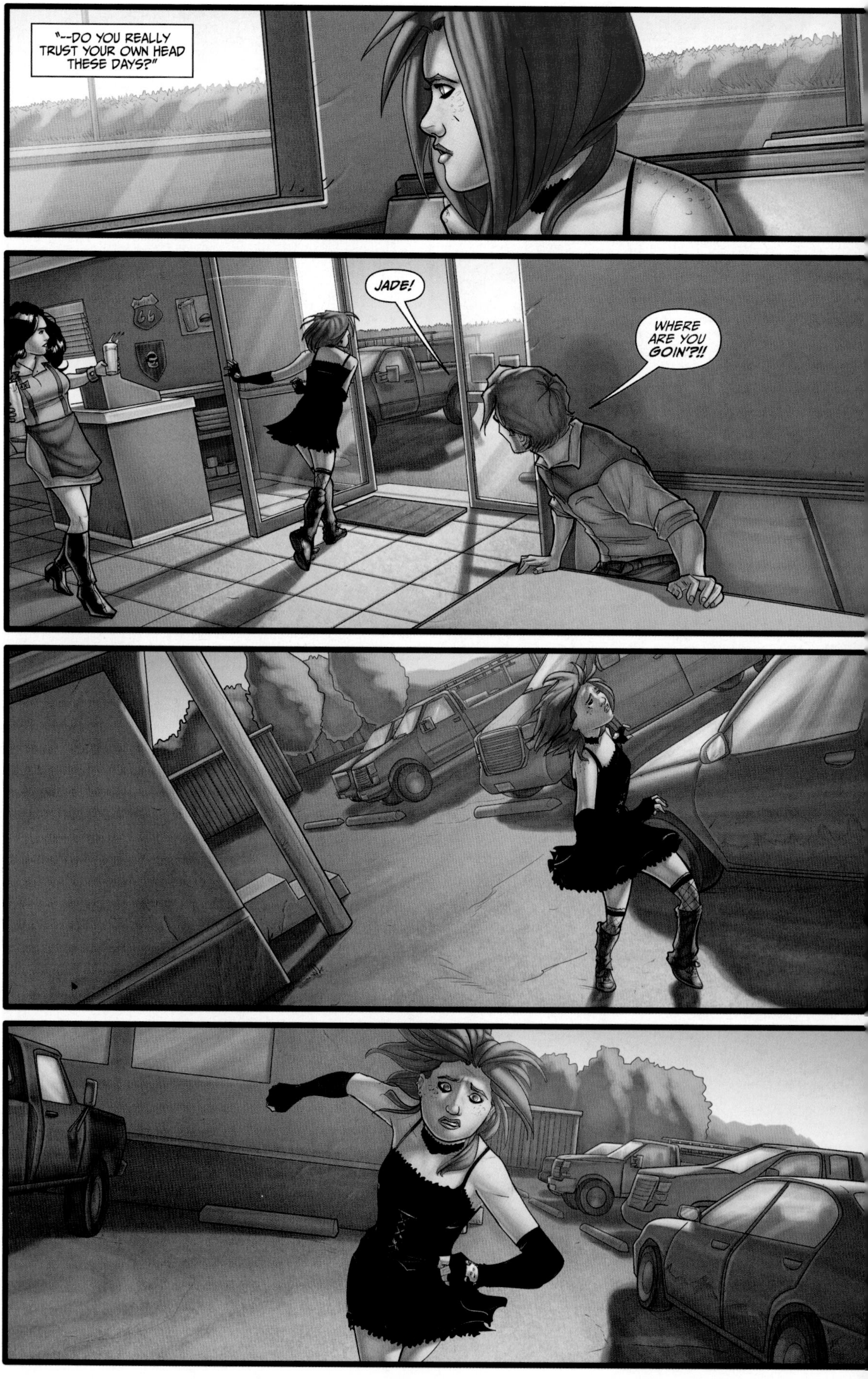
"--DO YOU REALLY TRUST YOUR OWN HEAD THESE DAYS?"
JADE!
WHERE ARE YOU GOIN'?!!

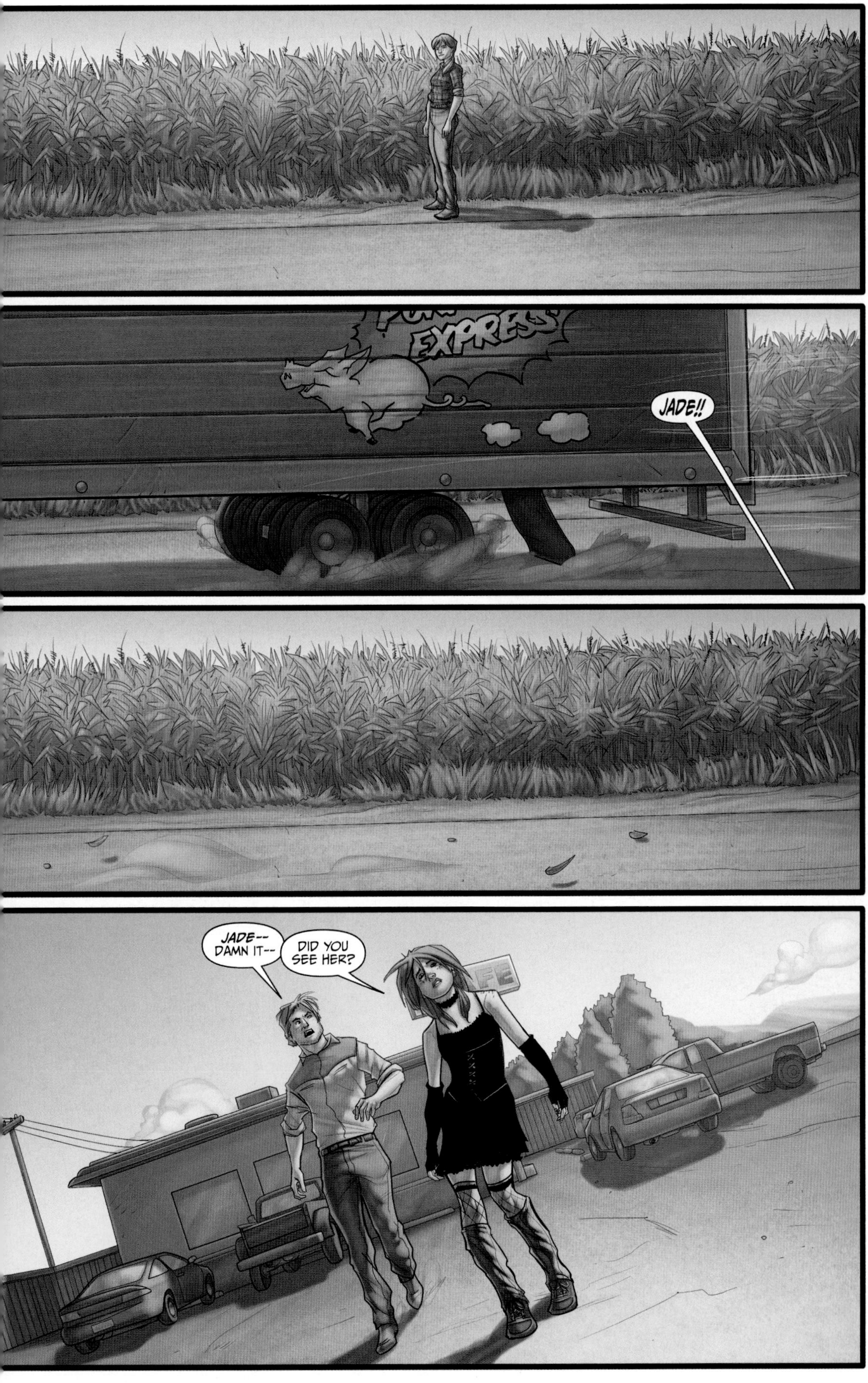
EXPRESS
JADE!!
JADE-- DAMN IT--
DID YOU SEE HER?

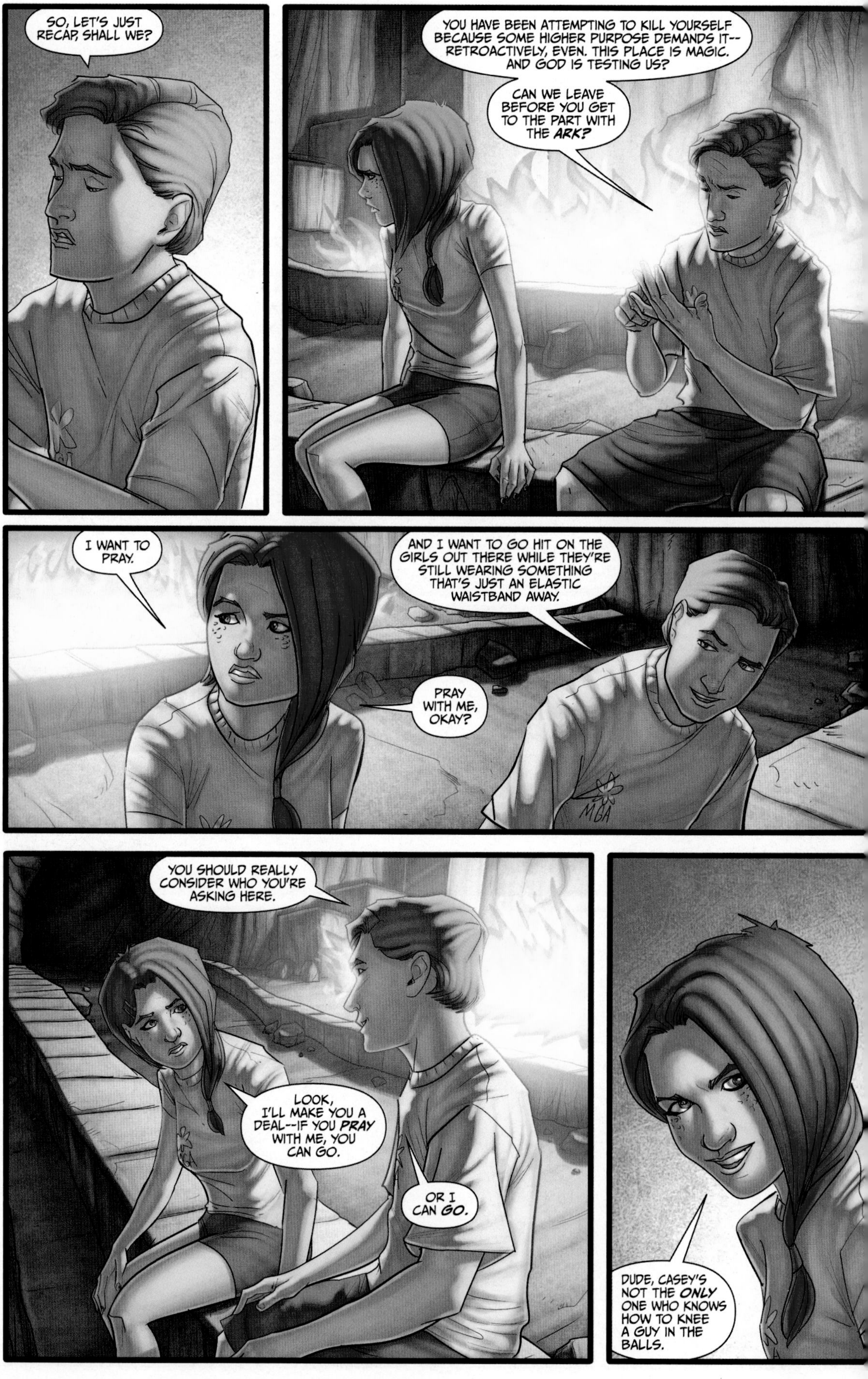
SO, LET'S JUST RECAP, SHALL WE?
YOU HAVE BEEN ATTEMPTING TO KILL YOURSELF BECAUSE SOME HIGHER PURPOSE DEMANDS IT-- RETROACTIVELY, EVEN. THIS PLACE IS MAGIC. AND GOD IS TESTING US?
CAN WE LEAVE BEFORE YOU GET TO THE PART WITH THE ARK?
I WANT TO PRAY.
AND I WANT TO GO HIT ON THE GIRLS OUT THERE WHILE THEY'RE STILL WEARING SOMETHING THAT'S JUST AN ELASTIC WAISTBAND AWAY.
PRAY WITH ME, OKAY?
MGA
YOU SHOULD REALLY CONSIDER WHO YOU'RE ASKING HERE.
LOOK, I'LL MAKE YOU A DEAL--IF YOU PRAY WITH ME, YOU CAN GO.
OR I CAN GO.
DUDE, CASEY'S NOT THE ONLY ONE WHO KNOWS HOW TO KNEE A GUY IN THE BALLS.

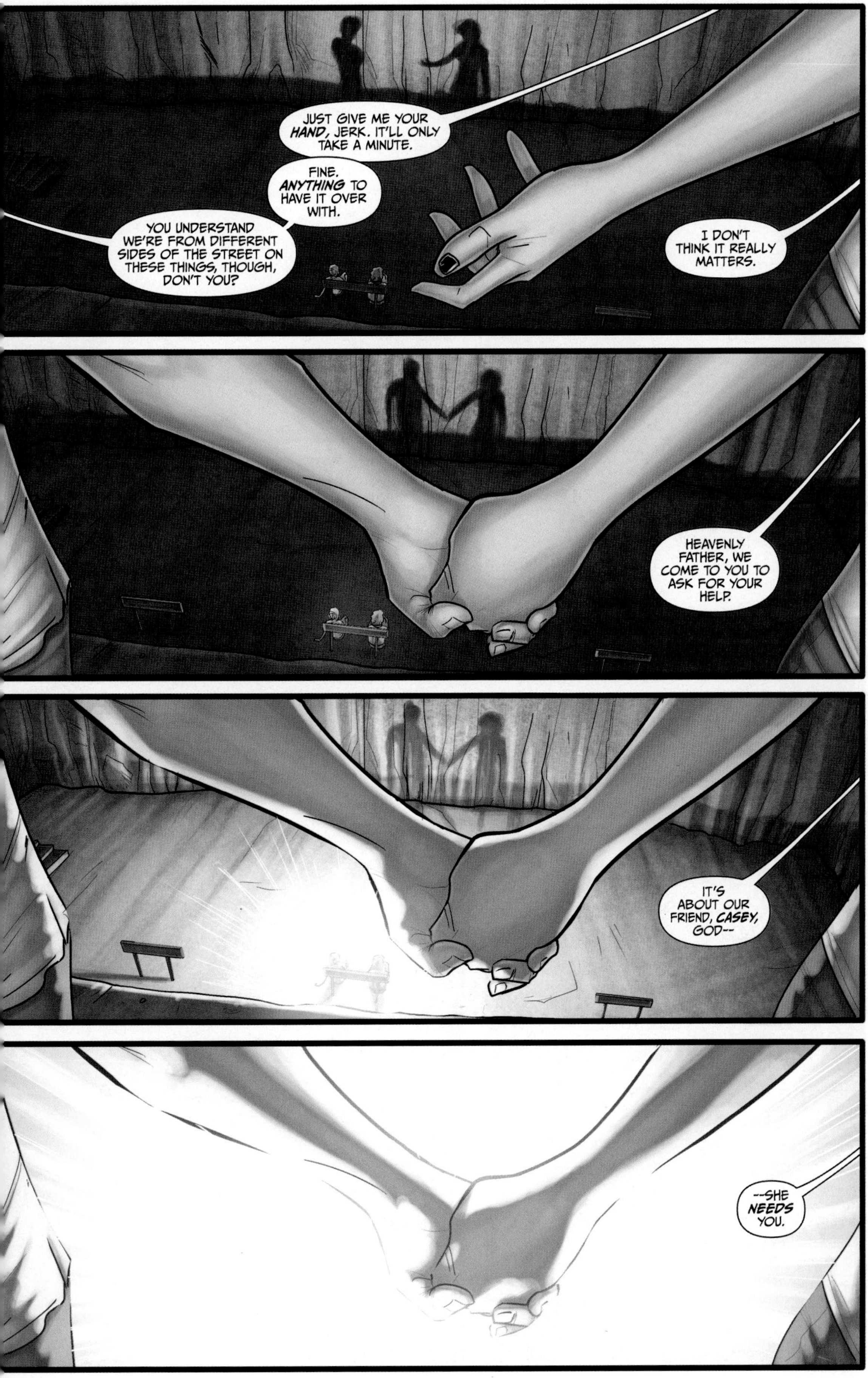

JUST GIVE ME YOUR HAND, JERK. IT'LL ONLY TAKE A MINUTE.
FINE. ANYTHING TO HAVE IT OVER WITH.
YOU UNDERSTAND WE'RE FROM DIFFERENT SIDES OF THE STREET ON THESE THINGS, THOUGH, DON'T YOU?
I DON'T THINK IT REALLY MATTERS.
HEAVENLY FATHER, WE COME TO YOU TO ASK FOR YOUR HELP.
IT'S ABOUT OUR FRIEND, CASEY, GOD--
--SHE NEEDS YOU.

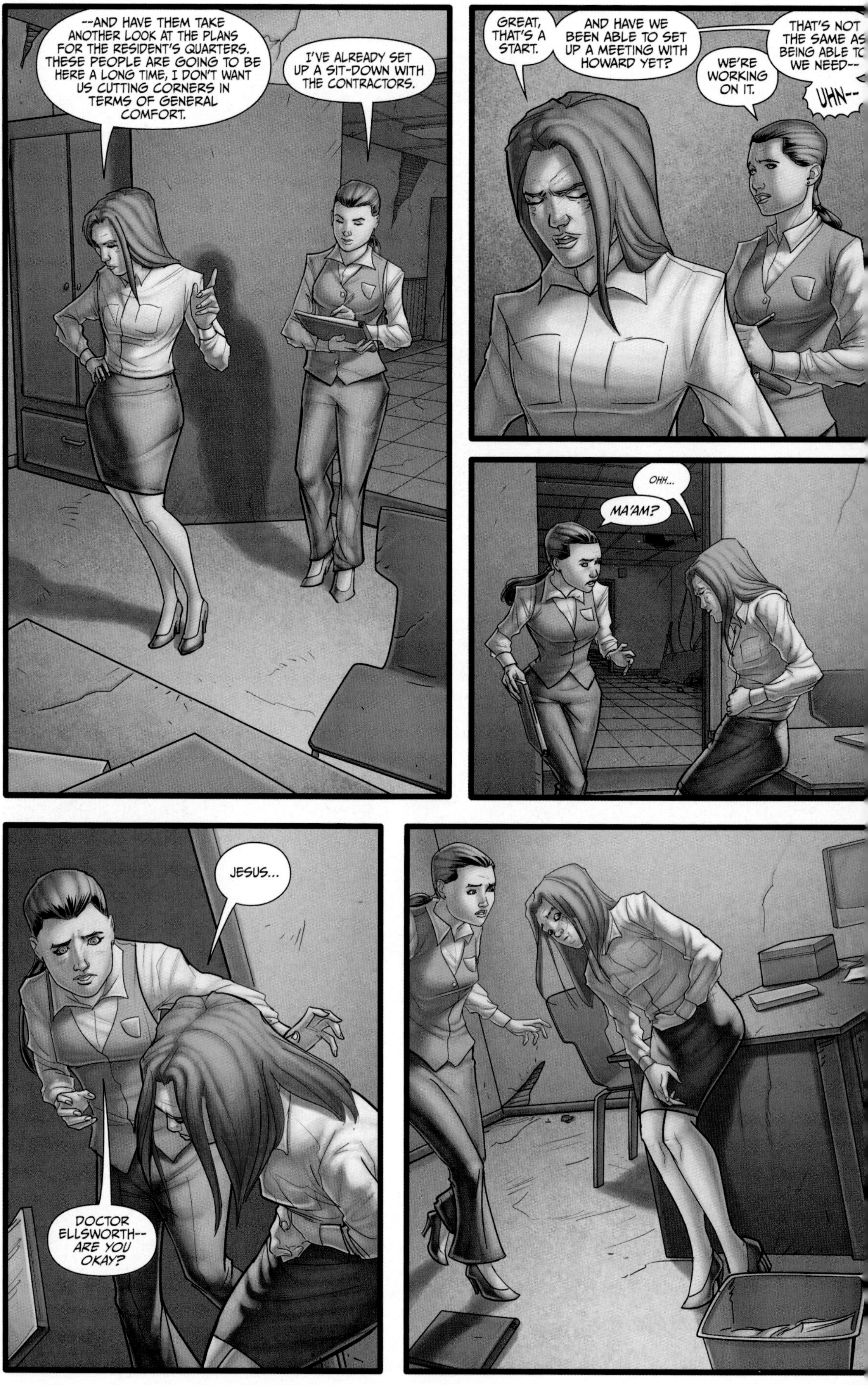
--AND HAVE THEM TAKE ANOTHER LOOK AT THE PLANS FOR THE RESIDENT'S QUARTERS. THESE PEOPLE ARE GOING TO BE HERE A LONG TIME, I DON'T WANT US CUTTING CORNERS IN TERMS OF GENERAL COMFORT.
I'VE ALREADY SET UP A SIT-DOWN WITH THE CONTRACTORS.
GREAT, THAT'S A START.
AND HAVE WE BEEN ABLE TO SET UP A MEETING WITH HOWARD YET?
WE'RE WORKING ON IT.
THAT'S NOT THE SAME AS BEING ABLE TO WE NEED--
UHN--
OHH...
MA'AM?
JESUS...
DOCTOR ELLSWORTH-- ARE YOU OKAY?

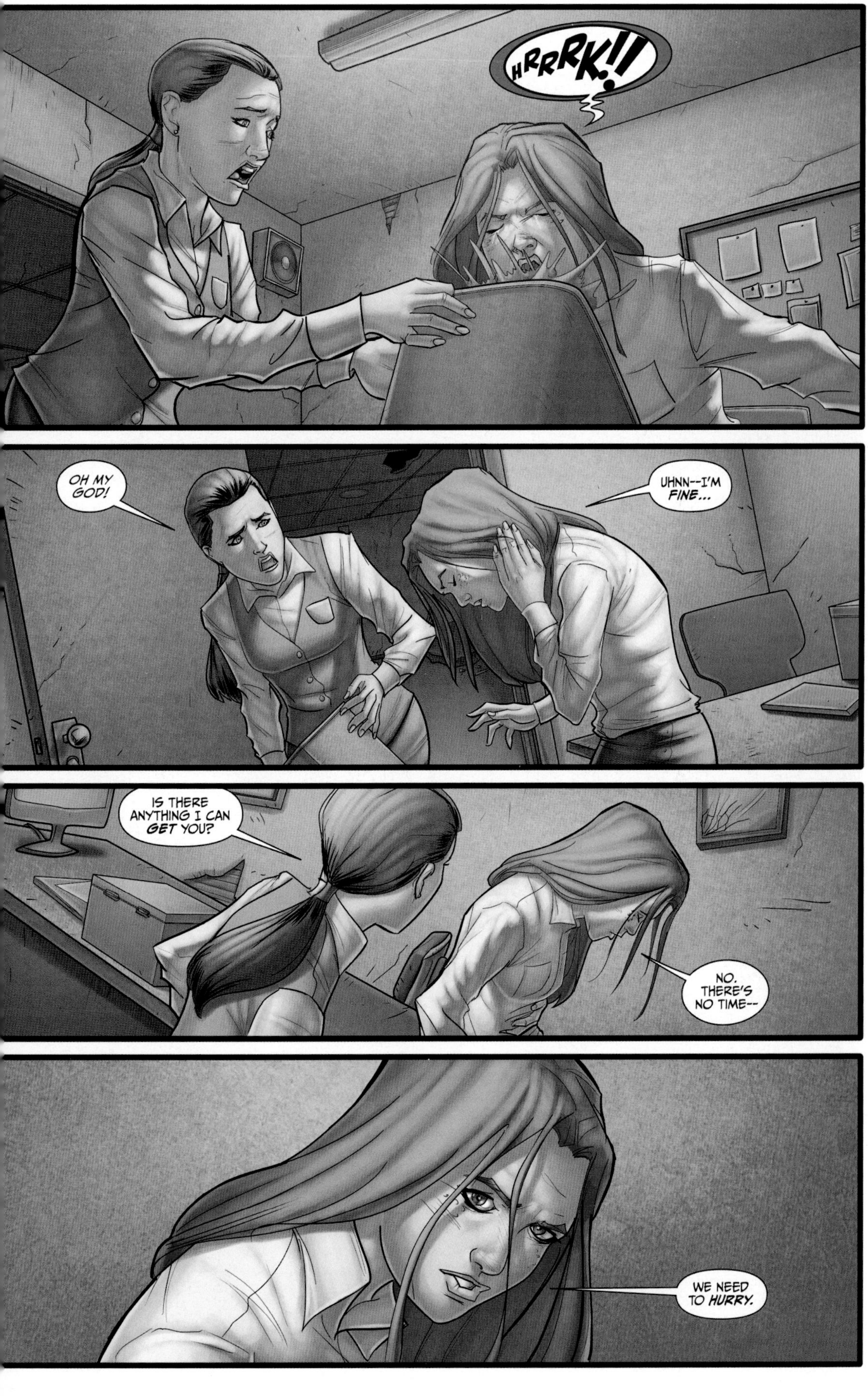
HRRRK!!
OH MY GOD!
UHNN--I'M FINE...
IS THERE ANYTHING I CAN GET YOU?
NO. THERE'S NO TIME--
WE NEED TO HURRY.

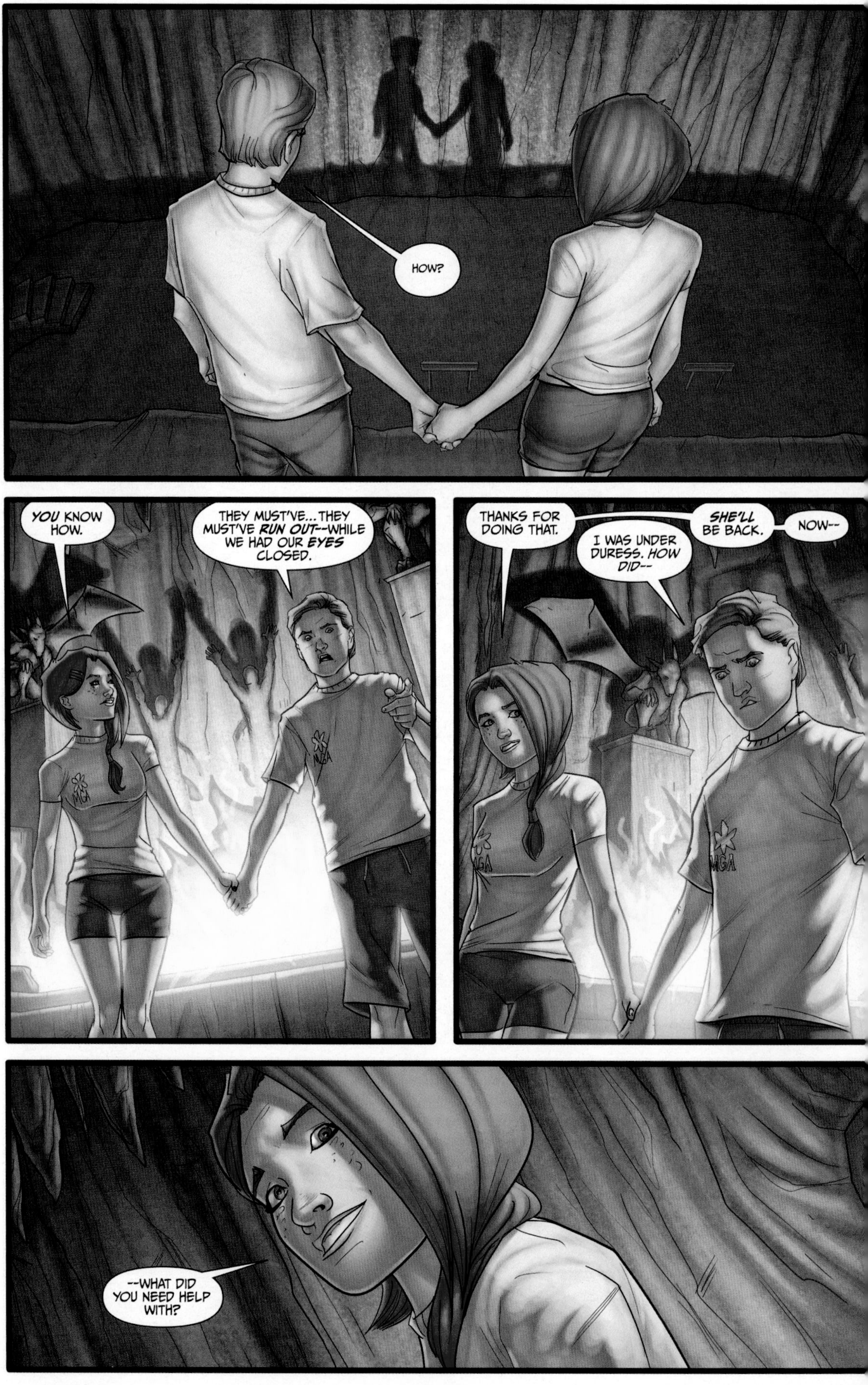
HOW?
YOU KNOW HOW.
THEY MUST'VE... THEY MUST'VE RUN OUT--WHILE WE HAD OUR EYES CLOSED.
THANKS FOR DOING THAT.
I WAS UNDER DURESS. HOW DID--
SHE'LL BE BACK.
NOW--
--WHAT DID YOU NEED HELP WITH?

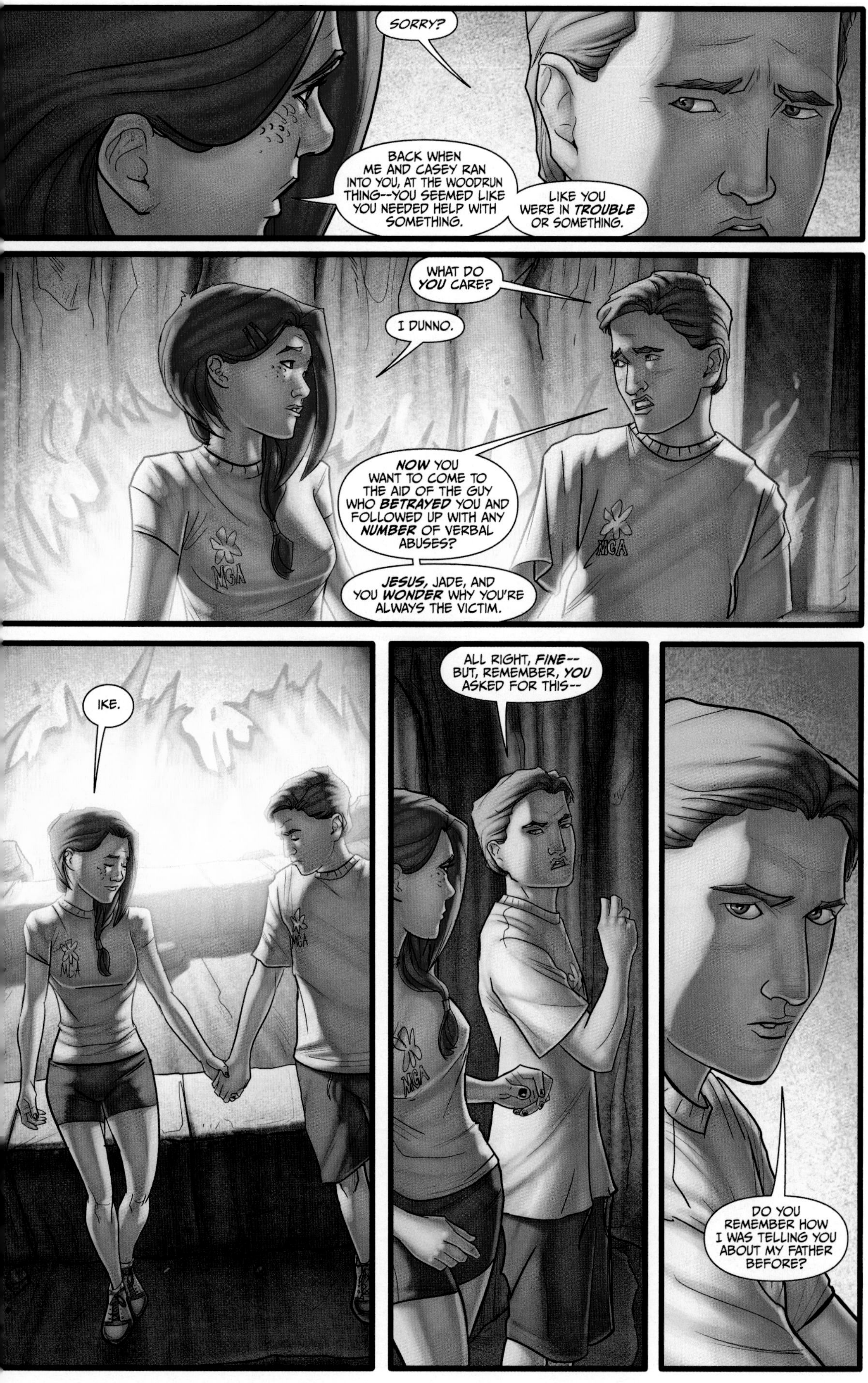
SORRY?
BACK WHEN ME AND CASEY RAN INTO YOU, AT THE WOODRUN THING--YOU SEEMED LIKE YOU NEEDED HELP WITH SOMETHING.
LIKE YOU WERE IN TROUBLE OR SOMETHING.
WHAT DO YOU CARE?
I DUNNO.
NOW YOU WANT TO COME TO THE AID OF THE GUY WHO BETRAYED YOU AND FOLLOWED UP WITH ANY NUMBER OF VERBAL ABUSES?
JESUS, JADE, AND YOU WONDER WHY YOU'RE ALWAYS THE VICTIM.
IKE.
ALL RIGHT, FINE-- BUT, REMEMBER, YOU ASKED FOR THIS--
DO YOU REMEMBER HOW I WAS TELLING YOU ABOUT MY FATHER BEFORE?

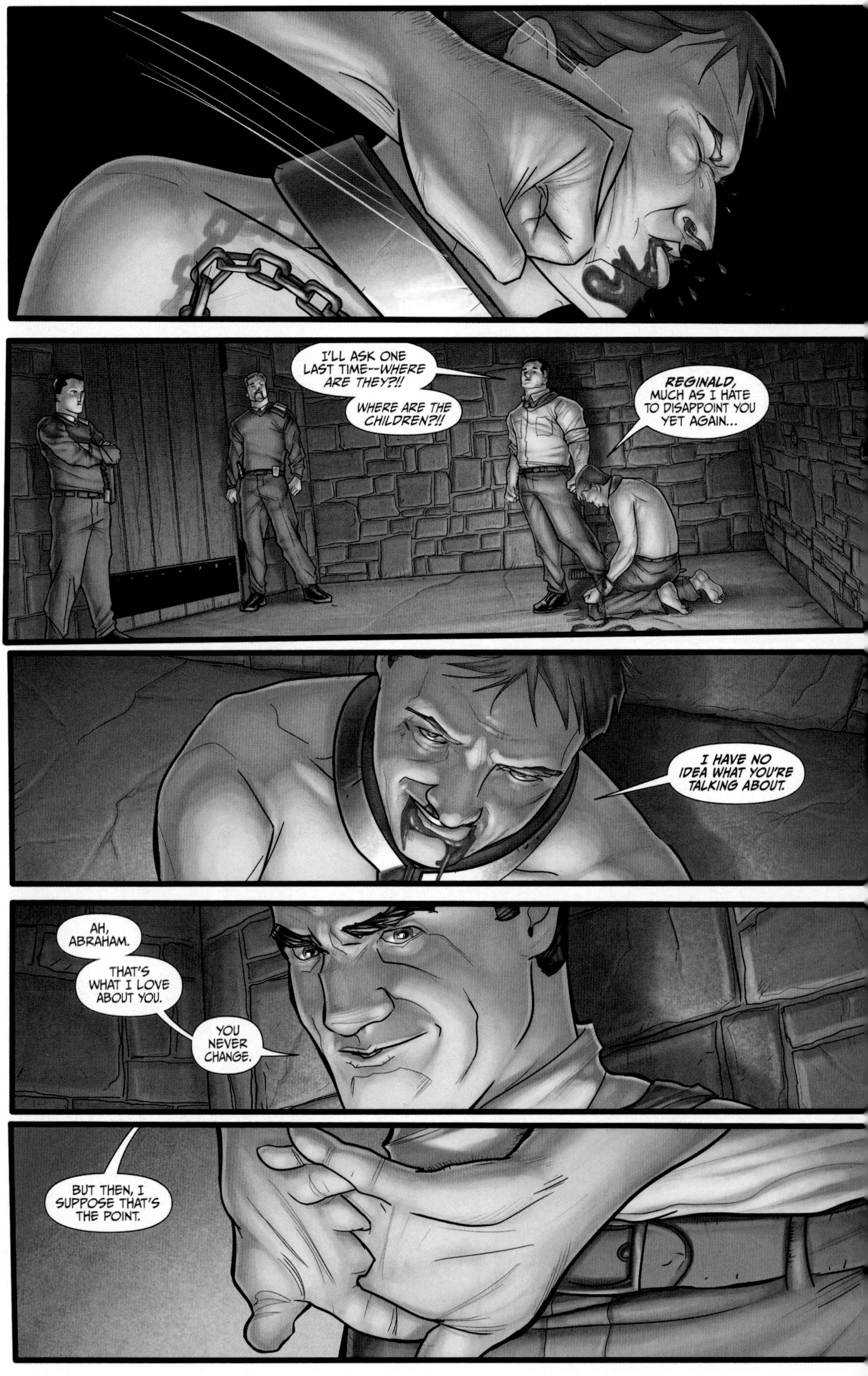
I'LL ASK ONE LAST TIME--WHERE ARE THEY?!!
WHERE ARE THE CHILDREN?!!
REGINALD, MUCH AS I HATE TO DISAPPOINT YOU YET AGAIN...
I HAVE NO IDEA WHAT YOU'RE TALKING ABOUT.
AH, ABRAHAM.
THAT'S WHAT I LOVE ABOUT YOU.
YOU NEVER CHANGE.
BUT THEN, I SUPPOSE THAT'S THE POINT.

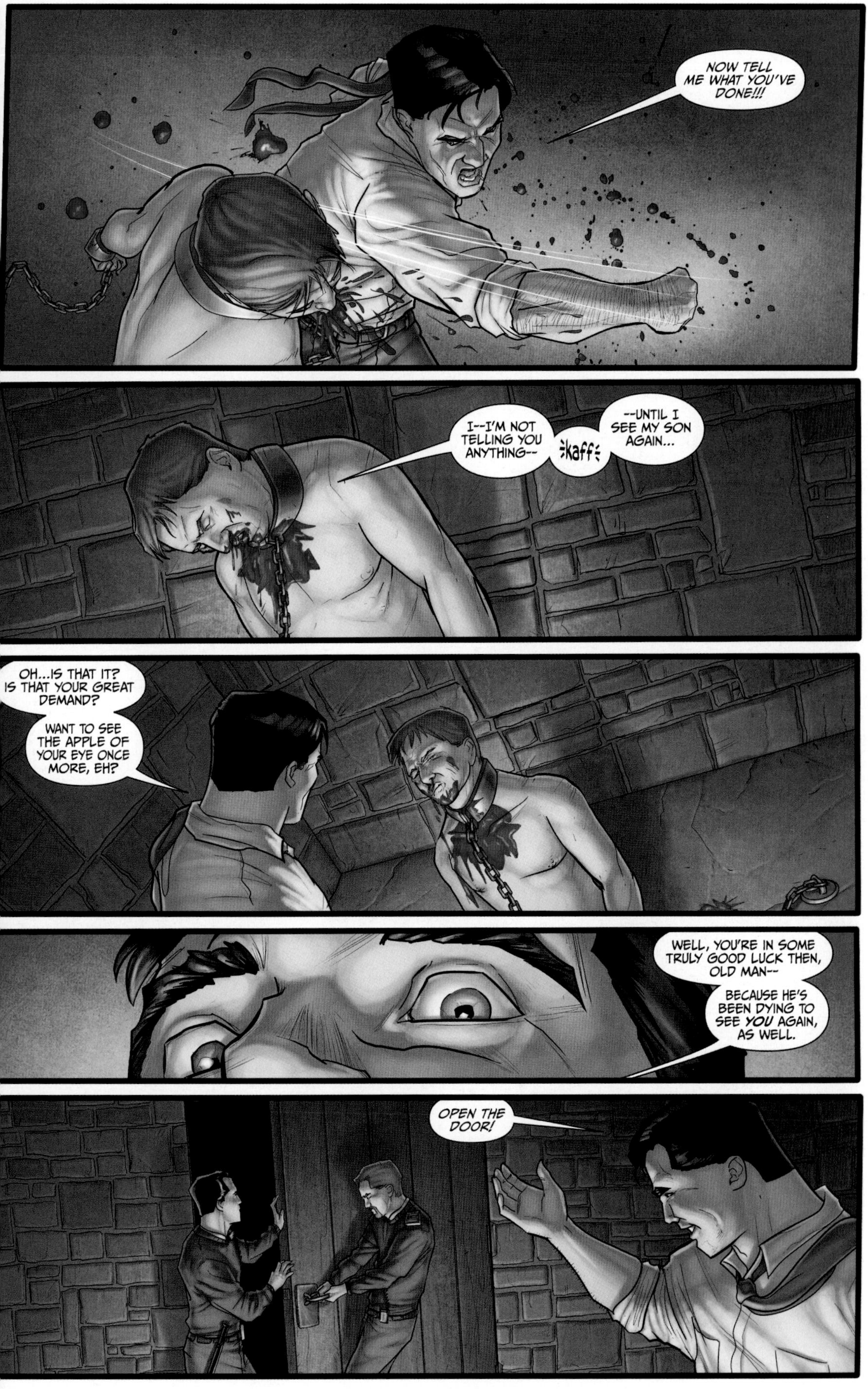
NOW TELL ME WHAT YOU'VE DONE!!!
I--I'M NOT TELLING YOU ANYTHING--
kaff
--UNTIL I SEE MY SON AGAIN...
OH...IS THAT IT? IS THAT YOUR GREAT DEMAND?
WANT TO SEE THE APPLE OF YOUR EYE ONCE MORE, EH?
WELL, YOU'RE IN SOME TRULY GOOD LUCK THEN, OLD MAN--
BECAUSE HE'S BEEN DYING TO SEE YOU AGAIN, AS WELL.
OPEN THE DOOR!

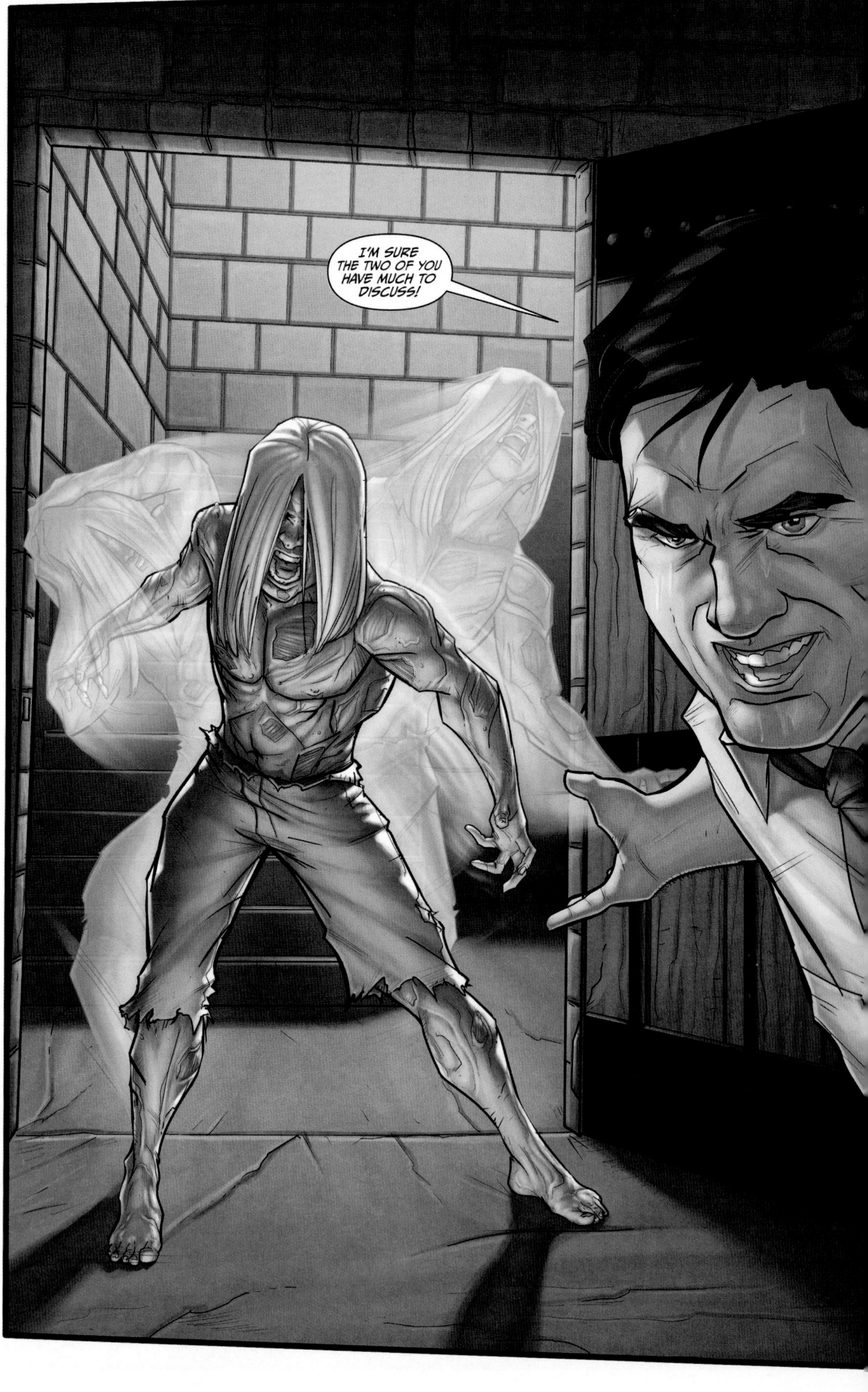
I'M SURE THE TWO OF YOU HAVE MUCH TO DISCUSS!

eighteen

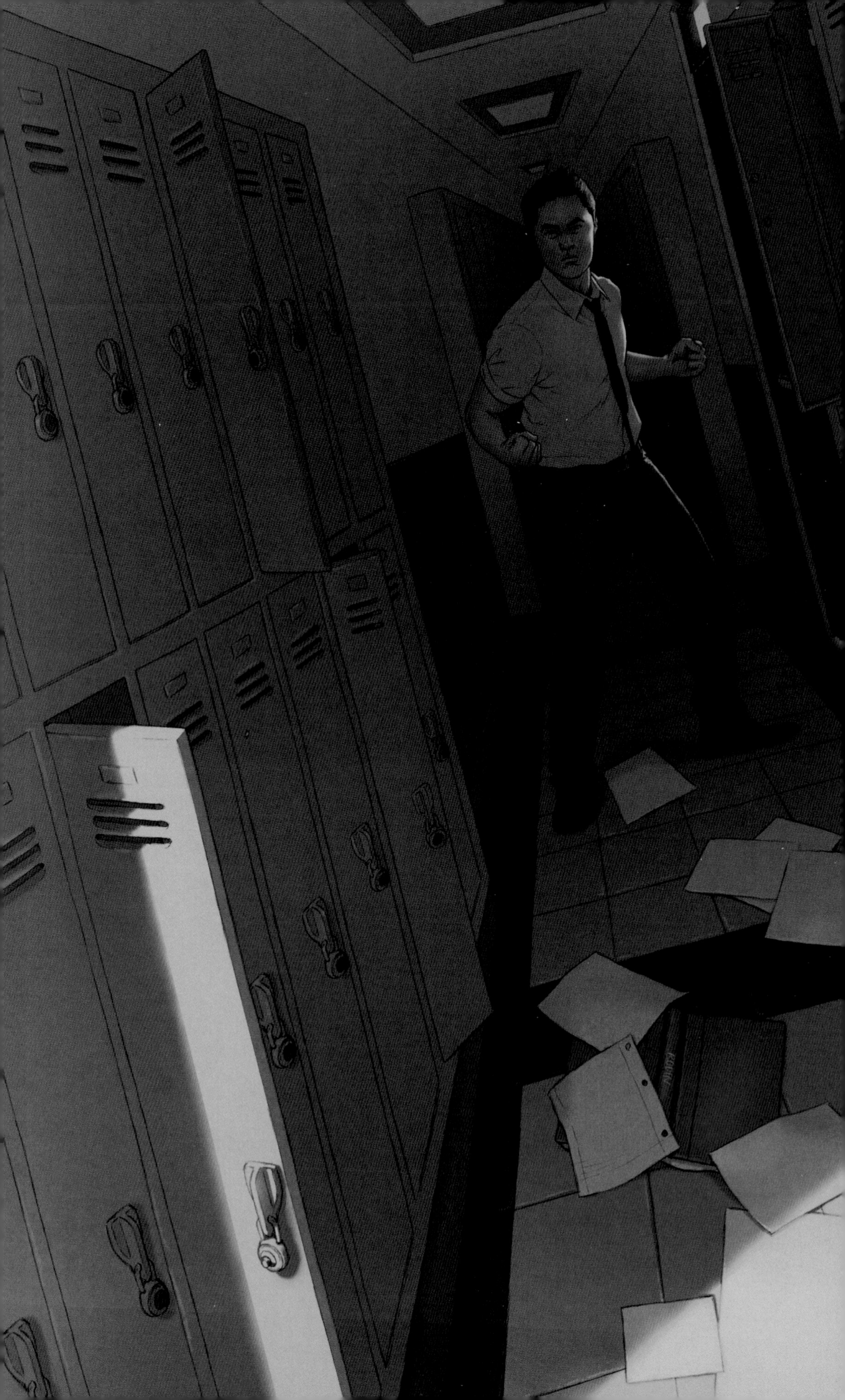

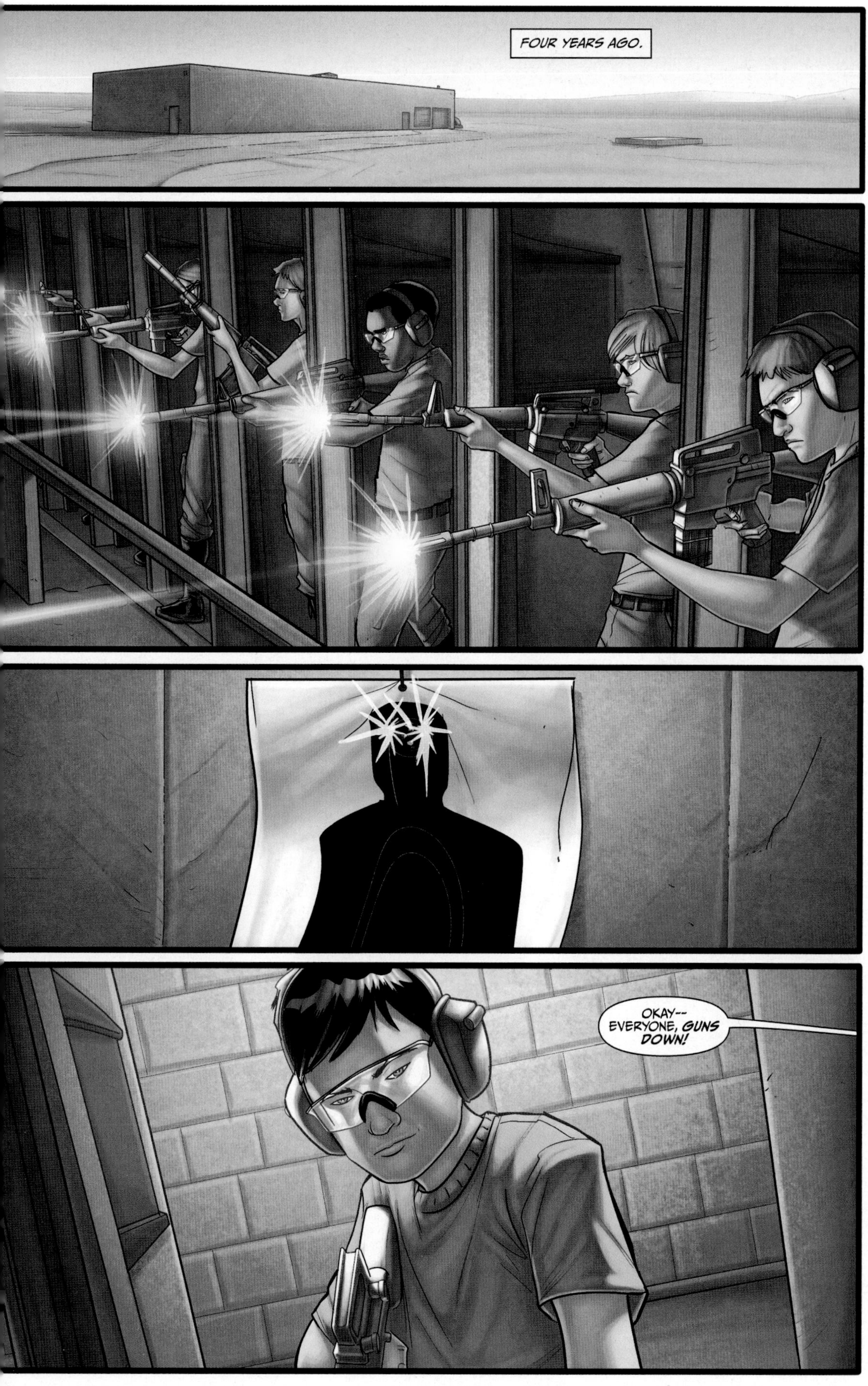
FOUR YEARS AGO.
OKAY-- EVERYONE, GUNS DOWN!

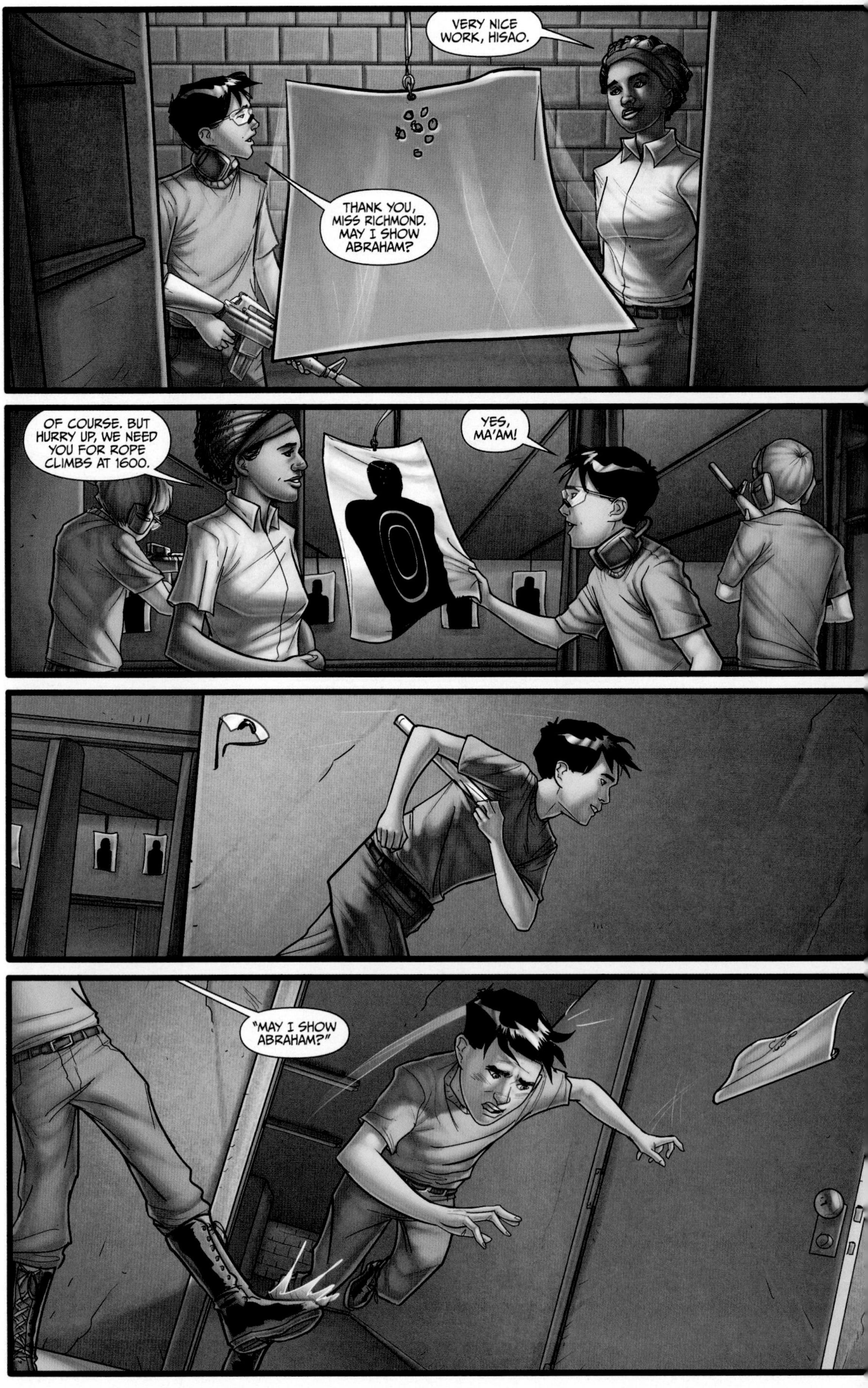
VERY NICE WORK, HISAO.
THANK YOU, MISS RICHMOND. MAY I SHOW ABRAHAM?
OF COURSE. BUT HURRY UP, WE NEED YOU FOR ROPE CLIMBS AT 1600.
YES, MA'AM!
"MAY I SHOW ABRAHAM?"

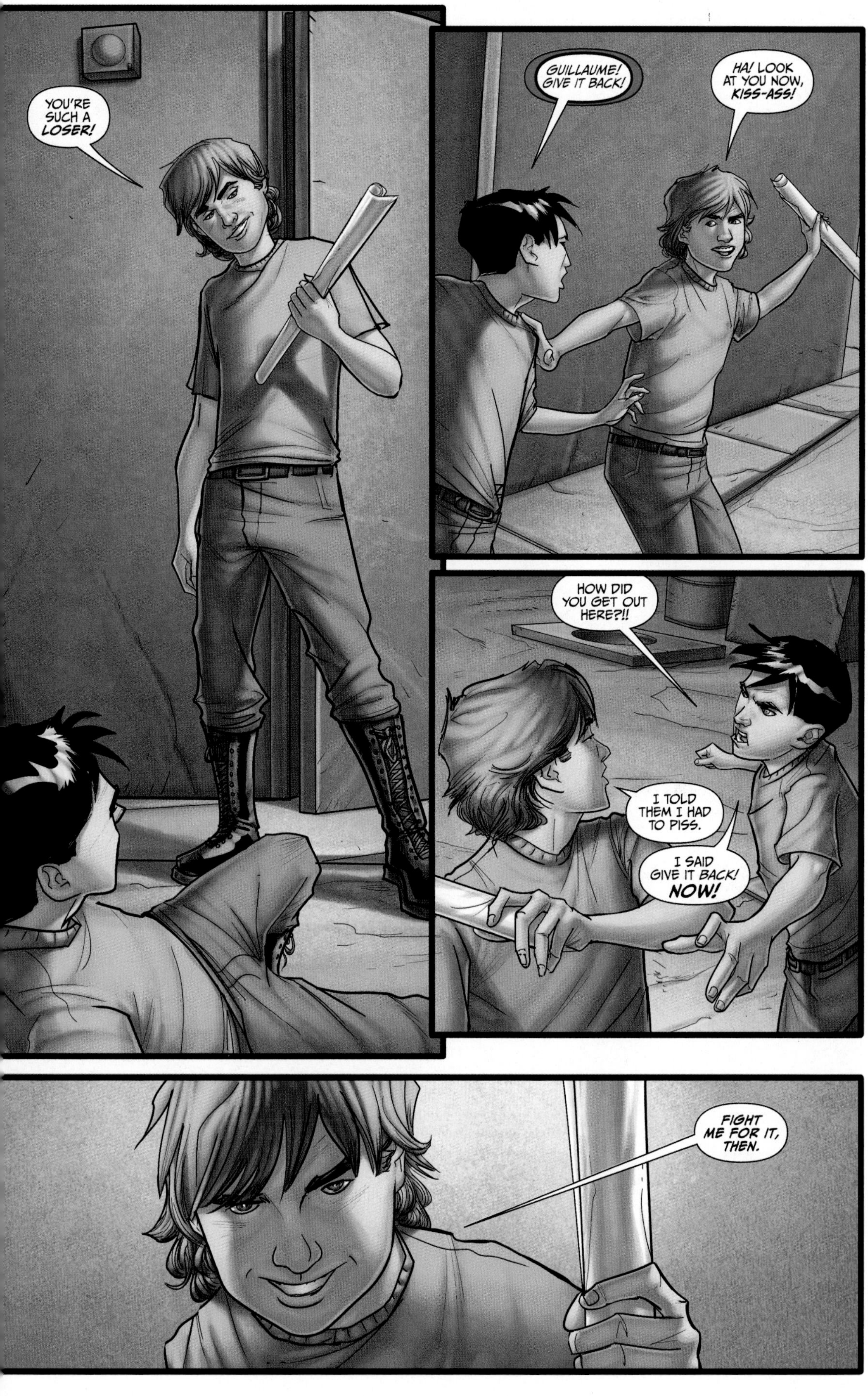
YOU'RE SUCH A LOSER!
GUILLAUME! GIVE IT BACK!
HA! LOOK AT YOU NOW, KISS-ASS!
HOW DID YOU GET OUT HERE?!!
I TOLD THEM I HAD TO PISS.
I SAID GIVE IT BACK! NOW!
FIGHT ME FOR IT, THEN.

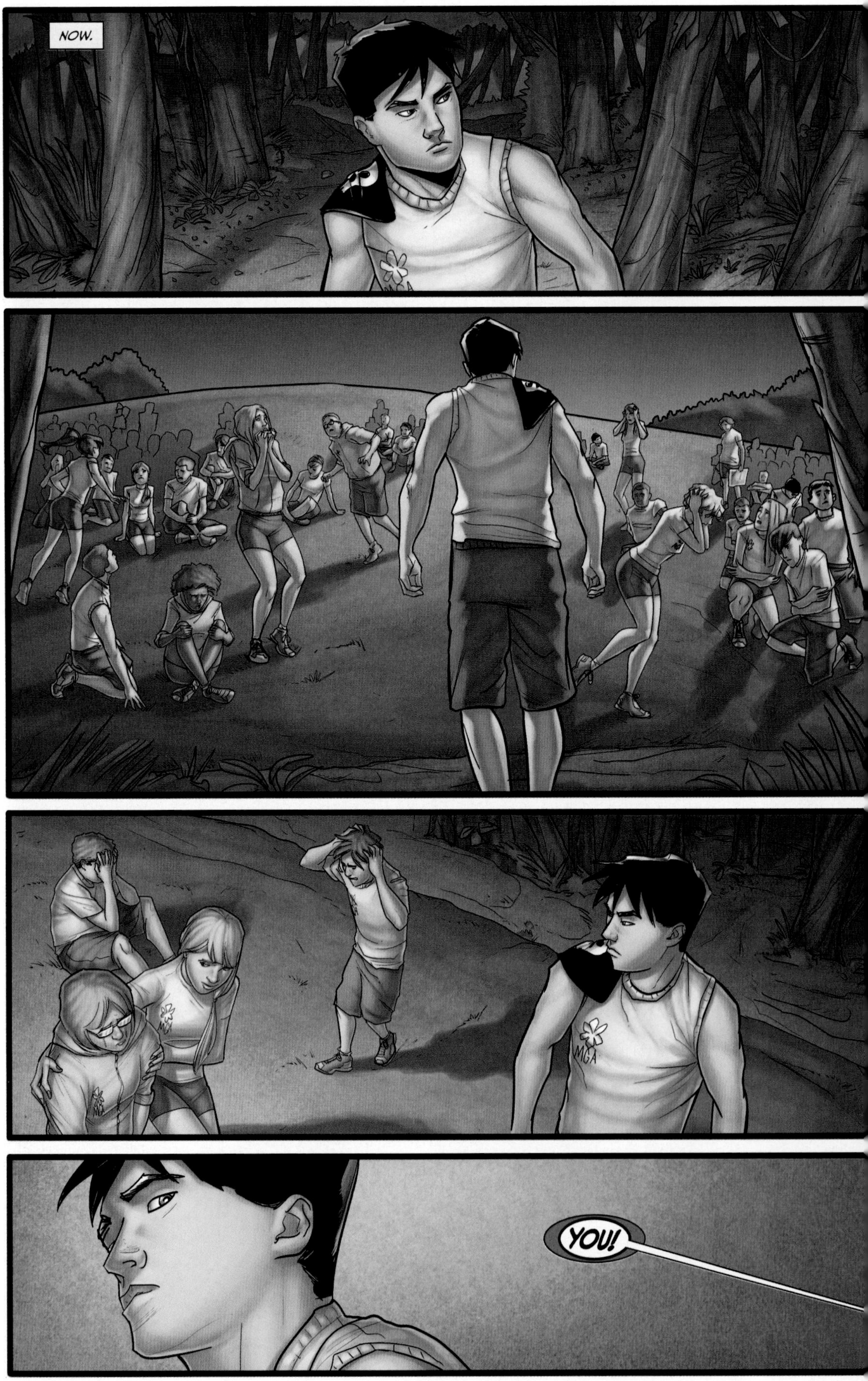
NOW.
YOU!

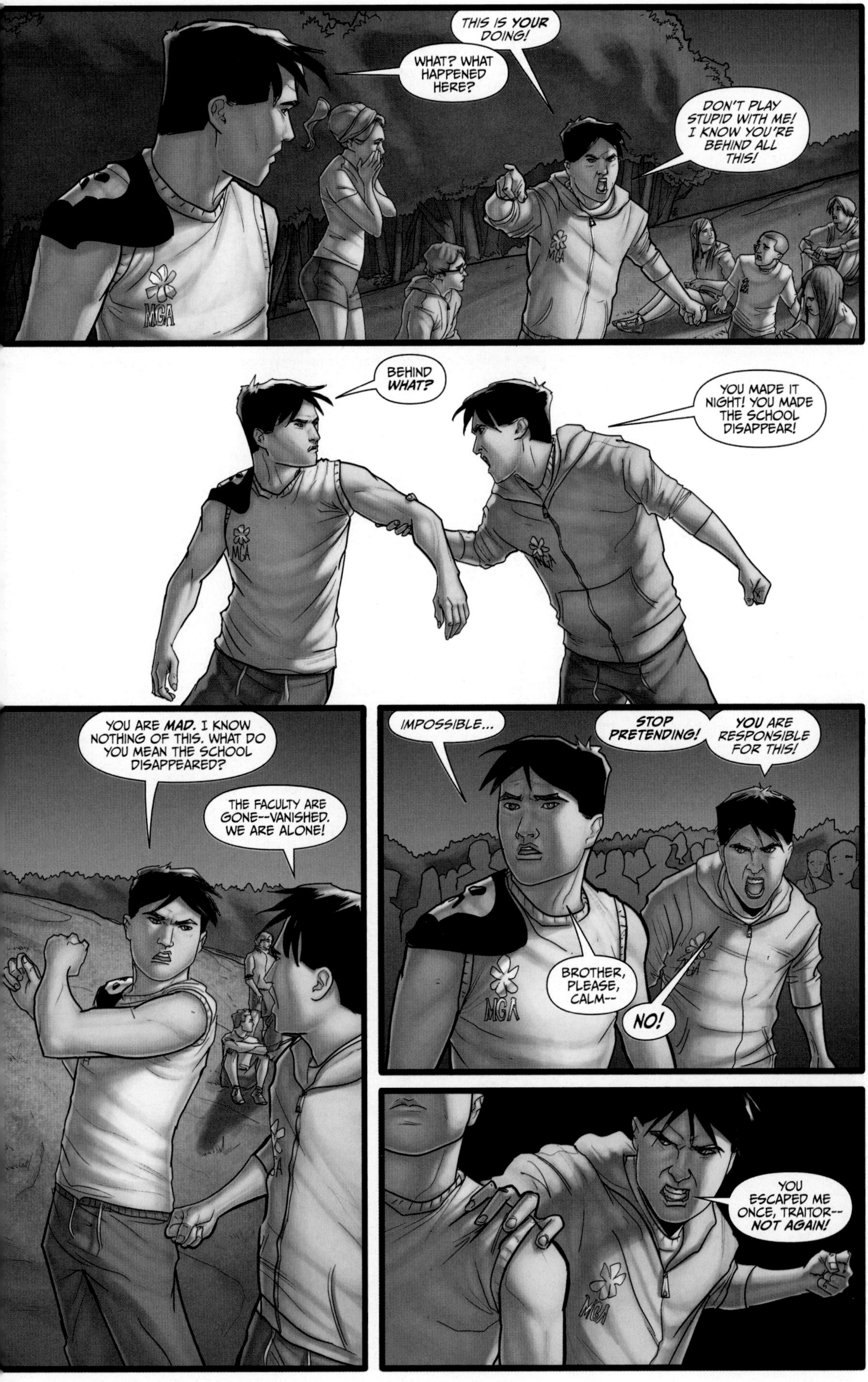
WHAT? WHAT HAPPENED HERE?
THIS IS YOUR DOING!
DON'T PLAY STUPID WITH ME! I KNOW YOU'RE BEHIND ALL THIS!
BEHIND WHAT?
YOU MADE IT NIGHT! YOU MADE THE SCHOOL DISAPPEAR!
YOU ARE MAD. I KNOW NOTHING OF THIS. WHAT DO YOU MEAN THE SCHOOL DISAPPEARED?
THE FACULTY ARE GONE--VANISHED. WE ARE ALONE!
IMPOSSIBLE...
STOP PRETENDING!
YOU ARE RESPONSIBLE FOR THIS!
BROTHER, PLEASE, CALM--
NO!
YOU ESCAPED ME ONCE, TRAITOR-- NOT AGAIN!

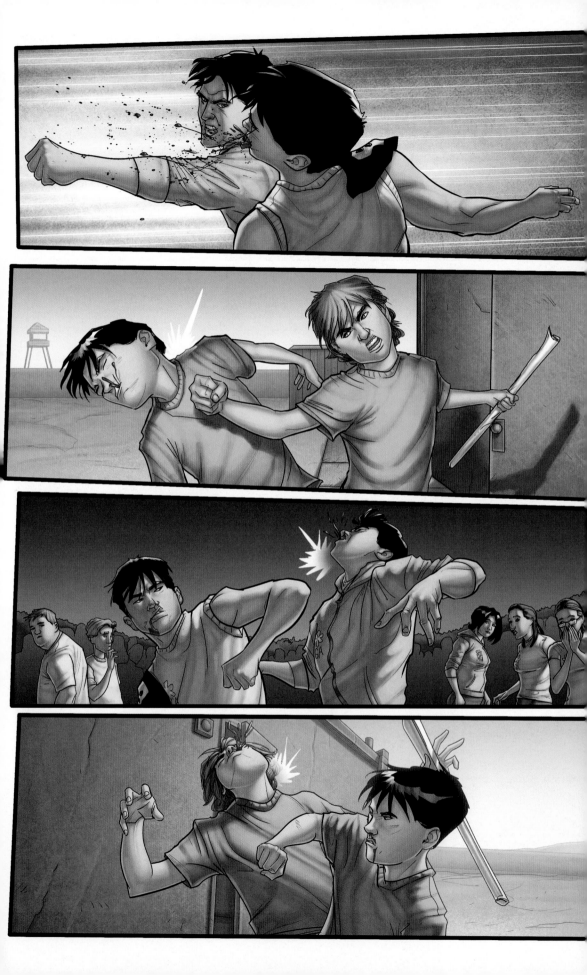

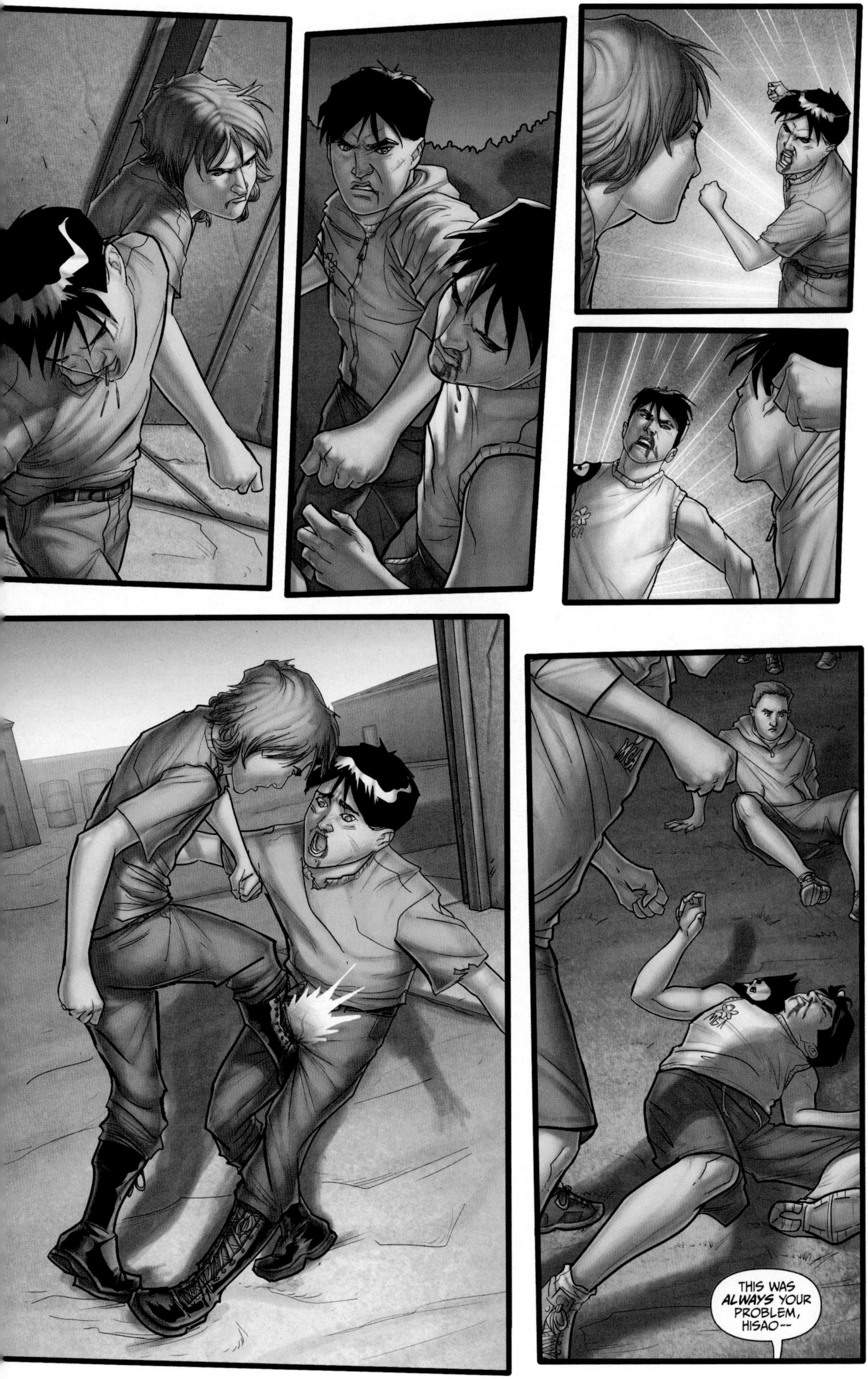
THIS WAS
ALWAYS YOUR
PROBLEM,
HISAO--

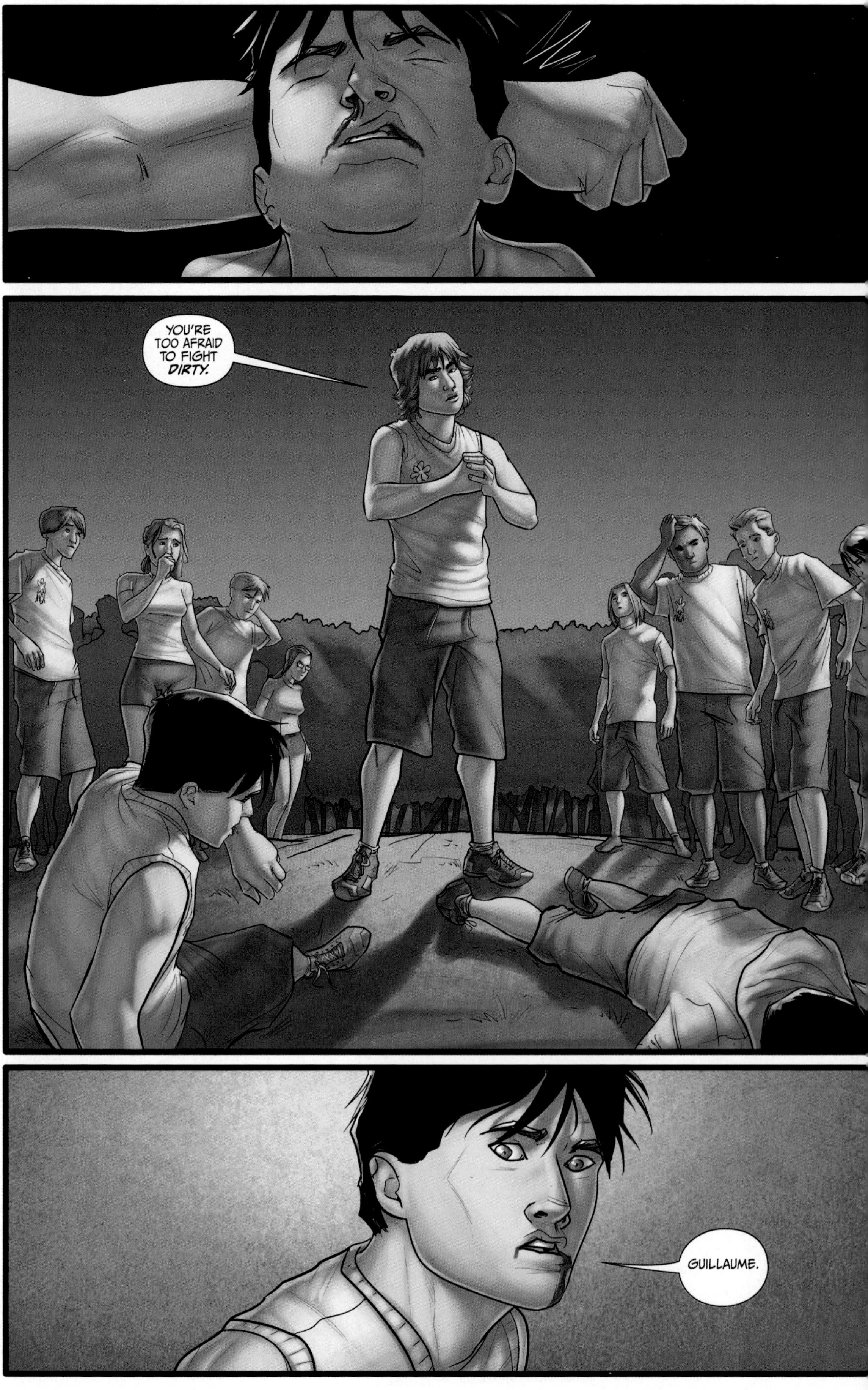
YOU'RE TOO AFRAID TO FIGHT DIRTY.
GUILLAUME.

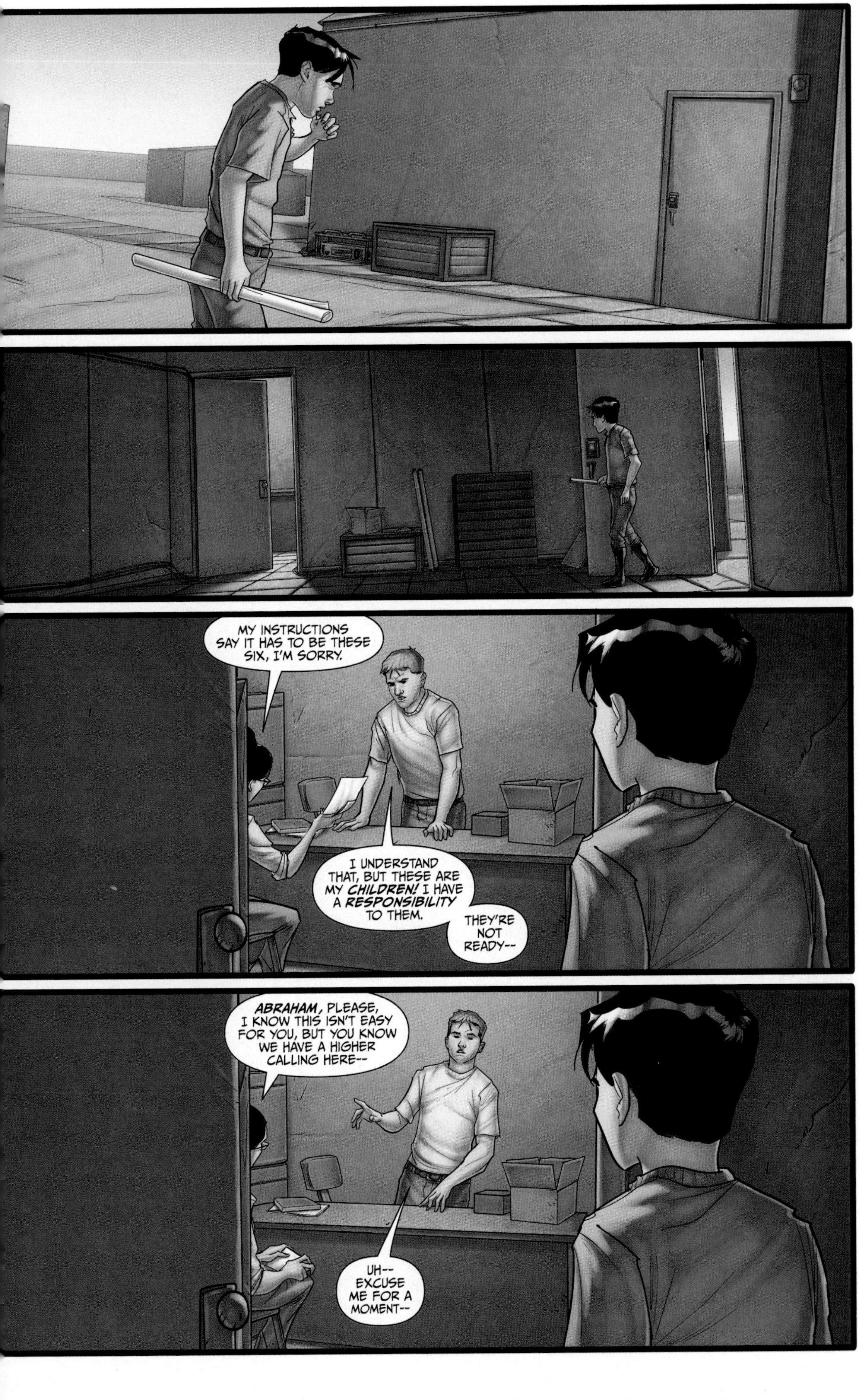

MY INSTRUCTIONS SAY IT HAS TO BE THESE SIX, I'M SORRY.
I UNDERSTAND THAT, BUT THESE ARE MY *CHILDREN!* I HAVE A *RESPONSIBILITY* TO THEM.
THEY'RE NOT READY--
ABRAHAM, PLEASE, I KNOW THIS ISN'T EASY FOR YOU, BUT YOU KNOW WE HAVE A HIGHER CALLING HERE--
UH-- EXCUSE ME FOR A MOMENT--

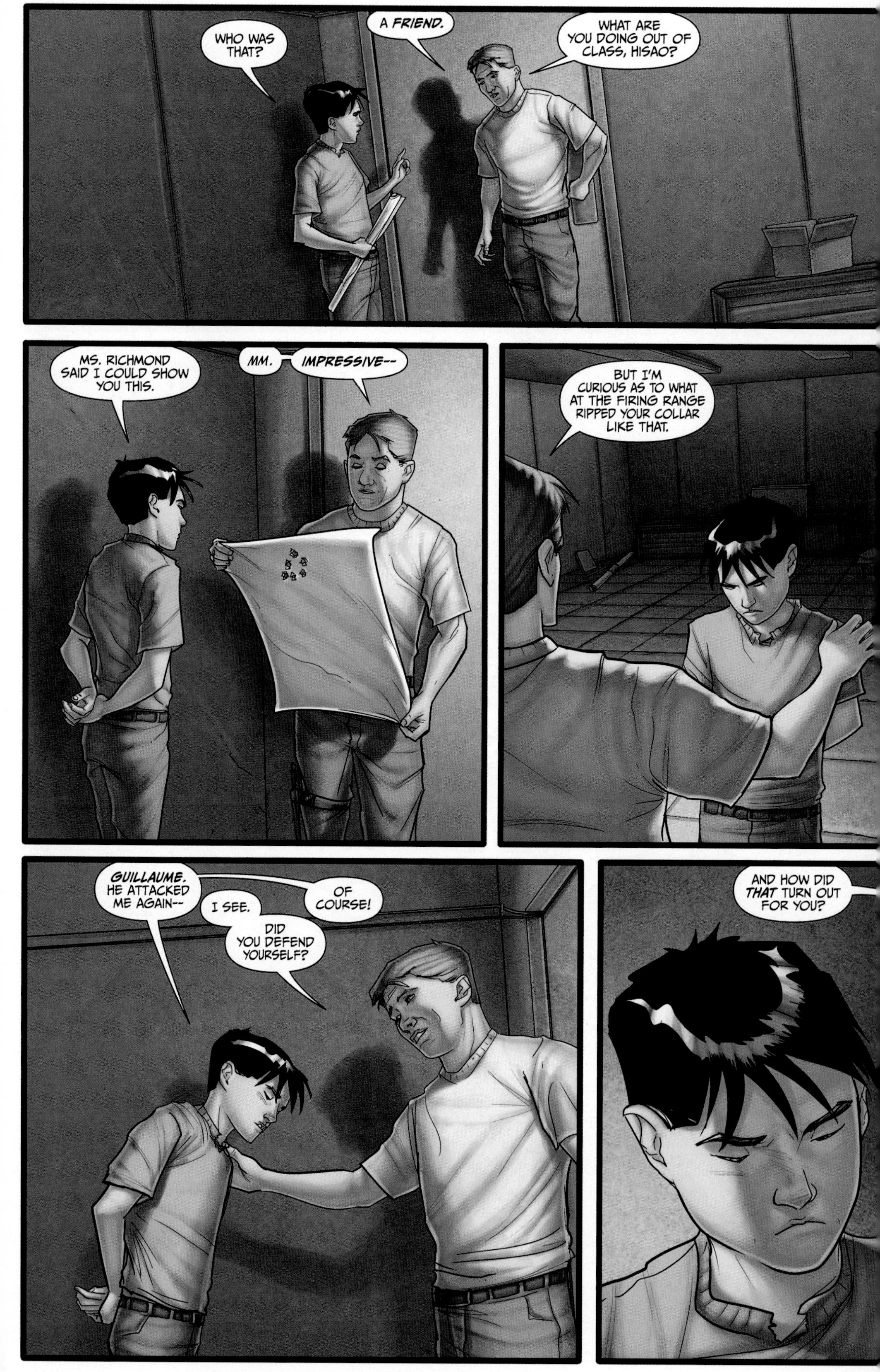

WHO WAS THAT?
A FRIEND.
WHAT ARE YOU DOING OUT OF CLASS, HISAO?
MS. RICHMOND SAID I COULD SHOW YOU THIS.
MM.
IMPRESSIVE--
BUT I'M CURIOUS AS TO WHAT AT THE FIRING RANGE RIPPED YOUR COLLAR LIKE THAT.
GUILLAUME. HE ATTACKED ME AGAIN--
OF COURSE!
I SEE.
DID YOU DEFEND YOURSELF?
AND HOW DID THAT TURN OUT FOR YOU?

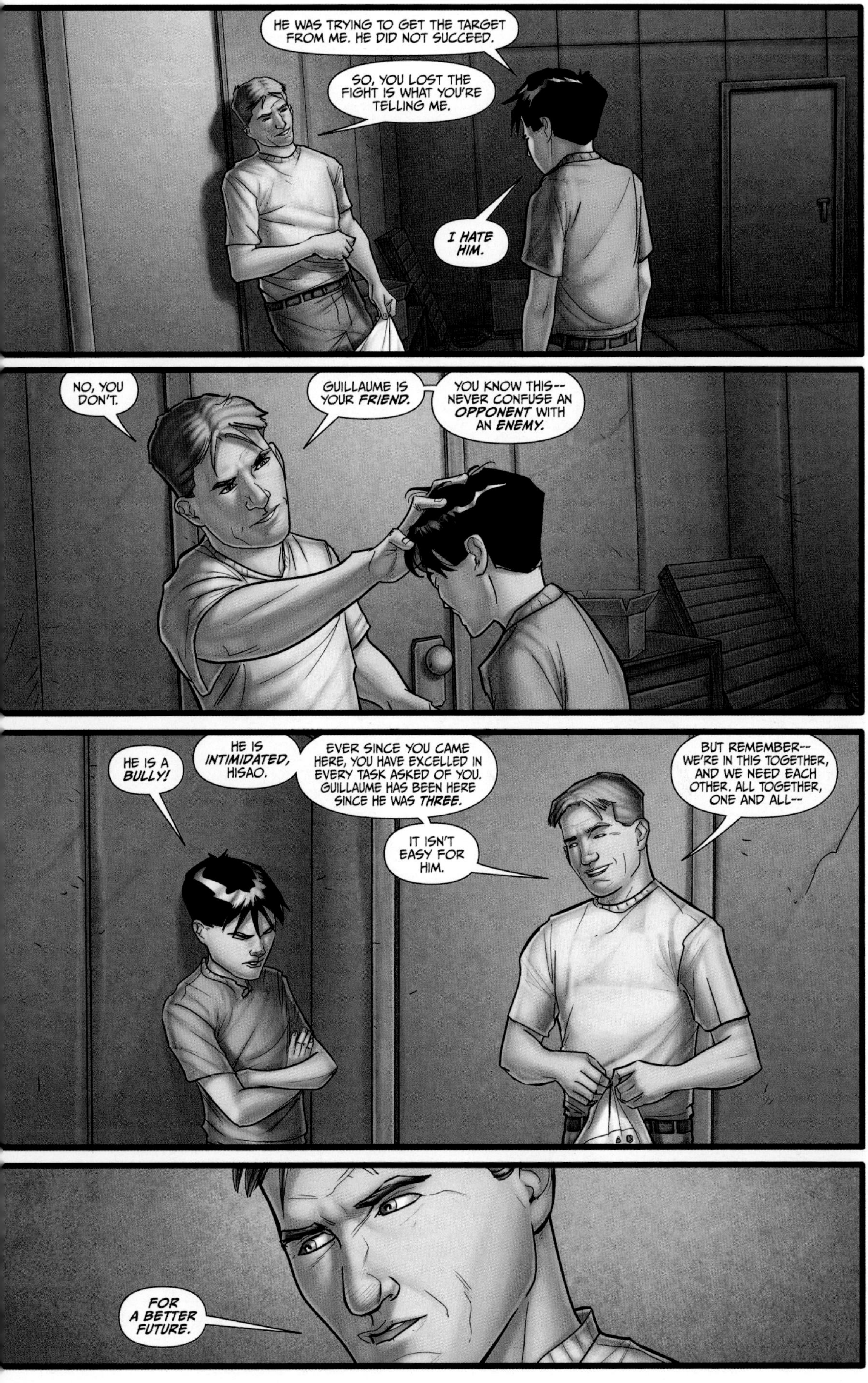
HE WAS TRYING TO GET THE TARGET FROM ME. HE DID NOT SUCCEED.
SO, YOU LOST THE FIGHT IS WHAT YOU'RE TELLING ME.
I HATE HIM.
NO, YOU DON'T.
GUILLAUME IS YOUR FRIEND.
YOU KNOW THIS--NEVER CONFUSE AN OPPONENT WITH AN ENEMY.
HE IS A BULLY!
HE IS INTIMIDATED, HISAO.
EVER SINCE YOU CAME HERE, YOU HAVE EXCELLED IN EVERY TASK ASKED OF YOU. GUILLAUME HAS BEEN HERE SINCE HE WAS THREE.
IT ISN'T EASY FOR HIM.
BUT REMEMBER--WE'RE IN THIS TOGETHER, AND WE NEED EACH OTHER. ALL TOGETHER, ONE AND ALL--
FOR A BETTER FUTURE.

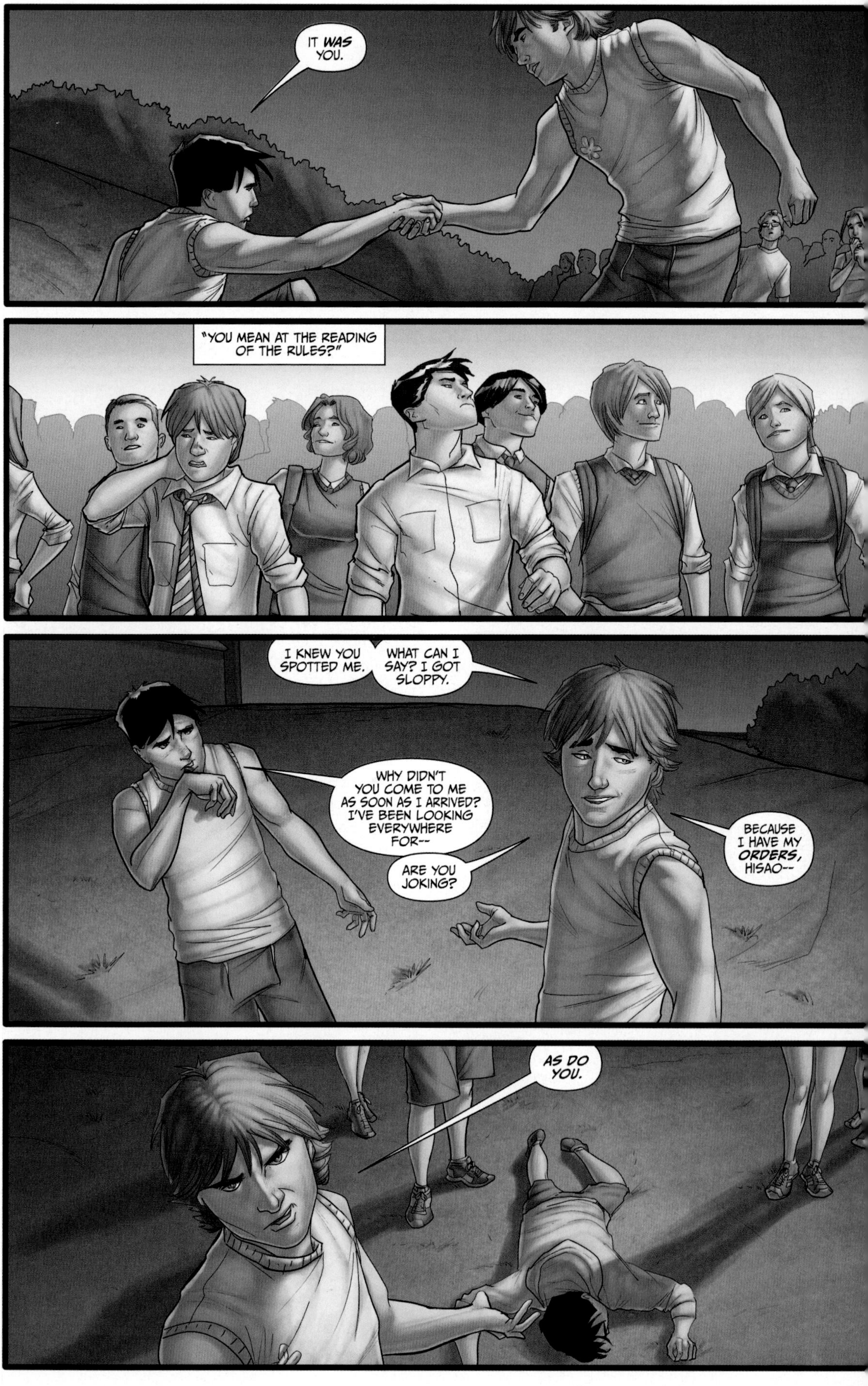
IT WAS YOU.
"YOU MEAN AT THE READING OF THE RULES?"
I KNEW YOU SPOTTED ME.
WHAT CAN I SAY? I GOT SLOPPY.
WHY DIDN'T YOU COME TO ME AS SOON AS I ARRIVED? I'VE BEEN LOOKING EVERYWHERE FOR--
BECAUSE I HAVE MY ORDERS, HISAO--
ARE YOU JOKING?
AS DO YOU.

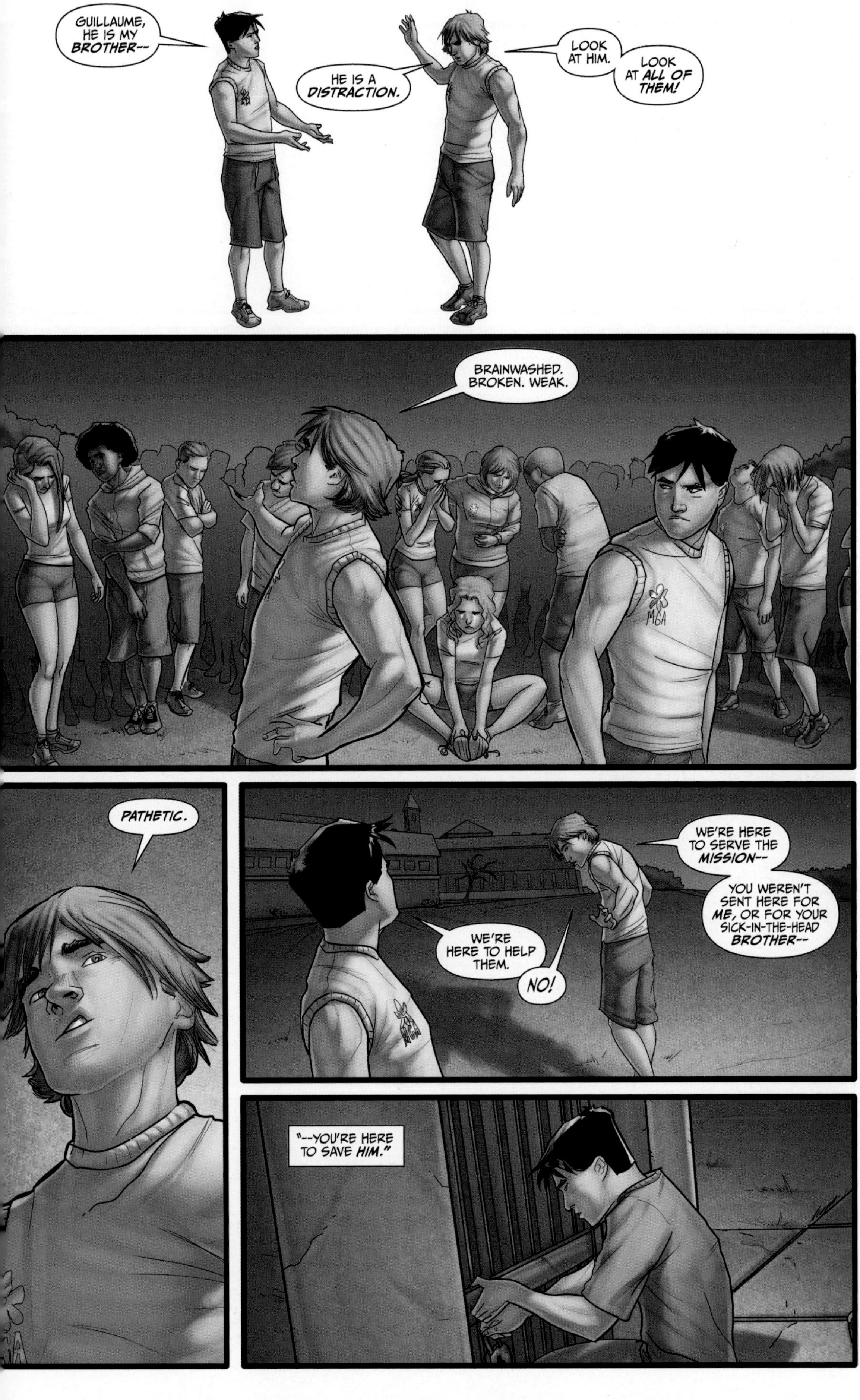
GUILLAUME, HE IS MY BROTHER--
HE IS A DISTRACTION.
LOOK AT HIM.
LOOK AT ALL OF THEM!
BRAINWASHED. BROKEN. WEAK.
PATHETIC.
WE'RE HERE TO HELP THEM.
NO!
WE'RE HERE TO SERVE THE MISSION--
YOU WEREN'T SENT HERE FOR ME, OR FOR YOUR SICK-IN-THE-HEAD BROTHER--
"--YOU'RE HERE TO SAVE HIM."

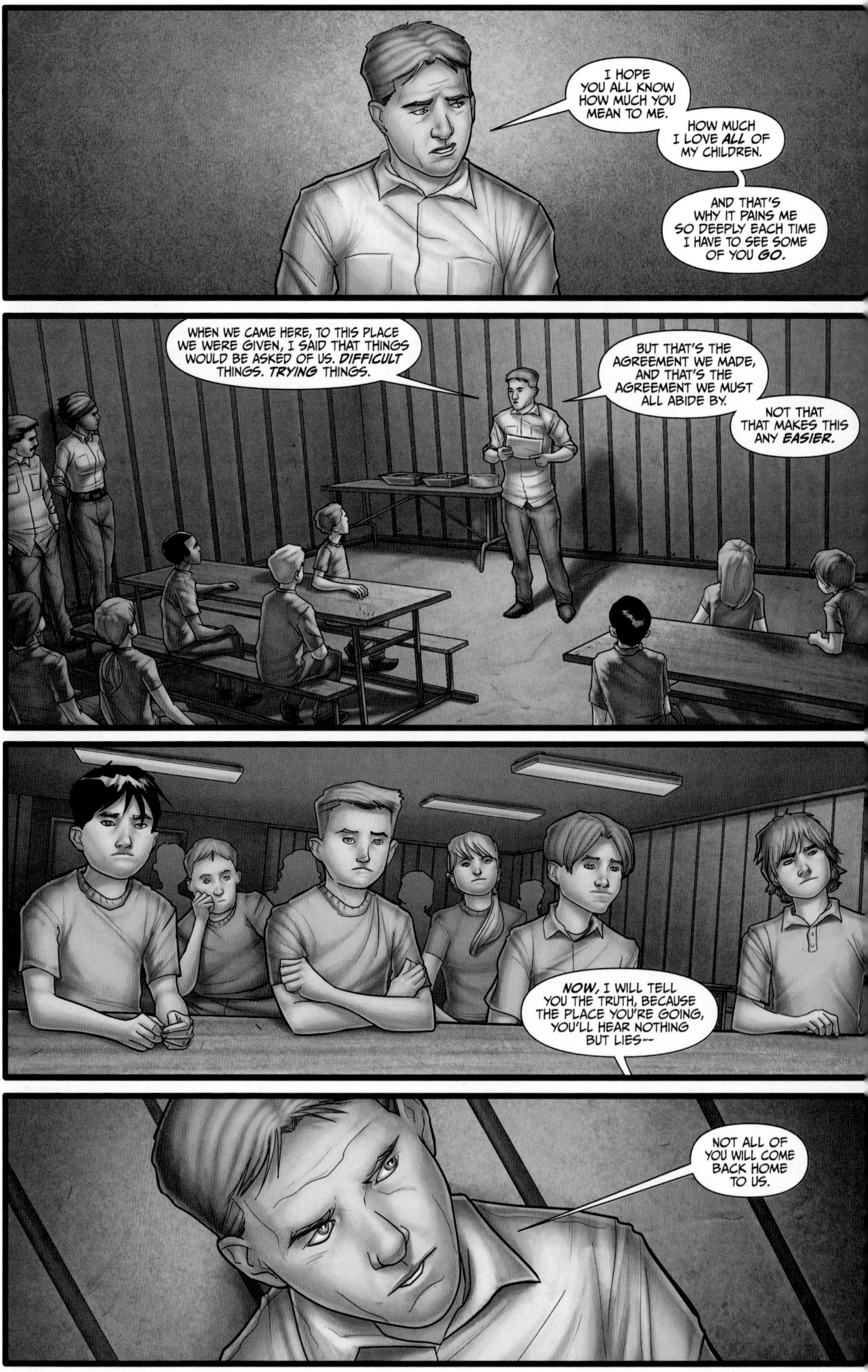
I HOPE YOU ALL KNOW HOW MUCH YOU MEAN TO ME.
HOW MUCH I LOVE *ALL* OF MY CHILDREN.
AND THAT'S WHY IT PAINS ME SO DEEPLY EACH TIME I HAVE TO SEE SOME OF YOU *GO.*
WHEN WE CAME HERE, TO THIS PLACE WE WERE GIVEN, I SAID THAT THINGS WOULD BE ASKED OF US. *DIFFICULT* THINGS. *TRYING* THINGS.
BUT THAT'S THE AGREEMENT WE MADE, AND THAT'S THE AGREEMENT WE MUST ALL ABIDE BY.
NOT THAT THAT MAKES THIS ANY *EASIER.*
NOW, I WILL TELL YOU THE TRUTH, BECAUSE THE PLACE YOU'RE GOING, YOU'LL HEAR NOTHING BUT LIES--
NOT ALL OF YOU WILL COME BACK HOME TO US.

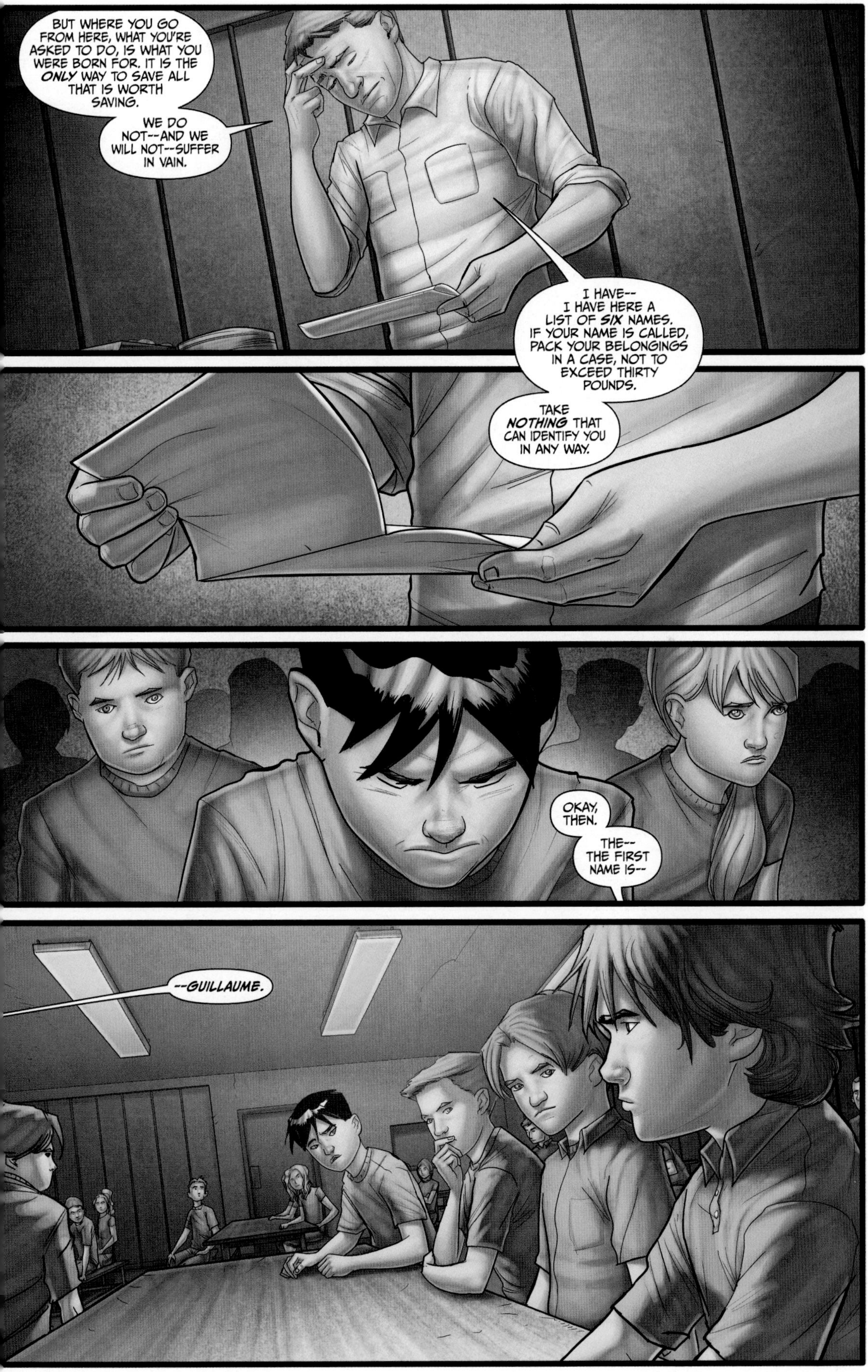
BUT WHERE YOU GO FROM HERE, WHAT YOU'RE ASKED TO DO, IS WHAT YOU WERE BORN FOR. IT IS THE *ONLY* WAY TO SAVE ALL THAT IS WORTH SAVING.
WE DO NOT--AND WE WILL NOT--SUFFER IN VAIN.
I HAVE-- I HAVE HERE A LIST OF *SIX* NAMES. IF YOUR NAME IS CALLED, PACK YOUR BELONGINGS IN A CASE, NOT TO EXCEED THIRTY POUNDS.
TAKE *NOTHING* THAT CAN IDENTIFY YOU IN ANY WAY.
OKAY, THEN.
THE-- THE FIRST NAME IS--
--GUILLAUME.

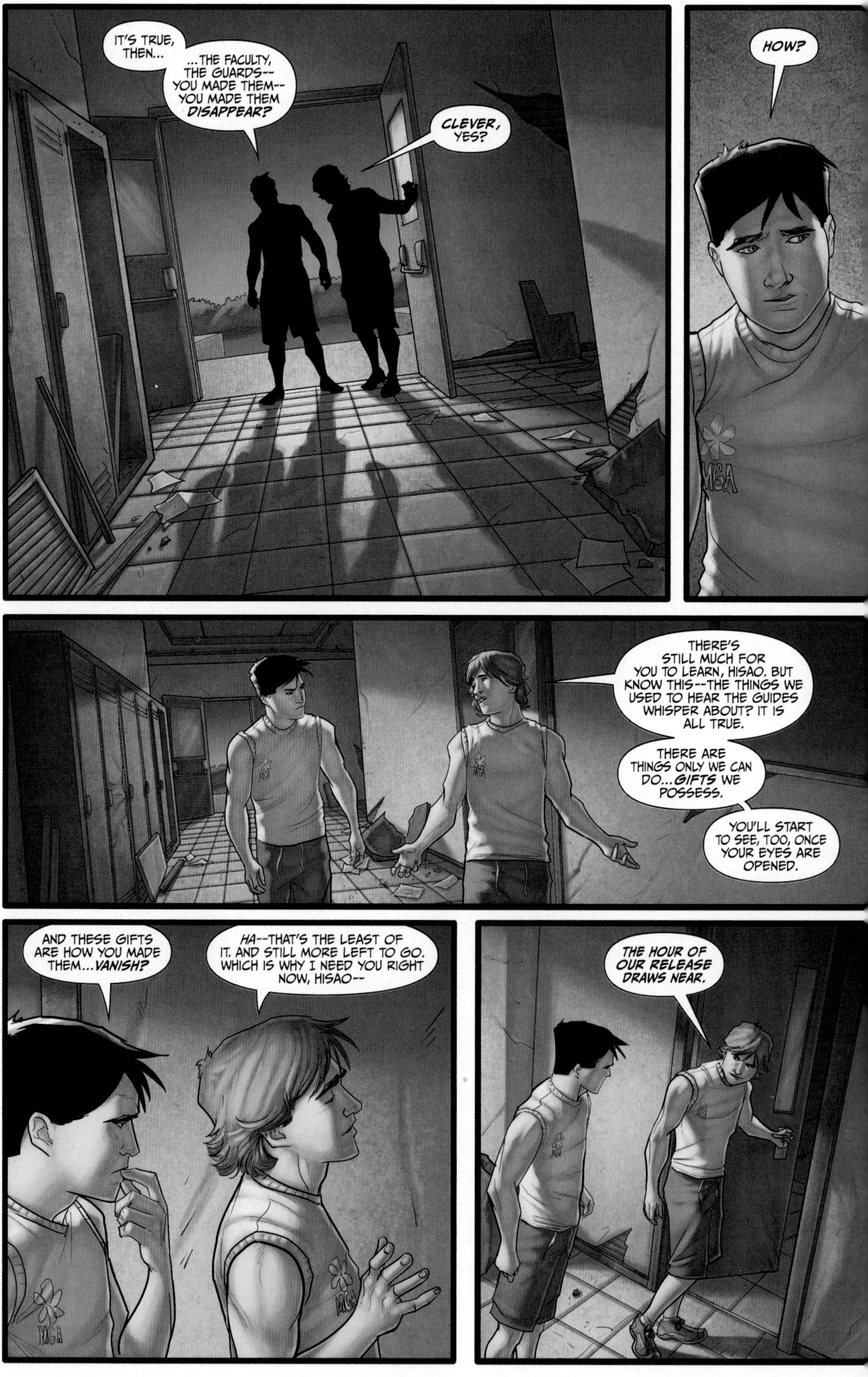
IT'S TRUE, THEN...
...THE FACULTY, THE GUARDS-- YOU MADE THEM-- YOU MADE THEM DISAPPEAR?
CLEVER, YES?
HOW?
THERE'S STILL MUCH FOR YOU TO LEARN, HISAO. BUT KNOW THIS--THE THINGS WE USED TO HEAR THE GUIDES WHISPER ABOUT? IT IS ALL TRUE.
THERE ARE THINGS ONLY WE CAN DO...GIFTS WE POSSESS.
YOU'LL START TO SEE, TOO, ONCE YOUR EYES ARE OPENED.
AND THESE GIFTS ARE HOW YOU MADE THEM...VANISH?
HA--THAT'S THE LEAST OF IT. AND STILL MORE LEFT TO GO. WHICH IS WHY I NEED YOU RIGHT NOW, HISAO--
THE HOUR OF OUR RELEASE DRAWS NEAR.

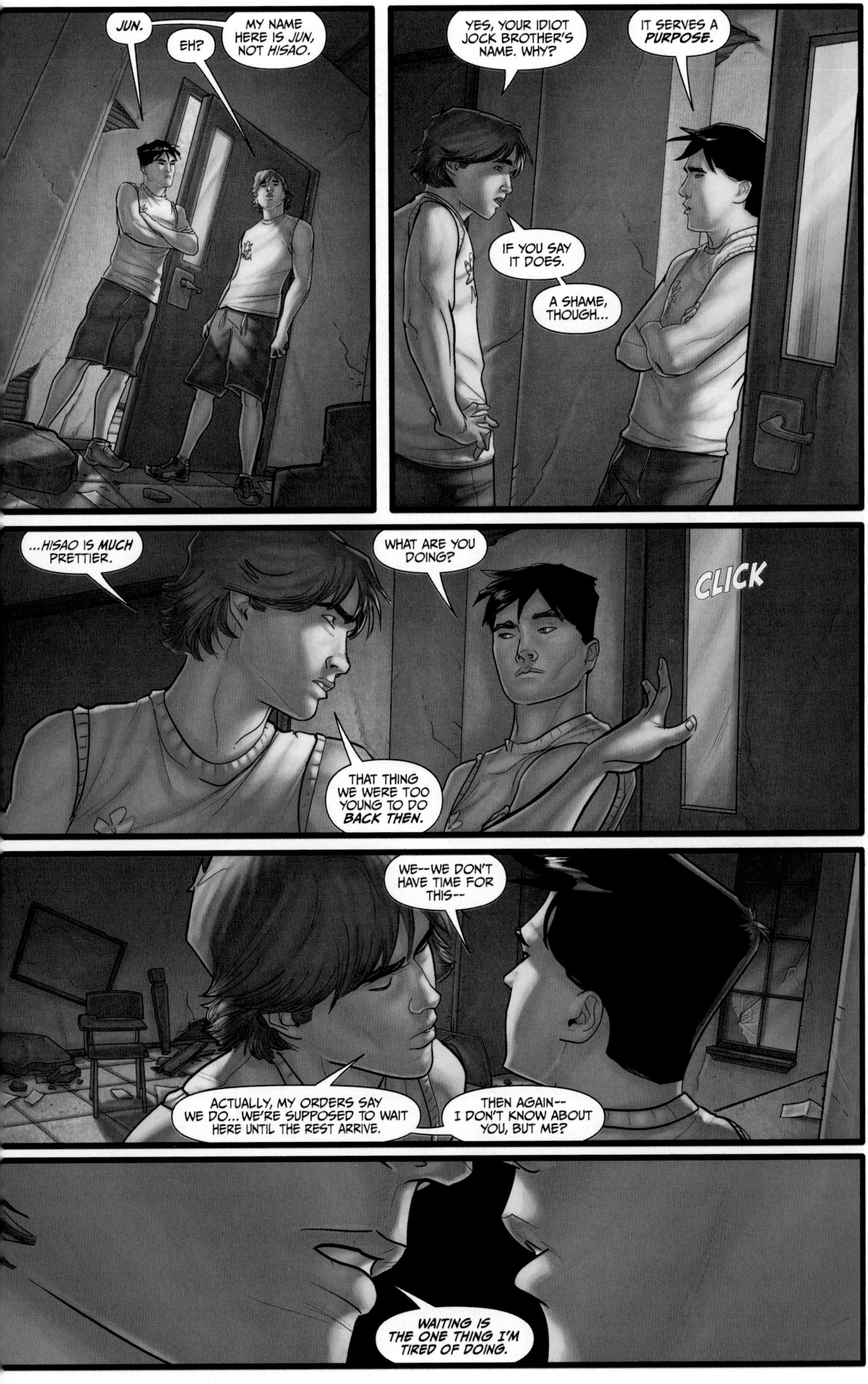
JUN.
EH?
MY NAME HERE IS *JUN*, NOT *HISAO*.
YES, YOUR IDIOT JOCK BROTHER'S NAME. WHY?
IT SERVES A *PURPOSE.*
IF YOU SAY IT DOES.
A SHAME, THOUGH...
...*HISAO* IS *MUCH* PRETTIER.
WHAT ARE YOU DOING?
CLICK
THAT THING WE WERE TOO YOUNG TO DO *BACK THEN.*
WE--WE DON'T HAVE TIME FOR THIS--
ACTUALLY, MY ORDERS SAY WE DO... WE'RE SUPPOSED TO WAIT HERE UNTIL THE REST ARRIVE.
THEN AGAIN-- I DON'T KNOW ABOUT YOU, BUT ME?
WAITING IS THE ONE THING I'M TIRED OF DOING.

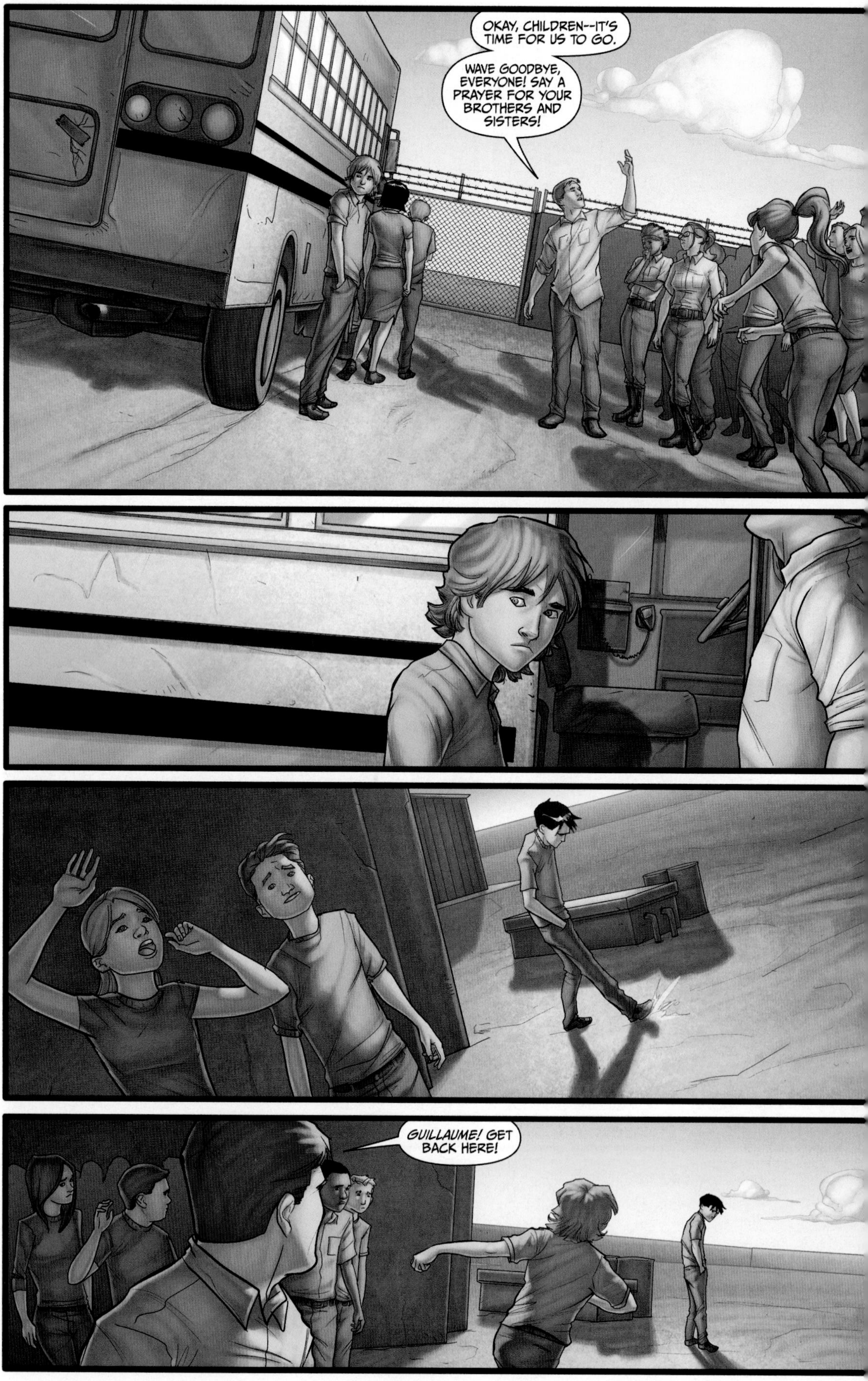
OKAY, CHILDREN--IT'S TIME FOR US TO GO.
WAVE GOODBYE, EVERYONE! SAY A PRAYER FOR YOUR BROTHERS AND SISTERS!
GUILLAUME! GET BACK HERE!

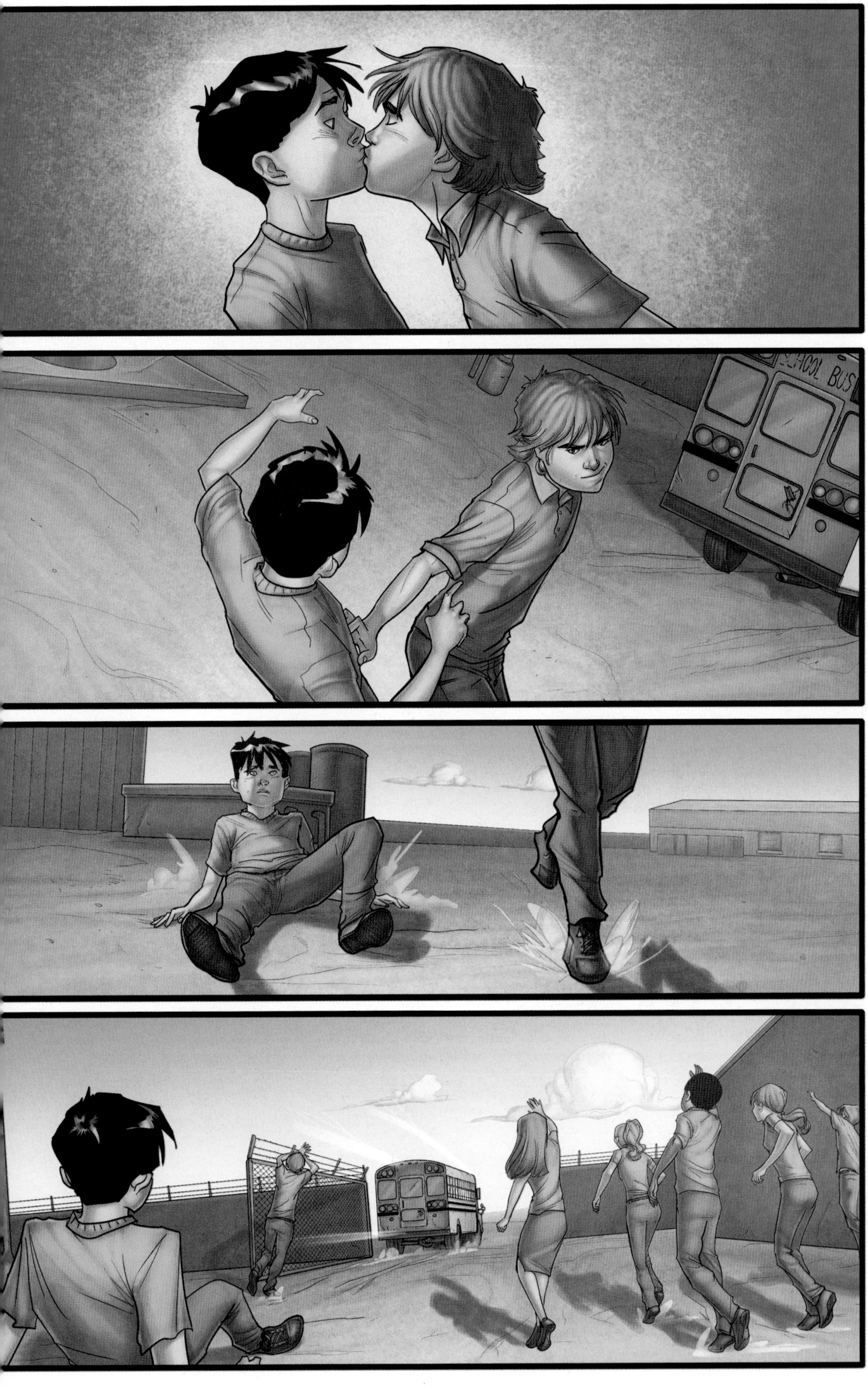
SCHOOL BUS

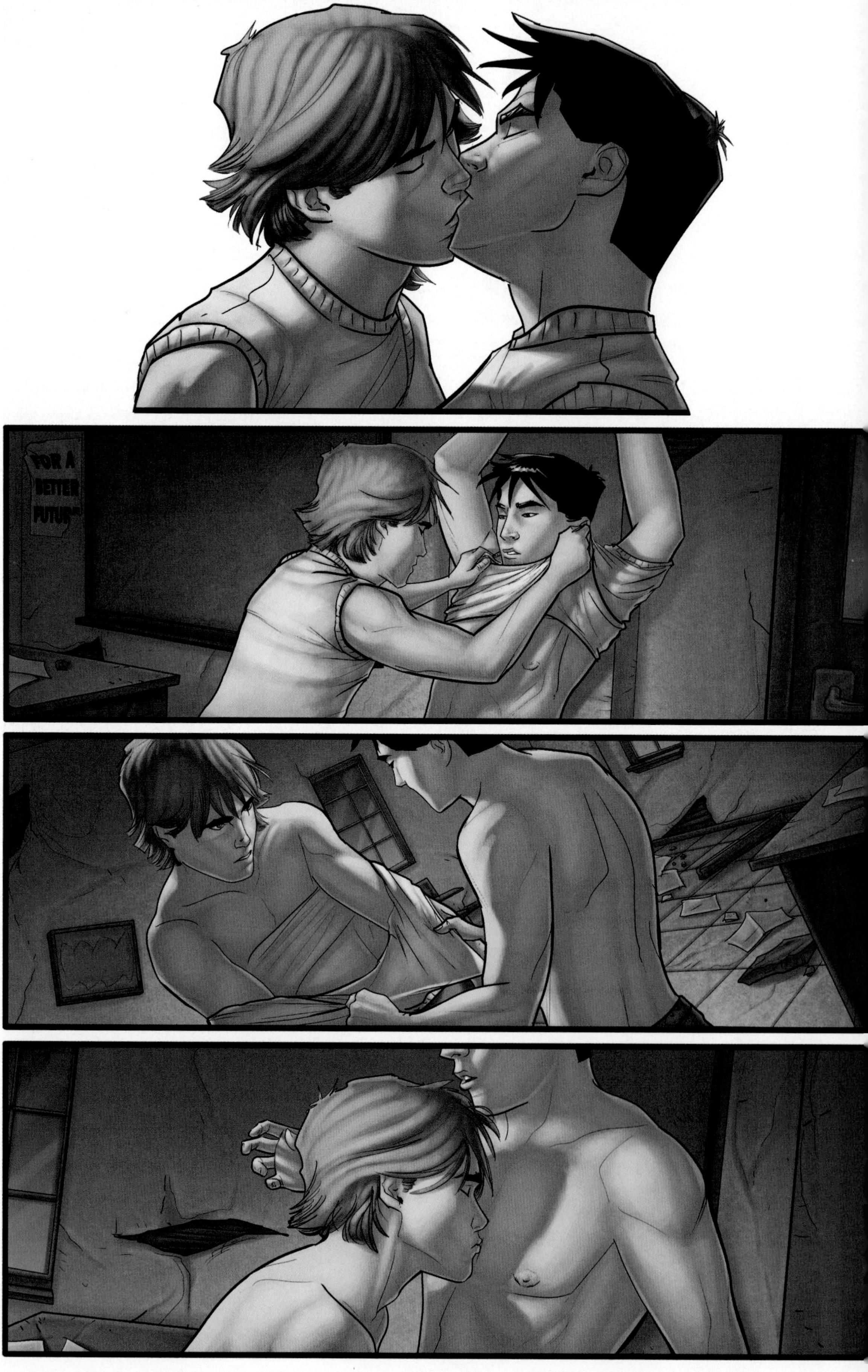
FOR A
BETTER
FUTUR

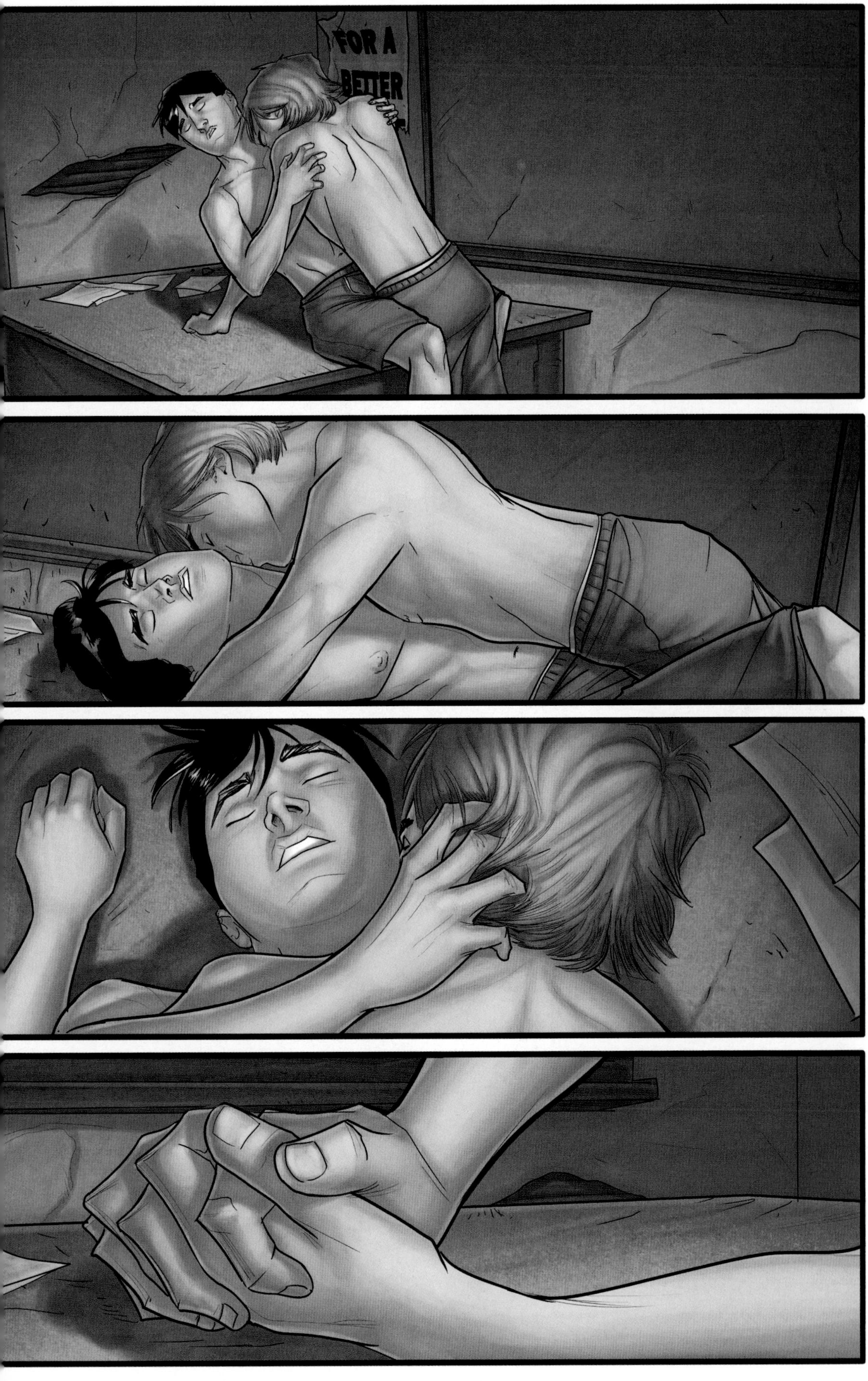
FOR A
BETTER

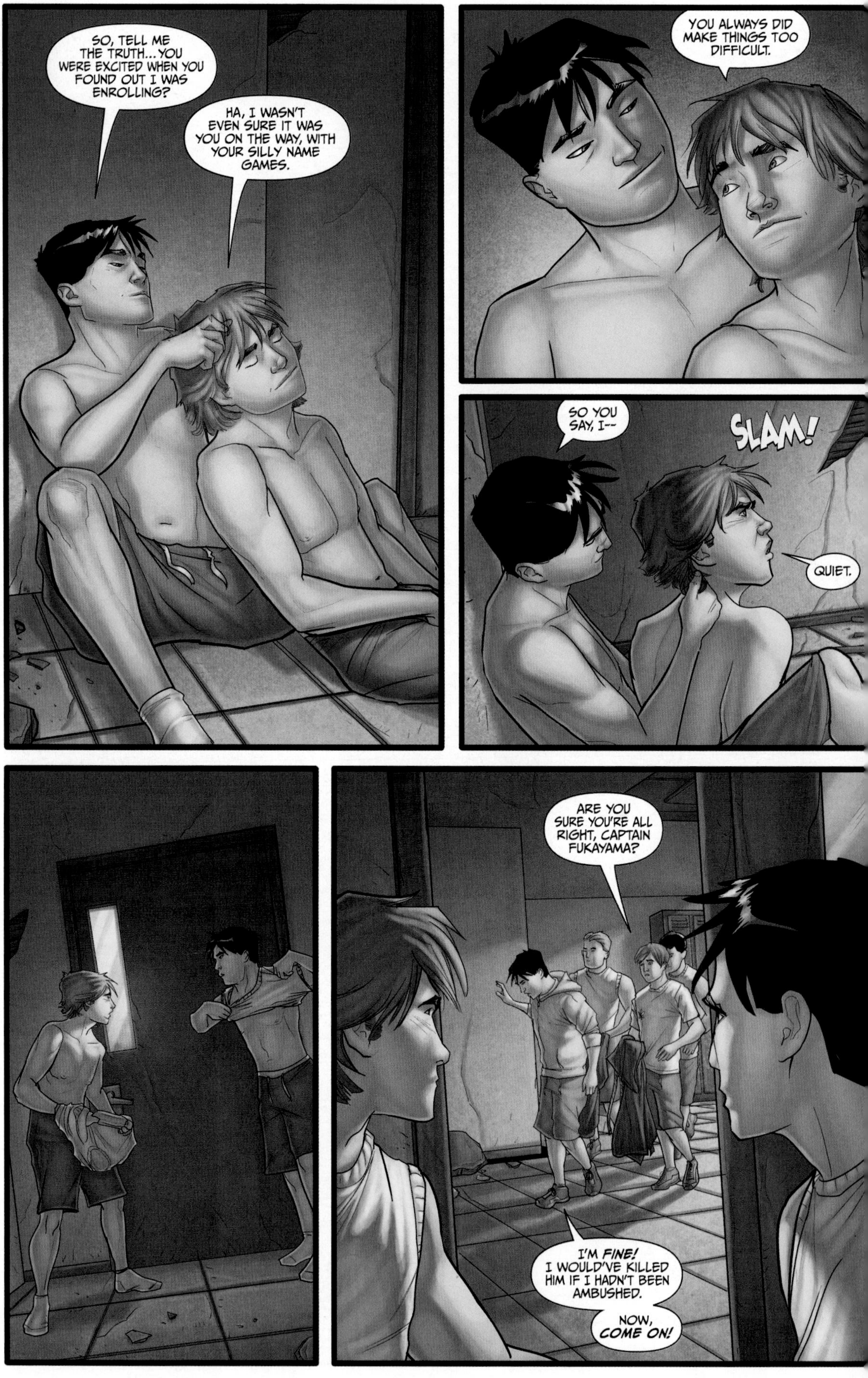

SO, TELL ME THE TRUTH... YOU WERE EXCITED WHEN YOU FOUND OUT I WAS ENROLLING?
HA, I WASN'T EVEN SURE IT WAS YOU ON THE WAY, WITH YOUR SILLY NAME GAMES.
YOU ALWAYS DID MAKE THINGS TOO DIFFICULT.
SO YOU SAY, I--
SLAM!
QUIET.
ARE YOU SURE YOU'RE ALL RIGHT, CAPTAIN FUKAYAMA?
I'M FINE! I WOULD'VE KILLED HIM IF I HADN'T BEEN AMBUSHED.
NOW, COME ON!

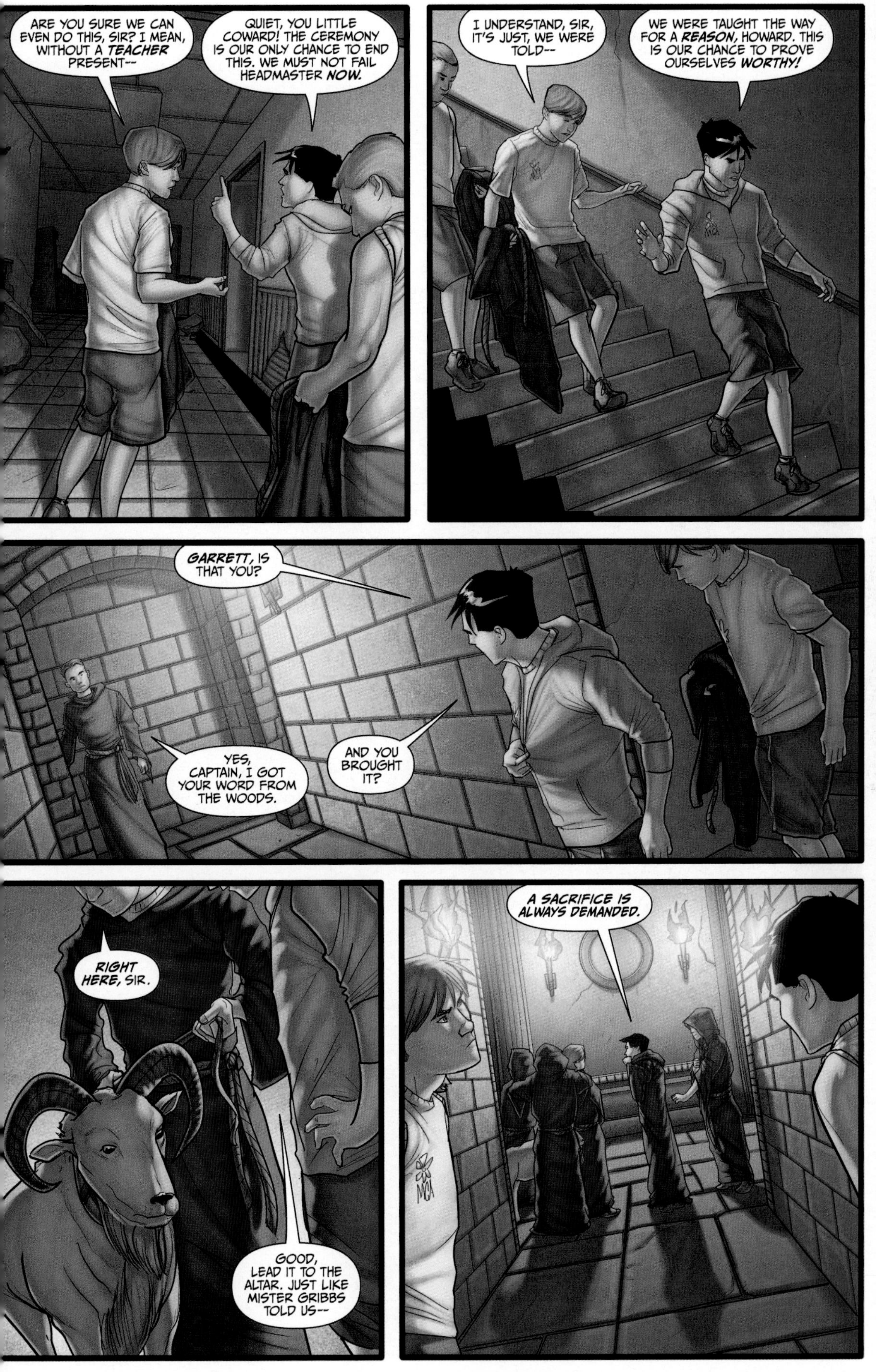
ARE YOU SURE WE CAN EVEN DO THIS, SIR? I MEAN, WITHOUT A TEACHER PRESENT--
QUIET, YOU LITTLE COWARD! THE CEREMONY IS OUR ONLY CHANCE TO END THIS. WE MUST NOT FAIL HEADMASTER NOW.
I UNDERSTAND, SIR, IT'S JUST, WE WERE TOLD--
WE WERE TAUGHT THE WAY FOR A REASON, HOWARD. THIS IS OUR CHANCE TO PROVE OURSELVES WORTHY!
GARRETT, IS THAT YOU?
YES, CAPTAIN, I GOT YOUR WORD FROM THE WOODS.
AND YOU BROUGHT IT?
RIGHT HERE, SIR.
GOOD, LEAD IT TO THE ALTAR. JUST LIKE MISTER GRIBBS TOLD US--
A SACRIFICE IS ALWAYS DEMANDED.

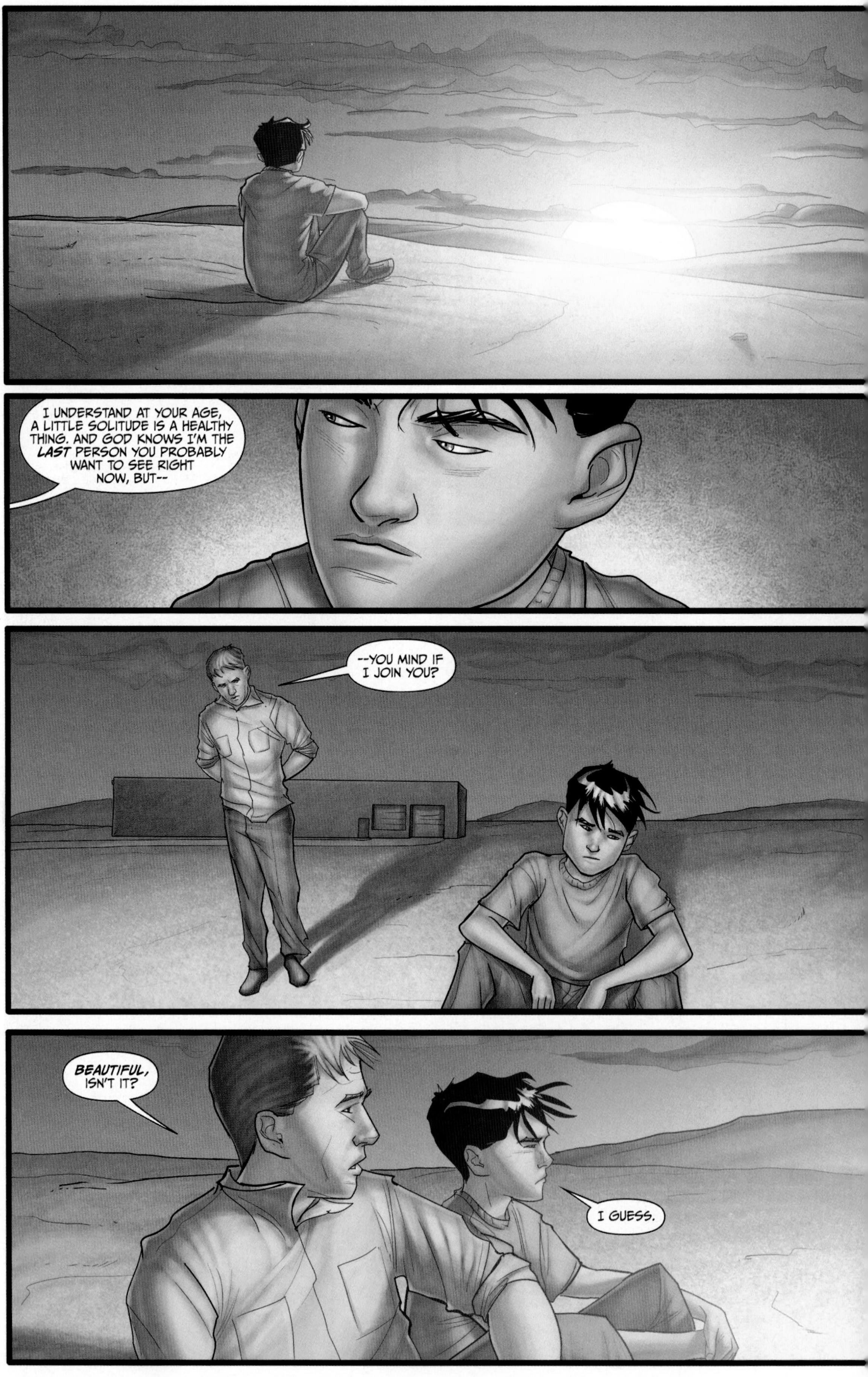
I UNDERSTAND AT YOUR AGE, A LITTLE SOLITUDE IS A HEALTHY THING. AND GOD KNOWS I'M THE *LAST* PERSON YOU PROBABLY WANT TO SEE RIGHT NOW, BUT--
--YOU MIND IF I JOIN YOU?
BEAUTIFUL, ISN'T IT?
I GUESS.

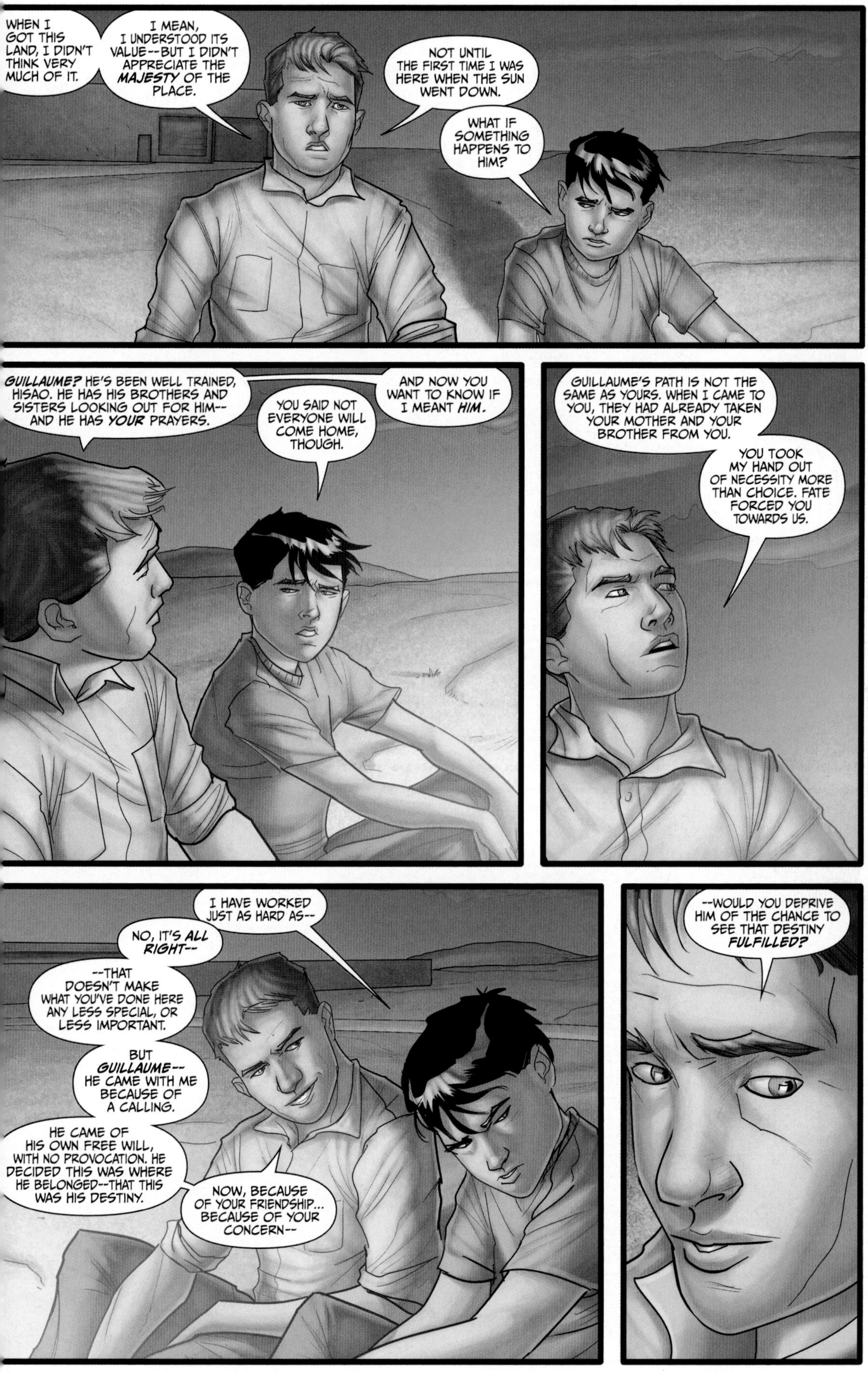
WHEN I GOT THIS LAND, I DIDN'T THINK VERY MUCH OF IT.
I MEAN, I UNDERSTOOD ITS VALUE--BUT I DIDN'T APPRECIATE THE *MAJESTY* OF THE PLACE.
NOT UNTIL THE FIRST TIME I WAS HERE WHEN THE SUN WENT DOWN.
WHAT IF SOMETHING HAPPENS TO HIM?
GUILLAUME? HE'S BEEN WELL TRAINED, HISAO. HE HAS HIS BROTHERS AND SISTERS LOOKING OUT FOR HIM--AND HE HAS *YOUR* PRAYERS.
AND NOW YOU WANT TO KNOW IF I MEANT *HIM.*
YOU SAID NOT EVERYONE WILL COME HOME, THOUGH.
GUILLAUME'S PATH IS NOT THE SAME AS YOURS. WHEN I CAME TO YOU, THEY HAD ALREADY TAKEN YOUR MOTHER AND YOUR BROTHER FROM YOU.
YOU TOOK MY HAND OUT OF NECESSITY MORE THAN CHOICE. FATE FORCED YOU TOWARDS US.
I HAVE WORKED JUST AS HARD AS--
NO, IT'S *ALL RIGHT*--
--THAT DOESN'T MAKE WHAT YOU'VE DONE HERE ANY LESS SPECIAL, OR LESS IMPORTANT.
BUT *GUILLAUME*--HE CAME WITH ME BECAUSE OF A CALLING.
HE CAME OF HIS OWN FREE WILL, WITH NO PROVOCATION. HE DECIDED THIS WAS WHERE HE BELONGED--THAT THIS WAS HIS DESTINY.
NOW, BECAUSE OF YOUR FRIENDSHIP... BECAUSE OF YOUR CONCERN--
--WOULD YOU DEPRIVE HIM OF THE CHANCE TO SEE THAT DESTINY *FULFILLED?*

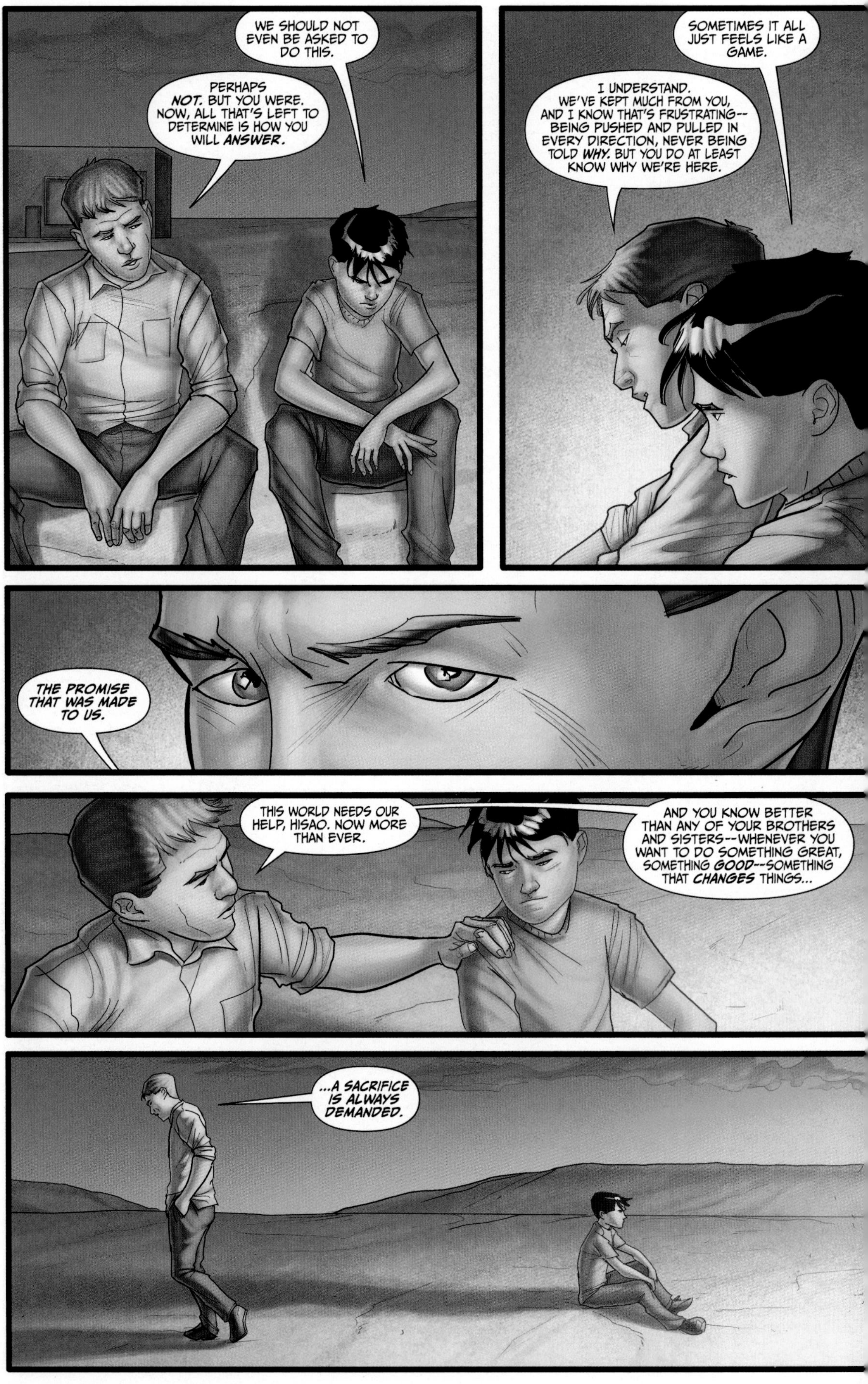
WE SHOULD NOT EVEN BE ASKED TO DO THIS.
PERHAPS NOT. BUT YOU WERE. NOW, ALL THAT'S LEFT TO DETERMINE IS HOW YOU WILL ANSWER.
SOMETIMES IT ALL JUST FEELS LIKE A GAME.
I UNDERSTAND. WE'VE KEPT MUCH FROM YOU, AND I KNOW THAT'S FRUSTRATING--BEING PUSHED AND PULLED IN EVERY DIRECTION, NEVER BEING TOLD WHY. BUT YOU DO AT LEAST KNOW WHY WE'RE HERE.
THE PROMISE THAT WAS MADE TO US.
THIS WORLD NEEDS OUR HELP, HISAO. NOW MORE THAN EVER.
AND YOU KNOW BETTER THAN ANY OF YOUR BROTHERS AND SISTERS--WHENEVER YOU WANT TO DO SOMETHING GREAT, SOMETHING GOOD--SOMETHING THAT CHANGES THINGS...
...A SACRIFICE IS ALWAYS DEMANDED.

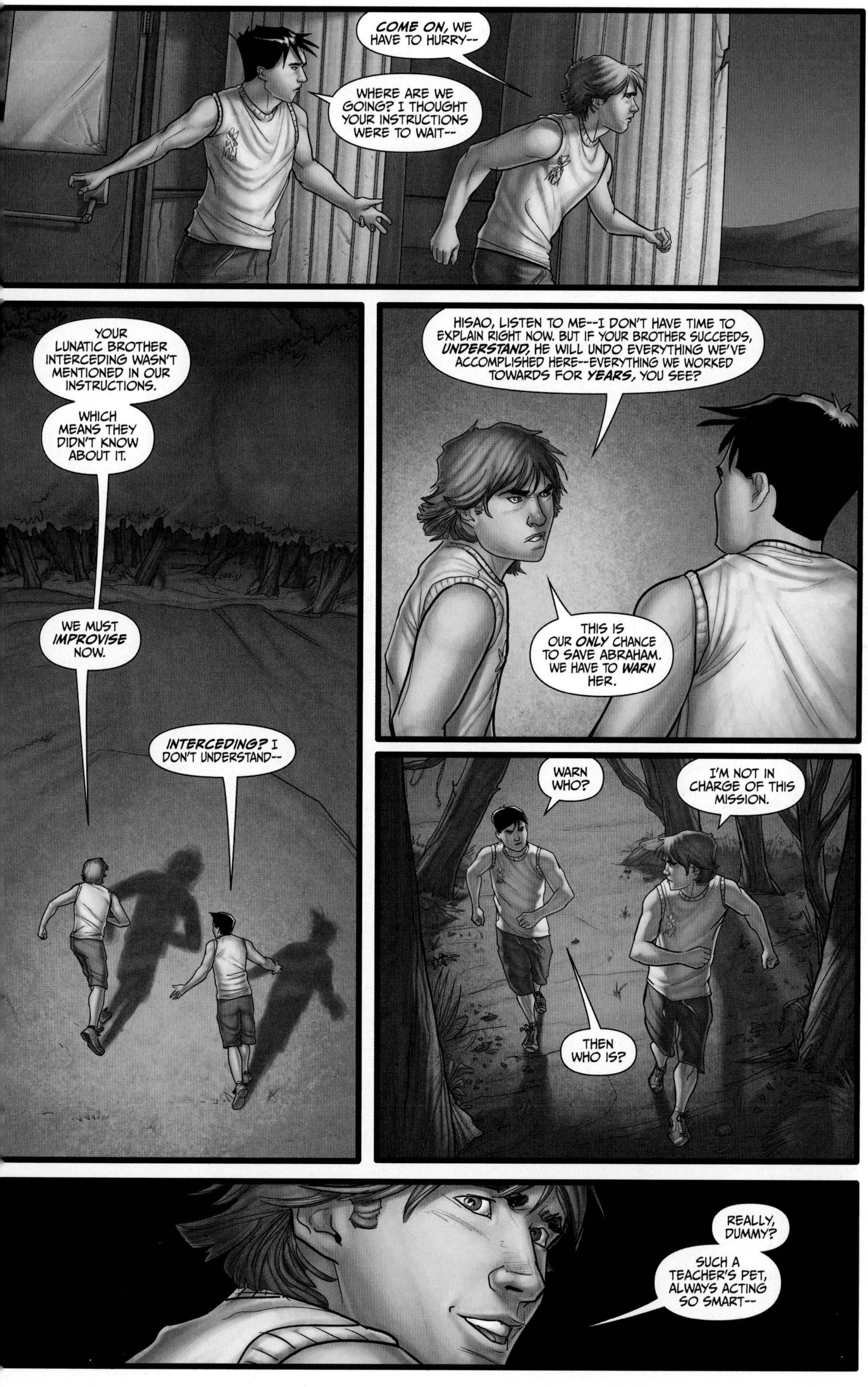
COME ON, WE HAVE TO HURRY--
WHERE ARE WE GOING? I THOUGHT YOUR INSTRUCTIONS WERE TO WAIT--
YOUR LUNATIC BROTHER INTERCEDING WASN'T MENTIONED IN OUR INSTRUCTIONS.
WHICH MEANS THEY DIDN'T KNOW ABOUT IT.
WE MUST IMPROVISE NOW.
INTERCEDING? I DON'T UNDERSTAND--
HISAO, LISTEN TO ME--I DON'T HAVE TIME TO EXPLAIN RIGHT NOW. BUT IF YOUR BROTHER SUCCEEDS, UNDERSTAND, HE WILL UNDO EVERYTHING WE'VE ACCOMPLISHED HERE--EVERYTHING WE WORKED TOWARDS FOR YEARS, YOU SEE?
THIS IS OUR ONLY CHANCE TO SAVE ABRAHAM. WE HAVE TO WARN HER.
WARN WHO?
I'M NOT IN CHARGE OF THIS MISSION.
THEN WHO IS?
REALLY, DUMMY?
SUCH A TEACHER'S PET, ALWAYS ACTING SO SMART--

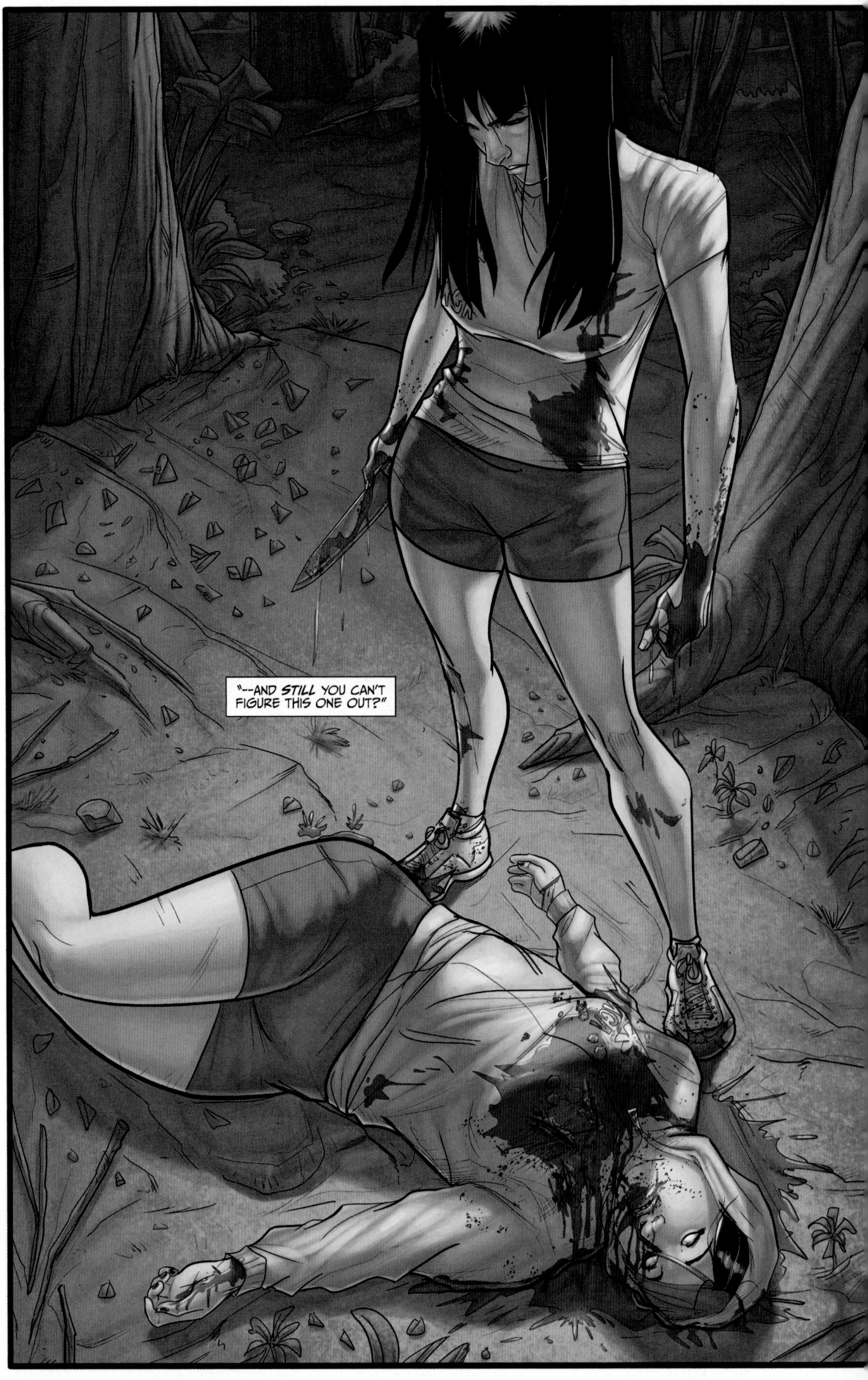
"--AND STILL YOU CAN'T FIGURE THIS ONE OUT?"

nineteen

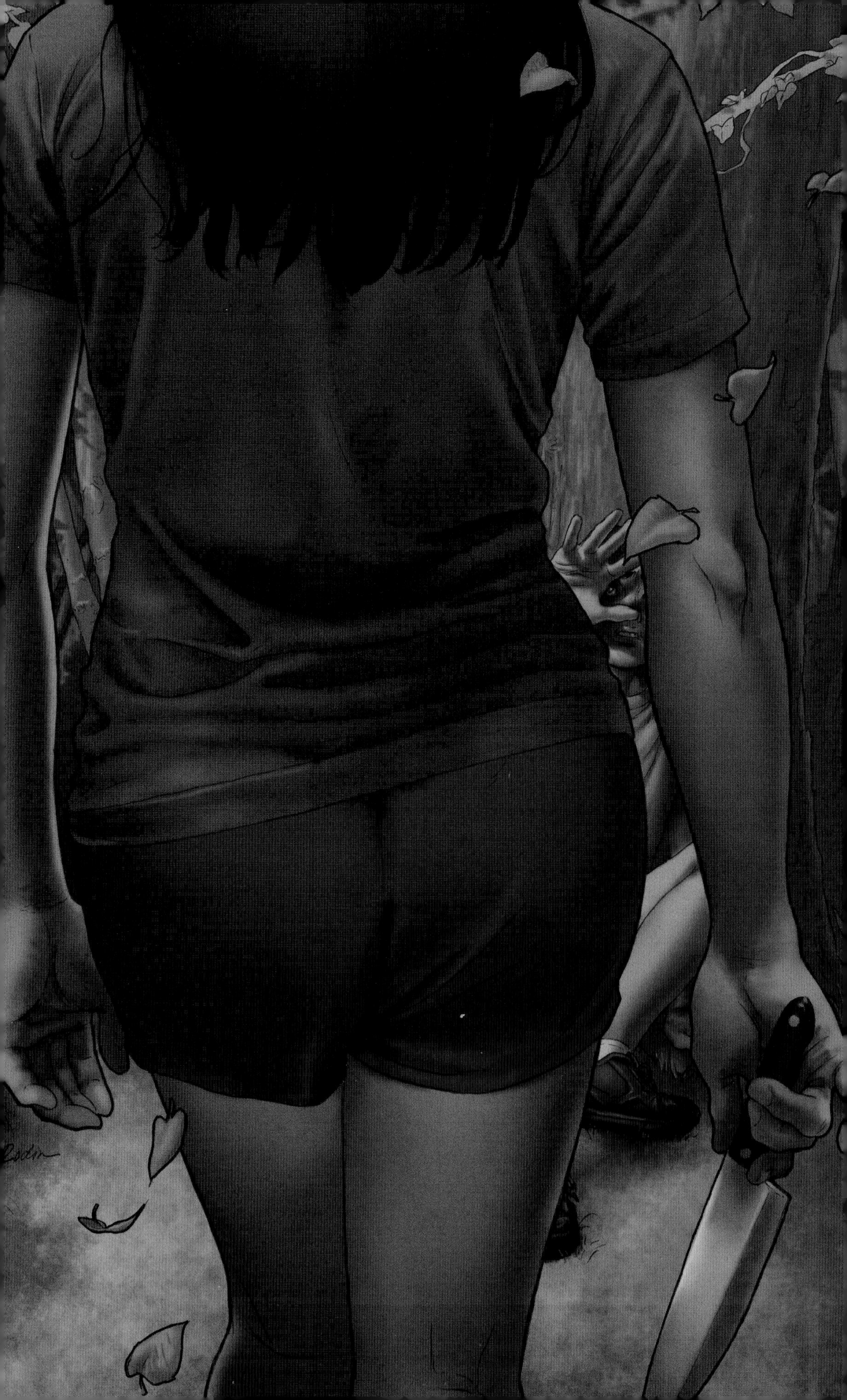

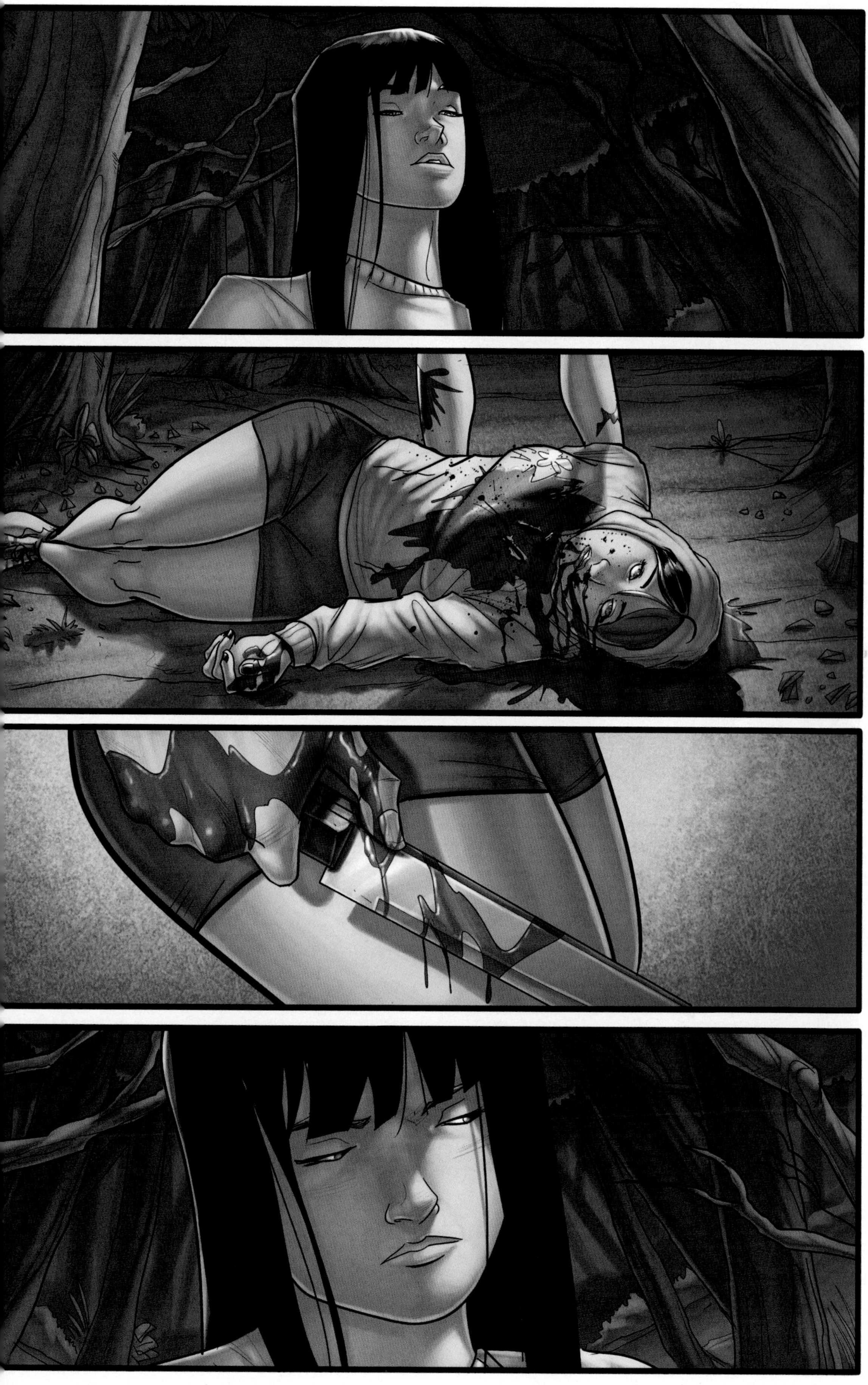

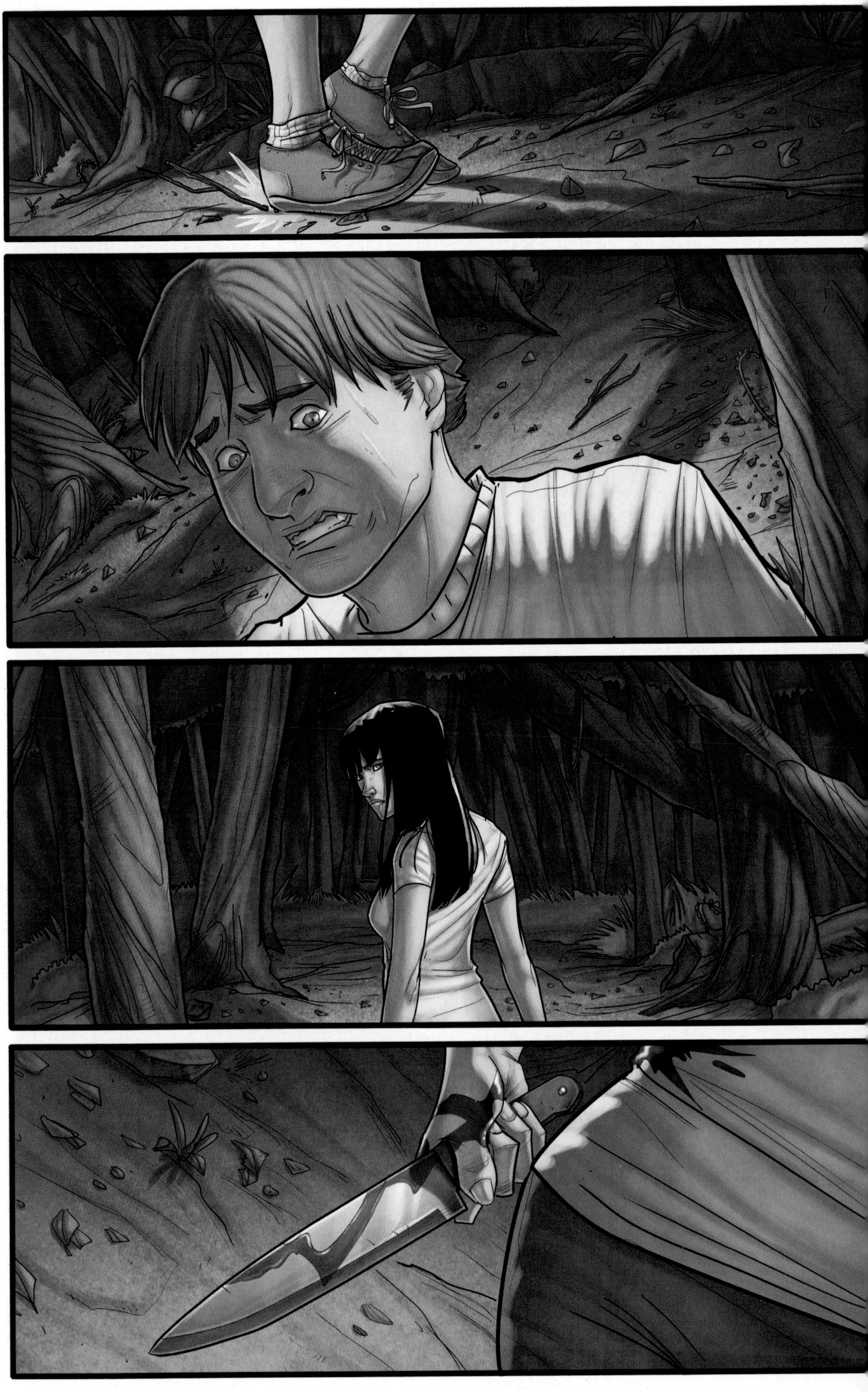

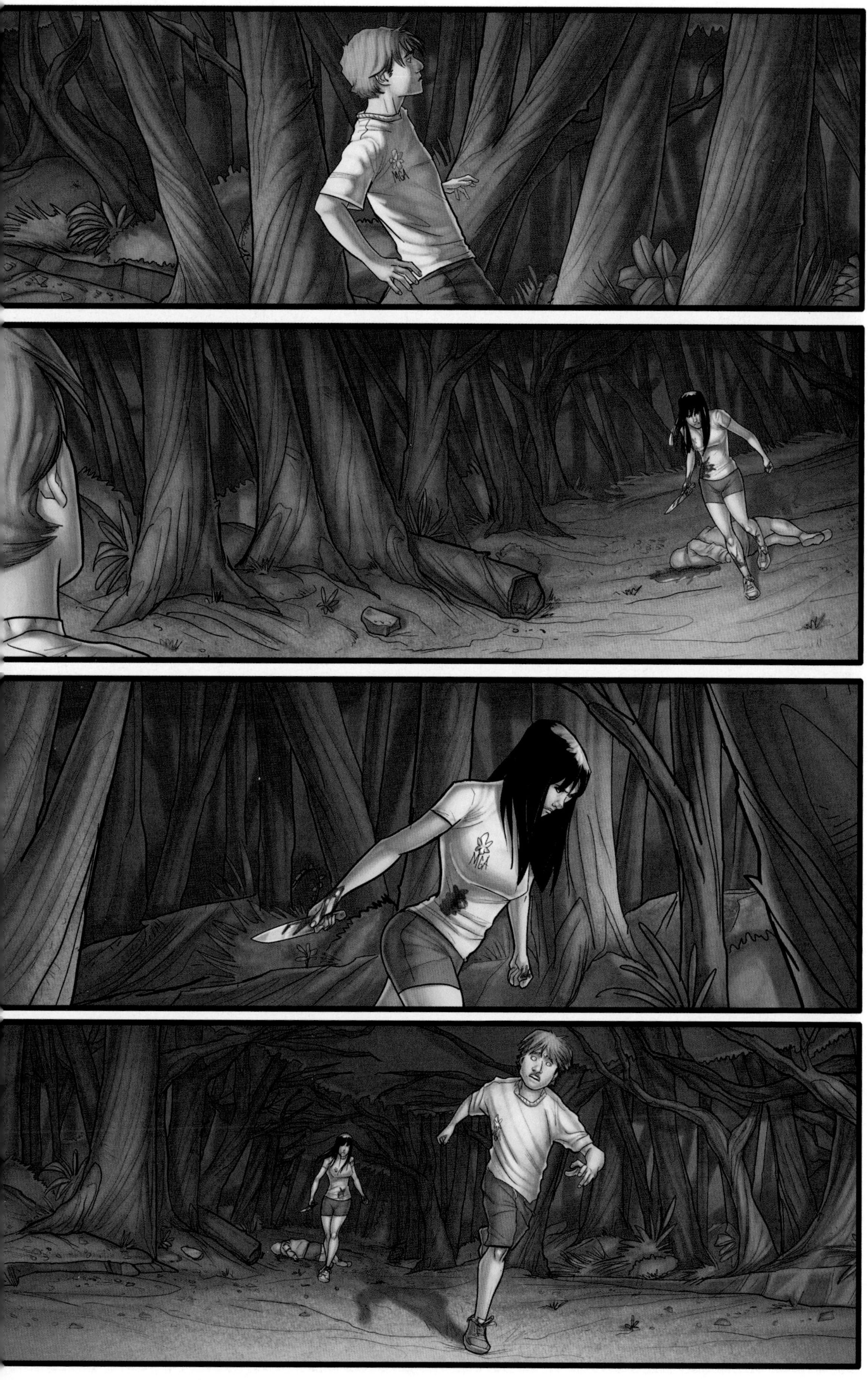

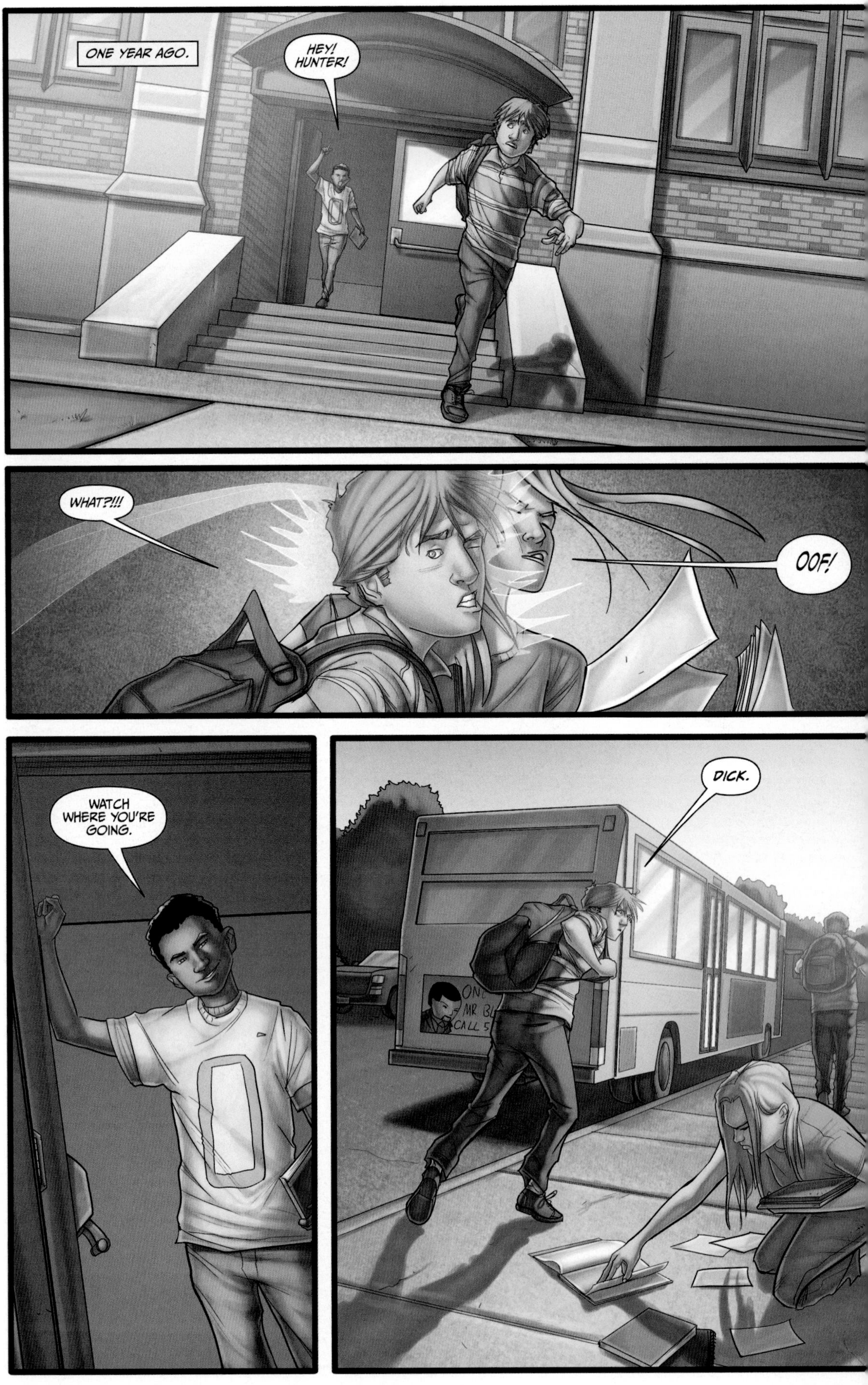
ONE YEAR AGO.
HEY! HUNTER!
WHAT?!!!
OOF!
WATCH WHERE YOU'RE GOING.
DICK.

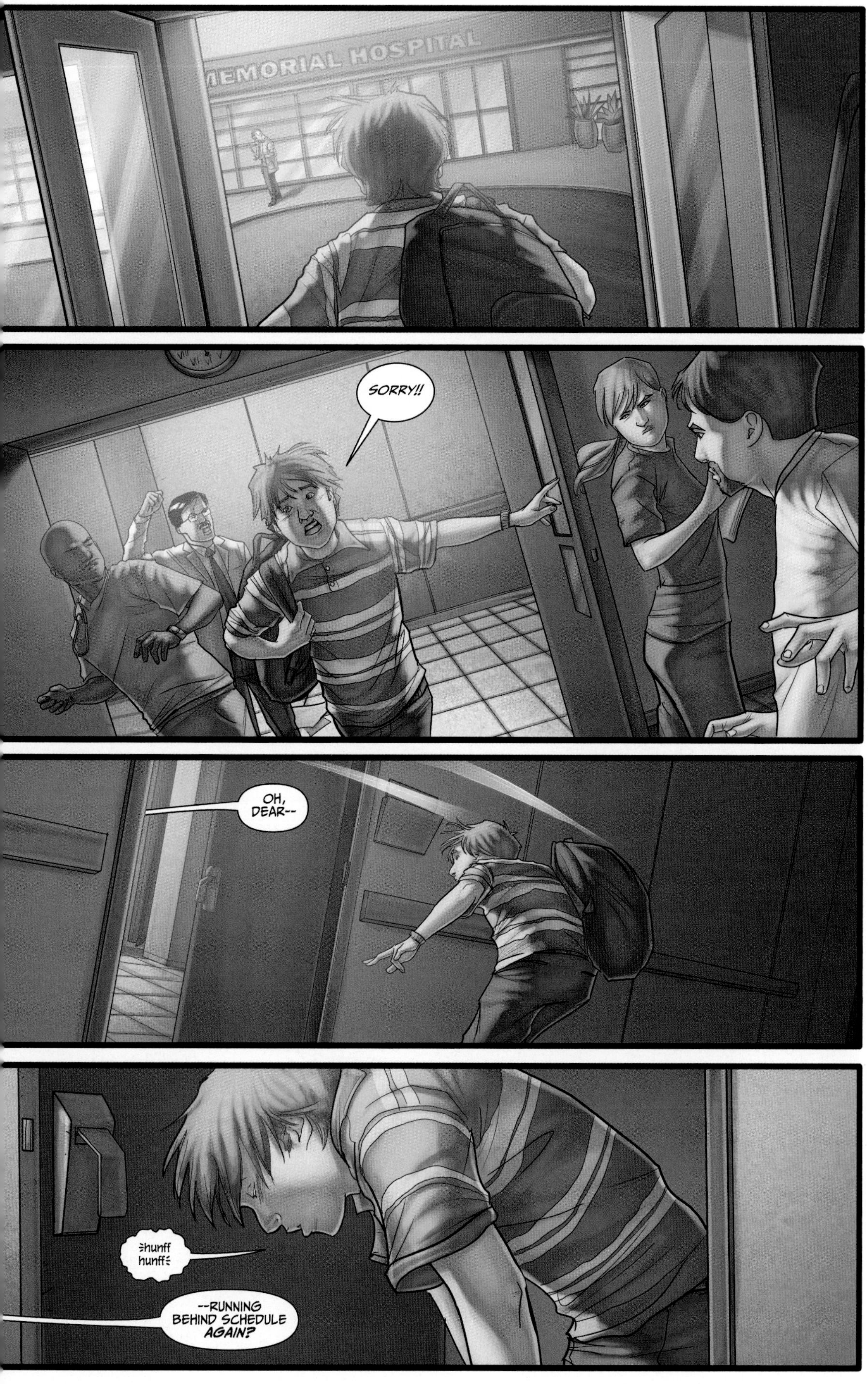
MEMORIAL HOSPITAL
SORRY!!
OH, DEAR--
hunff hunff
--RUNNING BEHIND SCHEDULE AGAIN?

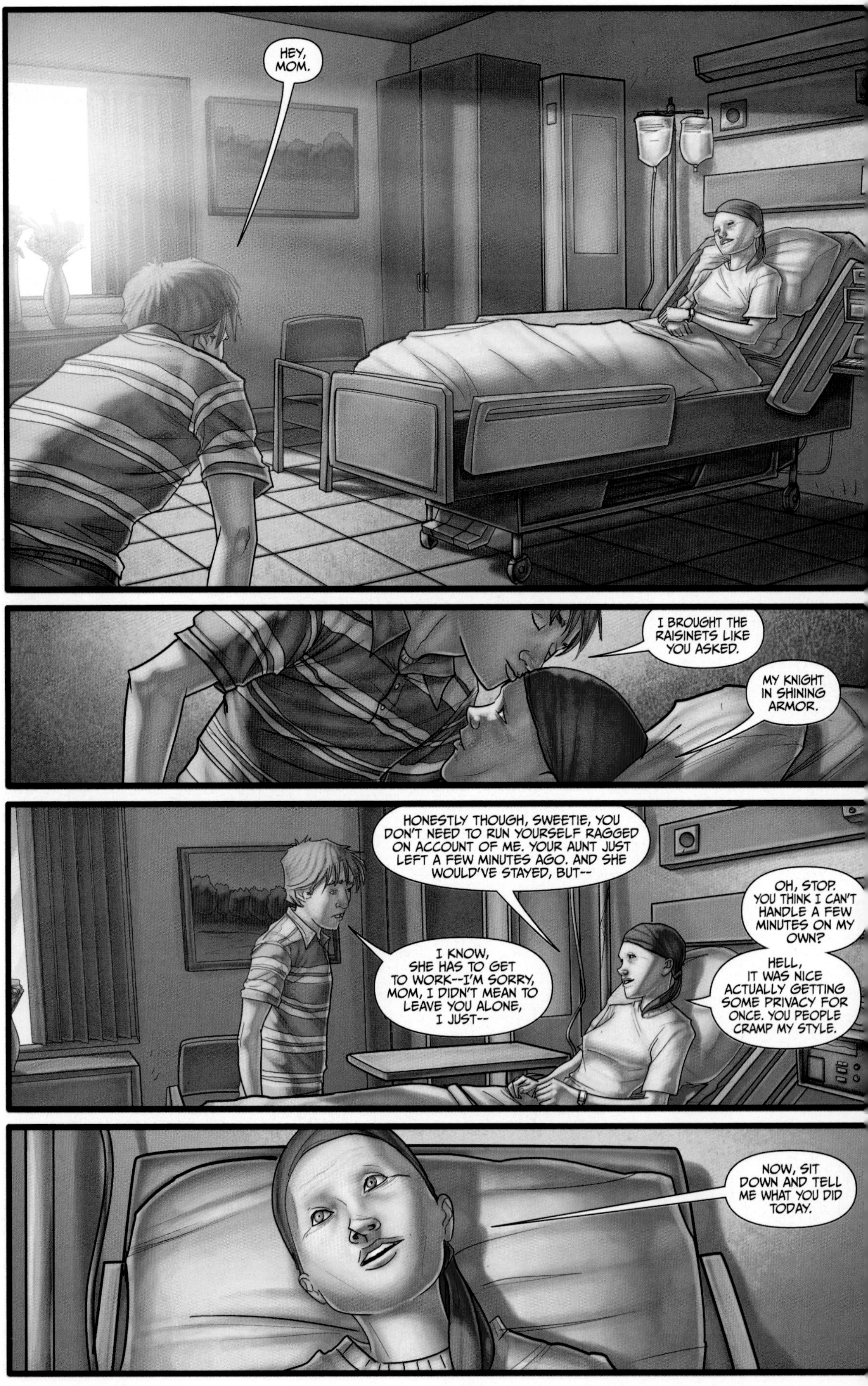
HEY, MOM.
I BROUGHT THE RAISINETS LIKE YOU ASKED.
MY KNIGHT IN SHINING ARMOR.
HONESTLY THOUGH, SWEETIE, YOU DON'T NEED TO RUN YOURSELF RAGGED ON ACCOUNT OF ME. YOUR AUNT JUST LEFT A FEW MINUTES AGO. AND SHE WOULD'VE STAYED, BUT--
I KNOW, SHE HAS TO GET TO WORK--I'M SORRY, MOM, I DIDN'T MEAN TO LEAVE YOU ALONE, I JUST--
OH, STOP. YOU THINK I CAN'T HANDLE A FEW MINUTES ON MY OWN?
HELL, IT WAS NICE ACTUALLY GETTING SOME PRIVACY FOR ONCE. YOU PEOPLE CRAMP MY STYLE.
NOW, SIT DOWN AND TELL ME WHAT YOU DID TODAY.

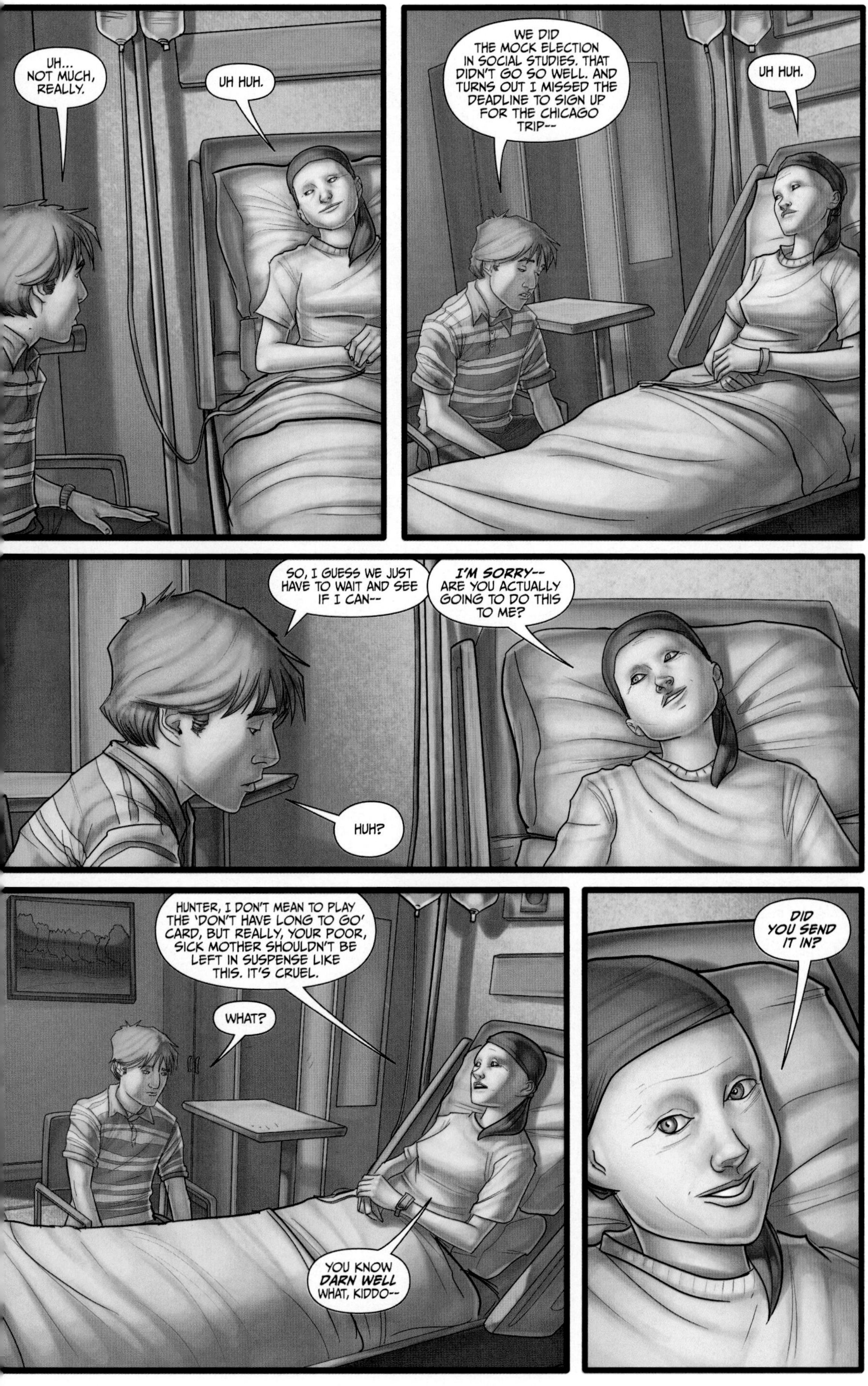
UH... NOT MUCH, REALLY.
UH HUH.
WE DID THE MOCK ELECTION IN SOCIAL STUDIES. THAT DIDN'T GO SO WELL. AND TURNS OUT I MISSED THE DEADLINE TO SIGN UP FOR THE CHICAGO TRIP--
UH HUH.
SO, I GUESS WE JUST HAVE TO WAIT AND SEE IF I CAN--
I'M SORRY-- ARE YOU ACTUALLY GOING TO DO THIS TO ME?
HUH?
HUNTER, I DON'T MEAN TO PLAY THE 'DON'T HAVE LONG TO GO' CARD, BUT REALLY, YOUR POOR, SICK MOTHER SHOULDN'T BE LEFT IN SUSPENSE LIKE THIS. IT'S CRUEL.
WHAT?
YOU KNOW DARN WELL WHAT, KIDDO--
DID YOU SEND IT IN?

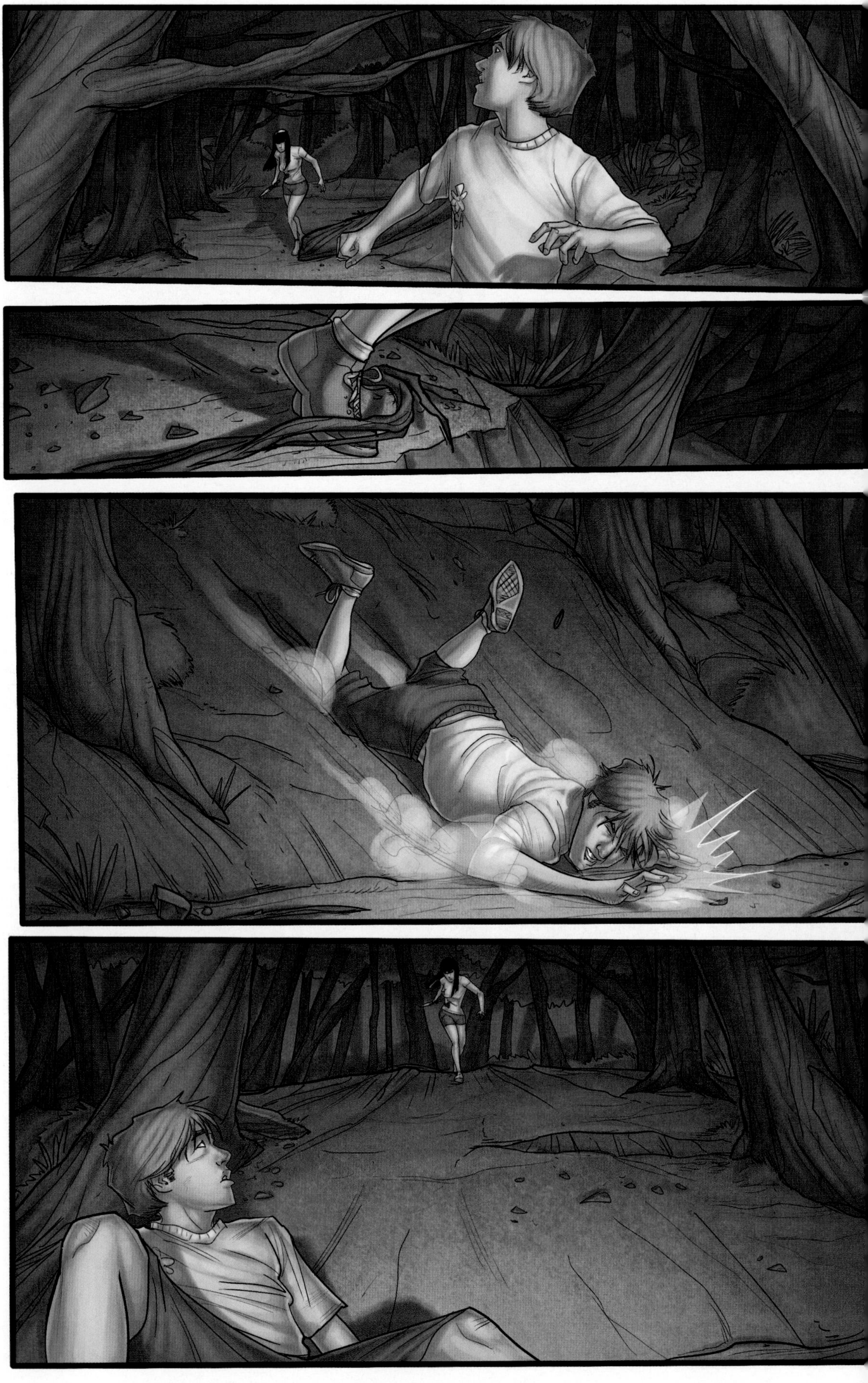

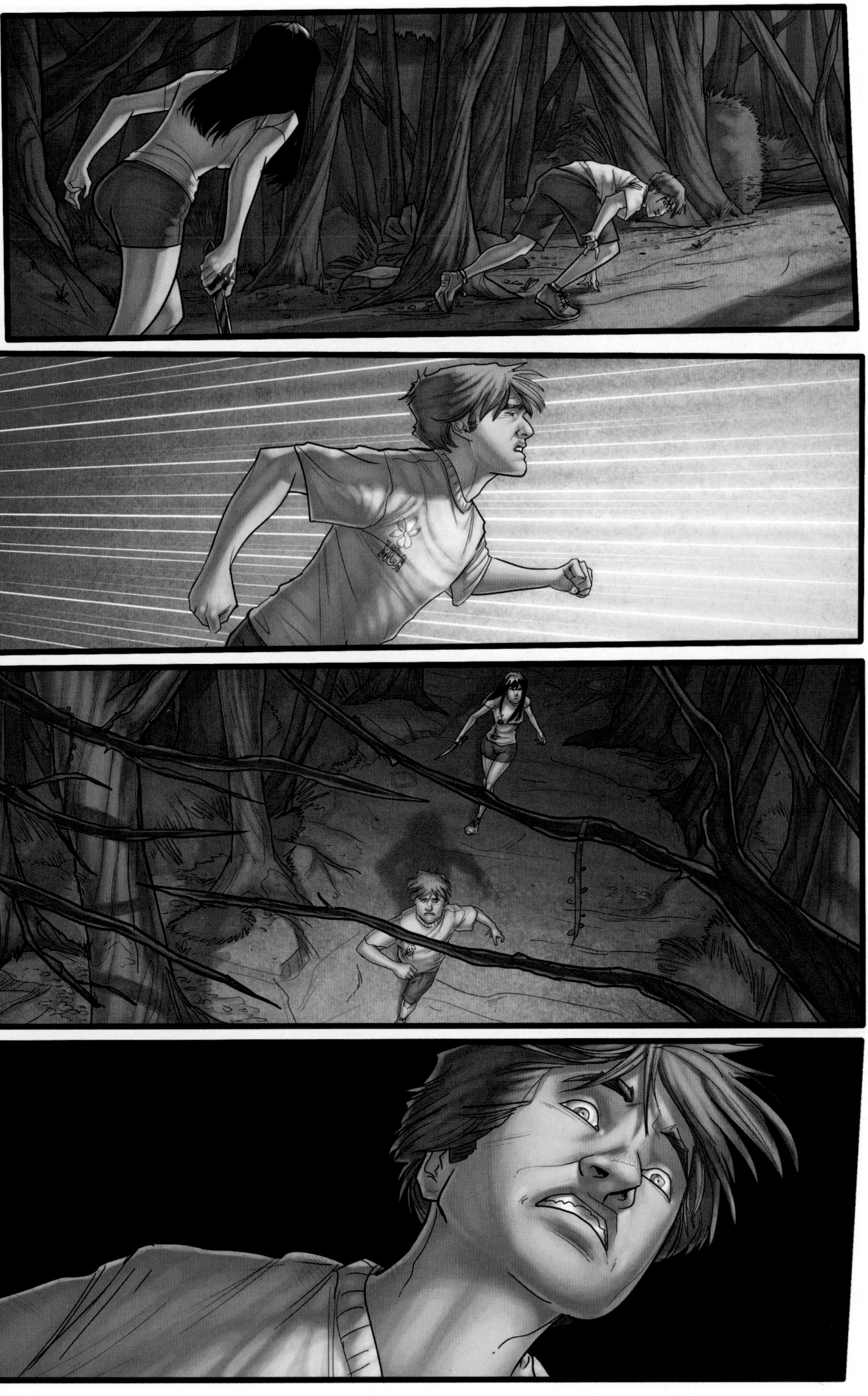

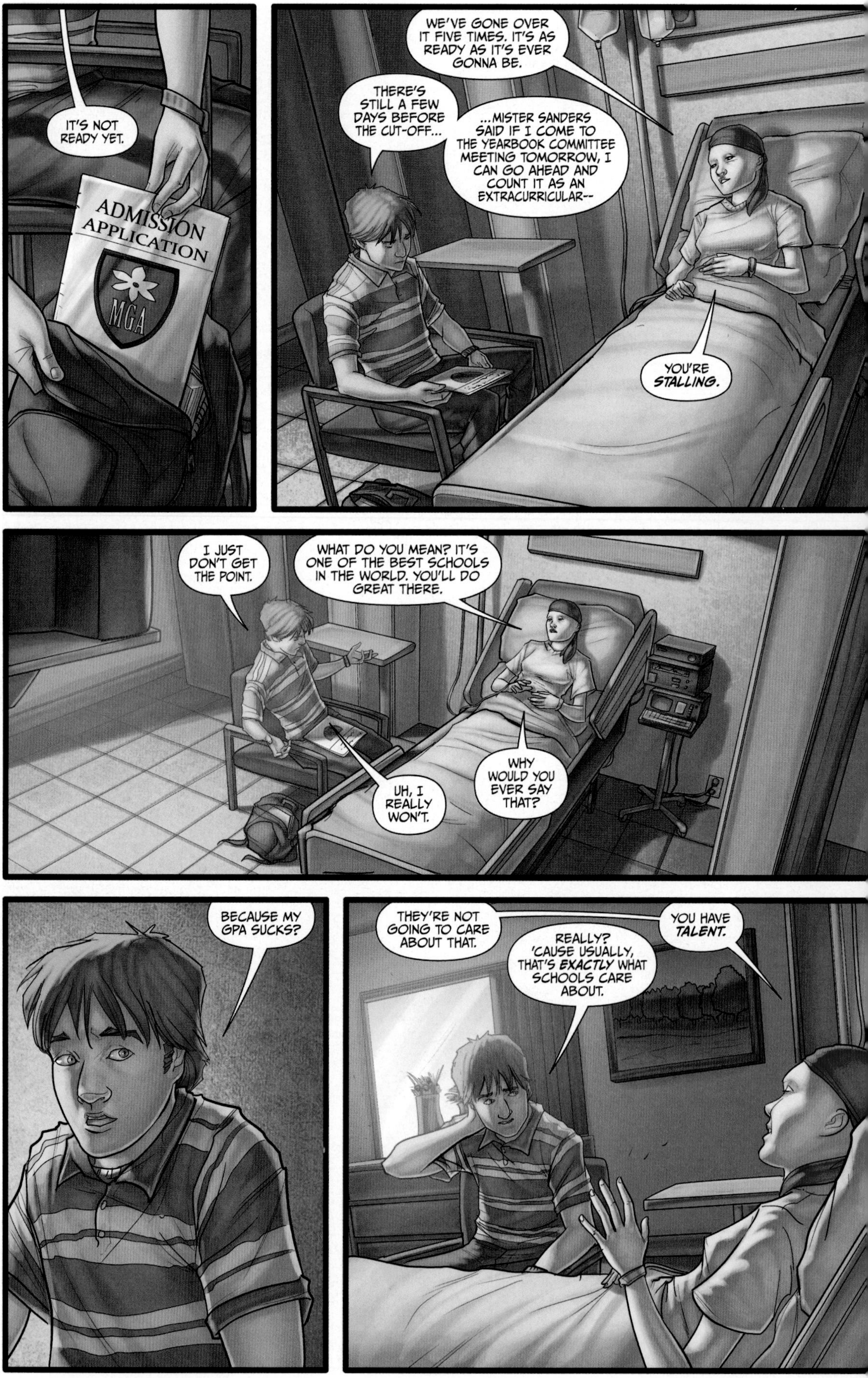
IT'S NOT READY YET.
ADMISSION APPLICATION
MGA
WE'VE GONE OVER IT FIVE TIMES. IT'S AS READY AS IT'S EVER GONNA BE.
THERE'S STILL A FEW DAYS BEFORE THE CUT-OFF...
...MISTER SANDERS SAID IF I COME TO THE YEARBOOK COMMITTEE MEETING TOMORROW, I CAN GO AHEAD AND COUNT IT AS AN EXTRACURRICULAR--
YOU'RE *STALLING.*
I JUST DON'T GET THE POINT.
WHAT DO YOU MEAN? IT'S ONE OF THE BEST SCHOOLS IN THE WORLD. YOU'LL DO GREAT THERE.
UH, I REALLY WON'T.
WHY WOULD YOU EVER SAY THAT?
BECAUSE MY GPA SUCKS?
THEY'RE NOT GOING TO CARE ABOUT THAT.
YOU HAVE *TALENT.*
REALLY? 'CAUSE USUALLY, THAT'S *EXACTLY* WHAT SCHOOLS CARE ABOUT.

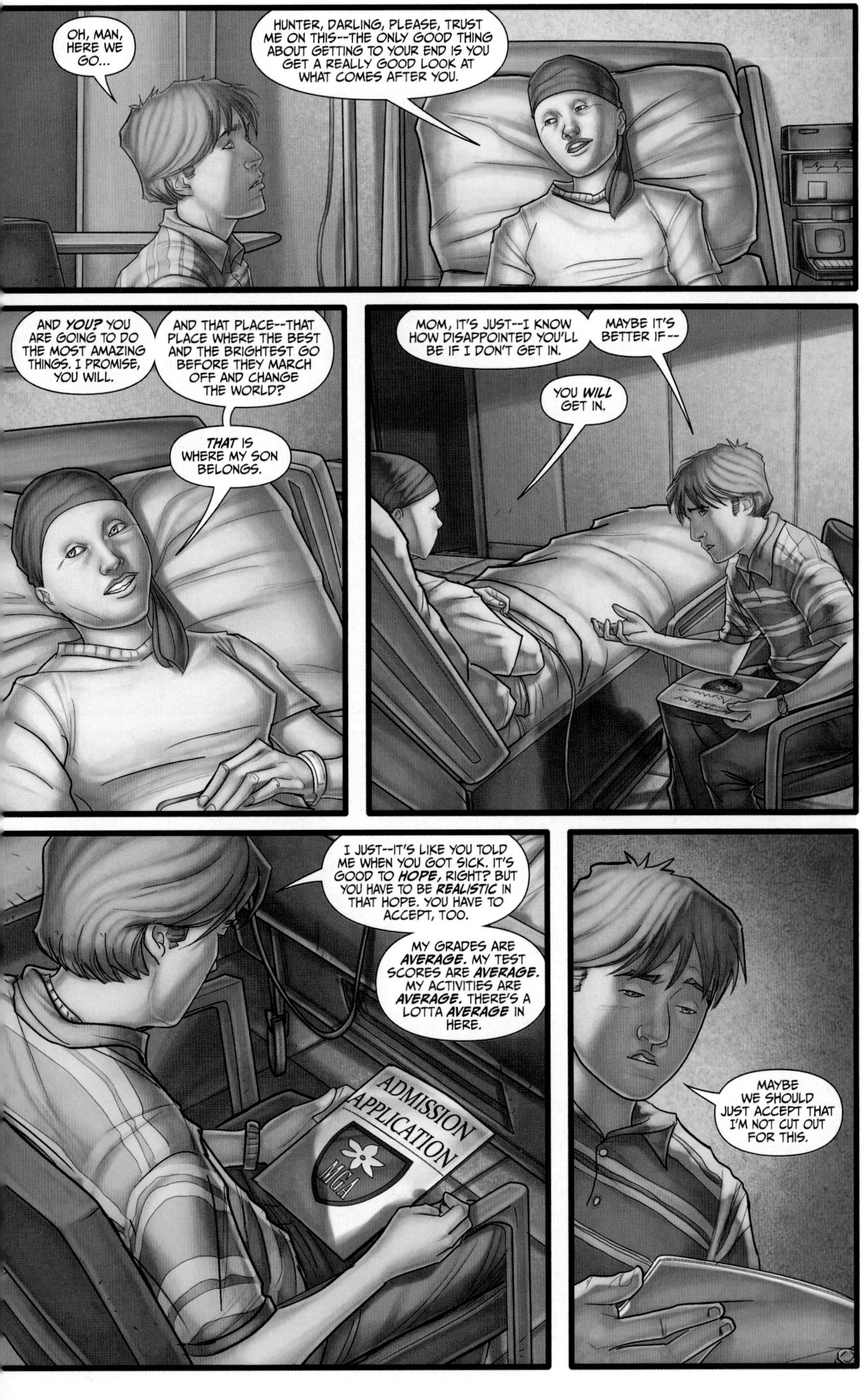
OH, MAN, HERE WE GO...
HUNTER, DARLING, PLEASE, TRUST ME ON THIS--THE ONLY GOOD THING ABOUT GETTING TO YOUR END IS YOU GET A REALLY GOOD LOOK AT WHAT COMES AFTER YOU.
AND *YOU?* YOU ARE GOING TO DO THE MOST AMAZING THINGS. I PROMISE, YOU WILL.
AND THAT PLACE--THAT PLACE WHERE THE BEST AND THE BRIGHTEST GO BEFORE THEY MARCH OFF AND CHANGE THE WORLD?
THAT IS WHERE MY SON BELONGS.
MOM, IT'S JUST--I KNOW HOW DISAPPOINTED YOU'LL BE IF I DON'T GET IN.
MAYBE IT'S BETTER IF--
YOU *WILL* GET IN.
I JUST--IT'S LIKE YOU TOLD ME WHEN YOU GOT SICK. IT'S GOOD TO *HOPE,* RIGHT? BUT YOU HAVE TO BE *REALISTIC* IN THAT HOPE. YOU HAVE TO ACCEPT, TOO.
MY GRADES ARE *AVERAGE.* MY TEST SCORES ARE *AVERAGE.* MY ACTIVITIES ARE *AVERAGE.* THERE'S A LOTTA *AVERAGE* IN HERE.
ADMISSION APPLICATION
MGA
MAYBE WE SHOULD JUST ACCEPT THAT I'M NOT CUT OUT FOR THIS.

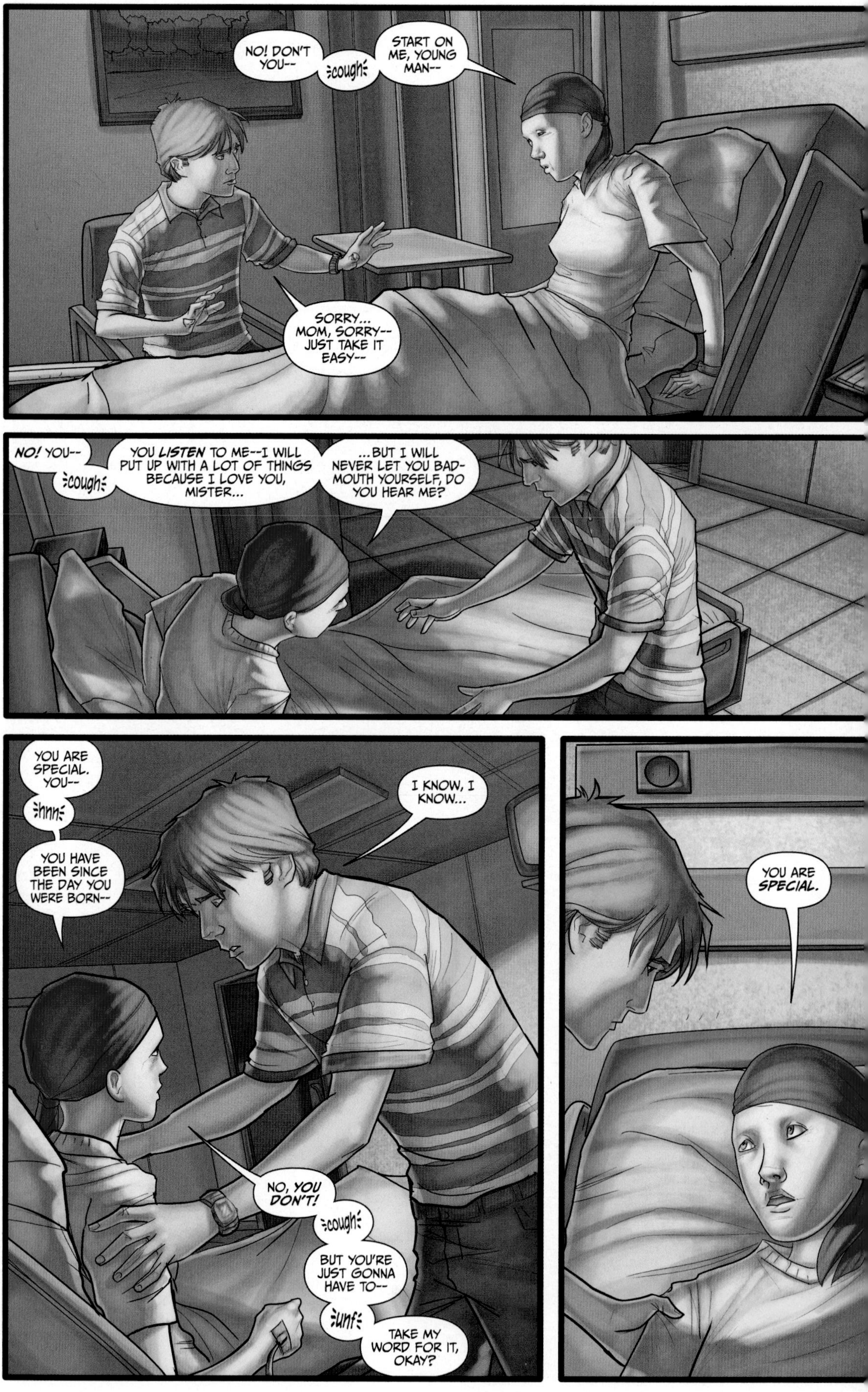
NO! DON'T YOU--
cough
START ON ME, YOUNG MAN--
SORRY... MOM, SORRY-- JUST TAKE IT EASY--
NO! YOU--
cough
YOU LISTEN TO ME--I WILL PUT UP WITH A LOT OF THINGS BECAUSE I LOVE YOU, MISTER...
...BUT I WILL NEVER LET YOU BAD-MOUTH YOURSELF, DO YOU HEAR ME?
YOU ARE SPECIAL. YOU--
hnn
YOU HAVE BEEN SINCE THE DAY YOU WERE BORN--
I KNOW, I KNOW...
NO, YOU DON'T!
cough
BUT YOU'RE JUST GONNA HAVE TO--
unf
TAKE MY WORD FOR IT, OKAY?
YOU ARE SPECIAL.

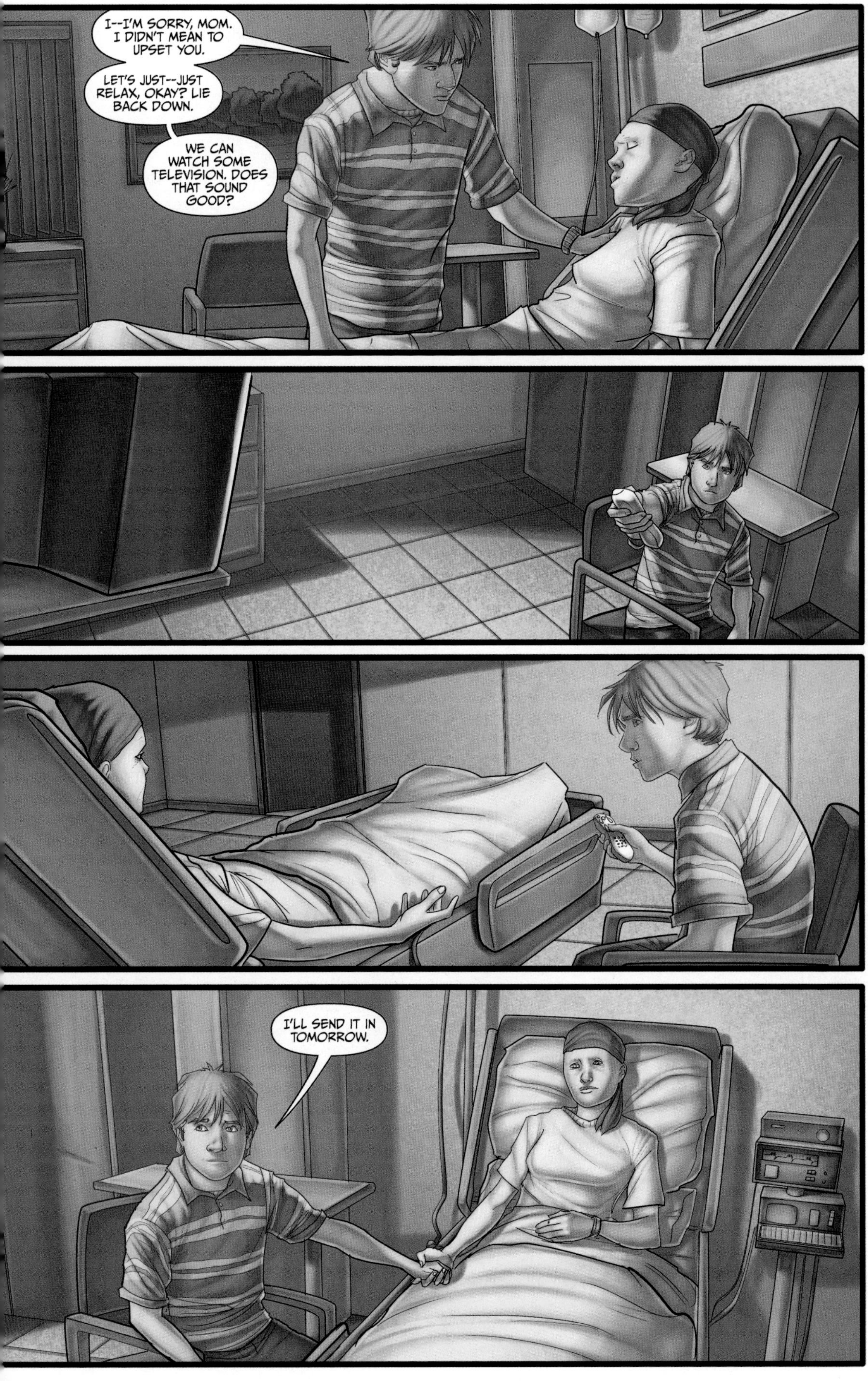
I--I'M SORRY, MOM. I DIDN'T MEAN TO UPSET YOU.
LET'S JUST--JUST RELAX, OKAY? LIE BACK DOWN.
WE CAN WATCH SOME TELEVISION. DOES THAT SOUND GOOD?
I'LL SEND IT IN TOMORROW.

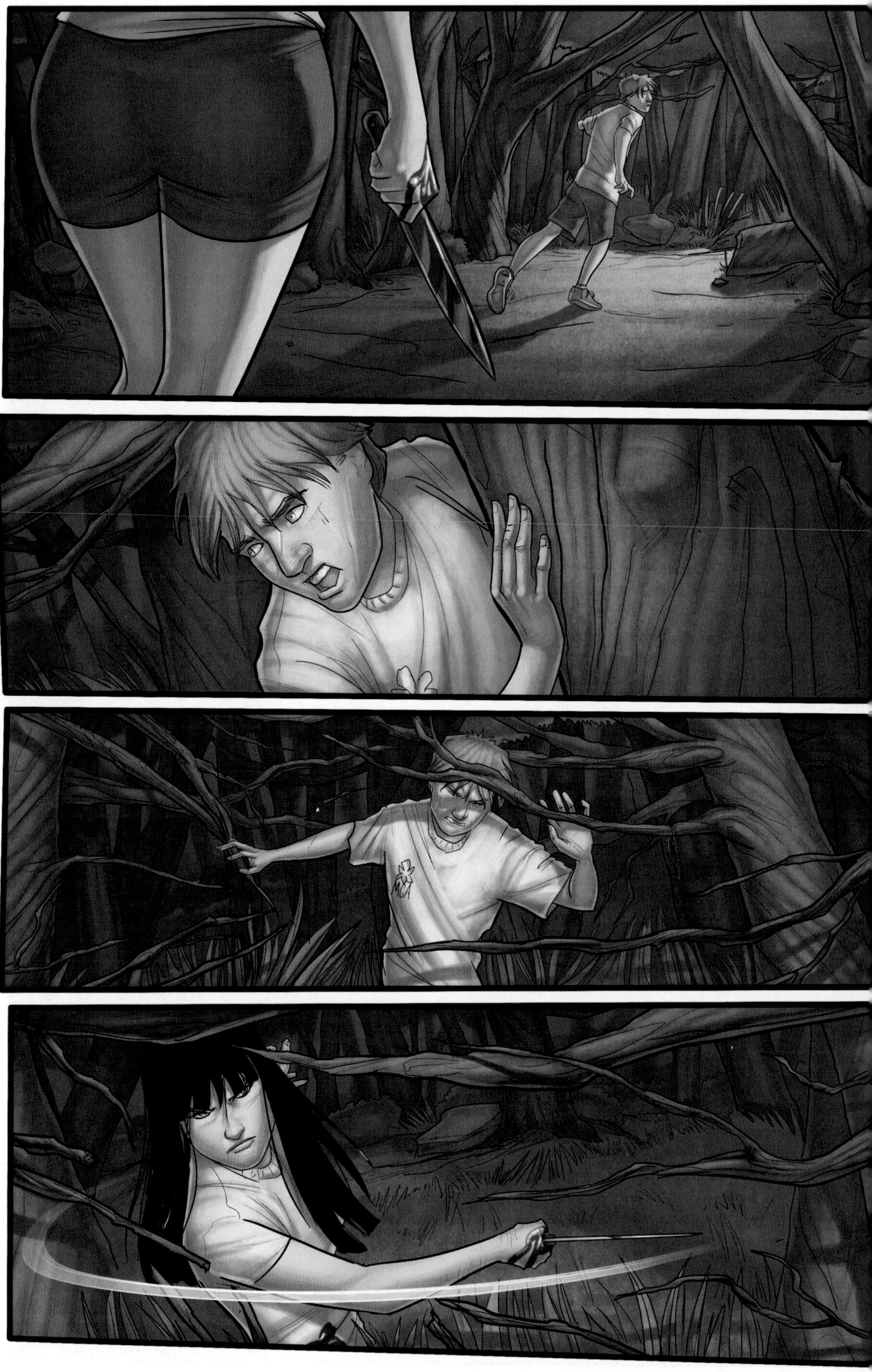

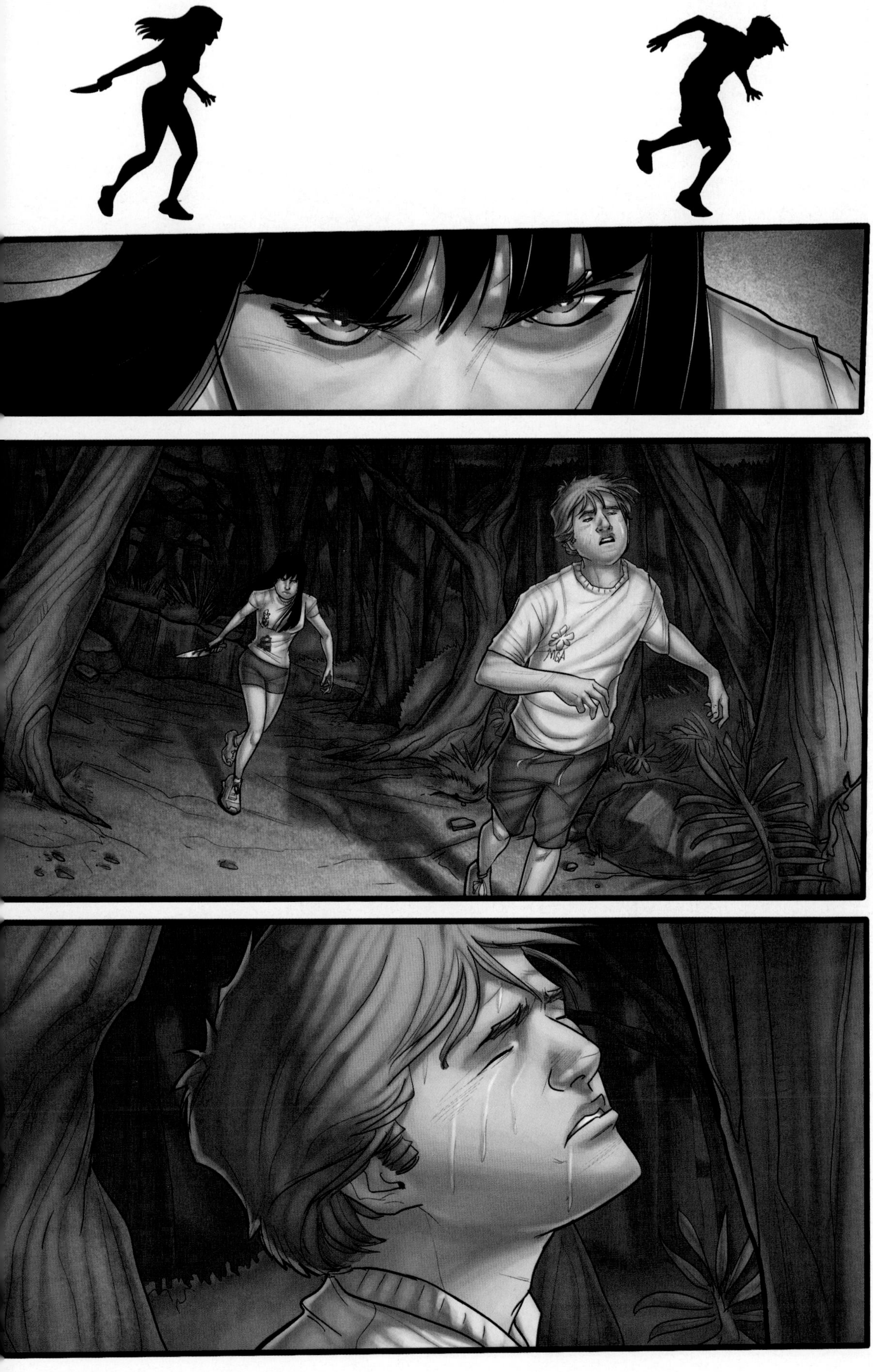

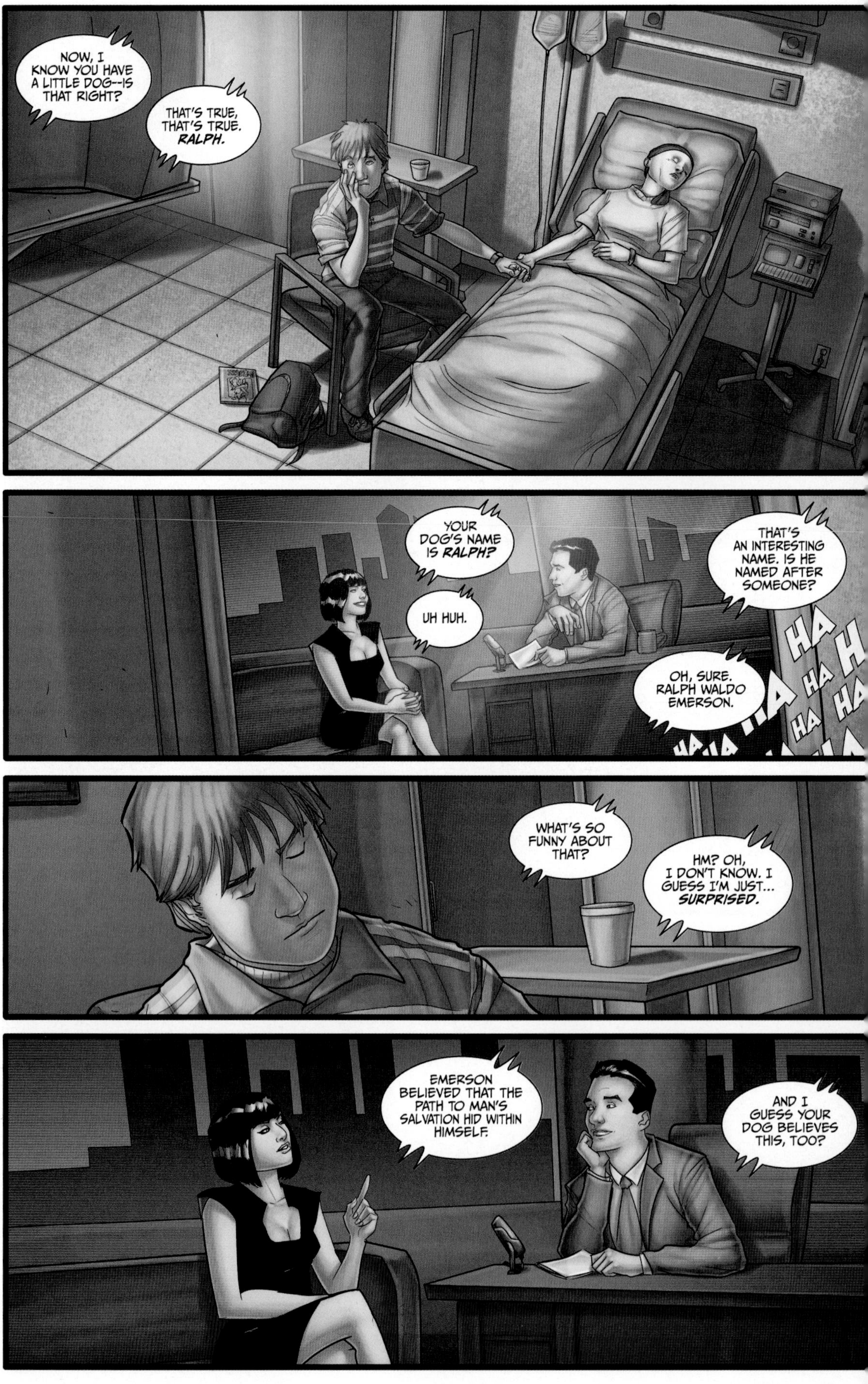
NOW, I KNOW YOU HAVE A LITTLE DOG--IS THAT RIGHT?
THAT'S TRUE, THAT'S TRUE. ***RALPH.***
YOUR DOG'S NAME IS ***RALPH?***
UH HUH.
THAT'S AN INTERESTING NAME. IS HE NAMED AFTER SOMEONE?
OH, SURE. RALPH WALDO EMERSON.
HA HA HA HA HA HA
WHAT'S SO FUNNY ABOUT THAT?
HM? OH, I DON'T KNOW. I GUESS I'M JUST... ***SURPRISED.***
EMERSON BELIEVED THAT THE PATH TO MAN'S SALVATION HID WITHIN HIMSELF.
AND I GUESS YOUR DOG BELIEVES THIS, TOO?

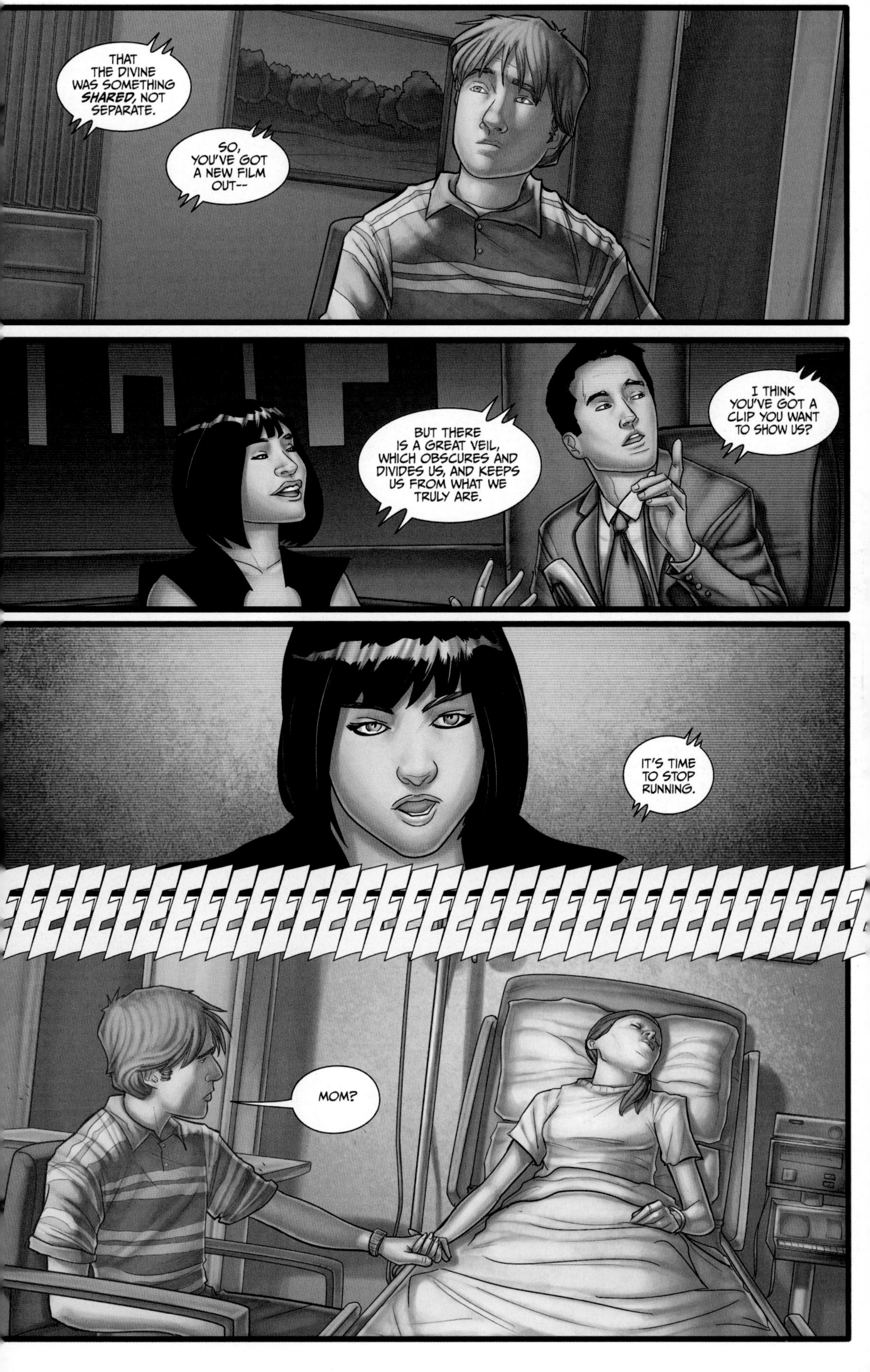

THAT THE DIVINE WAS SOMETHING SHARED, NOT SEPARATE.
SO, YOU'VE GOT A NEW FILM OUT--
BUT THERE IS A GREAT VEIL, WHICH OBSCURES AND DIVIDES US, AND KEEPS US FROM WHAT WE TRULY ARE.
I THINK YOU'VE GOT A CLIP YOU WANT TO SHOW US?
IT'S TIME TO STOP RUNNING.
EEEEEEEEEEEEEEEEEEEEEEEEEEEEEEEEEEEEEEEEE
MOM?

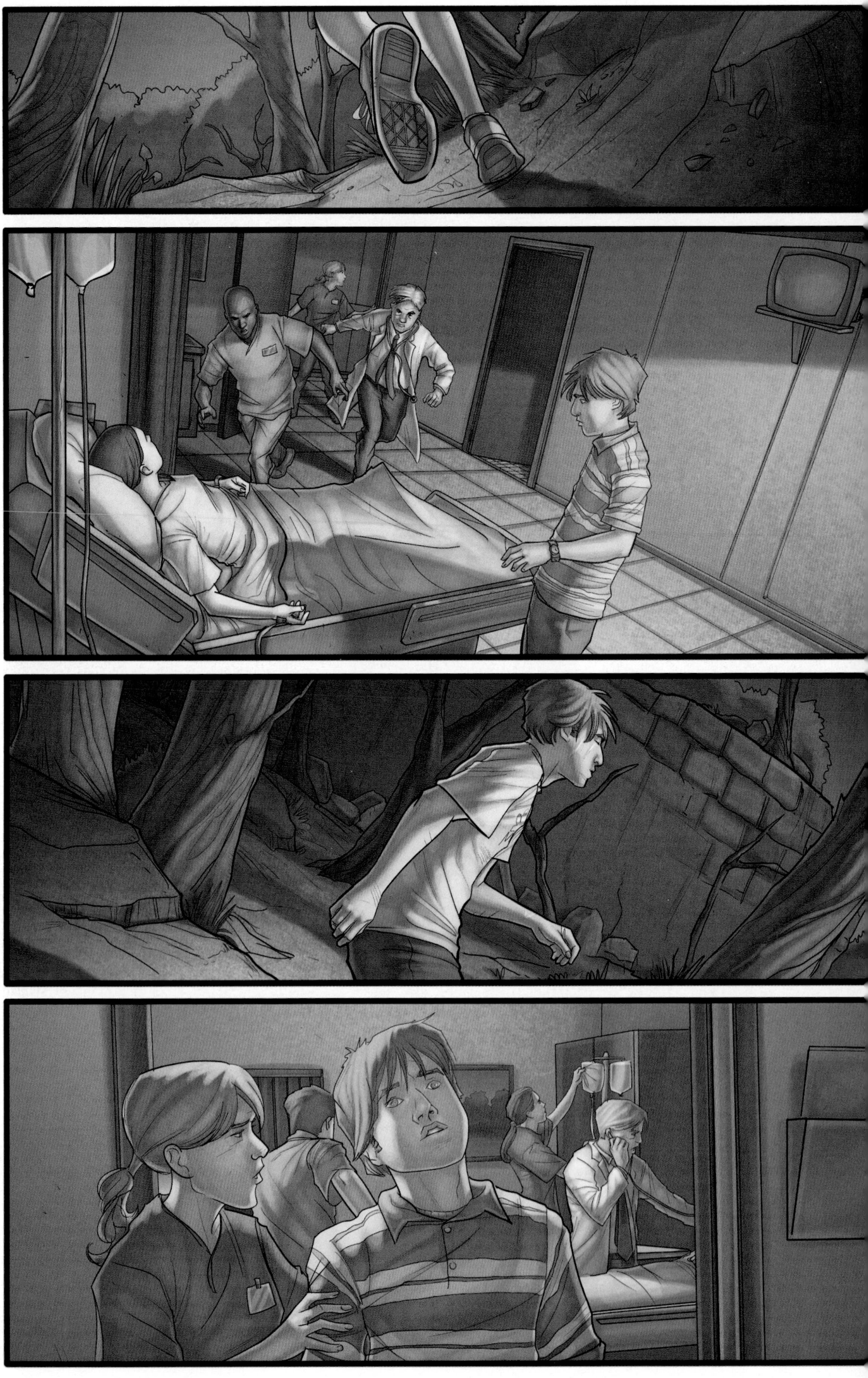

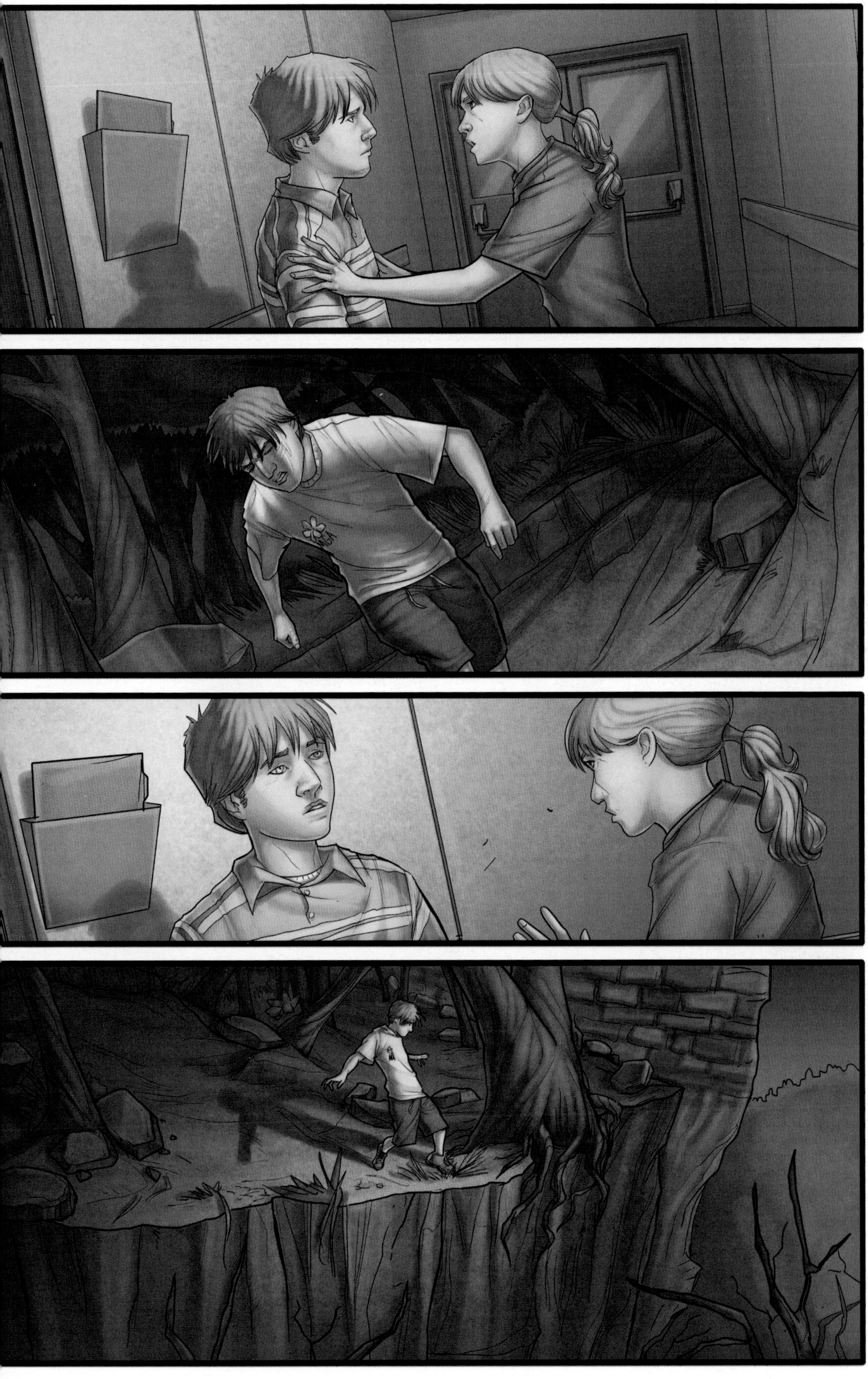

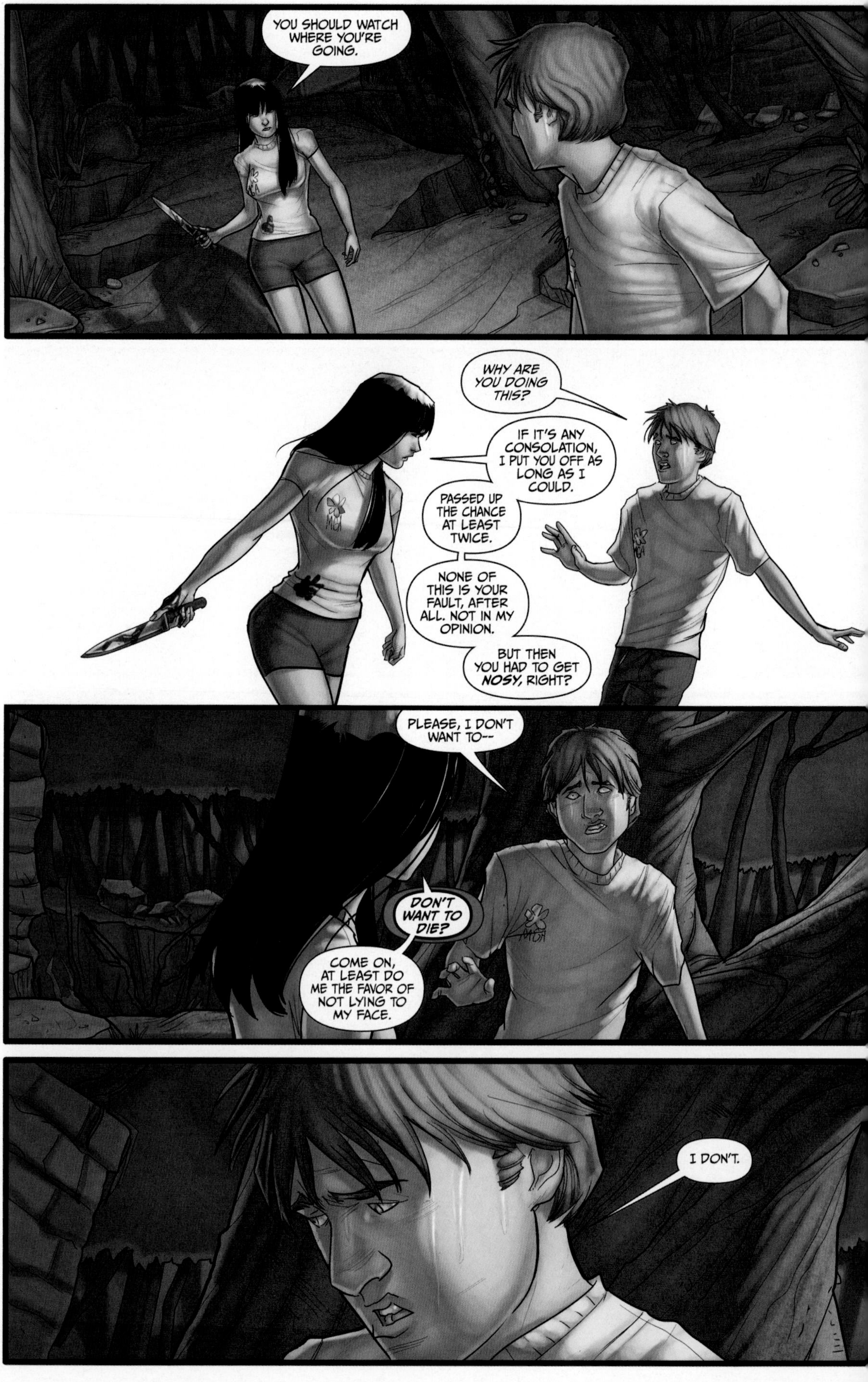
YOU SHOULD WATCH WHERE YOU'RE GOING.
WHY ARE YOU DOING THIS?
IF IT'S ANY CONSOLATION, I PUT YOU OFF AS LONG AS I COULD.
PASSED UP THE CHANCE AT LEAST TWICE.
NONE OF THIS IS YOUR FAULT, AFTER ALL. NOT IN MY OPINION.
BUT THEN YOU HAD TO GET NOSY, RIGHT?
PLEASE, I DON'T WANT TO--
DON'T WANT TO DIE?
COME ON, AT LEAST DO ME THE FAVOR OF NOT LYING TO MY FACE.
I DON'T.

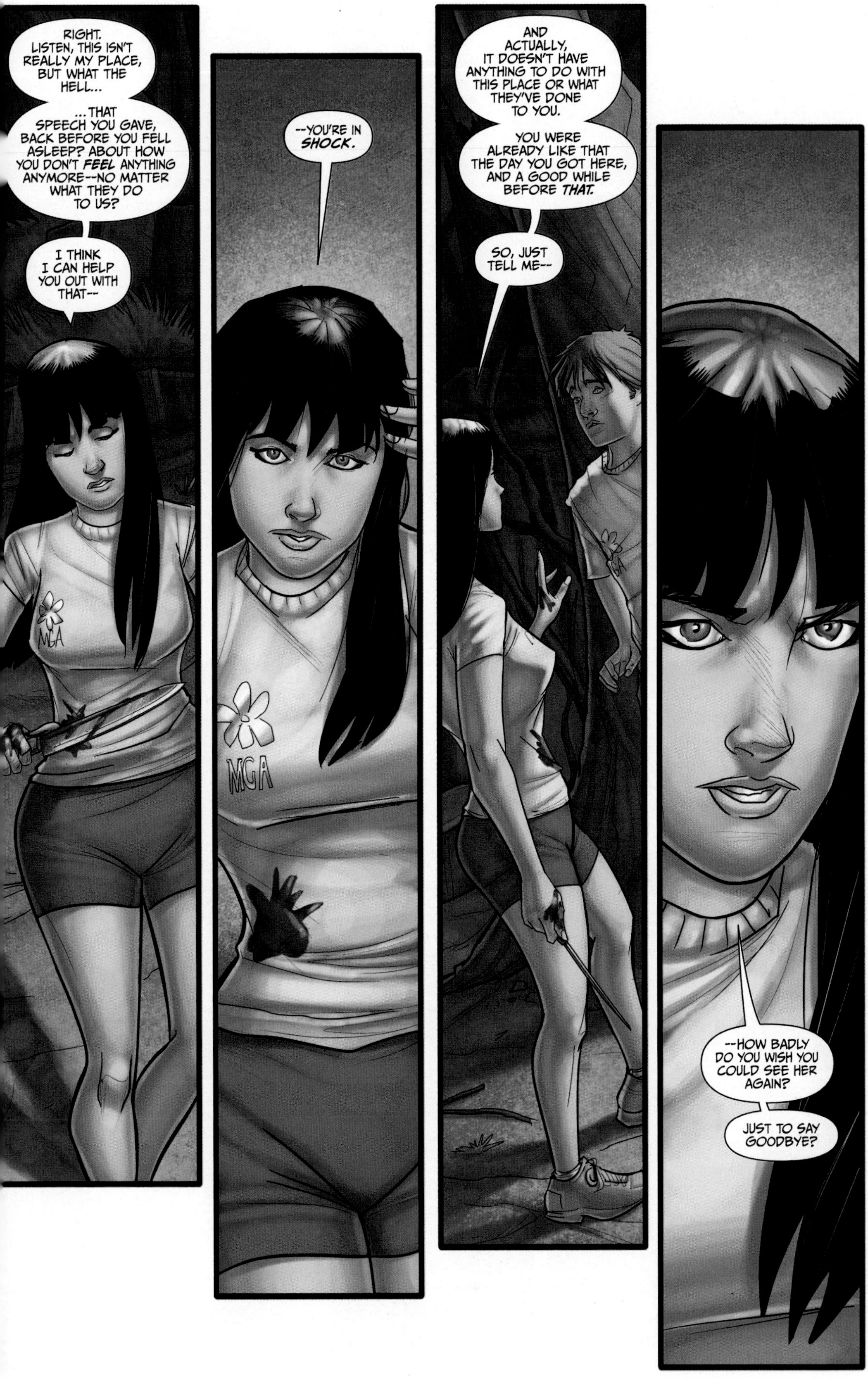
RIGHT. LISTEN, THIS ISN'T REALLY MY PLACE, BUT WHAT THE HELL...
...THAT SPEECH YOU GAVE, BACK BEFORE YOU FELL ASLEEP? ABOUT HOW YOU DON'T FEEL ANYTHING ANYMORE--NO MATTER WHAT THEY DO TO US?
I THINK I CAN HELP YOU OUT WITH THAT--
--YOU'RE IN SHOCK.
AND ACTUALLY, IT DOESN'T HAVE ANYTHING TO DO WITH THIS PLACE OR WHAT THEY'VE DONE TO YOU.
YOU WERE ALREADY LIKE THAT THE DAY YOU GOT HERE, AND A GOOD WHILE BEFORE THAT.
SO, JUST TELL ME--
--HOW BADLY DO YOU WISH YOU COULD SEE HER AGAIN?
JUST TO SAY GOODBYE?

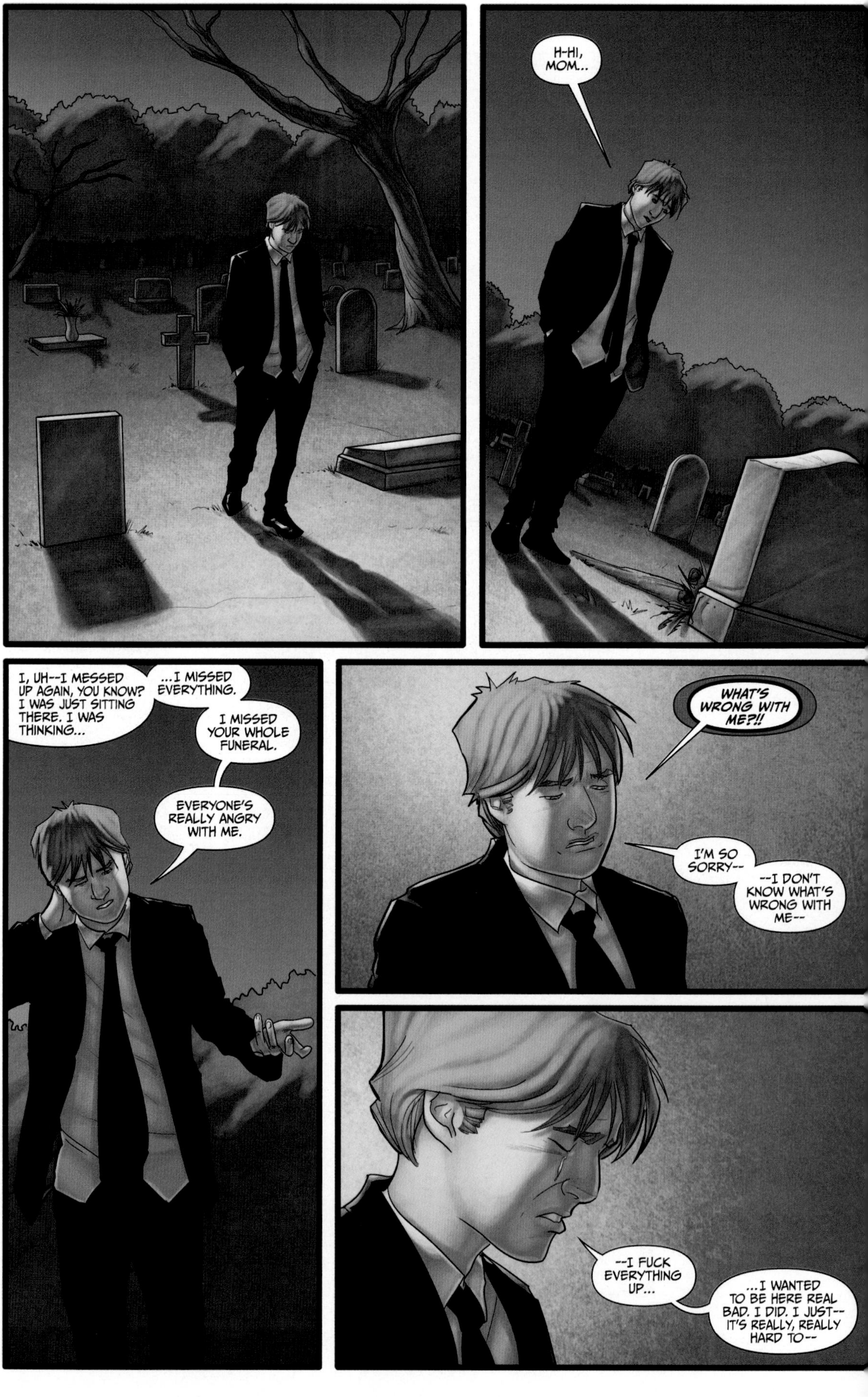
H-HI, MOM...
I, UH--I MESSED UP AGAIN, YOU KNOW? I WAS JUST SITTING THERE. I WAS THINKING...
...I MISSED EVERYTHING.
I MISSED YOUR WHOLE FUNERAL.
EVERYONE'S REALLY ANGRY WITH ME.
WHAT'S WRONG WITH ME?!!
I'M SO SORRY--
--I DON'T KNOW WHAT'S WRONG WITH ME--
--I FUCK EVERYTHING UP...
...I WANTED TO BE HERE REAL BAD. I DID. I JUST-- IT'S REALLY, REALLY HARD TO--

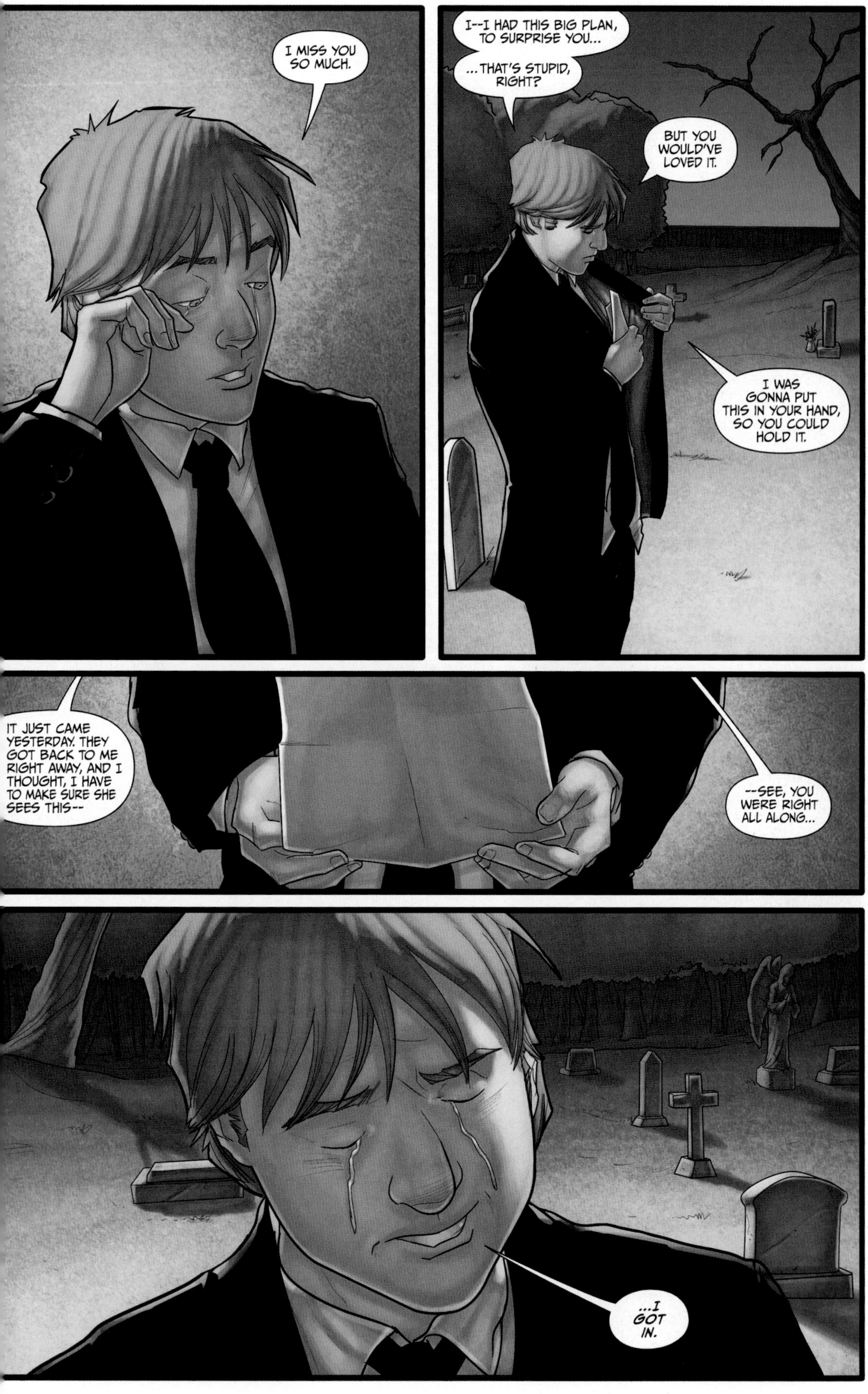
I MISS YOU SO MUCH.
I--I HAD THIS BIG PLAN, TO SURPRISE YOU...
...THAT'S STUPID, RIGHT?
BUT YOU WOULD'VE LOVED IT.
I WAS GONNA PUT THIS IN YOUR HAND, SO YOU COULD HOLD IT.
IT JUST CAME YESTERDAY. THEY GOT BACK TO ME RIGHT AWAY, AND I THOUGHT, I HAVE TO MAKE SURE SHE SEES THIS--
--SEE, YOU WERE RIGHT ALL ALONG...
...I GOT IN.

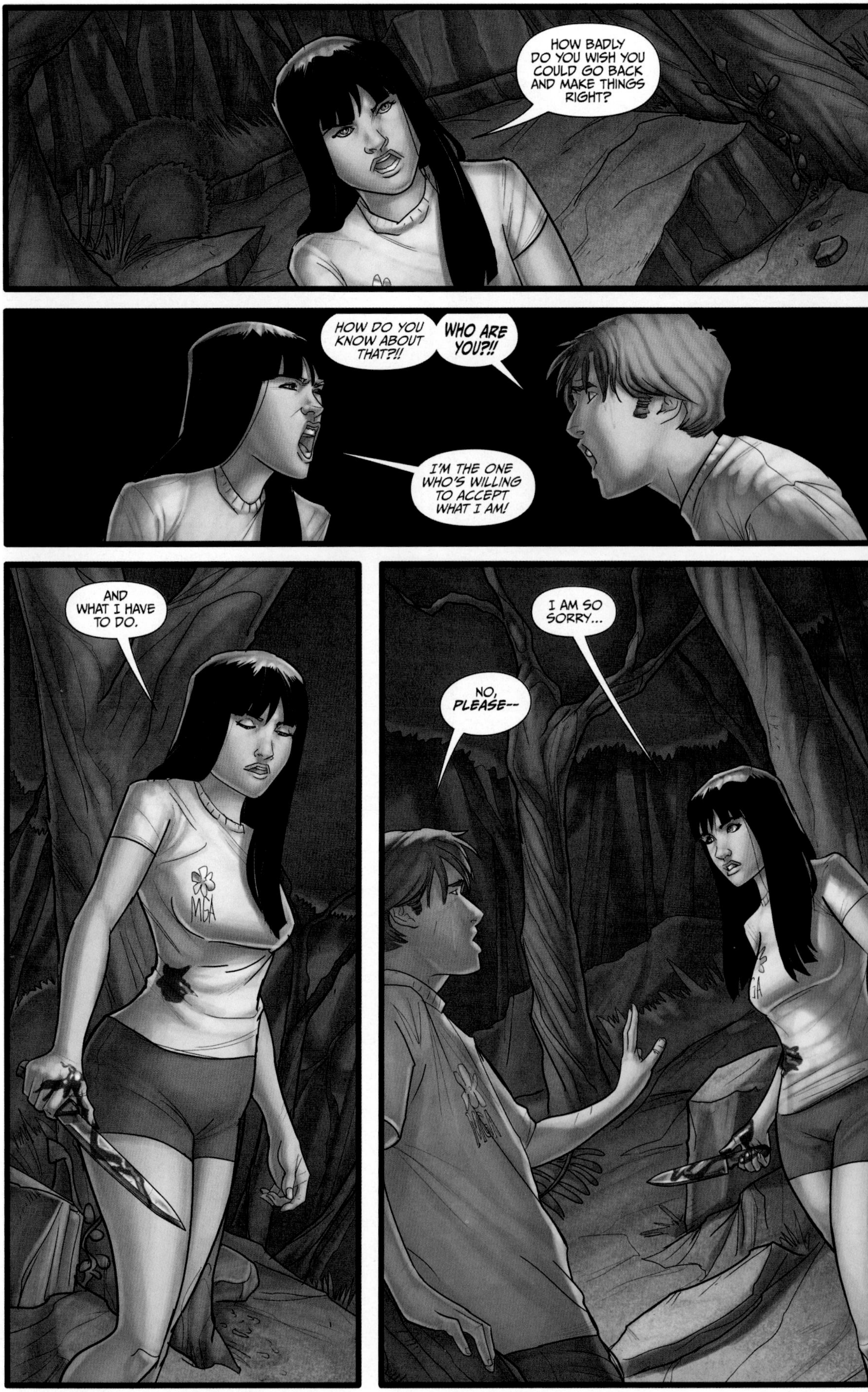

HOW BADLY DO YOU WISH YOU COULD GO BACK AND MAKE THINGS RIGHT?
HOW DO YOU KNOW ABOUT THAT?!!
WHO ARE YOU?!!
I'M THE ONE WHO'S WILLING TO ACCEPT WHAT I AM!
AND WHAT I HAVE TO DO.
I AM SO SORRY...
NO, PLEASE--

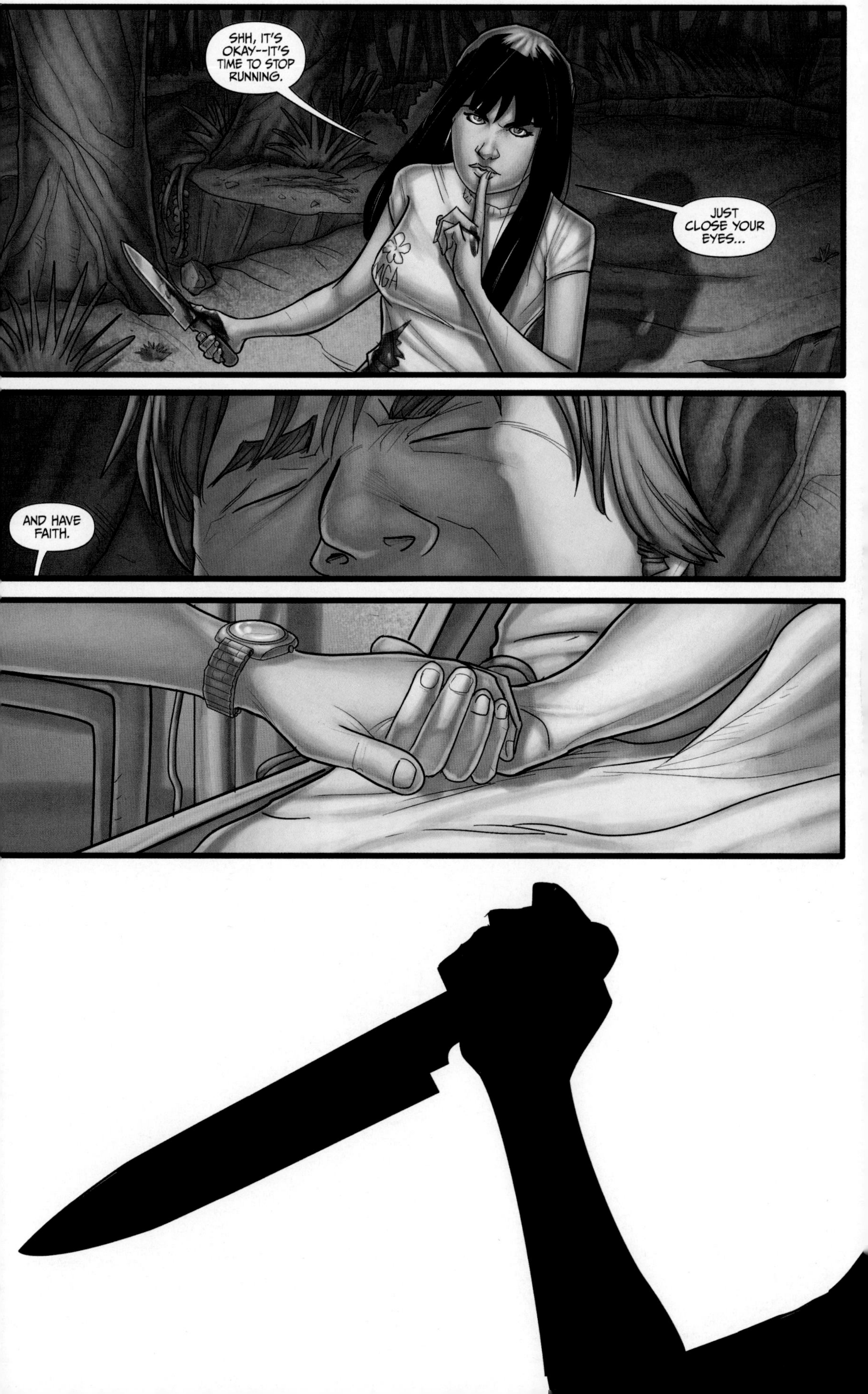
SHH, IT'S OKAY--IT'S TIME TO STOP RUNNING.
JUST CLOSE YOUR EYES...
AND HAVE FAITH.

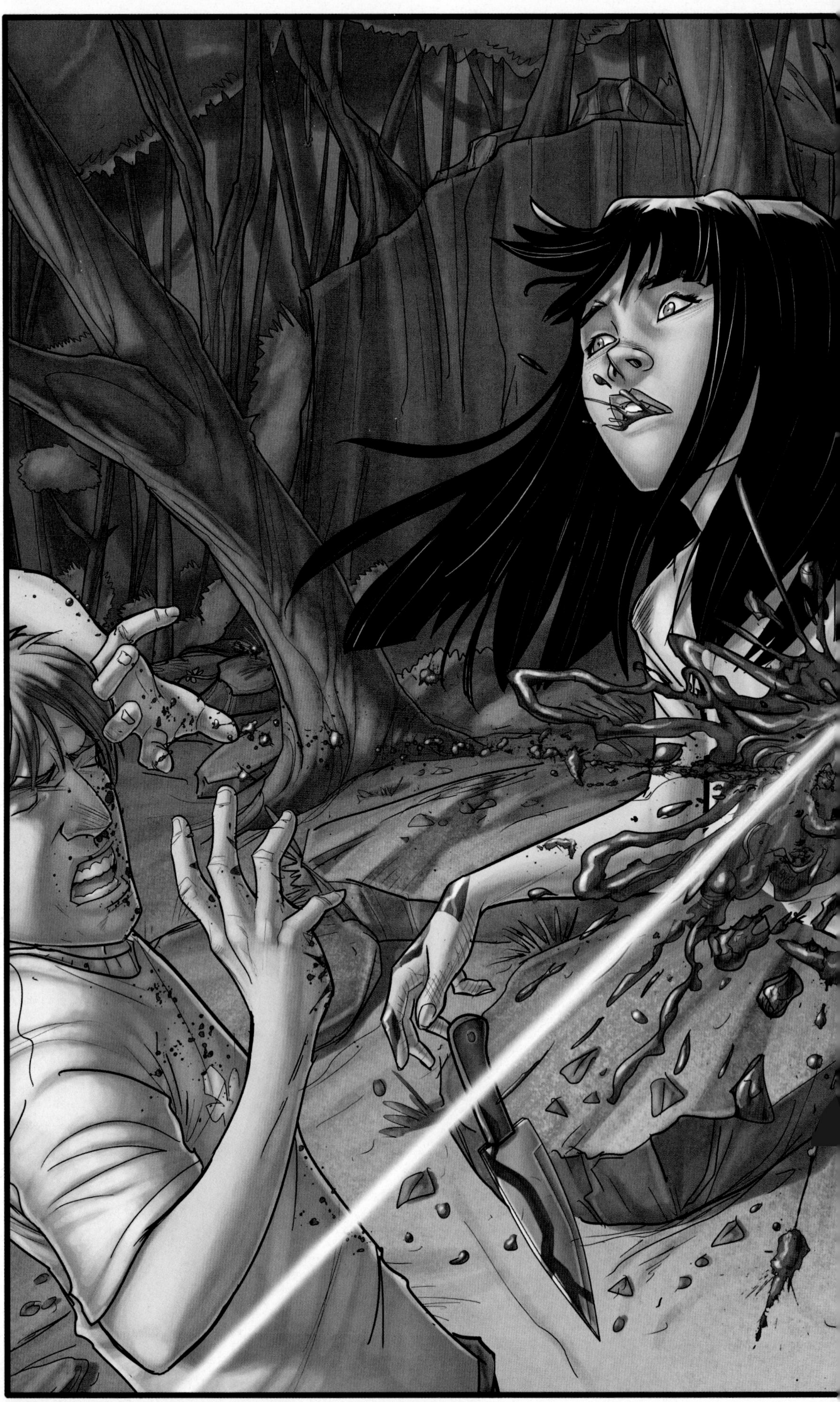

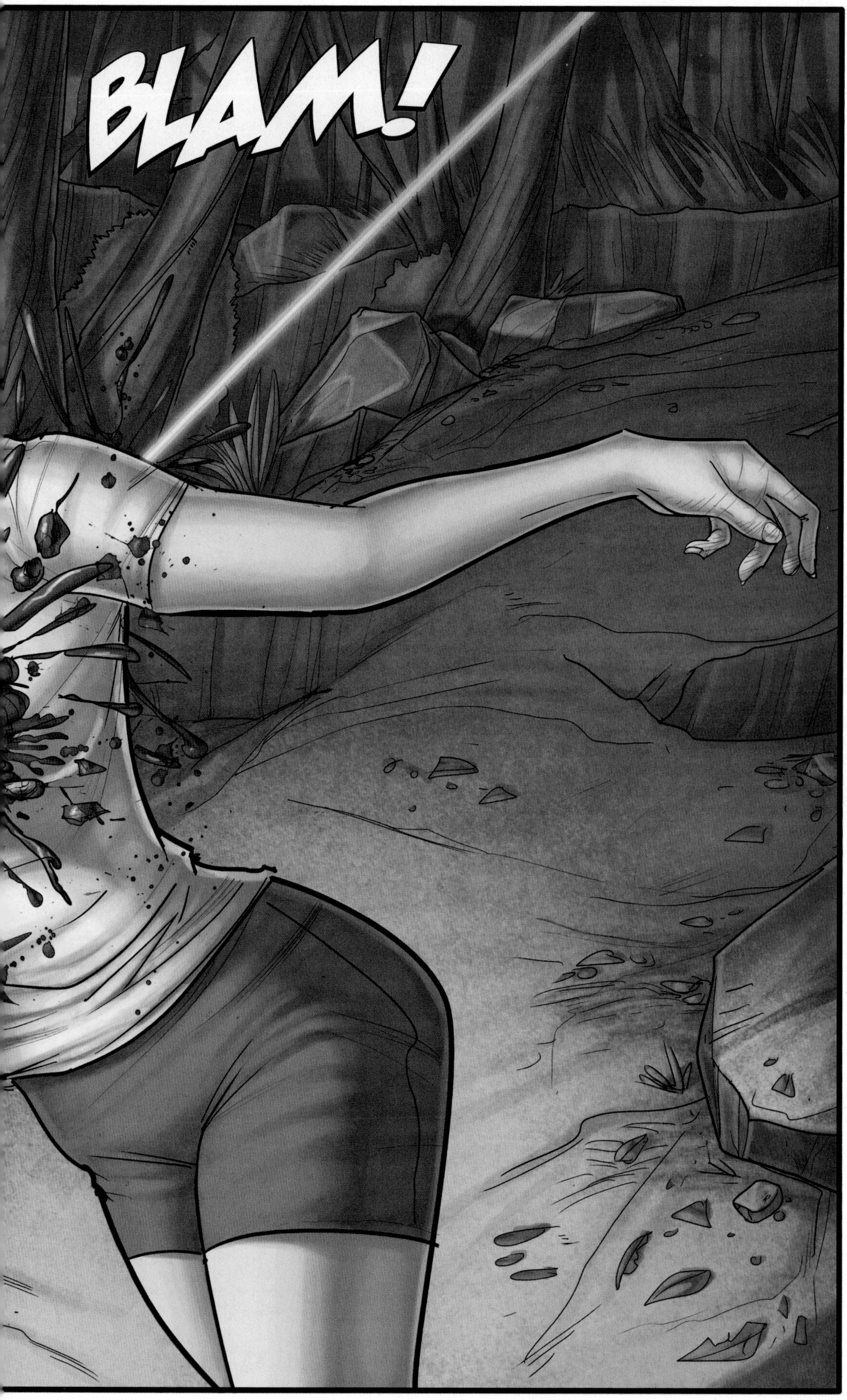
BLAM!

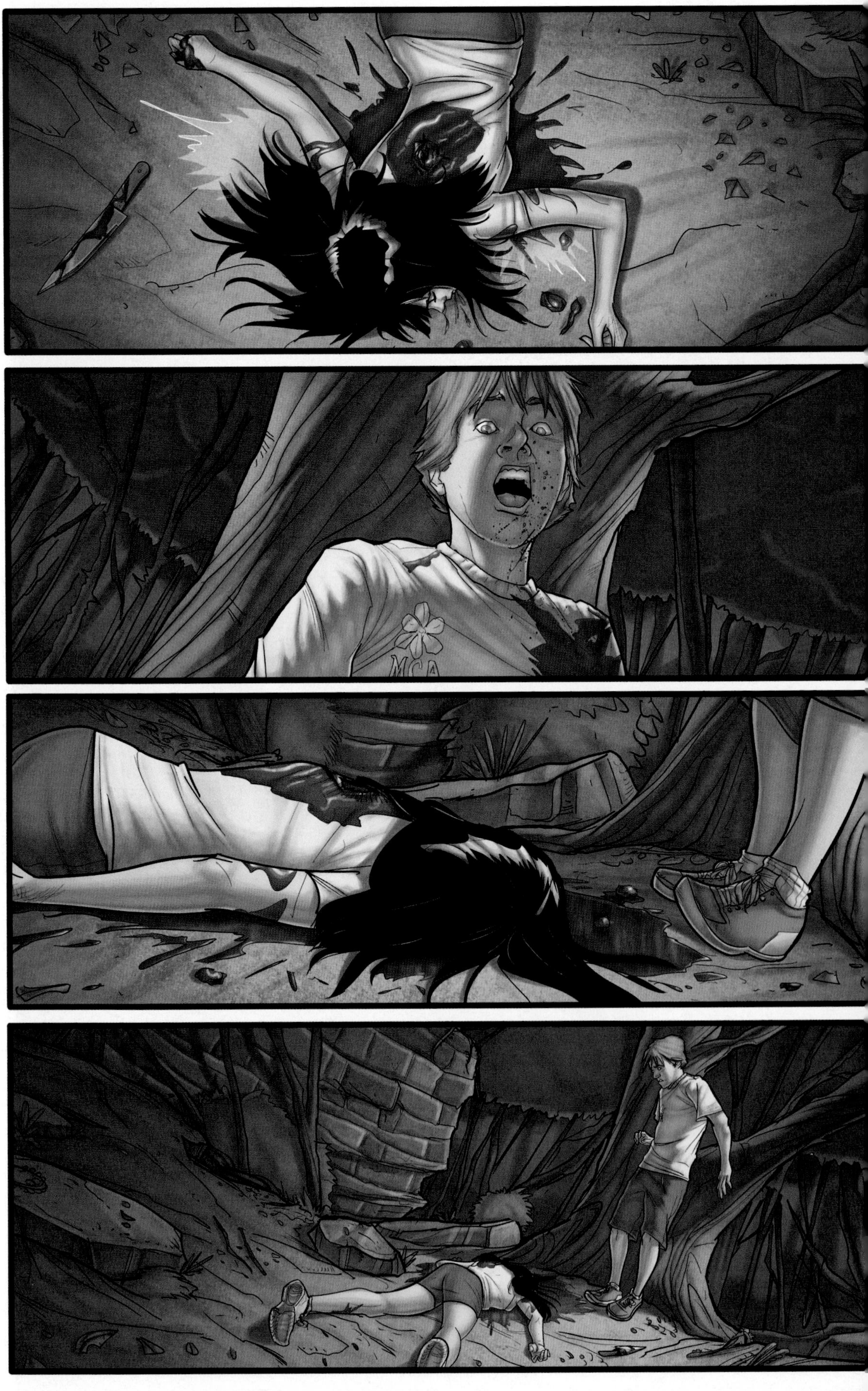
MCA

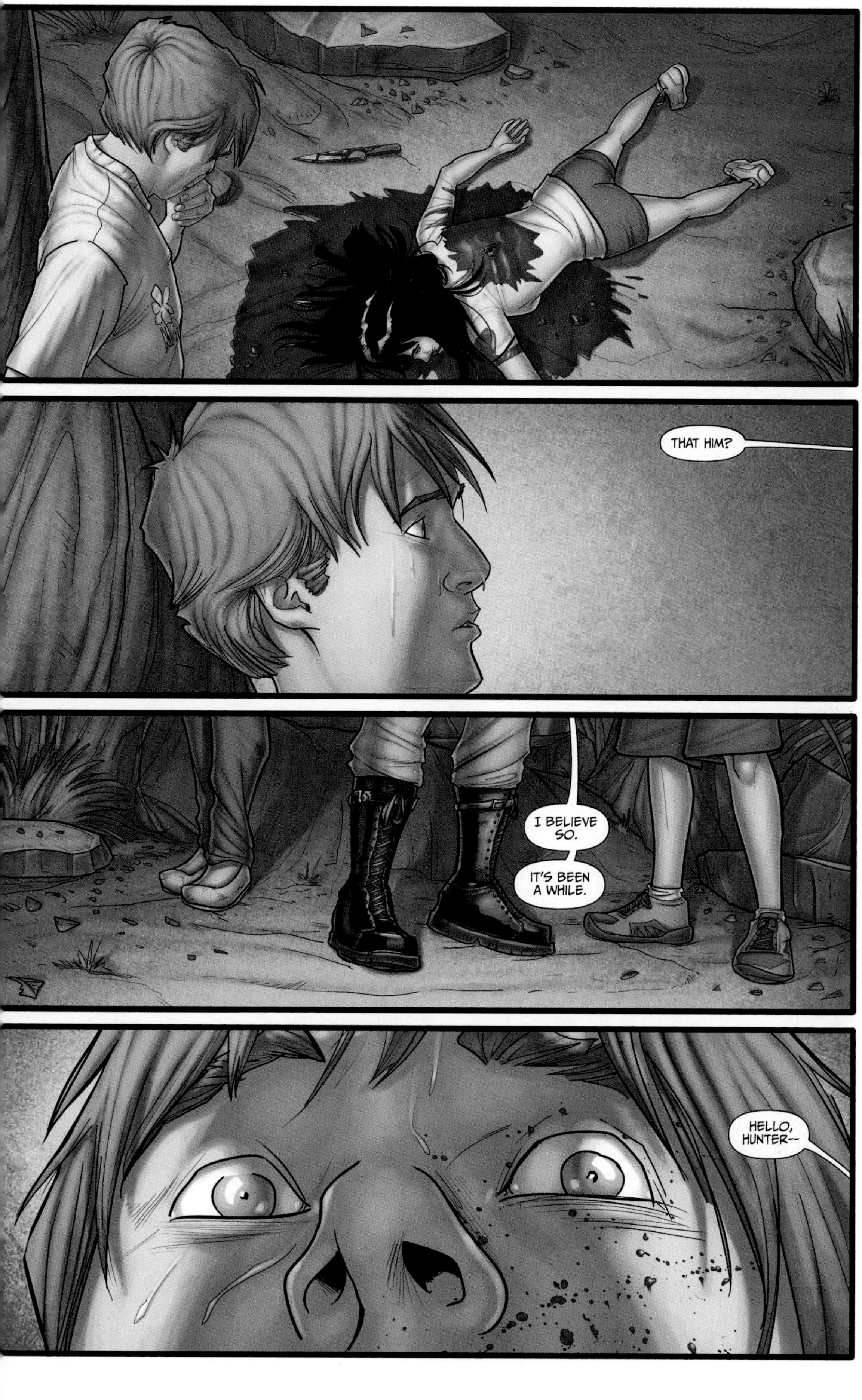
THAT HIM?
I BELIEVE SO.
IT'S BEEN A WHILE.
HELLO, HUNTER--

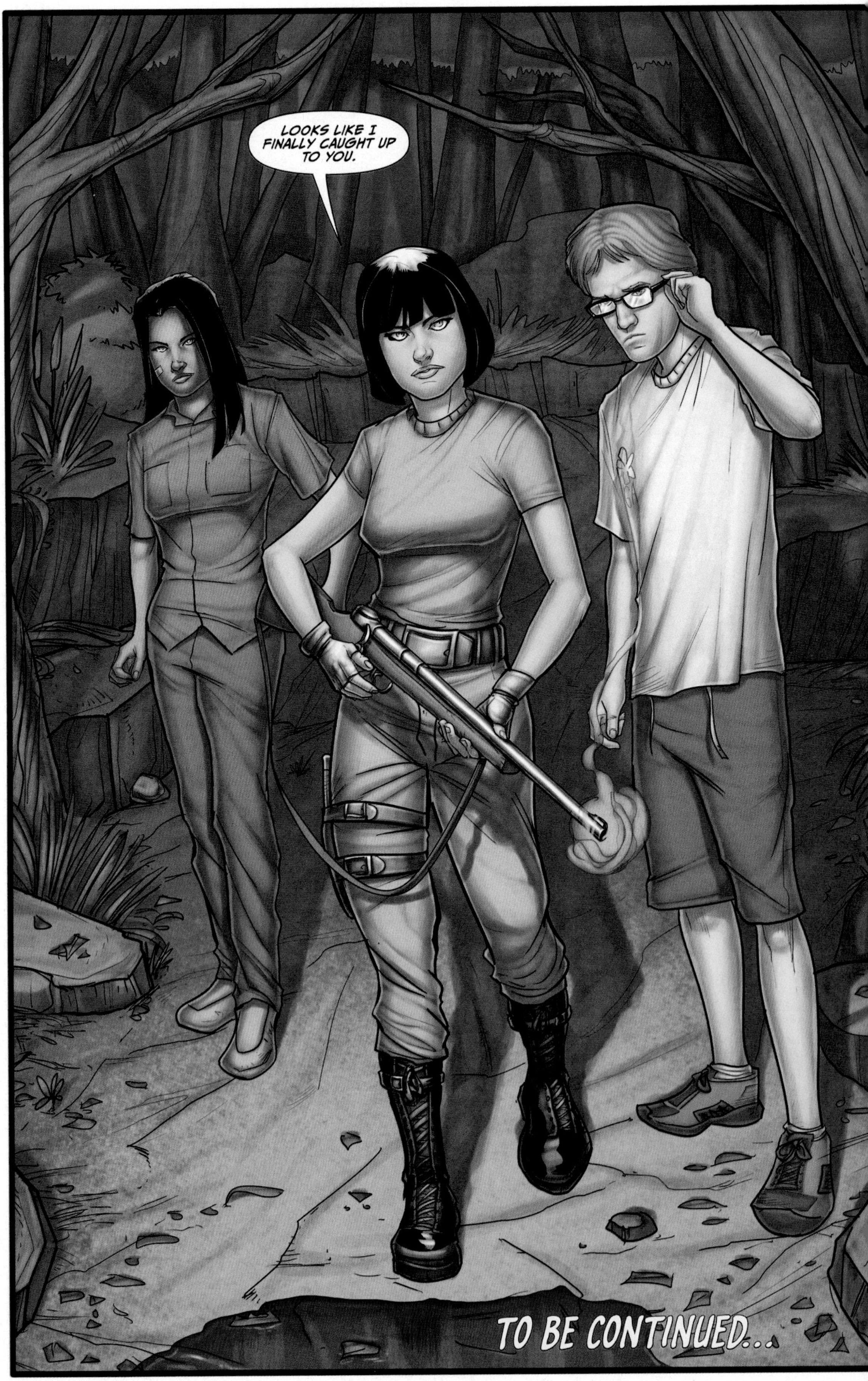
LOOKS LIKE I FINALLY CAUGHT UP TO YOU.
TO BE CONTINUED...

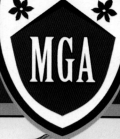

THE ART OF JOE EISMA

Issue after issue, Joe's artistry brings to life the world of Morning Glory Academy. Here's a look at some of his behind-the-scenes design work.

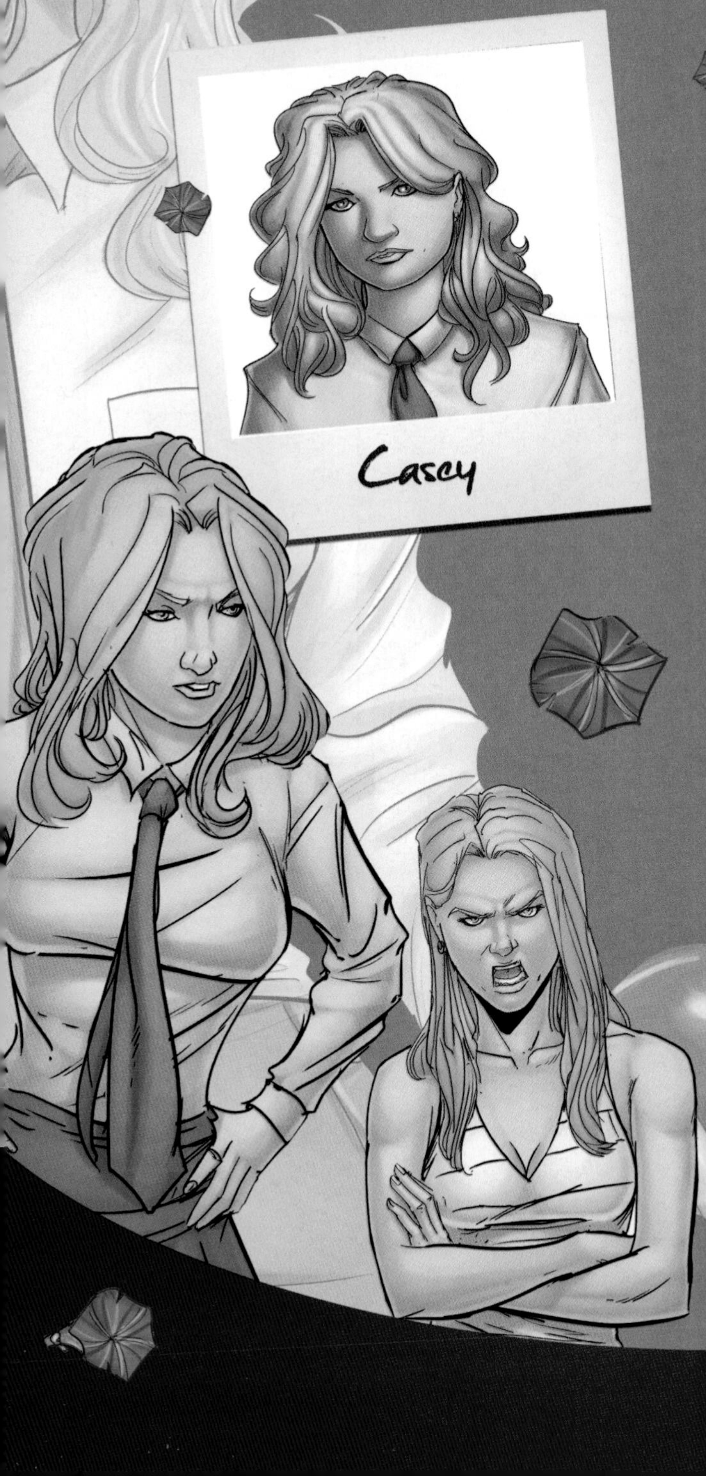
Casey

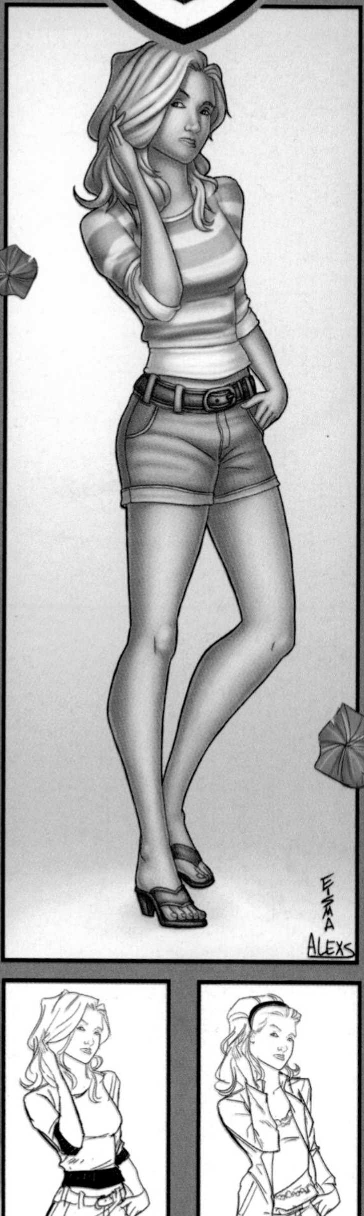
EISMA
ALEXS

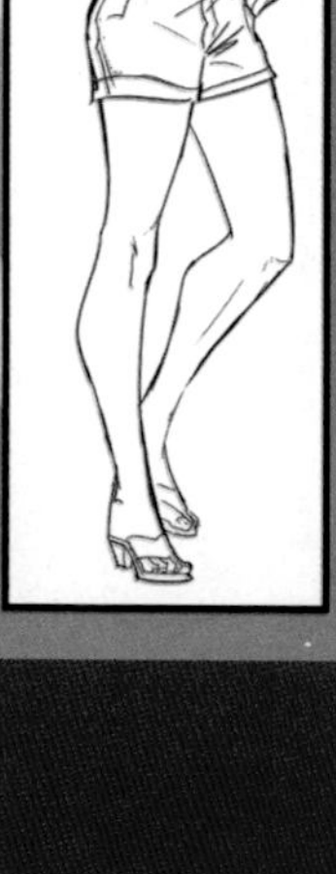

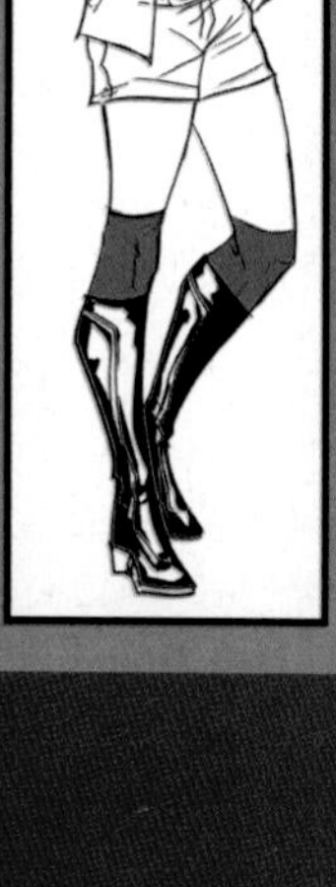

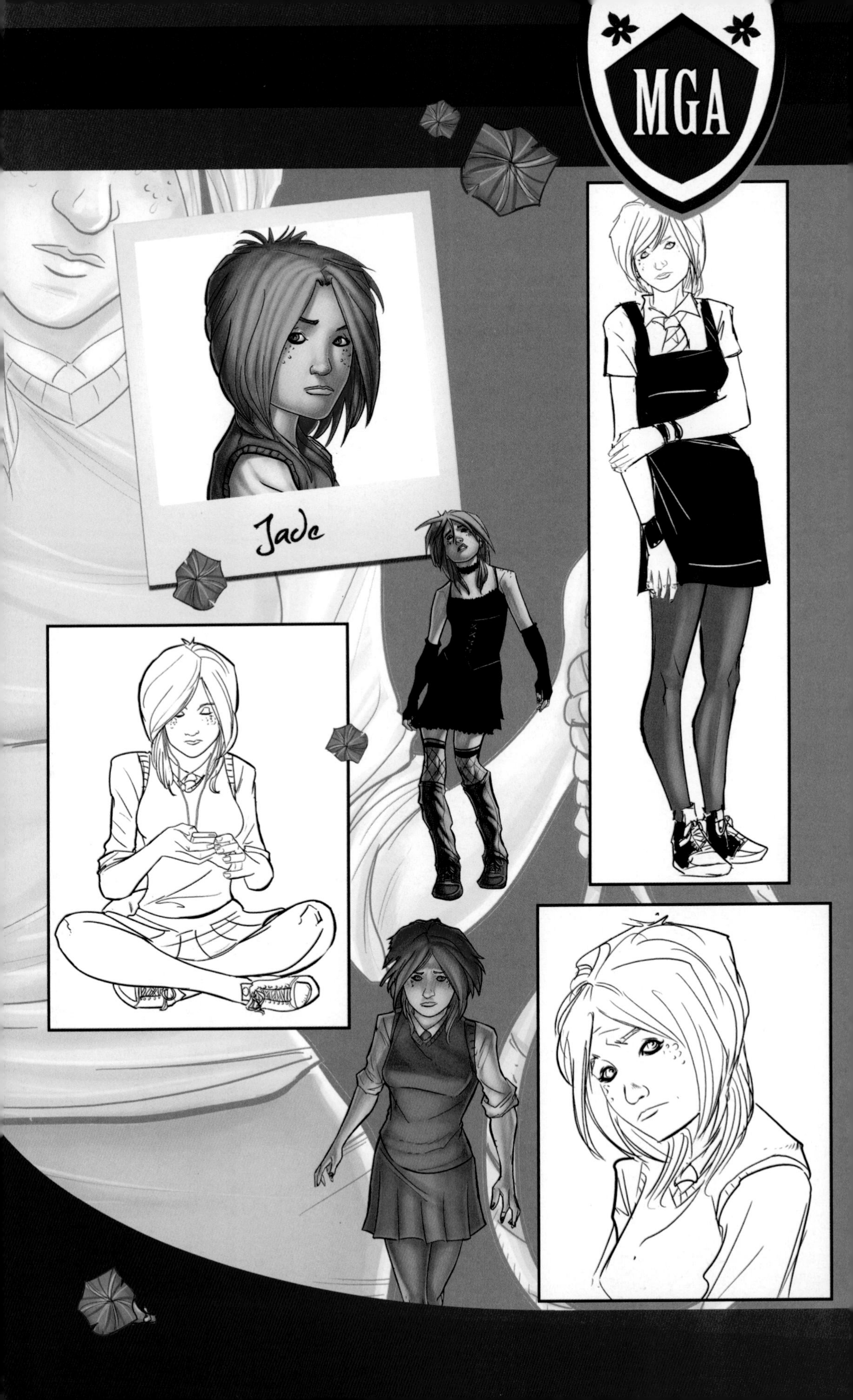
MGA
Jade

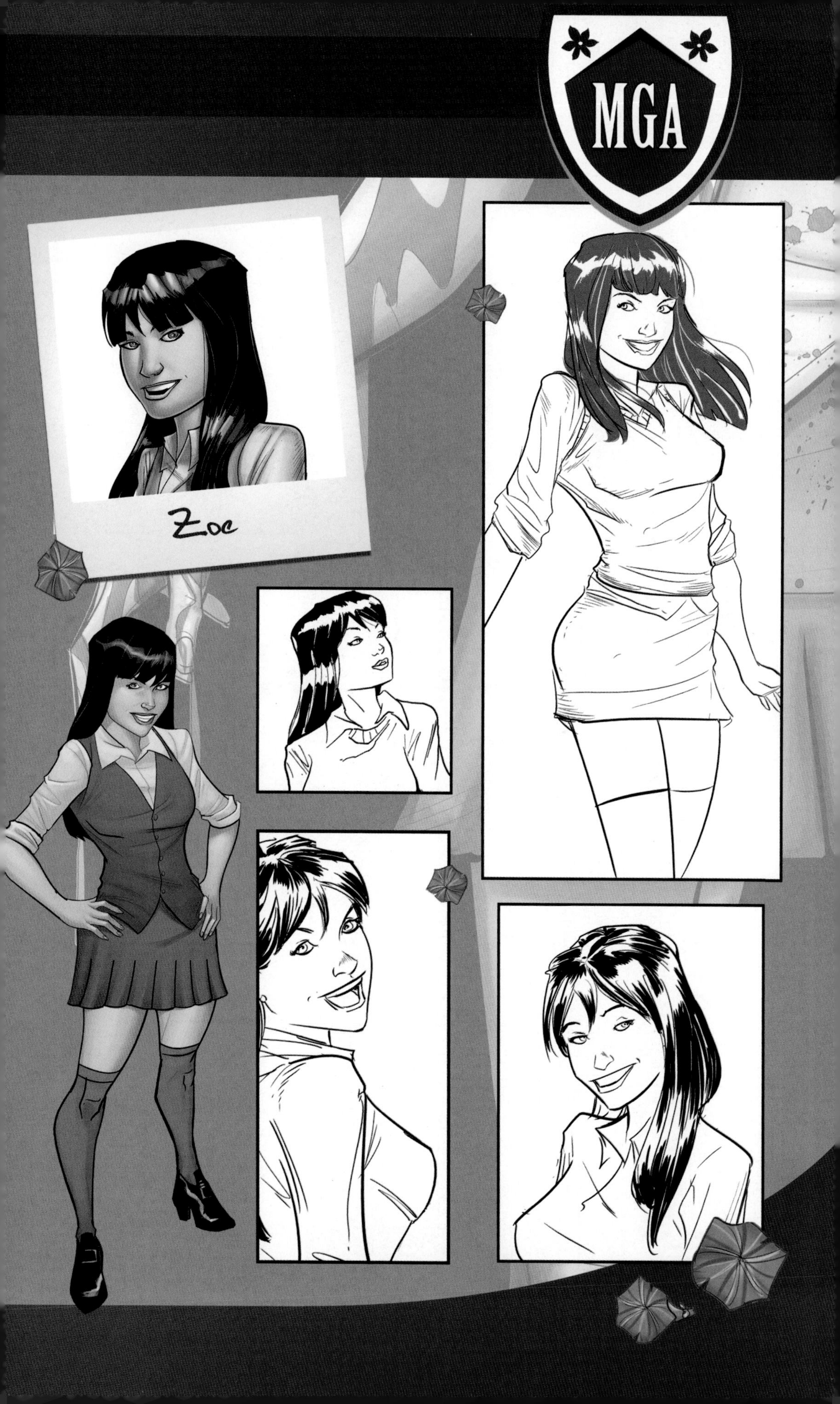
MGA
Zoe

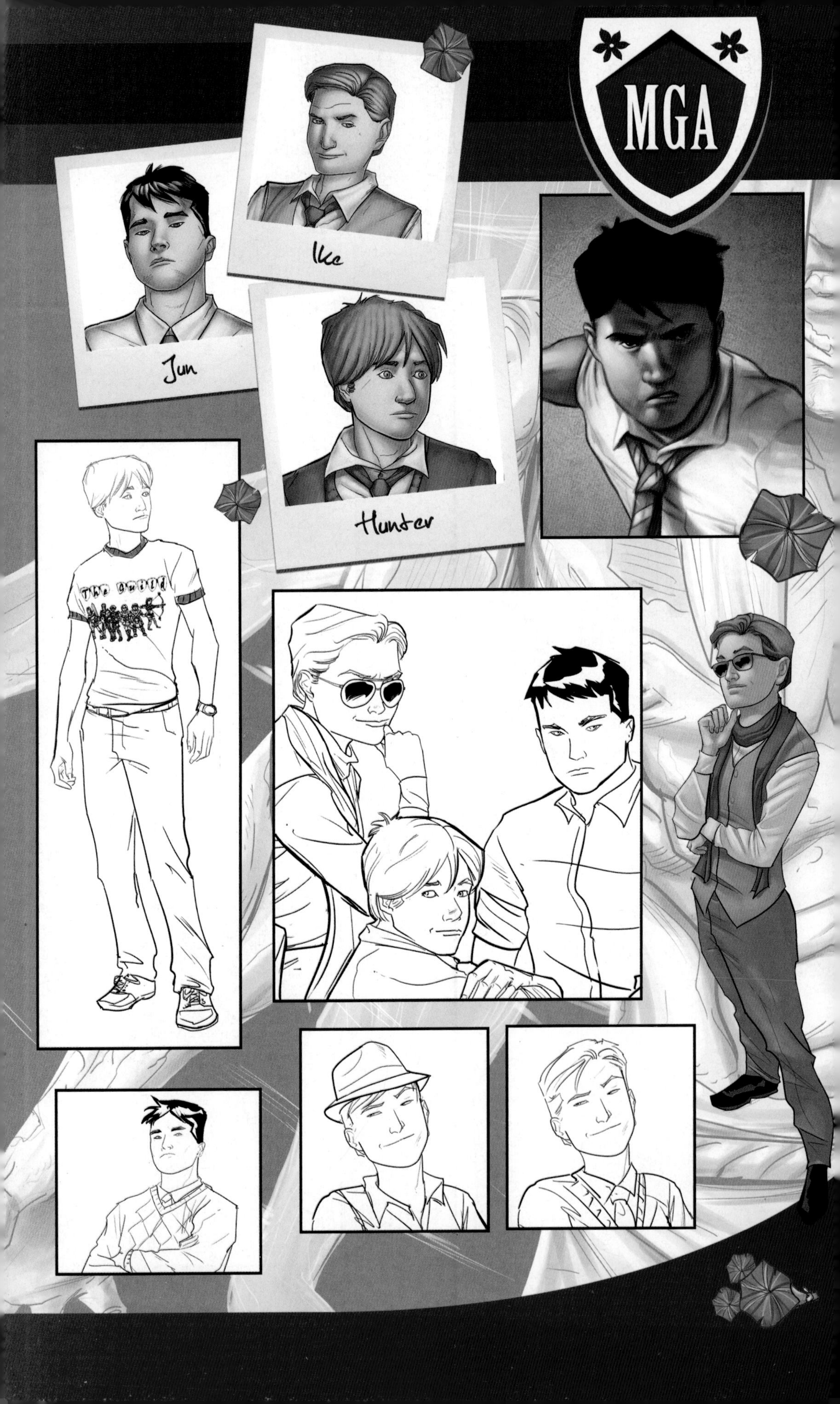

MGA
Ike
Jun
Hunter
The Guild